D0201218

Knight's
Modern Seamanship
SIXTEENTH EDITION

Knight's Modern Seamanship

SIXTEENTH EDITION

REVISED BY JOHN V. NOEL, JR., CAPTAIN, U.S. NAVY (RET.)

Assisted by **Frank E. Bassett,** Commander, U.S. Navy

 VAN NOSTRAND REINHOLD COMPANY

NEW YORK   CINCINNATI   ATLANTA   DALLAS   SAN FRANCISCO

LONDON   TORONTO   MELBOURNE

Van Nostrand Reinhold Company Regional Offices:
New York   Cincinnati   Atlanta   Dallas   San Francisco

Van Nostrand Reinhold Company International Offices:
London   Toronto   Melbourne

Copyright © 1977 by
LITTON EDUCATIONAL PUBLISHING, INC.

Library of Congress Catalog Card Number: 76-16277

ISBN 0-442-26049-0

Manufactured in the United States of America

Published by Van Nostrand Reinhold Company
135 West 50th Street, New York, N.Y. 10020

Published simultaneously in Canada by
Van Nostrand Reinhold Ltd.

15   14   13   12   11   10   9   8   7   6   5

Library of Congress Cataloging in Publication Data

Knight, Austin Melvin, 1854–1927.
  Modern seamanship.

  Includes index.
  1. Seamanship.   II. Noel, John Vavasour, 1912–
II. Bassett, Frank E.   III. Title.
VK541.K73   1976   623.88   76-16277
ISBN 0-442-26049-0

Preface to the Sixteenth Edition

This Sixteenth Edition takes Knight's *Modern Seamanship* to its 75th year. Fifteen editions have carried this work through two world wars and into the nuclear age.

There is no need to describe all the changes that have occurred since 1901. What is important for this book is the fact that much of the rapidly changing knowledge that the mariner needs today, and tomorrow, is being provided by books and journals in every major language. During the past decade alone dozens of periodicals about the sea, ships, boats, and various naval or merchant marine matters have come into existence. So much is happening—nuclear power, hydrofoils, hovercraft, super tankers, containerization, and the application of electronics and automation—that no one book can cover everything.

Accordingly, this edition has been prepared to be of special use to the mariner who has space for only one book on seamanship on his shelf or in his seabag; to the intermittent yachtsman who has time to read only one book and thereafter to use it as a presailing refresher; and to the naval and merchant marine students who need a readable and explanatory text as well as a handy reference book for their academy, college, or reserve training programs.

For these and other uses the 16th Edition of Knight's *Modern Seamanship* has been designed to provide both a general overview of modern seamanship and a practical guide for those who are actually going on or under the sea in a large ship or small craft.

The Rules of the Road have been substantially changed and this edition delineates and explains those that are now effective. Nomenclature of US Naval vessels has also recently changed—this is reflected herein. The world's growing realization that man may be irrevocably ruining his environment by pollution has resulted in a relatively simple but authoritative short section on *Pollution*.

This new edition has been prepared by a large team of specialists under the direction of Commander Frank E. Bassett, U.S. Navy.

Major contributors were:

Captain Edwin A. MacDonald, USN (ret.)
Lieutenant William H. Tate, USN
Lieutenant Commander Arthur J. Tuttle, USN
Professor John F. Hoffman, Ph.D., P.E.
Lieutenant Commander Howard L. Sipple, USN
Lieutenant Commander James E. Oertel, USN
Lieutenant Richard R. Hobbs, USN
Lieutenant Commander Richard A. Smith, Royal Navy
Mr. Joseph M. Frosio, Headquarters, Naval Weather Service Command
Captain Carvel Blair, USN (ret.)

Minor contributors were:

Mr. Bert C. Wylds
Lieutenant James R. Burkhart, USN
Lieutenant Commander James E. Millner, USN
CWO2 Wilbur J. Brown, USN
Lieutenant Commander Durward B. Mommsen, Jr., USN
Mr. Jerry P. Totten, Office of the Supervisor of Salvage, Naval Sea
    Systems Command
Lieutenant Commander Louis S. Hathaway, USN, Nautical Science
    Department, Maine Maritime Academy

John V. Noel, Jr.
Frank E. Bassett

Preface to the First Edition

An attempt is made, in the following pages, to cover a wider field than that covered by most of the existing works on Seamanship.

The admirable treatises of Luce, Nares, and Alston, originating in the days when Seamanship was almost wholly concerned with the fitting and handling of vessels under sail, have preserved through later editions the general characteristics which they naturally assumed in the beginning. These treatises will never be out of date until the time, still far in the future, when sails shall have been entirely driven out by steam. It will hardly be denied, however, that the Steamer has long since established its claim to consideration in Seamanship, and that there is room for a work in which this claim shall be more fully recognized than in the treatises above referred to. The excellent work of Captains Todd and Whall, *Practical Seamanship for the Merchant Service*, deals more fully than either of its predecessors with the handling of steamers; but its point of view is, as its name implies, primarily and almost exclusively that of the Merchant Service.

Shortly after the present work was begun, a circular letter was addressed to officers of the Merchant Service and extensively circulated through the Branch Hydrographic Offices at New York, Philadelphia, Baltimore and Norfolk, requesting the views of the officers addressed.

The answers received to these questions were unexpectedly numerous and complete. More than forty prominent officers of the Merchant Service replied, many of them writing out their views and describing their experiences with a fullness of detail far beyond anything that could have been anticipated.

The thanks of the author are due particularly to the following for letters or for personal interviews covering the above points: Capt. W. H. Thompson, *S.S. Belgenland;* Capt. T. Evans, *S.S. Runo;* Capt. J. Dann, *S.S. Southwark;* 1st Officer T. Anfindsen, *S.S. Southwark;* Capt. J. C. Jameson, *S.S. St. Paul;* Capt. H. E. Nickels, *S.S. Friesland;* Capt. G. J. Loveridge, *S.S. Buffalo;* Capt. F. M. Howes, *S.S. Kershaw;* Capt. T. J. Thorkildsen, *S.S. Trojan;* Capt. Otto Neilsen, *S.S. Pennland;* Capt. H. Doxrud, *S.S. Noordland;* Capt. C. O. Rockwell, Clyde S. S. Co.; Capt. S. W. Watkins, *S.S. Montana;* Capt. Anders

Beer, *S.S. Nordkyn;* Capt. J. M. Johnston, *S.S. Sardinian;* Capt. A. R. Mills, *S.S. Westernland;* Capt. J. S. Garvin, *S.S. Cherokee;* Capt. Robt. B. Quick, *S.S. El Cid;* Capt. Wm. J. Roberts, *S.S. New York;* Capt. T. Richardson, *S.S. Noranmore;* Capt. E. O. Marshall, *S.S. Maryland;* 1st Officer H. S. Lane, *S.S. Maryland;* Capt. W. F. Bingham, *S.S. Marengo;* Capt. R. Gowing, *S.S. Greatham;* Capt. H. J. Byrne, *U.S.A.T. McPherson;* Capt. Paul Grosch, *S.S. Stuttgart;* Capt. Geo. Schrotter, *S.S. Belgravia;* Capt. F. C. Saunders, *S.S. English King;* Capt. Chas. Cabot, *S.S. Venango;* Capt. Chas. Pinkham, *S.S. Queen Wilhelmina;* Capt. A. Traue, *S.S. München;* Capt. W. Thomas, *S.S. Quernmore;* Capt. H. O. Nickerson, Fall River Line; Capt. Geo. Lane, Baltimore Steam Packet Co.

Important assistance was received from Naval Constructor W. J. Baxter, U.S. Navy, who prepared Chapters I and XVIII; and from Lieutenant E. E. Hayden, U.S. Navy, who contributed several Charts and much valuable information upon Meteorology, for Chapter XIX.

Chapter V was suggested by a paper, "Mechanical Appliances on Board Ship," by Captain Thomas Mackenzie, issued by the London Shipmasters' Society as No. 29 of their valuable series of publications.

It would be impossible to mention all the naval officers who have assisted the author with criticism and suggestions; but acknowledgment is especially due to Lieut.-Commander A. W. Grant, Lieut. John Hood, Lieut. W. R. M. Field, Lieut. John Gow, Lieut.-Commander W. F. Worthington, Commander J. E. Pillsbury, Lieut. V. S. Nelson, Lieut. Ridgely Hunt, and Chief Boatswain W. L. Hull, all of the United States Navy.

Above all, acknowledgment is due to Chief Boatswain C. F. Pierce, U.S. Navy, who not only assisted in the preparation of many parts of the text, but prepared sketches for fully one-half the illustrations of the volume.

Austin M. Knight.

United States Naval Academy
April 1, 1901

Contents

PART III   OCEANOGRAPHY AND THE WEATHER

PART IV   RULES OF THE ROAD

APPENDICES

Knight's

Modern
Seamanship

SIXTEENTH EDITION

PART

I

Ships and Boats

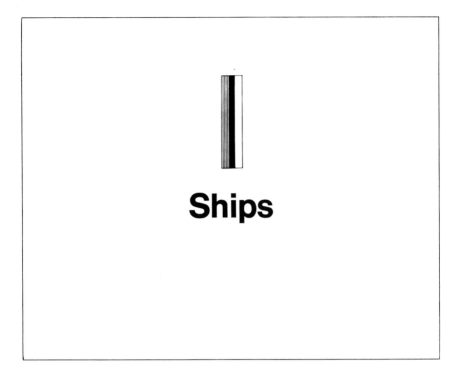

Ships

Ships are classified in several ways: by the materials of which their hulls are built, by their methods of propulsion, by their ownership, or by their uses. It seems handiest and most rational to classify them by their uses. Even in this method of classification we are limited by the fact that many ships are used for more than one purpose, and we must fit our grouping to the primary or principal use of each ship.

The broadest classification of ships by use distinguishes them as MEN-OF-WAR and MERCHANT SHIPS. These were originally the same; each vessel carried on its business of trade or transportation and was at the same time prepared to attack or to defend itself against any enemies encountered. As time went on, nations found it cheaper and more efficient to have certain public vessels designed and armed for warlike purposes only, and to give them the primary function of destroying hostile ships and the protection of their own unarmed merchantmen. Because of new concepts of war and of new inventions, such as the submarine and the airplane, the pendulum has now swung partly back to the point where some merchant ships are built to carry a certain amount of armament and do carry it in wartime.

Men-of-war and merchant ships together are major components of seapower—and upon seapower rests in large part the security as well as the prosperity of the United States of America and of the Free World. Seventy percent of the earth's surface is water; in one sense we and our allies in North America and in South America are islands, surrounded by vast oceans. We must control these oceans not only to provide ourselves with the raw materials for industry, which we need, but to provide weapons and food for our allies in times of emergency. The oceans are also our shield and bulwark: In their depths are concealed nuclear submarines armed with missiles, an invulnerable force to deter our enemies from attack.

It is well to remember that insofar as many important strategic raw materials are concerned the United States is a have-not nation. Only ships can bring us such metals as tin, cobalt, bauxite, and manganese, to mention but a few, that are so vital to our factories.

In keeping the sea trade routes open, in quelling local disorder, and in showing the Flag throughout the world, our country needs ships, both merchant and men-of-war. The Merchant Marine and the Navy are partners in maintaining American seapower.

1.1   Most U.S. Naval Vessels in an active status are commissioned ships, having been formally placed in commission. Such a ship flies a commission pennant (or command flag) to indicate her official status. Service craft are usually placed "in service," rather than "in commission." Ordinarily they have no names, being identified by designation and hull number.

1.2   Classification   The Navy's ships and service craft are officially classified in a list prepared by the Office of the Chief of Naval Operations. This listing has four major categories: combatant ships, combatant craft, auxiliary ships, service craft. Within the combatant ships are: warships (including aircraft carriers, cruisers, destroyers, frigates, patrol combatants, command ships, submarines), amphibious warfare ships, and mine warfare ships. Among combatant craft are: patrol, landing, mine countermeasures, and riverine warfare craft. The misson of auxiliary ships and service craft is to support the combatant ships. (See Table 1.1.)

Combatant Ships

1.3   Aircraft Carriers   The modern attack aircraft carrier (with its airplanes) and the task force built around it are the heart of the Navy's striking power. Features of an aircraft carrier include: island super-

Table 1.1   U.S. Navy Ships and Craft Designations (representative types)

A. Combatant Ships

1. WARSHIPS

Aircraft Carriers

CV	Aircraft Carrier
CVA	Attack Aircraft Carrier
CVAN	Attack Aircraft Carrier (nuclear propulsion)
CVN	Aircraft Carrier (nuclear propulsion)
CVS	ASW Aircraft Carrier

Surface Combatants

Cruisers

CA	Heavy Cruiser
CG	Guided Missile Cruiser
CGN	Guided Missile Cruiser (nuclear powered)

Destroyers

DD	Destroyer
DDG	Guided Missile Destroyer

Frigates

FF	Frigate
FFG	Guided Missile Frigate
FFR	Radar Picket Frigate

Patrol Combatants

PG	Patrol Combatant
PHM	Patrol Combatant Missile (hydrofoil)
PCE	Patrol Escort

Command Ships

CC	Command Ship

Submarines

SS	Submarine
SSN	Submarine (nuclear propulsion)
SSBN	Fleet Ballistic Missile Submarine (nuclear propulsion)
SSG	Guided Missile Submarine

2. AMPHIBIOUS WARFARE SHIPS

LCC	Amphibious Command Ship	LPD	Amphibious Transport Dock
LKA	Amphibious Cargo Ship	LPH	Amphibious Assault Ship
LPA	Amphibious Transport	LSD	Landing Ship Dock
LHA	Amphibious Assault Ship	LST	Landing Ship Tank

3. MINE WARFARE SHIPS

MCS	Mine Countermeasures Ship	MSO	Minesweeper Ocean
MSC	Minesweeper Coastal		

B. Combatant Craft

PCH	Patrol Craft (hydrofoil)	MSB	Minesweeping Boat
PGH	Patrol Gunboat (hydrofoil)	MSI	Minesweeper Inshore
PTF	Fast Patrol Craft	MSR	Minesweeper Patrol
LCM	Landing Craft, Mechanized	ATC	Armored Troop Carrier
LCU	Landing Craft, Utility	PBR	River Patrol Boat
LWT	Amphibious Warping Tug	ASPB	Assault Support Patrol Boat

Table 1.1 *(cont.)*

C. Auxiliary Ships

AD	Destroyer Tender	AOE	Fast Combat Support Ship
AE	Ammunition Ship	AOR	Replenishment Oiler
AFS	Combat Store Ship	AR	Repair Ship
AGS	Surveying Ship	ASR	Submarine Rescue Ship
AH	Hospital Ship	ATF	Fleet Ocean Tug
AO	Oiler	ATS	Salvage and Rescue Ship
AF	Store Ship	ARS	Salvage Ship

D. Service Craft

AFDB	Large Auxiliary Floating Drydock	YNG	Gate Craft
		YOG	Gasoline Barge
APL	Barracks Craft	YP	Patrol Craft
YD	Floating Crane	YTB	Large Harbor Tug
YG	Garbage Lighter	YW	Water Barge

structure and angled flight deck, catapults for launching aircraft, arresting gear for aircraft recovery, hangar deck where planes are stowed and repaired, and large elevators for the rapid transfer of aircraft from deck to deck. The newer CVNs are large enough to carry as many as 100 jet aircraft and accommodate over 4500 sailors of the ship's company and embarked air groups. (See Fig. 1.1.)

1.4 Cruisers Other than aircraft carriers, cruisers are the largest U.S. warships now active. They have a long cruising range, as the name implies, and are capable of high speeds. Guided missiles are the main

Fig. 1.1 The nuclear powered aircraft carrier USS *Nimitz* (CVN 68). (*Official U.S. Navy photograph.*)

weapons of a modern cruiser, enabling the ship to carry out its primary duty of providing antiaircraft defense to a task force.

Cruisers are also armed with conventional guns for use against enemy aircraft, ships, and shore installations—plus ASROC (antisubmarine rockets), helicopters, and torpedoes for use against submarines.

The *Long Beach,* commissioned in 1961, is the Navy's first ship since World War II to be designed and built from the keel up as a cruiser. She is also the world's first nuclear-powered surface ship. Armed with Terrier missiles forward and Talos missiles aft, she has automatic systems for handling and launching both types.

The latest cruiser type is the nuclear powered Guided Missile Cruiser *California* (CGN 36). In addition to surface to air missile armament California is the first warship to be armed with the 5 inch unmanned gun mount. (Fig. 1.2)

1.5 Destroyers Destroyers are not only the most versatile warships in the Navy, but also the most numerous. They are capable of speeds up to 35 knots, and depend on speed and maneuverability for protection. Their primary duty is antisubmarine warfare. However, they are useful in almost any situation—offensive or defensive action against surface

Fig. 1.2 The Navy's nuclear powered guided missile frigate *California* (CGN 36). (*Official U.S. Navy photograph.*)

ships, antiaircraft defense, gunfire support for amphibious operations, or patrol, search, and rescue missions.

The largest destroyer contract in recent years has been given to Litton Industries for the Spruance class (DD 963). These big destroyers have been designed not by the Navy but by civilians who are building them by modular methods in a very advanced assembly-line yard newly constructed in Mississippi. They are 565 feet long, displace 8700 tons, and are gas-turbine driven at over 30 knots. Armament includes missiles and guns for ASW and gunfire support of amphibious landings. (see Fig. 1.3)

Closely associated with destroyers are frigates. They have less speed and less gunfire capability than DDs and specialize in ASW in escorting merchant and naval convoys. The latest frigates are the Knox class.

The Guided Missile Frigate (FFG) is the latest development in the ship types closely associated with destroyers. This class meets the continuing need to replace retiring World War II vintage surface combatants in the 1970's and beyond. The first unit of this class is expected to join the fleet in 1977. These ships will be powered by gas turbines and will be armed with surface-to-surface, surface-to-air missiles, and a 76 MM gun. It will also be equipped to operate two manned helicopters. (Fig. 1.4.)

Fig. 1.3   The gas turbine powered destroyer USS *Spruance* (DD 963) underway during builder's trials. *Spruance* is the first of the Navy's latest class of destroyers and the first U.S. gas turbine large combatant. (*Official U.S. Navy photograph.*)

Fig. 1.4 An artist's conception of the FFG-7 class guided missile frigate. (*Official U.S. Navy photograph.*)

1.6 Submarines The SS, or submarine—often called *attack submarine*—locates and destroys ships, especially other submarines. Surfaced, an SS operates on diesel power; submerged, on battery power. A ship with the same mission is the SSN, a nuclear-powered submarine (or nuclear attack submarine.) It is an improved ship in many respects, not the least of which is the method of propulsion.

SSBN There are certain aspects of the fleet ballistic missile submarine that set it apart. It is not a part of the nation's general-purpose defense forces, rather, it is an element of the nation's strategic deterrence forces. Also, the SSBN has two crews, one to relieve the other following the 60-day submerged patrol. (Fig. 1.5.)

SSBNs range up to 525 feet in length and 7250 tons displacement, by far the world's largest submarines. Older ones carry the A-3 Polaris missile; newer ones, the Poseidon missile with its multiple warhead.

Latest in the SSBN class of submarines are those designed for the TRIDENT missile. The TRIDENT is the most recent of the line of submarine launched ballistic missiles and is capable of hitting strategic targets at ranges in excess of four thousand miles.

Fig. 1.5 The *U.S.S. George Washington* (SSBN 598) under way. *(Official U.S. Navy photograph.)*

1.7 Other Warships *Patrol ships* also come under the warship heading. Foremost among this type is the PG, or patrol gunboat, which interdicts and destroys coastal shipping and carries out patrol, blockade, and surveillance tasks. The hydrofoil gunboat has submerged foils that cause it to plane at higher speeds, that is, to become supported not by the hull but by the foils. Advantages of this are much higher speeds and a smoother ride. (Fig. 1.6.)

Fig. 1.6 Sharp lines of the patrol gunboat *U.S.S. Crockett* (PG 88) stand out in this view. *(Official U.S. Navy photograph.)*

1.8   Amphibious Warfare Ships   All ships of this specialty are designated with an initial *L:* LPA, for example, or LKA. The former is the amphibious transport, the latter is the amphibious cargo ship. The very names give an indication of the several missions: tank landing ship, amphibious fire support ship, amphibious command ship, and so on.

The newest type among the amphibs is the LHA, a general-purpose amphibious assault ship. It combines the individual tasks of other amphibious types, and its function is to transport and land troops and their combat gear by means of embarked helicopters, landing craft, and amphibian vehicles.

The LPH (Fig.1.7)—amphibious assault ship—resembles a small aircraft carrier. It lands troops with its embarked helicopters as does the amphibious transport dock (LPD). The LPD also launches assault craft from its floodable docking well as does the dock landing ship (LSD).

The LCC (Fig. 1.8)—amphibious command ship—is the flagship and co-ordination center for the Amphibious Force Commander and his staff. It has extensive communications and command and control facilities.

1.9   Mine Warfare Ships   These ships are concerned with the sweeping or the laying of mines. The MSC—coastal minesweeper—sweeps magnetic, acoustic, contact, and other mines in waters up to 5 fathoms deep. The MSO—ocean minesweeper—sweeps mines from the 5- to

Fig. 1.7   The amphibious assault ship *U.S.S. Iwo Jima* (LPH 2) under way off the coast of San Diego, California. *(Official U.S. Navy photograph.)*

Fig. 1.8 Amphibious command ship USS *Mount Whitney* (LCC 20). (*Official U.S. Navy photograph.*)

100-fathom curve. Both types use wood and nonmagnetic metals in their construction.

Combatant Craft

The vessels known as naval craft are smaller than ships, more restricted in range, and limited in crew facilities. Thus they are usually dependent on tenders (or mother ships) or on shore facilities.

There are four categories of combatant craft and some 25 different types. Three categories relate to already-mentioned forms of warfare: landing craft, mine countermeasurers craft, and patrol craft. The other category is riverine warfare craft. Among the latter are certain types that reached full development in the river-war of Vietnam: fast patrol craft, river patrol boats, monitors, and command and control boats.

Landing craft operate largely between ship and shore, and their titles commence with "landing craft"; for example: landing craft mechanized (LCM), landing craft utility (LCU), landing craft vehicle personnel (LCVP). An exception is the amphibious warping tug (LWT).

Five different types comprise the mine countermeasures group. These are the minesweeping boat and minesweeping drone as well as: inshore craft, river craft and patrol craft.

Table 1.2 Warship Data for Ships and Their Classes

Ship	Year of Completion, Conversion, or Commissioning	Overall Length (feet)	Full-load Tonnage	Maximum Speed (knots)	Features
COMBATANT SHIPS					
Aircraft Carriers and Cruisers					
CVN: *Nimitz*	1973	1092	95,100	30+	Initial fuel for 13 years; Sea Sparrow missiles and 2
CVN: *Kennedy*	1968	1048	61,000	35	Twin Terriers and Sea Sparrow missiles
CVN: *Enterprise*	1961	1123	83,300	35	Twin Terriers
CVA: *Kitty Hawk*	1961	1062	75,200	35	
CVA: *Forrestal*	1956	1039	78,000	33	
CVA: *Ticonderoga*	1944	895	41,700	33	
CGN: *Long Beach*	1961	721	17,400	35	First nuclear-powered surface warship
CGN: *California*	1972	596	10,200	30+	Missiles; 5-inch 54 guns; multi-purpose nuclear-powered
CGN: *Truxton*	1967	564	9200	30+	Missiles; guns; nuclear-powered
CGN: *Bainbridge*	1962	564	8700	30+	Terrier, 3-inch guns, ASROC
CG: *Belknap*	1964	547	7900	30+	Missiles and guns
CG: *Albany*	1962	673	17,500	33	Twin Talos; Twin Tartar
CG: *Little Rock*	1960	610	14,600	32	Twin Talos aft, 6-inch guns forward
Destroyers and Frigates					
DD: *Spruance*	1975	565	8700	30+	Gas turbine drive; highly automated weapons system

Table 1.2   (Cont.)

Ship	Year of Completion, Conversion, or Commissioning	Overall Length (feet)	Full-load Tonnage	Maximum Speed (knots)	Features
DDG: C. F. Adams	1960	432	4500	30+	
FF: Garcia	1964	415	3400	30+	Major function ASW
FFG: Brooke	1966	415	3400	30+	Major function ASW
Submarines					
SSBN: Lafayette	1966	425	7300	30	Both Poseidon and Polaris missiles carried this class
SSBN: Geo. Washington	1959	382	6000	30	Polaris missiles; 20 knots on surface as for all subs
SSN: Permit	1962	279	3700	30	
SSN: Skipjack	1959	251	3100	30	Torpedoes; antisub missiles
AMPHIBIOUS WARFARE SHIPS					
LCC: Blue Ridge	1970	620	17,000	20	Command and communications ship
LKA: Charleston	1968	575	16,000	20	Carries assault equipment and supplies
LPA: Paul Revere	1958	565	17,000	20	Carries troops and assault boats
LPD: Austin	1965	570	17,000	20	Carries both troops (1000) and equipment
LPH: Iwo Jima	1961	553	13,500	20	Helicopter ship for landing troops by air
LSD: Anchorage	1969	553	13,500	20	Carries landing craft inside in docking well

Designation	Year	Tonnage	Length	Number	Description
Mine Warfare Ships					
MCS: *Ozark*	1967	9000	440	20	Countermeasures, minecraft
MSO: *Agile*	1956	750	172	17	Wood and bronze nonmagnetic sweeper
MSC: *Bluebird*	1953	370	144	15	Sweeps mines in coastal waters
COMBATANT CRAFT					
PGH: *Flagstaff*	1968	60	75	50	Hydrofoil gunboat (prototype)
LCM: (numbered)	Various	55–170	55–75	9	Landing craft for amphibious landings
LCU: (numbered)	Various	375	135	11	Landing craft for amphibious landings
MSB: (numbered)	1951	39	57	12	Minesweeping boat
PBR: (numbered)	1967	8	31	25	River patrol boat
PCF: (numbered)	1966	22	50	28	Inshore patrol, a "swift" boat
AUXILIARY SHIPS					
AD: *Samuel Gompers*	1967	21,600	643	18+	Support ship, repairs, maintenance for DD types
AFS: *Mars*	1963	16,500	581	20	Underway supply ship for fleet
AE: *Nitro*	1959	17,500	512	21	Underway missile supply ship
AH: *Repose*	1945	15,400	520	20	Hospital ship, 800 beds
AO: *Truckee*	1955	40,000	655	18	Underway fuel oil supplier
AOE: *Camden*	1967	53,600	793	18	Underway fuel ammo, etc. supplier
AOR: *Wichita*	1969	38,000	659	18	Underway fuel stores, etc. supplier
AS: *Hunley*	1962	18,500	599	18	Support, maintenance for SSBN
ATS: *Edenton*	1971	3,117	283	16	Rescue and salvage Tug

Auxiliary Ships

There are more than 50 different types of auxiliary ships. Of these, the most dynamic are those that carry out underway replenishment such as: ammunition ships, combat stores ships, replenishment oilers, and fast combat support ships.

Some attend to the needs of other ships (destroyer tender, submarine tender). Some specialize in repair work (repair ship, cable repair ship, landing craft repair ship); or in rescue and salvage missions (fleet ocean tug, salvage tug, salvage ship, salvage lifting ship.) Some have duties of a scientific nature (environmental research ship, missile range instrumentation ship, oceanographic research ship, surveying ship); and some types do not come under any grouping (distilling ship, degaussing ship, and net laying ship).

Service Craft

The emphasis here is on *craft*—and for the greater part, these vessels are not self-propelled. The range of types is wide for it extends from floating drydocks capable of berthing aircraft carriers on down to water barges, floating pile drivers, and garbage lighters.

MSC Ships

1.10 Ships of the Military Sealift Command carry defense cargoes for all the armed forces. Part of this is done by U.S. Flag Merchant vessels under charter to MSC, and part is done by the "nucleus fleet" of government owned, civilian manned vessels. The nucleus fleet consists of freighters, tankers, special purpose cargo carriers, and oceanographic research/ scientific support vessels. MSC nucleus ships are considered to be "in service" and are designated U.S. Naval Ship the name being preceded by USNS (see Fig. 1.9).

Most MSC cargo type vessels are now of the specialized cargo carrier type. These special types include roll on/roll off vehicle carriers, heavy lift ships, and specialized ordnance carriers. The largest part of the nucleus fleet is now engaged in hydrographic/oceanographic work for the navy and in satellite tracking and other related aerospace research.

MSC has also undertaken to man several replenishment oilers of the T-3 class formerly manned by Naval Personnel. These ships with civilian crews are continuing to perform the same underway replenishment of the fleet services a they did when manned by the Navy. This project was undertaken to reduce the cost of operation of these vessels and to release Naval personnel to other duties.

Fig. 1.9 *U.S.N.S. Sea Lift*, a ship of the Military Sealift Command. Built in 1965, 12,000 tons, with roll on/roll off facilities for vehicles. *(Official U.S. Navy photograph.)*

U.S. Coast Guard Ships and Craft

1.11 Cutters Ships or larger craft in the Navy are collectively known as *cutters* in the Coast Guard's fleet. All contribute to one or more of the Coast Guard's primary missions. Principal cutter types are: high-endurance, medium-endurance, large patrol craft, small patrol craft, icebreaker, and buoy tender .

High-endurance cutters (WHEC) have the ability to stay at sea for extended periods, and to make mid-ocean rescues. Four classes of this cutter exist, the latest being the 385-foot class, which has a full load displacement of 3050 tons and a crew of about 165. Rated at 36,000 horsepower, they have a top speed of 29 knots, a cruising range of 12,000 miles at 20 knots. Tasks are search and rescue, oceanography, military operations, and law enforcement. (See Fig. 1.10.)

Medium-endurance cutters (WMEC) perform their missions in a zone extending to about 500 miles off U.S. coasts. Cutters of the 210-foot class have a 930-ton displacement and a diesel or diesel/gas turbine drive rated at 5000 horsepower. Cruising range is 5000 miles at 18 knots.

Patrol craft of the Coast Guard have law enforcement, search and rescue, and port security functions. There are more than 100 patrol craft (WPB) in two classes. Large patrol craft (95-foot—*Cape* names) displace from 98 to 106 tons and have a 15-man crew. Small patrol craft (82-foot—*Point* names) displace about 65 tons.

During 1965–66 the Navy transferred to the Coast Guard's icebreaker

Fig. 1.10   The 378-foot U.S. Coast Guard Cutter *Hamilton*, first built of her class of modern high-endurance cutters, heads out into the North Atlantic from her home port at Boston, Massachusetts. Her primary duties are long-range search and rescue, ocean station patrol, oceanographic research and gathering of meteorological data, and military readiness. (*Official U.S. Coast Guard photograph.*)

force its own five icebreakers. Thus the latter service now has the national icebreaking mission. Most icebreakers are of the *Wind* class: length 269 feet, beam 64 feet, displacement 6500 tons.

Other Government Ships

1.12   Other types of U.S. public vessels include ships and craft of the Army, and of the Interior and Commerce departments. The Army Corps of Engineers operates about 45 dredges (cutter-head, bucket, dipper, hopper, etc.) in channel-and-harbor maintenance. At Army Transportation Corps locations, a few hundred mechanized and utility landing craft, yard tugs, lighters, and other workboat types carry on in support of local transportation efforts.

Commerce Department ships are under the control of the National Oceanic and Atmospheric Administration. They carry the hull letters NOAA, an acronym you will see often in this volume.

These ships start with Class I ocean survey ships, "all oceans, all climates" vessels of the *Discovery* class, which measure 303 feet in length, 52 feet in beam. Then come medium survey and coastal survey ships. Next, auxiliary survey vessels—90-footers with limited range and capability. (Fig. 1.11.)

Interior Department ships and craft are equipped for biological and geological ocean research, and marine mining and fisheries development. Most measure 150 feet and upward, and were built during the 1950s and 1960s. Some are conversions, but the majority were designed and built for their specific research task.

Fig. 1.11 The NOAA *Oceanographer*, a research ship operated by the National Oceanic and Atmospheric Administration.

Merchant Ships

1.13   Merchant ships fall into these broad categories: freighters, dry bulk carriers, tankers, passenger ships, coastal and harbor craft. By methods of propulsion, they are either steamships or motorships. More specifically and in the order of their development, these methods are: steam reciprocating, steam turbine (low or high pressure), diesel, turbo-electric, diesel electric, gas turbine, turbo-charged diesel, and nuclear-powered (using a nuclear reactor for heat source).

Cargoes vary greatly—dry or liquid, low value (i.e., sand and gravel) or high value (automobiles and electronics parts). There are as many variations among merchant ships as among warships. As the years go by there is an increased tendency toward specialization.

Break Bulk Cargo Ship—Freighter   This is the ship that, making regular runs on regular schedules, carries a variety of commodities in its cargo holds. Break bulk cargo ships handle material in or out of holds by means of cargo nets, pallets, barrel slings, and other devices. A representative ship is the *S.S. American Ranger:* length, 507½ feet; beam, 75 feet; draft, 32 feet; deadweight tonnage, 13,264. It has a steam turbine drive and is rated at 20 knots.

Container Ship   In contrast to the freighter's "open" cargo, the cargo handled by a container ship is already stowed in containers— large boxes of various material: aluminum alloys, steel, plywood, etc.

Container ships tend to utilize containers of the same size (i.e., 8 × 8 × 20 feet or 8 × 8 × 40 feet), which provides for uniformity in handling and stowage. A recent development in ocean shipping and the key to inter-modal transport, container ships generally are larger and faster than freighters. Ships of the *Hawaiian Enterprise* class are a good example: about 1000 24-foot containers are carried—560 below decks and 456 on deck. These large ships can make the San Francisco–Hawaii run in 3½ days. (See Figs. 1.12 and 1.13.)

Most carriers involved in the container ship service now use computer loading in the major terminal ports to speed the loading process and to insure that cargoes in the containers are staged in the proper order for unloading in different ports and also for optimum weight distribution to insure ship stability and trim.

Ro/Ro and Lash   The "container revolution" has been accompanied by two other types. While neither has the impact of the container ship, they do have features that hold bright promise in ocean shipping. The roll on/roll off ships are essentially vehicle carriers. Vehicles of all types—along with trailer-mounted containers—are driven aboard ship

Fig. 1.12 Container ship *S.S. American Legion*, owned by United States Lines. Length, 700 feet; 22,000 tons; built in 1968.

Fig. 1.13 *G.T.S.* (gas turbine ship) *Euroliner*, the first private application of gas turbine power to ocean shipping, is the newest and most modern container ship. First of four ordered for Seatrain Lines, Inc., these 800-foot, 32,000-ton ships can do 26 knots and are driven by gas turbines. *Euroliner* can carry 960 40-foot containers.

through side and stern cargo ports. Then, through a system of internal ramps, they are spotted in position for the ocean crossing. Lash is short for *lighter aboard ship.* They are also known as barge carriers, but there is more to it than sealifting barges. Cargo-collecting barges service loading points at distances from the central ship—the Lash ship. Taken aboard, they are later discharged at the off-loading port. (See Fig. 1.14.)

Dry Bulk Carrier   Dry bulk carriers are limited in the range of items they carry. However, those they do carry are equally essential: grains, fertilizer, coal, sugar, iron ore, aluminum ore, dry chemicals, and so on. It is material without mark or count, and carried in shipload lots. Some bulk carriers are self-loaders, in that they have the capability of loading (and unloading) their own cargoes. Others depend on pierside facilities.

Tankers   In a sense tankers are also bulk carriers. But because of their great numbers in world shipping and their cargo product, they comprise a type of their own. Tankers carry POL products (petroleum, oil, lubricants.) Their main single cargo is bulk oil. The world's largest ships—of some 300,000 deadweight tons (plus) and 80-foot draft—are regularly employed in the transportation of oil from Middle Eastern oil fields to offshore discharge points in Europe and the Far East. (See Fig. 1.15.)

Liquid Bulk Carrier   Ships of this type resemble tankers, but their cargo products are different. They illustrate merchant shipping's ten-

Fig. 1.14 The *S.S. Acadia Forest*, a lash ship showing the barge-handling gear.

Fig. 1.15 The largest merchant ship ever built in the United States, the 225,000 deadweight ton tanker *Brooklyn* leaves New York harbor on her maiden voyage. The *Brooklyn* was built by Seatrain Building Corp. at the old Brooklyn Navy yard. The supertanker is 1,094 ft. (335m), and is capable of carrying 1.5 million barrels of oil. (*Courtesy U.S. Dept. of Commerce Maritime Administration.*)

dency toward specialization. Some of these ships are liquefied gas carriers, carrying gas (i.e., butane, propane) under refrigeration and great pressure. Some transport liquefied natural gas at −259°F. Others carry wine, orange juice, or liquid ammonia.

Combined Ore/Oil Regardless of type, merchant ships have compartmentalization—which means that one hold can be well sealed off from another. In essence, combined oil/ore carriers—and ore/bulk/oil carriers (OBOs)—utilize different holds for transport at one time of mixed bulk cargoes.

Passenger Ships Passenger ships, of course, carry people. As contrasted with cargo ships, they are few in number, their decline in past years having been attributed to rapid transoceanic air transport. The largest of the passenger ships, or ocean liners as they are sometimes called, also carry cargo. In contrast is a type of passenger ship that also stresses cargo: the passenger-combination ship. As a general rule, these accommodate between 12 and 40 passengers. Some characteristics of passenger ships are their larger size, higher speeds, hotel-like

Fig. 1.16 The SS *Manhattan*, after conversion, makes the first northwest passage by commercial vessel. She began her historic voyage at Chester, Pa., August 24, 1969, and returned to New York, November 12, 1969. More than 9,000 tons of steel and equipment were used to provide the tanker with ice-breaking capabilities. (*Courtesy U.S. Dept. of Commerce Maritime Administration.*)

Fig. 1.17   Drawing of the latest States Line RO/RO ship.

accommodations, special safety features, numerous lifeboats, and moderate capacity for baggage, mail, and special cargo. Most large passenger ships sail part of the time on round-trip cruises.

Towboats and Tugs

1.14   Towboats   These are a numerous and important type of specialized commercial craft. On rivers, canals, and other inland waterways they pull or push other vessels, providing the propulsion and direction to move them to their destinations. Some are designed to push long strings of barges ahead of them.

1.15   Commercial Tugs   Included here are harbor tugs, seagoing tugs, and salvage tugs. Like towboats, practically all are diesel-powered. Harbor tugs move lighters and railroad car floats from place to place and help to dock large ships. Seagoing tugs often tow strings of barges along the coasts. Some measure 100 feet in length and can handle transoceanic tows. Salvage tugs are built to render aid to the largest of ships, even under the most arduous conditions. A first-rate tug of this kind will exceed 280 feet in length and have a 17,500-horsepower drive. Her 25-man crew will handle elaborate navigation and firefighting equipment, large pumps, and automatic-tension towing winches.

Boats and Other Craft

2.1 Introduction Boats are waterborne craft capable of limited independent operation. In some cases they are designed to be hoisted aboard ships. When assigned to ships, boats are used for transporting supplies and people. At sea, such boats serve as lifeboats, one being designated as the "ship's lifeboat." It is maintained in a ready condition at all times for rescue operations, for the training of the crew in man overboard drills, and for general boat training (Fig. 2.1).

Landing craft are a special form of Naval boat used to transport troops, equipment, stores, fuel, and ammunition between the ship and shore during landing operations. They are designed to land directly on the beach. Amphibious tanks (LVT) are over-the-beach assault craft, carrying troops ashore and inland.

2.2 Boat Construction Metal, plastic, and wood are the three materials used in building boats. There is now considerable experience in ferro-cement, a combination of steel and cement. Plastic is being used increasingly for boats under 50 feet in length, while metal or wood is used for the larger boats. Many boats designed for a given purpose have proved successful for other purposes. For example, the 63-foot

Fig. 2.1 A 26-foot plastic-hulled motor whaleboat being lowered from gravity davits. (*Official U.S. Navy photograph.*)

Aviation Rescue Boat (as converted) is used as a gunboat, patrol boat, noise-measuring boat, personnel boat, and torpedo retriever—in addition to its original job of rescuing men from downed aircraft.

2.3   Materials   Marine plywood, plastic, and glass cloth are important materials for pleasure boat construction. Wood is now seldom used for military craft. Some commercial boats are built of molded plywood, in which thin strips, impregnated with glue, are diagonally bent over a mold to the shape of the hull desired, building up a skin of several layers thickness. The mold is then placed in an autoclave where, at increased temperatures, the strips are curved and formed into a one-piece hull—which is light, strong, seamless, and as with all wood hulls, inherently buoyant.

With metal boats, the shell and frames are of welded sheet steel or of aluminum.

Plastic and glass boats dominate current construction in lengths of 50 feet and under. Such boats are built of layers of glass cloth laid in or over a mold of the desired shape for the final hull form. Each layer of cloth is impregnated with either epoxy or polyester resin and the completed hull permitted to dry before being removed from the mold. Plastic boats do not have seams. Those less than 26 feet in length generally use bulkheads for athwartship stiffness rather than frames. Longitudinal strength is provided by plastic members built up inside the shell.

When built in quantity, the cost of plastic boats is comparable to that of wood or metal ones. Upkeep costs are generally less, though there are indications that minor repairs are needed more often. Secondary bonds are particularly troublesome. Plastic boats are impervious to ship worms. In contrast, they are quite susceptible to becoming fouled by marine organisms such as barnacles. These are difficult to remove on plastic hulls, for sand blasting cannot be done without damage to the hull. Therefore it is necessary that the antifouling bottom paint for such boats be renewed at regular intervals. Since paint removers attack the resin, it is difficult to avoid paint and, therefore, weight buildup.

2.4 Buoyancy Lifeboats and personnel boats, regardless of their construction material, are normally fitted with material (plastic foam) or with air tanks to provide sufficient buoyancy to float the craft fully loaded. Styrofoam or cellular cellulose acetate (CCA) are the most popular forms of buoyant material used in wood or metal boats. This material is available in "plank" form and is customarily installed as near the sheer level as possible. In plastic boats it is normal practice to use foam, sometimes mixed and sprayed into spaces, rather than built-in planks.

In self-bailing boats a watertight deck runs the length of the boat slightly above the load waterline. The space below thus becomes a watertight compartment. Water from this deck runs overboard through freeing ports or scuppers in the side of the boat. Water that leaks into the compartments below the deck is pumped out by a bilge pump.

If the buoyancy of a boat can be carried high, above the waterline, the boat will tend to right itself should it capsize. Self-righting boats are built in such a shape as to permit carrying the bow air tanks and stern air tanks high, and are also fitted with a heavy keel. Self-bailing and self-righting features are sometimes combined, as in the larger motor lifeboats used by the Coast Guard.

2.5 Nomenclature Figure 2.2 lists a number of parts for a wood hull. The names of these parts do not change to any marked degree regardless of the material used in building the boat.

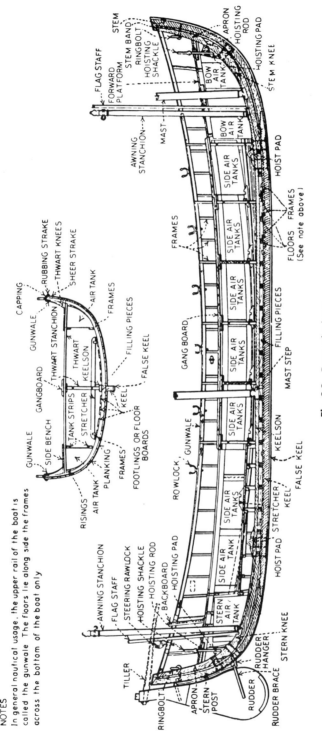

NOTES

In general nautical usage, the upper rail of the boat is called the gunwale. The floors lie along side the frames across the bottom of the boat only

Fig. 2.2 Parts of a boat.

FLAG STAFF
FORWARD PLATFORM
STEM
STEM BAND
RINGBOLT
HOISTING SHACKLE
APRON
HOISTING ROD
HOISTING PAD
STEM KNEE
BOW AIR TANK
AWNING STANCHION
BOW AIR TANK
MAST
SIDE AIR TANKS
HOIST PAD
SIDE AIR TANKS
FRAMES
FLOORS
FRAMES (See note above)
FILLING PIECES
SIDE AIR TANKS
KEELSON
MAST STEP
SIDE AIR TANKS
FALSE KEEL
KEEL
SIDE AIR TANKS
FALSE KEEL
KEELSON
STRETCHER
HOIST PAD
SIDE AIR TANK
STERN AIR TANK
HOISTING PAD
BACKBOARD
HOISTING SHACKLE
HOISTING ROD
STEERING RAWLOCK
FLAG STAFF
AWNING STANCHION
TILLER
RINGBOLT
STERN POST
APRON
RUDDER
RUDDER HANGER
RUDDER BRACE
STERN KNEE
GUNWALE
ROWLOCK
GANG BOARD
FRAMES
AWNING STANCHION
GANGBOARD
GUNWALE
CAPPING
RUBBING STRAKE
THWART KNEES
SHEER STRAKE
THWART STANCHION
THWART
AIR TANK
FRAMES
KEELSON
FILLING PIECES
FALSE KEEL
KEEL
STRETCHER
TANK STRIPS
FRAMES
PLANKING
FOOTLINGS OR FLOOR BOARDS
AIR TANK
RISINGS
SIDE BENCH
GUNWALE

2.6   Identification of Navy Boats and Coast Guard Boats   Reference to a particular boat in any detail should include both its length and type, for example: "26-foot motor whaleboat." Landing craft, however, are properly designated by the abbreviated name, such as "LCM." The hull registry number should also be cited. This number is engraved or bead welded on the hull during construction, and also appears on the hull label place. When boats are painted or repaired, care must be taken to keep the registry number in a legible condition. Coast Guard boats under 100 feet length are referred to by type. Their hull number, on the bow, shows length (first two digits) followed by boat serial number. For example, 44347 would be a 44-foot motor lifeboat, number 347.

2.7   Barges and Gigs   Navy boats assigned for the personal use of flag rank officers are barges (Fig. 2.3). Boats used by commanding officers and chiefs of staff not of flag rank are gigs. The following types of standard boats are often modified and assigned for use as barges or gigs: 26-foot, 28-foot, 33-foot, and 40-foot personnel boats; 35-foot and 40-foot motorboats; 36-foot LCPL. The exterior hull of a barge is painted black. Other Navy boats and craft are painted haze gray. Coast Guard working boats and vessels are black-hulled. Rescue vessels are normally white. All Coast Guard boats now carry the orange slash mark.

2.8   Upkeep and Maintenance   Wooden boats require special attention in providing ventilation and drainage, and in preventing leakage. To this end, all ventilation terminals should be kept open. The laza-

Fig. 2.3 An Admiral's barge underway in the Straits of Magellan. (*Official U.S. Navy photograph.*)

rette, stern, and bilge areas should be provided with a reliable means of ventilation. Standing fresh water, even in small amounts, is particularly harmful.

Deck seams, in the plank sheer area especially, must be carefully caulked and maintained. Decks must be sanded with care to retain the proper camber to allow water runoff and to prevent low areas where fresh water would tend to stand. During fair weather, hatches and deck plates of boats afloat should be opened to increase air circulation. Wet dunnage, rope, and life jackets in lockers and forepeak spaces should be removed and aired out.

Wooden boats should not be washed down with fresh water if there is a chance of water penetration into the wood. Salt water, which has some preservative value, should be used instead. For removing salt accumulations from varnished surfaces, chrome and brass fittings, and windows, the use of fresh water is recommended. Salt does attract moisture from the air, however, so its exclusive use for wooden boats' washdown is no cure-all for rot—which is caused by retention of dampness in timber.

Boat crews must be alert for any leaks beneath the covering board or the deckhouse. Moisture is trapped by thick coats of paint, so overpainting must be avoided. On some wooden boats the stem, stern, and bilge areas are purposely left unpainted. In such areas, wood preservative solutions rather than paints are used.

Metal boats call for added care in the matter of corrosion prevention. Proper upkeep of paint and other coatings in all interior and exterior surfaces is a necessity. The proper number of zincs must be installed in the stern area on steel hulls (as well as on some wood and plastic hulls) to prevent electrolytic corrosion.

2.9 Care of Equipment Propeller shaft alignment should be checked regularly. Crankcase oil should be changed after every 100 hours or so of running time. Boats alongside one another should be separated by boat fenders. When the boat is lifted from the water, the struts, propeller, sea suctions, and shaft bearings must be checked. Worn propellers or worn shaft bearings bring on heavy vibrations, eventually damaging hull and engine. Gear housings, steering mechanisms, and other moving parts must be kept well lubricated.

It is not possible to paint or caulk oil-soaked bottom planking in wooden boats. An oil-soaked bilge is a fire hazard in any boat. When draining or filling fuel tanks or engine crankcases, avoid spillage. Gasoline fumes in bilges are especially dangerous, since a spark from static electricity or ignition of the engine can set off an explosion.

Ashore and aboard ship, wooden blocking and wedges should support a stowed boat's overhang both fore and aft. Chocks should be located opposite frames or bulkheads. In order to spread the stress, the loads imposed by gripe pads should be distributed as widely as possible. Take-up devices on the gripes should be marked at the limit of the tightening required.

Hoisting and Lowering

2.10 Hoisting and Lowering Ships have devices for hoisting and lowering boats. When hoisted (or lowered) by a ship's crane, the boat's hoisting slings are used. When hoisted at the davits, the boat's fore-and-aft shackles are used. The Raymond releasing hook is a standard release device used for attaching or releasing the davit falls from the davit shackles installed in the boat. It is a swivel hook with a tripper hinged at the bill of the hook. The tripper is so weighted at its outer end that when the boat is waterborne and the load is removed from the hook, it automatically tumbles, thus throwing the boat shackle out of the hook and releasing the boat.

When the boat is not waterborne, the load on the hook prevents the tumbling of the tripping device. To speed up "hooking on" prior to lifting the boat, the weighted end of the hook is provided with a lanyard, which is passed through the shackle and held taut in order, first to prevent tumbling of the tripper, and second, to hold the shackle in the hook prior to hoisting. This is not difficult in a flat calm but normally the ship is rolling as the boat rises and falls. This is why many boat crews wear hard hats or helmet liners. The bow hook should be strong, agile, and steady in order to do his job and to avoid a swinging hook both while hooking on and after release.

2.11 Boat Davits Gravity, crescent, quandrantal, and radial or round bar are the usual types of davits. (Fig. 2.4) With the gravity-type davit, the boat is carried in two cradles mounted on rollers. The rollers ride along two parallel tracks at right angles to the ship's side. After the gripes are released, a brake is released. This action permits the boat and the entire assembly to roll down the tracks by gravity, stopping with the lifeboat suspended over the ship's side. Tricing lines swing the boat against the ship's side and hold it in position until frapping lines are passed around the falls and secured, thus holding the boat in position to receive people aboard. After this, the tricing lines are cast adrift by tripping the pelican hooks before the boat is loaded. The next action is that of releasing the brake, which causes the boat to be lowered to the water. A Falls Tensioning Device on modern gravity davits maintains a constant and safe tension on the boat during lowering and hoisting.

The crescent davit is a type of hinging-out davit used on all classes of naval vessels. In this type of davit the arms are crescent-shaped and are moved in and out from the ship's side by means of a sheath screw which may be operated by handcrank or by power.

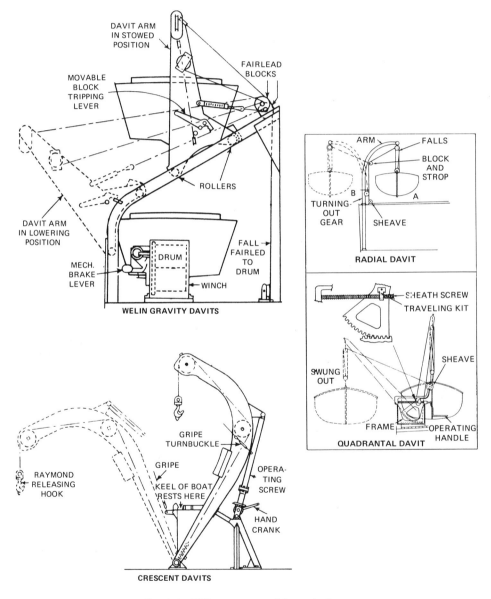

Fig. 2.4 Different types of boat davits.

With quandrantal-type davits, the boat is carried on chocks under the davits. The davits themselves stand upright with the tops curved in toward each other so that the ends come directly above the hoisting hooks of the boat. The davit, which pivots, is turned outboard by a crank operating a worm gear.

With radial or round-bar davits, the boat is carried in chocks, under the davits. Like the two preceding types, these also pivot. Chapter 12 includes a detailed description of the use of radial davits.

Two commercial davits are the Rottmer and the Steward. These feature releasing hooks in each end of the boat to which the falls are attached. Hinged on pins, the hooks are held engaged by a locking device. A jointed shaft running the length of the boat is connected to both locking devices or releasing devices. This can be so configured that each fall can be separately released, which is preferable when the boat is launched or recovered when the ship is underway. Upon throwing a lever attached to this shaft, the hooks are capsized and the boat is released.

The Mills chain-releasing mechanism is also common in the merchant navy. The gear-release handle is conveniently located on deck at the after end of the boat. When this handle is pulled, trigger hooks with ball weights (to which the boat falls are made fast) drop. The boat is then free fore and aft. Before the releasing gear can work, the boat must be waterborne.

2.12 Label Plate Boats in the Navy are fitted with a label plate, which provides data about its design, manufacture, and maximum capacity. The last is calculated in terms of carrying capacity of men (about 10 cubic feet of internal volume per man, based on an average weight per man of 165 pounds, fully clothed and wearing a life jacket).

2.13 Some Specific Boat Types A boat's design is determined largely by: mission or purpose, cargo or personnel capacity, speed, minimum maintenance, and weight in event shipboard stowage is required.

Dinghies are small boats (about 9 feet long) carried aboard somewhat larger craft, such as landing craft and rescue boats. They are a general tender, and can, on occasion, provide transportation for the crew. When equipped with sail, a dinghy is also used for recreation. It is normally equipped with a pair of oars.

Punts are general-purpose workboats, square-ended, and usually used for work along the ship's waterline. Though equipped with oars, they are usually propelled by sculling. Wherries are larger versions of dinghies, and used for the same general duties.

Motor whaleboats are built along the same hull lines as the pulling whaleboats of whaling days. They are necessarily heavier, and their weight makes them considerably less seaworthy. Originally made of wood, motor whaleboats are now made of plastic and are equipped with a wheel and rudder in lieu of a tiller or steering oar.

Personnel boats are similar to commercial cabin cruisers. They carry personnel and are largely replacing the officers' motorboats.

Utility boats are used to transport personnel and cargo. Assigned mainly to shore-based boat pools at first, they are now replacing the shipboard motor launch.

Inflatable lifeboats are carried aboard most Navy ships. They require periodic inspection and testing so that they will function properly when needed. A typical one is the 15-man liferaft, which contains food and other supplies needed in the event the ship is lost.

2.14 Amphibious Craft   See Chapter 1.

2.15 Nondisplacement Craft   The hydrofoil uses underwater foils to obtain lift just as wings lift an airplane in air. With the hull partially above water, resistance is greatly reduced and speed increased. Fixed foils are the most common and are used for ferries up to several hundred feet in length, particularly in Russia on the rivers and lakes. The Supermar PT series, made by Rodriguez in Italy, are used mainly in Europe in sheltered and semi-sheltered waters (Fig. 2.5). Boats with

Fig. 2.5 A Rodriguez (Italian) PT 50 type passenger-carrying hydrofoil. *(Courtesy of Leopoldo Rodriguez.)*

movable foils, controlled by a wave sensor and a computer, have been developed and are more seaworthy because the boat can rise and fall in response to the waves it passes over. Boeing and Grumman in the United States both sold movable-foil hydrofoil gunboats of advanced designs to the U.S. Navy and Boeing hydrofoils are now on order for NATO. These are powered by gas turbines whereas the usual fixed-foil boats use diesel engines. The succesful hydrofoils being built use water-jet propulsion instead of propellers.

Ground Effect Machines (GEM) or hovercraft ride over the waves, marsh, or land on a cushion on air, forward motion being gained by air propellers (Fig. 2.6). These are in service as ferries across the English Channel and are used as military craft and for exploring. A variation that uses water propellers driven by diesel engines for propulsion

Fig. 2.6   British hovercraft, SR N6. *(Courtesy of British Hovercraft Corporation Ltd.)*

is used only in the water. Examples are in service as ferries in the Mediterranean along the French coast. All GEM use gas turbines to provide the air cushion which is contained by a skirt. Large ocean-going GEM are under development as major seagoing merchant vessels. With GEM, greater size promises greater efficiency although problems of structural strength in the event of a forced landing at sea remain acute. Large hydrofoils are also being developed but not over 1000 tons.

2.16 Boat Capacity When people are carried, the designated carrying capacity should not be exceeded; in carrying stores, the load in pounds (of both men and stores) should not exceed the maximum allowable cargo load. Passengers, stores, and baggage should not be carried topside on motorboats. If stores and baggage are carried in motorboats, the number of passengers should be reduced. The man in charge of the boat, either the coxswain or the senior officer embarked, must make this judgment carefully, as several catastrophic accidents will attest. The factors of weather and sea conditions must not be ignored, despite inconveniences due to reduced loads.

2.17 U.S. Coast Guard Boats The Coast Guard develops and employs many boats. Some are used aboard ships; many are operated from shore stations. The 52-foot motor lifeboat is designed for rescue work in rough seas. A double-ender, it is steel-hulled with the superstructure and interior trim being made of aluminum alloy. The diesel engines drive twin screws. Other features are: fire and salvage pumps of a 500-gallon-per-minute capacity, improved visibility and protection at steering stations, power-driven windlass and capstan, forced ventilation and electric heating for the compartments.

The 40-foot utility boat is a general-purpose, twin-screw diesel-engined craft that meets requirements for light rescue, security, and offshore duty.

The 36-foot motor lifeboat is a heavy-duty, steel-hulled, self-righting nonsinkable lifeboat. Capable of action in heavy storms, this craft is a Coast Guard standby.

The 44-foot motor lifeboat is a larger, later, and more advanced craft than the preceding. It has a crew of 3, but a capacity for 40 men, with a 16-knot speed and a 150-mile cruising range. It is well suited for its search and rescue duties and is so designed that it handles well under heavy sea and surf conditions. (See Fig. 2.7.)

The 30-foot utility boat is similar to its 40-foot big brother, with many of its features. A diesel-powered, single-screw craft, it is designed for light rescue, security, and offshore work. The hull is of

Fig. 2.7 A 44-foot U.S. Coast Guard steel motor lifeboat, the CG 44303, rides the crest of a spurning wave at the entrance to Umpqua River, Oregon, near where the boat recently performed the awesome feat of rolling over in the dangerous curl of a series of high waves and kept on operating. *(Official U.S. Coast Guard photograph.)*

plastic. Developmental work for the 30-footer hull and the power package for the new 30- and 40-footers was accelerated by competition in several Miami-Nassau powerboat races. Diesel-powered rough-water craft, the test boats placed well.

The 26-foot pulling self-bailing surf boat is carvel-built and oar-propelled. It is steered by a sweep, and is light enough to be moved by trailer along the beach and launched on the beach. Even smaller is the 16-foot (plastic) outboard motorboat. Manned by a boarding team, this boat is powered by a 35-horsepower outboard, and is used chiefly on inland waters.

2.18 Merchant Marine Lifeboats Ships of the U.S. Merchant Marine are subject to the construction and safety standards administered by the Coast Guard in conformity with an international agreement among the world's maritime nations. Under this agreement, all large oceangoing cargo ships and tankers must provide a lifeboat capacity of 200 percent for all persons aboard. In contrast, the lifeboat capacity of an ocean-going passenger ship is reduced to 100 percent, because the ship's hull is built to higher standards of internal subdivision.

The most recently built lifeboats in this country are of steel, aluminum, or fiberglass construction with internal blocks of plastic foam to provide extra buoyancy. Each lifeboat is required to be equipped with a considerable inventory of survivial equipment, including food, drinking water, and pyrotechnic signals. Diesel-propelled and hand-propelled lifeboats are also in use. The hand-propelled mechanism consists of a propeller that is driven by a flywheel, that in turn is rotated by a hand lever-and-crank system operated by the occupants seated in the lifeboat.

2.19 Inflatable Liferafts   Inflatable liferafts supplement the lifeboats carried by passenger vessels in the merchant marine. These rafts are also the primary lifeboats on board Navy and Coast Guard vessels. A naval vessel such as a large carrier can not possibly carry sufficient boats to act as lifeboats in case the ship must be abandoned. The answer is the inflatable liferaft. Large aircraft carriers carry in some cases over two hundred of these rafts. Liferafts in the deflated condition are very compact and easy to stow. They can in most cases be launched by one or two men or

Fig. 2.8   Inflatable raft being launched from the side of a ship. (*Photograph courtesy of the Switlik Parachute Co., manufacturer of the raft shown.*)

Fig. 2.9   Inflatable raft shown fully inflated in the water. (*Photograph courtesy of the Switlik Parachute Co., manufacturer of the raft shown.*)

by hydrostatic action (Fig. 2.8). CO_2 bottles contained in the raft inflate the raft automatically after a tug on the seapainter. Modern rafts are extremely seaworthy and provide excellent protection for the occupants from the elements (Fig. 2.9). Rafts are available in sizes ranging from a small four man raft suitable for small boats or yachts up to rafts of twenty five man capacity. The most up to date rafts are shipped and stowed in cylindrical fiberglass containers which keep the rafts from exposure to the elements and to damage from the sun and stack sediment burns. The container permits the raft to be sealed, allowing prevention of pilferage of raft supplies.

Rafts for use on board merchant vessels, U.S. Coast Guard vessels, and private yachts must meet the construction requirements of the Coast Guard. Such rafts must also be reinspected by an authorized test facility at specified intervals.

Fishing Craft and Equipment

Commercial fisheries are of two general types: pelagic and demersal. Pelagic species are those which live at or near the surface of the sea; demersal species inhabit the sea bottom. Distinct craft and gear have evolved for catching each of these types of fish.

2.20   Craft for Pelagic Fishing   Pelagic fish include mackerel, herring, tuna, and shark. They habitually travel in schools that move rapidly through the upper layers of the ocean. The captain in quest of pelagic fish selects his fishing ground through past experience or sometimes from interpretation of sea temperature and other oceanographic data. He pinpoints his quarry by eye or by underwater sound. For visual search, pelagic fishing craft are equipped with a crow's nest and high-power optics. A helicopter or light airplane may be employed to extend search range. Fish-finding sound gear ranges from simple flasher type depth indicators through recording echo sounders to scanning-type "fish scopes." High sonic frequencies give sharp resolution which shows echoes from schools or even from single fish as well as from the sea floor.

Once located, pelagic fish are taken by purse seines, drift nets, harpoon, and hook and line. Purse seiners take much of the world pelagic catch. A purse seine is a long deep net of small mesh. The seiner, usually with the aid of one or more workboats, lays the net in a circle around a school of fish and joins the ends. The bottom is then closed by a purse line strung through eyes along the lower edge of the net. When hauled in, the purse line acts as a draw string, gathering together the bottom of the seine and preventing the escape of the fish. (See Fig. 2.10.) The net is then brought on deck—by hand in smaller or older boats, by power block in larger and more modern craft—until the catch is concentrated in a small pocket of remaining water. The fish are then taken aboard by dip nets or by fish pumps.

A typical New England mackerel seine measures 1500 feet along the cork line (upper edge) by 30 feet deep. Heavy and expensive, it includes nearly 3000 corks, 2000 leads, 30 six-inch purse rings, and 350 fathoms of steel, nylon, or manila purse line. Other seines are larger; a typical West Coast tuna seine is about twice as long and ten times deeper. The cost may range into tens of thousands of dollars.

Figure 2.11 shows an Alaskan salmon seiner. The net is stowed on the low, wide fantail on top of a rotating turntable. A power-operated roller and a heavy boom are used to handle the seine. The high bow and bridge give excellent sea-keeping qualities, and the crow's nest gives the lookout good visibility. The skiff is stowed atop the seine. Tuna seiners are larger, faster and longer-legged. The newest ships are 200 feet or

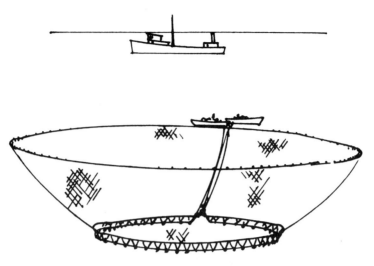

Fig. 2.10 Purse seine.

more overall, capable of 16 knots, with a long high seas endurance. They can fish the most distant grounds. Seiners based in California work grounds in the South Pacific and eastern tropical Atlantic.

Another pelagic fishing craft, the tuna clipper, uses hook and line. Like the tuna seiner, it was originally a Pacific type but has recently fished off

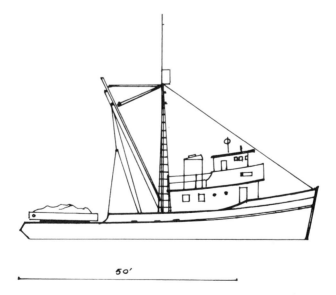

Fig. 2.11 Alaskan salmon seiner.

the Atlantic coast of Africa. In both oceans it ranges far beyond the continental shelf in search of large tuna, particularly the skipjack. After a school is located, the clipper attracts them alongside by throwing overboard bait fish. The tuna strike large feathered, barbless jig hooks, with two or three poles and lines attached to each jig. The hands swing the tuna on deck, shake them off the hook, and strike them below in refrigerated holds.

The tuna clipper in Fig. 2.12, like the purse seiner, is built for long voyages on the high seas. It has a high crow's nest for good visibility, and a low stern with outboard "racks" or stages for the pole handlers. A tank aft holds the live bait, and there are facilities to trim down aft so that the racks are nearly at sea level. Cold storage capacity may be as great as 1000 tons. Clippers carry lampara nets to catch bait and sometimes purse seines for taking the smaller varieties of tuna.

The drifter is another common type of pelagic fisherman. As illustrated by Fig. 2.13, drifting gear consists of long "fleets" of gill nets. Each net is about ten fathoms long by several fathoms deep. The mesh is larger than that of a purse seine, wide enough so that fish can pass only part way through. They are then entangled in the mesh until brought on board and pulled free by the fishermen. The drifter "shoots" up to 100 nets in a continuous line suspended near the surface by wooden or plastic floats. Nets are laid at dusk so that the fish cannot see the mesh. Moored to the leeward end, the boat drifts until dawn—whence the name "drifter"— then the nets are hauled and the catch recovered. Sometimes they are hauled by hand, to an increasing extent, by a powerful winch or reel.

The drifter is particularly important in European pelagic fisheries. A

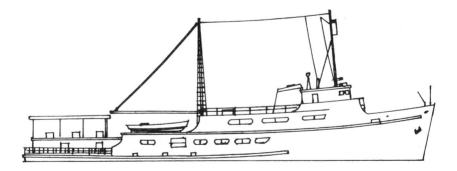

50'

Fig. 2.12 Tuna clipper.

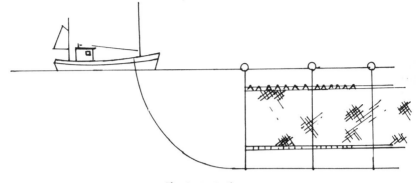

Fig. 2.13   Drift net.

typical North Sea drifter is shown in Fig. 2.14. Designed to work grounds close to port, the drifter brings in its catch fresh. Slow and rugged, it has limited accomodations and few comforts. The foremast mounts a long boom for handling the catch. The mast is often mounted in a tabernacle so that it can be lowered to increase stability. The short mainmast carries a steadying sail to reduce rolling and keep the boat headed into the wind. Drifters vary in size from small 20-footers to modern craft of over 100 feet.

In many parts of the world pelagic fish are taken by trolling. The Bay of Biscay tunny fishery was worked for many years by sailing craft called *thoniers.* Ruggedly built yawls and ketches, now replaced by power

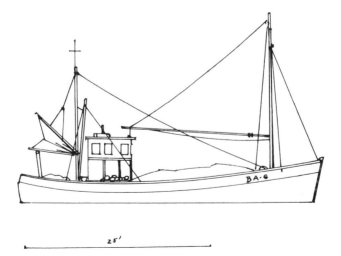

Fig. 2.14   North Sea motor drifter.

boats, they streamed their baits from long lines attached to *tagnons* or poles. The salmon fishery in the U.S. Pacific Northwest is also worked by trolling. A typical troller is shown in Fig. 2.15. Diesel powered, it is flush decked with mast and deckhouse forward. Six or eight lines can be handled, and a power winch or "gurdy" is fitted to pull in the hooked fish.

Whales, although mammals, comprise a pelagic fishery. Over-exploitation has reduced their numbers severely, and most countries except Japan and Russia have abandoned whaling. Highly organized flotillas of store ships, tankers, factory ships, whale catchers, carcass towers, and aircraft spend the season in the North Pacific in Antarctic

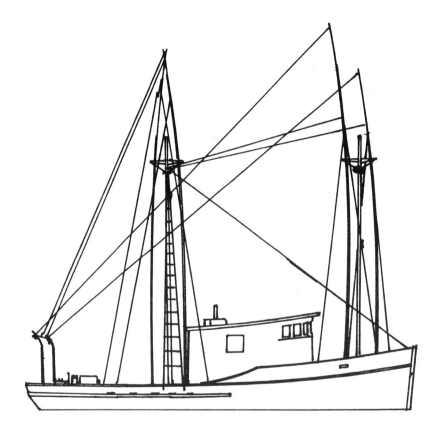

25′

Fig. 2.15 Salmon troller.

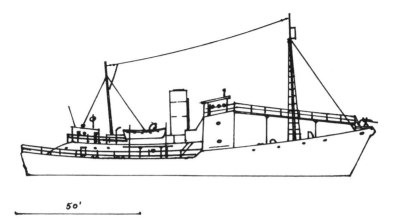

50'

Fig. 2.16 Whale catcher.

waters. A whale catcher is a fast, maneuverable craft mounting a harpoon gun. Its job is to pursue the whale, harpoon it, buoy the carcass, and set off after another whale. The carcass is towed to the factory ship where it is hauled aboard and processed.

A whale catcher is shown in Fig. 2.16. Steam propelled, it can make about 15 knots. A catwalk from forecastle to bridge allows the harpooner to man his gun even in heavy seas.

2.21 Demersal Fishing Gear   Cod, flounder, pollack, and shellfish are among the most important demersal fish. They are usually taken by trawling. The term "trawler," commonly applied to many types of fishermen, should properly be reserved for vessels that use trawls. An otter trawl is sketched in Fig. 2.17. A cone-shaped net bag, its forward end is spread open either by a beam, in the smaller sizes, or by a pair of otter boards or "doors." Weights in the form of steel bobbins or chains hold the lower edge of the mouth on the sea bottom, while steel or aluminum floats on a head rope support the upper edge. Otter boards are heavy flat sructures of steel or steel-reinforced wood. Rigged to tow at an angle like underwater kites, they can extend a trawl mouth 100 feet wide and 15 feet high. Long warps allow the trawl to be dragged along the bottom in water as deep as 200 fathoms. The rugged construction of a large trawl permits catches of 25,000 pounds or more. The midwater trawl, a recent develpment, is towed at an intermediate depth between bottom and surface. Fish finder sonar, either with a tilting hull mount or a towed transducer, tells the skipper the depth and direction of the school so that he can tow the trawl through it.

To stream his gear, the trawler lies to across the wind. He then lowers the trawl over the side and begins to circle around it. As he approaches

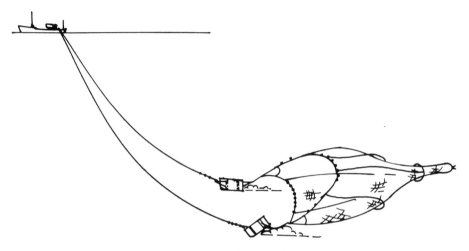

Fig. 2.17   Otter trawl.

the trawling course he lowers the otter boards. The warps are paid out as the trawl doors set properly. In 200 fathoms of water, about 450 to 600 fathoms of warp are used. The warps are led to a special hookup or towing block on the inboard quarter and the vessel steadies on course at two or three knots. After a run which may last several hours, the trawl is winched back on board. The cod end is opened to dump the catch on deck. If the ground is especially good, it may be marked with a buoy for future reference.

2.22   Craft for Demersal Fishing   Trawlers vary widely in size. Among the smallest are the New England "draggers." With good fishing grounds close by on the continental shelf, short and frequent cruises are feasible. The design which has developed is shown in Fig. 2.18. Normally of 100 feet or less, the typical dragger is diesel-propelled and mounts two masts with a steadying sail aft. Sturdy and seaworthy, they operate year around in the stormy North Atlantic. In the North Sea, whose shallow waters support an ancient and important demersal fishery, the trawler fleet is composed of craft generally similar to the New England draggers.

Distant ground trawlers are operated by most of the European countries and by Japan. Built for long trips and large catches, they are strong ships with heavy gear, complete freezing or processing equipment, and modern electronics. They range in size to over 200 feet and 500 tons. British trawlers work the Barents Sea, French craft operate on the Grand Banks, Russian distant water boats fish off the East Coast of the United States, and Japanese trawl in the Barents Sea. (See Fig. 2.19.)

An important fishery in the Gulf of Mexico and off the southeastern

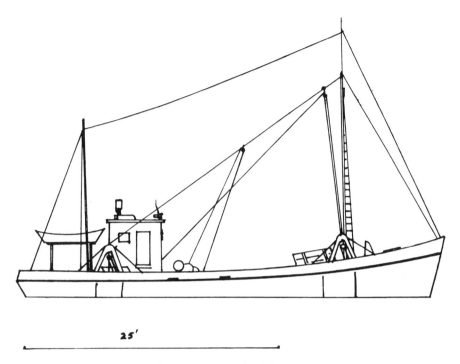

Fig. 2.18 New England dragger.

United States is shrimping. The double trawl rig developed there has spread to other shrimp grounds throughout the world from the Gulf of Alaska to the Indian Ocean. A typical shrimper is shown in Fig. 2.20. It streams two otter trawls, rigging the warps through blocks mounted at the ends of the port and starboard outriggers. Sometimes they tow a third

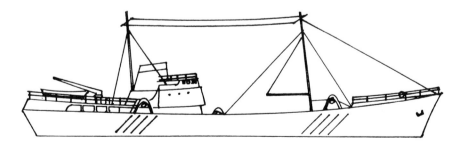

Fig. 2.19 Trawler (European).

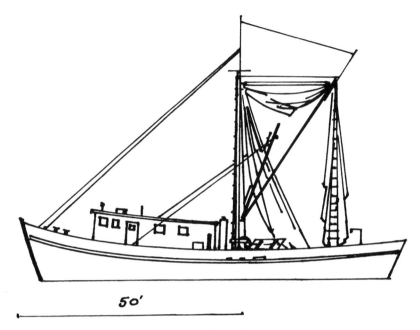

Fig. 2.20 Shrimp boat.

trawl directly over the stern. Motor driven, Gulf Coast shrimpers generally work shallow coastal waters but sometimes cross the Gulf of Mexico
to fish the fertile Campeche Bank.

A recent development in demersal fishing is the stern trawler. Net
handling over the side of a conventional side trawler is a slow procedure,
hazardous in heavy weather. Damage to gear and catch is possible and
automation of the operation is infeasible. By shifting the trawl to the stern
and installing a sloping ramp, it has become possible to reduce manhan-
dling and to locate the men in a safer position. The warps on a stern trawl
are run through blocks on the quarters, slung either from gallows or from
an inverted U-shaped gantry. A winch amidships hauls in the warps and
in some cases coils the trawl on a drum. The blocks, winches, rigging, and
deck fittings are designed for remote operation, often by a single man.
Some ships are fitted with an hydraulically operated door which can
close the after end of the slipway for added safety. Reduction of personnel and increased efficiency are important economic factors which have
led to an increase of the number of stern trawlers in most fishing fleets. A
Soviet bloc stern trawler and fish factory is sketched in Fig. 2.21. This class
has a long slipway and a novel stack arrangement with twin funnels located port and starboard of the fish deck.

Another technique of demersal fishing is pair trawling. In this system

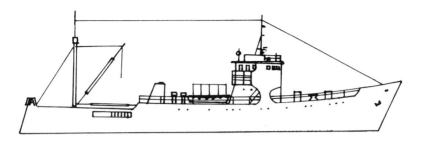

50'

Fig. 2.21 Stern trawler (Soviet bloc).

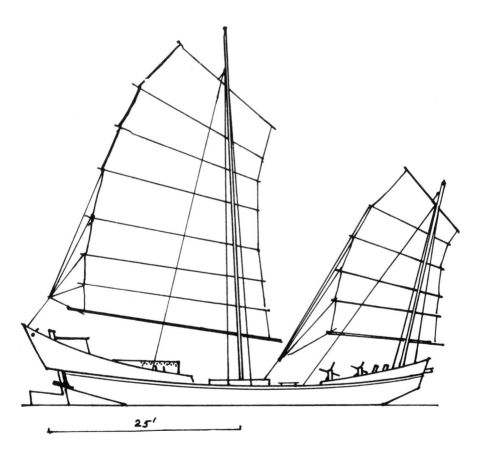

25'

Fig. 2.22 Yellow Sea fishing junk.

two craft steam on parallel courses, towing between them a trawl which may be as wide as 300 feet. Since each boat supplies only half of the total towing force, pair trawlers tend to be of small to medium size. They are fitted with winches but do not require gallows. Pair trawling is common in the Yellow and China Seas. The junk shown in Fig. 2.22 is a typical sailing pair trawler, a type giving way in some areas to motorized junks and sampans. Large hand powered windlasses, two masts, and a low silhouette distinguish it from larger, bulkier cargo junks.

Offshore trap fisheries take various species of shellfish, including king crabs in the North Pacific and lobsters on the Continental Shelf of the eastern United States. A "West Coast Combination design" has evolved and is numerous in the Alaskan crab fleet based in Kodiak. A raised forward deck with the pilothouse forward gives a long open main deck aft for handling pots or, when rigged for trawling, for working the trawl and sorting fish. The hull has pronounced sheer to keep bow and stern clear while allowing a low waist for easy gear handling. Fig. 2.23 shows a modern boat of this type. A somewhat similar although smaller craft has come into use in the New England offshore lobster fishery (Fig. 2.24). Both boats have high bow and low stern with cabin well forward in contrast to the typical houseaft dragger and drifter. New England offshore lobstermen range from 45 to 65 feet overall, half again as large as the older inshore boat. A two to three hundred horsepower diesel gives a

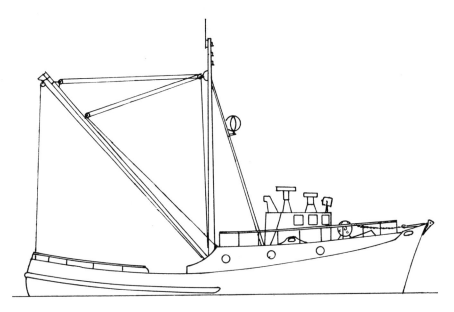

Fig. 2.23   West coast combination vessel rigged for King crabbing.

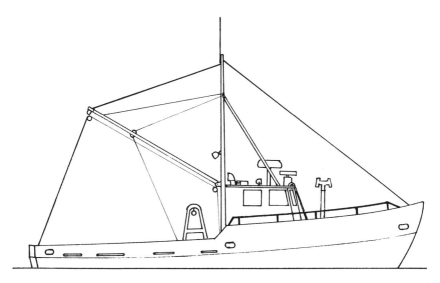

Fig. 2.24   New England offshore lobster boat.

speed of about ten knot with a full load of fifty or more traps on the after deck. A crew of two or three set the pots, ten to twenty to a string, in waters up to 50 fathoms. Individual pots are separated by ten or more fathoms to reduce the load on the pot hauler. A modern boat has extensive electronics including radar, loran, and VHF and Citizen's Band radiotelephone.

2.23   Long Line Fishing   The "long line" is used for demersal fishing the world over and in some fisheries for pelagic fishing. Baited hooks are secured every two or three fathoms to a heavy hemp, nylon, or wire line. (See Fig. 2.25.) After one end is buoyed and anchored, the boat plays out the line along a chosen track. For bottom fish the line lies on the bottom, for billfish and tuna it is buoyed every 50 fathoms to remain about 100 feet below the surface. When the entire line is set the far end is buoyed and anchored and the boat works its way along the line, removing the catch and rebaiting the hooks. Lines of 100 fathoms are handled by one or two men in an open boat. Farther seaward, medium sized vessels run lines up to 50 miles in length. They are fitted with power winches to bring the line on board. Distant water longliners sometimes handle lines and catch themselves or, in the case of "dorymen," from fleets of pulling boats. Similar in hull shape to long ranger trawlers, they carry nests of dories on deck. Among the last modern sailing fishermen are Spanish and Portuguese dorymen that work the Grand Banks. Utilizing their

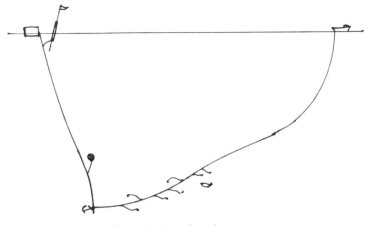

Fig. 2.25   Lone line (bottom).

diesels for the long voyages to and from the banks, they conserve fuel by using sail while on station.

There are many variations of the gear and craft dscribed above, and many have local names. Fishery research continues to produce new types of gear, and search for new profitable fisheries continues worldwide. Midwater trawls whose depth above the bottom can be controlled have entered the pelagic fishing picture. A trend continues towards combining several capabilities in a single hull for increased flexibility and greater profit per voyage.

Fishing vessels at work are often hampered in their movements. The Rules of the Road recognize their problem and prescribe special day marks and light. These are described in Part IV.

Unfortunately there is no such international concensus on the right to fish off foreign coasts. The facts of geography and of biology make for international disagreement. Small, densely populated countries want to catch fish not only along their own shores but also worldwide, wherever they can obtain this valuable source of protein. Such nations prefer minimum restrictions on their fishing fleets. At the other extreme are states whose chief resource is the fisheries of their adjoining high seas. These governments favor laws banning foreign craft from wide areas of ocean for the benefit of their own fishermen. Even within the United States opinions differ: the San Pedro tuna captain prefers narrow fishing limits so that he can get his seine close to the west coast of South America, while the Gloucester dragger seeks a 200 mile limit to keep the Russian fish factories off the New England banks.

Lacking treaty agreements to the contrary, present United States policy denies the right of any nation to regulate fishermen of other countries more than 12 miles offshore. Many such treaties exist, some bilateral and other multilateral. The United States has agreements on various aspects of fishing with Canada, Japan, U.S.S.R., and several other nations. Most maritime governments accept the 12 mile concept with the notable exception of Iceland, who claims 50 miles, and Chile, Ecuador, Peru, Costa Rica, Honduras, and El Salvador, who insist on a 200 mile limit. Many proposals for international regulations have been proposed and debated. The Third Conference on Law of the Sea, which met in 1974 in New York and in Santiago, Chile, ended in disagreement. Quarrels over fishery regulation remain a continuing international irritant, an uncompleted chapter in the law of the sea.

Yachts

2.24 Boating for Pleasure The growth in the number and variety of pleasure craft both power and sail is remarkable. Powerful and reliable outboard motors now drive pleasure craft from small rubber dinghies to large cabin cruisers and houseboats. In recent years a new engine, the inboard outboard, has appeared on the scene as well as adoption of high speed diesel engines with increased safety over gasoline designs. Hulls are made largely of plastic although recently ferrocement designs are becoming increasingly popular and are less expensive to produce. Tubular aluminum and light weight steel masts have replaced wooden masts in most sailing craft. In fact, many recent innovations in braided and plaited lines have evolved because of the needs of the yachtsman. There is a power or sailing pleasure craft available at an affordable price for nearly all income levels.

Fig. 2.26 A modern cabin cruiser with two cabins, 38 feet. *(Courtesy of Hatteras.)*

2.25   Powerboats   Small outboard-powered boats, often transported by trailers, are used for fishing, waterskiing, cruising in sheltered waters, and commuting. Larger powered boats, cabin cruisers (Fig. 2.26), usually have inboard engines and are used for pleasure cruising, commuting, and fishing. Special sport fishermen, 25 to 50 feet, have hulls that can be driven at high speed (30 knots) by large engines in order to travel long distances in search of fish. Cabin cruisers and sport fishermen are usually fitted with electronic navigation and depth-sounding gear, radar, and ship-to-shore voice radio.

Houseboats for use on rivers, canals, lakes, and sheltered waters have become increasingly popular. Some are fast enough to pull waterskiers and seaworthy enough to go to sea in calm weather. They are all comfortable and spacious in relation to conventional cabin cruisers and much less expensive.

2.26   Sailing Yachts   From tiny frostbite dinghies that are sailed in cold weather, to large ocean racers, the enthusiasm for recreational sailing has grown despite the popularity of powerboats. Small day sailors are usually built to standard class designs so their owners can race against each other. These can vary in size and cost from a Sailfish for several hundred dollars to an America's Cup Challenger that represents an investment of millions of dollars. Such sailing boats or yachts have no engines and rarely cruise overnight.

Many major colleges and universities as well as the U.S. Naval Academy, U.S. Coast Guard Academy, U.S. Merchant Marine Academy, and all of the state maritime academies carry on a vigorous inter-collegiate program of sail racing. In these races standard designs of Dinghies and larger sailing boats are used such as the well known "Shields Class" sloops. (Fig. 2.27.)

Powered sailing yachts for cruising and racing are built in all sizes and with a variety of rigs such as sloop, schooner, cutter, and ketch. They are also often built to standard designs, but sailing yachts of widely different sizes and rigs can race equitably under special handicaps or rating regulations that give certain boats a time advantage. Most sailing yachts are used for cruising and do not race since a successful ocean racer today must have a specially designed hull, a fairly large crew, a great taste for hardship, and such esoteric gear as special sail-handling winches that cost thousands of dollars each. (Fig. 2.28.)

Thousands of dollars worth of specialized and extra sails must also be carried by any boat that expects to be successful in the racing circuit.

Organizations such as the International Ocean Racing Committee and the North American Yacht Racing Union determine yacht racing rules.

Fig. 2.27   Typical intercollegiate racing dinghies. (*Official U.S. Navy photograph.*)

2.27   New Designs in Sailing Yachts   Catamarans and trimarans have achieved considerable acceptance as racing and cruising boats in recent years. Catamarans have twin hulls and trimarans have a main hull with two smaller hulls, one on each side. Multihulls are shallow draft, roomy, very fast if not overloaded, and considerably cheaper than single hulls. The latter must be built very heavy and strong with a keel to provide stability. They move through the water whereas a multihull moves for the most part over the water, depending on the wide separation of its hulls for stability.

Under very extreme and heavy storm conditions, when exposed to the occasional large freak wave with a vertical face, a multihull like any other vessel can capsize, but unlike a single hull cannot easily be righted. Multihulls, however, have been successful in ocean racing and are quite safe even in bad weather. They do not generally sail to windward as fast as a single hull but can easily reach superior speeds off the wind. Small catamarans have become popular for day sailing,

Fig. 2.28   A large sloop-rigged ocean racing yacht. (*Official U.S. Navy photograph.*)

racing, and surfing. Large multihulls often have small auxiliary engines, although the sensitivity of a multihull under sail to very light breezes makes auxiliary power less important.

2.28   Safety for Yachtsmen   Even in a sailing dinghy or an outboard-powered rubber boat you can lose your life in a sudden squall or maim a snorkeling swimmer with your propeller. Respect the water and rules, written and unwritten, that have been developed by the experience of seagoing people. Use lifejackets, be alert for bad weather, watch out for swimmers and other boats, be alert to sudden changes in weather. Cooperate with the Coast Guard, make way for large ships even though you may technically have the right of way, be considerate of fishermen, control pollution, and avoid drinking afloat if it affects your equilibrium or judgment.

Ship Structure, Stability, and Maintenance

The Hull

The main body of a ship exclusive of masts, superstructure, etc., is called the *hull*. For a steel ship it is made up of plates covering a framework which in many ways is similar to the framework of a building or a bridge. The hulls of various types and classes of vessels are basically similar, with certain modifications to suit the mission of the vessel.

A very important part of the framing of any vessel is the bottom centerline longitudinal, known as the centerline *keelson*. This assembly is generally made up of vertical and horizontal members, the vertical member being called the center vertical keel, the bottom horizontal member being called the flat-keel with the upper horizontal member being known as the keel rider plate. These three members form a deep girder type of structure of longitudinal continuity and strength which will withstand the various severe loadings to which the ship is subjected, as when it is drydocked or inadvertently grounded. This girder is often referred to as the backbone of the ship. All parts of the keelson are continuous from the forward end, where it joins the stem, to the after end, where it joins the stern post, or stern-post assembly if the stern post does not exist.

There are two major framing systems used in the construction of ships, the transverse and longitudinal framing systems. In reality most ships are built employing a combination of the two systems; however, one of the two systems will usually predominate. Both systems utilize transverse watertight bulkheads, from innerbottom to main deck, for watertight subdivision.

The transverse framing system employs closely spaced floors, side frames and deck beams, at right angles to the keel, with intercoastal longitudinal stiffeners. This system offers volumetric advantages in that hold areas are relatively uncluttered by hull structure. Fore and aft strength is provided mainly by shell plating and decks; with some contribution by longitudinal deck girders in the "normal mixing" of transverse framing with some longitudinal framing. Most merchant dry cargo ships and most naval auxiliary-type ships employ this mixed, but predominantly transverse, framing system. (Fig. 3.1.)

The longitudinal framing system consists of longitudinally placed strength members on the shell plating and decks, supported by widely spaced, deep transverse web frames. Such longitudinal strength members, effectively continuous through most of the length of the ship, add appreciably to the longitudinal strength of the hull as a structural girder. The merchant tanker and bulk carriers can successfully utilize this framing system; however dry cargo ships suffer loss of cargo volume due to the deep webs protruding into the cargo space. (Fig. 3.2.)

From the above, a general statement can be made that in merchant shipbuilding either the transverse or longitudinal framing system is utilized in a more or less "pure" form. Naval warship construction uses a basic longitudinal framing system, with some combination of the two systems to achieve greatest strength and least weight consistent with other design parameters.

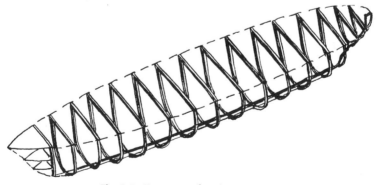

Fig. 3.1 Transverse framing system.

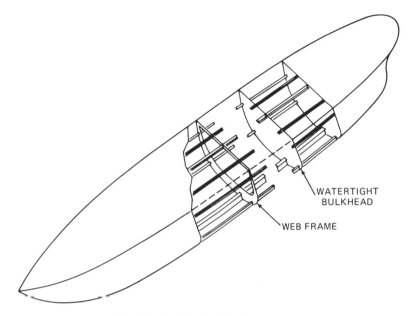

WATERTIGHT
BULKHEAD

WEB FRAME

Fig. 3.2 Longitudinal framing system.

Prior to the development of welding techniques, all portions of the ship's structure were joined by riveting. This practice has given way almost entirely to welding. There is a saving in weight of as much as 10 to 15 percent when welding is used. It gives a better surface that is better able to resist corrosion and to reduce skin friction in the underwater body of a ship. The use of welded construction does, however, call for a very carefully controlled assembly sequence in order to minimize locked-in stresses. Specifications for larger vessels sometimes call for a combination of welded and riveted construction. The riveted joints are located at the gunwale and bilge strake to act as crack arrestors.

Larger ships are usually fitted with inner bottoms which extend to the sides of the ship. Large combatant vessels are often fitted with heavy armor plate surrounding the machinery spaces and other vital spaces from slightly above the waterline to several feet below the waterline.

The ship is further subdivided into as many small compartments as is practical, consistent with the mission of the vessel, in order to minimize leakage and flooding if the outer shell is damaged.

3.1   Hull Shapes   The power characteristics, such as speed, of a ship depend to a great extent on the shape of her hull below the water-line, that is, the underwater body. The widest part of the hull is near the halfway point between the bow and stern, and the hull in this vicinity is called the middle-body section. The bottom and sides in the midship section are joined by a curve which completes an approximate right angle and which is called the turn of the bilge. From the middle-body section the lines of the hull slope smoothly to the bow and stern in what may become a hollow or reverse curve at some point before reaching them. The narrowing part of the underwater body forward of the middle-body section is called the entrance. The corresponding part aft is called the run. A ship that has a long and tapering entrance and run and a proportionally short middle-body section is said to have fine lines. A fast man-of-war generally has fine lines. (Fig. 3.3.)

A ship with a great extent of parallel middle body combined with a relatively short entrance and run—such as a large, slow bulk carrier—is said to have a full form. Her boxlike middle-body section is comparatively long to give her greater carrying capacity.

If the sides slope outward from near the turn of the bilge toward deck level, they are said to be flared. If they slope inward, the amount of the slope is called the tumble home. If a deck slopes from the centerline to the side, it is said to be cambered. (Fig. 3.4.)

There are as many refinements on this general scheme of the underwater body as there are ship designs and special uses for ships. Generally the run is somewhat longer than the entrance, and the after part of the run is narrowed for a greater distance to allow for the installation of rudder and propellers. The keel may be shortened aft, and the stern post may slant from the end of the keel to the waterline for the same reasons. These characteristics are known as reduced after dead-wood. Cutting away the after deadwood has an important effect on ship handling, which will be discussed in a later chapter. The lines of some ships, instead of coming to a sharp edge at the bottom of the

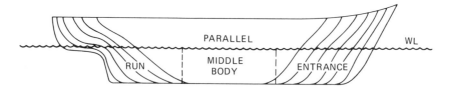

Fig 3.3   Sections of the hull shape.

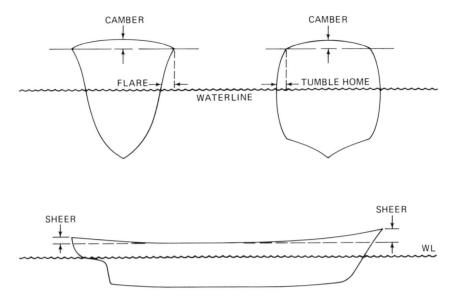

Fig. 3.4 Illustrations of sheer, camber, tumble home, and flare.

stem, expand at that point into a rounded shape extending from the keel to a few feet below the waterline. This shape is known as a bulbous bow and enables a vessel so fitted to attain greater speeds at or near full power than a vessel not so equipped. (The stem at and a few feet on each side of the waterline is a sharp edge.) In addition, bulbous bows can be used as oceanographic observation spaces or as fairings for sonar.

There are a wide variety of shapes for bows in addition to the bulbous bow. Most common on modern ships is the raked bow. The Meierform bow is that used on icebreakers. Illustrations of several types of bow and stern shapes are shown in Figs. 3.5 and 3.6, respectively.

The shape of a ship's underbody explains the great difference between shipbuilding and ordinary construction. Each frame member must be fitted to the desired contour of the hull, and side plates must be bent to the proper shape before being fastened to the frames in order that the completed ship may have her designed characteristics.

3.2 Submarine Hulls The hull of a submarine is distinctive in that it is made up of several parts. The pressure hull is the major part and is cylindrical with rounded, streamlined ends. In this main part are the submarine's vital machinery, living spaces, weapons, etc. Attached to

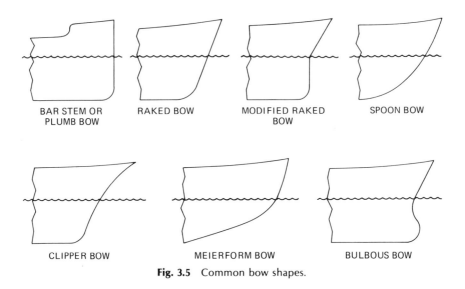

Fig. 3.5 Common bow shapes.

the pressure hull is the superstructure which may contain a conning tower, decks, etc. Only the conning tower is watertight. Mounted around and attached to the pressure hull are ballast and fuel tanks.

3.3   Decks   Decks are used primarily to provide structural strength, shelter, working spaces, and living quarters; secondarily they sub-

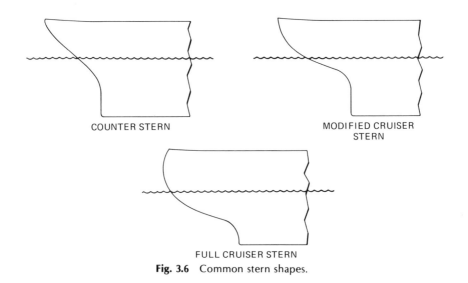

Fig. 3.6 Common stern shapes.

divide the hull horizontally into a greater number of compartments. For transversely framed ships the decks are supported by deep fore-and-aft members called deck girders, and by athwartship members called deck beams. Deck girders are in turn supported by stanchions which provide the decks with support additional to that afforded by the bulkheads. For longitudinally framed ships the decks are supported on longitudinal members that in turn are supported by transverse bulkheads and by athwartship beams. These extend between web frames on the side shell and have intermediate stanchion support. The highest deck extending from stem to stern is called the main deck. A partial deck above the main deck at the bow is called the forecastle deck; at the stern, poop deck; amidships, upper deck. The name upper deck, instead of forecastle deck, is applied to a partial deck extending from the waist to either bow or stern. A partial deck above the main, upper, forecastle, or poop deck and not extending to the side of the ship is called a superstructure deck. A complete deck below the main deck is called the second deck. Two or more complete decks below the main deck are called the second deck, third deck, fourth deck, etc. A partial deck above the lowest complete deck and below the main deck is called a half deck. A partial deck below the lowest complete deck is called a platform deck. Where there are two or more partial decks below the lowest complete deck, the one immediately below the lowest complete deck is called the first platform, the next is called the second platform, etc. Decks which for protective purposes are fitted with plating of extra strength and thickness are further defined for technical purposes as *protective* and *splinter* in addition to their regular names.

Fittings

3.4   Fittings   Fittings are various structures and appliances attached to the hull to assist in handling the ship or performing the ship's work, to provide for the safety and comfort of the crew, or merely for ornamental purposes. (See Fig. 3.7.) They may be affixed solidly to the hull or may be capable of a limited amount of motion. They may be operated by hand or by power. They may be found in any part of the ship, including the underwater body, although the commonest and most useful fittings are generally encountered around the weather decks.

Chocks are some of the most numerous and useful fittings found aboard ship. They generally take the form of castings, weldments, or forgings welded to the hull near the side along weather decks and are

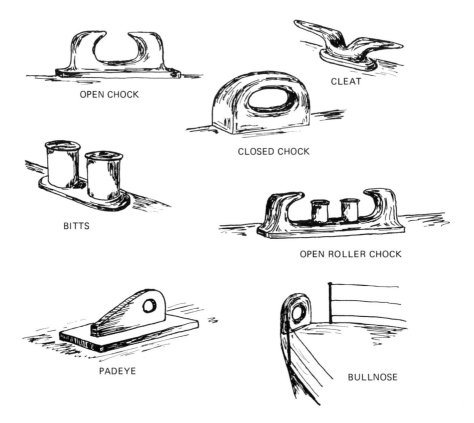

Fig. 3.7 Various hull fittings.

used for the purpose of guiding lines led aboard. The most common form is the open chock that has an opening on top through which the line is dropped and two curved parts called horns to hold it in. If the horns meet and the line must be led through the opening, it is called a closed chock. The heavy closed chock built at the extreme bow of destroyers and other light vessels for guiding a towline is commonly known as the bullnose. The inner surfaces of chocks are smoothed and rounded to avoid chafing the lines. Some have rollers fitted on each side for the same purpose, in which case they are known as roller chocks.

Bitts are usually found in the neighborhood of chocks and somewhat inboard of them. They are heavy vertical cylinders, usually cast in pairs and often used for making fast lines that have been led through the chocks. The upper end of a bitt is larger than the lower end or is fitted with a lip to keep lines from slipping off accidentally.

As bitts are often required to take very heavy loads, extra frames are worked into their foundations to distribute the strain. Bitts are sometimes built and installed ruggedly enough so that the ship may tow or be towed by them. When built in pairs, each bitt is sometimes called a horn.

Another common fitting is the davit. Davits are set in sockets which allow them to rotate. They are made of heavy pipe or plates and are angled so that the upper end or head of the davit will plumb some space below it at a distance from the davit's base. A tackle is rigged at the davit head so that weights can be lifted and swung as the davit is rotated. The most common use for davits is to carry lifeboats, but they are sometimes rigged to lift or lower weights over the side or out of trunks and holds.

There are numerous smaller but very useful fittings found about the weather decks. A plate with an eye attached, riveted to the deck to distribute the strain over a large area and to which a block can be hooked or shackled, is called a pad or padeye. An eyebolt serves the same purpose and may be attached to the deck or to a bulkhead or a frame overhead. If the eyebolt carries a permanent ring, it is called a ringbolt. Cleats are light, double-ended horns on which lines are made fast. Awning stanchions and lifeline stanchions are found at the ship's side on weather decks and are used to rig awnings and lifelines. Some of these are either hinged or set in sockets so that they can be cleared away when this is necessary. Sockets are often set in the deck for special purposes, such as setting the king post for a boom and topping-lift.

Ports are fixed or hinged, framed, heavy glass plates set in the ship's side or superstructure.

Winches and cranes are the most common and most useful power fittings found aboard ship. A winch consists of a heavy frame fastened solidly to the deck and an engine or motor that turns a horizontal shaft mounted in the frame, usually with a drum fastened to each end of the shaft. If the line is revolved around the drum for several turns and is tended carefully, it will withstand a heavy strain and can be accurately controlled. Blocks rigged to padeyes or eyebolts are commonly used to give lines a fair lead to the winch drums. In case a line has a limited and repeated travel, as when cargo is being handled in and out of a hold, and for heavy loads, the line is attached permanently to a winch drum and handled by winding and unwinding it on the drum according to the direction of the shaft's rotation. Winches take the place of an enormous amount of manpower and are invaluable in speeding up operations even when sufficient manpower is available. A winch that is used primarily to handle the anchor cables, but that usually has horizontal drums or a vertical capstan in addition, is called an anchor windlass.

Cranes may be regarded as large, power-driven davits. A crane may be built up as a solid structure or rigged with a boom that can be raised and lowered so as to plumb different distances from its base. The hauling part of a permanently rigged wire rope tackle for lifting weights is made fast to a drum. Motors or engines lift or lower weights by rotating the drum, rotate the crane, and lift or lower the boom. The crane is used primarily for hoisting and lowering heavy weights, such as boats and airplanes, over the side, but it can be used for many other purposes within its radius.

The location of fittings and other fixed objects on deck is normally identified by the numbers of the closest ship's frame. Certain frames, usually every fifth one, have their numbers cut or stamped in an accessible location near each side of the ship. Intermediate frames can be located by measuring from a marked frame in multiples of the frame spacing or the distance between frames, which is usually uniform. The number of frames in the hull and the length of the frame spacing are useful knowledge to have about any ship.

3.5 Compartment Designation for Warships Every space in a warship (except for minor spaces, such as peacoat lockers, linen lockers, and cleaning gear lockers) is considered a compartment and assigned an identifying letter number symbol. This symbol is placed on a label plate secured to the door, hatch, or bulkhead of the compartment. There are two systems of numbering compartments, one for ships built prior to March 1949, the other for ships built after March 1949. Both these systems agree, however, in one respect: Compartments to port have even numbers, those on the starboard side have odd numbers. The two systems resemble each other also in the fact that a zero precedes the deck number for all levels above the main deck. Figure 3.8 shows both systems of numbering decks. The older system uses 100, 200, 300, etc., series and always 900 for the double bottoms, while the new system uses 1, 2, 3, etc., and the double bottoms are given whatever number befalls them. For ships built prior to March 1949, the first letter of the identifying symbol is A, B, or C, and indicates the section of the ship in which the compartment is located. The A section extends from the bow of the ship aft to the forward bulkhead of the engineering spaces. The B section includes the engineering spaces, while the C section extends from the after bulkhead of the engineering spaces aft to the stern.

After the division letter, the deck designation comes next in the symbol. Main deck compartments are indicated by numbers such as

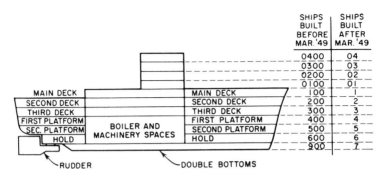

Fig. 3.8 Deck symbols for navy ships.

102, 109, 119. Second deck compartments run from 201 through 299, third deck compartments form a 300 series, etc. A zero preceding the number indicates a location above the main deck. The double bottoms always form the 900 series on any ship built before March 1949, regardless of the number of decks above.

What the compartments are used for is indicated by the following letters:

A—Supply and storage   M—Ammunition
C—Control   T—Trunks and passages
E—Machinery   V—Voids
F—Fuel   W—Water
L—Living quarters

Here is an example of a compartment symbol on a ship built before March 1949:

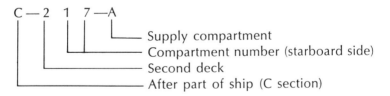

3.6 Ships Built after March 1949 For ships constructed after March 1949, the compartment numbers consist of a deck number, frame number, relation to centerline of ship, and letter showing use of the compartment. These are separated by dashes. The A, B, C divisional system is not used.

Deck Number Where a compartment extends down to the bottom of the ship, the number assigned to the bottom compartment is used. The deck number becomes the first part of the compartment number.

Frame Number   The frame number at the foremost bulkhead of the enclosing boundary of a compartment is its frame location number. Where these forward boundaries are between frames, the forward frame number is used. Fractional numbers are not used. The frame number becomes the second part of the compartment number.

Relation to the Centerline of the Ship   Compartments located on the centerline carry the number 0. Compartments completely to starboard are given odd numbers, and those completely to port are given

Table 3.1   Compartment Letters for Ships Built after March 1949

Letter	Type of Compartment	Examples
A	Stowage spaces	Storerooms; issue rooms; refrigerated compartments
AA	Cargo holds	Cargo holds and cargo refrigerated compartments
C	Control centers for ship and weapon-control operations (normally manned)	CIC room; plotting rooms; communication centers; radio, radar, and sonar operating spaces; pilothouse
E	Engineering control centers (normally manned)	Main propulsion spaces; boiler rooms; evaporator rooms; steering gear rooms; auxiliary machinery spaces; pumprooms; generator rooms; switchboard rooms; windlass rooms
F	Oil stowage compartments (for use by ship)	Fuel-oil, diesel-oil, and lubricating oil compartments
FF	Oil stowage compartments (cargo)	Compartments carrying various types of oil as cargo
G	Gasoline stowage compartments (for use by ship)	Gasoline tanks, cofferdams, trunks, and pumprooms
GG	Gasoline stowage compartments (cargo)	Gasoline compartments for carrying gasoline as cargo
K	Chemicals and dangerous materials (other than oil and gasoline)	Chemicals, semi-safe materials, and dangerous materials carried for ship's use or as cargo
L	Living spaces	Berthing and messing spaces; staterooms, sanitary spaces, brigs; medical spaces; and passageways
M	Ammunition space	Magazines; ammunition and missile handling rooms; ready service rooms; clipping rooms
Q	Miscellaneous spaces not covered by other letters	Shops; offices; laundry; galley; pantries; unmanned engineering, electrical, and electronic spaces
T	Vertical access trunks	Escape trunks or tubes
V	Void compartments	Cofferdam compartments (other than gasoline); void wing compartments
W	Water compartments	Drainage tanks; fresh-water tanks; peak tanks; reserve feed tanks

even numbers. Where two or more compartments have the same deck and frame number and are entirely starboard or entirely port of the centerline, they have consecutively higher odd or even numbers, as the case may be, numbering from the centerline outboard. In this case, the first compartment outboard of the centerline to starboard is 1; the second, 3; etc. Similarly, the first compartment outboard of the centerline to port is 2; the second, 4; etc. When the centerline of the ship passes through more than one compartment, the compartment having that portion of the forward bulkhead through which the center-line of the ship passes carries the number 0, and the others carry the numbers 01, 02, 03, etc. These numbers indicate the relation to the centerline and are the third part of the compartment number.

Compartment Usage   The fourth and last part of the compartment number is the letter which identifies the primary usage of the compartment. On dry and liquid cargo ships a double-letter identification is used to designate compartments assigned to cargo carrying. The letters are shown in Table 3.1.

The following example of a compartment number illustrates the application of these principles of compartmentalization for ships built after March 1949:

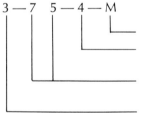

3 — 7   5 — 4 — M

         └─── Ammunition compartment
         ──── Second compartment outboard of the centerline to port
         ──── Forward boundary is on or immediately abaft frame 75
         ──── Third deck

Hull Piping Systems

Piping built into the hull which carries a liquid or a gas is known as a hull piping system. The principal hull piping systems are:

Firemain	Fresh water
Sprinkling	Drainage
Flushing	Compressed air
Damage control flooding	Fuel-oil
Ballasting	Aircraft fuel

3.7   Firemain System   The firemain system in large ships forms a loop throughout the greater portion of the ship. Cross-connections are installed between mains in most main transverse watertight subdivisions. The loop may be arranged in a horizontal or vertical plane. In aircraft carriers, a bypass main is installed below the uppermost service mains, thus incorporating the features of both the horizontal and vertical loop.

In small ships, such as ocean escort types, a single main is provided on the damage control deck.

In combatant ships, the firemain can be segregated into smaller independent sections so as to minimize loss of pumping capacity in event of localized system damage.

3.8   Sprinkling System   The magazines of a warship are divided into groups, according to location. Each group is supplied by a separate sprinkling system connection leading from the firemain at a convenient location and controlled by a group control valve. The group control valves are operated from remote control stations, hydraulically, or mechanically. Sprinklers may also be actuated automatically by a thermostat when there is a temperature rise in the magazine.

3.9   Merchant Ship Sanitary Piping   On merchant ships, separate sanitary piping systems are installed. Current regulations prohibit discharge of raw sewage overboard. Holding tanks and/or sewage treatment plants are therefore installed. This system is now effective for warships.

3.10   Flushing System   For sanitary spaces, flushing water at pressures around 30 psi is supplied. Present practice is to provide branches from the firemain, via stop valves and reducing valves, wherever flushing services are required.

3.11   Damage Control Flooding   In aircraft carriers, remote-operated, hydraulically controlled flood valves are installed in counter-floodable voids. The latest practice provides a single flood valve to service several such voids in order to minimize the number of openings in the hull. These valves permit rapid counter-flooding even when power is temporarily lost.

3.12   Ballasting System   It is often necessary to ballast fuel oil stowage tanks with salt water after the fuel oil is burned, in order to maintain proper list, trim, draft, torpedo protection, and stability. Fuel oil ballast tanks in such ships are flooded with salt water from the sea or from the firemain through a manifold. Removal of ballast water from the tanks is accomplished by eductors actuated from the firemain. Fuel oil service tanks should never be ballasted with water. Modern merchant ship practice is to provide separate stowage tanks for oil and ballast.

3.13   Fresh-Water System   Fresh or "drinkable" water, called potable water, is usually stored aboard ship in special tanks, low in the ship. From these tanks, it is delivered to necessary outlets, such as scuttle-butts, lavatories, galley sinks, and the like, through the fresh-water system. This consists of a pump and pressure tank or continuously operating centrifugal pumps, which maintain pressure in the system. Pumps are usually located near the freshwater tanks, and frequently in engineering spaces.

3.14   Drainage System   Each ship has some means provided for removing water from within its hull. Systems of piping, with or without pumping facilities installed for this purpose, are termed *drainage systems*.

Drainage systems are divided, on most ships, as follows:

1. Main drainage system
2. Secondary drainage systems
3. Plumbing and deck drains
4. Weather-deck drains
5. Feed drains in machinery spaces

In addition to the above systems, the following portable pumps are used to drain flooded areas not provided with drainage facilities:

1. Electric submersible pumps
2. "P-250-type" pump
3. Jet jumps (eductors)

The main drainage system runs throughout the main machinery compartments. However, on some ships it extends well into the bow and stern. On smaller ships the main drain consists of a single pipe running fore and aft, usually amidships. On larger ships it is a loop system, extending along both sides of the engineering compartments and joined at the ends. Main drainage systems may be used on many later types of ships to drain "floodable" voids used in counter-flood-ing, after such voids have been flooded, and to empty fuel-oil tanks which have been ballasted with seawater. Eductors, actuated from the firemain, are used to provide suction lift.

Secondary drainage systems serve to drain spaces forward and aft of the main machinery compartments. The piping is smaller in size than that used in main drainage systems. It may be a continuation of the main drainage system, but in many instances they are not connected.

Plumbing and deck drains are provided for draining fixtures and compartments within the ship by gravity. Gravity drainage piping is installed most extensively in compartments above the waterline. On large ships, some compartments near or below the waterline may be drained to compartments lower in the ship, where the water can be pumped overboard. These lower compartments are bilges and bilge wells, shaft-alley sumps, drain tanks, or sanitary drain tanks.

3.15 Compressed Air System Ships rely on compressed air for many tasks and services. Examples of tasks include starting of emergency diesel generators, launching torpedoes, and operating valves and controls. Examples of services include operating of pneumatic tools, servicing vehicles, and charging divers' tanks.

On the submarine the compressed air system is of major importance. This is because compressed air is used in blowing ballast tanks for maintaining the proper buoyancy. Other uses include the operation of control systems, torpedo ejection, and emergency breathing.

Compressed air is provided, normally, by shipboard compressors and stored in receivers or flasks for use as required.

3.16 Fuel-Oil System The fuel-oil pumping system in large ships consists of a loop serving all fuel-oil tanks and permitting transfer of fuel from storage tanks to service tanks and thence to fuel-oil service pumps. The latter pump the fuel oil to the fuel-oil heaters and thence to the burners in the boilers. Included in the system are topside fuel-oil filling connections, which lead down to the loop.

This system is also used for *transfer* of liquid for correction of list and trim, or improvement of stability or reserve buoyancy after damage, and furnishes a possible avenue for progressive flooding.

3.17 Aircraft Fuel Systems *Aviation Gasoline System* Ships carrying or tending piston-engine-type aircraft store and handle highly volatile aviation gasoline. Gasoline systems are designed to minimize the inherent fire and explosion hazard.

The majority of the gasoline systems installed are of the sea-water-displacement type. During aircraft fueling operations the gasoline pumped from the storage tanks is displaced with seawater which is supplied either from the firemain through reducing valves or from separate seawater pumps. When receiving gasoline the seawater in the tanks is displaced with the gasoline entering the tanks. This keeps the tanks full, eliminates dangerous pockets of gasoline vapor, and provides a positive suction head to the gasoline pumps.

Aviation Gas Turbine Fuel (JP-5) System Ships carrying or tending gas turbine-engine-type aircraft store and handle gas turbine engine fuel (JP-5). This fuel has a high flash point and is considered safe for storage aboard ships in unprotected tanks similar to ships' diesel oil tanks. The use of a high flash point fuel also allows elimination or reduction in the safety requirements associated with gasoline systems, such as explosion-proof equipment and special firefighting and ventilation requirements. However, because of the gas turbine fuel's affinity for water, special system installation requirements are necessary for quality control of the fuel, such as two-stage filtration.

The gas turbine fuel is stored in regular ship's tanks. The fuel is transferred via transfer pumps and purifiers or filter/separators to gas turbine fuel service tanks. Delivery of gas turbine fuel to aircraft fueling stations, such as hangar and flight deck stations on an aircraft carrier, is via service pumps and filter/separators. Gas turbine aircraft fueling stations are distributed along the hangar and flight deck areas to serve any aircraft parked in these areas.

Stability

The original stability of a ship and its ability to withstand hull damage and flooding is the business of her designers and builders, but the basic principles of stability and damage control are important to the seaman for his own safety and that of his ship. A ship has two principal kinds of static stability, longitudinal and transverse· The first tends to keep a ship from rolling end over end; the second tends to keep her from capsizing. Longitudinal stability is always enough to avoid danger, although poor longitudinal stability characteristics may cause discomfort by excessive pitching and make a very wet ship. The knowledge of the transverse stability of any ship, on the other hand, is important to the seaman in order to gauge the amount of roll allowable without danger of capsizing.

3.18 Moments and Forces Unless acted upon by some external force, a ship that is properly designed and loaded remains upon an even keel. A righting moment which develops when the vessel rolls tends to return the ship to an even keel. The righting moment is the product of the righting arm (defined later) and the force of buoyancy. The force of buoyancy is the sum of the vertical components of the hydrostatic pressure on the underwater body. It is also equal to the weight of the water displaced by the underwater body. The force of buoyancy also keeps the ship afloat, but it may be overcome and the ship sunk if too much weight is introduced, as is the case when too many holds or compartments are flooded. The righting moment tending to bring the ship back on an even keel may be overcome and the ship capsized if too much weight is introduced on one side of the centerline, as when all compartments on one side are flooded. A ship may also capsize when it is stranded and the righting arm becomes negative due to reduction of the underwater volume and the upward force acting at the point of stranding.

The foregoing examples are static forces tending to capsize a ship. The effects of wind and waves are dynamic forces. A smaller dynamic force than static force may be sufficient to overcome the righting arm and to capsize a ship because the effect of a dynamic force depends on the speed with which it is applied as well as on its magnitude. A common example is that a boat under sail may be capsized by a sudden squall when it might weather perfectly a wind of the same force that came up gradually.

3.19 Anti-capsizing Forces   An elementary idea of the forces tending to prevent a ship from capsizing can be obtained from (a) and (b) in Fig. 3.9. In (a), G represents the center of gravity of the ship. It is the point where the sum of the moments of all the weights of a ship with reference to any axis through this point are equal to zero. In other words, the ship acts as though all its weight were concentrated at this point. Because the loading is usually the same on both sides of the vertical centerline plane, G usually lies in this plane, and in ships of conventional form, near the waterline. The center of gravity does not shift vertically if weights are added or subtracted whose algebraic sum lies in the same horizontal plane as the center of gravity. It is raised if the sum of the weights added lies above this plane, or the sum of the weights subtracted lies below it. Conversely, it is lowered if the sum of the weights subtracted lies above it, or the sum of the weights

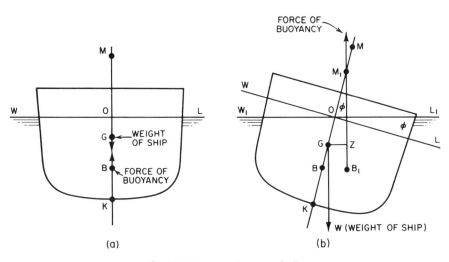

Fig. 3.9   Forces acting on a hull.

added lies below it. The pertinent formula is:

$$KG_1 = \frac{WKG \pm w_1 Kg_1 \pm w_2 Kg_2 \cdots \pm w_n Kg_n}{W \pm w \pm w_2 \cdots \pm w_n}$$

where KG_1 = new height of center of gravity above the keel

$\quad W$ = original displacement of ship

$\quad KG$ = original height of center of gravity above the keel

$\quad w_1$ = weights added or removed

$\quad Kg_1$ = height of w_1 above keel

3.20 Pressure Hydrostatic pressure on a submerged body, such as the hull of a ship, is proportional to depth and acts at right angles to the surface of the hull. Each square foot of surface of the hull is subject to a pressure of 1/35 ton for every foot of depth (or 64 pounds per foot of depth of seawater). This water pressure is applied to the hull and transmitted through the frames, decks, and bulkheads to the various parts of the ship. Although the horizontal pressures of water exerted on each side of the ship cancel each other, the force still acts on the hull. The decks and transverse framing and bulkheads prevent lateral crushing of the hull.

If the skin of the ship is ruptured, the hydrostatic pressures formerly exerted on the plating are now imposed on the bulkheads of the flooded compartments. This is why all bulkheads require stiffeners to prevent them from bulging, and why bulkheads well below the waterline are thicker, require more stiffeners, and are subjected to higher test pressures. Flooding water will exert a considerable *upward pressure* against the overhead deck of a flooded compartment if the deck in question is some distance below the waterline.

3.21 Buoyancy Factors The symbol B is used to indicate the ship's center of buoyancy, which may be considered that point through which the resultant of all upward forces is considered to act and which lies in the geometric center of the underwater form of the vessel. When the ship is on an even keel, B is in the vertical longitudinal centerline plane, and the upward force of buoyancy is directly under the point G where all the weight of the vessel is considered concentrated. When the ship lists or rolls, B moves to the lower side, and a vertical line drawn from B cuts the vertical plane of the centerline. The point M, where this line cuts for an infinitesimal angle of inclination, is called the metacenter, and distance GM is called the metacentric height. BM is called the metacentric radius and is mathematically equal to I/V, where I is the moment of inertia of the waterline plane and V is volume of displacement.

For any given condition of loading, G may be considered fixed, but both B and M move as the vessel heels. In (b) of Fig. 3.9 the ship has heeled to the right an angle of ϕ degrees, and B has moved to B_1, the center of gravity of the volume of liquid displaced in this new position. A vertical line through B_1 cuts the centerline at M_1, the new position to which the metacenter has moved. A perpendicular line drawn from G to the intersection of line B_1M_1 (point Z) is the righting arm and is indicated by the symbol GZ. As can be seen, it is the distance between the lines of action of the force of buoyancy B acting upward and the force of gravity acting downward. The righting moment is equal to the value of the couple set up by W and B. Its value is $W \times GZ$ or $B \times GZ$, where W is the weight of the ship.

As the ship heels over further, M_1 moves down the centerline, and the distance GM_1 decreases by an amount varying with the characteristics of the individual ship. Theoretically, M_1 could move below G and the righting arm GZ become negative, but in practice other factors could usually capsize the ship before this point is reached. The angle at which GZ becomes negative is the upper limit of the range of stability.

As the angle of inclination increases, the length of the righting arm increases for a time until it reaches a maximum, after which its length decreases due to the movement of M_1 down the centerline. The righting moment varies directly as the righting arm, since W remains constant; hence it, too, increases until it reaches a maximum after which it decreases sharply. This is called the point of maximum righting arm.

The preceding paragraphs give a very rough idea of the forces tending to prevent a ship from capsizing. All the factors involved are treated thoroughly under the science of naval architecture. Cross curves of stability show the ship's static stability characteristics (i.e., righting arms, range of stability, etc.) for different displacements at an assumed position of center of gravity. Curves of form show geometric characteristics for different drafts (such as displacement in fresh and salt water, and KM). GM may then be calculated from the relationship $GM = KM - KG$, provided the weight effects have been evaluated. Even more practical, a stability diagram may be solved. It is emphasized, however, that KG and KM must *both* be known, before an appraisal of ship stability is accurate.

For instance, an aircraft carrier is a very steady platform and has several times as great a metacentric height as a destroyer, but her range of stability is less, and consequently she cannot roll to as great an angle with safety. Because of the great displacement W of a carrier, the righting moment $W \times GZ$ is also large and would never be exceeded under any conditions, even after extensive damage to the watertight shell.

The addition of weight above the center of gravity decreases the metacentric height and consequently the range of stability. The same effect is caused by removal of weight below the center of gravity. The most common example of this is in ships when the fuel tanks are emptied without admitting water ballast for compensation.

Wind and waves are usually dynamic forces. Sudden strong gusts of wind or heavy seas, especially in shallow water, may build up a dangerous roll. A rough method of keeping out of trouble is to watch the period or time required for a complete roll from side to side. The period should remain approximately the same regardless of the magnitude of the angle or roll. Should the period increase appreciably, or the ship appear to hesitate at the end of the roll before coming back, she is probably approaching or past the position of maximum righting effect, and immediate steps should be taken to decrease the roll by changing course or speed or both.

3.22   The *GM* Formula   The seaworthiness of a ship is dependent on three things:

1. Its initial and overall stability. Initial stability is the resistance of a ship to initial heeling when on an even keel. Overall stability is the resistance of a ship to heeling caused by static forces throughout her range of stability.
2. Its range of stability. Range of stability is the total angle through which the righting arm is positive. It is the angle of heel either to port or to starboard through which a vessel tends to return to an upright position.
3. Its dynamic stability. Dynamic stability is the righting energy available to resist heeling through an angle not greater than the range of stability.

Initial stability is measured by the transverse metacentric height in feet, which is the distance from the center of gravity up to the metacenter. The center of gravity and the *KM* remain fixed for any particular condition of loading. Both may change for different loadings with a resulting change in the metacenter height (*GM*). Any change in this can be quickly estimated by the formula:

$$GM = \left(\frac{0.44B}{T}\right)^2$$

where GM = the transverse metacentric height in feet
B = ship's beam in feet
T = time in seconds of a complete roll; e.g., port to starboard to port

NOTE: The constant 0.44 represents an average for various hull forms.

Thus if the period of the roll is doubled, the *GM* is quartered, and in all probability the ship is in danger. The decision to abandon a ship or to attempt to save her is based greatly on this new calculated *GM*.

3.23 Applications of the *GM* This *GM* can be increased by lowering the center of gravity by completely flooding some of the lowest tanks and by casting overboard top hamper, boats, torpedoes, spars, and mast. The removal of any free surfaces by the complete flooding or pumping of fresh-water or fuel-oil tanks, and the removal of water in the bilges will increase the *GM*, especially if the tanks run athwartship.

A ship with a long, easy roll makes a good platform and a good passenger ship, but the very fact that she has an easy roll is a sign of a low metacentric height. A ship with a large *GM* will have a quick, jerky roll which is uncomfortable. Beam has a great effect on initial stability (*GM*) since the moment of inertia of the waterline plane is a geometric function of the beam.

Static stability for any angle is measured by the righting arm at that angle of inclination. As a ship is inclined, this arm increases until it becomes a maximum approximately when the main deck waterways are awash. Further inclining decreases this arm until, at about twice the angle at which the arm was a maximum, it becomes zero and the vessel will no longer right itself.

This last angle gives the range of stability of a ship and totals approximately twice the angle at which the main deck waterways are awash. Therefore, a high freeboard as compared to the beam is desirable. Between two different types of ships, the relative range of stability is measured by the ratio of freeboard and beam; whereas between two ships with the same ratio of freeboard to beam, the *GM* is the measure of the relative range of stability. Merchant ships with their high freeboard compared to their beam are very seaworthy, even though they have a low value for their *GM*.

The work utilized in the inclining of a ship is the measure of its dynamic stability. If the force of the sea acting on a ship becomes great enough to heel her over until the righting arm becomes zero, the ship will not be able to right itself. The apparent force of the sea is greatest when the period of the ship and that of the waves are in synchronism, thereby building up a much deeper roll. This force can be controlled by the ship's changing course or speed or both—which actions alter the apparent period of the waves relative to the ship.

3.24 Stability of a Submarine The principles presented above for surface ships apply equally to surfaced submarines. However, the rapidly increasing righting arm at moderate angles of inclination exhibited by surface ships, up to the point of deck edge immersion, is not experienced in submarines. This is true principally because, with their nearly circular cross-section, the waterplane area does not change appreciably when inclined. Because the center of gravity is normally very low in a submarine, they enjoy relatively good stability, both on the surface and when fully submerged. During the transition period while submerging, a submarine possesses the least transverse stability; due primarily to the free surface effect of water being flooded into the main ballast tanks. This free surface effect does not exist when the submarine is on the surface, except due to a small quantity of residual water in the tanks, and it does not exist when fully submerged, as the main ballast tanks are then completely filled.

3.25 Anti-rolling Devices   Certain artificial methods are sometimes used to reduce a ship's roll. Rolling keels or bilge keels are builtup structures of roughly triangular cross section attached outside the hull near the turn of the bilge and extending part of the length of the ship. These false keels have the function of damping the roll of the ship. Since their introduction in the late 1800's bilge keels have been installed on nearly all ocean-going ships, both commercial and military. Some large warships built during this period were built without bilge keels, their sheer bulk was presumed to provide enough resistance to roll; these ships were almost invariably fitted with bilge keels after service showed them to be heavy rollers.

Other anti-roll devices have been designed and installed on limited numbers of ships. These include anti-roll tanks, gyroscopic stabilizers and anti-roll fins. The first two share with bilge keels the advantage that they do not depend on ship speed for their effectiveness. All active-fin stabilizing systems are designed to take advantage of the hydrodynamic lift forces created by the fin at an angle to the water flow created by the ship's speed. Fin stabilization is ineffective when the ship is stopped or at anchor.

Although both anti-roll tanks and stabilizing fins, and gyroscopic stabilizers to a lesser degree, have proven very successful in reducing roll, their disadvantages in cost, weight and space required and power consumption (if required) have restricted their use. Bilge keels, of slight weight and cost, completely passive, requiring no power and installed on the exterior, requiring no internal space will undoubtedly remain the predominant form of anti-roll device.

3.26 Displacement   The weight of the volume of water displaced by a ship is called her "displacement" and is normally expressed in long tons. A cubic foot of seawater weighs 64 pounds, and of fresh water

62.4 pounds. Thus, a ton is equal to 35 cubic feet of seawater or 35.9 cubic feet of fresh water. Displacement tons are 2240 pounds in the British units now in general use. Metric tons, used by many nations, are equivalent to 1000 kilograms or 2205 pounds.

3.27 Measurement, Gross and Net Tonnages Under existing systems, gross tonnage is a volume measure of the total enclosed space of a ship (with certain space exemptions) expressed in tons of 100 cubic feet each. This unit of volume was originally used in the "Moorsom system," and this system, with some annoying variations in application, has been adopted by most maritime nations.

Net tonnage, which was intended to relate to the earning power of a ship, is derived from gross tonnage by deducting spaces that may have no earning capacity. Spaces such as engine and boiler rooms, shaft alleys, bunkers, and crew accommodations are generally considered deductible. Laws of the various maritime nations vary in the extent to which deductions are permitted.

A 1961 survey of the Inter-Governmental Maritime Consultative Organization (IMCO) of the United Nations determined that, among the 25 major maritime nations responding, there was considerable disparity in the ways that gross and net tonnage were used for charges, fees, and statutory purposes. Because of the differences, the International Convention on Tonnage Measurement of Ships (1969) developed a universal system subject to acceptance by member states of the United Nations. This Convention will come into force 24 months after 25 governments constituting 65 percent of the world's fleets have accepted it. Existing ships may be exempt from the new convention up to 12 years after it has come into force.

3.28 Tonnage Log Functions Under the 1969 Convention, the gross tonnage is a logarithmic function of the total enclosed volume of the ship without exemptions—and the net tonnage is a logarithmic function of the total cargo volume with adjustment for high freeboard ships and an additional function for the number of passengers when these number more than 12. The effect of the log function is to cause the former 100 cubic-feet-per-ton factor to vary from about 160 to 110 cubic-feet-per-ton as the volume increases. This adjustment was necessary in order to maintain numerical values of tonnage as reasonably close as possible to those determined under existing systems.

3.29 Load Line Markings In accordance with the International Load Line Convention (1966), which became effective in July 1968, load lines were established for all new vessels 79 feet or more in length and for all existing vessels of 150 gross tons or over, which engage in foreign voyages or international voyages by sea (other than solely on Great Lakes voyages) and fly the flag of a country adhering to the convention. (Exceptions to this are: ships of war; fishing vessels; pleasure craft [yachts] not used or engaged in trade or commerce; new vessels less than 79 feet in length; and existing vessels of less than 150 gross tons.)

Special load lines for vessels engaged in voyages on the Great Lakes and in coastwise voyages by sea are in conformity with the Coastwise Load Line Act of 1935 (as amended).

3.30 Meaning of the Markings Load line markings indicate the drafts at which, for various conditions and types or classes of vessels, there will still be left a sufficient percentage of reserve buoyancy to ensure the vessel's safety. On it are indicated the maximum safe drafts for salt and fresh water, for winter and summer, and for some indicated locations.

3.31 American Bureau of Shipping Responsibility As provided in the Load Line Act, the American Bureau of Shipping assigns load lines and issues load-line certificates. The authority by whom the load lines are assigned may be indicated by letters marked alongside the disk and above the centerline (**Fig. 3.10**).

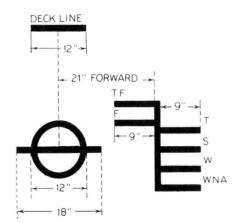

Fig. 3.10 Explanation of symbols of the load line mark for cargo ships and tankers:

TF—Tropical fresh water load line   S—Summer load line
F—Fresh water load line   W—Winter load line
T—Tropical load line   WNA—Winter North Atlantic load line

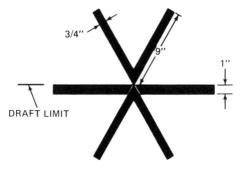

Fig. 3.11 U.S. Navy load line marking.

3.32 U.S. Navy Markings Although excepted from the International Load Line regulations, U.S. Navy warships display a draft limit marking, in addition to draft numerals. The mark, shown in Fig. 3.11, may be located either near the draft numerals or amidship.

3.33 Draft In Fresh Water The draft of a ship will be greater in fresh water than in sea water because fresh water is less dense (the total weight of water displaced by the hull must always equal the total weight of the ship's hull and all that it carries, the weight of displaced water is equal to the specific weight of the water multiplied by the volume below the waterline; if the specific weight is less (sea water = 64 pounds per cubic foot; fresh water = 62.4 pounds per cubic foot) then the displaced volume must be greater, to yield the same total weight of displaced water). Hence, as shown in Fig. 3.10, the fresh water load line "F" allows a deeper draft loading than that allowed by the summer load line "S," or the center of the marker disk, which is the limiting load draft in sea water, unless in tropical waters. The fresh water draft mark permits loading to a point exceeding the sea water mark in a fresh water port, a river or lake, and then proceeding out to sea without exceeding the sea water mark. Specific weight, or density, of the "fresh water" should always be checked, however; brackish water will have a specific weight between the values of fresh and sea water.

Hull Damage Control

The stability principles considered in this chapter are useful to the seaman to the extent that they explain in general why the undamaged, properly loaded ship remains upright in heavy weather. They also reveal the range and type of response that may be expected from the undamaged ship. If damage occurs, it is necessary to apply these principles quickly to save the ship. In the application of these principles it is important to realize how damage may reduce margins of buoyancy and stability. Damage sustained by vessels in peacetime accidents is often similar to the effect of wartime enemy action; a peacetime collision with possible attendant fires and explosions may be just as serious as enemy hits.

After serious damage or in heavy weather the captain must be guided by three factors if he is to save his ship: He must maintain *power, buoyancy,* and *stability.* The damaged ship sometimes may be able to survive in calm waters by maintaining only buoyancy and stability. But it may often be impossible to do this without power. Flooded engineering compartments or water reaching main switchboards (through flooding or through ventilators) are important causes of power loss.

3.34   Shipboard Fire   Uncontrolled fire aboard ship is the single greatest catastrophe that can occur to a ship that remains afloat. Although modern construction techniques and materials have reduced the danger of shipboard fire, consumable supplies, such as paint stores and dry and liquid cargo, pose an ever-present threat. Once started, shipboard fires are difficult and sometimes impossible to extinguish. Several classic examples of relatively small initial fires that eventually completely destroyed ships are the *S.S. Normandie,* which capsized at her berth as a result of added water used for fire fighting, the *U.S.S. Lexington,* and the *U.S.S. Franklin.* The *Lexington* was lost as a direct result of uncontrolled fire resulting from battle damage; and the *Franklin,* although saved from fire damage, cost about 2000 casualties. Small fires may disrupt essential circuits, causing a loss in power and communications. Except for carbon dioxide systems, all fire extinguishing systems add free-surface water and a resultant loss in stability during the course of extinguishing a fire.

3.35   Overall Consequences of Hull Damage   War experience has shown that whenever a ship suffers damage involving serious flooding, either the damage is so extensive that the vessel never stops listing or settling in the water, going down within a few minutes, or the vessel stops heeling, changing trim, and settling in the water shortly after initial damage.

Experience also shows that vessels which survive several hours after damage and then sink, suffer flooding the control of which requires proper training of the crew. This flooding usually comes about in the following manner:

As a result of a hit or collision a large hole is opened in the side.

Several bulkheads and decks may be carried away just inside this hole. Immediate flooding occurs through these large holes, giving the ship her initial list, trim, and reduced stability.

In addition to the large holes, there may be a certain amount of subsidiary damage, with riddled or warped bulkheads and decks, opened seams, leaking doors and hatches, etc. These permit slow leakage and progressive flooding past the boundaries of the damage. The slow flooding is aggravated if personnel escaping from the damaged area leave doors or scuttles open behind them.

3.36   Action Before and After Damage   Precautions before any damage is sustained will often determine whether or not efforts to save the ship afterward can be successful. As a rule, men-of-war are better able to cope with damage. They are usually more fully compartmented than merchant ships and have more men and equipment to rally against the damage. There has been an increasing tendency both to design and to operate merchant ships with a higher capacity to resist damage. And on both naval and merchant ships there has been a growing understanding that the captain or master has a vital primary role in insuring precautions against damage at sea. These consist generally of:

1. Utilization of designed hull safety features at all times when at sea (such as ensuring that watertight boundaries are faithfully maintained).
2. Ensuring that the ship is not overloaded.
3. Ensuring that deck loads are not exceeded.
4. Ensuring proper amount and distribution of liquid and other cargo and ballast.
5. Ensuring that crew members are trained to localize damage insofar as facilities of the ship permit.

The loss of the *Andrea Doria* is well known by mariners as an example of how improper liquid loading can doom a ship to sinking. When one of her huge, off-center, empty fuel tanks ruptured and filled, the *Andrea Doria* suddenly increased her list nearly 20 degrees.

There exists, in any situation where the vessel does not sink immediately, an excellent chance of saving her if slow leaks can be patched and plugged. Bulkheads that have not collapsed under the blast and onrush of water from the hit are not likely to collapse under hydrostatic pressure.

Immediately after serious damage TWO IMPORTANT DECISIONS must be made: (1) whether all hands should remain aboard, all but the salvage party should be evacuated, or all hands should abandon ship; and (2) what corrective measures will improve the situation instead of making it worse. The first of these decisions is made by the captain, but his conclusions must be based on information that he receives from the engineer. The second decision is frequently the problem of the engineer unless it involves ship handling or loss of military efficiency (as through jettisoning ammunition).

3.37   The Enemies of Stability   If a ship's tank or void is only partially full, the liquid contents may "slosh' 'back and forth with the motion of the ship. This effect is known as *free surface*. A similar effect is noted if a compartment is partially flooded.

If the hull is ruptured so that one or more compartments are open to the sea, *free communication with the sea* results.

Free surface and free communication with the sea are, when combined, the deadly enemies of stability.

There is little excuse for much free surface; tanks partially full should generally be ballasted. The captain who takes his ship into heavy weather with excessive or avoidable free surface in his tanks is foolhardy. The ship with initial free surface which is damaged so that it also acquires loose water and free communication with the sea will almost surely be in danger. Free surface should be avoided, since it always causes a reduction in GM and overall stability. (It should be remembered that a reduction in GM reduces a ship's stability.) Free communication with the sea not only reduces GM *but GZ as well.* Thus, not only is some initial stability lost, but since GZ decreases, there is a decrease in the ship's righting moment.

Maintenance

3.38   Care and Preservation   Without proper care, both wood and metal hulls deteriorate rapidly to the point where they are unsafe and unusable. Wooden hulls are subject not only to rot and deterioration when not properly protected from the atmosphere, but also to damage from marine animals and marine growths that attack the underwater body. Metal hulls must be protected from both corrosion and erosion in order to maintain their seaworthiness.

Marine animals and marine growths that damage the hull of a ship or retard its speed are natives of salt water and, in general, are more common and damaging in tropical waters than in colder climates. The greatest hazard to wooden hulls is the teredo or marine borer, a worm-like mollusk that eats its way through wood and riddles planks and timbers with small holes. Like all marine animals and growths, the teredo is poisoned by copper and its derivatives, and the standard protection for wooden hulls is to cover them with a copper base or similarly poisonous paint. Originally a tropical pest, the teredo has spread until it is now found in virtually all salt-water harbors of the United States.

The underwater pest which causes the most trouble on steel hulls is the barnacle, although mussels and marine grasses of various sorts are also found attached to the underwater body. The barnacle is a univalve mollusk which attaches itself tightly to the skin of the ship and forms a shell that is roughly cone-shaped. It propagates freely and if undisturbed will soon build up a layer several inches deep. Barnacles and other marine growths apparently do little damage to a steel hull, except to destroy the protective paint and allow seawater to promote corrosion, but they may reduce the speed of a ship as much as several knots by increasing skin friction between the water and the hull. Modern plastic paints, applied hot in drydock, protect a hull from barnacles for several years.

The greatest problem in the care and preservation of metals is corrosion. Corrosion is the gradual disintegration of a metal due to chemical or electrochemical attack by atmosphere, moisture, or other agents. There are many different types of corrosion. A technical discussion of the various types may be found in any standard reference work on the subject.

Although a ship does not encounter any corrosion problems which may not be found anywhere else, it does encounter virtually all types of corrosion. A bronze propeller secured to a steel shaft and turning in an electrolyte (sea water) introduces the possibility of electrochemical attack on the shaft and the ship's hull. The propeller itself may suffer from cavitation and corrosion-erosion attack. Pumps handling seawater are subject to similar conditions. Propeller and pump shafts are also subject to corrosion fatigue.

3.39 Corrosion The hull and superstructure of the vessel are usually of plain carbon steel, and any seaman knows the amount of chipping and painting necessary to combat the severe rust caused by a marine atmosphere. Some superstructures have been built of aluminum alloys which resist atmospheric corrosion.

The various means for preventing or minimizing corrosion may be classified under four headings:

1. The Use of Alloys that Resist Attack by the Particular Environment The resistance to atmospheric attack of such materials as the copper base alloys, stainless steels, and Monel metal are well known, but there is no single alloy that is immune to all corroding media. However, the addition of alloying elements in even small amounts may greatly improve the resistance of a particular material to a given environment. About 0.25 percent copper added to a carbon steel doubles its resistance to atmosphere corrosion. Copper-nickel is an excellent material for condenser tubes, but its resistance to seawater is greatly improved by the addition of 0.2 to 0.6. percent iron. Depending on environment, the corrosion resistance of stainless steels may be improved by small additions of manganese, silicon, columbium, titanium, molybdenum, or nitrogen.

2. *The Use of Galvanic Protection*   The electrochemical mechanism may be utilized for protecting a structural metal in contact with an electrolyte. This galvanic protection consists of attaching to the structure a metal, anodic to the one to be protected, thus sacrificing the added metal and protecting the structure. Zinc is commonly used to protect steel, cast iron, brass, and bronze. The zinc must be in good electrical contact with the metal to be protected and the electrolyte. Galvanic protection is used for propeller shafts, rudders, and hull plates by attaching zinc plates near the propellers.

3. *The Control of Environment*   Metals have very low corrosion rates in dry gases and in pure water free from air. An outstanding example of control of environment is the dehumidification done in the mothballing program carried out by the armed forces since the end of World War II. The sealed interiors of ships were kept dry with air-conditioning machines; guns, tanks, planes, etc., were completely sealed in moistureproof covers and provided with moisture-absorbing agents.

4. *The Use of Protective Coatings*   These may be divided into four classes: (a) chemical coatings, (b) organic coatings, (c) metallic coatings, and (d) inorganic coatings.

Chemical coatings are those formed by chemical reaction between the metal surface and an appropriate solution. The application of phosphate coatings to the ferrous metals is representative of this group. The part to be protected is dipped in or sprayed with a solution of phosphates, and the coating that forms not only is resistant to atmospheric corrosion but serves as an excellent base for paints. Some magnesium and aluminum alloys are similarly protected with chromate coatings. Oxide and silicate coatings may also be chemically produced on certain metals.

Organic coating materials include paint, varnish, plastics, natural and synthetic rubbers, bituminous, and petroleum products. In general, these materials form a mechanical film to exclude air and moisture from the metal surface. Their effectiveness depends on the initial cleanliness of the metal and on the film thickness. All of them may be satisfactory for prolonged periods of time, depending on environment and whether or not the surface is subjected to abrasion.

Inorganic coating products consist of inorganic zinc silicates. Depending on the composition, some adhere to the surface by a mechanical bond, while some adhere by a combination of mechanical and chemical bonding.

Metallic coating processes serve to cover a corrodible metal with a thin layer of another metal which is more resistant to attack. Sometimes the coating also provides galvanic protection, as is the case with zinc or cadmium coatings on the ferrous metals. Metallic coatings may be applied by electroplating, hot dipping, or metallizing.

Electroplating consists of making the clean base metal the cathode in an electrolytic cell containing a water solution of some salt of the metal being deposited. Close control of the process is essential to good nonporous plating. Copper, nickel, chromium, cadmium, and zinc are electrodeposited on iron and steel as corrosion preventives.

Hot dipping consists of immersing the cleaned base metal in a molten bath of the coating metal. The process is suitable for those metals that will wet each other. Zinc and tin coatings are commonly applied by hot dipping.

Metallizing is a metal spraying process in which a wire or powder of the coating metal is melted by an oxyacetylene flame in the presence of an air jet which atomizes the metal and sprays it onto the base metal. The base metal must have a roughened surface since the bonding is purely mechanical. Virtually all metals can be sprayed, and the process is used to build up worn parts and provide hard surfaces as well as for corrosion resistance.

The protective measures just described for the underwater hull cannot be used at discretion, as is done in the case of surfaces above water. The submerged hull is virtually inaccessible while the ship is waterborne. No protective coating that will last indefinitely under water has been devised. Damage to underwater fittings may occur that will remain undetected as long as the fittings remain submerged. The only practical method for preserving the underwater hull is to remove it from the water at intervals, make needed repairs, and give it the best protective coating available before refloating. This routine is generally known as drydocking.

Drydocking

3.40 Schedules and Routine This, for government ships, is done according to directives in force. Merchant ships, classed with the American Bureau of Shipping, are drydocked for special periodic surveys. The outer shell, stem and stern frames as well as the keel are cleaned and inspected. Tanks are tested under pressure. The rudder and its supports are checked for unusual wear and rebushed if necessary. The chain is ranged and inspected, and usually repainted. Every third year a merchant ship's tail shaft is drawn and inspected.

3.41   Types of Drydock   There are several methods of drydocking. The oldest and simplest is known as beaching or careening. This process consists of putting a ship on a shelving beach at high tide, working on alternate sides during periods of low tide. This method will never be seen in modern practice, except in the case of very small vessels. For the ordinary steel vessel the usual methods of drydocking are by the use of marine railways, floating drydocks, and graving docks.

A *marine railway* is an inclined shipway having a cradle on wheels that runs on rails. It is moved by means of a windlass and endless chain. Few marine railways will handle a ship larger than a moderate-sized destroyer.

The usual *floating drydock* (see Figs. 3.12 and 3.13) is made up of rectangular, open-ended section that can be fastened firmly together. Tanks are flooded with water to sink the dock far enough for a ship to enter the cradle and then are pumped out so as to raise the ship and the inner part of the dock clear of the water. By using enough sections of suitable dimensions, all ships can be docked. Sections of the dock also can be used to dock each other. One of the great advantages of float-

Fig. 3.12   The floating drydock U.S.S. ARD 30 is set up for the next ship to enter. All the positioning blocks in the ARD 30 are precut to fit each individual ship. *(Official U.S. Navy photograph.)*

Fig. 3.13 The medium auxiliary floating drydock six (AFDM 6) moves into its recently completed mooring facilities. *(Official U.S. Navy photograph.)*

ing drydocks is that they can be towed to the localities where they are most needed. Mobility of floating drydocks has been increased greatly in the types of construction developed by the U.S. Navy in the past few years. Floating drydocks for the smaller types of vessels are built in one piece with the usual ship-type bow and are equipped with a steering mechanism. For ease in towing, a section with a ship-type bow may also be provided for larger sectional floating drydocks. Most floating drydock sections are self-contained. They have pumps for emptying their ballast tanks, and power plants and other facilities for the storage and distribution of such services as oil, compressed air, steam, and electric current; and they may be equipped with machine shops and with quarters for their crews.

A *graving dock* (Fig. 3.14) is a permanent installation in a shipyard. It is a narrow basin having walls and a floor, usually built of reinforced concrete, into which vessels may be floated and from which the water may be pumped out, leaving the vessels dry and supported on blocks. It is used for repairing and cleaning the underwater hulls of ships and in some cases for building ships.

Graving docks are built at an angle to the shore line, and one end must be open to navigable water in order to allow the entrance of ships. This open end is usually closed by a caisson or gate, either floating or sliding. In some docks a double swinging gate is used. The most usual type, the floating caisson, is a self-pumping hollow gate which is floated and towed clear when the dock is flooded. After a ship enters the dock the caisson is moved into place and flooded with water, which causes its ends to sink into wedge-shaped grooves cut in the walls of the dock while its base fits against and is supported by the sill, which extends across the entrance of the dock and is raised somewhat above its floor. The depth of water over the sill at high tide

Fig. 3.14 Flooding begins in drydock #1 at the Long Beach Naval Shipyard prior to the entry of a ship. *(Official U.S. Navy photograph.)*

determines the greatest draft of any ship that can be docked. In a naval shipyard dock especially, it is desirable that this depth be greater than the ordinary draft of any ship it is expected to accommodate in order to allow for the increased draft due to battle damage.

The walls of a graving dock are usually built in steps which are known as altars. Power capstans and fixed bollards are installed to control the lines used in hauling the ship in and out of the dock. Blocks are heavy wooden structures used to build up the cradle in which the ship rests while in dock. The keel blocks, upon which the ship's keel is supported, are large cube-shaped, semi-fixed structures built up of concrete, hardwood, and soft pine caps. Other blocks, called bilge blocks or side blocks, are prepositioned in accordance with the individual ship's docking plan. Should bilge blocks not be available and a ship have insufficient flat bottom for the installation of enough keel blocks to keep her uptright, wale shores may be used. These are spars extending from the ship's side to the side of the dock and wedged in place as she settles upon the keel blocks. In case several small vessels are to be docked at once, blocks may be set up for them on appropriate sections of the dock floor.

3.42 Preparations for Docking   In preparing a dock to receive a vessel, the dockmaster or docking officer first refers to the ship's docking plan. This furnishes necessary information concerning the underwater hull for docking purposes. For United States men-of-war a copy will usually be found in the files of the ship's home yard, but every ship should carry its own docking plan. To place the blocks accurately and to build them up to the proper height and angle, the docking plan must give the following information:

1. Full extent of keel with flat and rising portions accurately delineated.
2. Peculiarities of stern post and rudder.
3. Sections, amidships and elsewhere, to show proper height and angle of bilge blocks, if these are necessary.
4. Shape and location of keels, docking keels, struts, propellers, underwater fittings, and projections of all kinds.

Further, since it is often necessary to provide more blocks than usual under heavy weights, the docking plan should show:

5. Location of boilers, engines, and other unusual weights.

To assist in locating sighting battens the plan should show:

6. The length on the load waterline.

Finally, in order to enable the dockmaster to determine whether or not the dock can take a ship, or to place her accurately in the dock, the plan must show:

7. The length overall, the beam, and all projections, such as blisters, increasing the normal beam.

3.43 Docking   The dockmaster of any particular dock, knowing the ship's draft, the maximum depth over the sill, and the current and tidal variations in the vicinity, decides on the time the ship should enter the dock and so informs the commanding officer. The commanding officer makes the necessary arrangements to ensure that at the time specified the ship is without any list to either side and with trim, if any, as specified by the dockmaster or docking officer.

The dock being already prepared, water is admitted, the caisson is floated and removed, and the ship is brought to the dock entrance, usually with the assistance of tugs. When the bow of the ship has safely crossed the sill of the dock, the responsibility for her safety rests upon the dockmaster, who hauls her into the dock, replaces and sinks the caisson, centers the ship, starts dock pumps, and proceeds with the docking until the ship is safely landed on the blocks and the dock is pumped dry.

Should any extraordinary conditions exist, such as those due to accident or battle damage to the ship, the special precautions taken in docking her must depend upon the judgment of the dockmaster.

During the period when the ship is in dock, no change of any kind in her weights should be made without the knowledge and consent of the dockmaster. Improper changes in weights may cause her to do serious damage to herself or the dock when she is floated, due to sudden changes in list or trim.

3.44   Routine Work in Drydock   The following routine drydock work is done in addition to any special underwater repairs or alterations.

1. Clean bottom, including scaling or wirebrushing of badly corroded parts.
2. Cut out and redrive all loose or badly corroded rivets.
3. Caulk leaky seams and rivets.
4. Overhaul underwater valves.
5. Repack underwater stuffing boxes.
6. Renew zinc and mild steel protectors as necessary.
7. Take propeller shaft clearances and rewood stern and strut bearings as necessary.
8. Check pitch of propellers, clean and polish them.
9. Examine rudder pintles and gudgeons and rudder shaft packing; take rudder bearing clearances.
10. Paint bottom; paint draft marks; paint boot-topping.
11. Inspect and repair bilge keels.
12. Clear all sea strainers.

3.45   Undocking   After all underwater repairs are completed and the bottom is painted, a time for flooding the dock is agreed upon between the commanding officer of the ship and the dockmaster. The former stations men at the outboard valves and elsewhere as he deems necessary, to ensure that water does not enter the ship. The latter stations men at the various shores and lines to prevent as far as possible any injury to the ship or dock from a change of weights or any unexpected alteration in tide or wind.

Water is admitted to the dock under the dockmaster's control. When all sea-valve openings are covered, flooding is usually stopped until their watertightness can be reported. When the water has risen to a sufficient height the ship lifts from the keel blocks. When the ship is safely afloat flooding is continued until the water level within the dock is the same as that outside. The caisson is floated as quickly as possible, then removed, and the ship is hauled out of drydock.

3.46 Elevator Drydocks The newest drydocks, especially for relatively small vessels, are the Syncrolift marine elevators that feature a rail transfer system. This permits movement of the vessels from the elevator platform to remote areas of the shipyard where repairs or building can be done leaving the elevator platform free to dock other vessels. Well over 100 Syncrolift drydocks are in use worldwide, from 70 to 12,000 tons capacity. Maximum size is 60,000 tons. The Syncrolift is basically an elevator type of drydock. The platform is lowered vertically and stopped at a predetermined depth. The vessel to be drydocked is floated over the submerged platform which is then raised until the vessel and platform are completely above the water level.

The platform that supports the vessel during the drydocking operation is raised and lowered by electrically controlled hoists with wire rope cables. The hoists are supported by fixed structures on both sides of the platform and are normally supported by standard marine piling of concrete or steel. The number of hoists, capacity of each hoist, and their spacing is varied to provide the required drydocking capacity. Each hoist consists of an electric motor, a reduction gear system, a wire rope cable drum and a double brake arrangement. The electric motor is a specially designed alternating current synchronous induction motor. It has operating characteristics necessary for the wide range of loads required in drydocking. The motors are designed to operate at a fixed rate of speed regardless of the load variations imposed by the ship's weight distribution. All the electric motors are interconnected and controlled at one central control point. In effect, the motors act as though they are connected mechanically and no variation in speed from one motor to the other is possible. This assures constant lifting speed at all hoists which in turn keep the elevator platform level.

The minimum number of hoists is four, and by varying their capacities, Syncrolifts capable of lifting 70 to 230 tons are constructed. As additional capacity is required, eight or more hoists are used.

Fig. 3.15   Aerial view of Syncrolift platform, transfer system, and workberths; Fisheries Development Corporation, Walvis Bay, South Africa. Platform is 260 ft long by 50 ft wide, operated by twenty-two 180-ton hoists. Rated capacity is 2310 long tons. (*Photograph courtesy of Syncrolift Pearlson Engineering Company.*)

The platform construction consists of steel structural members and wood planks for decking. Platforms using only four hoists have their steel members welded together to form a single structure. Syncrolifts using eight or more hoists have an articulated platform which consist of a series of main transverse lifting beams supported by a hoist at each end. They do not have to be connected to each other because the constant speed of each hoist assures that all beams will remain at the same level.

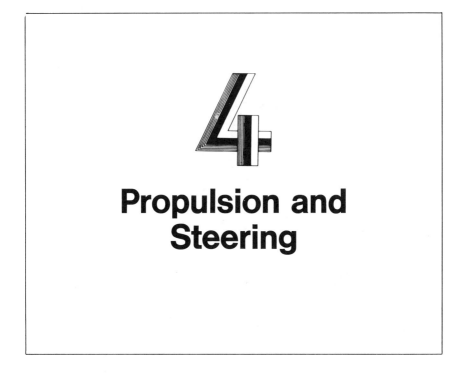

Propulsion and Steering

A knowledge of seamanship would not be complete without an understanding of the means available to maneuver a ship: the power plant and the steering mechanism. A ship's captain or deck officer must know the minimum and maximum responses of his ship to backing, accelerating, and rudder angle under all conditions. With this knowledge the expert shiphandler will always avoid putting his ship into such a situation that judicious use of his engine and rudder cannot extricate him. Regardless of the apparent complexity, any propulsion device is based on the fundamental principles of energy conversion. The energy available in a fuel, whether conventional fuel such as oil, or nuclear fuel, is converted to mechanical energy which is then used to give the ship kinetic energy or energy of motion.

4.1 Boilers Marine boilers supplying steam for propulsion are usually water tube boilers of the express (small tube) type. In this type of boiler, made possible by modern feed water treatment, the water is inside the tubes. The products of combustion change the water to steam by transfer of heat through the tube walls. The small tubes of the express type boiler provide the greatest heat transfer surface in a given space. This large heat transfer area allows the boiler to be brought up to full pressure from a cold start in about 2 hours. Pressures as high as 1200 pounds per square inch are used in naval vessels.

4.2   How the Deck Officer Can Promote Efficient Boiler Operation

Some deck officers seem to feel that the engineer's only reason for blowing tubes is to spread fine carbon dust over the clean topside, and consequently they refuse to allow tubes to be blown on their watch. An understanding of the reasons which make blowing tubes necessary may temper their reluctance to grant permission. When oil is burned in a boiler a layer of soot is deposited on the outside of the small water tubes. This soot layer is undesirable for the following reasons; (1) The soot acts as an insulator and slows heat transfer to the water within the tubes thereby reducing efficiency of the boiler. (2) If the soot is left in a boiler when fires are secured, it absorbs moisture from the air; the moisture activates the sulfuric acid in the soot, and this acid attacks the metal of the tubes and boiler drum. (3) If allowed to remain in the boiler too long the soot packs into a solid mass which can only be removed by tedious hand cleaning methods. To maintain maximum boiler efficiency, tubes should be blown once each four hour watch while under way and at least twice each day when in port. As a practical matter on merchant ships when under way tubes are blown two or three times a day instead of once every four hours. Blowing tubes requires that the steam used be replaced by an equal amount of water from the make-up system. This water must be replaced by the distilling plant.

When tubes are blown high pressure steam is admitted to the soot blowers (perforated tubes) which are permanently installed in the boiler. The soot blowers have steam admitted to them in a specific order which is designed to sweep the soot out the stack.

The officer of the deck should also be aware that a light brown haze from the stack usually indicates maximum engineering plant efficiency.

4.3   Nuclear Reactors

On nuclear powered ships the heat to generate steam for propulsion turbines, turbogenerators and auxiliaries comes from a nuclear reactor instead of a boiler. The reactor serves the same function as the furnace of a boiler in that it provides the heat to convert water to steam. The heat is supplied by burning a unique fuel which is capable of nuclear fission and is controlled by moving a neutron absorber (the control rods) in or out of the fuel area. The heat resulting from the controlled nuclear fission is used to heat water which is maintained under high pressure. This water, known as the coolant because it removes heat from the reactor, provides heat to a heat exchanger which is the steam generator.

First generation nuclear power plants, such as that shown in Fig. 4.1, consist of a primary and a secondary system.

Primary or Main Coolant System   The reactor gives up heat to the main coolant, highly pressurized water, which gives up this heat in the steam generator to form steam. The coolant is then returned to the reactor where it is again heated and the process is repeated. The coolant is kept under high pressure to ensure that it will not boil in the reactor vessel, which can cause the reactor to fail.

Secondary or Main Steam System   The secondary system is the main steam system. The coolant from the reactor gives up heat to the feed water of the secondary system in the steam generator. The steam formed by this process goes to the engine room where it is used in the same

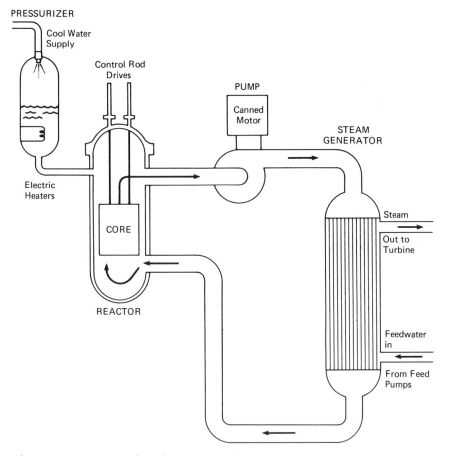

Fig. 4.1   Basic marine nuclear plant. Diagram shows, in simplified terms, a model nuclear plant. Once steam is generated in a marine nuclear plant, it is treated just like that produced from an oil-fired burner.

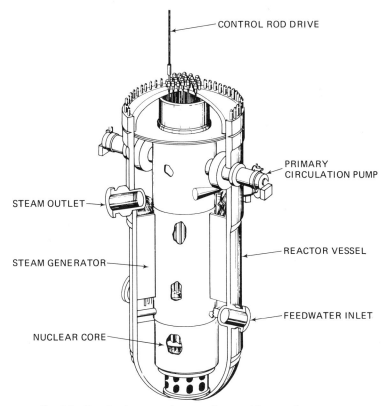

CONTROL ROD DRIVE

PRIMARY
CIRCULATION PUMP

STEAM OUTLET

REACTOR VESSEL

STEAM GENERATOR

FEEDWATER INLET

NUCLEAR CORE

Fig. 4.2 Sketch of a second generation maritime nuclear reactor.

manner as in an oil-fueled ship. The secondary system is completely isolated from the primary system in this type of nuclear plant and does not penetrate the reactor vessel.

Newer nuclear systems are now available wherein the secondary system (main steam) penetrates the reactor vessel and the heat transfer from the coolant to the main steam system takes place within the reactor vessel. The two systems are still isolated completely from each other within the reactor vessel in this type of nuclear plant. Figure 4.2 shows this second generation type of reactor.

4.4   The Steam Turbine   Steam enters a turbine through nozzles which direct the steam on to moving blades mounted solidly on a rotor. The rotor is enclosed in a casing and supported on bearings at each end of the casing. When the steam has passed through the first row of moving blades, making them spin, it enters a row of stationary blades attached to the casing which in turn direct the steam against a second row of moving blades attached to the same revolving rotor. Alternate rows of fixed and moving blades are located along the length of the turbine. The steam flows through the turbine because of the pressure difference between the point of entry and the point of exit. As it passes through each set of fixed and moving blades (known as turbine stages), the steam pressure and temperature drop as some of the energy is extracted to make the turbine rotor revolve. Theoretically the stages necessary to extract all the energy available between the entering and final steam pressures could be in one casing, but actually such a turbine would be too long, the shaft would tend to sag in the middle, and unequal expansion could take place. Actually the stages are divided between two turbines known as the high-pressure and low-pressure turbines. To provide backing power another turbine is required, designed to turn the shaft in the reverse directon. This backing turbine could be housed in a separate casing, but because of its small power requirement (requiring only two or three stages) in comparison to the ahead power requirement, it is more economical to mount it in the existing turbine casing of the low-pressure turbine.

Turbines are most efficient when running at high speed (3000 to 6000 rpm), whereas most propellers* are most efficient at slow speeds (up to about 200 rpm). To allow both to run at their most efficient speed, a reduction gear is used between the turbine and the propeller shaft. The reduction ratio varies but is in the neighborhood of 20 to 1 for large ships.

On merchant ships with single-screw propulsion, the propeller revolutions per minute may vary from 80 on large, slow tankers to 110 or so on higher-speed cargo ships. In these cases the gear reduction ratios may vary from 40 to 1 to 80 to 1; and may, in the future, necessitate the use of triple reduction gearing.

4.5 What the Deck Officer Should Know about His Turbines   When the officer of the deck gives permission to the engineers to start warming up the main plant he should know that the engines are slowly turned by the jacking gear. The jacking gear consists of an electric motor and a hand-operated gear clutch which can be connected to the reduction gear. The clutch is connected, and the electric motor is started, which turns over the turbines slowly and the propellers even more slowly. While no way is put on the ship by this, the OOD should make sure that nothing can foul the propellers in their slow revolving before he grants permission to warm up.

Approximately 15 minutes before the time set for getting under way, the engineer officer of the watch will request permission to "Spin main

---

* Propellers will be discussed in more detail in a later section of this chapter.

engines with steam and continue spinning at 3- to 5-minute intervals." The officer of the deck should realize that it is only the engines that are "spun" and not the propellers. A quick puff of steam sufficient to start the turbines rolling is admitted from the ahead throttle, and as soon as the turbines start, the ahead throttle is closed and the astern throttle is opened, stopping the spin. The propeller may turn only a fraction of a revolution, but no way should be put on the ship from this spinning.

The reason for spinning the turbines at 3- to 5-minute intervals is to prevent uneven heating of the turbine rotor with the possibility of its developing a change in shape. With the close fit of the rotor in the turbine casing a slight sag would cause the blades to scrape on the casing and possibly snap off. Before spinning the main engines with steam, the jacking gear must be disconnected. The purpose of jacking is the same as for spinning with steam. Whenever the engines are stopped, they should be spun every 5 minutes. When word is given to secure the plant, the jacking gear is again engaged, and the turbines are jacked over until cooled.

On some of the latest ships, the roll-over of the turbine is under bridge control and monitored by audible and visible alarms on a predetermined time cycle. In these cases, the deck watch actuates the bridge throttle which silences the audible alarms. A further sophistication may also be found wherein the turbines are automatically spun on a set time cycle whenver the bridge throttle is in the STOP position.

4.6 Locking a Shaft If one engine or propeller is damaged while a ship is under way, and the ship cannot be stopped, the damaged engine and shaft must be locked to prevent worse damage. If only the steam is shut off, the shaft will continue to turn as the water acts on the dragging propeller. To lock a shaft underway, the ahead throttle is closed and the astern throttle is opened enough (steam is admitted to the backing turbine) to stop the shaft from turning; then the jacking gear is engaged and a friction brake on the jacking gear is tightened. The other shaft (or shafts on a four-shaft vessel) are usually limited in their allowable revolutions when one or two shafts are locked. The limitation is required to avoid overloading the driving turbines and shafts. The limiting rpm's for naval ships are given in a technical manual which is provided to all ships.

4.7 Internal-Combustion Engines The fuel for an internal combustion engine is burned within the engine itself and the products of combustion pass directly through the engine. The transformation of heat to mechanical energy is thus completely contained with the engine. There are basic differences in the method used to initiate combustion in

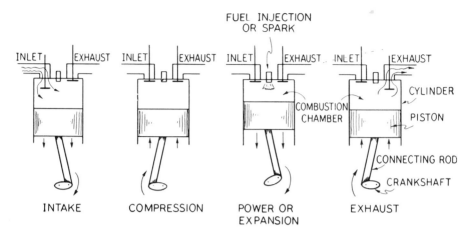

Fig. 4.3 One cylinder of a spark ignition engine (four-stroke cycle) showing the four phases in one complete firing cycle.

internal combustion engines. In the gasoline engine fuel and air are mixed in the carburetor and admitted to the combustion chamber by the inlet valve. This mixture is compressed and then ignited by an electrical spark. The burning fuel expands and converts heat energy to mechanical energy by driving the piston down. The products of combustion are then removed through the now opened exhaust valve. The gasoline engine is seldom used today in marine application because of the hazard present in the highly flammable fuel. The operation of a 4-cycle engine is shown in Fig. 4.3.

Large diesel engines used for marine applications are usually of the 2-cycle type shown in Fig. 4.4. In this type of engine air, which has been

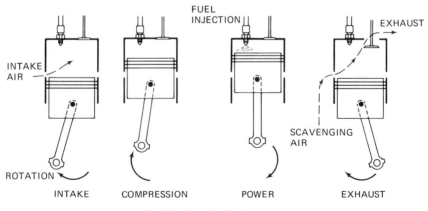

Fig. 4.4 2-cycle diesel engine.

increased in pressure by a blower, enters the intake port. This air is then compressed to a very small volume by the piston which causes the temperaure of the air to rise to nearly 2000 degrees. Fuel is then injected into the cylinder and is ignited by the high temperature air. The burning fuel–air mixture expands, driving the piston down, thus converting heat energy to mechanical energy. When the piston is at the bottom of the cylinder the products of combustion are swept out through the open exhaust valve by the incoming fresh air. By closing the exhaust valve before the piston closes the intake port the engine can be supercharged and thus develop greater power.

4.8 Use of Diesels In non-Navy service, diesel engine propulsion can be found in many foreign flag merchant ships as well as in many small craft worldwide—such as tugs, research vessels, fishing craft, small coastal craft, and workboats. Diesel propulsion for large American merchant ships has not received general acceptance.

The diesel can be connected either directly to the propelling shaft or through a reduction gear to the propelling shaft. Another method is to use the diesels to drive electric generators which supply electricity to drive motors which turn the propeller shafts. This will be discussed further at the end of this section.

The direct-connected diesel must be of slow speed in order to allow the propeller to operate at an efficient speed. However, to reduce weight and improve its own efficiency, the diesel should run at high speed. The reduction gear is the logical answer and allows the diesel to turn at its efficient high speed while the propeller turns at its efficient slow speed. Most diesels have a flexible coupling between the engine and the reduction gear of the propeller shaft to prevent engine vibrations from being transmitted to the gears of the shaft. The coupling can be hydraulic—similar in style but larger than those used in automobile automatic transmission—spring packs, or an electromagnetic device.

4.9 Gas Turbines The gas turbine is a lightweight, compact plant which can be warmed up and loaded in a matter of minutes. Figure 4.5 shows a schematic diagram of a gas turbine plant. The engine is started by an electric motor or by forcing air into the compressor section causing it to rotate.

When the gas turbine is running, air enters the compressor where its pressure is increased from about 2 to 20 (depending on the size of the engine) times the atmospheric pressure. This air then goes to the combustion chamber where it is mixed with the fuel and burned. While starting the engine an external spark is required as a source of ignition. Once the engine has been started combustion is continuous and is self

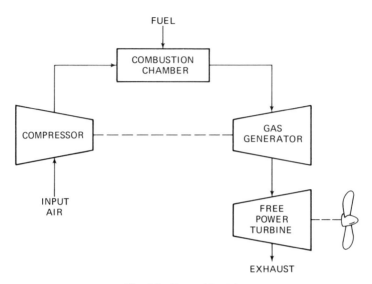

Fig. 4.5 Gas turbine plant.

sustaining. The combustion chamber, while a simple appearing device, must be carefully constructed to insure proper mixing of fuel and air, cooling, and freedom from flame "blow-out." The products of combustion enter the gas generator which usually consists of 4 to 6 simple turbine stages. The gas generator provides the power to drive the compressor and when it is generating sufficient power the starting device is disconnected and the engine is self-sustaining. The exhaust from the gas generator goes to the free power turbine which drives the propeller through reduction gears. This split shaft arrangement allows the compressor-gas generator to be operated at its most efficient speed while the free power turbine speed can be varied as required.

A simpler form of gas turbine does not have the free power turbine but takes its output from the gas generator shaft. This single shaft system is not as efficient for variable load operation but is used where a fixed speed (such as a generator) is required.

The gas turbine is an undirectional engine and means must be provided for backing down. This can take the form of gearing and a clutch or, as is more common, a controllable pitch propeller.

The U.S. Navy has built its newest destroyers, the Spruance class, 8700 tons, with gas turbine drive. New merchant ships are also using gas turbines for main propulsion.

4.10 Electric Drive Any of the propulsion engines mentioned so far could be used with an electric drive. In the electric drive these engines drive an electric generator at a constant speed. The generator or generators in turn supply electricity to electric propulsion motors which drive the propeller either directly or through a reduction gear. Reversing the propellers is accomplished by electrical switches which reverses the driving motors. The engine driving the generator can only turn in one direction. The electric switches can be located on the bridge and hence give the officer of the deck complete control of his speed and direction of travel. Diesel–electric tugboats are frequently fitted with this type of control.

4.11 Engine and Steering Control The bridge is the primary station for controlling the engines a well as for steering and navigating the ship. In large ships auxiliary control stations are provided with part or all of the bridge control instruments duplicated and with sound-powered telephone communication with the bridge and the engine rooms. In merchant ships an auxiliary control and steering station is generally located on or above the main deck, in the after part of the ship. In men-of-war, where the chance of battle damage is great, engine and/or steering controls may be found in secondary conning stations (located remote from the bridge) in central control stations or controlling engine rooms, in steering engine rooms, and possibly in other locations. These are discussed in Chapter 7.

4.12 Bridge Control of Propulsion Plant Newer ships are being fitted out with automated propulsion plants, and the bridges of these ships have installed (propulsion) bridge control consoles. This console enables the bridge officer to control directly the speed and direction of the propeller(s) by controlling the propulsion turbine throttle valves or the pitch of the propeller. Bridge control enhances the maneuvering response time of the ship in that it eliminates the time lag in transmitting sped changes from the bridge to the engine room by the engine order telegraph. It also results in marked personnel economies.

The bridge officer may move the throttle control in any manner (e.g., swiftly or slowly) because automatic controls are provided in the propulsion system that insure its safe operation under all operating conditions.

Since ship response is faster with bridge control than with conventional, the deck officer should familiarize himself with the throttle control operation and the response times for maneuvering speed changes and the response of the ship in executing emergency crash astern maneuvers. Normally, specific instructions for the bridge console operation are posted on the console as a guide for the operator. He should be thoroughly familiar with the instructions, especially those telling how transfer of control between the engine room and bridge is accomplished and those telling the purpose of all indicators and alarm lights on the console. Before assuming his first bridge watch, he should receive a check-out on the bridge control console by one of the ship's engineering officers.

4.13 Propellers After the energy of a fuel has been converted to heat and in turn the heat converted to mechanical energy, a way must be found to use the mechanical energy to drive the ship. The propeller is the device used to drive all large modern ships. The propeller in a fluid, such as a marine propeller, is a device to obtain a reactive thrust by increasing the velocity of the fluid through its disk. It thus changes the momentum of a mass and provides a propulsive force, or reactive thrust. One method of describing a propeller is by the number of blades it has. Normally a propeller with more blades will have a smaller diameter for the same "pushing" power than one with fewer blades.

Another method of describing a propeller is by the direction it turns when driving the ship ahead. Obviously we must specify the side from which we view the propeller in determining its direction or motion. By convention, a right-handed propeller is defined as a propeller that turns in a clockwise direction, viewed from astern, when driving the ship ahead. Similarly, a left-handed propeller turns counter-clockwise viewed from astern, when driving the ship ahead. Ships having one propeller are designated as single-screw ships; ships having two propellers are called twin-screw ships, while multi-screw ships may have three or four propellers. It is most common for ships to be equipped with one, two, or four screws. The blades of a propeller may be fastened to the hub with bolts or may be cast with the hub in one piece.

One type of propeller which can reverse the direction of a ship without requiring a change of direction of the shaft is the controllable pitch propeller. The hub of a controllable pitch propeller contains a mechanism which can change the pitch of the propeller as shown in Fig. 4.6. This change in pitch allows the vessel to be maneuvered without reversing the rotation of the engines. With the increased use of gas turbines, which are inherently non-reversable, as main propulsion engines this feature is required. The primary advantages of the controllable pitch propeller are its reversability and its ability to allow a constant engine RPM under varying power conditions. This latter feature allows the main propulsion plant to be run at its most efficient point.

Another type of propeller, the supercavitating propeller, has a special application for very high speed ships such as hydrofoils. Developed by the U.S. Navy, it reduces the effect of cavitation, if not the cavitation itself. Cavitation (Fig. 4.7) is caused by the lower pressure on the rear face

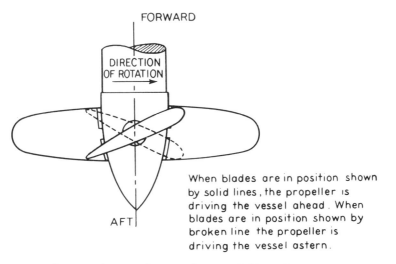

FORWARD

DIRECTION
OF ROTATION

AFT

When blades are in position shown
by solid lines, the propeller is
driving the vessel ahead. When
blades are in position shown by
broken line the propeller is
driving the vessel astern.

Fig. 4.6 Schematic diagram of a controllable pitch propeller.

of the propeller. This lower pressure, resulting from the air-foil like shape of the blade, causes some of the fluid in the low pressure region to vaporize. The vapor pockets thus formed both consume energy and cause erosion of the blades. The supercavitating propeller, operating at high speed, thus eliminating reduction gears in some installations, creates a vapor cavity along the trailing edge of the new type blade that results in a minimum of power loss and erosion.

Fig. 4.7 A conventional bladed propeller as it revolves. Note the turbulence or cavitation, which limits its speed and efficiency. *(Official U.S. Navy photograph.)*

4.14 New Forms of Propellers Some new propulsion concepts now in use are the shrouded propeller, the skewed propeller and the cycloidal propeller. The shrouded propeller (Fig. 4.8) has the propeller set into a nozzle. This arrangement can provide greater efficiency at speeds up to about 15 knots. Above these speeds the increased drag caused by the shroud overcomes the increase in efficiency and the overall result is a loss in total efficiency. Another disadvantage to the shroud is a reduction in backing power. This reduction is caused by the fact that a nozzle is basically a one-way device which is installed to improve ahead propulsion.

The skewed propeller provides a decrease in the vibration caused by the rotation of the propeller. However, as the skew of the propeller is increased the blades must be made thicker which causes a reduction in efficiency.

The cyclodial propeller provides great maneuverability but with a reduction in efficiency. This type of propeller can provide equal thrust in any direction. The blades change pitch as the system rotates to provide thrust in the desired direction. One example of successful use of cycloidal propellers is on tugs where this maneuverability and equal power in any direction make them desirable.

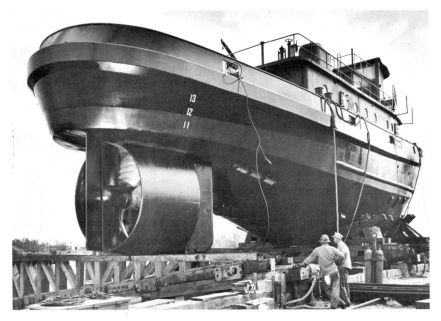

Fig. 4.8 The Dravo *Pioneer*, a tug fitted with Kort Nozzle or shrouded propeller.

4.15 Steering Steering implies the ability to change and to hold a course, and for this there must be an adequate combination of fixed or movable stern control surface (skegs or rudders respectively). For turning, the rudder is of major importance with some complex interaction with skegs or other fixed structure.

The usual method of changing the heading of a ship underway is by putting the rudder over to one side or the other. The action of the water on the rudder forces the stern of the vessel sideways, and the vessel changes course. Until saturation of rudder area is reached, the larger the rudder, the tighter the ship will turn, because there is a larger area on which the water can act.

Besides the area of the rudder, the speed of the water past the rudder also effects the response of a ship to putting the rudder over; the faster the water is traveling, the better the response. Because the water is traveling faster directly astern of the propellers, rudders directly abaft the propellers permit getting rudder forces at zero and low speeds. We can see then that if a ship is to be very maneuverable and have a small turning circle, the rudder should be as large as possible or two rudders should be provided, preferably abaft the propellers.

Rudders are of three general types: balanced, semi-balanced, and unbalanced, as shown in Fig. 4.9. When part of the rudder area is located forward of the rudder stock, the rudder is easier to turn because the action of the water on that part tends to help the rudder turn. The unbalanced rudder is the hardest to turn. The choice of rudder is determined by the shape of a vessel's stern, the number of propellers, and the speed the vessel will develop. To turn the rudder a steering gear is required.

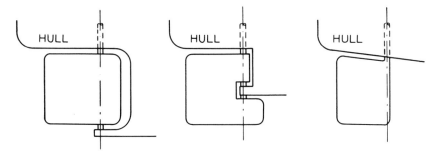

BALANCED   SEMI-BALANCED   UN BALANCED

Fig. 4.9 Common types of rudders.

4.16   The Steering Engines   The electrohydraulic type of steering gear (Fig. 4.10) is used on all modern naval ships. The hydraulic power is furnished by a variable-stroke hydraulic pump driven by a continuously running constant-speed electric motor. There are many variations of the number and arrangement of the hydraulic rams, pumps, and driving motors, and of the method of transmitting the motion of the rams to the rudder cross-head, but the schematic drawing shown in Fig. 4.10 illustrates the essential principles of this type of steering gear. As shown in this plan, movement of the control mechanism E in one direction causes the pump S to take suction from one pipe leading to it and to discharge to the other. Movement of the control mechanism in the opposite direction causes the direction of pumping to be reversed. When the control mechanism is in the neutral position, a hydraulic lock is placed on the rams, and no fluid is pumped. The rate of pumping in either direction depends on the amount of movement of the control mechanism, which is constructed so that small movement will produce the maximum available rate.

The electrical self-synchronous type of control is used by all modern naval ships. Briefly, the system consists of a synchro transmitter controlled by the motion of the steering wheel, suitable electric leads, and a synchro receiver connected to the control mechanism at the steering gear. Synchro transmitters and receivers are alternating current electric motors designed so that the rotor of the receiver follows, in speed and amount of angular displacement, the motion of the transmitter rotor. Motion of the steering wheel, which is carried on an extension of the shaft of the synchro transmitter rotor, is, therefore, transmitted directly to the control mechanism which acts to cause the steering gear to produce the desired rudder angle.

With all types of steering gear control, provision is made on all naval ships and on most other ships for quickly shifting control from station to station. The practice of making this shift of steering control part of the daily routine offers valuable training for handling a casualty in any ship control station.

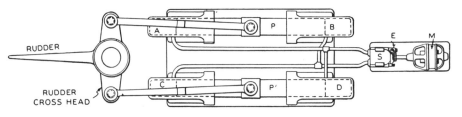

Fig. 4.10   Diagrammatic plan of electrohydraulic steering engine.

When twin rudders are provided, they both turn the same amount in the same direction if steering control is on the bridge. However, on some ships, when control is shifted to the steering engine room (some large ships have separate steering engines for each rudder), each room can independently control the motion of its own rudder. In a ship where this is true, the old adage that a ship has no brake is proved false. While the design was not made expressly to permit this, both rudders can be turned outward, thus slowing the ship just as air brakes slow an airplane. Even though it is not recommended that officers of the deck make a practice of slowing down by using the rudders in this manner, and it involves using sound-powered telephones to give orders to the steering engine room, the OOD should know if such a method of slowing is available in his ship for use in unusual situations. For example, a ship may have way on and power to the steering engines but cannot back down.

4.17 Recent Steering Devices New devices for steering now being used are a variety of rudder and propeller mechanisms that give certain ships improved handling qualities. Some ships have an active rudder that has a small propeller with its own power source installed with it as an integral unit. Ships fitted with Kort nozzles or shrouded propellers may have a steering rudder abaft the propeller and a pair of flanking rudders forward of the propeller. The steering rudder is used in the usual manner for ahead operation. The flanking rudders are for operation astern, and generally hard-over angles are used.

Another common device is the bow-thruster unit. This can be a propeller in a fixed transverse tunnel at the bow, or a retractable, swiveling propeller unit, or a cycloidal unit. Bow thrusters are primarily used as maneuvering assist devices in low speed operation.

Ground Tackle

Windlasses

A ship's windlass is designed primarily for handling anchor chain. The chain is guided over a fairlead and then around the capstan where it rides on a collar called a *wildcat*. This wildcat is essentially a sprocket designed to engage the links of the chain. The sprocket can be keyed to the capstan shaft and thus to the windlass motor, or it can be allowed to run free. A brake is also incorporated to control the wildcat when it is running free. Windlasses are arranged in many ways and combinations on various vessels, and are often provided with warping heads for handling line. There are four general classes, depending on the kind of drive: steam, electric, electric-hydraulic, and hand. (See Fig. 5.1.)

Anchors

When an old-fashioned anchor (Fig. 5.2) is let go in fairly deep water, it strikes the bottom crown first and immediately falls over until it rests on the end of the stock. From this position any drag on the chain to one side "cants" or capsizes it, pulling the stock down horizontally

Fig. 5.1 The anchor windlass of the attack transport *U.S.S. Cambria* (LPA 36). *(Official U.S. Navy photograph.)*

upon the bottom and pointing the flukes fair for biting. As the drag continues, the fluke is forced into the ground. If the anchor is well designed and enough scope of chain is used so that the pull is approximately parallel to the bottom, the heavier the pull, the deeper the fluke digs in. To obtain this effect a long enough scope of chain must be used so that the pull of the anchor will be approximately along the bottom. Use of too short a scope will lift the shank of the anchor and break out the fluke in a series of jumps.

Stockless anchors present an enormous advantage in ease of handling and stowing. On account of the absence of a stock, they can be hoisted directly into the hawse-pipe and stowed there ready for letting go quickly. Some features common to stockless anchors are:

1. The arms are pivoted upon the shank and can swing from 30 to 45 degrees on either side.
2. The palms are in the plane of the arms instead of at right angles to it.
3. As a result of this construction, both flukes should bite if either one does.
4. The arms carry a shoulder with a sharp edge at the crown which takes on the bottom and throws the arms downward to ensure the flukes biting.

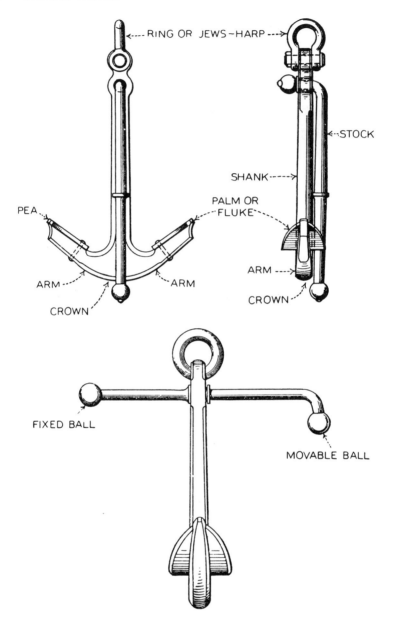

Fig. 5.2   Old-fashioned anchor.

The stockless anchors most commonly encountered are the Baldt, the Dunn, or the Norfolk (Fig. 5.3) which is a Navy-manufactured anchor of the Dunn type. The Navy stockless is used on most men-of-

Fig. 5.3   Large Navy stockless, 40,000-pound bower anchor on *U.S.S. Midway* (CVA 41).

war on account of its convenience in handling. Stockless anchors do not, however, have as much holding power as an old-fashioned anchor of the same weight or of the same fluke area, which is a better measure of holding power than weight. With too short a scope of chain or even under a steady pull, a stockless anchor has a tendency to disengage its flukes by gradually turning over and rolling them out. It also has a tendency to clog or ball with mud in a muddy bottom. If this occurs and the anchor breaks out, the arms may pivot to an angle where it is impossible for the flukes to bite again. It can then offer no resistance to dragging except its weight.

A new anchor developed by the British for very large ships such as the big tankers is the A.C. 14 anchor. (See Fig. 5.4.) Because of improved design this anchor has more than twice the holding power of a conventional anchor of the same weight and it is more stable under extreme stress.

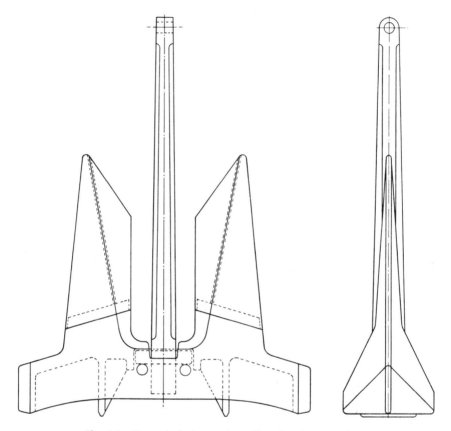

Fig. 5.4 General design and profile of A.C. 14 anchor.

5.1 Anchor Gear *Chain Cable* Chain is made to Navy and commercial link standard dimensions which are the same, 6 wire diameters long by 3.6 diameters wide. Anchor chains furnished in time of war are of all types: die-lock, forged and welded, stud-link, and cast steel. Die-lock and high-strength welded steel types of chain are considered standard and will replace other types. (See Fig. 5.5.)

Connecting Shackles Detachable links are used for connecting the shots of anchor chain. They have replaced the old Navy standard U-shaped shackles and also the Kenter connecting shackle. Detachable links of commercial design are also furnished for use with cast-steel chain. (See Fig. 5.6.)

Bending Shackles Bending shackles for use with cast-steel chain (conforming to American Bureau of Shipping requirements) and with die-lock chain are used for attaching the anchor to the chain cable. (See Fig. 5.7.)

Fig. 5.5 Swivel-shot, large-chain, 3½-inch heavy-duty die-lock. *(Official U.S. Navy photograph.)*

***Mooring Swivels* Forged-steel swivels with two detachable links attached at each end are for use in mooring. (See Fig. 5.8.)**

Housing Chain Stoppers Navy standard housing chain stoppers are used for holding the anchor taut in the hawse pipe or for riding to an anchor or holding the anchors when the anchor chain is disconnected for any reason. The large chain stopper wrenches are used for equalizing the strain on the stoppers when riding to an anchor with more than one stopper in use and for securing the anchor in a hawse pipe. (See Fig. 5.9.)

Mooring Shackles Forged-steel shackles are used for attaching the anchor chain to mooring buoys. An additional special lightweight mooring shackle, not possessing the full strength of the anchor cable, is used for some ships.

Shackle Tool Sets Tool sets including spare taper pins and locking plugs are provided for use in assembling and disassembling detachable links.

Clear Hawse Pendants A wire rope pendant, 5 to 15 fathoms long, fitted with a thimble at one end and a thimble length of open link chain and a pelican hook at the other end, is used in clearing a hawse which has been fouled by the anchor cables.

Dip Ropes A fiber rope pendant fitted at one end with a thimble and a dip shackle large enough to engage a link of the anchor chain is provided for use in mooring or clearing a hawse.

Outboard Swivel Shots Standard outboard swivel shots consisting of detachable links, regular chain links, a swivel, end link, and bending shackle are fitted on most vessels to attach the anchor cable to the

LEAD PELLET

FORELOCK PIN
(NOTE TAPER)

NOTICE
LUGS

LUGS OVERLAP AND
WILL BE HELD
TOGETHER BY
FORELOCK PIN

MARK TO
ASSIST IN
CORRECT
ASSEMBLY

ASSEMBLED

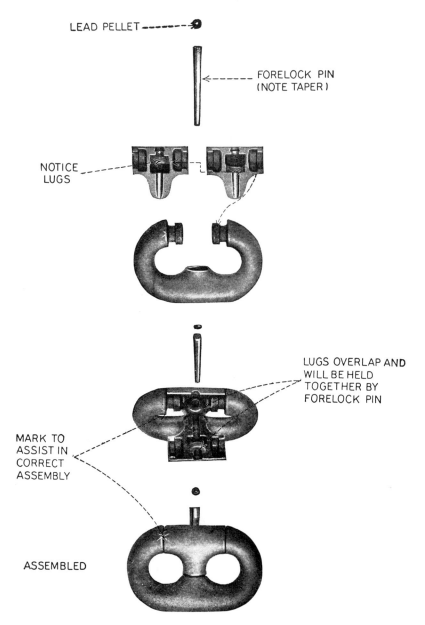

Fig. 5.6 Detachable link.

anchor. These vary in length up to approximately 5 fathoms and are also termed bending shots. The taper pin in the detachable link in the outboard swivel shot is additionally secured with a wire-locking clip.

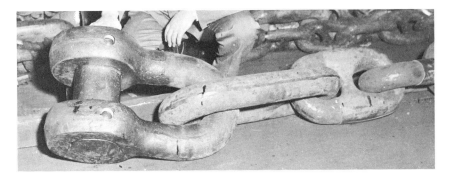

Fig. 5.7 Large-sized bending shackle for 3½-inch heavy-duty die-lock chain. *(Official U.S. Navy photograph.)*

Fig. 5.8 Mooring swivel, large size. *(Official U.S. Navy photograph.)*

Fig. 5.9 Chain stopper. *(Official U.S. Navy photograph.)*

Chain Cable Jacks A cable jack consisting of a lever mounted on an axle and two wheels is used for handling anchor chain of 2¾-inch size and larger. An anchor bar of the pinch-point crowbar type is used for smaller-sized chain.

Mooring Hooks These hooks are used on destroyers and smaller ships for facilitating mooring to a buoy.

5.2 Die-Lock and High-Strength Welded Steel Stud-Link Chain Die-lock and high-strength welded steel chain are standard. Cast-steel, die-lock, and high-strength welded steel chain are capable of withstanding great shock and have uniform dimensions, and the elastic limit of the links is high.

Under the usual service conditions, the links of these types of chain do not stretch or become deformed, and the chains will operate smoothly over the wildcat during the period of their entire useful life. Cast-steel chain can be distinguished by the fact that the studs are solid and an integral part of the links, and each common link in the shot is identical. High-strength welded steel chain in some types is made up with alternate solid-forged links having integral studs. Every other link has the stud welded in place. In one type of high-strength, welded steel chain which is constructed of alternate solid-forged and welded links each welded link is reforged after welding, and the entire chain has the appearance of being made of solid-forged (or cast-steel) links with integral studs throughout. The studs of the die-lock chain are also an integral part of the link; they are, however, split through the middle. The fact that the studs of cast-steel, die-lock, and high-strength welded steel chain cannot fall out is a great advantage because this eliminates the danger of the chain kinking and the pounding of links on adjacent links.

Die-lock links are made of two-forged pieces, both roughly U-shaped. Two stems of one piece contain a series of paralleled indentations, giving them the appearance of screws. The socket piece has holes at each end of the U. In joining the two pieces to form a link, the pierced socket section is heated, then the stems of the other section are thrust into the holes. The socket section is then pounded with a drop hammer, forcing its material around the indentations in the stems in die blocks.

5.3   Chain Identification Marks   Each shot of the chain usually bears a serial number that is stamped, cut, or cast on the inner side of its end links at the time of manufacture. In the case of cast-steel chain this number is preceded by the letters C.S. If an end link is lost or removed from a shot, this identification number should be cut or stamped on the side of the new end link of the altered shot. Cast-steel and some types of high-strength welded steel chain have these markings on the studs of alternate links only.

Each shot of die-lock chain has a serial number and date of manufacture stamped on the inner side of the end links. The studs of such chains are marked "U.S.N." on one side of the stud and the wire diameter of the chain on the other side.

5.4   Anchor Identification Marks   Every anchor, except small boat anchors and lightweight type (LWT) anchors 100 pounds and less in weight, when purchased for Navy use and before delivery to respective naval shipyards, has cast or cut in its crown a serial number. This serial number should not be confused with the weight number which also appears on the anchor. It is the practice on stock or old-fashioned anchors for one side of the crown to be marked with the initials of the inspector, the name of the manufacturer or commercial name of the anchor, and the serial number of the anchor. In the case of lightweight type anchors, this legend may appear on the shank.

On the opposite side of the crown the weight of the anchor in pounds, the year of fabrication, and "U.S. Navy" are cast, stamped, or cut by the manufacturer. The same practice is adhered to in regard to the stockless anchors, except that the markings appear on each side of the flat of the crown.

Ground Tackle

Ground tackle consists of all of the anchors and anchor chain in a vessel as well as the necessary gear. The sizes, weights, and amounts supplied to vessels in service are determined after consideration of the characteristics and operating conditions of the vessels and of past experience.

5.5   Navy Type Detachable Link (Fig. 5.6)   The Navy detachable link has been adopted as standard for use as a connecting link for joining shots of anchor chain on naval vessels.

The Navy Type Detachable Link consists of a C-shaped link with two coupling plates which form one side and the stud of the link and a taper pin which holds the parts together and is locked in place at the large end by a lead plug.

When assembling detachable links, care should be taken to ensure that the parts are correctly matched. Detachable link parts are not interchangeable, and matching numbers are stamped on the C-link and on each coupling plate to enable proper identification for correct assembly. The matching surfaces should be slushed with a mixture of 40 percent white lead and 60 percent tallow by volume prior to final assembly. Vessels outfitted with cast-steel anchor chain are furnished detachable links of Navy and also commercial manufacture, such as E-Z joining links (Naco), Esco connecting links, and riveted (Naco) connection links.

5.6   Riding and Housing Chain Stoppers (Fig. 5.9)   Riding and housing chain stoppers consist of a turnbuckle inserted in a short section of chain, a slip or pelican hook attached to one end of the chain, and a shackle at the other end. The stopper is secured by the shackle to a permanent pad on the vessel's deck. When in use, it is attached to the anchor chain of the ship by straddling a link with the tongue and strong back of the pelican hook, and a certain number of standard chain stoppers are supplied to naval vessels as a part of their equipment. It is the latest practice in the case of destroyers to fit one stopper in the way of each chain cable. On auxiliary vessels and vessels of merchant type, two in the way of each chain cable are fitted if it is practicable to do so. On destroyers, the stopper is made of the same strength as the anchor chain. Because the windlass on these vessels has only one wildcat, it is intended that one chain will be held by the windlass and the other by its chain stopper. In the case of other vessels, chain stoppers are furnished of such size that the strength of each is equal to about 40 percent of the chain cable with which it is used. The stoppers should not be solely relied upon for holding the anchor. Upon anchoring, the wildcat brake band should first be set up tight, and the stoppers then used to back up the brake band. The wildcat should then be disconnected from the engine.

5.7 Purposes of Chain Stoppers   The purposes for which chain stoppers may be used are as follows:

1. To ride to when at anchor, in addition to the use of the brake band on the windlass.
2. For letting go the anchor more quickly than can be done by the brake band.
3. **As an emergency fitting in case the brake band of the windlass should become inoperative.**
4. To hold a chain from running out, while it is being taken off the wildcat, to permit another chain to be put on for heaving in. On destroyers, to hold a chain being bitted or unbitted or brought to the windlass.
5. To hold the anchors taut in the hawse pipes when housed, except in cases where the end of the anchor shank or the anchor shackle projects above the deck line (nonstandard).
6. To hold an anchor chain when disconnected for the purpose of attaching the mooring swivel. Lashing can be resorted to in addition.

5.8 Anchor Chain Marking   *Painting*   Anchor chain in the Navy is painted as follows to serve to identify the length of chain paid out:

One link on each side of the 15-fathom detachable link shall be painted white.
Two links on each side of the 30-fathom detachable link shall be painted white.
Three links on each side of the 45-fathom detachable link shall be painted white, etc.
Detachable links shall be painted as follows: 15-fathom D link, red; 30-fathom D link, white; 45-fathom D link, blue; 60-fathom D link, red, etc.

The exception to the foregoing is that all of the links in the last 15-fathom shot inboard shall be painted red, and all of the links in the next adjoining 15-fathom shot shall be painted yellow.

On auxiliary vessels where the distance between hawse pipe and wildcat is short, and consequently, only a short time is available for painting the chain while it is being heaved in, it may be desirable to limit the number of painted links on each side of the detachable link to one.

Marking   Anchor chain shall also be marked by turns of wire on the studs of certain links. The number of links counting away from the detachable link is used as a marker for that shot. Thus:

The first link at each side of the 15-fathom detachable link has one turn of wire around the stud.

The second link at each side of the 30-fathom detachable link has two turns of wire around the stud.

The third link at each side of the 45-fathom detachable link has three turns of wire around the stud, etc.

It is the practice in the Merchant Service to mark the anchor chain in the same manner, that is identify the links on either side of the 15 fathom detachable links (shackles) with white paint and turns of wire. The detachable link itself may or may not be painted.

5.9   Care to Prevent Bending Chain   Anchor chain when being used should not be subjected to short bends. Care should be taken to ensure whenever possible that anchor chain is not subjected to bending, such as may occur when the cable is lying across a vessel's stem, when a vessel is riding to a single anchor in a strong wind or current and is *"horsing"* or tacking back and forth, or when the cable is rove through a buoy ring or passed over a bolster of small radius. Chain is not as strong when subjected to such transverse bending. This is especially true in the case of die-lock detachable links, and therefore extra precaution should be taken to prevent subjecting these links to transverse bending.

5.10   Care of Ground Tackle by Ship's Force   Anchors, chains, and appendages should be kept in good condition by the ship's force. The chain cables should be overhauled whenever necessary and precautions taken to see that the various shots are properly marked and in good order. As the chain comes in when getting under way, each link should be examined for cracks and for other defects.

5.11   Periodic Inspection and Painting of Ground Tackle in Service by Ship's Force   Once each quarter and more often if necessary, all anchor cables in sizes up to and including 1½ inches should be ranged on deck and examined throughout their entire length. If necessary, they should be scaled and cleaned of rust and other foreign matter. Detachable links should be disassembled and examined for excess wear or corrosion, and where conditions warrant, the links should be replaced by new ones. Before reassembly, the links should be white-leaded. The detachable link located in the outboard swivel shot is fitted with a corrosion-resisting steel locking wire which serves to hold the taper pin in position. Disassembly of this link requires the removal and probable destruction of the locking wire, and the availability of replacement wire of the same type should be established prior to removal for inspection. Shackle bolts, locking pins, and swivels should be carefully examined and put in order, and such parts as require it should be coated with the special black chain paint furnished vessels for this purpose. In cold weather it is desirable to apply some heat to counteract the natural thickening of this paint. This may be done by an immersion electric heater or a steam coil. Experience has also shown that, when left standing for a considerable period, the turpentine substitute may evaporate to a considerable extent, with the resultant thickening of the paint. Vessels receiving anchor chain coated with green paint from stores should leave this coating intact and cover it with black chain paint.

Chain of sizes in excess of 1½-inch wire diameter should be overhauled, wirebrushed, and placed in a good state of preservation as often as is necessary. At least once each 18 months all anchor chain cable, regardless of size, including shackles and shackle pins, and detachable links, should be examined, overhauled, and placed in a good state of preservation. Shackles and shackle pins and detachable links should be refitted and greased or white-leaded, and identification marks should be restored if necessary. To distribute the wear uniformly throughout the entire length of the cable the shots should be shifted to a new position as necessary. In the case of vessels having cable the shots of which are connected with detachable links, 40- or 45-fathom shots may be shifted to any position in the cable which, in the commanding officer's opinion, will tend to distribute the wear evenly throughout the cable. In the case of vessels the shots in the cables of which are connected with U-shaped shackles, the 40-fathom shot should remain the first shot inboard of the outboard swivel shot regardless of wear. If serious defects are discovered during this overhaul of the anchor cables, the defective shots should be shifted to the bitter end of the cable until replacement can be accomplished. See the *NavShips Technical Manual* for complete instructions for maintaining anchor equipment as well as for instructions on securing the bitter end of the anchor chain to the ship's structure.

Cargo Handling
and Underway
Replenishment

Cargo handling is common to both merchant and naval ships. Cargo handling while under way is commonly accomplished by naval forces. This chapter will describe the most common techniques and devices as well as the latest procedures for handling cargo in port and while underway at sea.

Cargo Handling

6.1 Winches Winches are the primary power source for cargo handling. They are used for topping and swinging booms, for controlling whips, and for replenishment-at-sea rigs. Older ships generally have either direct current (D.C.) winches which are speed controlled through resistor banks, or steam winches. Newer ships which use alternating current as ship service power, may use direct current winches powered through a motor generator set, alternating current winches with step control, controllable stator winches, or electrohydraulic winches. Some winches are self-contained and draw their power from gasoline or diesel powered prime movers.

Whatever the type of winch, familiarize yourself with operating instructions and the winch controls before lighting-off. Inspect the equipment, make sure that rigging is clear, brakes are operable, and clutches function. Inspect and assure the operation of all safety devices installed in the winch.

Hydraulic winches need to be warmed up for about 30 minutes prior to use. Make sure that winch controls are in the proper mode, that is, tension or speed control. With two-speed winches assure that the gear shift lever is in the desired gear range.

For a steam winch, set the brake drum, disengage the clutch, and lock the control lever in neutral, then open the drain cocks. Move the throttle lever to admit steam slowly until the engine is warmed up and the cylinders are free of condensate. Close the drain cocks and return the control lever to neutral.

6.2 Booms and Cranes Booms used in the Navy and in the Merchant Marine are rated differently. Thus a Navy 10-ton boom and a Merchant Marine 10-ton boom, while both rated to *lift* 10 tons, are tested or overloaded to different factors. For replenishment-at-sea operations when booms are used, a Navy rated 10-ton boom is the minimum acceptable. Boom ratings are generally 3, 5, 8, 10, 15, 20, 30, etc. tons. Booms of 15 tons to 60 tons were formerly called "jumbo booms." Now "jumbo booms" generally refers to the largest boom on a ship. Boom lengths are generally 60 feet, the criterion for boom length being the ability to reach far enough over the side to spot cargo when topped to its most efficient angle. In Navy ships this works out to a 25 foot outreach when topped to an angle of 60 degrees.

A heavy lift boom is one of 50 or 60 tons to 150-ton, 200-ton capacity and even more. Representative heavy lift booms are the two 60-tonners found on the *U.S.S. Paul Revere* class of attack transports. As a case in point, the range of boom sizes in this class shows the variety of booms which may be found on a single ship. The *U.S.S. Paul Revere* has two 3-ton or 5-ton booms, two 8-ton, three or four 10-ton, one or two 30-ton, and a pair of 60-ton booms. Two Military Sealift Command cargo ships have a special "heavy lift" designation and each carries a pair of 150-ton booms. A few U. S. merchant ships and new Navy LKAs also have a heavy lift capability. Usually these are configured with a Steulchen or similar rig, described later in this chapter.

There are several methods of raising and lowering booms. The standard practice is to apply the topping lift wire directly to the drum of the winch. This is the safest method, but the time required may be prohibitive. Many ships now have special topping lift winches installed on the masts and king posts. These winches offer greater speed in raising and lowering booms.

Another method of topping and lowering single topping lift booms is by means of the cargo whip which is led from the head block through a fairlead block at the base of the mast, then shackled to one of the top links of the bull chain. By taking in on the whip, the boom is raised; by slacking off, the boom is lowered. This is the least desirable method and should not be considered unless the other methods cannot be used.

Tending the gypsy is the key job in topping or lowering booms; five or six round turns about the gypsy are recommended when working with wire ropes. Fewer turns are likely to slip, and more turns are likely to form slack in the wire. These slack turns may fall over the edge of the gypsy and cause the boom to drop. It is a good practice to assign one or two men to back up the man on the gypsy. These men can keep the wire from kinking, keep it clear of the winch, and aid the man on the gypsy in case of trouble. Assign one man to overhaul the whip as the boom is topped. Raise the boom to the desired height. Secure the topping lift as follows:

Single Topping Lift Shackle the bull chain to the padeye as shown in Fig. 6.1 and slack off on the bull line until the bull chain takes the strain. Throw the bull line off the gypsy head and secure it to the topping lift cleat with a minimum of three round turns and three figure eights.

Multiple Topping Lift Apply the stopped chain to the topping lift wire, using a stopper (rolling) hitch and two half hitches. Take turns around the wire with the remainder of the chain and hold it. Surge the topping lift wire until the stopper takes the strain and belay it as described for the single topping lift. Remove the stopper.

6.3 Yard-and-Stay Method In the yard-and-stay method of cargo handling, two booms are used. One of these booms plumbs the hatch and is called the hatch boom. The other is called the yard boom and it is rigged out over the side so that it plumbs the dock or pier. (See Fig. 6.2.)

The cargo whips coming from the hatch and the yard winches are rove through their respective heel and head blocks and are shackled to the same cargo hook.

If the whip has a thimble spliced in the end in the usual manner, it may be impossible to reeve the whip through the block, making it necessary to remove the whip from the winch drum so that the winch end may be rove through.

Another method is often used by Navy ships on which cargo operations are not the rule and where cargo-working gear is struck below until needed. A large eye is formed by turning back the end of the whip upon itself and securing, with wire rope clips, the eye thus formed. It is thus an easy matter to remove the clips, reeve the whip through the blocks, and replace the clips.

Booms are spotted in a working position by hauling on the guys. The yard boom is positioned over the pier, clear of the ship's side. The hatch boom is spotted slightly past the centerline over the hatch.

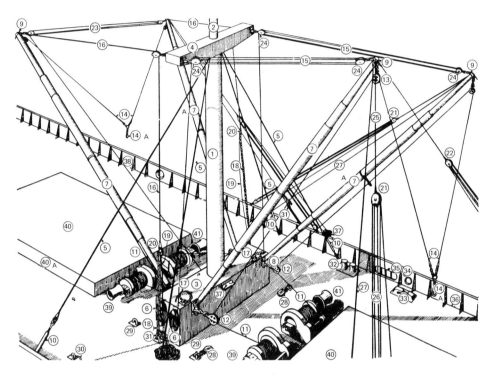

Fig. 6.1 Cargo handling gear.

NOMENCLATURE FOR FIG. 6.1

1. Mast	14A. Cargo hook	29. Padeye
2. Topmast	15. Topping lift (multiple)	30. Padeye and ringbolt
3. Mast table	16. Topping lift (single)	31. Shackle
4. Crosstree	17. Stopper chain	32. Bitts
5. Shroud	18. Bull chain	33. Open chock
6. Topping lift cleat	19. Bull line	34. Closed chock
7. Hatch boom	20. Bale	35. Freezing port
7A. Yard boom	21. Outboard guy	36. Scupper
8. Gooseneck	22. Inboard guy	37. Cleat
9. Linkband	23. Midship guy	38. Bulwark
10. Turnbuckle	24. Topping lift block	39. Hatch winch
11. Cargo whip	25. Guy pendant	40A. Hatch coaming
12. Heel block	26. Guy tackle	41. Yard winch
13. Head block	27. Preventer	
14. Cargo whips	28. Snatch block	

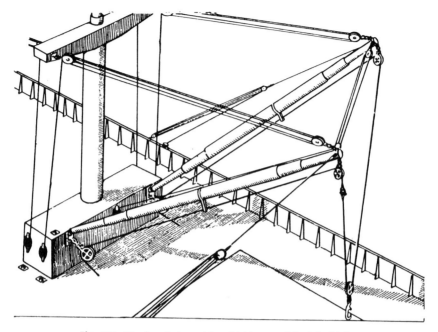

Fig. 6.2 Yard-and-stay with midship guy (block-in-bight).

The booms are set up on outboard guys and preventers. Guys should be slightly more taut than preventers. The inboard or midships guys are set as taut as possible by hand. The cargo whips coming from the hatch and yard winches are rove through their respective heel and head blocks and are shackled to the same cargo hook. If the whip has a thimble spliced in the end in the usual manner, it may be impossible to reeve the whip through the block, making it necessary to remove the whip from the winch drum so that the winch end may be rove through. Cargo whips are shackled to the cargo hook and a load is picked. The load is raised until the angle formed by the whips is about 120 degrees. Now the outboard guys and preventers are equalized by easing off the guy tackles. As outboard guys and preventers are being equalized, all slack is taken in in the inboard or midships guys. It is a good practice, when originally spotting the booms, to swing them slightly wider than desired. When guys and preventers are equalized, the booms will move inboard into position.

The winch controls for the yard and stay are usually located such that one man can operate both winches and have an unrestricted view of the hold. A load is moved from hold to pier in the following manner: The yard whip is kept slack as the hatch whip hoists the load from the hold and clear of the coaming. Then, by heaving around on the yard whip and paying out on the hatch whip, the load is moved across the deck and over the side. When the load is plumbed under the yard boom, the hatch whip is slacked off and the yard whip lowers the load to the pier.

Most yard-and-stay rigs use ¾-inch wire; therefore a block with at least a 12-inch sheave must be used for a runner block. Larger whips, of course, will require larger runner blocks (¾-inch wire requires a 14-inch block).

6.4   Yard-and-Stay Double Purchase   Nearly all methods of rigging yard-and-stay cargo handling gear for heavy lifts require that the cargo whip be doubled up and a block used. Doubling up the whip accomplishes two things: It doubles the load that may be lifted by the whip, and it reduces the load on the winch by half. The only difference between this rig and the ordinary yard-and-stay is that both cargo whips are doubled up and the runner blocks shackled to the cargo hook.

The end of the whip may be secured in several ways. The best method is to shackle the eye of the whip to the upper end of the boom. This tends to keep the bight of the whip from turning on itself and becoming wrapped up. It has the advantage of steadying the swing of the load in a fore-and-aft direction.

The chief advantage of the yard-and-stay double purchase is that lifts as heavy as the safe working load of the cargo booms can be handled at nearly the same rate as ordinary 1-ton or 1½-ton drafts. Light filler cargo can be handled with scarcely any loss of time.

6.5   Single Swinging Boom with Double Purchase   The single swinging boom with double purchase is considered one of the best methods of rigging for handling loads beyond the capacity of a single whip up to the capacity of a single boom. It is quickly and easily rigged and has the added advantage of flexibility. Loads may be placed at any point in the square of the hatch or on the deck.

The yard boom will be the one to be rigged, so the hatch boom is topped up and secured out of the way. (See Fig. 6.3.)

1. Strip the hatch whip from its drum and replace it with the yard boom's topping lift wire. Make sure the topping lift wire has a fairlead. This can only be done with a boom which has a multiple topping lift.
2. See that the yard whip is long enough to permit doubling up (250 to 300 feet).
3. Double up the whip.
4. Remove the preventers from the yard boom, and lead the guys to the proper fittings.

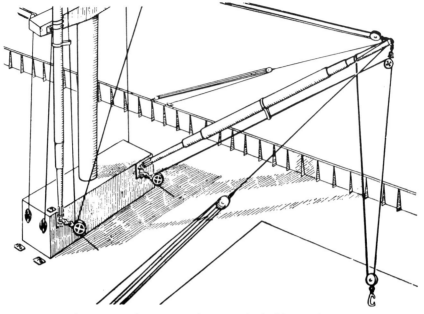

Fig. 6.3 Single swinging boom with double purchase.

5. Top up the boom and swing it into position by hauling on the guy tackles. The hauling part of the guys may be fairled to winches at adjacent hatches or men may be assigned to haul on the guys when swinging a load.

6.6 Two Swinging Booms   A load greater than the capacity of a single boom may be handled by using two booms working together as a single swinging boom. In this case, the whip of the two booms should be fastened to opposite ends of a lifting bar or strongback. As illustrated in Fig. 6.4, the lifting bar serves to equalize any difference in winch operation.

To move a load from the hold to the pier, it is first hoisted clear of the coaming. Then by using the guys, both booms are swung in unison until the load is over the pier. The load is then lowered to the pier. Swinging the load is a difficult operation, and it may be necessary to set the load on deck to change the position of the booms. Because this rig is cumbersome and difficult to handle, it should be used with great caution.

6.7 Block-in-Bight Method of Rigging a Double-Ganged Hatch
Many ships have double-ganged hatches, that is, they are equipped

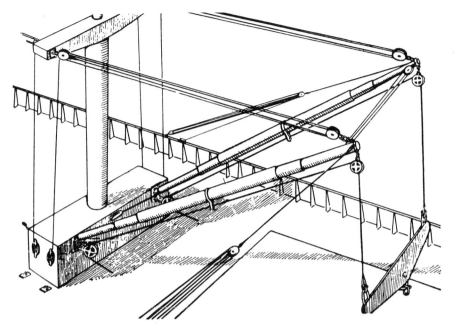

Fig. 6.4 Two swinging booms.

with two pairs of ordinary cargo booms. Handling heavy lifts at a hatch in this manner is facilitated by rigging all four booms as illustrated in Fig. 6.5.

The rigging procedure is as follows:

1. Reeve the forward hatch whip through a runner block, and shackle the eye to the eye of the after hatch whip. Reeve the forward yard whip through a runner block, and shackle it to the after yard whip.
2. Run the shackles joining the two sets of whips to within a few feet of the head blocks of the after booms.
3. Shackle the two runner blocks to the cargo hook.
4. Heavy lifts slightly less than the sum of the safe working load of two parts of the cargo whips may now be loaded or discharged by the usual yard-and-stay method.

This rig has the advantage of being rigged quickly without the necessity of lowering the booms, and only two winches are required for its operation. In addition, the gear may be readily singled up for ordinary light loads.

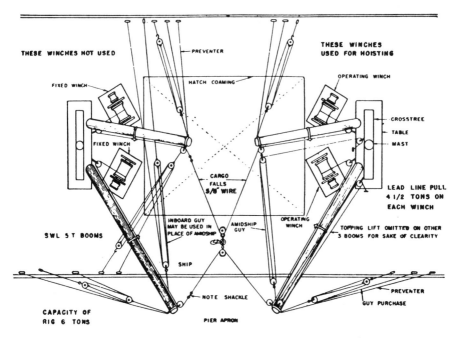

Fig. 6.5 Rigging a double-ganged hatch (block-in-bight).

6.8 Unrigging and Securing for Sea

1. Assign men to the winches, guys, whip, topping lift, and gypsies.
2. Cast off the preventers.
3. Remove the topping lift wire from the cleat as described below.

a. Single Topping Lift Remove the bull line from the cleat, place it in a snatch block, fairleading it to the gypsy. Take five or six turns around the gypsy in the same direction as the whip (over the top), and top up the boom until the bull chain is slack. Unshackle the bull chain and lower the boom to its cradle.

b. Multiple Topping Lift Pass the stopper chain on the topping lift wire and remove the figure eights from the cleat. Surge the topping lift wire until the stopper takes the strain, then shift the wire to the gypsy. Heave around on the wire until the stopper is slack. Remove the stopper and lower the boom. If the cleat is large enough and conditions warrant, the boom may be lowered to the cradle by surging the wire around the cleat instead of transferring it to the gypsy. However, only experienced men should attempt this.

Regardless of the type of topping lift, men on the guy tackles must keep all the slack out of the guys to prevent the boom from swinging while it is being lowered and cradled.

While the booms are being lowered, cargo whips should be tended to prevent turns from piling up on the drum of the winch.

When both booms are cradled, all gear should be secured. Whips are rewound smoothly on the drum of the winch and the cargo hook is secured to a ring or cleat with a slight strain. Guys are secured to the heel block, or fittings on the mast table, then set taut. The hauling parts of the guys are coiled over the guy tackles and tied off. Topping lift wires or bull lines are secured to cleats with the remainder of the wire coiled and hung on a cleat. Bull chains are shackled to padeyes on deck. If the ship is being made ready for sea, all running rigging and cargo handling gear is secured.

6.9 Rigging for Heavy Lift Heavy lift booms are normally carried in an upright position, collared to the mast, and fully rigged with topping lift, load purchase, and guy tackles already secured. The first step in rigging a heavy lift is to lead all purchases to power, four sources of power being required. Load purchase and topping lift wire are led through heel blocks to the winches at the hatch to be worked. Guy tackles are led to proper fittings, and the hauling parts of the guys are led to adjacent power sources. While it is preferable to use the anchor windlass or the after warping winch, the winches at the next hatch may be utilized, depending on the boom's location. If the hatch equipped with the boom is double-ganged, the additional two winches can be used for the guys.

Freeing the boom requires release of the collar that secures it to the mast. On some ships the weight of the boom may be taken off the collar by heaving around on the topping lift wire. On others it is necessary to use a tackle or a special breasting-up line. This line is hitched to the boom, clapped in a snatch block on the mast, and led to the gypsy. Take a strain on it until the collar can be released; then slack off the line until the weight of the boom is on the topping lift.

Prior to making a hoist with a heavy boom, all gear should be checked to ensure that all blocks are running free and none of the lines are chafing. Wire on the winch drums should lay tight and even. Guy tackles should be free of twists; hauling parts of guys fairled to power sources; hasps and hooks of snatch blocks moused securely with seizing wire. Stays, shrouds, and preventers must be checked and, if necessary, tightened.

Swing the other cargo booms at the hatch clear of the working area. Ordinarily it is sufficient to swing these other booms outboard against the shrouds and secure them with guys. In working deck cargo, it may be necessary to top them very high to clear the deck space.

6.10 Heavy Lift Boom—Operation Position the head of the boom directly over the load, with the slings carefully slung and shackled to the lower purchase block. Hoist the load a few inches off the deck, checking for any indication of undue strain; then hoist the load carefully until it is clear of the hatch coaming. By heaving around on the guy tackles, the boom is swung over the ship's side, and the load is ready to be lowered away.

In working a heavy lift boom, the handling of the guys requires special attention. When the boom is topped, the guys must be slacked off; when it is lowered, they must be taken in. Swinging the boom calls for heaving in on one guy and paying out on the other. This requires good coordination by the men handling the guys. One guy serves as a "hauling guy," the other serves as the "following guy." The "following guy" gives more difficulty. Be sure to ease off on the following guy smartly; otherwise it could part, causing much damage. It is good seamanship to allow a small amount of slack in the following guy but not enough slack to permit the boom to slap about.

A heavy lift boom suspended outboard with its load could cause the ship to develop a considerable list, placing undue strain on the guys. The natural tendency is for the boom to swing outboard in the direction of the list. Smart handling of guys to maintain control of the swinging boom is absolutely essential.

6.11 Precautions—Heavy Lift All that has been said about safety awareness and common sense precautions applies doubly when working with heavy lifts. Here are a few rules with special application to heavy lifts:

Do not overload. Be sure that the rig will make the lift safely. Rig carefully, checking each piece of gear as it is rigged. Check stays and shrouds. Before picking up the load, check each part of the rig. Hoist the load a few inches off the deck, and then check for indications of undue strain.

Hoist, swing, and lower the load slowly and smoothly. Jerking places undue strain on the rig. Hoist loads only high enough to clear the coaming and bulwarks.

When a load is being moved, keep every part of the rig under observation. Be alert for any change in sound: Normally a wire or natural fiber rope will hum under strain, but if it starts to squeak, squeal, or smoke it means danger. Also faulty blocks can give warning by squeaking or groaning.

6.12   Steulchen Rigs   Many merchant ships and a few Navy ships now have the Steulchen rig, or a variation of it. It consists of two supporting masts (usually inclined outboard at their tops) and a heavy lift boom. The topping tackle is fastened to swivel heads at the tops of the masts and to pivots at the boom head to prevent twisting of the tackle. Four winches are provided: two for hoisting the load and two for each of the topping tackles. The boom is raised by hauling on both topping winches. The boom is swung by hauling on one and paying out on the other topping winch.

Among the advantages of the Steulchen rig are its greater lifting capacity, less deck gear, and the increase in speed of the cargo hook. Its main advantage and chief characteristic is that the boom head, when fully raised, can be flopped forward (or aft) between the support mastheads allowing the boom to work the adjacent hatch. (Fig. 6.6.)

6.13   Containerized Cargo   The customary shipboard arrays of booms, winches, masts, and king posts do not suffice for the efficient handling of containers. Container ships operate between major ports which have facilities for the movement of the container from the truck or railroad car alongside onto or into the ship.

Fig. 6.6   This photograph of *USS Mobile* (LKA 115) clearly illustrates the Steulchen heavy lift boom rig. This boom serves both hatches forward and aft of it. The boom is capable of lifting the LCM-8 on deck adjacent to it. (*Official U.S. Navy photograph.*)

The most common rig used to handle containers is a rail-mounted crane, either gantry type or variable topping lift, having a three-direction motion that can spot the load to a precise shipboard location. Other rigs presently in use are the side loader and the straddle carrier, which are massive trucks with an extra capability for lift. Many container ships have one or more gantry cranes as an integral part of the ship's structure. Supported by rails running fore-and-aft, and with a further capability for vertical lift and horizontal swing, ship gantries are able to place containers in their assigned locations.

6.14 Roll On/Roll Off The roll on/roll off or "Ro/Ro" ship is a highly specialized type that accommodates trucks and trailers, passenger cars, military vehicles, and other rolling stock. The ship is so configured that loaded vehicles can be driven aboard through ramps at the stern and sides. Utilizing a system of interior ramps, vehicles are driven to their proper position, either below decks or topside. At the ship's destination they are driven off the ship in a reverse operation to the manner of loading.

6.15 Safety Precautions Great forces and stresses are involved when working with winches, booms, cargo whips and heavy loads. For example, the stopper chain of the topping lift must be properly secured or serious accidents may result. A rolling hitch and two half hitches with several round turns are recommended.

Topping lift wire should be secured around the topping lift cleats with a minimum of three round turns followed by three figure eights. To prevent the last few turns from slipping off the cleat, mouse the last two figure eights. Never half-hitch a topping lift wire around a cleat. It may tighten and become virtually impossible to remove. When a boom is lowered by surging, the mousing and the three figure eights are removed, after which the three or four turns are gradually surged. This should be done only by an experienced man.

When shackling a bull chain to a padeye, insert the shackle beneath the first slack link in the chain. Otherwise, this loose link and the shackle may crowd the bottom of the chain, thus causing dangerous distortion and strain.

Some commonsense precautions in cargo handling are:

1. Do not overload. Make certain that the rig will make the lift safely: Carefully rig and check each piece of gear as it is rigged. Check stays and shrouds.
2. Place the load directly under the boom head. Sling carefully and

use dunnage or other suitable chafing gear at points where there may be chafing.

3. Check every part of the rig before picking up the load. Hoist the load a few inches off the deck, and check the rig for indications of undue strain.
4. Hoist, swing, and lower the load slowly and smoothly. Jerking causes terrific strain in the rig and can easily cause portions of the rig to carry away. Hoist loads only high enough to clear the coaming and bulwark. A particularly heavy load raised too high will affect the stability of the ship and may cause considerable list. Listing increases the strain on the guys and preventers and, therefore, the danger of parting.
5. Watch while a load is being moved, and keep every part of the rig under constant observation. Listen for any change in sound.
6. Keep unnecessary personnel out of the area; those concerned with the operation must keep alert.
7. LOOK ALIVE AND STAY ALIVE.

All safety precautions should be strictly observed by all hands at all times. The following list contains commonsense precautions that all cargo handlers must observe.

1. Wear safe clothing and shoes. Do not wear trousers that are too long, and do not wear rings while at work.
2. Use the accommodation ladder or brow for boarding and leaving the ship. Don't ride the load.
3. Climb ladders in the hold only when the hoist is not in motion.
4. Use the walkway on the ship's side away from the side on which the hoist is operating.
5. Secure hatch rollers properly.
6. Lower blocks, crowbars, chain slings, bridles, etc., into the hold by cargo falls or other lines.
7. Pile hatch covers in an orderly manner.
8. Lay strongbacks flat so they will not tip over on personnel or be dragged into hatches or overboard by slingloads.
9. Stand in the clear when strongbacks and hatch covers are being handled on the deck above.
10. Stand in the clear away from suspended loads.
11. When steadying loads, do not stand between the load and any fixed object.
12. Stand clear of slings being pulled from under loads by cargo falls.

13. When using a dragline to move cargo, stand out of the bight and clear of the throw of the block and hook.
14. Be especially attentive when handling objects with sharp or rough edges.
15. Learn to lift properly to prevent straining.
16. Always use a light when entering dark places.
17. Never walk backwards while working with or around cargo on board ship.
18. Step down from elevations—never jump down.
19. Bend projecting nails in dunnage to prevent puncture wounds.
20. Report to your supervisor any defect in tools, materials, appliances, and gear.
21. When short pieces of dunnage are required, use only the proper cutting tools.
22. Report all injuries (even scratches, cuts, and splinters) to your supervisor and get immediate first aid or medical attention.
23. Know the location of fire-alarm boxes and fire-fighting equipment.
24. Do not engage in horseplay, practical jokes, or arguments.

Replenishment at Sea

The United States Navy has, over the years, developed techniques and procedures of transferring consumables from logistic support ships to combatant ships while under way at sea. Since World War II, the U.S. Sixth Fleet operating in the Mediterranean and the U.S. Seventh Fleet operating in the Pacific have resupplied themselves by utilizing underway replenishment (UNREP) techniques. The British, French, and Canadian Navies have adopted replenishment-at-sea techniques that are similar to those used by United States Fleet units. Underway replenishment has proved useful to Naval forces and may well have economic impact in commercial practice as ship size and operational costs warrant. The first significant replenishment operation at sea in the U.S. Navy was in 1899, when the collier *U.S.S. Marcellus,* while being towed, transferred coal to a warship, the *U.S.S Massachusetts.* Since that time, many methods have been tried and abandoned. Those described in this chapter have been adopted as the most feasible and are currently used in the fleet. Although reference herein is to booms, most modern UNREP ships rig their replenishment stations directly from fixed king posts and sliding blocks. Otherwise, the rigging is identical.

6.16   General Discussion   The cargo of the UNREP ship is determined by one of the following considerations: (1) requisitions prior to loading, (2) anticipation of fleet requirements, or (3) need for issuing provisions and stores in standard units. A package or kit which contains a specified grouping of items in fixed quantities, usually pallet loaded, is considered a standard unit.

There are four general principles for the loading of UNREP ships to ensure maximum efficiency in unloading.

1. Lots of homogeneous cargo should be stowed, if possible, in several holds, so that they may be off-loaded at as many transfer stations as possible.
2. Provision must be made for adequate passageways and working areas in and around the cargo to permit quick segregation of lots, checking, and separate handling of heterogeneous types of supplies. Loading must be planned so that the remaining cargo can be readily reshored at the completion of replenishment to reduce the danger from shifting cargo.
3. Bulky and heavy items must be placed near loading areas and in holds that can accommodate their transfer most readily. The hatch opening, the height of the hold, and the fact that certain types of receiving ships can receive bulky items only at certain stations must all be considered.
4. Replenishment must be accomplished at the highest possible tonnage rate per hour and in the shortest practicable time consistent with safety.

There are several methods which can be used to transfer cargo at sea. The tabulation below provides the load capacities of these methods under normal operating conditions. These figures must be reduced when transferring in rough or heavy seas.

Method	Maximum Capacity per Load (pounds)
Burton	6000
Housefall	2500
Double housefall	2500
Modified housefall	3500
Wire highline	3500/800[a]
Manila highline (5 inch)	600
Manila highline (3 inch)	300
STREAM	6000 plus[b]
Double burton	up to 12,000

[a] Load capacity with manila outhaul.
[b] Load capacity of STREAM depends upon preset tension in the highline wire.

6.17 Ship Formation for Underway Replenishment Normally the receiving ship maneuvers to take station alongside the delivering ship and adjusts course and speed as necessary to maintain station during the process. Except for the gear that is rigged aboard the receiving ship, such as fairlead blocks and riding lines, the delivering ship normally provides all the equipment for the operation. Large combatants usually take station to port of the delivery ship, small combatants to starboard. Formation course is selected on the basis of wind and sea conditions as well as tactical situations affecting the naval units. During UNREP, a "lifeguard" ship takes station astern of the delivery ship should a "man overboard" occur. Course changes by ships connected alongside can be accomplished by skilled personnel. Care must be exercised not to change the speed of the delivery ship, unless a speed change is ordered. A speed of 10 to 15 knots is advisable during UNREP operations. A combination distance-phone line is rigged between ships operating alongside. This line enables rapid bridge-to-bridge communication and indicates closing or opening of the distance between ships.

6.18 Burton Method While there are various ways of rigging the delivering ship, it is usual practice for the boom on the side adjacent to the receiving ship to be used for the transfer, and the boom on the opposite side to be used to hoist the loads from the hatch. The following method is the most efficient way of burtoning cargo when only one set of booms and winches is available at the active hatch. Normally, each ship furnishes its own burton whip, one whip from each ship being lead to the swivel fitting above the cargo hook. In some cases, the delivery ship supplies both whips, one fairled to a high point on the receiving ship which approximately plumbs the load landing area of the receiving ship. The burton whip sizes range from ¾ inch to 1 inch 6 × 37 or 6 × 31 high-grade plow steel (IWRC) between 600 and 800 feet in length.

Setting Up The procedure for rigging a burton station on the delivering ship, using the port boom for transfer (burtoning), and using the starboard boom as the hatch boom (hoisting cargo out of the hold) (Fig. 6.7) is as follows:

1. Secure the thimble eye of the burton whip (running from port boom) to the triple swivel and hook. Reeve the bitter end of this wire through to the boom head and heel blocks and lead it to the winch. Secure the bitter end of the whip to the winch drum and spool the whip onto the drum.
2. Fashion a lizard of 3-inch manila with a large shackle at the

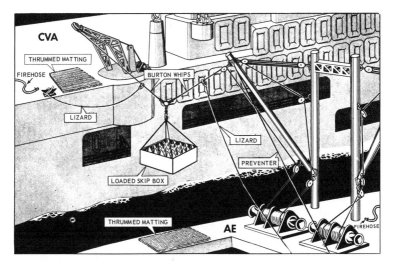

Fig. 6.7 Burton rig.

bitter end (optional). Place the shackle over the whip outboard of the head block.

3. Secure a heavy preventer of suitable length and strength to the inboard side of the boom head.
4. Secure shackle pins with seizing wire.
5. Top up the boom in such a manner that the whip plumbs the desired loading point on the port side of the main deck.
6. Set up and belay the guys.
7. Lead the preventer to the starboard side of the ship at an angle as close to 90 degrees from the boom as possible, or to the fixed position provided. Take a strain and belay the preventer.
8. Rig the starboard boom (hatch boom) so that its whip plumbs the center of the hatch. Attach a 3-inch manila lizard to the whip. This done, the starboard boom is then ready for hoisting loads from the hold to the loading point on the main deck's port side.

The Receiving Ship   Burtoning stations are rigged in accordance with ship plans and specifications which designate specific fittings for this application. The burton whip block is secured to the burton fitting. The burton whip bitter end is rove through the whip block and led to the drum or gypsy head. A 3-inch manila lizard may be shackled around the whip (optional).

The thimbled eye of the burton whip should be on deck ready for passing when the burton whip messenger from the delivering ship with attached snap hook is received on board.

Operation When the ships are steaming alongside, the delivery ship passes a messenger to the receiving ship. The receiving ship bends its burton whip to the messenger, allowing the delivery ship to haul in the burton whip. The rig is ready for use when the ship is attached to the triple swivel.

Actual transfer is as follows:

Beckets or the sling of the load are placed into the cargo hook. The delivering ship heaves in on the burton whip and hoists the load clear of the deck and rail. The receiving ship takes a strain on its burton whip and as the delivery ship slacks away on her burton whip, the load is thus worked across. When the load is hanging from the receiving ship's burton point, the delivery ship slacks her whip and the receiving ship lowers the load to the deck. Successful burtoning requires teamwork between winchmen on both ships.

Stress in rigging may be reduced to a minimum by keeping the load as low as possible (consistent with sea conditions) and hoisting it just high enough to clear the rails of the two ships. As the load crosses between ships, it should be kept as low as possible, yet be maintained at a sufficient height to prevent immersion. Upon completion of transfer, the rig is disconnected in reverse order of connection.

6.19 Housefall Method While burton methods require power sources on both ships and teamwork between the ship's winchmen, housefall methods utilize the power sources of the delivering ship only. Rigging for housefall transfers can be done in several ways, making use of one or two booms. The housefall boom and whip can be plumbed over the center of the hold, thus serving the twofold purpose of lifting cargo to the deck and then transferring it to the receiving ship. This method, however, reduces the rate of transfer because of the longer distance the hook travels. Rigging procedure requires two booms, as shown in Fig. 6.8.

Setting Up Rigging the normal housefall as described below requires the use of two booms of the delivering ship, one boom located at the active hold and one boom at the hold forward of the active hold:

1. Secure the thimbled eye of the cargo whip to the triple swivel and hook, reeve the bitter end of this wire through the head and heel blocks of the boom at No. 2 hold and spool it onto the winch drum. The position of the boom, the guys, and the preventer are the same as for burtoning.
2. Secure temporarily the housefall block (a runner block of about 20 inches) to the bulwark with a short piece of 2-inch manila line outboard, opposite the center of the hold.

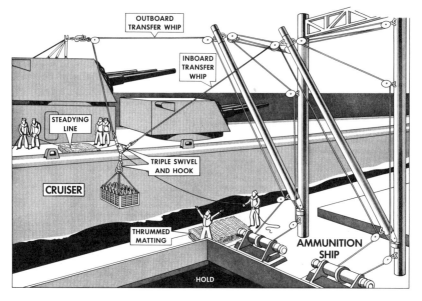

Fig. 6.8 Housefall rig.

3. Secure the thimbled eye of the transfer whip to the triple swivel and hook. Reeve the bitter end of the whip through the housefall block (outboard of all projections and rigging), walk it forward, reeve it through the head and heel blocks of the boom at No. 1 hold, and then spool it onto the winch drum.
4. Secure galvanized preventer wire (at least 1½-inch) to the inboard side of each boom head. Top up the booms so that its whip clears all standing rigging projections when making transfers to the receiving ship.
5. The remaining steps in rigging the delivering ship are the same as for burtoning.

Operation   The receiving ship secures a gin block to the suspension point (same as for burton). A wire pendant with a thimbled eye is run up through this block. The thimbled eye remains on deck for attachment to the pelican hook of the housefall block.

During receiving, the hook is secured to the thimble of the housefall block eye. A strain is applied to the wire pendant until the housefall block is two-blocked, and the hauling part is then secured.

The housefall block messenger is detached from the bridle and used to haul the housefall block over as the delivering ship pays out on the housefall transfer whip. The block is then secured to the wire pendant and made ready for cargo transfer.

On the delivering ship, the load is hoisted clear of the rail with the housefall cargo whip. The strain is taken on the housefall transfer whip, and the load is worked over to the receiving ship.

On completion of the transfer operation, the lines are passed back to the delivering ship in the usual manner. This type of rig proves advantageous when the receiving ship cannot keep good fore-and-aft position.

When loads must be kept higher above the water than is normally possible in housefalling, the housefall rig can be modified by the addition of a trolley block on the transfer whip. This trolley rides on the outboard transfer whip. Rigging is the same as for the basic housefall except attachment points must be close together, one over the other, so the trolley will ride in an upright manner.

6.20   Double Housefall   The double housefall speeds transfer of cargo to ships that do not have sufficient suspension points to handle more than one rig. However, double housefalling is somewhat slower than housefalling to two separate receiving stations.

In a double housefall operation to delivering ship uses two adjacent housefall rigs. Both housefall blocks are passed over the receiving ship simultaneously. In operation, one housefall rig alternately passes a loaded net to the receiving ship while the other returns an empty net to the delivering ship. The separation of the two housefall rigs on the delivering ship must be a minimum of 25 feet to prevent the outboard whips from fouling.

6.21   Wire Highline Method   The wire highline method uses a wire suspended between the ship on which a trolley rides. The load, attached to the trolley, travels along the highline. The loaded trolley is pulled to the receiving ship by an outhaul line and is pulled back to the delivery ship by an inhaul line.

Setting Up   To use the wire highline, the receiving ship must have a high attachment point. This is usually a padeye welded to the ship's structure. There is also an additional padeye of 1-inch diameter located below about 12 to 18 inches from the first padeye. The block used to fairlead the inhaul line is attached to this second padeye. Sufficient deck space must be provided in the vicinity of the padeyes to handle cargo being received.

The highline passes from a winch on the delivering ship through a block on a boom head and then across to a padeye on the receiving ship (**Fig. 6.9**). A trolley rides the highline and is moved toward the receiving ship by an inhaul line (manually handled) and is brought back to the delivering ship by an outhaul line (winch operated).

A boom is normally used to provide a satisfactory lead for the wire

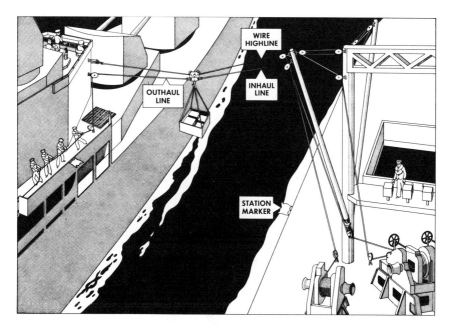

Fig. 6.9 Wire highline rig.

highline. However, any other point of suspension on the ship's structure will serve if it is sufficiently high and strong. The highline is normally 600 feet of ¾-inch wire (high grade plow steel) with a thimbled
eye on its outboard end. A highline is boom rigged as follows:

1. Reeve the inboard end of the wire through a trolley block,
   through the head and heel blocks of the boom, and then spool
   onto a winch drum.
2. Attach a pelican hook to the thimbled eye with a ⅞-inch shackle.
3. Shackle the manila outhaul line (2½-inch) to the inboard end of
   the trolley block and then run it through an 8-inch wooden block
   and a swivel attached to a becket on the underside of the head
   block. The outhaul line is finally taken through a fairlead to the
   gypsy head of a winch.
4. Equip the manila inhaul line (2½-inch) with a snap hook attached
   to bridle. Fake down the center section of the line on the deck
   clear for running and shackle the standing end to the outboard
   side of the trolley block.

Little preparation is required on board the receiving ship for the
highline method. Below the highline padeye, an 8-inch snatch block
is secured to take the manila inhaul line. Additional snatch blocks are
rigged to fairlead the inhaul line clear of the landing area.

Operation   When the inhaul line comes on board the receiving ship, it is detached from the birdle and led into the blocks provided for it. The pelican hook or shackle is secured to the highline padeye, establishing the highline connection.

The load is now hooked to the trolley block and a strain is taken on the highline, thus lifting the load clear of the deck and rail. The load is hauled across to the receiving ship by slackening the outhaul line and taking up the inhaul line. When the load is suspended over the landing area, the delivering ship slacks off on both the highline and outhaul line, setting the load on the receiving ship's deck.

It is important always to keep a good catenary in the highline to avoid unnecessary strain when a load is suspended.

6.22   Manila Highline Method   The manila highline can be used in transferring provisions, personnel, and light freight. Preparation for rigging is essentially the same as for a wire highline, and a 12-inch snatch block attached to a padeye at the delivering station is sufficient. It is kept taut during transfers either by manpower or by a capstan. The entire rig is relatively easy to set up and is the safest method now available for transferring personnel.

To transfer personnel singly or in pairs, the only safe rig is the manila highline with all lines tended by hand. Heaving in lines by hand, with a sufficient number of men standing by for emergency, is the best method to insure against the highline parting from sudden strains caused by rolling ships.

6.23   Vertical Replenishment (VERTREP)   Vertical replenishment utilizes helicopters to transfer goods between ships. This method does not often replace conventional methods, rather it augments them. It reduces the time required to replenish ships in a dispersed formation.

6.24   STREAM   Underway replenishment techniques continue to advance with the introduction of systems and equipment of recent design. STREAM incorporates these advances into a standard, highly effective transfer system. The STREAM transfer rig utilizes a wire highline connected between ships. A trolley rides the highline. Inhaul and outhaul whips originating in and tended from the delivery ship haul the trolley, or a wire whip or manila outhaul tended on receiving ship can be used. The fundamental difference between STREAM and the conventional methods described previously is the preset and con-trolled tension in the highline wire which allows STREAM to handle loads up to 9000 pounds. A brief description of the major STREAM equipment follows.

Ram Tensioner The ram tensioner maintains the present tension in the highline wire. It consists of a very large hydraulic cylinder, the piston of which acts as the ram, an air compressor, an accumulator, and air flasks. The highline is rove through a movable block on the piston and a fixed block on the cylinder, then to the highline winch. Air from nearby flasks keeps pressure on a piston in the accumulator cylinder from which the pressure is transmitted to the ram. As tension on the highline or span wire is relaxed, pressure in the system causes the ram (piston) to extend, taking up the slack. (**See Fig. 6.10.**)

Sliding Block The sliding block is an elevator which travels vertically on a king post of the delivery ship. The sliding block lifts the transfer load above bulwark obstructions before transfer. The highline is rove through the sliding block. (**See Fig. 6.11.**)

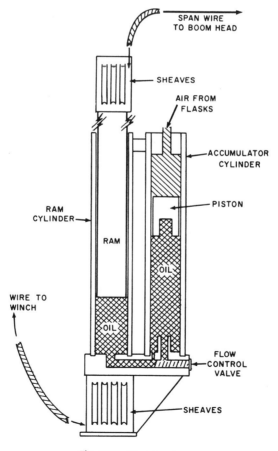

Fig. 6.10 Ram tensioner.

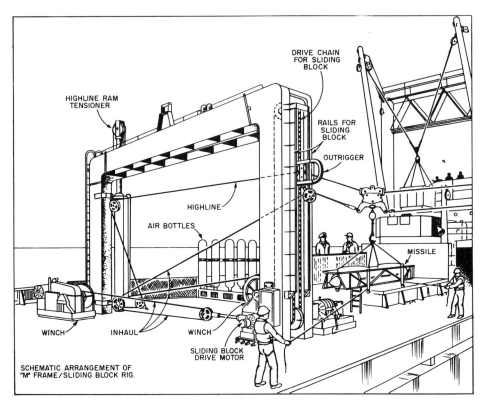

Fig. 6.11 Sliding block.

Sliding Padeye   The sliding padeye is an elevator traveling vertically on a king post on the receiving ship. The highline bitter end is fixed in the sliding elevator. Its function is to lower loads to the deck of the receiving ship. Other devices are available with STREAM that can perform a similar function.

Various items of specialized equipment have been designed for the STREAM system. These are used to handle missiles and other large or delicate ordnance. STREAM equipment in this category includes Terrier/Tartar receivers, Talos receivers, missile strongbacks, and specialized wire rope fittings.

6.25   Fueling at Sea   Fueling at sea is normally accomplished by using either of two accepted rigs, span wire or the close-in. The method is determined by the kind of ship delivering the fuel and the conditions under which the delivery must be made. The main difference between the rigs lies in the method of extending the hose to the receiving ship. Of the two, the span wire is preferred and requires the more elaborate rig. Ships not equipped to transfer by span wire must do so by the close-in method.

6.26   Close-in Method—Setting up for Delivery   (Fig. 6.12.) The hose in the close-in rig is supported by boom whips and bight lines leading from saddles (at least three) on the hose to booms or other high projections on one or both ships. A description of equipment and arrangements that may be used as a guide in making up the hose and lines for close-in fueling follows.

The span of hose usually consists of seven 35-foot lengths of lightweight, collapsible hose 6 or 7 inches in diameter (4-inch hose for destroyers) and flow-through saddles. To the outboard length of the hose are attached:

1. a flow-through riding line fitting;
2. a 4-foot length of hose;
3. another riding line fitting;
4. a 9-foot length of hose;
5. end fittings for the hose.

The saddle whips attach to the flow-through saddles. Three saddle whips are used. The first of the three consists of 300 feet of ¾-inch wire rope or 5-inch manila, fitted with a thimble eye and ⅝-inch

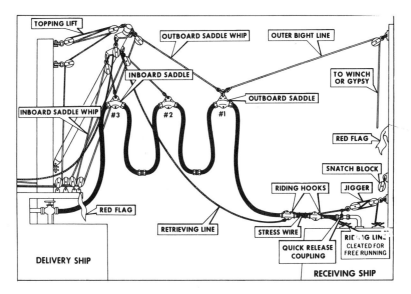

Fig. 6.12 Close-in rig.

shackle at one end. The whip is shackled to the outboard saddle, rove through the appropriate size block shackled to a padeye below the head block, and then through a fairlead to a winch. Saddle whips No. 2 and No. 3 consist of 240 feet of ½-inch or ¾-inch wire rope or 5-inch manila, fitted at one end with a thimble eye and ⅝-inch shackle. Shackled to saddles 2 and 3 respectively, these whips are rove through blocks on the king post or boom, then through fairleads to winches.

An outer bight line is used only when fueling vessels larger than destroyer types. It is a 5-inch manila 50 fathoms long, with a thimble eye and a 1-inch shackle at one end. To the other end is taper-spliced a 15-fathom length of 2½-inch manila, then 15 fathoms of 21-thread manila, and to that 30 fathoms of 6-thread or 9-thread manila. The thimbled eye of the outer bight line is shackled to the outboard end of the outboard saddle whip.

The retrieving line consists of 50 fathoms of 3½-inch manila, with a thimble eye and a ¾-inch shackle at one end. The thimble eye is shackled to the inboard riding line fitting and the line is rove through a 12-inch or 14-inch snatch block on the forward side of the boom head, then through a fairlead to a gypsy head. This gypsy head may be used alternately for both the retrieving line and the inboard saddle whip.

The hose messenger is a 3½-inch manila line 40 fathoms long, with a thimble eye and a ¾-inch shackle at one end. To the other end is taper-spliced a 15-fathom length of 21-thread sisal. The thimble eye of the messenger is shackled to the outboard riding line fitting. The messenger is seized to the outboard end of the hose at 3-foot intervals with two turns of 21-thread.

The fueling boom is positioned 90 degrees to ship centerline and so that the head of the boom is just outboard of the ship's rail. In rigging, the hoses hould be topped up inboard to outboard as follows:

1. Two-block the inboard saddle.
2. Hoist saddles No. 1 and No. 2 to a point just below the inboard saddle.
3. Using the retrieving line, hoist the inboard riding line fitting to a point just below the outboard riding line fitting just outboard of the No. 1 saddle.
4. Lead the hose messenger to the superstructure deck and fake it down athwartships.

Receiving Ship—Setting Up   A 12-inch snatch block, through which the hose line messenger is led, is provided at each fueling station. This block is placed inboard of the ship's side and about 6 feet above deck. To expedite hauling in the hose, a line with a snap hook on the end should be led through the snatch block, ready to attach to the hose messenger. In some ships additional blocks are necessary to fairlead the messenger.

On ships larger than destroyers, a 14-inch snatch block is secured at the highest convenient point above where the hose will be taken aboard. This is used to fairlead outer bight line, which helps support the outboard hose saddle.

A riding line about $3\frac{1}{2}$ to 7 fathoms long, made of 4-inch or 5-inch manila, is provided at each fueling station. One end of this line is eye-spliced and secured to the hook or shackle of a jigger tackle. The other end is left free until the hose is aboard, when it will be secured to a cleat.

Operation As the receiving ship completes her approach and steadies alongside, bolos, or line-throwing gunlines, are sent over from each station on the delivering ship to corresponding stations on the receiving ship. Using these lines, the telephone cable; distance line messenger, hose line messengers, and outer bight lines are started over.

If the delivering ship has difficulty getting her gunlines across, the receiving ship may use her own line-throwing guns if so requested by the delivering ship. In all cases, gunlines must be passed back at the earliest convenience to the ship furnishing them. As soon as telephone jackboxes reach the deck of the other ship, connections must be made and communications established. Tending of the distance line and the telephone cable seized to it is undertaken at the same time.

The delivering ship pays out the hose messenger by hand as the other ship draws it on board. On the receiving ship the hose messenger is led to the snatch block provided about 6 feet above the deck and, finally, to a winch; or it is fairled on deck for heaving in by hand. The delivery ship pays out on the retrieving line and saddle whips, allowing the hose to be hauled across by the messenger. Assistance can be rendered by men heaving on the outer bight line, if such a line is being used. As the end of the hose comes on board, the stops securing it to the messenger are cut, one by one, until the bight of the riding line is slipped over the riding hook and the riding line is set taut. The hose end is now ready to be coupled to the receiving ship's hose or to be lashed in the fueling trunk. After this is done, the messenger is restopped to the hose and removed from the snatch block, and the bitter end is returned to the delivery ship.

When an outer bight line is used, as is normal when the receiving ship is larger than a destroyer, the receiving ship takes it to the 14-inch snatch block provided at some convenient high point and tends it carefully. This line is important. As the ships roll, the hose bight may dip in and out of the water unless the outer bight line is used to raise and lower the outboard hose saddle. When the ships roll in opposite directions, the hose rises suddenly, and the bight line as well as the delivery ship's saddle whip, which is also helping to support the saddle, stretch out horizontally. If these lines are not slackened immediately, they will break under the tension.

The outer bight line, tended by the receiving ship, and the outboard saddle whip, tended by the delivery ship, need constant handling by alert, intelligent men. High-speed winches must be used. The winchmen on both ships must work together, keeping their eyes on the outboard saddle, and should try to maintain the two lines in the form of an upright V.

When the outer bight line is not used, the outer hose bight is controlled by the outboard saddle whip alone.

When fueling is completed, the engineer force on the receiving ship gives the "Stop Pumping" signal, disconnects the hose after a back suction has been taken or the hose blown clear, and closes the necessary valves or replaces the end flanges or hose caps. The hose is eased out on the bight of the riding line, and as the outer bight line is being eased out, the delivery ship heaves in and two-blocks the inboard and outboard saddles. The delivery ship stops off the inboard saddle whip, removes it from the gypsy head, and belays it to a cleat. The retrieving line is placed on the same gypsy, and with it the hose is hauled aboard. Finally, the receiving ship returns the outer bight line, the telephone lines, and the messengers. The delivery ship returns the distance lines.

6.27 Span Wire Rig (Fig. 6.13.) This method permits ships to open out to between 140 and 180 feet and, when ram-tensioned, to 240 feet. The hose is extended by use of a single span wire stretching between the two ships, the hose hanging from trolley blocks that ride along the wire. The greater separation is safer, and conducive to easier maneuvering and better station-keeping. These factors not only allow commanders a wider latitude in choosing a fueling course, but they also facilitate the use of antiaircraft and antimissile weapons should the need for them arise. The span wire method, with its higher suspension, also affords protection for the hose in rough weather.

Setting Up for Delivery The hose and end fittings are coupled together as specified for the close-in rig, except that a ¾-inch galvanized stress wire is shackled between the inboard riding line fitting and the outboard saddle.

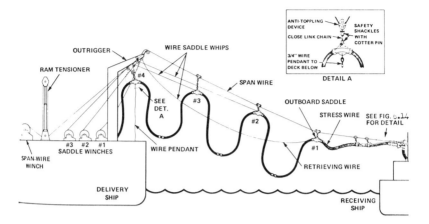

Fig. 6.13   Tensioned span-wire rig.

The saddle whip is made up and rigged as in the close-in method, except that wire is normally used instead of manila and the whip controls both the inboard and center saddles (No. 3 and No. 2). The whip is shackled to No. 2 saddle and rove through a block on the forward side of the boom, through a runner block secured to No. 3 saddle, through another block on the boom, and then is fairlead to a winch.

The runner is an antitoppling block, part of an antitoppling device that keeps the runner from toppling when waves hit the hose. A 70-foot, ¾-inch wire pendant running from a fitting on deck to the bottom of the saddle prevents the saddle from being two-blocked.

The retrieving line is ½-inch or ¾-inch wire, 450 to 800 feet long, fitted with a thimble eye at one end. This end is shackled to the outboard saddle and is rove through a block on the after side of the boom head and then is fairled to a winch.

The hose messenger is 3½-inch or 4-inch manila line 35 fathoms long, fitted on one end with a thimble eye and a ⅞-inch shackle. Taper-spliced in succession to the other end are 15 fathoms of 2-inch manila, 10 fathoms of 21-thread, and 20 fathoms of 6 or 9 thread. The messenger is secured to the outboard end of the hose by shackling the eye to the outboard riding line fitting and seizing the line to the hose at 3-foot intervals with 21-thread sisal.

The span wire is ¾- or ⅞-inch wire rope a minimum of 600 feet long (800 feet for tensioned span wire). The hose is suspended from

the span wire by trolley blocks shackled to the center and out-board saddles and to the two riding line fittings. Two free trolleys are attached by sisal stops to the outboard end of the hose. A pelican hook is secured to the outboard end of the span wire. To facilitate securing the span wire to the messenger, padeyes are welded to two wire clamps that are bolted to the wire approximately 2 and 4 feet from the shackle. About 200 feet from the end of the messenger (which is secured to the hose), two heavy-duty snap hooks are seized about 2 feet apart. These hooks are snapped into the padeyes on the wire clips. This method prevents the wire from sliding down the mes-senger as it might if stopped off with small stuff. A single turn of small stuff, run through the bale, supports the pelican hook. Some span wires and highlines are tensioned, which gives better control of the rig and permits wider ship separation. Such span wires may be up to 800 feet long. The boom is topped and the hose hoisted as in the close-in method.

Receiving Ship—Setting Up On the receiving ship, the 12-inch snatch block, riding line, and fairlead blocks are rigged as for close-in fueling. The 14-inch snatch block is not rigged, because there is no necessity for the outer bight line. A length of small stuff for hauling in the messenger is rove through the fairlead and snatch blocks.

Operation When the end of the messenger comes across, the re-ceiving ship attaches it to the line rove through the snatch and fairlead blocks. The delivery ship pays out the messenger by hand as the other ship hauls it in. When the span wire comes aboard, the stop holding the pelican hook is cut and the hook is attached to the long link in the padeye provided. Then the two snap hooks are unfastened and hauling is recommenced. The delivery ship starts tending the span wire and positions the saddles so that the span wire carries the weight and the hose is kept from the water as it is hauled across.

When the hose end comes within reach, the trolley supporting the end is cut loose, permitting the hose to be hauled farther inboard. As soon as possible, a bight of the riding line is slipped over the riding line hook and the riding line is set taut and secured.

When the delivery ship is a fleet oiler, the hose messenger is de-tached and returned to the oiler, using the hose messenger retrieving line provided. When the delivery ship is a carrier, however, the hose messenger is left shackled to the riding line fitting and the bitter end only is returned. The receiving ship retains a bight of the messenger.

Upon completion of pumping and blowdown, the receiving ship disconnects the hose and secures the valve in the closed position (or replaces the hose cap or end flange). If the delivery ship is a carrier and the receiving ship has retained a bight of the messenger, it is re-stopped to the hose in at least two places.

The receiving ship slacks the riding line, easing the hose over the side, while the delivery ship heaves in on saddle whips and hose retrieving line.

When the hose has been retrieved, the span wire is slackened, and upon signal from the delivery ship, the pelican hook is tripped and the wire is eased over the side by an easing-out line. NOTE: In any tensioned rig, tension must be taken off the highline or span wire prior to tripping the pelican hook.

6.28 Astern Fueling Method   Normally the U.S. Navy does not use this method. Agreements between NATO nations call for all escort-type ships to be able to receive fuel from designated merchant tankers by alongside and by astern methods.

The rig consists of a towed marker buoy, twenty 30-foot sections and a 15-foot section of 6-inch buoyant fuel hose. The receiving ship takes position off the quarter of the delivering ship. A shot line and hose messenger are passed to the receiving ship. The receiving ship pays out fuel hose, and the delivering ship drops back until her bridge is opposite the marker buoy. Then she hauls aboard the discharge end of the hose.

6.29 Special Hose Fittings   A key part of any underway fueling rig is that section at or near the receiving ship's fueling trunk. Improved devices that bring together the end of the hose and the fueling trunk can speed the processes considerably. One such device is the breakable-spool quick-release coupling. Another is a combined quick-release coupling and valve. Perhaps the best of these devices is the probe fueling unit. This assembly has two main parts: a male probe attached to the end of the delivering ship's hose, and a receiver (that leads to the fueling trunk) supported by a swivel fitting on the receiving ship. A pelican hook for securing the span wire is an integral part of the swivel fitting. Key to the whole device is a sliding sleeve valve that opens when the probe is engaged properly but that automatically closes when disengaged. Mounted on either side of the receiver are indicators showing when the probe is seated. As the probe mates, indicators rise to the vertical and then drop back to a position about 30 degrees above the horizontal. When the probe is properly engaged, a latch mechanism prevents its being withdrawn under normal pull and strain, unless it is disengaged by means of a pull on a lever on the receiver. However, the probe will also be disengaged by a pull of about 2500 pounds of the inhaul.

Passing the Probe Fueling Unit The probe fueling system employs a span wire which is passed in the same manner as the span wire rig discussed previously. After the span wire has been connected and with a ship separation not greater than 140 feet, the fueling hose with probe is eased down the span wire until the probe is within reach of personnel on the receiving ship. A remating line is then attached to the hook on the outboard end of the probe trolley by the receiving ship and the probe is hauled in to engage the receiver. A pull of from **300 to 500 pounds on the remating line will seat the probe. (Fig. 6.14.)**

When ships are more than 140 feet apart, and at all times when fueling carriers, an outhaul must be used to haul the probe across to the receiving ship. From five to eight men, depending on the fairlead arrangement, should be used on the outhaul or remating line.

6.30 Additional Reference Sources Not all methods of underway replenishment have been discussed here. For greater coverage the reader is referred to *Boatswain's Mate 3 and 2,* NavPers 10121 series, and *Boatswain's Mate 1 and C,* NavPers 10122 series. *Naval Warfare Publication (NWP)* 38 has information on methods and techniques followed when only U.S. Navy ships are involved. *Allied Tactical Publication (ATP)* 16 describes procedures to be followed when ships of NATO nations are involved in underway replenishment.

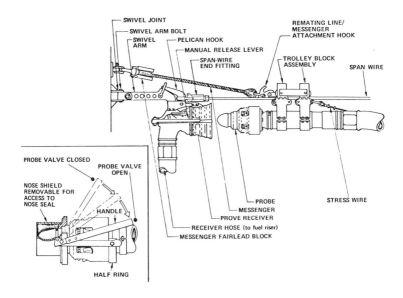

Fig. 6.14 Single probe fueling rig.

6.31   General Safety Precautions for Transfer and Fueling

1. Personnel assigned to transfer stations must be adequately trained in all phases of safety procedures and precautions. They should wear safety helmets and clothing of the prescribed color.
2. Because transfer stations on receiving and delivering ships are in exposed locations, personnel working close to ships' sides where solid bulwarks are not installed must wear kapok-type life jackets. If it is necessary to use inflatable-type life jackets, they must be inflated.
3. During heavy weather, personnel working on weather decks should wear life jackets.
4. Personnel must be cautioned to keep clear of suspended loads whenever possible.
5. Ample provision must be made to prevent the shifting of cargo, with its risk to both personnel and material.
6. Wire highline may not be used to transfer personnel. When manila highlines are used to transfer personnel, a capstan may not be employed to haul the line; it must be tended by manpower.
7. In handling ammunition, it must be remembered that carelessness and haste, in addition to causing accidents, often result in rendering ammunition unserviceable even when in containers.
8. In the transfer of personnel where water temperatures are low, "immersion suits" should be worn.
9. Whenever practicable, a rescue ship or helicopter should be stationed astern of ships replenishing at sea for the purpose of rescuing personnel lost overboard.
10. During night replenishment flashlights (life jacket-type) should be pinned to the left breast of each life jacket in use. They are not to be lighted unless the order is given to do so.
11. Plastic police whistles should be issued to each man wearing a life jacket during night replenishments. They are worn on a lanyard around the neck, with the whistle tucked inside the life jacket to prevent fouling in lines or gear.
12. A lifebuoy watch should be stationed in the after part of the ship with a buoy fitted with an automatic float light.

Ship
Communications

Communications is the act of exchanging information; the ways and means of doing so, and the information so given. Shipboard communications are of two types: internal and external. The latter is meant to imply rapid and reliable communications at a distance, for example, visually by signal flags or electronically by radio. A ship also has internal or interior systems of communications, such as public address, telephone, engine-order telegraph, and dial or sound-powered telephone systems.

7.1 Interior Communications A ship's interior communications (IC) equipment is normally less complicated than that used for exterior communications. IC equipment is essential for the orderly perfor-mance of both emergency and routine shipboard functions. IC systems are generally classed as either an indicating or a sound system.

7.2 Interior Indicating Systems There are usually one or more sound systems to provide alternate or backup communications for the indi-cating systems between vital locations, such as between the bridge and main engine control. IC systems normally employ a synchronous motor system to transmit information or orders.

Engine order telegraphs (annunciators) provide the conning officer a rapid and reliable means of ordering (and receiving acknowledgment of) changes in engine speed or direction. This is accomplished with two sections. The engine-order section controls the speed range ("standard," "full," etc.); the propeller order section controls speed within a range.

Rudder angle indicators, which show the actual position of the rudder, are a valuable aid in maneuvering the ship.

Course-to-steer indicators provide the conning officer and helmsman the course to steer, as directed by navigational or weapons-control devices. Gyrocompass repeaters, the pitometer log, and the wind direction and force indicators are also forms of interior indicating systems.

7.3   Interior Sound Systems   While indicating systems communicate only raw facts or orders, sound systems can amplify and make recommendations on the information that has been transmitted by the indicating systems. Since the voice is used, the scope of information is almost infinite.

Multichannel and Public Address Systems   Multichannel systems use electronic amplifiers and push-button selector switches, allowing one or more stations to communicate directly. Public address systems are announcing systems only.

Telephones   On larger ships the standard telephone is used. Normally it serves routine administrative purposes; however, in emergencies it serves as an alternate system for operational purposes. Unlike the sound-powered phone system, the number of stations that can communicate directly is determined by the type of equipment.

Voice Tubes..One of the oldest IC methods, voice tubes are still found in the most modern ships. This system of metal tubes connecting various stations is the least susceptible to battle damage.

Sound-powered phone systems constitute the mainstay of internal communications in Navy ships. These phones require no external power. Speaking into the mouthpiece generates an electrical signal that is reproduced as sound on other phones on that circuit. Circuits may be (1) direct—a line connecting one or more outlets in the ship; (2) switched—lines passing through a switchboard, which allows one or more circuits to be connected together; or (3) phone type—lines between points with both a selector switch to select the desired station and a hand-crank growler or push-button buzzer to alert the station being called. Some systems pass through an amplifier to increase the volume. An automatic cutout will bypass the amplifier should the latter fail.

7.4 Closed Circuit Television Television facilitates the rapid display of a fast-changing or complex picture. Examples of use aboard Navy ships include the briefing of pilots and plane crews, using the tactical displays from the combat information center. Some ships mount a TV camera on the pierside bow to facilitate docking. Television also facilitates training aboard ship and assists communications between captain and crew. Closed circuit TV transmits over wires the picture signal from the camera to the picture tube. In contrast, the commercial (or home) TV system transmits the signal through the air.

7.5 External Communications In sharp contrast to the foregoing internal systems are those that provide rapid and reliable external communications. They break down into three major classes: sound, electrical, and visual. The latter two are further broken down into:

Electrical Communications	*Visual Communications*
1. Radiotelegraph	1. Flaghoist
2. Teletypewriter	2. Flashing light
3. Radioteletypewriter	3. Semaphore
4. Radiotelephone	4. Pyrotechnics
5. Computer/Digital	5. Colored lights
6. Satellite	
7. Facsimile	
8. Television	

7.6 Sound Signaling Rules of the Road call for the use of a ship's whistle, siren, and foghorn for sound signaling. Navigational aids such as lighthouses and whistle, bell, gong, or horn buoys emit noises, another form of sound signaling. The procedure for sound signaling is described in International Code of Signals (H.O. 102)—1969. It is normally limited to one-letter signals of the international code—signals that have an urgent or important meaning, or are in very common use. (Table 7.1.)

7.7 Electrical Communications Radiotelegraph, often called CW for "continuous wave," is a system for transmitting Morse code that has been in use by the Navy since as early as 1903. Although the use of radiotelegraph in today's modern complex communications systems is limited, CW is still considered one of the most trustworthy systems available to achieve reliable communications to a system which would be placed in use when all else fails.

The teletypewriter provides instantaneous point to point printed communications between a sender and a receiver and can be utilized with either a landline or radio mode of operation.

Table 7-1 Single Letter Signals

A I have a diver down; keep well clear at slow speed.

*B I am taking in, or discharging, or carrying dangerous goods.

C Yes (affirmative or "The significance of the previous group should be read in the affirmative").

*D Keep clear of me; I am maneuvering with difficulty.

*E I am alterng my course to starboard.

F I am disabled; communicate with me.

G I require a pilot. When made by fishing vessels operating in close proximity on the fishing grounds it means: "I am hauling nets."

*H I have a pilot on board.

*I I am altering my course to port.

J I am on fire and have dangerous cargo on board: keep well clear of me.

K I wish to communicate with you.

L You should stop your vessel instantly.

M My vessel is stopped and making no way through the water.

N No (negative or "The significance of the previous group should be read in the negative"). This signal may be given only visually or by sound. For voice or radio transmission the signal should be "NO."

O Man overboard.

P **In harbor.**—All persons should report on board as the vessel is about to proceed to sea.
At sea.—It may be used by fishing vessels to mean: "My nets have come fast upon an obstruction."

Q My vessel is "healthy" and I request free pratique.

*S My engines are going astern.

*T Keep clear of me; I am engaged in pair trawling.

U You are running into danger.

V I require assistance.

W I require medical assistance.

X Stop carrying out your intentions and watch for my signals.

Y I am dragging my anchor.

Z I require a tug. When made by fishing vessels operating in close proximity on the fishing grounds it means: "I am shooting nets."

*Notes: 1. Signals of letters marked by an asterisk (*) when made by sound may only be made in compliance with the requirements of the International Regulations for Preventing Collisions at Sea.
2. Signals "K" and "S" have special meanings as landing signals for small boats with crews or persons in distress. (International Convention for the Safety of Life at Sea, 1960, Chapter V, Regulation 16.)

Landline communications are used by shore-based military and commercial activities. In landline operations the sending and receiving stations are connected by cable, such as are telephones. Switching and relay centers function to complete the landline system and make possible rapid and reliable communications from originators of messages to the intended addressees.

Radioteletype, as its name might imply, utilizes radio waves in its mode of operation and is not dependent upon cables. Radioteletype is primarily intended for use by mobile stations and is capable of transmitting

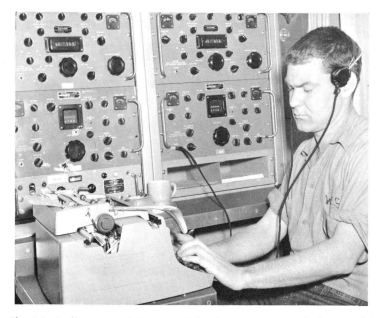

Fig. 7.1 Radioman receiving CW. *(Official U.S. Coast Guard photograph.)*

automated high speed long range communications over either land or ocean areas. The Navy uses radioteletype for ship to ship, ship to shore, and shore to ship communications. Today, radioteletype is the primary method of communications used by ships, both for outgoing and incoming messages. Radioteletype provides the means to send or receive traffic at the rate of 100 words per minute, and higher, in contrast to the 18 to 25 wpm speed of CW.

Traffic handling capacities are further increased by the use of multi-channel teletype systems aboard some of the larger ships. These circuits are designed to provide a large capacity for circuits between stations and are attained by the utilization of multiplex equipment. Signals from several teletypewriters are multiplexed into one signal for transmission. This signal is then broken down at the receiving station and distributed to the various teletypewriters as appropriate. The Navy uses a maximum of sixteen channels in any multiplex system operation.

Radiotelephone provides the most rapid and convenient means of exercising command and control as information can be exchanged directly and instantaneously between personnel concerned. The advent of single side band (SSB) has greatly enhanced long range voice communications, providing real time communications between an on-scene commander and a higher headquarters. The majority of voice circuits are controlled by key personnel from remote stations such as the bridge, the pilot house, or from within the combat information center.

With the advantages of radiotelephone go some disadvantages. Transmissions may be unreadable because of static, enemy interference, or a high local noise level. Additionally, wave propagation characteristics of radiotelephone frequencies are sometimes erratic, allowing transmissions to be heard at great distances, but not by the intended nearby addressee. Whereas nearly all teletypewriter circuits are protected by security, or cryptographic devices, which make their signals unintelligible to all but the authorized recipients, few long range voice circuits are presently capable of providing secure voice transmissions. Consequently, in order to maintain privacy, or security of information, radiotelephone operations must be severely restricted in its use to unclassified information. This restriction applies to both short and long range communications, however, short range tactical circuits, for the most part, are now secure circuits.

Computer, or digital communications, are in use aboard some of the larger ships. Several kinds of information can be translated into digital data, however this data must be recorded and processed to become useful. Several types of terminals that can be connected to the control unit of a data terminal include magnetic tape, teletypewriter, and computer terminals. These terminals are used to extract and transmit information to the data terminals. Supply requisitions and formatted routine reports such as Defense Energy Information System (DEIS) reports are examples of information transmitted through digital communications.

Satellite communications systems are in the process of being installed and utilized on many of the larger ships in the Navy. Basically, orbiting satellites act as relay stations for transmitting stations, relaying their signals back to earth to intended receiving activities. This system will ultimately provide the advantages of reliable long range communications between any point or points on the earth.

Facsimile (FAX) gives a receiving station a printed display of transmitted information and is especially useful for promulgating such matter as photographs and weather charts. The image to be sent is scanned by a photoelectric cell and transmitted via a radio wave. The transmitted picture is simultaneously reproduced on a recorder at the receiving activity. Facsimile requires several minutes to complete the transmission of a picture twice the size of this page.

Television has present and future applications, some of which are listed below:

1. remote guidance of missiles;
2. reception of reconnaissance data from aircraft;
3. remote inspection of underwater salvage operations;
4. simultaneous briefing of many commanding officers or aviators of a task force when the tactical situation is too urgent to permit duplication of weather data, charts, or other pictorial information.

7.8 Shipboard Communications Facilities As it pertains to personnel on the ship's bridge, communications mainly takes the form of visual signaling. Navy ships are provided with these basic publications: *Allied Naval Signal Book; International Code of Signals; Wartime Instructions for Merchant Ships.* U.S. merchant ships carry the *International Code* under all conditions—and are provided with the *Wartime Instructions* by the Navy under wartime conditions.

The *International Code of Signals* is the basic signaling publication, and serves most methods of communications—whether visual, electrical, or sound. First published in 1857, it is used today by ships of all nations. The U.S. edition is further identified as "H.O. 102...U.S., Naval Oceanographic Office." (Since named Defense Mapping Agency Hydrographic Center) The one volume contains both instructions for use, and one-, two-, and three-letter codes and their meanings, allowing for thousands of combinations of information units.

Language barriers are overcome by the code by virtue of its multilanguage printings. Thus, as a simple example, the signal NF—"you are running into danger"—conveys that meaning regardless of the language used. In addition to the English-language version (of which H.O. 102 is one form), the *International Code* is also published in French, Italian, German, Japanese, Spanish, Norwegian, Russian, and Greek.

By their nature, Navy ships and merchant ships have considerable differences in their requirements. This, in turn, is reflected in the relatively large number of Navymen with shipboard communications duties and by the variety of equipment of a Navy ship. For rapid exterior communications, Navy ships normally have two main stations where messages and signals are sent, received, and processed. These stations are known as the radio station and the visual station. Coordination of both stations in large warships takes place in the communications center under the supervision of the communications watch officer (CWO). The communications center is usually located in the vicinity of the main radio room or radio central.

At the visual station there are semaphore flags, portable signal lights, and a loud hailer ("bull horn" or electric megaphone). Signal flaghoists and flags are in the vicinity. A ship's bell and whistle are nearby. Running lights and other navigational and anchor light fixtures are located on the masts, superstructure, and above the main deck; controls are near the visual station—usually in the pilothouse. Signals searchlights are in the superstructure in the vicinity of the visual station; blinker lights are installed on the yardarms with keying controls at the visual station. Pyrotechnic devices are located near the signal bridge.

The radio station facilities are concentrated mainly at radio central. Radio antennas are located throughout the superstructure. Radio transmitters and receivers are found not only in radio central but in special transmitter rooms and separate radio rooms. Portable and emergency radio equipment is located in a number of places. Remote-operated radiotelephone units—send/receive facilities—are found on the bridge, in the pilothouses, in CIC, and in radio spaces. Radio-teletype and radiotelegraph facilities are normally operated at the main radio station.

A number of interior communications systems are employed to link the bridge and pilothouse with the key shipboard communication facilities. Regular telephones as well as sound-powered telephones are used. Voice tubes are also used, and on some ships pneumatic tubes are installed to send messages quickly. Amplifier-type announcing systems (often referred to as "squawk boxes" or "intercom units") are widely employed also.

7.9   Visual Telecommunications   Visual communications systems have been in use since men first sailed the seas and are often the best means for communicating at short range (Fig. 7.2.)

Fig. 7.2 Navy signalman reads visual signals on a distant ship. *(Official U.S. Navy photograph.)*

The most important visual systems are flaghoist, flashing light, and semaphore. Pyrotechnics and colored lights have important wartime and emergency uses.

Flaghoist is a method whereby various combinations of brightly colored flags and pennants are hoisted to send messages. It is the primary means for transmitting brief tactical and informational signals to other ships nearby. Signals are repeated by addressees, thus providing a sure check on the accuracy of reception. Texts of messages which may be sent are limited to those found in signal books.

Directional flashing light is a visual telegraphic system in which an operator opens and closes the shutter of a searchlight to form the dashes and dots of the Morse code. The light is pointed and trained to be seen only from the viewpoint of the receiver.

Nondirectional flashing light is sent out from a lamp on a yardarm. Dots and dashes are made by switching the lamp on and off. Since the light is visible in every direction, this method is well suited for messages which are for several addressees.

Semaphore is a communication method in which an operator signals with two hand flags, moving his arms through various positions to represent letters, and special signs. It is especially suitable for long administrative messages because of its speed. It is not readable much farther than two miles, even on a clear day.

Pyrotechnics have a wide variety of uses. Often their use can be a matter of life or death. Examples are identification of own ship or attracting attention when in distress. Coastal lifesaving stations also emply pyrotechnic flares to signal to vessels in distress.

7.10 Semaphore Facilities Semaphore requires little equipment— the two hand flags attached to staffs are all that is needed (Fig. 7.3). The standard semaphore flags are usually 15 or 18 inches square, and each staff is long enough to enable the sender to grasp it firmly. The flags are similar to the *oscar* alphabet flag. The *papa* flag is sometimes substituted. Most semaphore flags issued to the fleet today are fluorescent and are made of sharkskin cloth.

7.11 Searchlights Light sources are incandescent or mercury-xenon lamp, xenon-arc or carbon-arc. Control of the light is by means of a shutter. This is illustrated in Fig. 7.4. The front and rear doors are hinged to the searchlight case to permit access to the interior for relamping and cleaning. There is usually a handle on the rear of the case to elevate and depress the light or turn it in azimuth.

7.12 Nancy Facilities Nancy is a system of visual communications using infrared light, which is visible only with the aid of equipment designed for this purpose.

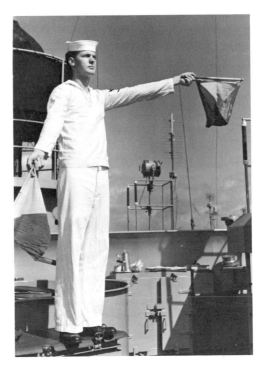

Fig. 7.3 A signalman sending semaphore. *(Official U.S. Navy photograph.)*

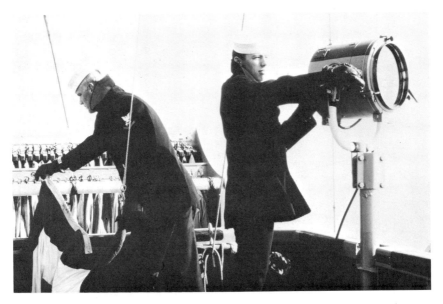

Fig. 7.4 Signalmen man the signal bridge. *(Official U.S. Navy photograph.)*

7.13   Flaghoist Signaling   The flags of a hoist are always read from the top down. When a signal is too long to fit in one halyard—when, in other words, more flags are required than can be made into a single hoist—the signal must be continued on another halyard and read outboard to inboard. When a signal is broken into two or more hoists, it must be divided at points where there can be a natural space without affecting the meaning of the signal.

Flags are kept in flagbags. Such storage permits rapid makeup of the hoist. The signal is hoisted as soon as each flag is attached.

Flags used on board ship are shown in color in the signal books. More flags are used on men-of-war than on merchant ships; 40 flags on merchant ships, 68 flags on Naval men-of-war (Figs. 7.5, 7.6, 7.7, and 7.8.)

7.14   Other Signal Light Facilities   Men-of-war carry a number of lights which may be used to signal not only the status of the vessel according to the requirements of the Rules of the Road but for other purposes as well.

The boom lights, portable towing lights, and minesweeper polarity signal lights (red and green) are energized from various local lighting circuits.

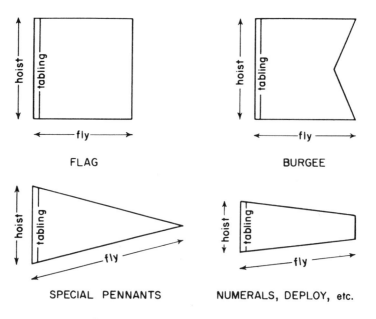

Fig. 7.5 Types of flag, and flag terms.

Fig. 7.6 Signalmen aboard the guided missile frigate *USS Talbot* (FFG 4) hoist signals. *(Official U.S. Navy photograph.)*

The masthead light, range light, side lights, white stern light, and permanent towing lights are usually controlled from the running light switch box on the bridge.

The signal and anchor light switch box on the bridge controls the following lights (when installed):

Aircraft warning lights	Underwater task lights
Forward and after anchor lights	Speed lights
Blinker lights	Station-keeping lights
Breakdown and man-overboard lights	Steering light
Minesweeping lights	Wake light

Due to the wide variety and uses of ships' lights, a brief description of the most important ones is included here:

Aircraft Warning Lights One red light is installed at the truck of each mast and extends more than 25 feet above the highest point in the superstructure. Where it is impossible to locate this light so that

Fig. 7.7 A signalman mans the flag bag aboard the guided missile destroyer *USS Coontz* (DDG 40). *(Official U.S. Navy photograph.)*

it is visible from any location throughout 360 degrees of azimuth, two lights are installed.

Blinker Lights These lights are installed only on the signal yardarm outboard, one port and one starboard. On ships with more than one mast they are located only on the forward yardarm. Screens are fitted at the base of these lights to prevent glare or reflections from interfering with the navigation of the ship. Lights are operable from signal keys located on the bridge; intensity may be varied by energizing the upper bank, lower bank, or both banks.

Boom Lights Boom lights are permanently installed on the outboard end of each boat boom and are energized from receptacles on the ship's service lighting system.

Breakdown and Man-overboard (Not Under Command) Lights These are mounted on brackets extending abaft, and offset from, the

Fig. 7.8 Signalman aboard dock landing ship *U.S.S. Alamo* (LSD 33) runs signal flags up hoist as ship steams in South China Sea. *(Official U.S. Navy photograph.)*

mast or structure to permit all-around visibility insofar as is practicable. To facilitate pulsating these lights as a "man-overboard" signal, the rotary snap switch in the signal light switch box which controls them is fitted with a crank handle.

Minesweeping Light   These lights are installed on all minesweepers (or ships fitted to sweep mines) to warn other ships to keep clear of the sweep gear. The signal consists of a triangular display of three 32-point green lights, one on each forward yardarm and on the foremast. Lights on the yardarm are at least 3 feet outboard of the mast and the light on the mast is at least 3 feet above the lights on the yardarms. The light on the mast is installed on a bracket extending forward of the mast and offset to ensure visibility ahead and astern.

Polarity Signal Lights   Two lights, one red and one green, are installed close together to each side of minesweepers to indicate polarity or direction of magnetic field. These lights are mounted to be visible from 20 degrees forward to 20 degrees abaft the beam on each side of the ship. They are pulsed by contacts in the minesweeping control panel.

Speed Light   This light is installed in ships of frigate (FF) size and larger to indicate the ship's speed. It is located at the truck of the mast. If it is impracticable to locate this light so that it is visible throughout 360 degrees of azimuth, two lights are provided.

Station-keeping Lights   Two lights are installed on all minesweepers required to give sweep information at night. They are located in a vertical plane perpendicular to the keel so that accurate observations may be taken. These lights are mounted to be visible from 20 degrees forward or 20 degrees abaft the beam on each side of the ship. If it is impossible to locate the lower light so that it can be seen on both sides of the ship, two lights are used, one on each side.

Steering Light   This light is installed on specified ships and on ships where the pilothouse is more that 100 feet abaft the bow, unless structural interferences make use of this light impracticable. The light is located on the jackstaff or other centerline structure and is visible to the helmsman.

Stern Light, Blue   This light is installed near the stern of ships likely to be engaged in convoy operations. It is mounted to show throughout a total azimuth of 12 points—from astern to 6 points on each side of the ship.

Towing Lights   Minesweepers, tugs, and other ships normally engaged in towing operations have permanently installed towing lights. Other ships have two portable towing lights, each of which is equipped with sufficient cable and a plug connector to permit energizing these lights from the nearest lighting receptacle connector.

Underwater Task Lights   These lights are installed on all ships engaged in underwater operations, such as minesweepers. They consist of three lights in a vertical line one over the other not less than 6 feet apart. The highest and lowest of these lights is red, and the middle light is white. The red lights are the same fixtures as those used for breakdown and man-overboard lights, whenever practicable, and the switching is arranged accordingly.

Wake Light   This light is installed on the flagstaff or after part of the ship to illuminate the wake, and is so mounted that no part of the ship is illuminated by it.

Aircraft carriers have a complex arrangement of night-flight operations lights. These consist of such lights as deck edge lights, homing lights, parking lights, and takeoff lights.

7.15   Messages and Signals   In naval communications, a message is a formal type of communication; like a postal letter, it is addressed to a certain destination(s) and has a text and an ending. The address is known as the heading. The form of the signal (or sign) is abbreviated or modified, but conveys a meaning nevertheless. Signals may be used in the process of transmitting messages; examples of this are message handling signals and call signs.

On Navy ships, the commanding officer must authorize all communications sent from the ship; both signals and messages. Some signals are made as a part of the ship's routine without this specific authorization in each case: An example of this is the running lights which are always turned on at sunset when underway. Messages, on the other hand, are authorized and released by the captain. Messages which have been released are delivered to either the ship's radio or visual station for transmittal. At either place call signs, internal handling instructions (signals), are added: The recipient is then "called" and the message is transmitted and receipted for. The ship maintains complete files of communications transmitted and received.

7.16   Special Merchant Ship Considerations   Few vessels of any size go to sea without some radiotelegraph or radiotelephone capability. Coast Guard and Federal Communication Commission requirements are quite specific on that point. For vessels less than 300 gross tons, no radio equipment is required; for those 300 to 1600 gross, radiotelephone equipment and a qualified operator are required; for those 1600 gross and over, radiotelegraph and a qualified operator(s) are required.

If the ship is a passenger type (more than 12 passengers) a 24-hour radio watch is required. The great majority of merchant ships normally have but one radio operator, the radio officer. He is on watch 8 hours out of 24. An automatic alarm system is required when a 24-hour watch is not maintained. (This is the alarm that responds to another ship's radiotelegraph signal on a frequency of 500 khz.) If the alarm system goes out of order, it gives a signal that is audible in the radio room, in the operator's cabin, and on the bridge.

Deck officers, the watch officers of the merchant marine, must have proficiency in visual signaling as there is no one else on the bridge to do the signaling. They must be able to read signal flags and to have a general competence in other visual signaling methods, including the ability to read flashing light at 10 words per minute and transmit at 6 words per minute. Usually there are but two men on a merchant ship's bridge: the watch officer and the helmsman. (The lookout is stationed at the bow.) With other duties to perform, the watch officer is often unable to respond immediately to another ship's call-up for an exchange of visual signals.

7.17 Distress Signals A ship in distress can so indicate by visual, sound, or radio means. The various ways of doing this are briefly described in the rules of the road. The radiotelegraph signal "SOS," transmitted in Morse code (. . . - - - . . .), or the radiotelephone signal "Mayday," transmitted by voice, both reveal that the sending vessel is threatened by grave and imminent danger and requests immediate assistance. The first two sections of general code combinations in the International Code of Signals deal with: distress–emergency–casualities–damage.

A merchant ship in distress may use the radiotelegraph alarm signal to secure attention to distress calls and messages. This alarm signal is designed to actuate the radiotelegraph alarms of other ships so fitted. The emission consists of a series of 12 dashes sent in one minute, the duration of each dash being 4 seconds, the duration of interval between dashes being one second.

Mayday is only one of the three radiotelephone safety messages, the other two being PAN and SECURITE ("saycuritay"). Pan (for urgency) indicates that the sender has an urgent message to transmit concerning the safety of a ship, aircraft, other vehicle, or a person. Sécurité (for safety) indicates that the sender is about to transmit a message concerning the safety of navigation or giving important meterological warnings.

A ship receiving a distress signal (SOS or MAYDAY) from a nearby ship acknowledges receipt, but only after first ascertaining that it will not interfere with messages from ships in a better position to render assistance.

Navigation

Navigation is the process of directing the movement of a craft from one place to another. The earliest form of navigation probably was *piloting,* the determination of position relative to landmarks, natural or man-made.

When man became brave enough to venture out of sight of objects that could be used for guiding him on his way, a new form of navigation was born: *dead reckoning.* This involved keeping an account of the direction and distance traveled, however crude the determination, so that one could reverse his travel back to familiar surroundings.

The earliest compass was the wind, waves, sun or other celestial body, or perhaps the flight of birds. For the measurement of direction, the horizon circle surrounding the observer was divided into 12 or 16, and later 32, "points," a custom which continued in some quarters to the present century. A common unit of distance was the "day's journey." Speed or distance was estimated.

Many of the early efforts to improve navigation centered around attempts to develop means of determining more accurately the direction and speed of progress of the craft. Thus, the magnetic compass was among the earliest instruments provided to the navigator.

Celestial navigation in the sense of determining the position of the observer by means of celestial bodies had to await not only the development of instruments for observation, but also the ability of astronomers to predict and publish future positions of the bodies observed, the development of mathematics, and the invention of a means for keeping accurate time of a reference meridian before longitude could be determined. Before the time of a reference meridian was available at sea, it was common practice to sail first to the parallel of the destination and then to "run down the latitude" until landfall was achieved.

The application of electronics to navigation is, of course, a much more modern development, being a product of the twentieth century. Early attempts at navigation by use of radiobeacons became known as *radionavigation;* today the use of the term has been extended to include all forms of navigation by an electromagnetic wave. The term *electronic navigation* has been applied to all navigation systems involving use of electronic components, including radionavigation systems, sonar, satellite navigation, and inertial navigation systems. The most recent development in navigation is *space navigation,* concerned with the direction of a craft through interplanetary space.

It is sometimes convenient to class all marine surface navigation under two headings: dead reckoning and position-fixing. Because the uncertainty of positions determined by dead reckoning increases with time or distance traveled, some method of periodic updating by position-fixing is needed. Piloting is position-fixing relative to points on the earth. Celestial navigation utilizes celestial bodies for the determination of position; radionavigation uses a lattice pattern established by means of one or more radiated electromagnetic waves; and various advanced electronic navigation systems utilize features of the ocean bottom, or a system of gyros and accelerometers, or satellites for the same purpose.

Fundamentals

Navigation is concerned in large measure with position, direction, distance, speed, and time.

8.1 Position is generally expressed by the navigator in terms of geographical coordinates: latitude and longitude. Although astronomers, surveyors, and geodesists define various forms of latitude and longitude, the navigator invariably uses geodetic coordinates. The geodetic latitude of a place is the angle between the plane of the equator and the normal to the ellipsoid of revolution assumed to be the figure of the earth. Geodetic longitude is the angle this same normal makes with a plane containing the rotational axis of the earth and an arbitrary reference point on its surface, almost universally the old Greenwich Observatory at London, England. It is true that position determination by celestial navigation yields astronomical coordinates, but the difference between these and the geodetic coordinates shown on navigational charts, while important to surveyors and geodesists, is seldom of operational significance to the navigator. Consequently, except in unusual circumstances, the navigator assumes all positions determined by him to be in geodetic coordinates. Geographical position is usually stated in degrees, minutes, and tenths of a minute (a precision of approximately a tenth of a nautical mile or better), although the uncertainty of positions out of sight of land is seldom less than a small number of *miles*.

In pilot waters, when landmarks are used for piloting, position may be stated in terms of direction and distance from an object such as a lighthouse or buoy. While traversing a buoyed channel, the navigator may indicate position in terms of progress along the channel, using numbered buoys as the reference. Thus, the position may be stated as "abeam buoy 8," or "between buoys 9 and 11."

8.2   Direction is involved in navigation with respect to motion of the vessel, sometimes in stating its position, and frequently with respect to objects (e.g., landmarks, celestial bodies, radio transmitters, etc.) used in the determination of position.

As used in navigation, direction is usually expressed as the horizontal angle between a line pointing in some reference direction and a second line extending in the "direction" desired. If the progress or orientation of the vessel is involved, direction is usually stated to the nearest whole degree or half degree. The same is generally true of observed directions of landmarks. Computed directions of celestial bodies are usually stated to the nearest tenth of a degree. In most cases, direction is expressed as the total angle from the reference direction clockwise through 360 degrees, using three figures plus the decimal, if any. Thus, a course due east is stated 090 degrees, and one **30 degrees west of true north, 330 degrees. Occasionally direction each side of the reference direction, through 180 degrees, is stated. In this case, the direction of measurement must be indicated if ambiguity is to be avoided.**

Several different reference directions are in common use in navigation. A *true* direction is based upon true north, or the northerly direction along a geographical meridian. This is the direction nearly always used in computations and plotting.

True north differs from *magnetic* north by the angle between the geographical meridian and the magnetic meridian, defined as the direction of the horizontal component of the lines of force of the magnetic field of the earth. Magnetic north is the direction indicated by a magnetic compass not subject to disturbing forces. The angle between true and magnetic north is termed *variation* by navigators and *magnetic declination* by certain earth scientists. Designated east or west, through 180 degrees, to indicate the northerly direction of the magnetic meridian with respect to the true meridian, it varies with geographical position on the earth. Variation changes slowly with time; this *secular* or *annual change* is usually shown on charts. There is, additionally, a daily fluctuation called *diurnal change*, which is generally too small to be of navigational significance except in polar regions.

Compass north is the direction north as indicated by a magnetic compass. This is seldom the same as magnetic north because of the influence of local magnetic forces associated with ferrous metal or electric currents in the immediate vicinity of the compass. The difference between magnetic and compass north is termed *deviation*. It is designated east or west, through 180 degrees, to indicate the direction of the north end of the compass axis with respect to the magnetic meridian. Deviation varies with the vessel, the position of the compass in the vessel, the direction in which the vessel is pointed, and sometimes the geographical position of the vessel and the length of time the vessel has been on the same heading. It also changes when structural alterations are made to the vessel (especially if electric welding takes place near the compass), electrical wiring is changed, or when the vessel is struck by lightning or takes on a cargo of magnetic material. The algebraic sum of variation and deviation is termed *compass error*.

North as indicated by a gyrocompass is called *gyro* north; it usually differs by only a small amount from true north in the lower and mid-latitudes in which most ships operate. The difference between gyro and true north is termed *gyro error*, designated east or west to indicate the direction of the north end of the gyro axis with respect to the true meridian. Gyro error is a function of vessel speed, heading, and latitude; it is usually greatest on easterly or westerly headings unless velocity compensation is applied. Most general purpose gyrocompass systems are unusable beyond 70° latitude, as their corrective forces are derived from the speed of the earth's tangential rotational velocity.

In some areas, particularly in high latitudes, a navigational grid is superimposed on the navigational chart, usually because of the rapid convergence of the geographical meridians. The "north–south" grid lines are all parallel *on the chart*. By convention, *grid* north is the direction of the north geographical pole from Greenwich. This is true in both the arctic and antarctic, so grid north is continuous along both the Greenwich and 180th meridians, completely around the world. Grid north differs from magnetic north by an angle known as *grid variation* or *grivation,* designated east or west through 180 degrees as the magnetic meridian points to the east or west of grid north, respectively.

A *relative* direction is the horizontal angle between a line extending in the forward direction along the longitudinal axis of the vessel and a line extending from the vessel toward a second point. It may be expressed as a direction from 000 degrees dead ahead clockwise through 360 degrees or as an angle of 0 degrees through 180 degrees right or left of the bow. In British usage relative direction is designated green or red to agree with colored side lights carried in accordance with the International Rules of the Road. An older practice sometimes still used to indicate an approximate relative direction is to state the direction as so many "points" (of 11¼ degrees) on the starboard or port bow or quarter, or forward or abaft the starboard or port beam.

A number of directions are involved in navigation. The *heading* of a vessel is the horizontal component of the direction in which it is pointed. The term is used to indicate both the instantaneous direction, which may change from moment to moment, or the average direction over a period of time.

Unless there is no wind or current, the heading is not the same as the *course,* which is defined as the intended direction of travel. The difference between the two is termed *leeway* or *drift angle,* although the terms leeway and drift are often applied to the amount and rate, respectively, of motion to leeward. The *course line* is a line extending in the direction of the intended course.

Course made good is the single direction from some point of departure to some point of arrival, not necessarily the origin of the voyage and the intended destination. There is only one course made good between any two given points, regardless of how many changes of course may have been involved.

Track is the path followed by the vessel, and sometimes the direction of that path. When used as a direction, track, like heading, may refer either to the instantaneous value or to the average over a period of time, but only between changes of course.

Bearing is the direction of one terrestrial point from another, usually the direction of an object as viewed from the vessel.

Azimuth is the direction of a celestial body. Azimuth is occasionally used as a synonym of bearing, but seldom by navigators.

Any of the reference directions can be used with any direction, although relative directions are customarily confined to bearings and azimuths. If the context leaves any reasonable possibility of ambiguity or confusion, the reference direction should be stated, for example as "bearing 137 degrees true," "B 137 degrees T," "course 264 degrees per steering (magnetic) compass," or "C 264 degrees p stg. c."

8.3 Distance is involved in navigation in such applications as determining speed, the time needed to travel a given distance at a given speed, the position of a vessel relative to landmarks, and the probable time of sighting a landmark.

Distance is usually expressed in nautical miles, although yards, feet, or meters may occasionally be used. A nautical mile is exactly 1852 meters, a little more than 6076 feet. Its convenience stems from the fact that, for ordinary purposes of navigation, it can be considered equal to one minute of arc of a meridian or any other great circle. Over short distances it is sometimes considered equal to 2000 yards.

This measure of distance is particularly convenient because the expansion and distortion of the Mercator projection commonly used for nautical charts varies with latitude; that part of the latitude scale at the mid-latitude of operations can be used as a distance scale. Also convenient is the fact that computations related to celestial navigation as well as those involved in great circle sailing include an arc of a great circle that is converted to distance. With a conversion factor of unity, no computation is needed. Distance is customarily stated to the nearest tenth of a mile.

8.4 Speed of a vessel is nearly always stated in *knots,* one knot being defined as one nautical mile per hour. The origin of the name "knots" is interesting. The Dutchman's log required a supply of floating objects which, dropped overboard near the bow, passed along the ship's side in a number of seconds related to ship's speed. Some unknown ingenious seaman tied a line to the object so that it could be retrieved and used again. This led to a modification in the technique whereby the object was thrown over the stern and the amount of line paid out during a fixed period of time was calibrated directly in nautical miles per hour. The measurement was simplified by tying a number of knots in the line at intervals equivalent to one nautical mile per hour during a given time period measured by a chant or sand glass, allowing an initial unit for the object to enter and become firmly embedded in the water. Thus, the number of knots that passed through the seaman's hands after the initial amount of line was released was a direct measure of speed in nautical miles per hour, or "knots" (not "knots per hour," a unit of acceleration).

8.5 Time is needed in navigation for many purposes, including the reckoning of the hour of the day, the estimation of time of arrival (ETA) at some point, the computation of speed, the identification of navigational lights, the labeling of a position or single line of position, and the determination of the time of an observation of a celestial body. The last use requires an accuracy considerably greater than that needed for other applications. This is so because the earth turns on its axis at a rate of one minute of arc (one nautical mile near the equator) each four seconds. Thus, an error of one second of time can introduce an error of as much as a quarter of a mile. In celestial navigation and timing of lights, time is usually stated to the nearest second. For other uses the nearest whole minute is adequate.

Time of day is customarily stated in four digits, without punctuation, from 0000 at the start of a day through 24 hours to 2400 at midnight ending the day. The A.M. and P.M. designations are not used, nor is the addition of "hours" necessary or correct. When seconds are used, the time is stated $18^h24^m07^s$ or sometimes 18-24-07.

Several different "kinds" of time are used by the navigator, each of which is distinguished by the basis by which the passage of time is measured. *Mean solar time* is commonly used to regulate the affairs of man, including the navigator. It is based on the average speed of apparent motion of the sun in a westerly direction, the hour of the day being a measure of the position of this "mean sun" relative to a reference meridian. For *Greenwich mean time* (GMT), the reference meridian is the geographical meridian through Greenwich. This time is used for tabulation of ephemeridal information in the nautical and air almanacs. For this reason, and the fact that no adjustment of time is needed as one changes longitude, with the consequent risk of a blunder, some mariners prefer to use Greenwich mean time exclusively for navigation, even though zone time may be used to regulate ship affairs. When a nearby meridian (at sea the nearest meridian divisible by 15 degrees a whole number of times) is used, as the reference, *zone time* (usually called "standard time" ashore) results. During summer, it is common practice to adjust all clocks ahead one hour to the standard time kept in the next adjacent time zone to the east; this is called *daylight savings time*. When the meridian of the observer is used as the reference, *local mean time* (LMT) is the result. Times of sunrise, sunset, twilight, moonrise, and moonset are tabulated in the almanacs for, LMT at the Greenwich Meridian, which in most instances can be considered the LMT of the phenomenon at the local meridian. The LMT of the phenomenon can be converted to zone time by applying the difference of longitude between the two meridians, converted to time units by using the relationship that one minute of longitude equals four seconds of time, the meridian to the east having the later time.

A similar set of *apparent solar times* is based upon the position of the actual sun observed in the sky. The difference between mean and apparent solar time is cumulative, reaching a maximum in one direction, then decreasing to zero, reaching a maximum in the opposite direction, and then again returning to zero. Two such cycles, differing somewhat from one another, occur each year. This difference, called *equation of time*, reaches its greatest value of nearly 16½ minutes in November.

When a reference point among the stars is used instead of the sun, *sidereal time* results. Sidereal time differs from solar time in that the sidereal day starts when the reference point crosses the *upper* branch of the reference meridian (sidereal "noon") rather than the lower branch (midnight), and there is no sidereal *date*. A sidereal day is about 3^m56^s *shorter* than the mean solar day because of the annual revolution of the earth around the sun. Consequently, there is one more sidereal day than there are solar days per year. Sidereal time is useful for star charts and other designations of positions of celestial bodies relative to one another.

Equipment

8.6 Charts   Because navigation is concerned with going from one place to another, the navigator's *chart,* a map intended primarily for navigation, is perhaps his most fundamental item of equipment. Today the chart is nearly always printed in several colors by offset lithography on special chart paper which is not subject to excessive distortion through unequal shrinkage or expansion, but is sturdy and will withstand repeated erasures of medium soft pencil plots without damage or defacement of the printed features.

The portrayal of a curved surface such as that of the earth results, of course, in some distortion. Maps intended for different purposes need somewhat different properties. Accordingly, a number of different methods of depicting the earth's surface on a plane have been devised. These methods are called *map* (or chart) *projections.* Those projections used by navigators can be grouped in three classes, as follows:

Cylindrical, in which the surface of the earth is conceived as transferred by one of several methods to a cylinder tangent to the earth at some great circle. The cylinder is then cut along a line parallel to its axis and spread out flat.

Conic, in which the earth's surface is conceived as transferred to one or more cones tangent or secant to the earth. The cone, like the cylinder, is then cut along an element and spread out flat to form the map.

Azimuthal, in which the earth's surface is projected directly onto a plane tangent to the earth at a point.

The word "projection," when used relative to charts, in most cases does not refer to geometric or perspective projection. Of the various properties of chart projections, the following are of principal interest to navigators:

Conformality, also called *orthomorphism,* the correct portrayal of angles. A conformal chart has the same scale for an infinitesimal distance in all directions around any point.

Uniformity of scale over the entire chart.

Portrayal of a rhumb line, a line having the same directional relationship to all meridians, as a straight line.

Portrayal of a great circle, the intersection of the surface of the earth with a plane through its center, as a straight line.

The following chart projections are those used most commonly by navigators:

Mercator, also called *equatorial cylindrical orthomorphic,* which describes it well. The cylinder is tangent to the earth at the equator; the projection is conformal; meridians are parallel, vertical lines; the parallels of latitude are perpendicular to the meridians and spaced increasingly far apart as one proceeds north or south from the equator; a rhumb line appears as a straight line; and a great circle, other than the equator or a meridian, appears as a curve. This is the projection commonly used for nautical charts. Distortion is small near the equator, increasing with higher latitude. For this reason, two variant forms of this projection are sometimes used. In the *transverse Mercator* projection the cylinder is tangent along a meridian, giving constant scale along this meridian. This projection is used principally in polar regions and by surveyors.

In the *oblique Mercator* projection the cylinder is tangent along a great circle other than the equator or a meridian. The projection is useful in portraying, without distortions, the path along a great circle between two planes widely separated.

Rectangular, a cylindrical projection similar to the Mercator but with uniform spacing between parallels. It is not conformal and distortion is great in high latitudes, but the projection is useful for showing the declinations and sidereal hour angles of stars.

Lambert conformal, a conic projection with two standard parallels. The cone intersects the earth along two parallels of latitude. Between these parallels, the earth's surface is compressed, and beyond them it is expanded. Meridians appear as straight lines converging toward the nearest pole, while parallels appear as arcs of circles with a common center at the point of convergency of the meridians. The projection, as indicated by its name, is conformal. A great circle appears as nearly a straight line, and a rhumb line as a curve. The Lambert conformal projection, particularly useful for portraying an area having a relatively narrow spread of latitude and a great extent in longitude, is widely used for aeronautical charts, but little used for nautical charts.

Gnomonic, an azimuthal projection with points on the surface of the earth geometrically projected to the plane by rays from the center of the earth. Meridians appear as straight lines converging toward the nearest pole, and parallels of latitude, other than the equator, appear as curves. The projection is not conformal except at the point of tangency. Its principal value to the navigator is the fact that great circles appear as straight lines. Its use is primarily to plot a great circle course line between two places. Points at convenient intervals along the line are transferred by latitude and longitude to a Mercator nautical chart and connected by a series of straight lines to approximate the great circle. A rhumb line appears as a curve on a gnomonic chart.

There are many other types of projections, including stereographic, orthographic, and azimuthal equidistant, but most have little application to the practice of marine navigation.

Information on nautical charts is given principally by symbol. Charts produced by various nations adhere quite well to the standard symbols approved by the International Hydrographic Bureau. However, there are some differences, and for this reason one should familiarize himself with the differences of a chart of an origin other than those to which he is accustomed. Useful information may also be conveyed by notes on the chart. The principal United States sources of nautical charts are the National Ocean Survey of the National Oceanic and Atmospheric Administration, formerly known as the Coast and Geodetic Survey, and the Defense Mapping Agency Hydrographic Center (formerly the U.S. Naval Oceanographic Office). *Chart N.O. 1,* issued jointly by both these agencies, lists the symbols and abbreviations used on all charts produced in the United States. These agencies have representatives at all principal U.S. ports.

It is important that charts be kept corrected up-to-date. The principal means by which this is accomplished is the *Notice to Mariners* published weekly by the Defense Mapping Agency Hydrographic Center.

At sea the chart may be replaced by a *plotting sheet,* a type of blank chart showing only the graticule of latitude and longitude lines and one or more compass roses for measuring direction. Plotting sheets provide an inexpensive, uncluttered surface for the dead reckoning plot and for plotting the results of celestial observations in areas remote from shoal water.

8.7 Publications   A great many publications of interest to mariners are available through agents of the organizations mentioned and of the U.S. Government Printing Office and the U.S. Coast Guard, as well as from comparable foreign sources. The following is a sample of some of the more important publications used frequently by navigators:

tide and tidal current tables;
light lists;
coast pilots and sailing directions, listing detailed information of coastal waters and ports throughout the world;
The Nautical Almanac;
The Air Almanac;
sight reduction tables, for solution of problems of celestial navigation,
American Practical Navigator, a reference book containing a wealth of information on virtually any subject related to navigation.

8.8 Plotting Equipment is also important to the navigator. This includes some type of drafting machine; parallel rulers, triangles, a protractor, or a plastic plotter of the navigator's preference; dividers, compasses; and medium hardness pencils and a good soft eraser.

8.9 Instruments   In addition to charts, publications, and plotting equipment, various instruments are needed for measuring the quantities required for navigation, discussed earlier. The sophistication and cost of these instruments vary considerably in the different classes of vessels.

Direction Heading is indicated by a compass. Nearly all larger vessels now carry a *gyro compass,* sometimes in multiple installations. This device uses one or more gyroscopes installed in such manner as to remain essentially horizontal and to seek the true meridian. This instrument is subject to several errors. In the best modern gyro compasses these errors are essentially eliminated in the design or by manual setting. In any instrument a small residual *gyro error* can be expected. This error tends to increase with higher latitude, as the directional force of the compass becomes weaker with decreased earth rotational speed. At some latitude, usually **70** degrees or beyond, the uncertainty becomes unacceptably large. *Gyro repeaters,* to indicate at remote locations the reading of a gyro compass, may be located at convenient places throughout a ship.

A *magnetic compass* is generally located in view of the steersman whether or not a gyro compass or repeater is available. This is called the *steering compass*. Additionally, a *standard* magnetic compass may be placed at a location relatively free from disturbing magnetic influences. A magnetic compass is subject to variation and deviation errors, as discussed earlier. The *binnacle,* the housing for a magnetic compass, is provided with means for applying equal but opposite magnetic influences to offset the various components of the magnetic force arising from magnetic material in the vessel. This process is called *compass adjustment.* Some error, varying with the heading, can be expected to remain. After adjustment of a magnetic compass, the vessel is placed successively on various magnetic headings and the deviation is measured and recorded in a *deviation table,* sometimes called a *magnetic compass table.* The process is called *swinging ship.* Residual deviation is applied as a correction to a compass direction. Variation, being independent of the vessel, is applied without reduction, as the second component of compass error.

Attached to the directive element of either form of compass is a *compass card,* a circular disk graduated with directions, now invariably from 0 degrees at north clockwise through 360 degrees. A *lubber's line,* a vertical mark on the case, is aligned with the longitudinal axis of the vessel. This mark turns with the vessel, indicating, by its position relative to the graduations on the compass card, the heading of the vessel.

Bearings or azimuths may be measured by means of a compass, repeater, or *pelorus.* The last, sometimes called a "dumb compass," is similar in appearance to a compass, but has no directive element. The compass rose can be set by hand to the true, magnetic, compass, gyro, or grid heading of the vessel, depending upon the kind of bearing desired. Any error in the heading at the time of observation introduces an error in the bearing if a correction is not applied. If 0 degrees of the pelorus card is set at the lubber's line, relative bearings are indicated. For measuring bearings or azimuths, a *bearing circle* or *azimuth circle,* respectively, is placed over the compass or pelorus to provide suitable sighting vanes or prisms for making the observations. For greater accuracy through magnification, a telescopic alidade may be used.

Speed and Distance   Devices for measuring progress of the vessel have evolved from the primitive Dutchman's log, mentioned earlier, through mechanical logs which were introduced about the middle of the seventeenth century, to various modern devices attached to the hull of the vessel and providing remote indications electrically. A typical modern device is the electromagnetic log. A rodmeter attached to the bottom of the ship has an electromagnetic sensing element that produces a voltage proportional to the speed of the vessel through the water. Any motion of the water over the bottom, however, introduces an error in the speed relative to the solid earth under the water. Of course, speed and distance can be determined indirectly by comparison of fixes at known times.

Depth   One of the oldest devices used by the mariner is a *sounding pole* for determining depths of water. In deeper water this was replaced by a *sounding lead,* consisting of a weight attached to a line. Sometimes a recess in the bottom of the lead was *armed* with tallow so that a sample of the material of the ocean floor could be obtained. Posidonius, an early stoic philosopher, speaks of obtaining soundings of 1000 fathoms in the Sea of Sardinia as early as the second century B.C. The early mariner measured the amount of line used by counting the number of times a portion of it extended between the ends of his outstretched arms as he hauled it in. This was considered to be six feet, the unit that became known as the fathom, indicating the amount of line the mariner could "fathom" at one time. The lead line later was graduated by the attachment of various indicators, such as bits of colored rag or leather, or a knot in the line, to provide an immediate indication of depth. The nom de plume Mark Twain, adopted by Samuel Clemens, originated from the oft-heard report of Mississippi River seamen announcing the measurement of a depth at the two-fathom mark. Later, greater depths were measured by means of a *sounding machine* that used a hollow glass rod, inserted in a recess in the lead. The rod was coated on its inner surface with a chemical or with scribings that changed color when wet. The distance to which the water penetrated the tube (closed at its upper end), compressing the air trapped inside, was calibrated in depth of water. Nearly all modern devices for determining depth are *echo sounders.* A *transducer* attached to the bottom of the vessel converts electrical energy into sonic or ultrasonic energy. The time needed for a signal to travel to the bottom and its echo to return is proportional to depth. The indication may be flashing light, cathode ray tube, or recording on paper.

Time   For many centuries man has realized that the difference in local time between two places is a measure of the difference in longitude between them. The problem was to determine time at a longitude different from that of the observer. Many persons, some of note, wrestled with this problem. The Royal Greenwich Observatory was established to help in the determination of longitude. Some degree of success was achieved through measure of "lunar distances" (the angular distance between the moon and another celestial body near the ecliptic), and by noting the time of occultation or emergence of the satellites of Jupiter. But these methods were difficult, time consuming, and generally beyond the comprehension of mariners. Several countries offered handsome prizes to anyone who could devise a practical solution to the problem of "discovering" longitude at sea. As might be expected, many and varied were the solutions proposed. A practical solution finally came in the eighteenth century through the development by John Harrison, a Yorkshire clockmaker, of a successful marine chronometer, after a lifetime of effort.

The marine chronometer is characterized by a nearly uniform *rate*. The instrument is not reset while in use, but a careful log is kept of its error, and a correction is applied to its indications. Because of the importance of accurate time in navigation, it was common practice long after radio time signals became available to carry three chronometers, so that if one developed an excessive error, it could be identified by comparison with the others. The daily winding of the chronometers was a ritual invariably reported to the commanding officer. Timepieces throughout the vessel, including *comparing watches* for timing celestial observations, are still set by means of the chronometer. However, the availability of radio time signals and the emergence of electronic means of determining longitude without recourse to celestial observations have resulted in some lessening of the importance of the role of this device.

Altitude The mariner's sextant, developed independently by John Hadley in England and Thomas Godfrey in the United States in 1730, has been widely used as a symbol of navigation. Earlier, the common quadrant, astrolabe, cross-staff, backstaff, and nocturnal had been used for measuring altitude (elevation angle) with some success, but these left much to be desired. A modern sextant, little changed in principle from the originals, is shown in Fig. 8.1. The double reflecting principle, upon which the device is based, permits the use of an arc of the instrument of only half that of the angle measured. The common practice for many years of using an arc of 60 degrees, a sixth of a circle, gave the instrument its name. Most modern instruments have arcs somewhat in excess of 60 degrees, and because of the optical principles involved, are capable of measuring angles in excess of 120°; whether an octant, sextant, quintant, quadrant, or of some other measure, all such intruments are now generally called sextants. As noted earlier, sextants are sometimes used to measure horizontal angles between terrestrial objects. Even in modern times, when electronic navigation has eclipsed celestial navigation to some extent, many navigators still carefully safeguard their sextants and take great professional pride in their ability to keep them in adjustment and to use them skillfully.

Electronic Equipment. The electronic equipment used for navigation

Fig. 8.1   A marine sextant. (*Courtesy of Weems & Plath, Inc.*)

takes many forms and degrees of complexity. Instructions for its use generally accompany the equipment and electronic technicians are usually needed to maintain it. As with other instruments, results with electronic equipment can usually be enhanced by study, experience, and analysis.

Basic Kinds of Navigation

8.10   Dead Reckoning   It is sometimes stated that dead reckoning is the basic form of surface navigation, always being available in some form, however crude, and that the role of position-fixing is to update the dead reckoning plot from time to time. Whatever the method of navigation used, prudence dictates maintenance of an up-to-date dead reckoning plot. It is the only means of determining the present and projected future positions of a moving vessel, and it provides a safeguard against large errors in position-fixing.

With the wide availability and low cost of modern nautical charts, it has become the usual practice for the navigator to perform dead reckoning by plotting directly on the chart or a plotting sheet. A typical dead reckoning plot is shown in Fig. 8.2. Note the conventions in labels and symbols. Those which relate to the course line are placed parallel to the line, above and below it; the course being steered is printed above the

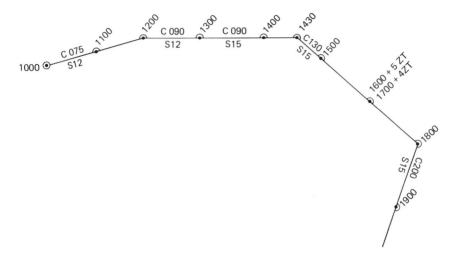

Fig. 8.2 Dead reckoning (DR) plot. The plot starts with the 1000 fix position on 4 July, with the vessel on course 075 degrees true, speed 12 knots. At 1200 the course is changed to 090 degrees true, at 1430 to 130 degrees true, and at 1800 to 200 degrees true. At 1300 the speed is changed to 15 knots. At 1600, the nearest integral hour to entering a new time zone, the time is changed one hour. Note that DR positions are marked and labeled each integral hour and at each change of course or speed. Labels relating to a *line* are along the line, those relating to a DR position are at an angle to the line, and those relating to a fix are horizontal.

line, and the speed is indicated below the line. No units are shown unless there is a reasonable possibility of misinterpretation. Dead reckoning positions are indicated by a semicircle, and fix positions by a circle. Note the double label at 1600 + 5ZT and 1700 + 4ZT, denoting a change in the standard zone time being kept.

Dead reckoning positions are plotted according to a set of rules which have become established through long and repeated usage, called the *Six Rules of DR:*

1. A DR position is plotted every hour on the hour.
2. A DR position is plotted at the time of every course change.
3. A DR postion is plotted at the time of every speed change.
4. A DR position is plotted for the time at which a fix or running fix is obtained.
5. A DR position is plotted for the time at which a single line of position is obtained.
6. A new course line is plotted from each fix or running fix as soon as it is plotted on the chart.

Some vessels are equipped with some form of mechanical device for plotting the dead reckoning, the position of the pen at any time representing the dead reckoning position of the vessel at that time. The output of any mechanical or electrical device should be checked periodically as a protection against defective operation.

Dead reckoning may also be performed by computation. This was the method commonly used before accurate charts became readily available at nominal cost, and is the method still favored on some few small vessels where plotting may be difficult because of lack of adequate protected space or because of excessive motion of the vessel. A number of methods of computation have been developed. Collectively, they are known as "the sailings." *Parallel sailing* is applicable when going due east or due west along a parallel of latitude. *Plane sailing,* based upon the assumption that the earth is flat, is adequate over relatively short distances. *Middle latitude sailing* takes into account the curvature of the earth by using a mean value of latitude for the area. Several methods of determining the "middle latitude" have been devised. *Mercator sailing* allows for expansion of a meridian as shown on a Mercator chart. *Great circle sailing* is applicable to computation relating to great circles, assuming the earth to be a sphere. *Composite sailing* is a combination of great circle and parallel sailings, used when it is desired to limit the maximum latitude to some value less than that of the vertex of the great circle. Formulas and sample computations for the various sailings are given in the *American Practical Navigator,* by Nathaniel Bowditch.

8.11 Piloting   Before electronics was applied to navigation in the first part of this century, piloting was confined principally to a narrow strip within sight of land or marks placed in the sea for the guidance of mariners. Any prominent object—a mountain summit, a headland, a conspicuous tree—served the purpose if it could be identified and its position was known. Centuries before Christ, man added additional marks known as *aids to navigation* at convenient locations. The lighthouse of Alexandria, built on the Mediterranean coast of Egypt in the third century B.C., with its log fire, was considered one of the seven wonders of the ancient world. Today, numerous lighthouses, lightships, beacons, buoys and daymarks are to be found at convenient points along the various coasts and navigable inland waterways of the world. Additionally, easily identifiable, prominent cultural features intended for other purposes are available. Examples are a factory chimney, a distinctive dome of a building, and a radio tower.

A common method for determining the position of a vessel relative to identifiable external objects is illustrated in Fig. 8.3. The true bearings of two or more objects are determined simultaneously or nearly so, and the reciprocals are plotted from the charted positions of the

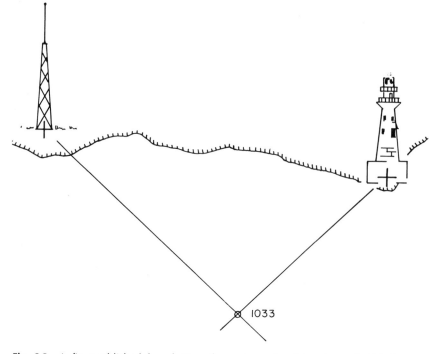

Fig. 8.3   A fix established by plotting the reciprocals of bearings of 310 degrees true on a tower and 046 degrees true on a lighthouse, observed simultaneously at 1033.

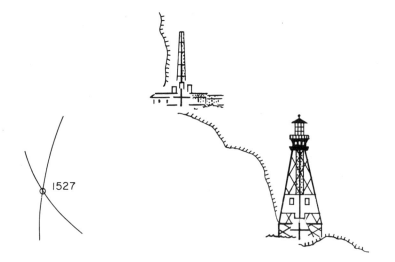

Fig. 8.4   A fix established by plotting arcs of distance circles of 3.6 miles from a chimney and 5.7 miles from a lighthouse, observed simultaneously at 1527.

objects. The common intersection of the bearing lines is the position
of the vessel, called a *fix*. Although a third bearing adds little if anything to the accuracy of the position determination, it does provide
some protection against a significant recording or plotting error.
Other methods include the determination of two or more distances,
illustrated in Fig. 8.4, and distance and bearing of the same object,
illustrated in Fig. 8.5. Distance may be determined by radar, range
finder, or by measuring the elevation angle to the top of an object
of known height (or the angle subtended by the object itself).

Each bearing or distance measurement provides one *line of position*.
(LOP). If lines are not obtained simultaneously, or nearly so, it is necessary to *advance* or *retire* one or more of them a distance and direction
equal to that of the estimated motion of the vessel between observations, with a loss of accuracy equal to the uncertainty of the motion of
the vessel during the period involved. A position thus determined is
called a *running fix* (*R. Fix*), because the vessel has run a certain distance
along her track during the interval between the times at which the two
LOP's were obtained.

Position may also be determined by means of horizontal sextant
angles between three objects not on a circle through the position of
the vessel. A *three-arm protractor,* called a *station pointer* by the
British, or its equivalent is used to determine position. If two observers

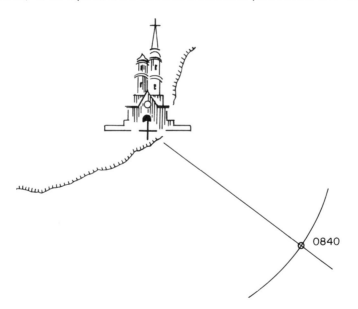

0840

Fig. 8.5 A fix established by plotting a distance of 4.2 miles and the reciprocal of
a bearing of 306 degrees true of a church steeple, observed simultaneously at 0840.

are not available for simultaneous observation, satisfactory results can usually be obtained by observing, in quick succession, one angle, a second angle, and then the first again, using the average of the two readings of the first angle and the time of the second angle.

Soundings may also be used in a well surveyed area with a distinctive pattern of depth contours. The method involves plotting, on transparent material, a line representing the course line of the vessel, and marking off, to the scale of the chart, a series of positions a few minutes apart and labeling each mark with the depth of water measured at that time. The line is then placed over the chart and adjusted until it fits the depths shown on the chart, making any allowance needed for tide or calibration of the sounding device used.

Some channels are provided with *ranges,* consisting of two beacons so placed that when they appear in line, the vessel is in the center of the channel. Most of these beacons have lights for use at night. When following a range, one must, obviously, turn to the next course at the appropriate time to avoid grounding.

Another means of avoiding danger without determining the position of the vessel is the use of a *danger bearing* on a single prominent object. Any bearing greater or less, as the case might be, than a certain safe bearing indicates possible danger. Maximum or minimum horizontal or vertical *danger angles* between two objects or the top and bottom of one object, respectively, may be used in a similar manner in an area where rocks and shoals are a potential hazard.

Piloting may also involve electronics, discussed next, and advanced systems, covered later in this chapter.

Electronic Navigation

Probably the first application of electronics in navigation, in 1904, was for broadcasting time signals to ships at sea so that chronometers might be checked between visits to ports. This was followed, in 1907, by the broadcasting of navigational warnings; in 1921, by the development of the radio direction finder; and in 1922, by the echo sounder. During and following World War II a number of electronic navigation systems were introduced, and a great many more were proposed.

8.12 Techniques   Various techniques are employed in the use of electronics for navigation. Direction, distance, and distance-difference are all measured in a variety of ways.

Direction   A vertical loop antenna of appropriate design has the property of receiving stronger signals from some directions than from others. When the signal is traveling perpendicular to the plane of the loop, the signals received by the two sides of the loop tend to cancel each other, and minimum signal is transmitted to the receiver, while a signal received from a direction parallel to the plane of the loop is strongest. This principle is used in the *radio direction finder* aboard ship or at *direction finder stations* ashore. An accompanying vertical *sense antenna* resolves the approximately 180 degree ambiguity that would result without the additional antenna. Radio bearings are used in piloting in the same manner as visual bearings. Radio, as well as optical, signals travel great circles. If they are to be plotted as equivalent rhumb lines on a Mercator chart, a correction may be needed, depending upon latitude and both the direction and the distance between transmitter and receiver. However, except in polar regions, where meridional convergence is maximum, visual bearings are usually observed over such short distances that the correction is negligible and can be ignored. This is often not true of radio bearings, for which a convergence correction may be needed at any latitude. A radio bearing is also subject to error because of refraction when the signal crosses a coastline or mountain range at an oblique angle.

Radio ranges, intended primarily for use by aircraft, utilize other techniques for directional transmission of radio signals. *Consol*, available in Western Europe, transmits a rotating pattern of dots and dashes which the user can convert to directional information by references to a special chart or table.

Radar, which depends upon the reflection of radio signals from an obstruction, similar to the reflection of light by a mirror, generally uses frequencies sufficiently high to permit employment of a reasonably sized hyperbolic antenna for both transmission of the outgoing signal and reception of the returning echo. Direction is determined by noting the orientation of the antenna. Distance is determined by transmitting very short bursts of radio energy, called *pulses,* and timing the interval between transmission of the signal and return of the echo in microseconds (millionths of a second). The interval between pulses is sufficiently long to permit return of an echo before another signal is transmitted. Some aids to navigation, notably important buoys, have been fitted with radar reflectors to return a stronger signal, to extend the range at which the aids can be observed, and to assist in distinguishing the returns from them when sea clutter (return from sea waves) is present. Direction and distance determined by radar are used in the same manner as visual measurements. The distance is usually not sufficiently great to require a correction for plotting on a Mercator chart. The position of the vessel relative to its surroundings can sometimes be determined by comparing the echoes appearing on the radarscope with the nautical chart, a technique also useful in the identification of points from which bearings and ranges are measured. Shore-based radar is used in some ports to provide guidance to ships entering and leaving port.

A number of longer-range systems are based upon the measurement of the difference in distance between the observer and two or more transmitting stations sending out synchronized radio signals. The resulting line of position from a pair of stations is a hyperbola. The families of hyperbolic lines of position associated with three stations operating together are shown in Fig. 8.6. By using a special chart or table, the user is able to identify the hyperbola, from each pair, passing through his position. Their common intersection marks the location of his ship. The geometrical contribution to accuracy, as indicated by the spacing of hyperbolas from a pair of stations, decreases from maximum accuracy along the *base line* joining the two stations, to lesser accuracy with distance from the base line, reaching minimum accuracy along the *base line extension* beyond either station.

Loran-A uses pulsed transmission similar to that of radar, but at frequencies of 1750 to 1950 kilohertz. Within a distance of some 500 to 900 miles from the farthest station, groundwaves are received. Typical accuracy in a favorable part of this coverage area is 1 to 2 miles. At greater distances, where only skywaves are received (to a maximum of about 1400 miles), an uncertainty of 5 to 7 miles is typical. As with other hyperbolic systems, a special receiver is needed.

Loran-C is similar to loran-A but uses lower carrier radio frequency (about 100 kilohertz) and a more sophisticated, phase-lock receiver to compare both the pulses from the two stations and the phase of individual waves within the pulses. This results in increased ground-wave accuracy to a maximum distance of about 1500 miles from the more remote transmitter.

Decca, a British system, is in the same general frequency range as loran-C. In this system, excellent accuracy is achieved by the phase-comparison technique, to a useful range of about 240 miles from a group of stations operating together. As in all pure phase-comparison systems, Decca is subject to ambiguity in relatively narrow lanes, typically about ½ mile wide. In this system, lane identification is achieved by periodic measurement on a much coarser pattern, with wider lanes.

Omega, another phase-comparison, hyperbolic system uses very low frequencies (in the 10 to 14 kilohertz band) to permit worldwide ground-wave coverage with only eight stations, when fully implemented, and nearly equal accuracy everywhere. Lanes are typically about 8 miles wide. Lane identification is provided by using additional

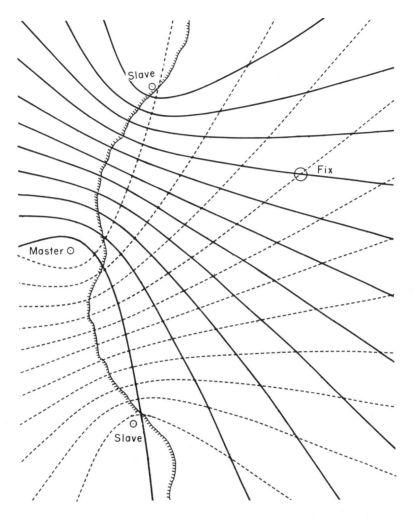

Fig. 8.6 A fix established by identifying the hyperbolic lines of position determined by measuring the difference in time of reception of synchronized signals from a master and two slave transmitters.

frequencies, with different lane widths, or by receiving signals from additional transmitters. Accuracy of the system is typically about ½ to 1 mile by day, and double this error by night.

Additional hyperbolic systems are used principally for survey operations within approximately 200 miles of the shore. *Lorac* and *hyperbolic Raydist* are typical of these systems.

Celestial Navigation

Celestial bodies can be used to establish *celestial lines of position*. The usual method involves timed observations, a form of computation called *sight reduction,* and plotting.

For purposes of navigation, all celestial bodies are imagined as being located on the inner surface of a *celestial sphere* of infinite radius concentric with the earth. The "fixed" stars are imagined to be virtually stationary on this vast sphere, and bodies of the solar system to be in relatively slow motion across its inner surface. The sphere itself is pictured as rotating once each sidereal day on its axis, the extension of the earth's axis of rotation. It is this diurnal apparent motion that is of primary interest to the navigator.

Two sets of celestial coordinates are commonly used in navigation. Sight reduction consists essentially of converting coordinates of one set to those of the other.

In the *celestial equator system* the plane of the equator of the earth is extended until it intersects the celestial sphere along a great circle called the *celestial equator.* The intersections of the extended axis of rotation of the earth with the celestial sphere mark the north and south *celestial poles.* The intersection over the terrestrial pole nearest to the observer is also called the *elevated pole,* because it is above the observer's horizon. Angular distance from the celestial equator to any point on the celestial sphere, a quantity similar to latitude on the earth, is called *declination.* A quantity similar to longitude is called *hour angle.* Hour angle is further identified by noting the origin of measurement, the Greenwich celestial meridian (*Greenwich hour angle,* GHA), the local celestial meridian (*local hour angle,* LHA), or the hour circle through the vernal equinox, a reference point on the celestial sphere, (*sidereal hour angle,* SHA). A *celestial meridian* remains fixed with respect to a point on earth, being the intersection of the celestial sphere and the meridional plane through that point. An *hour circle* is similar to a celestial meridian but rotates with the celestial sphere, relative to a point on earth. A circle parallel to the plane of the celestial equator is a *parallel of declination.* Unlike longitude, hour angle is reckoned westward through 360 degrees. *Meridian angle* is similar but reckoned eastward or westward from 0 degrees at the local meridian to 180 degrees in each direction. Thus, declination changes slowly (very slowly for "fixed" stars), but hour angle and meridian angle change at the rate of approximately 15 degrees per hour. Coordinates of the celestial equator system are tabulated at frequent intervals in the nautical and air almanacs.

The second set of celestial coordinates commonly used by the navigator is similar but based upon the position of the observer, and so are unique for each person. The primary great circle of this system is the *celestial horizon,* which gives the system its name, *horizon system of coordinates.* The pole directly over the observer is the *zenith* and the opposite pole is the *nadir.* Great circles joining the two poles are called *vertical circles.* The vertical circle through the north and south points of the horizon is also the local celestial meridian (a convenient relationship in sight reduction), and the vertical circle through the east and west points is the *prime vertical circle* (PV). Angular distance above the horizon, similar to latitude, is *altitude,* while circles joining all points of equal altitude are called *parallels of altitude.* True *azimuth* is reckoned from true north clockwise through 360 degrees. *Azimuth angle* is reckoned clockwise and counterclockwise through 180 degrees starting from north or south to agree with the latitude of the observer (also the horizontal direction of the elevated pole).

Coordinate conversion (sight reduction) is based upon solution of the *navigational triangle,* shown in Fig. 8.7. Its vertices are the elevated pole, the observer's zenith, and the celestial body. Its sides are the colatitude of the zenith (90°-observer's latitude), the polar distance of the body (90° ± declination of the body), and the coaltitude of the body (90°-

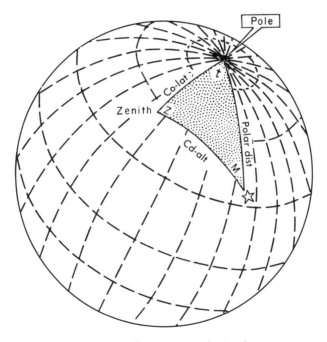

Fig. 8.7 The navigational triangle.

observed altitude), sometimes called the zenith distance. Its interior angles are the meridian angle of the body (t), the azimuth angle (Z), and the parallactic angle; the latter angle has no significance in the ordinary practice of celestial navigation.

To establish a celestial line of position, the navigator observes the altitude of a celestial body with a sextant and notes the time of observation to the nearest second. Certain corrections are applied to the *sextant altitude (hs)* to obtain the equivalent *observed altitude (Ho)* of the center of the body, without refraction, as it would be observed from the center of the earth. From the almanac he determines the declination and Greenwich hour angle. Using an assumed position near his actual position he converts the GHA to the LHA and t. With meridian angle (t), declination (d), and latitude of the observer (L), he solves the navigational triangle for computed altitude (Hc) and azimuth angle (Z), which he converts to true azimuth (Zn). He then compares Hc with Ho to determine *altitude difference (a)*.

He is now ready to plot the celestial line of position. Refer to Fig. 8.8. The locus of all points on the surface of the earth having the same altitude is a circle with the *geographical position* of the body (the earth point having the body in its zenith) as its center and radius equal to the *coaltitude* or *zenith distance* (90 degrees minus altitude). This radius is usually much too large to plot on a nautical chart of the area of the ob-

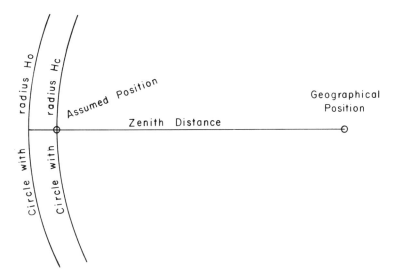

Fig. 8.8 Arcs of circles of equal altitude of a celestial body. In this illustration the observed altitude is less than that computed for the assumed position. Therefore, the zenith distance is greater than at the assumed position, and the actual circle of equal altitude is farther from the geographical position of the body.

server. Because of the curvature of the earth, the altitude of the body at a point closer to its geographical position is *greater* than that at a point further away. The difference, assuming the earth to be a sphere, is exactly equal to the great circle distance between the points, if they are both on the azimuth line to the body. Refer to Fig. 8.9. The computed altitude identifies the circle of equal altitude through the assumed position used for the computation. The observed altitude identifies the circle of equal altitude through the actual position of the observer, to the accuracy of measurement and computaton. The azimuth indicates the great circle direction of the geographical position. By starting at the assumed position and measuring the altitude difference toward or away from the body, as the observed altitude is greater or smaller, respectively, than the computed altitude, the navigator establishes one point on the circle of equal altitude, on some point of which the observer is located, within the accuracy of observation. At this point he erects a perpendicular to the azimuth line. Over several miles this tangent to the circle of equal altitude can be considered the circle of position itself, and constitutes the celestial line of position. A second line, from another observation at the same time, or adjusted to the same time, establishes a celestial fix. Additional lines provide protection against gross errors and some reduction of probable error. Different solutions based upon unique relationships may be used if a celestial body is near the zenith of the observer, if it

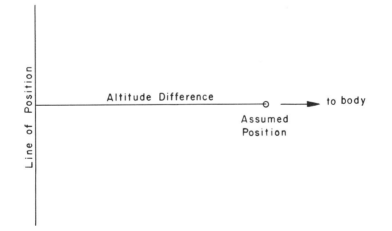

Fig. 8.9 Plotting the celestial line of position of Fig. 8.8. From the assumed position, the altitude difference is measured toward or away from the celestial body as *Ho* is greater or smaller, respectively, than *Hc*. Through the point thus determined, a line of position, the tangent of the circle of equal altitude at this point, is drawn perpendicular to the azimuth line.

is on his celestial meridian, if he is near the geographical pole, or if Polaris is the body observed.

It is important, of course, that the celestial body observed be identified. The sun and moon constitute no problem. Stars and planets can be identified by their positions relative to other bodies (a star chart is helpful), by computation, or by a device called a *star finder* or *star identifier*.

Advanced Systems

Several advanced navigation systems have been developed for special applications. The high cost of these systems, maintenance requirements, and lack of operational requirements preclude the wide adoption of such systems for general navigation at sea. Accordingly, the discussion of them will be brief, but the fact that such systems are in limited use justifies some mention of them.

8.13 Inertial The inertia of a mass at rest or moving at a constant velocity can be used to determine direction and distance traveled. Acceleration is involved whenever a body changes its velocity vector. Integration of acceleration with respect to time produces velocity; a second integration produces distance. Basically, a typical inertial navigator consists of accelerometers mounted perpendicular to each other on a horizontal platform, sometimes with another mounted vertically. Each accelerometer measures the component of acceleration in the direction of its longitudinal axis. High-grade gyroscopes are used to keep the platform horizontal and to provide a reference direction. The platform is precessed at earth rate.

In operation, the system is set to the coordinates of the point of departure and aligned with true north and the horizontal. As the vessel moves from one place to another, its progress is measured relative to "inertial space." Thus, the output is a form of dead reckoning relative to the surface of the earth, independent of motion of the water over the ocean floor. The system is subject to cumulative error that increases with time, and thus needs periodic realignment and updating from an independent source of positional data. It is also subject to oscillations, the principal ones having periods of 84.4 minutes (the *earth rate*) and 24 hours.

Inertial navigators are particularly applicable to missiles and fast aircraft, where flight time is measured in minutes or a small number of hours. They are also needed in spacecraft during short periods of powered flight. Their principal application at sea has been in fleet ballistic missile submarines. More recently, they have been introduced in geophysical exploration vessels, as indicated below.

8.14 Doppler Sonar   Progress relative to the ocean floor can be measured by means of the Doppler effect of acoustic energy. If a beam of acoustic energy is transmitted downward at an angle from the hull of a moving vessel, the frequency of the return echo differs from that of the transmitted signal by an amount proportional to the component of speed in the direction of the beam. A measure of components in different directions, with a good heading reference, provides a means for determining the velocity vector of the vessel. If four beams are used, one each directed forward, aft, to starboard, and to port, (the so-called "Janus" configuration, after the Roman god represented with two opposite faces) or at a known angle to these directions, errors resulting from tilt of the platform are largely eliminated. Some error remains as a result of a coupling effort of the components of the dynamic motions of roll, pitch, and heave.

In water to a depth of approximately 600 feet, echoes from the ocean floor provide a measure of progress independent of ocean currents. In greater depths, return is from the water itself, providing a dead reckoning relative to the water rather than to the ground. Doppler sonar thus provides a measure of progress from a known point. It is subject to cumulative error with distance traveled, and needs updating periodically. Because of its depth limitation, Doppler sonar is used principally in operations on the continental shelf. An outstanding example is oil exploration, which is confined largely to this area.

8.15 Satellites   One of the first practical applications suggested for artificial earth satellites was for navigation. A great many schemes have been proposed, and several are being actively investigated. Only one system is in operational use, the U.S. Navy Navigation Satellite System, Fig. 8.10.

Nominally, the system consists of four satellites in circular polar orbits at a height of 600 nautical miles above the surface of the earth. Each satellite is tracked by four ground stations in the United States. Orbital data are updated at a computing center, and at intervals of approximately 12 hours these data are transmitted from one of two injection stations to each satellite. At intervals of exactly two minutes, the orbital data applying to that period, the three previous periods, and the four succeeding ones are transmitted by the satellite on highly stable frequencies of approximately 400 megahertz and 150 megahertz.

The user with an appropriate receiver and another stable oscillator

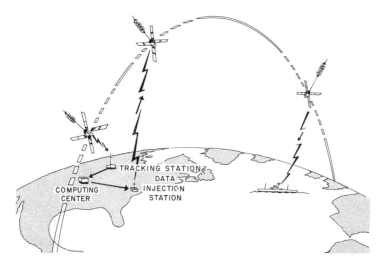

Fig. 8.10 The Navy Navigation Satellite System. Each satellite is tracked by four tracking stations in the United States. The data are sent to a central computing center where the orbital information is updated and transmitted from one of two injection stations to the satellite. There it is stored and transmitted at two-minute intervals. These data, with the Doppler counts measured by the user, provide him with his position and an accurate time signal.

receives the signals at both frequencies and counts the cycles received during each observation period. Because of the Doppler effect, this count changes from period to period as the satellite makes a pass above the observer's horizon. A minimum of three, but for best accuracy at least four, two-minute counts are needed to compute a fix. A good pass may provide as many as eight such counts. Very high passes provide a good indication of latitude but an unreliable indication of longitude. The reverse is true of very low passes, but these are usually rejected altogether because of excessive noise and sometimes for lack of a sufficient number of Doppler counts. The use of two frequencies makes possible the reduction to generally acceptable levels of the error resulting from ionospheric refraction. Tropospheric refraction is negligible except in the most exacting applications. The north or south component of the ship's speed must be taken into account if the accuracy of which the system is capable is to be realized, each knot of error in this component introducing a positional error of about a quarter of a mile. The number of good passes per day varies with the latitude and the spacing of the satellites, which is not uniform, but 10 to 12 is a good average.

The system was developed primarily for use by fleet ballistic missile submarines, to update their inertial system. It is little used commercially, a notable exception being vessels engaged in geophysical exploration.

8.16   Hybrid Systems   In some installations more than one type of system is used. For example, a Doppler sonar system may be used with a satellite receiver for periodic updating.

The development of reasonably small, reliable digital electronic computers suitable for use at sea has made possible the development of synergistic integrated systems, so designed that the errors tend to cancel or reduce each other, resulting in an output better than the sum of the individual components. These systems are very expensive and are used only where high accuracy and the economics of the application justify.

The Practice of Navigation

8.17   The Navigator   The prudent navigator is well informed on both the principles of navigation and their application. He continually studies to learn more of his subject, and makes a habit of analyzing his performance and results to improve his technique. He understands the principles of operation of his various items of equipment and checks frequently to be sure all is in good working order, giving prompt attention to any need for repair or servicing.

Well before the start of any voyage the navigator makes a careful check of all charts, publications, and equipment, correcting any deficiencies and making certain that all updating corrections have been made. He studies the charts and sailing directions, noting all hazards and unusual conditions. He makes notes on his chart, or at another conspicuous place, of items that will be useful. In areas where it is appropriate, he determines a danger sounding and traces this prominently on his chart, being careful not to use a red pencil if his chart will be illuminated by a red light. He studies the light lists and draws in the circular limit of visibility, at eye level from his vessel, for each light at a critical location. He studies the tide and tidal current tables to be thoroughly familiar with conditions to be encountered. He organizes his navigation team, if others are available to assist, to be certain that each person understands his responsibility and is competent to carry it out.

All of these details are taken care of in advance. Once the vessel is under way, he will be fully occupied with navigating the vessel. The time for preparation will have passed.

Several hours before the vessel gets under way, the gyro compass is started, if it has been turned off previously, and given sufficient time to settle on the meridian. Other equipment needing warm-up is turned on in plenty of time to insure reliable operation when needed.

Once the ship is moving, the navigator sees that a continuous dead reckoning plot is maintained and an accurate log kept of all bearings, distance measurements, etc. While proceeding out of the harbor, he checks off each buoy and landmark as it is sighted and passed. In the event of sudden onset of fog or other source of poor visibility, he will need to know his position accurately. This procedure is particularly important for vessels not equipped with radar, or ships so equipped but operating in areas where ample radar targets are not available. All available means of insuring the safe navigation of his vessel should be employed, using such redundancy as may be available to provide a check.

As the vessel leaves pilot waters, a last position is carefully determined and thoroughly checked as a point of departure for the deepwater portion of the voyage. The equipment used in piloting is then secured for sea and the more leisurely routine of navigation away from land is set.

During this portion of the voyage a position by an electronic system, such as loran, is obtained at regular intervals, perhaps hourly if available. Near the time of sunset or sunrise more frequent fixes may **be desirable, if the system used is subject to skywave contamination, for these are the periods of greatest change in the relative strength of groundwaves and skywaves, and frequent fixes will be helpful in** interpretation. Each time a fix is obtained by any method, the set and drift of the current are determined as a guide to the future, as well as an indication of a possible major error in the navigation or of the existence of an unusual condition. Inconsistent results should be accounted for, if possible. If they cannot be reconciled, one is at least alerted to a possible anomalous condition.

If celestial navigation is used, the daily routine, called the "day's work in navigation," usually consists of the following steps:

1. Morning twilight observations and sight reduction for a fix.
2. Winding the chronometers and determination of chronometer error.
3. Morning sun line, preferably when the sun is on or near the prime vertical, as a check on longitude, with an azimuth observation to check the accuracy of the compass.
4. Noon sight of the sun for a check on the latitude, with a running fix by advancement of the morning sun line, or a fix with a line of position from an observation of the moon or Venus.
5. An afternoon sun line, preferably when the sun is on or near the

prime vertical, for a check on the longitude, with an azimuth observation to check the accuracy of the compass.

6. Computation of the time of sunset and the approximate altitudes and azimuths of celestial bodies available for observation during evening twilight.
7. Evening twilight observations and sight reduction for a fix.
8. Computation of the times of sunrise and the beginning of morning twilight and the approximate altitudes and azimuths of celestial bodies available for observation during morning twilight.
9. Computation of the times of moonrise and moonset on the following day.

Variations of this routine are dictated by the weather, the availability of the moon or Venus in a favorable position for a daylight celestial fix, and other conditions.

As the time of landfall approaches, the navigator uses extra care in the determination of position. He turns on the radar and radio direction finder and breaks out the other equipment for piloting and prepares for this form of navigation. After landfall, he is careful to identify accurately the landmarks and aids to navigation sighted. He further verifies his position by soundings. During the passage to the pier or anchorage he uses all the care exercised at the start of the voyage, leaving nothing to chance.

The prudent navigator is at all times throughout a voyage alert to the uncertainty of position of his vessel, and to all opportunities to insure its safe navigation. He requires a frequent comparison of the magnetic and gyro compasses, perhaps half-hourly. He uses the radar, if available, in clear weather so as to develop an understanding of its limitations as well as its usefulness, so that he will be able to interpret results with confidence when other means of checking it are not available. Similarly, he uses all means available to him to acquire experience with each piece of equipment.

Navigation is far from a mechanical process. A reliable navigator is one who has developed good judgment through experience and constant analysis of results. The good navigator invariably asks himself, "are the results reasonable, are they consistent with other data"? The real test of a navigator comes when the safety of his vessel is at stake and inconsistent data are being obtained. It is then that his ingenuity and judgment are tested to the limit, and the long hours of comparison, analysis, and study to understand his equipment and its limitations pays off. As stated in the report of the Court of Inquiry investigation of the Point Honda disaster off the California coast in 1923, "The price of good navigation is constant vigilance."

PART

III

Shiphandling

General Principles
of
Ship Control

Many naval and merchant ships are twin or multiple screw and some have twin rudders. The ability to handle these ships can be improved by a thorough understanding of the forces set up in a single-screw ship when the propeller revolves, the rudder is "put over," and the ship moves through the water. We shall discuss, first, the propeller and rudder forces in a single-screw ship and then go on to consider these forces in a twin-screw ship.

9.1 Forces that Affect Maneuvering in a Single-Screw Ship* The action of a propeller in a single-screw ship brings into play many unsymmetrical forces. In order to understand these, it is necessary to have some idea of the manner in which a propeller generates forces. As a ship moves through the water, she experiences skin friction due to the viscosity of the water and tends to drag some of the water with her. If we measure the velocity of this water relative to that of the ship at increasing distances from the hull, we find that close to the hull the relative velocity is small because the water clings to the ship. The relative velocity increases as the distance from the hull increases

*Based, in part, on *Propeller Action in a Single Screw Ship.* Courtesy of the Director, David Taylor Model Basin.

until a point is reached where the water has no motion with respect to the surrounding sea. Its velocity relative to the ship equals the velocity of the ship. The boundary layer includes the water from the hull to the point where the relative velocity equals that of the ship. The width of this layer varies in some cases from zero at the bow to several feet near the stern. The net effect is that the boundary layer, a body of water, is given a forward motion by the passage of the ship.

Owing to this frictional drag upon the surrounding water, there is found aft, in the vicinity of the ship, a following current or wake called the *frictional wake*. The frictional wake is, in most cases, greatest at the surface in the vertical plane through the keel and abaft the ship. It decreases downward and outward on each side, as shown in Fig. 9.1. Streamline and wave patterns affect the velocity of the wake, but their effect is small.

The propeller revolves in this wake. Since the wake water is moving forward relative to the sea, the propeller, in effect, is advancing into a moving body of water. Its speed is less than that of the ship. Thus, if a ship is moving at 15 knots and dragging a wake with it at 3 knots, the propeller is only advancing at 12 knots *relative to the wake*. The ratio of the wake speed to the ship's speed is called the *wake fraction*: in this case $\frac{3}{15} = 0.20 = w$.

The speed of the advance of the propeller through the wake is given by

$$V_A = V(1 - w)$$

where V = ship's speed in knots. In the preceding case,

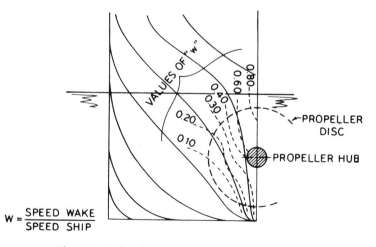

Fig. 9.1 Wake distribution for single-screw ship.

$$V_A = 15(1 - 0.20) = 15 \times 0.8 = 12 \text{ knots}$$

The wake speed of 3 knots is only an average speed and actually varies from place to place. Behind shaft struts, skeg, or rudder, the wake speed may equal that of the ship. It is this variation in wake pattern which causes the unsymmetrical propeller forces.

The wake pattern has been measured on many models. A typical wake distribution appears in Fig. 9.1. The curves on the right side are similar to those on the left. The figure shows by contours of w values the distribution of the wake velocity (the fore-and-aft components) over the propeller disc. Along the line labeled $w = 0.60$, the speed of advance of the propeller through the wake is only 40 percent of the ship's speed.

In addition to the fore-and-aft motion, the water moving aft alongside the ship has an upward and inward flow under the counter due to the general rise of the water as the stern moves forward.

Analysis of Propeller Action   The maximum thrust is developed at about 0.7 of the radius from the centerline of the shaft. We shall consider the forces generated at this point. The velocity of the blade section relative to the water is the resultant of two component velocities:

1. A forward motion through the water at velocity V_A or ship speed minus wake velocity.
2. A rotational motion of the propeller which is given by $2\pi RN$, where R is the radius under consideration (0.7) and N is revolutions in a unit of time.

The resultant velocity of the water V_0 is a combination of the forward and rotational motions. (See Fig. 9.2.) The effect of V_0 striking at the angle of attack α is to develop lift and drag just like the forces on an airplane wing. The direction of V_0 to the face of the blade section at the angle of attack produces forces which can be resolved into two components, a fore-and-aft force, the thrust T, and a torque Q. The former, T, propels the ship and the latter, Q, *generates a reaction or transverse force through the shafting which tends to force the stern to port or starboard.* If we look at Fig. 9.2 in another way, we could consider V_0 as one of the forces, all acting in the direction of the arrow and on the after surface of the blade. In fact, the forces act on both sides of the blade. If the angle of attack α between V_0 and the surface of the blade is small, the component forces T and Q will be small. If the angle is large, that is, when wV, the forward wake speed, is great, the force V_0 will strike the surface of the blade at a more effective angle. T and Q will be large; wV, the wake speed, varies as shown in

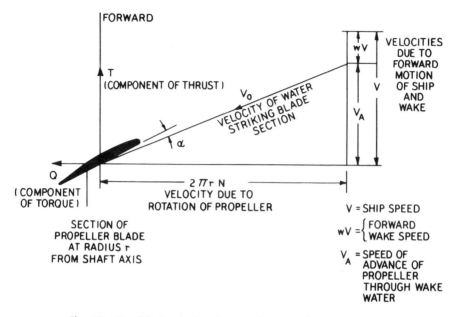

FORWARD

T
(COMPONENT OF THRUST)

V_0
VELOCITY OF WATER
STRIKING BLADE
SECTION

α

Q
(COMPONENT
OF TORQUE)

$2\pi r N$
VELOCITY DUE TO
ROTATION OF PROPELLER

SECTION OF
PROPELLER BLADE
AT RADIUS r
FROM SHAFT AXIS

wV
VELOCITIES
DUE TO
FORWARD
MOTION
OF SHIP
AND
WAKE

V

V_A

V = SHIP SPEED

$wV = \begin{cases} \text{FORWARD} \\ \text{WAKE SPEED} \end{cases}$

V_A = SPEED OF
ADVANCE OF
PROPELLER
THROUGH WAKE
WATER

Fig. 9.2 Simplified velocity diagram for propeller blade section.

Fig. 9.1, which explains the unsymmetrical forces acting on the hull. The amount of work done by each blade of the propeller will vary with its position in the disc.

There are four regions where the maximum change in force occurs:

1. As blade A (Fig. 9.3) approaches the vertical point, Fig. 9.1 shows it will pass through a region of relatively high wake speed and

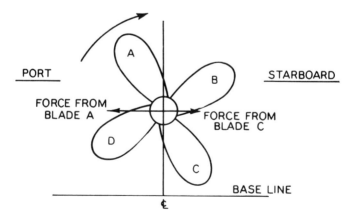

PORT

A

B

STARBOARD

FORCE FROM
BLADE A

FORCE FROM
BLADE C

D

C

BASE LINE

₵

Fig. 9.3 View from astern showing force on shaft axis.

therefore low values of V_A. (Figure 9.2 shows that α will increase as V_A drops in value. V_0 will act on the blade at a larger, more effective angle of attack. T and Q will increase.) The increase of the torque Q *reacts* through the shafting on the stern of the ship, forcing it to port with a right-hand propeller. If we revert to our explanation of V_0 above, it is clear the V_0 is acting from starboard to port against the rear side of the blade A. Because a right-handed propeller is being considered, V_0 will have two components: T, the thrust propelling the ship through the water; and Q, which generates a transverse or athwartship *force* now directing the stern to port.

2. Blade C will pass through an area opposite to that of blade A. A transverse force to starboard will be exerted. (But as the wake speed in the lower part of the disc is much less than in the upper, the angle of attack is smaller than on blade A, and the force to starboard will not be as great as that to port. The resultant force of these two forces is to port.)
3. Blade B will move downward against the upward flow of water under the counter. This flow is equivalent to an increase in N in the formula $2\pi RN$. The angle of attack α, velocity, thrust, and torque increase.
4. Blade D moves up with the flow and experiences a decrease in the above factors.

It is clear that B overbalances D, and the ship's head tends to fall off to port. When going astern the propeller turns in the reverse direction. The forces then act in the opposite direction from when going ahead and the ship's head will fall off to starboard. There are two more factors that affect the steering of the ship:

1. The propeller imparts a helical motion to the slipstream which impinges on the rudder even when amidships. That part of the helical slipstream above the axis of the propeller tends to move the stern to starboard, and the part below the axis tries to move the stern to port. The resultant force depends on the area of the rudder above and below the centerline of the shaft and the uniformity of the slipstream.
2. The next factor is the submergence of the propeller. If the ship is in ballast or at light displacement or plunging in heavy seas, the propeller may break surface, causing a decrease in the transverse effect of blade A. When the ship has little or no speed, Blade A, which is near the surface, may draw air and again decrease the transverse force.

The ship is therefore subject to several opposing, variable forces. Her actual behavior will depend on the magnitude of these forces. General experience shows that many single-screw ships with a right-hand propeller turning ahead tend to fall off to port. There are exceptions, and no hard and fast rule can be laid down. Observe your own ship.

9.2   Getting Under Way   With the ship stationary or just starting to move, the wake does not exist or is negligible. The top blade A may break the surface and thus lose some of its usual transverse force to port. If it does not break the surface, air may be drawn down with the same effect. The lower blade still acts to force the stern to starboard. The rudder, even when amidships, receives the helical slipstream at an effective angle high up on the port side. If the rudder has a larger area above the axis of the propeller than below, that force tends to move the stern to starboard. The result of these forces may be that the stern will move to starboard.

When backing, the forces due to blades A and C are reversed. Blade A may break the surface, but regardless, C, acting to port, will predominate. There is no helical slipstream thrown against the rudder. Most of the water which passes through the propeller disc comes from the free surface, and the rudder exerts no steering force until the ship gains sternway. The upper part of the discharge flow from the propeller strikes the starboard underwater body of the ship at a good angle. The lower part strikes the keel on the port side at a poor angle. It is probable that the force due to the upper part predominates, and the result of these forces tends to push the stern to port.

9.3   Handling Ships with Controllable Pitch Propellers   Many small ships, such as LSTs, tugs, and the Navy's nonmagnetic ocean minesweepers (MSO), have controllable pitch propellers. The blades of the propellers are rotated by a hydraulic mechanism in a plane parallel to that of the propeller shaft. Thus the blades can be adjusted to take more or less bite, or can be reversed in pitch. It is this latter feature particularly that adds maneuverability; some minesweepers, for example, can be stopped in less than two ship lengths when going ahead full power.

The forces acting on the controllable pitch propeller are the same as those described above for conventional propellers. The shiphandler uses his rudder and engines in the conventional way except, instead of speeding up, slowing, or reversing his engines, he adjusts or reverses the pitch of his blades by a control mechanism on the bridge. Since the response to change in propeller blade pitch is instantaneous the shiphandler must become accustomed to this disappearance of dead time when backing. Another novelty to the seaman trained to handle conventional ships will be his ability with controllable pitch propellers to move the ship quickly with high power. This was done by keeping the shaft revolutions high and the propeller pitch low. An increase in propeller blade pitch then applies power to the ship very suddenly.

9.4   Steering a Twin-Screw Ship, Single Rudder   A twin-screw ship has two propellers, one on either side of the centerline. Generally, they are out-turning, that is, the starboard one is right-handed and the port one left-handed. They turn in opposite directions to balance the propeller forces and enable the ship to steer a straight course with no rudder.

A multiple-screw ship normally has four propellers, two on a side, out-turning and so controlled that those on a side go ahead or astern as a unit. As the action of a multiple-screw ship is similar to that of a twin-screw ship, only the latter will be discussed.

The steering of a twin-screw ship is considerably simpler than that of the single-screw ship. The strong tendency of the single-screw ship to back stern to port does not hold with the twin-screw, and the latter backs with equal facility in either direction, barring the effect of wind, waves, and currents.

The various forces affecting the action of the single-screw ship are still present to a degree in the case of a twin-screw. In many cases they are considerably less because the forces from one screw are balanced by similar but opposite forces emanating from the other screw. In addition, there is a new force due to the movement of the screws around the centerline. It will readily be seen that with one screw going ahead and the other astern, there results a turning moment that tends to throw the *bow* to the side of the backing screw.

One powerful force should not be overlooked. It is the momentum of the ship, ahead or astern, acting through the center of gravity. If a twin-screw ship is going ahead and one screw is backed, two opposing forces are set in motion, namely, the force of the backing screw acting in one direction at a certain distance from the centerline and the weight of the ship acting in the opposite direction. These are in addition to the forces due to the action of the wake on the rudder if it is "put over."

The steering of the twin-screw ship will be considered under the following headings, no wind or sea:

1. Ship and Screws Going Ahead.
2. Ship Going Ahead, Screws Backing.

3. Ship Going Astern, Screws Backing.
4. Ship Going Astern, Screws Going Ahead.
5. One Screw Going Ahead, Other Screw Backing.

9.5 Ship and Both Screws Going Ahead, Single Rudder   In this case, with the rudder amidships the ship will steer a steady course. The transverse forces of the two propellers are equal and opposite in direction. As the shafts are offset equally, no turning moment is felt.

When the rudder is put over, it will receive some of the discharge flow from the propeller on that side but not as much as in a single-screw ship. The principal force which turns the ship is that set up by the wake against the forward side of the rudder.

If one screw is stopped with the rudder amidships, the turning moment of the revolving screw will take charge, and the ship will turn toward the side of the stopped screw. The discharge flow of the revolving screws does not strike the rudder.

9.6 Ship Going Ahead, Both Screws Backing, Single Rudder   The steering effect of the rudder is the only force turning the ship from a straight course. All other forces are equalized. The effect of the rudder is reduced as the headway is lost until there is no steering control when the ship is stationary.

If one screw only is backing and the other stopped with headway on, the turning moment of the backing screw added to the momentum of the ship going ahead will swing the stern away from the backing screw. If there is deadwood forward of the screw, the discharge flow will strike the underwater body and increase the swing.

9.7 Ship Going Astern, Both Screws Backing, Single Rudder   If the rudder is amidships, the various forces are equalized, and a straight course can be steered. If the rudder is put over, the pressure of the water that the ship is backing into against the back side of the rudder will enable a course to be steered. However, most of the water which passes through the screws comes from the free surface and thus has little effect on the rudder.

If one screw is stopped, the turning moment of the backing screw is added to the effect of the rudder when it is put over away from the revolving screw. The swing may be slowed or stopped if the rudder is put over toward the screw. The effect of the rudder is to counteract the effect of the screw, and how effective it is will be dependent upon the size of the rudder and speed of the engine.

9.8 Ship Going Astern, Both Screws Going Ahead, Single Rudder
The ship will respond to the rudder, that is, a left rudder will throw

the stern to port unless excessive sternway is on. The transverse forces of the screws will be equalized. The steering effect of the rudder when going astern will be reduced gradually as the ship loses headway, until all steering control is lost before the ship has lost sternway. This is because the discharge flow from the propellers will interfere with the flow of water against the back of the rudder.

9.9   Ship Stationary, One Screw Going Ahead, Other Screw Backing, Single Rudder   The rudder will have little effect until head or sternway has been gained. The turning moments of the two screws will be additive, but they may not be great when the shafts are close together. If the ship has no deadwood, she may turn easily. In narrow waters the two screws should be operated at such speeds that the ship does not gain headway or sternway when going ahead and backing at one-third or two-thirds speed. This balancing of forces will enable the captain to move the ship ahead or astern as desired by varying the speed of the backing or ahead engine. As a general rule with one engine ahead the same amount as the one astern, the ship will slowly make headway. The rudder may be used to increase the swing when some steerageway has been gained.

9.10   Twin Rudders on Twin-Screw and Multiple-Screw Ships   Twin rudders are installed on many vessels, large and small, and vary in position, shape, and size. The rudders on destroyers receive most of the upper half of the discharge flow of the propellers when going ahead. The lower half passes under the rudder. The installation of twin rudders has improved the maneuverability of ships. The general rule when handling twin-screw destroyers with one rudder is to order the proper rudder after the ship has gained headway or sternway. The installation of twin rudders has changed this rule, and the shiphandler should now order right or left rudder before the engines are moved. The rudder should be put over to take advantage of the discharge flow from the ahead propeller. This flow acts against the forward side of its rudder and thus creates a powerful force to turn the ship.

The improved turning characteristics of destroyers are appreciated when turning in narrow channels and going alongside a nest or tender where large angles of approach must be used. The maneuvers to shove off from a nest, tender, or pier under awkward conditions of wind and tide are also facilitated.

The key to all these ordinarily difficult maneuvers is the decisive effect of the discharge flow from the ahead propeller on the rudder astern of it. If the other propeller must be operated astern, it may do so without affecting the turn adversely because the water passing through its disc comes from the free surface and does not impinge on the rudder to any great extent. Hence, the ship can be turned to port from dead in the water, for instance, by ordering "left full rudder, ahead two-thirds," on the starboard engine and "back, two-thirds," on the port engine. The speed of the port engine can be varied thereafter to allow the ship to gain steerageway as and if desired. The rudder and the starboard engine need not be changed until the turn is completed.

9.11 Turning Characteristics The standard method of finding any ship's turning characteristics is to turn her in a number of complete circles under varying conditions and to record the results for each turn. The variables used are: right or left rudder of various degrees;

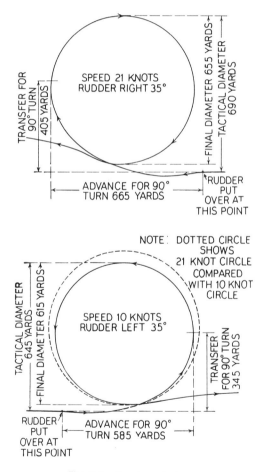

Fig. 9.4 Turning circles.

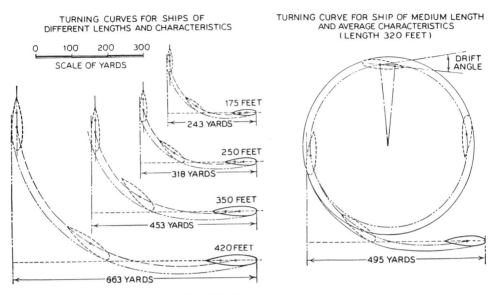

Fig. 9.5 Turning curves.

steady speeds of different value; and differences in draft and trim. When taking turning data, the effects of wind and sea are noted and allowed for. Most changes, of course, are not as much as 360 degrees, but by studying the complete turning circle the ship's behavior for turns of any extent can be determined. In considering the track actually followed by a ship during a turn, certain terms must be defined. These terms may be understood more easily by a simultaneous study of Figs. 9.4 and 9.5. Figure 9.4 shows actual turning circles of the *U.S.S. New Mexico.* One figure is the circle made at 21 knots with 35 degrees right rudder; the other, the circle made at 10 knots with 10 degrees left rudder. Figure 9.5 illustrates some differences in the turning curves made by ships of different lengths and characteristics.

9.12 Definitions *a. Turning Circle* The path followed by the *pivoting* point of a ship in making a turn of 360 degrees or more. For the ordinary ship the bow will be inside and the stern outside this circle.

   b. Advance The distance gained in the direction of the original course. The advance will be a maximum when the ship has turned through 90 degrees.

   c. Transfer The distance gained at right angles to the original course when the ship has turned through 90 degrees.

   d. Tactical Diameter The distance gained to the right or left of the original course when a turn of 180 degrees has been completed.

e. Final Diameter   The distance perpendicular to the original course between tangents drawn at the points where 180 and 360 degrees of the turn have been completed. Should the ship continue turning indefinitely with the same speed and rudder angle, she will keep on turning in a circle of this diameter. It will always be less than the tactical diameter.

f. Kick   The distance the ship moves sidewise from the original course away from the direction of the turn after the rudder is first put over. The term is also applied to the swirl of water toward the inside of the turn when the rudder is put over to begin the turn.

g. Drift Angle   The angle at any point of the turning circle between the tangent to the turning circle at that point and the keel line of the vessel.

h. Pivoting Point   That point about which the ship turns when the rudder is put over.

The turning circle is the path followed by the pivoting point during the turn. The pivoting point is in the horizontal centerline of the ship, and its position on that line depends on the shape of the underwater hull and especially on how much the after deadwood is cut away. The pivoting point moves forward if the ship is trimmed down by the head and aft if it is down by the stern. This characteristic is illustrated by the standard motor launch. When light, it pivots well aft on account of the weight of the engine, and when heavily laden it pivots well forward. The pivoting point may also move aft along the keel line to some extent if the ship is deep in the water and forward if she is light. It is normally in the forward one-third length of the ship. When its position is once determined, it does not vary enough in the ordinary ship under different conditions of load and trim to cause any difficulty in ship handling.

9.13   Other Forces Affecting Turning   Every seaman knows that the wind effects turning. The freeboard and superstructure act as a sail area whose effect must be considered, especially at low speeds. As the pivot point is well forward when a ship is moving ahead, the pressure acting on the greater exposed area abaft this point tends to turn the ship into the wind. Ships with high freeboard, such as a carrier, tend to turn into a wind much more rapidly and turn out of a wind much more slowly than under zero wind conditions. When going astern, the pivot point moves aft and there is a marked tendency for the stern to seek the wind. The stronger the wind, the stronger the tendency to back into the wind. This tendency can be used to facilitate a turn when maneuvering in restricted waters. In the case where the sail area of a ship's superstructure and freeboard (high bow, low stern) is concentrated forward the effect of the wind on the ship going slowly ahead is lessened. However, a ship with these latter characteristics will back into the wind even more rapidly.

The condition and relative direction of the sea affect both the progress and the steering of the ship by their effect on the underwater body. Any sea forward of the beam will retard the motion of the ship over the ground to a greater or less extent, while any sea from abaft the beam will accelerate it. The general effect of the sea on steering is to cause a ship to seek the trough. If the sea is on the bow or quarter, it may be necessary to carry a definite amount of either right or left rudder in order to maintain the course.

Current affects the underwater body of the ship. It is especially important because its existence may not always be realized. Known ocean currents may be shifted, accelerated, diminished, or even reversed by winds steadily in one direction over a long period of time. Currents in harbors, straits, and bays are caused by the action of the tides. The currents at the entrances to certain harbors (the Golden Gate) are strong at times and run at an angle with the entrance course. The current may be reduced or reversed by the tide. The direction and probable force of currents in ports and along the coasts may be determined approximately by the study of tide tables and current charts, but every effort should be made to verify the data found in these publications because the effects of wind and weather may make them inaccurate. Observation of the shape of the shore line and of the direction in which buoys and other anchored navigational aids are leaning will give a good check on the force and direction of the current running at any given time.

The general effect of a current on the underwater body of a ship is to move her bodily in the same direction in which the current is running. When turning in a current, the ship, at the completion of the turn, may be well down in the direction of the current from her position when the turn was started. When held at any point, as by an anchor, the ship usually assumes the position where the current has the least underwater area on which to act. For this reason, an anchored ship heads into the current unless the wind or sea is strong enough to overcome its effect. For the same reason, a ship at anchor will swing with the change of the tidal current. By means of spring lines, current can be used to cant a ship or to move her toward a dock. Steering is always easier when heading into a current than when going with it, except in narrow channels.

Shallow water will modify the normal action of screws and rudder in steering or turning a ship. She may be sluggish in answering her rudder or she may take a sudden sheer to one side. High speeds can be made in shallow water by the use of excessive power, but large waves are formed, which causes destruction to shipping and water-front facilities. The best seamanship in harbors and rivers is constant watchfulness, foresight, slow but steady speed, having an anchor ready for letting go, and some consideration for other craft.

When maneuvering at slow speed or turning at rest in a confined space in shallow water, the expected effects from the rudder and pro-pellers may not appear. Water cannot flow easily from one side of the ship to the other, so that the sideways force from the propellers may in fact be neutralized. Eddies may build up that counteract the propeller forces and the expected action of the rudder. If the attempt to turn at rest in shallow water with ahead revolutions on one shaft and astern on the other fails, or the turn is very sluggish, the situation will almost certainly become worse if the revolutions are increased. Stopping the engines to allow the eddies to subside, and then starting again with reduced revolu-tions, is more likely to be successful. In many harbors there is an ex-tremely small clearance between keel and bottom where such a situation is not unlikely.

9.14   Casting in a Narrow Channel   The expression to *cast* means to turn a ship to a particular heading in her own water. Ships turn in this manner when getting under way together in a crowded anchorage and when headed in the wrong direction. Single vessels in restricted anchorages often have to turn in their own water too because of nearby anchored vessels or a restricted maneuvering space.

The problem of turning twin-screw ships and a single rudder is not a difficult one. Go ahead on one engine and back on the other, using the rudder when head or sternway has been gained. If the ship is fitted with twin rudders which are directly behind the propellers, order *"hard over"* rudder before going ahead on one engine. Back the other engine at such speed as necessary to prevent headway or sternway being gained.

Single-screw ships can be turned quite easily in light winds in re-stricted waters. Take advantage of the tendency of most ships to back to port. The first move is to go ahead full with hard right rudder but reverse the engines before much headway is made. Shift the rudder after headway has been lost and back down a short distance and then go ahead *full*. The rudder should be ordered *right* full before the engines ahead begin to turn over. In stronger winds it is advisable to turn so that the tendency to back into the wind can be used to in-crease the turn. See Fig. 9.6.

Most seaman know that an anchor can be used to facilitate and expedite a turn in a restricted space. High-powered vessels generally use their twin screws and powerful engines to turn in places where a single-screw, low-powered steamer uses an anchor.

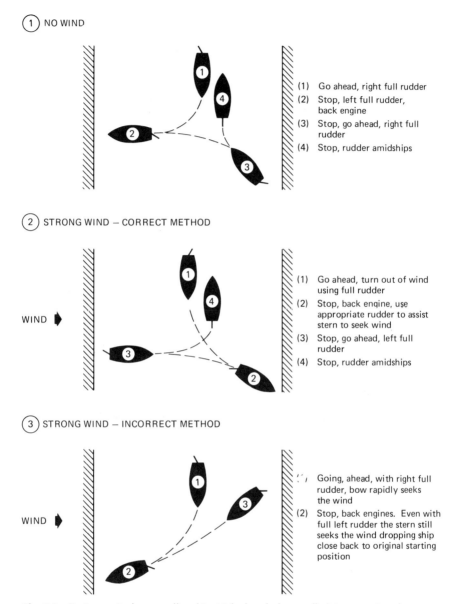

(1) NO WIND

(1) Go ahead, right full rudder
(2) Stop, left full rudder, back engine
(3) Stop, go ahead, right full rudder
(4) Stop, rudder amidships

(2) STRONG WIND — CORRECT METHOD

WIND

(1) Go ahead, turn out of wind using full rudder
(2) Stop, back engine, use appropriate rudder to assist stern to seek wind
(3) Stop, go ahead, left full rudder
(4) Stop, rudder amidships

(3) STRONG WIND — INCORRECT METHOD

WIND

(1) Going, ahead, with right full rudder, bow rapidly seeks the wind
(2) Stop, back engines. Even with full left rudder the stern still seeks the wind dropping ship close back to original starting position

Fig. 9.6 Casting a single-propeller ship (right-handed propeller) in a restricted space.

The anchor is dropped underfoot at short scope. If low powers are used, the anchor will drag somewhat, but the strain on the chain will not be injurious. The engines can be operated ahead and astern as before, but only slow speeds should be used and little steerway gained. The turn should be made to starboard by pivoting on the anchor when going ahead and by the tendency of the stern to swing to port when backing. A careful check of the chart should be made to ensure that a dragging anchor does not foul a submarine cable.

9.15 Navigating in a Narrow Channel A ship will be set off the nearer bank when proceeding along a straight, narrow channel, especially if the draft of the ship is nearly equal to the depth of the water. This effect is particularly noticeable in narrow reaches with steep banks such as certain sections of the Panama Canal and is called *bank cushion.* As the ship moves ahead, the wedge of water between the bow and the nearer bank builds up higher than that on the other side, and the bow is forced out sharply. The suction of the screw, especially with a twin-screw ship, and the unbalanced pressure of water on the quarter, lower the level of the water between the quarter and the near bank and force the stern toward the bank. This is called *bank suction.* The combined effect of bank cushion and bank suction may cause the ship to take a sudden and decided sheer toward the opposite bank. If a single-screw steamer traveling at very low speed with her starboard side near the right bank takes such a sheer, she may be brought under control by going ahead full with right full rudder. The added steering effect may overcome the bank suction. A twin-screw ship under similar conditions has a fair chance to recover from such a sheer by going ahead full on the port engine, stopping or backing the starboard screw, and putting the rudder full right. Should the sheer carry the ship across mid-channel, the starboard anchor should be dropped and snubbed if necessary. All engines should be reversed as the first anchor is dropped.

9.16 Turning in a Bend There are several factors which affect a ship trying to turn in a sharp bend in a narrow channel. Two of these have been described, *bank suction* and *bank cushion.* Both are strong when the bank of the channel is steep; they are weakest when the edge of the channel shoals gradually and extends into a large shallow area. The tendency of the ship to continue along her original course when the rudder is put over will be felt in the shoaling case. If the bank of the channel is abrupt and the ship deeply laden, a bank cushion will act against the tendency to continue on her course. The river or canal currents are strongest *in the bend,* and there may be eddies or counter currents on the lee side of the point. Turning in a bend requires a knowledge of how these forces act. Use the forces which are favorable and avoid those which are opposed.

A head current is the safest because a ship can be stopped very quickly, but a following current enables the ship to proceed at good

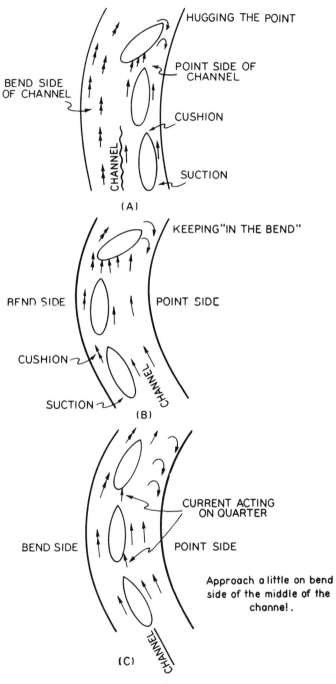

HUGGING THE POINT

POINT SIDE OF CHANNEL

BEND SIDE OF CHANNEL

CUSHION

SUCTION

CHANNEL

(A)

KEEPING "IN THE BEND"

BEND SIDE

POINT SIDE

CUSHION

SUCTION

CHANNEL

(B)

CURRENT ACTING ON QUARTER

BEND SIDE

POINT SIDE

Approach a little on bend side of the middle of the channel.

CHANNEL

(C)

Fig. 9.7

speed with very little speed on the engines. Bank suction increases with engine speed. Bank cushion increases with the ship's speed. The force of the current against the quarter can be used to turn the ship; therefore it is advantageous to proceed with the current.

. If the current is ahead, the best position to start the turn is from the middle of the channel. The eddy under the point and the increased current in the bend are both avoided. Proceed at a very slow speed over the ground so that the ship can be stopped quickly by the engines and the current, and perhaps an anchor or two.

There are three choices in *making* a sharp bend with a following current:

1. *Hug the point.*
2. *Stay in the bend.*
3. Proceed on the bend side of the middle of the channel.

If the ship *hugs* the point (Fig. 9.7 (A)), the helmsman will require a small amount of rudder toward the bank to steer a straight course. Less rudder will be necessary as the channel begins to bend and the ship moves away from the bank. This signal "less rudder" is a great help in determining when to begin the turn in clear as well as in foggy weather. However, slack water or eddies may be encountered around the turn. These may make it very difficult to prevent a sheer toward the near bank, particularly in shallow water when laden. The stern may feel the current under the quarter and thus increase the sheer.

If the master decides to make the turn *in the bend,* that is, away from the point (Fig. 9.7 (B)), the question arises when to turn. If he starts too late, the ship may ground on the bank *in the bend.* If he starts too early, there is a danger that the bank suction on one quarter added to the force of the current on the other may give the ship a rank sheer. The bank cushion under the bow will increase the sheer. If the bow should enter the eddies under the point, the ship may pivot and eventually ground on both sides of the channel at the same time.

Perhaps the safest way to turn with a following current is to approach the turn on a course a little to the bend side of the middle of the channel (Fig. 9.7 (C)). The eddies under the point and the increased current *in the bend* can be avoided, and the force of the current against the quarter can be used to assist the turn.

Two ships should not attempt to pass in a narrow channel in a bend. The ship which has a head current should stop and wait for the other to clear the bend.

9.17   Orders to the Wheel (Under All Conditions)   Orders to the wheel and to the engine room telegraph must be given firmly and distinctly and repeated by the steersman or engine order telegraph operator in the exact words given as a check to show that they are understood and are being obeyed. A standard phraseology should be used to ensure a uniform result for changes in course and speed. In giving many of the commands to the steersman, the first word gives the direction so that the wheel can be started immediately, and the second gives the amount of rudder to be used.

"Right (left) standard rudder!" Standard rudder is the amount used to turn with a certain tactical diameter.

"Right (left) full rudder!" This is used when it is desired to make as short a turn as possible. The number of degrees to use for full rudder is always greater than that used for standard rudder. As the full throw of the rudder is about 35 degrees to each side, full rudder is set a few degrees less in order to ensure that the rudder will not jam hard over against the stops.

"Right (left) 5 (10, etc.) degrees rudder!" This command is used when a more gradual turn is desired than would be the case if either standard or full rudder were used.

"Right (left) rudder!" This order starts the wheel over in the desired direction immediately and must be followed by other orders as an obscure situation develops. It should seldom be necessary to use this order.

With an experienced steersman all the foregoing orders may be followed by an order to steady on a certain compass course. The steersman will carry this out without further orders and report when steadied on the new course. With an inexperienced steersman or when the new course cannot be determined beforehand, the following orders are used:

"Rudder amidships!" This further slows the swing and is a warning that the new course is being approached.

"Meet her!" This order requires opposite rudder to stop the swing.

"Steady!" or "Steady as you go!" These are given to the steersman when it is desired to keep the ship on the heading she has at that instant.

The object of these orders is to steady the ship on the new course without letting her swing past it with consequent loss of position and unnecessary use of rudder. The exact times at which the various orders should be given for each ship must be determined by trial and experience. One valuable point to note is that a ship with heavy weights near the bow and stern requires more rudder to start and is harder to stop due to the momentum acquired during the turn.

Certain other orders to the wheel are used on occasion.

"Shift the rudder!" This is an order to change an equal amount from right to left rudder or vice versa. It is often used while going ahead and backing in restricted waters to assist in a turn.

"Right (left) handsomely!" This order is used for small rudder angles to make slight changes of course. It is rarely used today and probably is unfamiliar to most steersmen.

"Nothing to the right (left)!" This is given when the course to be made good is a shade off the course set, and all small variations in steering must be kept to the right (left) of the compass course. It is frequently used to avoid obstructions, buoys, or passing ships.

All orders to the steersman in regard to the course must refer to the compass by which he is steering at the time and must be in the form "Course, zero, zero, five." The steersman is not concerned whether the course is true or magnetic and must never be required to apply compass corrections of any kind. The officer of the deck should check the compass course upon assuming a new course and frequently thereafter.

The steersman must repeat all orders exactly as given and must report when they have been carried out. When he is relieved, he must report the fact to the officer of the deck and report the course being steered.

9.18 Orders to the Engine Order Telegraphs (Annunciators) Orders to the engine order telegraphs are in three parts:

1. The first part designates the engine, as "Starboard (port) engine" or "All engines." This puts the annunciator man on the alert.
2. The second part of the command gives the direction in which the engine order telegraph is to be moved, as "Ahead" or "Back."
3. The third part of the command gives the speed at which the engine is to be moved.

Thus: "All engines ahead full"; "Port engine back two thirds"; "Starboard engine ahead standard!"

Every order to the engine order telegraphs must be repeated word for word by the operator. When the engine room has acknowledged the order by the repeat back system on the telegraph, and the shaft revolution indicators show the engines are in the process of carrying out the order, the operator should then report what the engine is doing. Thus, upon the order from the officer of the deck, "Starboard engine, back one third," the operator repeats, "Starboard engine, back one third, sir." At the same time he rings up "back one third" on the starboard engine order telegraph. When this is repeated back from the engine room on the engine order telegraph, he reports, "Starboard engine answers back one third, sir."

9.19 Man Overboard   Over the years, the cry "Man Overboard" has become one of the most dreaded utterances to the ear of the mariner. For without quick action on the part of the ship's officers and crew, a man's life might well be lost. Therefore, the prudent watch officer, upon assuming his duties on the bridge, will rehearse in his own mind the actions he would take if such an event were to occur during his watch. The proper actions to be taken in the event of a man overboard depend on many factors. These would include:

1. The individual officer's experience and preferences for recovery techniques.
2. The ship's maneuvering characteristics (single screw, double screw, turning radius, etc).
3. The status of the engineering plant.
4. The side on which the ready life boat is rigged.
5. The visibility.
6. The wind direction and sea state.
7. The proximity of other ships.
8. The ship's location with respect to hazards to navigation.

Depending on the circumstances, one of the recovery methods outlined in Fig. 9.8 might be used. Simultaneously, there are several routine actions which are taken immediately when a man is reported overboard.

One or more, preferably more, life buoys should be thrown over at once. If a little presence of mind is exercised here, it is often possible to throw one of these very close to the man and, if possible, between the man and ship. At the first alarm a number of men (previously instructed through drills, etc.) go aloft to try to keep the man in sight; and as quickly as possible a quartermaster tracks the man with a pair of good binoculars.

The ordinary life buoy is so small that often the man in the water cannot see it, and it is of little or no assistance to the lookouts who are trying to keep him in sight. This is a serious and often fatal defect. It is well to keep a number of these small life buoys about the deck to be thrown overboard on the instant by anyone who may be near them; but in addition there should be available packets of sea dye marker for daytime use and battery-operated water lights for nightime. The latter are necessary to serve as markers not only for the man but to keep the spot in sight from the ship. At least 50 percent of all life buoys kept about the deck should be equipped with the battery-operated lights mentioned above. The sea dye markers should be kept handy to each life buoy.

Method and Primary Use	Diagram (ship on course 090; numbers refer to the explanation)	Explanation	Analysis	
			Advantages	Disadvantages
WILLIAMSON TURN 1. Used in reduced visibility because it makes good the original track.	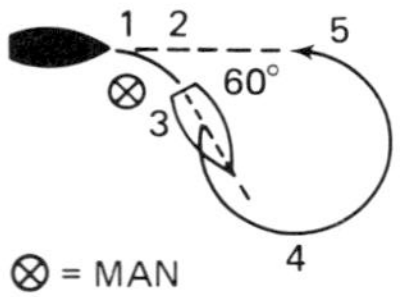	1. Put the rudder over full in the direction corresponding to the side over which the man fell. 2. When clear of the man, go ahead full on all engines, continue using full rudder. 3. When heading is 60° beyond the original course, shift the rudder without having steadied on a course. 60° is proper for many ships, however, the exact amount must be determined through trial and error. 4. Come to the reciprocal of the original course, using full rudder. 5. Use the engines and rudder to attain the proper final position (ship upwind of the man and dead in the water with the man alongside, well forward of the propellers).	1. Simplicity 2. Makes good the original track.	1. Slow 2. Takes the ship a relatively great distance from the man, when sight may be lost.
ONE TURN ("Anderson") Used by destroyers, ships which have considerable power available and relatively tight turning characteristics.	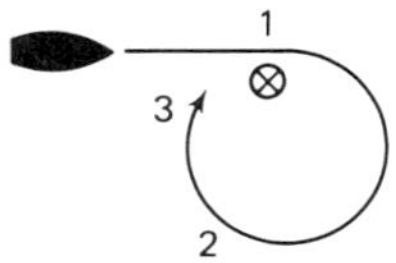	1. Put the rudder over full in the direction corresponding to the side over which the man fell. Go ahead full on the outboard engine only. When about two thirds of the way around, back the inboard engine 2/3 or full. Order all engines stopped when the man is within about 15 degrees of the bow, then ease the rudder and back the engines as required to attain the proper final position (as for the other methods). Many variations of this method are used, differing primarily in respect to the use of one or both engines, and the time when they are stopped and backed to return to the man and tighten the turn. The variation used should reflect individual ship's characteristics, sea conditions, personal preferences, etc.	The fastest recovery method.	1. Requires a relatively high degree of proficiency in shiphandling because of the lack of a straight-a-way approach to the man. 2. Often impossible for a single propeller ship.
TWO TURN (Race Track) Used in good visibility when a straight final approach leg is desired.	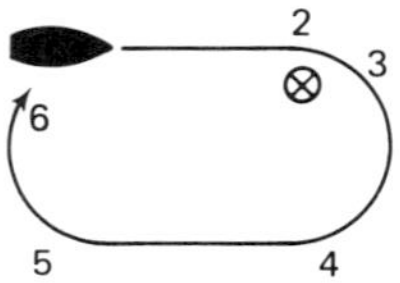	1. A variation of the one turn method which provides a desirable straight final approach to the man. 2. Put the rudder over full in the direction corresponding to the side over which the man fell. 3. When clear of the man, go ahead full on all engines, continue using full rudder to turn to the reciprocal of the original course. 4. Steady for a distance which will give the desired run for a final straight approach. 5. Use full rudder to turn to the man. 6. Use the engines and rudder to attain the proper final position (ship upwind of the man and dead in the water with the man alongside well forward of the propellers).	1. The straight final approach leg facilitates a more calculable approach. 2. The ship will be returned to the man if he is lost from sight. 3. Reasonably fast. 4. Effective when the wind was from abeam abeam on the original course.	Slower than the one turn method.

Fig. 9.8 Different methods of man overboard recovery.

Ships fitted with a Dead Reckoning Tracer should mark the trace at the time the man goes over. A course to steer back to this point on the chart can then be obtained.

Motor whaleboats are kept ready at sea for instant lowering for use as lifeboats. Whatever the recovery method selected, while the ship is maneuvering to approach the man, the boat crew should be readying the boat to be put in the water as soon as the ship has slowed sufficiently. In most sea conditions, a boat may be lowered with reasonable safety from a ship at a speed of four knots.

One method of maneuvering to recover a man overboard is to go full speed astern as soon as the man is clear of the screw and to lower the boat as soon as speed has been reduced sufficiently. This method is especially effective when the ship was originally at a slow speed. The boat goes back in search of the man and is guided by signals from the lookouts aloft by semaphore flags or hand held radios, provided they have succeeded in keeping the man in sight. Failing this the boat cannot go far wrong if it goes back on a course opposite the original heading of the ship, (down the ship's wake) for although the ship in backing will probably throw her head to one side, she will not usually gain a great amount of ground in that direction before coming to rest.

In weather too heavy to admit of lowering a boat the one method that can give hope of saving a man is to attempt to pick him up with the ship. With this method men should be standing by with heavy lines and additional life rings. In addition, the use of cargo nets over the side, attended by strong swimmers wearing immersion suits and with safety lines attached, is of great value.

Special rules are laid down for cases of man overboard in formation. All officers concerned must be familiar with these. In general, they provide for the necessary maneuvers to keep clear of other ships while picking up the man and for signals notifying other ships of the situation.

There are several different methods which ships may use to apprach a man in the water to pick him up, either directly, or with the boat. Three of the more common methods are discussed in Fig. 9.8.

9.20 Handling Very Large Ships No special techniques are needed in handling a 300,000-ton supertanker, but an appreciation of the mass and power of such ships is important. Very large ships, especially when loaded, cannot be expected to stop quickly or to turn nimbly when changing course. Thus, efficient lookouts, assisted by new automatic acoustic or radar detection and alarm devices, are required to avoid collision or grounding. Oil spills of massive proportions that happen today are such a serious catastrophe to man's environment that they must be prevented by the most elaborate and even expensive devices. For those who meet such monsters at sea it is well to remember their lack of maneuverability and not to put too fine an interpretation of the Rules of the Road upon a crossing or meeting situation even when theoretically the privileged vessel.

Handling Steamers in Heavy Weather

In the days of sail and in the early steam vessels, most of which also had after sails, the conventional way to handle a ship when the weather was too heavy for her to proceed on her course was to bring her head up until she had the sea on the bow and to hold her there with the rudder and sail, with little or no resultant headway. If she fell off—as from time to time she did—and started to gather way, the hard down helm and after sail would bring her promptly back to meet the sea. Thus she came up and fell off making some little way through the water, but none of it against the sea, in the main, drifting steadily to leeward. For such bluff-bowed ships, this was and is the ideal way of riding out a gale. But a modern steamer, whether a man-of-war, liner, or tramp, carries no sail and is commonly long and sharp. The propeller acts as a drag, tending to hold her stern-up to the sea, and this tendency is assisted by the excess of draft which such steamers usually have aft. To hold such a steamer bows-on to the sea, she must be forced into it—not at great speed, perhaps, but sufficiently great to maintain steerageway. This can strain the ship severely and causes grave doubt as to the wisdom of such a method of lying to. The opinion of late years is that a steamer should run slowly before a sea or lie to with the sea astern or on the quarter; and this view is supported both by theoretical considerations and by a convincing amount of practical experience.

9.21 The Approach of a Tropical Storm When a master is fore-warned of the approach of a tropical storm, his first thought must be the location of the center and the estimated track of the storm. The geographical position of his vessel with respect to the proximity of land or shoal water, and whether his vessel will be in the dangerous or navigable semicircle (see Chapter 20) of the storm, must be determined at once.

He should make an early decision and use all necessary speed to gain the safest possible geographical location before the storm is upon him. Once the center of the storm is near him, he should then be free to reduce speed, to avoid damage to his vessel. It may then be desirable to proceed at dead slow engine speed, barely maintaining steerageway, or even lie to for several hours until the storm passes. It might be desirable and safe to maintain a fair speed downwind.

If a master is unable to gain a satisfactory position with respect to shoal water, with the winds he can expect in a tropical storm, he may be forced to oppose the winds with appreciable engine speed, accepting risk of damages, to avoid being pushed into shoal waters.

On the other hand, if arrival in the navigable semicircle of a tropical storm before the storm is upon him is his only concern, he should not force his vessel in any continued effort to do so, but should ride out the storm as best he can.

9.22 Controlling a Ship in Very Heavy Weather The easiest position for a ship in a very heavy sea would be that which she would herself take if left at rest and free from the constraint of engines, helm, and sails. A ship, if left to herself in a seaway will usually fall off until she has the sea abaft the beam, the propeller acting as a drag and holding her stern-up. In this position she will roll deeply, but easily, and will drift to leeward, leaving a comparatively smooth wake on the weather beam and quarter.

If a ship rolls dangerously, she may be kept away more from the wind and sea by using a drag over the stern, or by turning over the engines just fast enough to give her steerageway; for it seems to be established, as the result of experience, that a steamer may safely run with the sea aft or quartering, *provided she runs very slowly.* Clearly this is not "running" in the old sense of that term, according to which a vessel going before the sea was forced to her utmost speed with the idea of keeping ahead of the waves, which were expected to "poop" her if they overtook her. It is evident from the statements of a large number of shipmasters who have tried the experiment of slowing down or stopping when running before a heavy sea, that this maneuver, so far from resulting in the disaster which many seamen would expect from it, had an extraordinary effect in easing the ship and keeping her dry.

The explanation of this seems to be that a ship running at high speed through the water draws a wave after her which follows under her counter and rolls along toward the waist on either side, tending continually to curl over and break on board. This wave is reduced to insignificant proportions in running dead slow.

9.23 Roll and Pitch Another point which enters into the behavior of a vessel going before the sea is that as she rolls and pitches she buries first one bow and then the other, increasing the pressure on the bow so buried. If she is being driven through the water, her head will be forced off, first to one side and then to the other, causing her to yaw badly with a continual tendency to broach to. This cannot be met by the rudder because, at the very time the bow is buried, the stern is lifted more or less out of the water, and the rudder loses, for the moment, its steering power. As the stern is lifted, there also comes a racing of the propeller which is in itself a serious danger at high speed. There seems no question that the dangers connected with running, so far from being increased, are greatly reduced, if not altogether removed, by slowing or stopping.

It will of course be understood that in this matter, as in all others connected with seamanship, due regard must be had for the peculiarities of the individual ship and that the maneuver which is safest for a majority of ships may be dangerous for certain ones. Thus a ship whose cargo may shift should not be allowed to roll excessively; nor should a warship whose heavy guns or missiles are carried high above the center of gravity. On whatever course the vessel may be kept, this rule may be regarded as of universal application; that, other things being equal, *the lower the speed at which she is run, the easier she will ride.*

9.24 Relationship between Ship and Waves   Attention is invited here to an important relationship, not always recognized, between a ship and the waves in which she floats. For every ship (in a given condition as to trim, etc.) there is a perfectly definite "rolling period"; a period in which she will make a complete roll, *without regard to whether she is rolling 10 degrees or 40.* So, also, in the case of a seaway, there is usually a fairly regular interval of time between wave crests passing a given point. If the point is a ship in motion, her motion may increase or decrease the interval between the waves so far as she herself is concerned; but this will not change the *regularity* of the interval. If it happens that this interval coincides with that required for the ship to complete a roll, each wave as it passes her will add its rolling impulse to the accumulated effect of those which have preceded it, and the ship will roll more and more deeply until she reaches *the maximum roll of which she is capable.* She will not capsize (if properly designed and undamaged) because there are forces at work to resist the rolling, and these increase as the depth of roll increases, until the rolling forces and the resisting forces balance. But she will continue to roll to the maximum limit until something is done to break up the synchronism between her period and that of the sea. This can be accomplished, *provided the ship has headway,* by changing the course or the speed, thus changing not the real, but the apparent, period of the waves. By running more nearly into the sea—meeting the waves—the apparent period is shortened; by running more nearly before it, the period is lengthened; but in either case it is *changed* and will no longer agree with the rolling period of the ship. The same effect is produced by a change of speed. If, therefore, it is judged from the violence of the rolling on a given course that the period of the waves is coinciding with that of the ship, the course or speed or both should be changed.

A ship making high speed in the direction of a heavy sea or swell may take a sheer and roll very severely. This has happened to destroyers during high-speed trials, with men being washed overboard and lost, as the ship, without warning, took a maximum roll. A moderate following sea, accompanied by a less obvious swell from a slightly different direction can occasionally coincide or harmonize, producing a very large sea astern which, if the helmsman is not alert and experienced, can produce the sudden roll mentioned above. Vigilance by the conning officer and good steering are the obvious preventions in addition, of course, to keeping men off the weather decks.

The length of the ship as compared with that of the waves is also a very important factor in the behavior of the ship, especially when she is running more or less with the waves or meeting them. It often happens that a small ship in a long sea will be perfectly comfortable where a larger and longer ship may be less so. The small craft climbs up and slides down the waves, accommodating herself to their slopes, and pitching only as the slope changes; but the longer craft, partially spanning the crests and the hollows of the waves alternately, one end being poised on the crest of one wave while the other end is buried in the adjoining one, may be making very heavy weather. A few years ago a large aircraft carrier in the Philippines was badly battered by a typhoon, but a destroyer escort, which passed through the same gale at very nearly the same place, was perfectly comfortable.

9.25 Bringing a Ship Bows-On   If, when a steamer is before the sea or in the trough, it is decided to bring her up to it, bows-on, she should first be slowed until she has barely steerageway, and should then be brought up as gradually as possible. To put the wheel over with considerable speed on and bring her up with a rush—slapping the sea in the face, as it were—could result in serious damage. After getting her up to the sea bows-on, the greatest watchfulness is required, first, to avoid falling off into the trough of the sea, as she will try to do the moment she loses way; and second, to avoid driving into the heavy, breaking seas, which will threaten her now and again. There is reason to believe that many of the phenomenal "tidal waves" reported as having suddenly overwhelmed steamers in mid-oceans have been simply the exceptionally heavy waves which build up from time to time in any long-continued gale; and that their destructive power was due to the fact that the vessels were driven into them instead of being allowed to drift before them and ride over them unresistingly. An officer should always be kept at the engineroom telegraphs, in lying to bows-on, and an engineer standing by below, to **obey bridge signals instantly. So long as she heads up to it, the more** slowly she turns over, the better. If a heavy sea is seen bearing down upon her, she should be stopped altogether. If she falls off, it will be necessary to increase the speed a little to bring her up, but she must be slowed again as soon as possible.

9.26 Using a Sea Anchor With small ships, and especially with yachts, a sea anchor has been used with good results. Such a ship, riding to leeward of a sea anchor of fair size with an oil bag hauled out to a block on the hawser well clear of the stem, and drifting slowly astern, will ride out almost any gale with safety and comfort. Indeed, as has been said above, this is the ideal position, in very bad weather, for any vessel which can be made to take and keep it. It is doubtful if a large steamer could be made to do this without the use of an anchor too unwieldy to be handled conveniently in a heavy gale.

9.27 Practical Sea Anchors In cases where a light drag is needed and no sea anchor is available, a boat may be used, with a hawser made fast to a span from the bow and stern ringbolts, and to a belly band amidships. A long spar (or a number of spars lashed together) may be used, also slung by a span. If a heavy awning can be added to such an improvised anchor, it will help to break the sea.

There are cases recorded of vessels having been kept head to sea by paying out their chain cables, unbent from the anchors. Where the water is shallow enough for the chains to drag on the bottom, they are especially helpful. A good-sized manila hawser, paid out *on the bight,* both ends being kept on board, makes a very convenient drag—perhaps the most convenient that could be devised. With both ends leading in through the stern chocks, it would be extremely helpful for holding her stern-on, and with one end at the stern and the other at some point near the beam, she could be held with the sea on the quarter. A block on the hawser would admit of reeving a line for hauling oil bags out and in.

In twin-screw ships, the propellers have not as much drag as with single screws, and such ships can sometimes be held up the sea without being driven into it dangerously, by turning over the lee screw very slowly. This is often the best way to lay a twin-screw ship to, although there is nothing in the nature of the case to prevent such a ship from riding easily with the sea astern or quartering.

9.28   The Calming Effect of Oil   The effect of oil in calming a rough sea has been known from the earliest times. The action of the oil is not only to prevent the breaking of waves, but to a considerable extent also to prevent them from forming. Its effect, when used on an angry sea, is described by all who have tried it as magical. Even in a surf, while it cannot altogether prevent the waves from breaking as they are driven in upon the shoals, it greatly reduces their violence and will often enable a boat to land when otherwise this would be out of the question.

Almost any kind of oil will give good results, but some kinds are very much better than others. Animal and vegetable oils are best; for example, sperm, porpoise, linseed, olive, and cotton seed; and fairly thick and heavy oils are better than lighter ones. Oil of turpentine is probably the best of all. Mineral oils are much less effective; however, a very thick sticky oil, or one that tends to thicken or congeal in cold weather, may be improved by thinning with petroleum. Soapsuds has a remarkable effect in preventing the formation of waves, but it does not keep them from breaking when formed.

Any method will answer for dispersing the oil which produces a slow and steady flow. A convenient way is to fill the closet bowls with oakum and oil, or to place a slightly opened can where it will give a slow drip into the bowls and out through the waste-pipes. A still simpler way and one frequently used is to fill a canvas bag, 1 to 2 feet square, with oakum and oil, and punch a number of holes through the canvas with a sail needle. Such a bag may be hung over the side at any point where it is found to give the best result. The quantity used need not exceed a few gallons—4 or 5 at most—even for a large ship riding out a prolonged gale.

It should be noted that the rate at which the oil spreads is slow in comparison with the speed even of a vessel drifting. Thus a vessel lying with engines stopped can make a "slick" to windward but not to leeward—except, perhaps, very close alongside—because she drifts faster than the oil can spread. So, in running, a vessel can leave a slick astern and to some extent on either hand, but can do nothing to calm the waves ahead of her. She can, therefore, avail herself of the benefits of oil if she is running more or less before the sea, but not at all if steaming into it.

9.29   Summary   We may sum up the various methods of handling a ship in heavy weather with the statement that the ship will usually be safest and most comfortable when stern-to, or nearly stern-to, to the sea, and *drifting before it.*

If, by the use of sails, a drag, or any other means, she can be held bows-on, *while being still allowed to drift,* this is probably the best way to lay her to; but if she cannot be held up without being forced into the sea, it will be because of the natural drag of the stern and propeller, and in this case advantage should be taken of this drag to hold her more or less directly stern-on, letting her drift in this way.

Even if the position she takes up in drifting is nearly in the trough of the sea, it will usually be found that she is easier in this position than in any other; however, the use of oil, as described above, is especially important in such cases.

If the position which she takes in drifting proves to be one in which she rolls dangerously, then she may run fast enough to steer, *but no faster,* and so keep the course which is found most comfortable.

Remember that it is the occasional large storm wave with the vertical face that presents the greatest danger. These waves are much bigger than their fellows and can pitchpole a yacht or small steamer end over end or roll it over. A few people have survived this experience, which has been reported most often in the immense waves of the Roaring Forties in the Southern Hemisphere. These freak waves occur even in moderate seas.

One final word of caution. The effect of "free surface" water in bilges and compartments is particularly important during heavy weather when a ship's stability is severely tested. Pumps must be kept operable to remove water; electrical switchboards must be kept dry. This points up to the need for making watertight closures well in advance of the onset of the worst part of the gale. To minimize free surface effect (see Chapter 2) it is advisable, particularly when bad weather is expected, to keep all tanks containing liquid either full or empty.

Docking, Mooring, and Anchoring— Handling Alongside

Mooring Lines

The lines used to secure the ship to a wharf, pier, or another ship are called *mooring lines*. Five-inch manila or smaller nylon is used for mooring lines in destroyers or smaller vessels. Larger ships may use 8-inch or even 10-inch lines. The manila lines may be reinforced or replaced by heavier lines or wire hawsers when the ship is finally securing alongside. Nylon lines are common now for all types of ships.

The mooring line which runs through the bull nose or chock near the eyes of the ship is called the *bowline*. The corresponding line aft is the *stern line*. These lines should lead well up the dock to reduce the fore-and-aft motion of the ship. Other mooring lines are either *breast lines* or *spring lines*. They are called bow, waist, or quarter breasts and springs, depending on the part of the ship from which they are run. Breast lines are run at right angles to the keel and prevent a ship from moving away from the pier.

Spring lines leading forward away from the ship at an angle with the keel are forward (bow, waist or quarter) springs. Those leading aft are aft (bow, waist or quarter) springs. Springs leading forward or aft prevent a vessel from moving aft or forward, respectively.

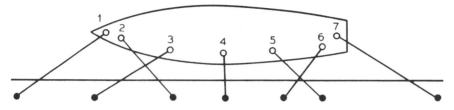

Fig. 10.1 (1) Bowline; (2) after bow spring; (3) forward bow spring; (4) waist breast; (5) after quarter spring; (6) forward quarter spring; (7) stern line.

If a ship moves ahead or astern with lines out, a breast may become a spring, and spring lines may change their leads. In the U.S. Navy, to prevent confusion and to add to the efficiency of line handling, lines are numbered from forward aft, according to the position where they are secured aboard ship. A ship may use fewer or more lines as necessary in which case the numbers are changed accordingly. The names are used after the ship is secured and the use and lead of each line becomes definite. Figure 10.1 shows the names and numbers for seven mooring lines.

Lines can be of the greatest assistance in making or clearing a pier. Prior to a ship coming alongside, the required lines with eye splices or bowlines in the ends should be led through the chocks up and over the lifelines. Heaving lines that have been successfully passed should be made fast near the splice and not at the end of the bight where they will become jammed when the eye is placed over the bollard. Heaving lines should be passed as soon as possible; then the heavy lines, the bights of which are necessarily hard to handle, may be run later when the vessel is farther up the pier and nearer her berth.

As a large ship works her way up the pier or into the slip, the lines should be *fleeted* up the pier in short steps, thus keeping them in position for use.

If two bights or eye splices are to be placed over the same bollard, the second one must be led up and through the eye of the first and then placed over the bollard. This makes it possible for either to be cast off independently of the other. This is called *dipping the eye*.

The ship in Fig. 10.2(a) is lying off a pier with a bow breast line secured to a bollard. If the line is led to a winch and a strain put on it, the bow will swing toward the pier, and the stern will move out. It should be noted, however, that the stern does not go out as much as the bow comes in. Because the ship is not held rigidly at the pivoting point, the mass as a whole will respond to the force acting on the bow, and the resultant motion will be like that shown in the figure.

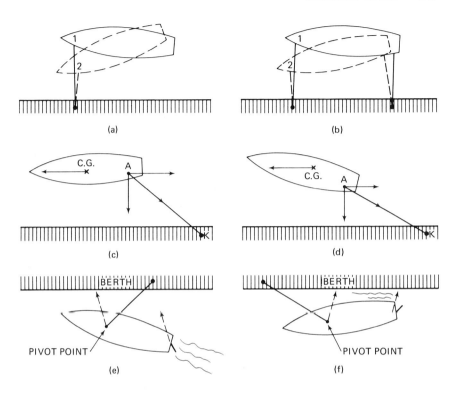

Fig. 10.2 Handling ship around a pier.

If, in the above case, the stern is held by a line to the pier as shown in (b), the pivot is transferred to the stern, and the whole ship moves toward the dock. This requires much greater effort than to turn the ship near her natural pivoting point as in (a).

If the bow and quarter breasts are hove in at the same time, the ship will be breasted in bodily but at greater expenditure of work than in the preceding cases.

If the ship has way on, either ahead or astern, her momentum **enters into the problem of her behavior. In Fig. 10.2(c), the ship** is moving forward parallel to the face of the pier (with engines stopped and rudder amidships). The after quarter spring AK is taut. The motion of the ship will be that resulting from her momentum along the original course and the tension along AK. The tension on AK may be resolved into two components. One retards the ship along the line of her original course and thus directly opposes the momentum, and the other moves her toward the pier. The stern will swing in and the bow out. It is important to note, however, that the momentum which is concentrated at the center of gravity forward of the pivot (A) opposes the turning and tends to keep the ship parallel. Thus, as a matter of fact, the ship does not turn much but comes in nearly parallel to the pier as shown in Fig. 10.2(d).

The vessel in Figs. 10.2(c) and (d) could go ahead on her engine(s) and put her rudder left to throw her head in. Since the steering effect of the rudder is due to the discharge current against the rudder and since the stern cannot move to starboard because it is held by the spring, left rudder can have comparatively little turning effect. Right rudder, on the other hand, will help to throw the stern in.

If in Fig. 10.2(a) the rudder is put left, it will throw the stern out and increase the rapidity with which the bow turns in. If put right, it will oppose the turning but not enough to overcome it.

In any case, if the line is made fast at the ship's natural pivoting point, and the engine(s) are turned over ahead or astern, the ship will spring in bodily. Her heading can be controlled by putting the rudder over, which throws the stern to either side, as desired. The ship swings under the influence of the rudder while coming bodily in on the spring, and it is often possible to come alongside quickly and smartly **by using this line only as shown in Fig. 10.2(e) and 10.2(f).**

In securing alongside a dock, wharf, or pier, special attention must be paid to the state and range of the tide. When securing at high water, enough slack must be left in the lines to ensure that at low tide they will not part, carry away bollards, or in extreme cases list the ship to a dangerous degree or even capsize small vessels.

10.1 Making Landings The names *dock, pier, and wharf* are used almost interchangeably. These are all structures connected to the shore with enough water up to them for vessels to come in or alongside. A pier is built at right angles to the shore; a wharf is parallel. Both are sometimes called docks, although strictly speaking a dock is a structure used for drydocking a vessel. The space between neighboring piers is called a *slip*.

Wharves and piers may be built on piles which allow a fairly free flow of water under them and in the slips between them. Their underwater construction may be solid, in which case there will be no current inside the slips, but eddies of various sorts may be found. Warehouses or other buildings may be built on them which may result in varying the effect of the wind on the upperworks of a vessel.

Wind and current at right angles to a pier are always more dangerous than when they are blowing or running respectively along its face. In coming alongside the conditions of wind and current existing

Orders to the Men at the Lines

Command	Meaning
Pass one (or number one)	Send line number one over to the pier. Place the eye over the bollard or cleat but do not take a strain.
Slack (slack off) the bowline (number one):	Pay out the line specified, allowing it to form an easy bight.
Take a strain on one (or number one):	Put number one line under tension.
Take in the slack on three (or number three):	Heave in on number three line but do not take a strain.
Ease three:	Pay out number three enough to remove most of the tension.
Avast heaving:	Stop heaving (taking in).
Check three:	Hold number three line but not to the breaking point, letting the line slip as necessary.
Hold two:	**Take enough turns so that the line will not slip.**
Double up and secure:	Run additional lines or bights of lines as needed to make the mooring secure.
Single up:	Take in all lines but a single standing part to each station, preparatory to getting under way.
Stand by your lines:	Man the lines, ready to cast off or moor.
Take in one (or number one):	Retrieve line number one after it has been cast off. When used by the conning officer it means to slack one, cast it off, and then pull it back abroad. When used by the officers in charge on the forecastle it is preceded by the commands "slack one" and "cast off one" and means merely to retrieve line number one and bring it back on deck.
Cast off:	A command *to those tending the mooring lines on the pier or on another ship* to disengage or throw off the lines from over the bollards or cleats.

should be observed carefully, and they should be used to assist when possible. Several cases of going alongside under different conditions of wind and current will be discussed.

It is of initial importance in making landings to make a plan in advance, showing the approach course and the point at which to reduce speed and/or stop engines, in order to avoid making the final landing with too much headway. This applies particularly if the wind or current are from astern.

10.2 Going Alongside—No Set On or Off the Pier (Single-Screw Vessel) A single-screw (right-handed) vessel can make a landing to port with little difficulty under these conditions. The ship should be headed for a point a short distance outboard of the place where the bridge will be when the ship is secured. The course of the approach should be at an angle of 10 or 15 degrees with the face of the pier. Slow speed should be used, and the engines should be stopped when there is sufficient headway to reach the berth. Enough headway to steer should be retained when the ship is almost abreast of her berth; the engine can be backed to stop the ship and to swing her stern to port and then parallel the pier. The ship can then be breasted in by the mooring lines and winches. If a single-screw ship must go alongside to starboard, the angle of approach should be about 10 degrees. The speed should be less than that used for a port landing but still enough to keep the ability to steer. As the bow approaches the pier the rudder should be put over to port (and, if necessary, the engine be given a kick ahead) to swing the bow away from, and the stern towards, the pier. Just before the ship is parallel to the pier the engine should be backed and the sideways force from the propeller should then counter the ship's swing so that she is stopped parallel with the pier abreast her berth. The point for which the ship should be headed during the approach should be the final position of the bridge when secured.

The port anchor may be dropped at short stay during the early part of the approach. The anchor is then dragged over the ground. The anchor will add to the steering ability, reduce the speed of the ship, and give the master better control of the bow and the stern when the final landing is being made. The difficulty at that time is that reversing the engine will force the stern away from the pier and the bow toward the pier when a *close* landing is contemplated.

The engines should be stopped later than would be done with a port landing. The dragging anchor will enable the ship to be stopped without backing with much power or for a long time. The anchor will probably enable the master to lay the ship alongside her berth without backing at all or perhaps with just a touch astern.

Every effort should be made to get a stern line out as soon as possible so that this line can be held when the engine is backed and the stern prevented from swinging away from the pier.

10.3 Going Alongside, Port Side To—Being Set On to the Pier The point for which the ship should be headed at the start of the approach should be farther away from the pier than the one used with no set. The angle of approach should be 20 to 30 degrees, and the speed of approach should be higher than above without attempting a high-speed landing. The amount of set ought to be watched constantly. If it is apparent that the set is more than anticipated and that, if the ship continues, she will strike the pier, there are four choices:

1. Head farther away from the pier.
2. Back clear and try again.
3. Stop with the ship parallel to the pier while there is still some open water between the ship and the pier.
4. Proceed at greater speed in order to reduce the time during which the ship is subject to the wind and current.

The conditions near the berth, the proximity of the berth, and the course will determine what action is advisable. If there are ships alongside of the pier ahead and astern of the allotted berth, it is probably wise to head up or back clear and try again. If there is a clear space astern of the berth, it may be possible to make a landing short of the correct berth and, once alongside, move up to the berth. There is always the fourth choice in which case the discharge current from the backing screw may cushion the impact somewhat, if the pier is solid, as opposed to pile, construction. The aim should be to stop the ship, preferably by backing the outboard engine only, parallel to the berth and about 30 feet from it, if the wind is blowing strongly on shore. If she is brought up much further out she may gather excessive leeway before touching.

10.4   Going Alongside, Starboard Side To—Being Set On to the Pier
If a single-screw ship attempts a starboard landing with a set on to the pier and finds that she is too close, the four choices of action are still available but number 2 should be changed to: Stop with the ship heading slightly away from the pier. In this position she can back, and in so doing, the stern will swing away from the pier. The ship will parallel the pier, lose her headway, and the discharge current will cushion the impact. The first choice, to head up, is not as satisfactory as before because the original approach course should make a smaller angle of about 10 degrees with the face of the pier. There is not as great an angle through which to head up as was available in a port landing.

10.5   Going Alongside a Pier—Being Set Off   If the wind is blowing off the berth it is essential to keep the bows well up to the pier until a line is passed. Once the bow has drifted outside the throw of a heaving line the situation can seldom be recovered except by a tug. It is therefore better to approach at a rather greater angle than in calm weather, to head initially for the nearer end of the berth and to get the bowline passed at the first opportunity. Should it be seen that the vessel is being set off the pier, the ship's head can be pointed well up into the pier and the approach made with more speed. The bowlines are gotten out, and when close to the pier, the rudder is put away from the pier. For a single-screw vessel, port side to, the landing is easily made by backing down on the screw. For a single-screw vessel making a pier to starboard, the approach should be made by snubbing the port anchor as previously described. In addition to snubbing the port anchor, a starboard quarter breast can be used to hold in the stern as the ship forges slowly ahead on it. In a twin-screw vessel, the outboard engine is backed.

10.6 Going Alongside—Current from Ahead When a current is running parallel to a wharf, the ship should be headed into the current and then brought alongside. Slack water is the most favorable condition; yet the current, if not too great, can be used and the berthing accomplished without trouble, except in the case of the largest vessels. With current from ahead, a vessel can use more speed through the water without increasing its speed relative to the wharf; therefore, the ship will have better rudder control.

The ship, making little headway along the face of the wharf, is brought in fairly close and parallel. The vessel must not be canted in because she might come in too fast and cause damage. A forward bow spring is sent well ahead and up the wharf.

When the ship is in position relative to the pier, all forward motion relative thereto is stopped, and the vessel is slowly dropped back on the spring. The amount of tension on this spring determines the rapidity with which the ship drifts in to the wharf. The rudder may be used to swing the stern.

Should the current be very strong, the ship should go a little way above the wharf and drop the outboard anchor. A forward bow spring should be run ashore. By veering chain and holding the spring, the ship will swing slowly in toward the wharf. By using the rudder and adjusting the strain on the anchor chain, perfect control can be maintained. When alongside, a bow breast and forward quarter spring are got out as soon as possible.

10.7 Going Alongside—Current from Astern Making a pier or wharf with a fair current is difficult and should be avoided when possible. If there is swinging room and if other reasons do not forbid, much time and fuel will be saved and danger avoided by dropping an anchor, swinging with the tide, and making the pier as previously described with the current from ahead. If this is not practicable, tugs should be used if available. If a tug is not available, the approach should be made as slowly as possible and as near to the pier as is safe. When about in position, the bow is canted out a few degrees from the pier. An after quarter spring is got out as soon as possible and the engines backed to keep from parting the line. Backing on the inboard engine of a twin-screw ship forces more water between the pier and the ship, thus cushioning her as she comes in. Care must be taken to prevent the stern from swinging away from the pier. The use of after spring lines and stern lines with the outboard engine backing will prevent this movement.

10.8   Clearing a Pier—No Wind and No Current   Clearing a pier is less difficult than making a pier. The first step is to slack all lines carefully and observe the effect. If the ship does not drift out, it will be necessary to force the stern away from the pier.

In a single-screw ship with the starboard side to the pier, the engine is backed. This swings the stern rapidly to port. If the bow is forced into the pier, right rudder is used to clear it as the ship goes astern. When the stern is about 50 feet out, the bow will be pointed in toward the pier. A quarter breast which becomes a spring as the ship continues to go slowly astern is now held. This action will bring the bow out. When pointed fair, the ship casts off and goes out ahead.

If the port side is to the pier, an after bow spring is used as the ship goes ahead slowly on it. Left rudder throws the stern well out. The ship is cast off and backed down slowly with right full rudder until clear. As the stern will gradually turn in toward the pier, it will be necessary to stop when parallel to the pier and several beams' width out from it. The vessel now goes ahead with right rudder, and the bow falls off as required.

A twin-screw vessel can shove off from a pier easiest by holding the after bow spring and slacking off all other lines. The outboard engine is turned over, slow ahead, until the inboard propeller is clear of the pier. Fenders can be used as necessary on the bow. Once the inboard propeller is free, let go all lines, and back both engines slow. The discharge current from the inboard propeller will breast the vessel out, particularly if the pier is a solid one. The officer conning should glance aft to note any tendency of his ship to start swinging either way. He should use the engines for steering until sufficient sternway is reached when the rudder can be used. The distance between the pier and the bow should be noted and the rate of turn regulated to prevent touching. The inboard screw discharge current when it reaches the bow tends to keep the bow off.

10.9 Clearing a Pier—Being Set On This is a difficult situation. To go out ahead without the use of tugs or an outlying anchor is risky. The ship must be taken out astern. A single-screw ship with her starboard side to the pier should go ahead on an after bow spring, and when the stern is well out, cast off and go astern full. If she is port side to, it is advisable to wait for a change in conditions.

If no tugs are available, and no anchor has been dropped, and the after bow spring proves ineffective, it is possible for a small ship to cast her stern well out by running a line from right forward to a point well inside the pier. When the engine(s) are backed the bow will be hauled into the pier and the ship will pivot on them as she tries to align herself with the pull of the line. She will gather sternway more rapidly on slipping than she would do if the after bow spring was used and she is therefore less liable to scrape her bow heavily on the pier before getting clear.

If only one tug is available to get the ship away from the pier in an onshore wind, she should tow outwards from a point fairly well forward, between the stern and amidships. As the tug begins to haul off, the ship should work her engines and rudder as necessary to swing the stern out. The ship then moves bodily outwards. In a single screw ship some headway will be gained by the need to go ahead with the rudder hard over towards the pier.

A twin-screw vessel should first go ahead on the outboard engine, holding the after bow spring. This will throw the stern out against the set. Then the ship should cast off the spring and back immediately on both engines. The wash of the inboard engine will tend to keep her off, and the speed of the inboard engine can be varied to keep the bow clear.

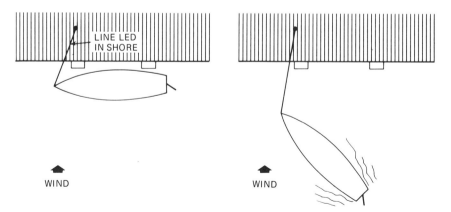

Fig. 10.3 Clearing a pier—being set on.

10.10   Clearing a Pier—Being Set Off   If the ship tends to drift out when all lines are slacked, the clearing of the pier is very simple. Continued slacking away on the lines will ease the ship off the pier. All lines are then cast off and the ship can proceed.

10.11   Clearing a Wharf—Current from Ahead   Ease off on all lines except the forward quarter spring. The stern will come in and the bow will go out where it will catch more of the current. While going ahead very slowly to keep the stern and the propellers away from the wharf, the bow will continue to swing. When far enough out, the ship may cast off all lines and proceed.

Should the stern not be clear to go ahead on the engines, a bow breast should be kept under a light strain, and when the ship is headed correctly, the breast should be checked while slacking the quarter spring. The stern will swing out and clear, and all lines can then be cast off and the engines put ahead. To use the bow breast in this manner, the bow must be farther out than the stern; otherwise the ship will come back alongside.

Should the wind prevent the bow from falling off, it will be necessary to go out astern as previously described for a ship being set on to the wharf.

10.12   Clearing a Wharf—Current from Astern   Holding an after bow spring and easing out on a quarter breast will let the stern swing outward. When pointed correctly all lines are cast off, and the ship goes out astern.

10.13   Working into a Slip   The best time for entering a slip is when the water is slack. The procedure is the same as in making a pier. In entering, an anchor under the forefoot for snubbing is of great assistance, since it gives greater steering control.

Should there be a good current running, the docking should be done with tugs; but if they are not available, the ship can make a landing on the end of the pier, heading into the current.

The ship is then warped into the slip. The springs for this purpose should be as short as possible to reduce the radius of the swing and should be as nearly perpendicular to the keel lines as practicable to produce the best springing effect. To protect the ship's side and the pier, a camel or suitable fenders are placed at the knuckle of the pier where the pressure is localized. The camel will distribute this pressure over many of the ship's frames, thereby preventing the crushing of them. The ship goes slowly ahead until the knuckle of the pier is amidships. Then the after bow spring is held and the rudder is thrown hard over toward the pier, aiding in the turn. After entering the slip, if being set off, the lines should be got out and walked up the pier in short steps and used as necessary to hold the ship in. If being set on, lines are run to the opposite side of the slip.

When backing into the slip the same principles of using the springs apply. The lines, especially the bow breasts, must be very strong, and good seamanship dictates that more than one be run. The additional ones are preventers and are used as alternates in the shifting of the lines for better leads. The vessel is dropped back until the knuckle of the pier is amidships, and with the quarter spring held the bow breast is eased. When the ship is pointed correctly, the engine is backed slowly. Deck winches are a help and almost a necessity in the case of a single-screw ship backing to starboard.

The most difficult problem is making a landing on the upstream side of a slip, with the wind and current from the same direction and at right angles to the pier, its underwater structure solid, and a large warehouse built upon it. Under these conditions entering the slip at slow speed will invariably result in the ship's stern being swept across to the other side of the slip before it can be controlled, with almost certain damage to the ship, the pier, or other shipping. Such a landing is sometimes possible with a high-powered vessel by entering the slip at a high enough speed so that the stern will be out of the effect of wind and current before it can be swept across the slip and then backing full to kill the headway. Such a maneuver requires expert judgment as to the instant of backing and perfect coordination with the engine room in order to avoid ramming the head of the slip.

10.14   Mooring to a Buoy   The ship should approach slowly with the current from ahead, and the buoy should be kept on a constant bearing. The buoy should be picked up on the lee bow if there is any wind so that the bow will drift toward it rather than away. It may be wiser to pick it up on the starboard bow in the case of a single-screw ship because of the tendency of her bow to drift to starboard when the engine is backed.

Most large ships moor by shackling the end of the chain, unbent from an anchor, to the ring of the buoy. Small ships may pass the end of the chain through the ring, haul it in, secure it on deck, and ride to the bight, but this is not recommended because the chain can be damaged where it is passed through the ring. In case the mooring is made habitually, a heavy wire mooring pendant with an eye and shackle on the end may be made up. In any case a hook rope is first passed to hold the bow in position while the moor is being made, and a man is placed on the buoy to handle lines and shackle up. Under favorable conditions, the man can be lowered over the bow and the hook rope passed down to him, but it is better to send him to the buoy in a boat. The same boat can carry the hook rope and a messenger fastened to the end of the chain. The hook rope is secured first. Care should be taken not to put too much strain on it or the buoy may be capsized and the man working on it thrown into the water. Next the messenger is run from underneath through the ring and brought back on deck to the capstan. The messenger is used to haul the end of the chain down to or through the ring. The shackle and pin, if used, can be taken in the boat or preferably lowered from the bow with lines, thus making it easier for the man on the buoy to handle them.

Some destroyers send out the bight of a heaving line in a boat. The bight has been cut and a ring and snaphook inserted. The man in the boat reeves one end of the heaving line through the ring on the buoy and snaps the ends together. The mooring party on the forecastle hauls the heaving line through the ring rapidly. A heavier messenger follows as the ship approaches the buoy. The anchor has been secured and enough chain roused up to allow the end to be reeved through the bull nose and to hang down to the water. As the ship gets closer to the buoy, the messenger which is made fast to the end of the chain is hove in. The chain reeves up through the ring on the buoy and is hove up on deck and secured. Such a mooring can be made in 1 to 2 minutes. It is important in all moorings to bring the ship up to the buoy and not attempt to pull the buoy to the ship.

Large ships, such as cruisers, with heavy chains usually moor close to the buoy with a wire. The anchor chain is then shackled to the wire and slides down the wire where it is made fast to the ring on the buoy.

A buoy can be picked up with a fair tide under some circumstances. It will require skillful shiphandling and speedy work by the man on the buoy unless the ship has twin rudders. When the vessel swings, it may put a severe strain on the moorings. In some cases, time will be saved if it is possible to drop an anchor, swing, and pick up the buoy with the current from ahead.

The need for veering chain when moored to a buoy during adverse weather is most important. If the ship is snubbed up close, the pull is generally upward, tending to break the buoy loose from its moorings. In addition, the lack of substantial weight of chain permits the transfer of the ship movements to the buoy to be horizontal with the weight of chain providing a cushion for the surges. Scopes as great as 45 fathoms have been used to good advantage, and where circumstances permit, the chain to the mooring buoy should be veered to produce a catenary such that the chain is never straightened out by the ship's movements. The Hammerlock Moor can also be used at a buoy to control "horsing," but care must be exercised to veer adequate chain before dropping the anchor to ensure that it is dropped well outside the anchor clump to which the buoy is secured. (Paragraph 10.27.)

10.15 Slipping a Mooring   A strong manila line or flexible wire is run through the buoy ring and back on deck to use as a slip rope. A strain is taken on it, and the chain is unshackled. Should the ship be riding to a bight of the chain, an easing-out line is used to ease the chain through the ring while the chain is hauled in. The ship is now riding to the slip rope, and unmooring is completed by letting the end of the slip rope go and reeving it through the buoy ring.

10.16 Mooring to Buoys, Bow and Stern   It is sometimes necessary to moor bow and stern to two mooring buoys in order to avoid any swing in a restricted space. When possible, the approach should be made against the current and on the side from which any wind or current present will tend to set the ship down on the line of buoys. The bow is moored to the upstream buoy in the usual manner. Meanwhile another boat should be used to carry a line to the second buoy to hold the ship's stern from swinging off. This line should be no heavier than necessary so that it can be handled easily, and care must always be taken to keep it way from the screws. The end of a wire of sufficient strength may then be carried out and shackled to the buoy ring. The first line may be taken in or kept as a preventer and for use in unmooring. The final moor should be taut in order to prevent the vessel from ranging ahead or astern. This may be ensured by heaving in on the stern line with an after winch or by veering on the buoy chain, taking in the required amount of stern line, and then heaving taut on the chain.

10.17 Winding Ship   It is seldom necessary to wind ship at a pier. When it must be done, the most satisfactory method is by the use of tugs, especially in the case of large ships. Tugs give better control and assist the engines to turn the ship. With a small ship or when no tugs are available, it is quite possible to wind ship by the use of the engines or by taking advantage of the current.

It is safer to pivot on the bow and thus avoid possible damage to the rudder and screws against the pier. An after bow spring should always be held and the stern lines slacked or let go. With a current from astern the stern will usually start out by itself. With a single-screw ship, starboard side to, backing down slowly will usually start the stern out. If port side to, going ahead dead slow on the after bow spring will have the same effect. With a twin-screw ship, backing the inboard screw or going ahead on the outboard one or a combination of the

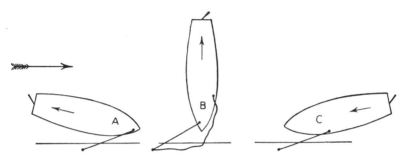

Fig. 10.4 Winding ship.

two should start the stern out. The swing is made on the after bow spring, but a forward bow spring on the other bow should be led from well aft to assist in controlling the swing and to take the strain after **the swing is past 90 degrees, as shown in (A) and (B) of Fig. 10.4. The** bow is kept clear of the pier by backing a little as needed. Should a strong current be running, a long after breast may be used to slow down the first part of the swing. During the latter part of the swing the engines may be used to slow the swing and to prevent the ship from slamming into the pier. After the winding is completed, the ship can be spotted in position with the engines or by hauling her ahead of the vessel's original position.

Anchoring

Letting go a single anchor is perhaps the simplest method of securing a ship to the bottom, and if the holding ground is good she should ride easily in bad weather provided ample scope of chain is used. The disadvantages are that in a strong current or in a gale she may sheer considerably, and also when a ship is anchored, it swings to the combined effects of the wind and current. Therefore it is necessary to have an unobstructed area equal to a circle whose radius is the length of the ship plus the scope of chain used. If, for some reason, the anchorage does not afford such an area, the ship must be moored.

10.18 Letting Go In modern ships with heavy ground tackle, the anchors are commonly housed in the hawse pipe and secured by chain stoppers which engage the chain by a slip or "pelican" hook. (See chapter 5.)

To ensure that an anchor will let go *immediately* after the housing chain stopper is released, prepare as follows: Connect up windlass wildcat, slack and release the outboard housing chain stopper and then engage the pelican hook of this housing chain stopper to the first horizontal chain link abaft the link previously engaged, release friction brake, heave in until windlass wildcat has the strain, cast off the after chain stopper(s), walk out anchor until the outboard housing chain stopper has the strain and there is one link of slack chain abaft stopper, set up friction brake lightly to prevent the slack chain from going into the chain locker, and disconnect windlass wildcat.

If the drift between the hawse pipe and the chain locker is considerable, it is well to rouse up a few links of chain and lighten the slack forward to a point just abaft the stopper. Care must be taken that all is clear below decks and in the chain locker.

To let go, the bale shackle pin is pulled out, and then the bale shackle of the chain stopper is knocked off the pelican hook with a sledge.

Always bear in mind that the anchors may be required unexpectedly when on soundings, in narrow channels, in restricted waters, or working around docks, etc. If they are ready for *instant* use, they may save worry and trouble. The anchor should always be let go with the ship moving slowly either ahead or astern, to avoid paying the chain down on top of the anchor.

10.19 Anchoring in Deep Water Where it becomes necessary to anchor in very deep water, it is absolutely essential that the ship should be going dead slow. As the anchorage is approached at very slow speed, the usual practice is to walk out the anchor to within 5 to 20 fathoms from the bottom at the proposed anchorage, fasten the stopper to the chain, and disengage the windlass, making the anchor ready for "letting go," and then let go. Maintain only enough headway to avoid paying the chain down on top of the anchor. The details of handling the windlass for anchoring in this way will vary with the type of windlass used, but it will be found that even where the ship is dead in the water and where the anchor is let go with only a few fathoms of drop, the weight of the chain alone will cause it to run out violently. In extreme cases, where the depths run to 40 and 50 fathoms, it may be advisable not to "let go" but to "walk out" the chain by the windlass engine until the anchor is on the bottom and the necessary scope of chain is out.

10.20   Anchoring at High Speed   If obliged to let go at a higher speed, or if for any reason it does not seem safe to check the ship with a short scope, the chain should be allowed to run until the ship loses her way sufficiently to make it safe to snub her. There is no great harm in running out 75 or even 90 fathoms of chain and afterward heaving in to a shorter scope; and it should be remembered that, in cases where the headway has to be checked by bringing up on the chain, the danger is less with a long scope than with a short one.

The danger connected with letting go while under considerable headway is often overlooked because the damage resulting does not necessarily show itself at once. The excessive strain may distort and weaken the links of the chain without actually parting them. The result is that the chain may give way at some time under a comparatively moderate stress. The practice of reducing the ship's headway by means of her ground tackle may introduce strains sufficient to cause fracture and will in any event be very apt to strain the chain beyond its maximum safe load equal to the proof load.

10.21   Scope of Chain for Maximum Holding   The scopes given in the following table are the "optimum" scopes for maximum holding. If longer scopes are used, the chain may be stressed beyond its safe service working load; if shorter scopes are used, the anchor will tend to drag before developing the full safe load on the chain. These figures apply substantially, regardless of the size of the ship, provided the ship is furnished with a properly balanced outfit of ground tackle and is given a safety factor of 4 on the ultimate strength of the chain. The scopes shown for the greatest depths could be obtained only by bending additional shots to the standard lengths of chain cable.

Scope Table

Chains	Depth in Fathoms (outboard lip of hawse pipe to bottom)									
	5	7½	10	15	20	25	30	35	40	45
Cast-steel chain (fathoms)	64	78	91	110	127	142	155	166	178	188
Die-lock N.E. steel chain or 1.25 manganese steel chain (fathoms)	74	90	104	127	146	164	178	192	204	216
Die-lock nickel steel chain (fathoms)	78	95	109	133	154	174	188	202	216	228

It is a common rule under ordinary circumstances to use a length of chain equal to five to seven times the depth of the water. This is satisfactory in depths of water not exceeding 18 fathoms. This amount of chain is perhaps enough for a ship riding steadily and without any great tension on her cable. On the other hand, if conditions necessitate, the chain should be veered when anchored in shallow depths to the maximum indicated in the scope table.

If greater holding power than that given by one anchor with the scope of chain shown in the table is necessary, it is better practice to drop a second anchor even with moderate scope of its chain than to rely upon the one anchor with a longer scope. Of course, in the case of extreme necessity when the greatest holding power is necessary, all anchors should be dropped and the chain veered the greatest possible scope. If there is ample sea room, it would be better to reduce the scope to the amounts shown in the table and accept the possibility of dragging anchor rather than risk breaking the chain.

10.22 Weighing Anchor   In heaving in, the windlass and chain can be relieved of considerable strain by a judicious use of the engines and rudder. To do this, the forecastle detail must keep the bridge fully informed as to how the chain "tends"; whether the chain is "taut" or "slack"; when the anchor is at "short stay"; when the chain is "up and down"; and when the anchor is "aweigh." As the anchor is hove in, the report is made to the bridge, "Anchor in sight, sir," "Clear or foul anchor," as the case may be; "Anchor clear of the water, sir," "Anchor is up, sir." The captain will then direct, "Secure the anchor" or "Make the anchor ready for letting go."

In case the chain tends across the bow, it may be cleared by stopping the windlass and going astern.

10.23 Foul Anchor   While modern double-fluke anchors are much less likely to foul than the old type, they occasionally give trouble in this way. A ship whose anchors house in the hawse pipes may be greatly embarrassed by the lack of facilities for lifting the anchor to a point where it can be hung securely and where the chain can be handled conveniently. As a rule in such cases, put a chain stopper on the chain, disengage the wildcat and let anchor go, engage wildcat, and heave in.

Under conditions such that the anchor may be expected to foul, it is a good rule to "sight" it frequently; and indeed this is advisable under any conditions when a ship remains at single anchor for a long time. It is especially important if bad weather is found to be approaching after lying for some time under circumstances which make it probable that the anchor may be foul. For sighting, the anchor may be weighed and another let go when the chain of the first one is "up and down."

An anchor sometimes becomes so well dug in or so fouled in rock or coral that it cannot be raised in a normal manner. Here the use of a wire strap around the crown may be needed. Anchorage charts often reveal locations where anchors have been lost, such as St. George's Channel, Bermuda. If necessary to anchor there it might be wise to consider fitting a crown strap and a buoyed work wire to the anchor before letting go. An anchor that has been lost with some chain attached can usually be recovered by the use of grapnels or an *anchor hawk*.

10.24   Riding to a Single Anchor   A vessel at single anchor in a strong tideway is likely to sheer considerably. This movement brings the current first on one side and then on the other and drives the vessel across the stream until brought up by her chain often with a violent shock. This may be prevented in a great measure by holding her with a steady sheer away from her anchor, by putting the rudder over as far as may be necessary, and keeping it there. The stern is driven over to one side and she is canted across the current and held there.

A ship is never in greater danger of dragging her anchor or parting her cable than when driving down with a slack chain, broadside on or partially so to wind or tide. Such a situation may of necessity arise in anchoring or may come about in sheering, as described above. It frequently happens in squally weather, where a ship swings in one direction during a lull just in time to be caught by a strong squall on the beam and be driven bodily off. It may be brought up with the chain taut across the stem.

In lying at an anchorage where such situations may arise, the greatest watchfulness should be exercised. Steam must be kept on the steering engine, a man must be at the wheel, an ample scope of chain should be veered, and a second anchor should always be ready for letting go at a moment's notice, even though there seems no chance of its being needed.

When the conditions are such that there is a possibility of dragging the anchor, a lookout should be posted to ensure instant notice if she begins to drag. The drift lead is useful, though not always to be trusted. This is a heavy lead kept on the bottom with its line made fast to some place well forward convenient for observation and left hanging with considerable slack. If the ship drags, the line tautens and tends ahead.

As long as a ship is fairly steady, a drift lead will usually give notice in case of dragging, but if she sheers about considerably, it cannot be relied upon. The farther forward it is used, the better, because the bow moves much less than the stern in sheering.

Good bearings of objects on shore are more reliable than the drift lead, and a range is best of all. Both of these are less trustworthy when the ship is sheering about than when she is steady because a range will open out when the ship swings and may seem to indicate that she is dragging. Its indications may be checked by watching the heading. Radar ranges to fixed objects ashore may also be used to detect dragging.

There are times when unexpected and unusual swells, seas, and currents set in toward an anchorage. In such cases the only thing to do is to get up steam promptly and shift to a safe anchorage or stand out to sea. The sailing directions should always be carefully read and every effort made to obtain the latest weather reports. There are also times when nearby ships will swing in opposite directions when there is little current or wind. In such cases each ship may heave in sufficient chain to avoid fouling; at other times one or more boats placed at the stern will exert sufficient power to push the ships clear or hasten their swing.

It is always advisable to keep a detachable link on deck where it can be reached conveniently for slipping suddenly if an emergency arises and to be sure that the pins can be driven out without difficulty. Tools for unshackling should be kept in a convenient place and never removed. A buoy and a buoy-rope at hand complete the preparations for slipping at short notice. In an exposed anchorage subject to sudden gales, these precautions are, of course, especially important.

If a vessel or other danger is seen drifting down upon you when lying at anchor in a tideway, by giving the ship a cant with the rudder thus bringing the current on the bow, and veering the anchor chain roundly, you may sheer well over across the tide and probably be clear of danger.

If an anchor is known to have dragged in a clay bottom, it should be picked up as quickly as possible; for it is certain to be "shod" (balled in mud) and to have lost much of its proper holding power. In letting go where the bottom is of this kind, it is important to give a good scope in the very beginning to prevent even the little dragging that is commonly to be expected as the anchor digs down to get its hold.

The plan of bending two cables together to obtain a "long scope" is not recommended if such a scope would result in exceeding the safe limit in the scope table. The fact must not be overlooked, however, that a defective link or shackle may result in disaster where a single cable is in use, and this may make it wise to let go a second anchor in cases where no chances can be taken. The vessel would then be moored.

Mooring with Anchors

A ship is moored when she has two anchors down at a considerable distance apart and with such scope of chain on each that she is held with her bow approximately midway between them. A ship so moored requires an unobstructed area reduced to a circle with a radius only slightly larger than the length of the ship.

10.25   Reasons for Mooring   There are two basic reasons for mooring: (1) To reduce the radius of the circle of the unobstructed area in which the ship will swing, by using an ordinary moor. Since it is desirable to make a taut moor under these conditions, the anchors should be so placed with respect to any current that a straight line connecting the two anchors would be parallel to the direction of current flow. (2) To snub the bow of a ship and prevent it from sheering in a current, gale, or hurricane, by using a bridle or hammerlock moor. Under these conditions, it is necessary to use a slack moor so the angle between the chains is about 90 degrees, and to place the anchors so that a straight line joining them would be perpendicular to the direction of current flow or expected wind.

10.26   The Ordinary Moor   In the ordinary moor the ship stands against the current (wind) to the proper position and lets go the first anchor which must always be the riding (upstream) anchor at that time. She veers on the riding chain, carefully laying out the chain so as to keep it taut and tending ahead as she drops down with the current (wind) to the position for letting go the lee or downstream anchor. When that position is reached, the second anchor is let go. She now veers on the lee chain and heaves in on the riding chain, taking care to lay the lee chain out properly until she is riding midway between both anchors with the desired scope of chain to each.

A mooring swivel is frequently used to prevent the anchor chains from fouling one another when a moored ship swings to the wind or current. When the mooring swivel is used, it is impossible to veer both chains.

10.27   The Bridle or Hammerlock Moor   In riding out a gale or hurricane, a vessel will often sheer violently back and forth across the wind (Fig. 10.5) and here the rudder has little effect in holding her with a steady sheer. This tacking back and forth is often called "horsing." Violent horsing can be cut in half by dropping a second anchor under foot with minimum scope out to it to act as a snubber, but even

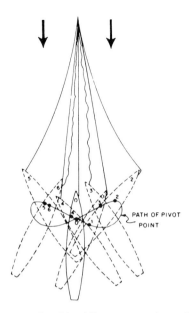

Fig. 10.5 Horsing movement of a ship riding to a single anchor. This diagram shows the violent figure-eight horsing motion of a ship riding with a long scope of chain out to a single anchor during a high wind.

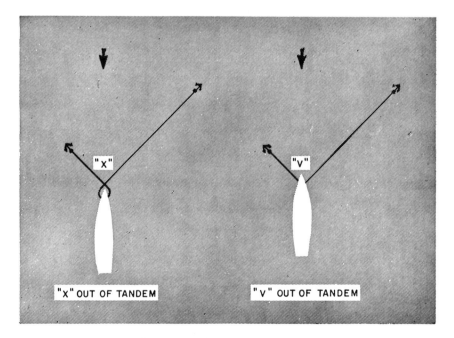

Fig. 10.6 Anchors acting as a bridle.

such reduced horsing may become excessive in a violent storm. In such cases, it is well to pick up the second anchor and redrop it at one extreme reach of a sheer, still using only a short scope, and then ride to this bridle (Fig. 10.6). The two chains will now work together to snub the bow and hold it steady. The "horsing" will be almost completely eliminated and the main engines can be used with precision to offset the greater portion of the wind. Should the wind be from a hurricane or typhoon, and should the bottom be sand or mud, it is sometimes feasible to permit the short-scope anchor to drag around as the wind veers or backs so that the open "X" or "V" of the bridle moor always faces the wind (Fig. 10.6). This bridle moor can be used whether the chains lead from the hawse in an open "V" or whether they cross the stem in an "X" (Fig. 10.7). Either position is satisfactory, but with preplanning as the hurricane approaches, it is naturally preferable to figure out which anchor should be used as the riding (long-scope) anchor in order to ride out the entire wind shift with an open "V" hawse as the short-scope anchor drags around.

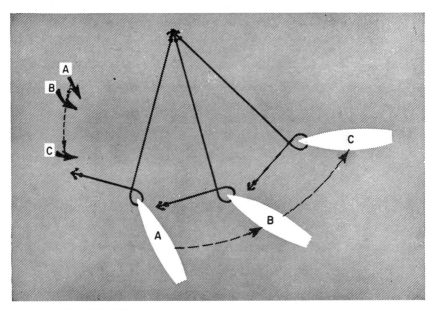

Fig. 10.7 Effect desired as short-scope anchor drags properly.

10.28 Going Alongside Another Vessel   In going alongside another ship at anchor or at a mooring buoy, the same general rules apply as for going alongside a pier. The anchored vessel may be riding to the current. Her stern should be watched carefully during the approach, as it may yaw, and allowance must be made for the effect of the wind. On the windward side, the ship coming alongside may expect to drift down fast on the anchored vessel. On the leeward side, a close approach must be made or the landing may be missed.

There is a double possibility of damage when going alongside another ship. Projections, such as bridge wings and sponsons, must be watched carefully to make sure they do not foul. There should be no **headway or sternway on the vessel coming alongside when she** finally touches. Fenders or puddings should be used by both ships and, if possible, should extend far enough horizontally to cover several frames.

In clearing from alongside another vessel, the same precautions should be observed. If the wind is favorable it may be possible to drift away from the anchored ship and go out ahead or astern as desired. If this cannot be done, it is usually handier to spring the stern out and back away, but when going out astern care must be taken not to rake the anchored vessel's side with the bow.

10.29 Destroyers and Destroyer Types   More naval officers learn practical shiphandling in destroyers than in any other type of vessel. This is especially true of coming alongside, as destroyers are often required to dock, go alongside tenders, or secure in nests at a mooring buoy. For this reason, it is well to note carefully some of the peculiarities of the type.

They are high-powered in comparison to their displacement and respond quickly to the engines. They have plenty of backing power. With one engine going ahead at one-third or two-thirds speed and the other backing, at the same speed, they will normally make headway if the backing revolutions have not been standardized. Destroyers have a narrow beam compared to their length; consequently the propeller shafts are close together. The fact that most of the after deadwood has been cut away gives these ships a small turning circle.

Most destroyers have more surface exposed to the wind forward than aft. This construction acts as a permanent head sail and gives the bow a tendency to fall off before the wind and the stern a tendency to back into it. The light construction of destroyers makes it imperative to avoid heavy pressures and sharp blows on their hulls when coming alongside. There is an understandable fascination in handling destroyers which often leads to the taking of unnecessary chances. A good destroyer officer is one who handles the power at his disposal daringly when he needs to do so, but does not invite disaster by rashness. It happens occasionally that an engine will not follow the signal through fault of personnel, and engine order telegraphs have been known to break down while on full speed ahead or astern. Should such an accident happen when the commanding officer is charging into a landing at high speed and trusting to his backing power to stop in time, merely to show himself to be a smart shiphandler, the result may be a smashed bow or some worse accident caused not by an effort to perform some important service but merely by bravado. Situations are sure to occur when the extra power available must be depended upon. It is the height of folly to invite more of them than necessary. Handle a destroyer with caution normally, and with boldness when necessary.

The light fittings, large power, and small lines make it especially important to exercise care in warping or springing around piers. It is often necessary to work the engines in opposite directions with great power, but great strain must not be brought on the lines by imparting motion to the vessel.

The speed to be used in approaching a pier should be in keeping with the space available ahead or astern of the landing and with weather and harbor conditions. It often happens that the landing must be made when other vessels are moored ahead and astern of the assigned berth.

The pier should be approached at a slight angle (10 to 20 degrees) slowly but steadily, and the engines stopped with sufficient headway to overrun the landing slightly. When it is certain that the ship's momentum is sufficient to carry the bow into heaving line distance, the engines are stopped. Heaving lines are passed as soon as possible, and the mooring lines hauled ashore. The engines are worked to bring the ship in to a securing position, care being taken that springs and breasts are properly led and that neither bow nor stern is brought in too sharply, because any localized pressure may result in damage to the thin shell plating.

When the current is running strong and parallel or nearly parallel to the pier, the wind may be considered of secondary importance, for the destroyer is long and narrow and when placed at an angle to the axis of the current will rapidly be carried toward or away from the pier, depending upon that angle.

If the current is forcing the ship on to the pier, as will often happen if piers are athwart the stream, it is important that engines be maneuvered to keep squared up with the pier as the ship drifts in with the current. Under such circumstances sufficient fenders must be ready in place to avoid serious local damage that may be caused to the shell plating.

If the current is running away from the pier, speed must be used, and lines must be got out smartly. Once the lines are out, the stern must be brought in by springing on the bowline and by skillful use of engines and rudders.

To make a landing with a fair tide is very difficult, as the slightest cant toward the pier will bring the current under the inboard quarter. This force will require two-thirds or full speed of engines and lines to bring the stern in, especially if strain be brought on a forward line, which is an error commonly made (every destroyer officer learns that it is useless to attempt to spring in on a bow spring with fair tide). The ship should be brought as nearly parallel to the pier as possible, preferably with a slight cant outward, and the after lines got out smartly and held. If a line can be secured aft, it will act as a spring, and the current will bring the ship in readily. The bow will take care of itself.

Going Alongside a Ship at Anchor   This is very similar to going alongside a pier except that conditions of wind and current to be met are usually more favorable. The destroyer must keep clear of an overhanging stern or of any projections from the side of the vessel approached and if possible select a part of the ship's side where there are no projections. A whaleboat or a triced-up accommodation ladder may inflict serious damage to the destroyer's upper works. The greatest danger is the yawing of the vessel at anchor. Destroyers yaw very freely when anchored and riding to wind or current.

There is rarely any difficulty in going alongside another vessel at anchor. The fact that she is at anchor makes it reasonable to suppose that there will be ample maneuvering room astern, except when she rides with her stern close to the beach. The approach should be made fairly well clear with a slight cant inward, and the stern should be brought in and the bow carried out by backing the outboard screw and by use of the rudders as forward lines are passed. Here a spring leading forward from the after forecastle chock of the destroyer can be held and the ship breasted in easily by the current. Care must be exercised not to get the current on the inboard bow. Unlike the situation in going alongside a pier, the forward lines are the more important, for the stern will be taken care of by the wind or current to which the anchored vessel is riding. The engines and rudder can be used to assist in paralleling the two vessels as they draw together.

If a destroyer must approach a nest or tender at a wide angle, the bow should be placed about the width of the destroyer from the bow of the outboard destroyer or tender. The destroyer should then be stopped. A bowline should be sent across and held as a pivot, but not hove in until the ships are parallel. The approaching destroyer now goes ahead one third or two thirds on the inboard engine after the rudder has been put over, hard, away from the nest. The powerful turning force of the discharge flow from the ahead propeller against its rudder is to be utilized. The outboard engine is backed at the same speed and changed as necessary to prevent gaining head or sternway. After the ship is parallel to the nest, the bowline can be hove in assisted by a stern line, and a gentle landing made.

10.30 Tugs and Pilots   Normally a ship's master or commanding officer will have a pilot aboard when tugs are used to assist in ship-handling. There may be times, however, when the commanding officer must direct the tugs himself. For this reason Fig. 10.8 is shown. These tug signals are those officially adopted as standard by the Navy, although some local variations will undoubtedly persist. It is always advisable to confer, when practicable, with the tug skipper before the operation, agreeing on the signals to be used, methods of making fast the tug, etc.

10.31 The Mediterranean Moor   The Mediterranean Moor (Med Moor) is essentially a method of mooring a ship perpendicular to a mole or pier using lines to secure the stern and two anchors to hold the bow in place. As the name implies, the Med Moor is used almost exclusively in many Mediterranean ports where pier space is at a premium.

This type of moor has several advantages. First, it saves space in a harbor or port where pier space is small. Second, it provides a strong moor for high winds and rough weather. Third, it eliminates many of the problems associated with mooring alongside in nests. Fourth, each ship has its own brow to the pier. The Med Moor has two major disadvantages. There is a strong possibility of anchors becoming fouled with other ships when trying to get under way. For this reason it is often advisable to get under way in inverse order of entering port. The second disadvantage stems from the first in that it is difficult to get under way quickly in a crowded harbor.

This discussion will be limited to the destroyer. Cruisers and merchantment also utilize the Med Moor. Carriers, however, usually anchor outside the harbor due to limited maneuvering space.

Since the Med Moor is made perpendicular to the pier, it is important that the conning officer determine how far from the pier the anchors will be dropped. The first consideration is the length of the ship. The destroyer is about 390 feet long—130 yards. Next, it is necessary to determine the scope of chain to be used. The shortest chain on a destroyer is 105 fathoms. In making the Med Moor, it is necessary to choose a scope of chain that will allow enough room from the pier for the ship to maneuver freely but allow a margin for error while using the anchor. In general, 75 fathoms is chosen for a destroyer and

HAND WHISTLE (Police Type)

FROM STOP TO HALF SPEED AHEAD	1 BLAST
FROM HALF SPEED AHEAD TO STOP	1 BLAST
FROM HALF SPEED AHEAD TO FULL SPEED AHEAD	4 SHORT BLASTS
FROM FULL SPEED AHEAD TO HALF SPEED AHEAD	1 BLAST
FROM STOP TO HALF SPEED ASTERN	2 BLASTS
FROM HALF SPEED ASTERN TO FULL SPEED ASTERN	4 SHORT BLASTS
FROM HALF OR FULL SPEED ASTERN TO STOP	1 BLAST
CAST OFF, STAND CLEAR	1 PROLONGED 2 SHORT

Notes:

1. A blast is 2 to 3 seconds in duration.
   A prolonged blast is 4 to 5 seconds in duration.
   A short blast is about 1 second in duration.
2. In using whistle signals to direct more than one tug, care must be exercised to ensure that the signal is directed to and received by the desired tug. Whistles of a different distinct tone have been used successfully to handle more than one tug.
3. These signals may be transmitted to the tug by flashing light. However, flashing light signals should be restricted to use only when hand whistle or hand signals cannot be used.
4. Normally these whistle signals will be augmented by the hand signals given below.

HAND SIGNALS

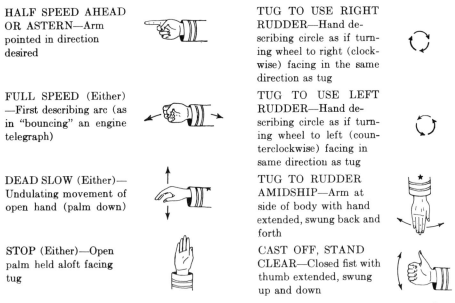

HALF SPEED AHEAD OR ASTERN—Arm pointed in direction desired

TUG TO USE RIGHT RUDDER—Hand describing circle as if turning wheel to right (clockwise) facing in the same direction as tug

FULL SPEED (Either) —First describing arc (as in "bouncing" an engine telegraph)

TUG TO USE LEFT RUDDER—Hand describing circle as if turning wheel to left (counterclockwise) facing in same direction as tug

DEAD SLOW (Either)— Undulating movement of open hand (palm down)

TUG TO RUDDER AMIDSHIP—Arm at side of body with hand extended, swung back and forth

STOP (Either)—Open palm held aloft facing tug

CAST OFF, STAND CLEAR—Closed fist with thumb extended, swung up and down

Note: Tug shall acknowledge all of the above signals with one short toot (one second or less) from its whistle, with the exception of the backing signal which shall be acknowledged with two short toots and the cast-off signal which shall be acknowledged by one prolonged and two short toots.

Fig. 10.8 Tug signals.

this allows a reserve of 30 fathoms. Thus we find that the drop distance from the pier is equal to the length of the ship plus the scope of chain (75 fathoms equals 150 yards)—280 yards.

With this distance determined, the conning officer takes a course approximately parallel to the pier. Speed is reduced so that when the ship is approximately 50 yards short of the position abreast of the berth, it has only bare steerageway. At this point the outboard anchor or the one opposite the pier is dropped from the wildcat. If the starboard anchor is dropped, RIGHT full rudder and a twist on the engines is applied so as to keep the anchor chain clear of the ship. The starboard anchor chain is veered until the ship reaches a point 50 yards on the opposite side of the berth. At this time, the other anchor is dropped. Since a destroyer has only one wildcat, the first anchor is dropped from it so that the scope of chain may be shortened at any time and the other is dropped from the compressor. The compressor is a movable constriction in the chain pipe which serves to check the anchor chain. Then the second chain is veered and the first taken in while the ship twists and backs into the berth. To obtain its final position the ship backs gently against the catenary of the anchor chain which is on the wildcat. When the moor is completed, there should be an equal amount of chain to each anchor, and in an optimum situation, an angle of about 60 degrees between the anchor chains. When the ship is close to the pier, the conn is generally shifted to the fantail where the distance to the pier can be obtained more accurately. The stern is secured to the pier with a stern line and quarter lines which are crossed under the stern. A stronger moor may be obtained by using the towing line as the stern line and reinforcing the quarter lines with wire. Once the stern line is secure, the moor is tautened by heaving in and equalizing the anchor chains. There should be moderate strain on the anchor chains and they should be standing well out of the water so that a wind from the bow will not damage the ship. (See Fig. 10.9.)

When getting under way and when the brow and after lines are taken in the second anchor dropped is heaved on in. Lateral movement of the ship's stern, if other ships are close aboard, can be controlled by a line to the pier aft and/or by the ship's engines. With one anchor aboard, the second anchor is heaved on and as it comes in the bow is usually headed fair for leaving port. Harbors requiring the use of a Mediterranean Moor are crowded and small; thus a pilot and necessary tugs are not only available but usually mandatory.

Destroyers often moor in a Med Moor nest. This is accomplished by having the first ship drop her inshore anchor only and then back into a stern first position against the pier. Remaining DDs moor

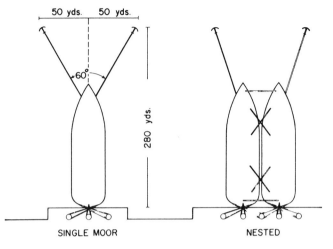

Fig. 10.9 Mediterranean Moor.

alongside with standard mooring lines to the other ships. The last ship in drops her offshore anchor only and twists into the stern first position. **The final result is a nest which is moored in a Med Moor. (See Fig. 10.9.)**

In some harbors, such as Barcelona, Spain, a gale which sends seas into the harbor entrance will cause a rapid rise and fall of the sea level within the port. A firmly moored ship under these circumstances may part her lines to the wharf, and the resultant fore-and-aft surging may carry away the brow. It is recommended that, if circumstances warrant, the brow be removed and all lines to the wharf be eased or taken in. A line or two tended on a winch will usually keep the stern under control as the ship surges. Nylon lines with their greater elasticity should be of help.

There is one important precaution to take when Med-mooring a large ship. The stern line, holding the stern in close to the pier against the strain of the anchor chain, must never be led from the aftermost chock straight down to the pier. In bad weather, as the stern rises and falls, a straight, short lead to the pier either will part or will pull out or rupture the bollard. Instead, lead tow stern lines aft from each quarter chock well forward of the stern chock. These lines will be longer, have more "give," and will make a smaller angle with the pier. In addition, of course, after spring lines should be led out from the stern chock, crossed, and secured well down the pier on each side, preventing the stern from moving side to side.

10.32 Handling Alongside Under Way   Shiphandling alongside for
the transfer of material and personnel is common in most big navies
and is used to some degree between merchant tankers. It presents no
special problems but there are a few techniques and guidelines that
may be helpful.

In approaching from astern another ship which is maintaining a
steady course and speed it is wise to measure her course as read by
your compass. Gyro compass differences of several degrees are not
uncommon and it will be an advantage to know if there is one.

Depending on weather, direction of sea and swell, and your own
degree of confidence you should make your approach smartly and at
100 to 200 feet from the delivering ship. In general, the closer the
better in order to facilitate and expedite passing lines across. When
hooked up you should maintain a reasonably close distance, under
good sea conditions, of 80 to 120 feet.

Follow the guide's wake, moving out a reasonable distance, perhaps
100 feet, and maintaining this distance as you go alongside. Imagine
that the guide ship is in the wake alongside as you approach and it will not
be difficult to select the proper distance. If you are making 5 knots more
than the guide as you approach, a rough thumb rule is to reduce to her
speed as your bow passes her stern. It is better to overshoot a bit than
to be short since the lines can start over as you range ahead and then
fall back to your station. However, if you have overshot considerably and
end up on the bow of the supplying ship, great care must be exercised.
If you reduce speed, without some alteration of course outwards to
counteract the inward turning moment caused by interaction then you
are liable to gain inwards and fall across the bow of the supplying ship.

It goes without saying that you should have your best man on the
wheel and a reliable officer to watch him and double check the ex-
ecution of your commands, and that casualty procedures should be
known and have been rehearsed.

In maintaining station, give your steersman an exact course to steer
in degrees. He will soon find the amount of rudder he must carry to
maintain a given course. Wind and sea and the pull of the replenishment lines between the ships are all factors that vary widely.

The use of modern constant-tension wire highlines that exert a pull
of 6 to 10 tons, often at considerable distances from the ship's pivot
point, introduces a few special factors but no great problems for the
shiphandler. If the difference between receiving and delivering ships
is great in respect to size and if a heavy tension is exerted far abaft or
far forward of the ship's pivot point a considerable deflection of course
is experienced by one or both ships. This can be countered by carry-

ing as much as 10 degrees of rudder in maintaining course by the ship keeping station, and in some cases, a ship may have to steer a course 2 or 3 degrees off the guide's course. The guide may also be required to carry rudder in order to maintain its specified replenishment course.

When tension is applied during "hooking-up" between replenishment ships commanding officers should keep each other informed of any special deflection experienced. Remember that casting off constant-tension rigs (tripping pelican hooks or unshackling) should not be done until tension has been released.

Remember the possible effect of bow wave and stern suction as you pass close aboard a large ship. As your bow approaches the guide you may feel the effect of your submerged bow wave meeting the guide's hull or wake. This tends to force your bow out; a good helmsman will expect this and counter it easily. The opposite effect, an attracting force between ship hulls due to stern suction caused by water being pulled into the propellers, is also a possibility if you permit your stern to get in too close to the guide. If this should happen do not stop or back your engines; it is important to maintain a minimum relative speed in relation to the guide. Just coach the helmsman into bringing your ship out gradually.

In maintaining station in regard to speed you may find that your small ship is affected by head seas and swells while a larger guide is not so affected. If an occasional large head sea tends to slow you down all you can do is to crank up a few turns each time it happens, taking them off as you begin to move forward again.

As replenishment is concluded and all lines are reported clear, increase speed quickly with gradual course changes to move you away from the guide's course. Watch your stern until you are well clear of the guide and, of course, do not cross his bow until no possibility exists of embarrassing him.

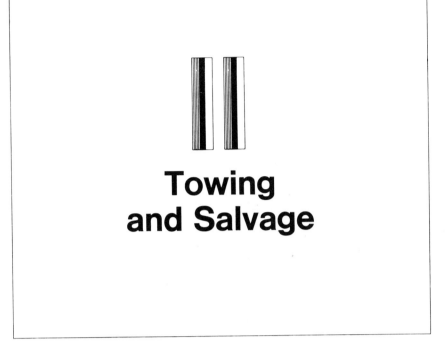

Towing
and Salvage

The rescue of ships in distress and the refloating of those which have grounded is a highly specialized calling to which men devote their lives, but every seaman should have a basic knowledge and understanding of towing and salvage.

Salvage tugs equipped to tow, fight fires, pump out ships, and assist in groundings are on call near all the major shipping lanes and routes of the world. Sometimes they are at sea on station waiting for their clients. Their work is highly specialized, usually hazardous, and often profitable. Very long range towing of huge floating offshore oil drilling rigs is another specialty that can only be mentioned in passing.

This chapter provides all that the average seafarer need know in order to tow or be towed in an emergency or to meet the emergency of a sudden grounding.

Towing

11.1 The Towline Generally speaking, the longer and heavier the towline, the easier the towing will be. A decided dip or catenary gives the same advantage here as in the case of a vessel at anchor riding with a good scope of chain. The weight of the catenary acts as a spring, preventing variations in the tension from being thrown upon the towline in sudden jerks.

Wire rope has proved very satisfactory for heavy sea towing. The advantages of using wire rope are that it is convenient for casting off, takes up comparatively small space when stowed, and does not deteriorate if properly dried and oiled before stowing.

Nylon is satisfactory for light or moderate towing. It is heavy enough to give a good dip when used in sufficient length, but it is not too heavy for convenient handling. Nylon is popular for relatively light towing because of its resiliency, ease of handling, and long life.

For towing a ship as small as 3000 tons in rough weather—and it must not be overlooked that rough weather may be encountered in almost any towing operation—the full length of an 8-inch nylon hawser or a 1½-inch diameter wire rope will be none too much.

Where the tow is a vessel whose displacement is comparable with that of a cruiser or aircraft carrier, the towline should be made up of 2½-inch or 2¼-inch diameter wire rope connected to a good length of her own anchor cable. The length that is needed will vary with circumstances, but it is far better to have too much than too little.

A point of some importance in towing in a seaway is to keep the ships in step. In other words, use such a length that they will meet the waves and ride over them together. If the length of the line is such that one vessel is in the trough of the sea as the other is on the crest, the line will slacken for a moment and then tauten with a sudden jerk; whereas if they meet the waves at the same time, the tension of the line will remain comparatively steady.

11.2 Securing on the Towing Ship In securing the towline, consideration must be given to letting go in an emergency.

For convenience in letting go, it is desirable to have a break in the line near the stern. It would be advisable to have a shackle connecting two parts of the line at or near this point, together with some arrangement like a pelican hook for slipping quickly. The possible whip of towlines and bridles when released at any point may be overcome by the use of preventers.

If the towing ship is comparatively large and has a chock at the stern, the line should be brought in through it. It is a good plan to use a short length of chain for the lead through the stern chock, shackling outside to an eye in the end of the towing hawser and inside to a towing bridle. The chain through the stern chock not only takes the chafe, but by its flexibility does away with the dangerous nip which might be thrown into wire if the tow chanced to take a rank sheer onto the quarter.

Where the chain is not used for taking the chafe in the stern chock, the towline must be fully protected by chafing gear which should be a long and bulky pudding. The stiffness of such a puddening reduces the sharpness of the nip which, without the pudding, would be thrown upon the towline from time to time by the sheering of the ships. A towline leads down, not up. Worm, parcel, and serve manila. Use canvas, hides, burlap, and old rope on wire towlines.

Where the strain is not too heavy to be taken by one pair of bitts, the towing line may be secured as shown by Fig. 11.1. Figure 11.1(A) shows how a towrope should not be secured. Here the greater strain comes on the left bitt, which might result in the left bitt lifting and being torn out.

In Fig. 11.1(B) the greater strain is taken by the after bitt, and though the forward bitt has some strain, they should hold under ordinary conditions.

When one pair of bitts is not strong enough, the line can be taken to as many as three sets of bitts if available. To divide the strain it is advisable to take one turn around the first bitts, two around the second, and three around the third, thus leaving the line free to render slightly and so equalize the strain.

Where pelican hooks are used for letting go, as shown by Fig. 11.2, the strain is taken momentarily on the hook, relieving the shackle so that it can be disconnected and towing hawser slipped when ordered. This arrangement entails practically no delay. An arrangement with a pelican hook taking the steady strain of towing offers the quickest emergency release.

Where pelican hooks are not used, a strap may be used on the wire or chain outside the shackle, and a heavy purchase hooked to the strap and taken to a winch. For letting go, the strain is taken by the winch long enough to disconnect at the shackle, after which the strap is cut as ordered (Fig. 11.2(C)). A preventer must be used to prevent a dangerous whip upon letting go.

There are some conditions under which it is convenient to use a span on the towing ship. The two parts are brought in through the quarter chocks. Generally, this makes it rather easier for the towing ship to steer, and the advantage gained in this respect may become important in cases where a small ship is dealing with a heavy tow. Where the line leads from a chock directly over the rudder, it binds the stern so that it can only swing in obedience to the rudder by dragging the tow with it. A large ship can take care of this situation by the power of her steering gear, assisted if necessary by the propellers; but a small ship with a heavy tow and with the line leading through the stern chock will steer very sluggishly if she steers at all. Tugs which are specially fitted for towing have their bitts well forward of the rudder

(A)

AFT →

(B)

Fig. 11.1 Lead to tow. (A) The wrong way to secure a towrope. (B) The right way to secure a towrope. (Direction of tow →.) *(Official U.S. Navy photograph.)*

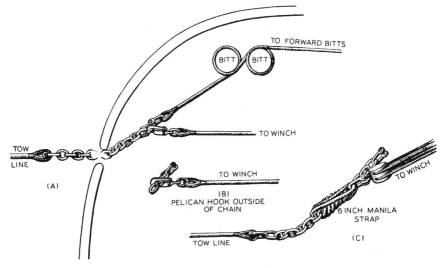

Fig. 11.2 Towing by bitts.

to allow the stern to swing; the fittings abaft the bitts allow the line to sweep freely across from one quarter to the other.

Where a span is used, it may be of chain, wire, or line. In this as in other cases, arrangements must be made for letting go quickly in emergencies.

A convenient plan is to bring the towline in through a quarter chock and bend a hawser from the other quarter to it at such a point outside that the two parts shall form a span of convenient length. The lines may be secured around bitts as previously described. This plan has the advantage that by letting go the second line we get rid of the span at once and have to deal only with the towline itself.

11.3 Towing Engines Vessels designed especially for towing, such as seagoing tugs, are fitted with towing engines which carry the towline on a drum and pay it out and haul it in automatically to keep the towing tension constant. For a steam towing engine this tension is controlled by a differential valve which is set to remain centered with any desired strain on the towline. If the tension rises momentarily, the valve moves in one direction. The drum revolves and pays out line until it has the required strain, and then the valve centers itself and the drum stops revolving. If the tension decreases, valve and drum move in the opposite direction, reeling in the line until the proper tension is restored. With electric towing engines an automatic controller accomplishes the same result. In this way the line is payed out or reeled in just enough to meet the condition prevailing at any given moment, and the average length of towline remains virtually constant. The drums of towing engines must be very rugged and are fitted to heavy foundations built into the frame of the ship. They are placed at a distance from the extreme stern, the pivoting point, in order to lessen the interference with the steering of the towing vessel. Guiding chocks and bollards and a long quadrantal chock for the towline extending along both quarters of the ship at deck level are installed for the same reason.

The standard towline for vessels fitted with a towing engine is 300 to 350 fathoms of wire rope 2 to 2½ inches in diameter. It is stowed on the drum of the towing engine when not in use. When towing is finished, the towline is cast off by the towed vessel and automatically reeled in by the towing engine. The eye of the towline is generally fitted with a plate shackle for securing aboard the tow.

11.4   Securing the Tow on Board   On board the tow the hawser is usually secured to the anchor cable, although there may be many conditions under which some other arrangement will be provided. If the anchor cable is not used, it is desirable to use at least a short length of chain to take the chafe in the chock in the same manner as already described for securing on the towing ship.

Where the anchor cable is used, the hawser is secured or shackled to it and the cable veered away to the desired length, after which the windlass brakes are set up and springs or chain stoppers are used to take the real strain of towing, as in Fig. 11.3. It is well to have a shackle between the windlass and the point to which the springs or chain stoppers are secured and to keep tools at hand for unshackling if it becomes necessary to let go in an emergency. Generally, the tow

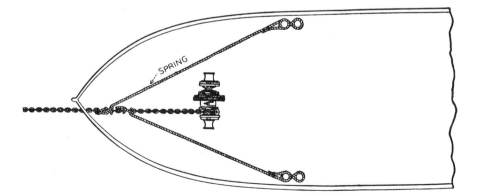

Fig. 11.3   Bow of ship towed.

should not let go in this way except in case of extreme emergency, because the line weighted with a considerable length of heavy anchor cable would sink immediately, hanging as a dead weight from the stern of the towing vessel. In this position it would be extremely difficult to handle and would be in danger of fouling the propellers. This applies only to cases where the tow is a vessel of some size and where she is towing by her anchor cables. It is evident that, where a large ship is towing a small one, the natural way of casting off is for the tow to let go, which leaves the line to be handled by the large ship.

11.5   Taking a Disabled Vessel in Tow at Sea   In good weather, this maneuver presents no special difficulty and calls for no extended discussion. The lines are run and secured as already described. The towing vessel starts ahead slowly on the course upon which the disabled vessel happens to be heading and uses every precaution to prevent a jerk on the line. It waits before changing course until both ships have gathered way and are moving steadily with a good tension on the towline.

In bad weather, towing should not be attempted unless exceptional circumstances make it necessary. The running of lines in a heavy sea is attended by considerable difficulty, especially if the vessel to be towed is unable to assist by placing herself in a favorable position. Moreover, in really heavy weather, it would be necessary to proceed so slowly that little or no time would be lost by waiting for the weather to moderate.

Disabled vessels lie in different positions relative to the wind, depending on the size and position of the superstructure, the trim, and, perhaps, drag due to damage. If there is more superstructure forward than aft, the vessel will lie with the wind from abaft the beam to astern. Vessels with much superstructure amidships will lie with the wind abeam and those with superstructure aft, such as tankers, lie head into the wind. All such vessels make leeway of 1 to 3 knots and, if lying at angle to the wind, headway or sternway. Vessels down by the head tend to head into the wind and vice versa.

If a tug with a deckhouse forward and a flat stern is the towing vessel, she should approach downwind and just clear of the bow, except when the vessel lies head into the wind. In this case, the approach of the tug is still downwind but just ahead of the vessel, using her engines to keep position and clear. The sketches in Fig. 11.4 show that the tug is able to work close to the disabled vessel and still keep clear by a kick ahead at intervals.

It will be considered in the discussion which follows that one vessel is going to tow another and that the weather is rough enough to call for the use of all reasonable precautions but not rough enough to

282 TOWING AND SALVAGE

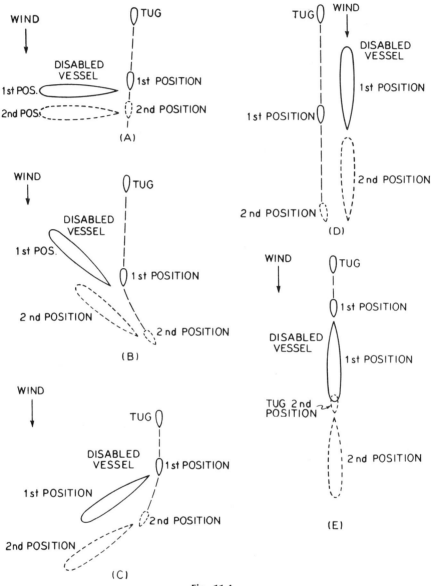

Fig. 11.4

make towing impracticable. It may be assumed that the disabled vessel
will be lying with wind and sea a little abaft the beam, this being the
position which a ship usually takes when lying in a seaway with
engines stopped. The other vessel places herself on a parallel heading
either to windward or to leeward. In considering which of these positions is to be preferred, we must remember that considerable time

will be required to run the lines; and that during this time both vessels will be drifting. A vessel which is light will drift faster than one which is loaded, and the drift of a vessel in ballast-trim often amounts to several knots. If the lighter vessel is to leeward, she will drift away from the other and make it very difficult to run the lines. It may be said that, as a general rule, if there is any important difference in the rate of drift of the two vessels, the lighter one should be to windward when the work of running the lines is begun. The towing vessel then places herself to windward if she is drifting faster than the other vessel and to leeward if she is drifting more slowly and on the same heading as the disabled vessel.

Where the difference in the rate of drifting is considerable, the time available for running the lines after the work is once begun will be short at best. Every precaution should be taken to prevent delay, with a clear understanding being established between the ships and all preparations made before the towing ship takes her position. In communicating between two ships, megaphones are of the greatest value. Under any except the most unfavorable conditions they should make it possible to perfect a thorough understanding of what is to be done and how. To a great extent they also may take the place of signals between the two ships after the towing begins, although a code should by all means be adopted and will be useful under many conditions. It is an excellent plan when feasible to send an officer on board the tow to remain there. First acquaint him with the plan to be carried out and provide him with a list of whistle and sight signals for handling the lines and the ships. If no boats are to be used, a paper may be floated across to the tow giving full instructions and a list of the signals. This may be sealed up in a bottle and attached to the rope or the float. Whistle signals are preferable to flags because they can be used at night or in a fog.

The following is suggested:

Code of Sound Signals for Towing

A short blast must not exceed 2 seconds in length.
A long blast must not be less than 6 seconds in length.

I am putting my rudder right.	1 short blast
I am putting my rudder left.	2 short blasts
Go ahead.	2 long
Stop.	1 long, 2 short
All fast.	2 long, 1 short
Haul away.	2 short, 1 long
Let go.	2 long, 5 short
Pay out more line.	1 short, 2 long
Avast hauling.	3 short
I am letting go (emergency).	5 short, 5 short, 5 short

11.6   Handling Lines and Getting Under Way   The first line to be run will be a light one by means of which the heavier ones can be hauled across. A 3-inch manila is a convenient size to begin with and, if new, so much the better because it will float freely. If a boat is to be used, it should be lowered with the crew and the greater part of the line in it and made clear as quickly as possible. The line should be payed out as the boat pulls away for the other ship.

The line may be floated alongside the disabled ship without much difficulty. The best way to do this will depend upon circumstances, but a common way is to float a good length of the line by life belts, casks, or any other means and to steam slowly around the disabled vessel, dragging this astern and causing it to foul the disabled vessel. If proposing to take up a position on her weather bow, it is a good plan to steam along the leeward fairly close aboard, cross the stern, and come around parallel to her heading. This will cause the line to foul her stern, which entails a little trouble in shifting it forward, but it leaves the towing ship in position without further maneuvering. Similarly, if proposing to take a position on the lee bow, pass along to windward, cross the stern, and come around to leeward. The line should be picked up without difficulty.

There may be special circumstances which will make it desirable for the disabled vessel to run lines, but under ordinary circumstances it is more convenient for the towing vessel to run them. Having got the first line across, the heavier lines are run and made fast to the anchor cable for the vessel to be towed where possible. A good length of cable is paid out—20 to 45 fathoms is none too much for heavy work —and the line made secure on both ships as has been described. Chafing gear is used liberally wherever it is needed. In the meantime, full instructions about starting are given to the chief engineer, and when all is ready, the engines are started ahead as slowly as possible and stopped the moment the line begins to tauten out. Then a few more turns are made and so on until the inertia of the tow is overcome and both ships are moving slowly with a steady tension on the line. The revolutions are then increased little by little, and the course changed gradually as may be necessary. When the tow is finally straightened out and moving steadily, the speed is worked up to that at which it is thought wise to continue.

In all changes of course the tow puts her rudder at first to the side opposite that of the leader and so steers around into the leader's wake.

After settling down to a steady rate of towing, the lines should be examined, the strain divided as evenly as possible, chafing gear renewed wherever necessary, etc. Hands should be stationed night and day to watch the lines on both ships, with axes and unshackling tools ready for slipping hurriedly if necessary. It is well to have a light messenger line between the ships for hauling messages across and for use in running a new line in case of necessity. This line should be left slack and should have ample length to allow for the fact that if the towline parts the leading ship will forge ahead considerably before she can be stopped.

Salvage

11.7 Groundings   Salvage in its broadest sense includes the salvage (recovery) of cargo, the removal of wrecks and the refloating of grounded ships. Only the matter of grounded ships will be discussed here since the salvage of cargo and the removal of wrecks involve highly specialized techniques not of major interest to seafaring men generally.

The first thing to do when you go aground is to think through your problem and avoid taking hasty action. Do not back full for a prolonged period and do not lighten ship before you have made a careful plan. In the meantime have your people make ready to lay out an anchor. Hasty disposal of weight may result in your being driven further up on the beach and/or may cause your ship to broach. It is often wiser to add weight by flooding certain compartments. Using your engines unwisely can foul your intakes and condensers and can wash more sand under your hull. If possible lay out an anchor to seaward and wait for a salvage vessel with beach gear. Next sound all around the ship to determine what part of the ship is grounded and the loss in draft. The average loss in draft times the tons per inch immersion as taken from the ship's curve will give the total loss in buoyancy in tons. This weight is the problem. The loss in buoyancy must be reduced to the point where the pull of beach gear and tugs will be sufficient to refloat the ship.

Salvage men have calculated that a pull of about 30 percent of the remaining lost buoyancy is required to refloat a ship aground on a sandy bottom with a gentle slope; 50 percent when the bottom is hard or gravelly; 60 to 80 percent for coral; 80 to 150 percent for rocky bottom. A large amount of weight will probably have to be removed from the ship to reduce the lost buoyancy to a manageable amount.

Personnel, fuel, and water can be removed more easily and quickly than stores, cargo, ammunition, spare parts, and guns. The decision to remove any or all of these weights, as well as when to move them, will depend on a number of factors. In all probability the determining factor will be the weather for offshore groundings, although the state of the tide at grounding and the time of the next tide or perhaps the next spring tide may be equally important. In some parts of the world the range of the tide is so great that ships grounding at part tide are refloated at high tide. Where the rise and fall of the tide is not that great, the time and date of the next spring tide may be the deciding factor as far as time is concerned.

Some other physical conditions must be known and weighed also. Was the ship fully loaded? What compartments, bottoms, and tanks have been holed? What kind of bottom is under the ship? Currents can scour the sand from under a ship in one place and pile it up in another. While all the physical conditions are being compiled and analyzed, it is wise to send out additional anchors to hold the ship in her grounding position.

11.8 Planning and Methods The planning must be done carefully so that the weights to be moved, the equipment to be used, and the dredging to be done will be coordinated and completed at the end of the time available. Some fuel and water will be required for engines. All of the weight removed cannot come from the double bottoms and fuel tanks or the stability of the ship may be adversely affected. Many men are required to handle stores, spare parts, cargo, and ammunition. These men must have deck space to handle these items and space alongside for the barges to receive the stores, fuel, etc. The plan must coordinate the times for removing weights, for laying out the beach gear on deck, for dredging alongside, and for receiving barges.

The following measures may be available and used:

1. Remove fuel.
2. Remove water.
3. Remove cargo.
4. Remove stores.
5. Remove spare parts.
6. Remove ammunition.
7. Remove guns or missiles.
8. Transfer some men.
9. Dredge and scour alongside.
10. Tunnel under the ship.
11. Rig beach gear.
12. Expel water from holed compartments.
13. Services of salvage vessels.
14. Services of tugs.
15. Twist the ship.

When large ships are stranded, a trench can be dredged along each side of the ship if the bottom is sandy or muddy. The trench should be made deep enough to receive a large part of the sand and mud upon which the ship is resting. If this sand and mud will crumble and move into the two trenches, the ship may be floated in her grounded position. This method has been successful occasionally.

European salvage men have had some success with scouring the bottom from under the ship. A small vessel with her propeller well immersed is secured to the grounded ship in such a position that the discharge current from her propeller scours the sand from under the ship. In some cases the engines of the ship itself have been used to remove sand and mud from under the ship. Care must be taken that a new shoal is not formed astern. The engines cannot be operated in the other direction, that is, astern, for very long because sand may be washed under the ship and the problem of refloating made more difficult.

Divers with high-pressure hoses are used, after trenches have been dredged, to start the movement of sand and to wash away the remaining sandy supports. Divers are used also to tunnel under the ship so that the chains which hold the pontoons in place can be rigged.

It is probable that certain compartments were flooded when the ship grounded. These compartments can be nearly freed of water by forcing air into the compartment. Care must be taken that the pressure of the air does not rupture the compartment. The pressure of the air should be a little higher than the pressure of the water due to the distance below the surface.

11.9   Beach Gear   One of the most useful pieces of equipment now available to a grounded ship is beach gear. It is in reality a development of the older methods of laying out anchors and cables for salvaging ships. The present-day beach gear consists of:

1. an 8000-pound Ells anchor fitted with a crown line and buoy for breaking loose and recovery
2. 15 fathoms of 2¼ inch chain attached to the anchor
3. two or three 100-fathom wire cables of galvanized plow steel
4. shackles
5. wire stoppers
6. a four-sheave wire tackle.

The anchor, sometimes backed by a second one, is planted well out and in the direction the ship will have to move when it is refloated. The end of the second wire is led through a chock or an opening cut in the side of the grounded ship. The tackle is laid out on deck and aligned with the wire so that the pull when applied will be straight with no nip or bend in the wire. The hauling part of the tackle is now led to a ship's winch or to a salvage winch installed to supplement the ship's gear. In the salvage of the *Missouri*, nine sets of beach gear were used in addition to three sets laid out from each of two salvage vessels which were pulling too. Each set of beach gear can exert a pull of 45 to 60 tons. Such gear kept under heavy strain has been a large factor in salvaging many vessels.

The services of salvage vessels are valuable because they have a large amount of gear, including beach gear, which can be used. The personnel are trained for salvage work and their anchor gear and winches are oversized.

There is a tendency to use any tug which is near when a ship grounds, under the impression that prompt, energetic action is desirable. Often this is not true because small tugs are of little use for pulling on large vessels aground. Tests of the pulling power of tugs have been made, and it has been found that they exert a pull of about 1 ton per 100 horsepower. Large seagoing tugs have a pull of 10 to 15 tons and Naval Fleet tugs about 30 to 35 tons.

It is very probable that the lost buoyancy of a large ship is so great that she exerts a pressure of hundreds of tons on the bottom. The sand under her has been packed so tightly that it has a consistency of low-grade concrete. We may say that the ship exerts a powerful suction on the bottom. One of the ways of breaking this suction has already been mentioned, namely, the crumbling of the sand under the ship into dredged trenches alongside. After much of the weight of lost buoyancy has been removed, and all preparations completed to refloat the ship, large tugs are used occasionally to twist the ship and thus break the suction. Small tugs are useful now to hold large tugs and salvage vessels in position to exert their best pull. In these operations cross currents can be very annoying.

The salvage plan should include the measures necessary to ensure the safe voyage of the refloated ship to the nearest base or shipyard. Anchors and chains must be returned, the holed compartments should be patched and shored, and the stability and trim of the ship must be satisfactory. If her engines cannot be used, she will have to be towed. These measures may require the reloading of fuel, water, stores, and even ballast in order that a further disaster may not occur.

11.10   Rescuing the Crew of a Wreck at Sea   There are no hard and fast rules which can be laid down for rescuing the crew of a wreck; only what is considered the best practice by experienced and capable seamen may be stated. So many elements control the application of the general rules, such as sea, wind, urgency of immediate assistance, maneuverability of the assisting ship, and the training and experience of the boat crews, that each case must be decided according to circumstances.

After having made contact and established communications, find out how urgent the case is and how much help may be expected from the crew of the wreck. If it is at night and weather conditions indicate an improvement or at least no worse weather, and the master of the disabled ship feels he can hold on and you feel you can maintain contact, wait for daylight.

Under any circumstances, when the rescue begins, determine the comparative drift of the two ships and whether or not there is any wreckage about the disabled ship. If there is wreckage, discern how it will hamper your boat work. If your ship drifts faster than the disabled ship, go to windward; but if the opposite is the case, go to leeward. Both ships should distribute oil freely. If for any reason the wreck cannot use oil, the rescuing ship should steam around her and run oil freely to create a slick into which the wreck will presently drift.

Before the rescue work begins, the boat should be equipped with two sharp hatchets in brackets, one at the bow and one at the stern; one ring life preserver with stout heaving lines made fast; two spare life jackets stopped with sail twine under each thwart; two spare oars; two small oil bags; and a small tin of storm oil.

If the weather is very rough, extreme precautions will be called for in lowering the boat and getting her clear. The ship should be held with the sea on the bow to give a lee for the boat and to reduce rolling as much as possible. The crew, with life belts on, is lowered in the boat. Frapping lines are used around the falls to steady the boat, and fenders are rigged to prevent the boat from being stove in if she swings in heavily.

Assuming that the boat gets off and makes the trip to the wreck in safety, the officer in charge must decide how he will establish communication and take off the passengers and crew. It is out of the question to go alongside to windward; and if he goes alongside to leeward, not only is there a risk of being stove by the wreckage which is likely to be found floating under the quarter, but there is the much more serious danger of being unable to get clear of the side again. A ship lying in a seaway with engines stopped drifts to leeward at a rate which is always considerable and may amount to several knots. A boat alongside such a ship to leeward is in exactly the same position as if she were alongside a dock against the face of which a strong current is setting. As a rule the boat must never be brought actually alongside the wreck. She may either lie off to windward and keep well clear and hold up head to sea or to leeward and hold on with a line from her bow to the wreck. If obliged to go alongside, the stem may be allowed to touch, with all being ready to back off if the boat shows a disposition to get broaside-on. The people on board the wreck put on the life belts, go down a line one at a time, hand over hand, and are hauled into the boat. In most cases the most favorable point for working will be under the lee quarter or the lee bow. This depends upon the way the wreck is lying with reference to the sea. It is sometimes possible for people to lower themselves or be lowered to a boat from the head booms or from an overhanging main boom when they could not be rescued in any other way. So serious is the question of avoiding actual contact with the wreck that many officers consider it best for the rescuing ship to go to windward and drop the boat down with a line, putting only two or three men in the boat.

Boat Handling
and Helicopter
Operations

Boat Handling

As ship's boats are normally designed for a variety of purposes, their handling will be discussed under the various conditions in which they are used.

The powerboats of a ship, including landing craft, do the greatest part of their work in port or off the beach, running from ship to shore. Under these circumstances it is normally a safe and simple matter to hoist and lower them with a crane or boom. When hoisting or lowering at sea or at anchor during rough seas, certain precautions must be observed in order to prevent the boat from being stove in, swamped, or the crew thrown overboard. If these precautions during operations in rough seas are understood and observed at all times, there should be no difficulty in hoisting and lowering boats under more favorable sea conditions.

With the exception of those boats which are provided with their own davits, large boats and heavier landing craft are hoisted and lowered by means of boat cranes or booms which hook on the slings rigged in the boat. The slings are attached to hoisting eyes which are built into the strongest sections of the boat. Davits which are used for many of the smaller boats can be considered as nothing more than two cranes which perform the same job in a slightly different manner.

Davits are used to swing the boat to the lowering position and then after it has been hoisted to swing it back on board. The actual raising and lowering could be done by manning the boat falls with sufficient men. However, the falls are generally taken to some source of power to accomplish raising the boat and then to a belaying point, such as a cleat or the gypsy head of a winch, for lowering.

The various types of davits used have been described in Chapter 2 and will not be discussed further here, with the exception of the radial davit, which is the most common aboard small combatant ships and is also the most difficult to use.

Prior to swinging the boat out, the boat plug is checked and reported to the man in charge as being in place. If the boat is resting in chocks, it is hoisted clear of the deck and all preparations are made to swing it out. When it is clear of the deck, the boat is shifted aft so that the bow will clear the forward davit. This davit is rotated and the bow pushed out so as to clear the side. The rear davit is then rotated and the stern pushed over the side. The boat is then ready for lowering. This type of davit provides a rapid and simple method of swinging out small boats such as the motor whaleboat.

Care must be taken in hoisting the boat out of the chocks. In hoisting it clear, it is advisable to hoist the stern of the boat first to avoid any danger of striking the propeller or rudder against the deck. After the stern has been hoisted clear, the commands are "avast heaving" and next "pass the stopper." The hauling part is then stopped-off as shown in Fig. 12.1 by means of a rolling hitch, a half hitch, and two or more turns against the lay, and by holding the bitter end of the stopper and the fall firmly together by hand. When the stopper has been passed and secured, the command "walk back" is given, and the strain is gradually released on the hauling part and taken up by the stopper. When all the strain has been transferred to the stopper, the order "up behind" is given. The men on the hauling part move forward with the slack of the fall to the davit where the line is belayed on a cleat or crucifix at the command "belay." Figure 12.2 shows the proper manner of doing this. Emphasis is placed upon passing a round turn first and a half hitch last. It is well to mention here that many seamen prefer to pass two round turns first, in lieu of one, for added protection. This procedure places the weight of the boat on the whole cleat rather than on just one of the horns which could conceivably shear off. When the after fall is properly belayed, the bow of the boat is raised and secured in like manner.

After the boat has been lifted clear of the chocks, the order "launch

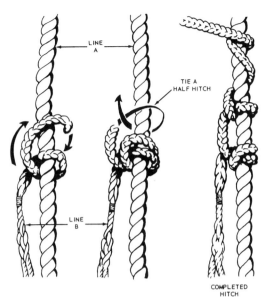

Fig. 12.1 Stopping-off the fall.

aft" is given and the boat is moved aft far enough to let the bow or stem of the boat clear the forward davit. When it is clear, the order "launch forward and bear out" is given. Then, as the bow is pushed out, and the boat is pushed forward, the bow passes over the side and between the davits. When it is far enough forward for the stern to

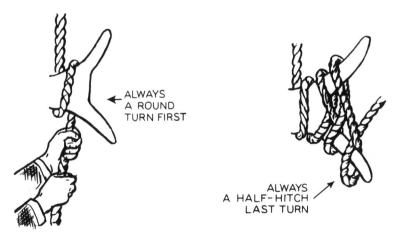

Fig. 12.2 Securing the fall to the cleat.

clear the after davit, the command "bear out aft" is given, and the stern is pushed over the side of the ship. The davits are then placed at right angles to the ship, and the boat is ready for lowering. The davits are fixed in their outboard position by guy lines to the davit heads.

12.1 Lowering and Hoisting Boats by Radial Davit *Lowering Away* Because the placing of the boat in the water when anchored or moored is normally a simple operation of lowering it until it is water-borne, lowering away will be discussed only while under way, as this is the most dangerous and difficult. The proper use of the sea painter and the rudder or sweeps bar is essential to keep the boat from being thrown against the side of the ship. The use of the sea painter will be described later in this chapter. In lowering a boat in heavy weather, steadying lines called *frapping lines* (Fig. 12.3) must be used. In using frapping lines, one end is secured to something solid on deck. The bight is passed around the falls and the end is brought back on deck and tended by a turn or two. The purpose in using the frapping lines is to keep the boat from swinging wide as the ship rolls. Another means of keeping the boat from swinging out as the ship rolls is the use of *traveling lizards* (Fig. 12.3). The traveling lizards are kept in hand in the boat, after a turn is taken around a thwart. Under no

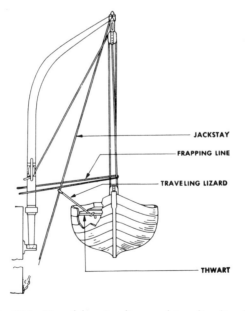

JACKSTAY

FRAPPING LINE

TRAVELING LIZARD

THWART

Fig. 12.3 Use of frapping lines and traveling lizard.

circumstances are the lizards to be secured in the boat. Frapping lines and lizards are also used together.

When ready to lower, the man in charge of lowering takes a position between the davits. When lowering by means of radial davits, only the most experienced men should be used on the cleats when slacking the falls. Care must be taken to prevent the lines from jumping the cleats. At the command "lower away together" the men on the cleats remove all the turns but the round turn (leave two turns if falls are nylon) and then gradually pay out the falls hand over hand. The boat should go into the water on an even keel or slightly by the stern. If the sea is rough, the boat should be held clear of the water until a trough appears in which to set it down. If the boat is set down on the crest of a wave, the hoisting gear will be subjected to a heavy strain when the sea drops out from beneath the boat. As soon as the boat is waterborne, the command "up behind" is given. At this order the men on the cleats remove the final turns and slack the lines so that the boat will ride immediately to the sea painter.

The coxswain of the boat must require his crew to wear lifejackets and hardhats and to keep both hands on the monkey (safety) lines in case the boat should fall. Small boat fenders should be rigged between the boat and the ship. He will have his engineer start the engine during lowering to be sure that it is warmed up. As soon as the boat is waterborne, the man in charge orders the *after* falls cast off, followed by the *forward* falls. The coxswain then sheers off and orders the bow hook to let go the sea painter.

To prevent the lower block from tumbling, a nontumbling block is used; that is, one designed to keep from turning over as it is hoisted back on board and the weight of the boat is no longer on it. However, even with this type of block, care must be taken in bringing it back on board. If the hauling part is pulled, the parts of the falls will not pass through the sheaves, and the block will turn over. Another safety factor is the swivel hook attached to the lower block. This swivel permits the removal of twists in the falls. If an attempt is made to raise the boat without removing the turns, the grind of the turning block may shear the shank off the hook. If not, the friction on the parts of the falls will be so great as to increase materially the difficulty of raising the boat. The block is of the automatic releasing hook type described in Chapter 2.

One thing to be stressed is the necessity of using the lanyard in hooking and releasing so that the hands are kept clear of the block. In addition to the danger of fingers being caught between the hook and the ring, there is the danger of a hand being mauled between the heavy block and the boat as a swell raises the boat unexpectedly. In hooking on, always lead the lanyard through the hoisting ring and then use the lanyard to draw the ring on the hook. The hook should then be held closed by means of the lanyard until the boat is clear of the water and the weight of the boat is on the hook. To prevent the hook from accidentally tripping, the lanyard should be bent around the shank of the hook.

Hoisting In   Assuming that the boat is approaching the side of the ship to be hoisted in, all preparations should be made in advance for receiving it. The davits should be swung out over the side at right angles, and the blocks should be lowered near the water from the davits, crane, or boom. The sea painter should be dropped by means of a light line. The most important point is to be sure that the painter is secured to the boat at the proper time.

When in position the boat coxswain should order his men to hook on the blocks, being sure to hook on with the forward block first. When this has been accomplished, he reports this to the man in charge of the "hoisting-in detail." The man in charge must not commence hoisting until it is reported by the coxswain that the blocks are hooked.

When all is in readiness for hoisting, the man in charge gives the command "set taut." The men on each winch then take the slack out of the falls. Because it is often difficult for the winch men to tell when the slack is out of the falls, the order "heave around together" and then "avast heaving" is given when the slack is out and the falls are taut. When the slack is out, the proceedings are stopped, and the man in charge checks to see that all is in readiness for hoisting, that is, there are no dips or turns in the falls. When everything is ready, he gives the order "heave around together." If one end of the boat is hoisted faster than the other, the command is given, "avast heaving forward (aft)"; then "heave around together" when the boat is again level.

If possible the boat is stopped at deck level to disembark the personnel. When the boat has been hoisted high enough to clear the rail, the order is given "avast heaving," then "pass the stopper." When stoppers are passed and secure, the tension on the hauling part of the falls is eased off by the command "walk back together," at which the men on the winches slack the falls by rotating the turns around the gypsy heads. When the stoppers have taken the strain, the command "up behind and belay" is given. On this command the men at the winches throw off the turns and quickly take the slack to the cleats, where it is belayed. Speed is essential, for at this time the weight of the boat rests entirely on the stoppers. When the falls are belayed, the stoppers are removed and the boat swung in.

12.2   Lowering and Hoisting Boats by Crane or Boom   A lee is first
made and it is preferable in this case to have no way on the ship.
Steadying lines are secured to the bow and stern of the boat and are
tended by the boat handling detail on deck. The safety runner is also
rigged. The boat is then lowered until just clear of the water, and at
the proper moment lowered quickly into the water. As soon as the
boat is waterborne, the ring of the slings is run clear of the hook by
a pull on the safety runner. Figure 12.4 illustrates the use of this safety
runner. When the ship is rolling or pitching, steadying lines should be
used on the crane blocks. The boat's engine should be running before
the boat takes the water. Round fenders should be hung over the bow
and quarter of the boat.

When all preparations have been made for hoisting, including handling the slings from the bight of the safety runner, the boat is worked
up under the crane. The bowline, stern line, and steadying lines are
passed, and the crane block lowered. The slings hang slack in the
bight of the runner while the legs are shackled to the hoisting chain
bridle of the boat.

When hoisting in a seaway using a crane or boom, there are three
principal difficulties to be overcome.

First, after hooking on and hoisting has commenced, the boat may
retouch the water, as the ship rolls, with a violent jerk which may
prove destructive to hoisting gear. To avoid this, advantage is taken
of a quiet moment. When the ship has begun to roll toward the boat
or the boat is on the crest of a wave, the block is quickly lowered, the
ring of the slings is run onto the hook by the safety runner, and
hoisting is commenced.

Second, the rolling of the ship may cause the boat to swing into the
side of the ship as it is being hoisted. This danger is met by the use of
fenders hung over the side of the boat. By properly tending the steadying lines, taking in and holding the slack as necessary, the swing will
be somewhat reduced. The action of the steadying lines is similar to
that of frapping lines. Where the boat is making headway through the
water or the ship is pitching badly, a long bowline and stern line
should be used to help reduce the surge fore and aft as the boat is
being hoisted.

Third, after hoisting and swinging in, difficulty is sometimes encountered in plumbing the boat into the chocks. It is advantageous,
especially where the boats stow close to the side of the ship, to have
four steadying lines, two forward and two aft. These lines should lead
from opposite sides of the boat at the bow and stern so as to cross
each other, thus providing a better lead for steadying the boat into
position.

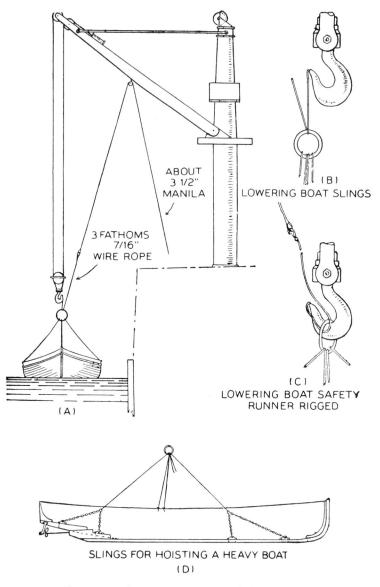

ABOUT
3 1/2"
MANILA

3 FATHOMS
7/16"
WIRE ROPE

(A)

(B)
LOWERING BOAT SLINGS

(C)
LOWERING BOAT SAFETY
RUNNER RIGGED

SLINGS FOR HOISTING A HEAVY BOAT
(D)

Fig. 12.4 Safety runner in use with boat sling.

Figure 12.5 shows a motorboat being hoisted aboard using a gravity davit. With this type of davit, the problem of plumbing the boat directly into its chocks is eliminated. Many other problems encountered when using either cranes or booms are also eliminated when using this type of davit.

Fig. 12.5 Motorboat hoisted aboard using a gravity davit. *(Official U.S. Navy photograph.)*

12.3 Use of the Sea Painter   The sea painter is made fast by toggle for quick release close to the center of the inboard side of the forward thwart and leads out over the gunwale on the inboard side of the boat. It is rigged so to facilitate sheering the boat off from the side of the ship when it is necessary to get away. On many occasions it is necessary to hold the boat alongside the ship in order to embark additional personnel. Many seamen recommend that a lanyard be attached to a bow shackle or ring at the stem which can be passed around the painter and then hauled tight to facilitate holding the boat alongside during this operation.

12.4 Handling a Powerboat   A Navy powerboat crew usually consists of a *coxswain*, a *boat engineer*, a *bow hook*, and a *stern hook*.

The coxswain is in command of the boat, subject to the supervision of any regularly assigned boat officer, or the senior line officer present in the boat. The engineer operates and cares for the engine. The bow hook handles forward lines and falls when making fast or letting go, casts off the sea painter, and acts as forward lookout when under way. The stern hook handles the stern lines and falls and keeps an eye out aft when under way.

12.5 Handling a Powerboat Under Way Steering a powerboat is much the same as handling a single-screw ship, although the reactions of the boat to the engines and rudder are more pronounced. When under way in choppy seas, speed should be reduced somewhat, not only to avoid shipping seas, but also to reduce the strain on the hull and on the machinery due to the racing of the screw when the stern rides clear of the water. Boats may be swamped by running them too fast against the seas. When heading into the sea, it is possible to make fair speed by careful nursing, that is, watching the seas and slowing, or even stopping for a moment as heavier seas bear down upon the boat. As in ships, the boat sometimes may be made to ride much easier when, instead of plunging head-in into the sea or running directly before it, a course is made with the sea on the bow or quarter. If running more or less across the sea, it is well to head up momentarily to meet heavy waves.

A large motor launch or landing craft has a high bow, and turning against the wind and sea is difficult. A large turning circle therefore may be expected and should be allowed for in confined waters.

Attention should be paid to weight distribution, especially in a head sea. Too much weight forward may cause the bow of the boat to plunge into the waves and possibly swamp; too much aft will cause the boat to fall off. When running before a heavy sea, weights aft will reduce yawing, but too much weight aft will cause the bow to ride too high. Wind and current should be observed and allowed for when leaving the ship or landing, as well as the compass course and time to destination, in order that the proper course may be steered in reduced visibility. In approaching any object in the water which may be damaged or injured by contact, such as a seaplane or target drone, always maneuver for a position that, when stopped, the boat and the **object will be separated. A coxswain should be careful to slow in** passing small open craft, men working on floats, or divers and swimmers, so as not to give them his wash. Neglect to do this can often prove dangerous to the other personnel near or in the water. Never pass a pier head, a bow, or stern of an anchored ship too closely.

12.6   Making a Landing   In making a landing, whether at a pier or a ship's accommodation ladder, it is a common mistake to keep too much way on the boat (conditions of load and trim materially affect momentum). The landing should be approached at such an angle and at such a speed that, should the engine fail to back, control of the boat is still maintained and it can be sheered away by rudder action alone without damage. The engines may, and often do, fail to respond promptly. The backing throws the stern off to port (in a right-handed screw) which should be taken into consideration when determining the angle of approach. In coming alongside a ship's accommodation ladder in a current or in a heavy sea, care must be taken not to catch the current or sea on the outboard bow, as this will sweep the bow in forward and perhaps underneath the lower platform of the accommodation ladder. Under these circumstances the boat may be swamped or damaged (Fig. 12.6(a)). The landing should be made by the aid of a boat line from forward, the boat being kept off a little from the side until the line is fast and then eased in by the rudder.

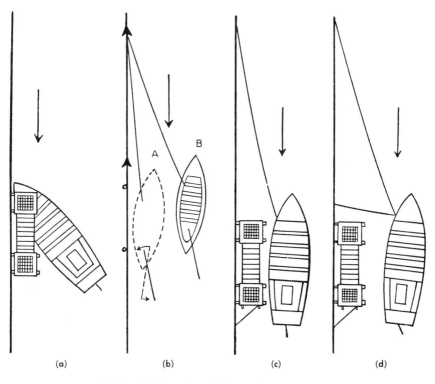

Fig. 12.6 Landings. Action of sea painter.

A powerboat coming alongside in a rough sea or in a strong current should always be required to take a boat line. Crews of powerboats frequently make their landings at an accommodation ladder by the aid of boat hooks alone. This is done by taking hold of anything that is within reach, and holding on, often with great difficulty and with the ever-present danger of a man falling overboard between the ship and the boat. A boat, lying at the accommodation ladder in a current and secured by a boat line made fast to a cleat on the inboard bow of the boat, can be controlled by a touch of the rudder, which sheers the stern out or in and thus catches the current on one bow or the other (Fig. 12.6(b)). Where a ship is rolling in an open roadstead or riding with the wind ahead with swells surging aft alongside the ship, the boat rises and falls dangerously at the lower platform and contact with it may damage or capsize the boat. The need of a long boat line, in effect a sea painter, is here emphasized. By using the boat line in combination with the breast line and by judicious use of rudder and engines, the boat may lie alongside the accommodation ladder without coming into contact with it (Figs. 12.6(c) and (d)). Fenders should always be carried and used freely. See Fig. 12.7 for a rigged accommodation ladder.

12.7 Embarking and Disembarking It is sometimes impossible, because of heavy seas, to make a landing at the accommodation ladder. In this case the passengers may come in over the boat boom. The rudder of the ship is put over to one side or the other, preferably to the side opposite that of the anchor. The ship will yaw back and forth but will usually yaw more on the side away from the rudder, thus creating a partial lee under her quarter. During each weather yaw of the ship, the boat pulls under the quarter by means of a long bowline previously rigged and boat passengers can climb up cargo nets hung for this purpose from the boat boom or from the ship's side. As the ship yaws back, the boat drops back on the painter and awaits the next lee.

Another method of embarking is by a cargo net rigged under a crane or boom. As the boat comes under the crane or boom, the net is lowered and seized by the passenger, who is then swung aboard. When the ship is so equipped, the airplane whip of a crane with its fast hoisting speed should be used. This method is applicable under way in a heavy sea. It should be used only as a last resort, however, because timing must be precise and great danger is always present to the disembarking passengers.

The cargo net is also used in the embarkation of a large number of persons or troops at sea from the ship to a number of boats or landing

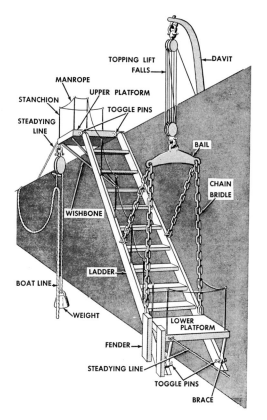

TOPPING LIFT
FALLS
DAVIT
MANROPE
UPPER PLATFORM
STANCHION
TOGGLE PINS
STEADYING
LINE
BAIL
CHAIN
BRIDLE
WISHBONE
LADDER
BOAT LINE
WEIGHT
LOWER
PLATFORM
FENDER
STEADYING LINE
TOGGLE PINS
BRACE

Fig. 12.7 Accommodation ladder.

craft. Cargo nets of sufficient length are hung over the side to reach into the boats. The boat comes alongside and is held there, while the foot of the cargo net is hauled into the boat and kept there while troops or personnel embark. The men who are already hanging on the net then drop into the boat.

Personnel may in like manner be transferred from the boat to the ship, but care must be taken in a heavy sea that the foot of the cargo net is taken into the boat to prevent personnel from falling between the boat and the ship and being crushed.

In the event of an emergency, such as recovering a number of people struggling in the water, cargo nets hung over the side of the ship may expedite their recovery.

12.8 Securing Boats Boats are usually secured to boat booms (Fig. 12.8), bows to guess warps, and sterns to a boat securing line which

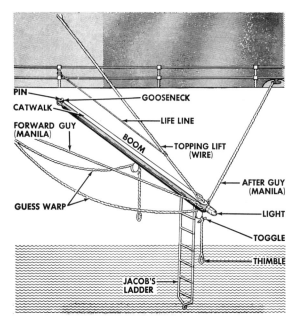

Fig. 12.8   Boat boom.

leads from the end of the boom well aft to the ship's side. This assists in holding the boats apart and in keeping them parallel to the ship. Sufficient slack should be allowed for roll and pitch when securing the boats.

In a heavy sea or storm, the boat boom may become unstable due to the roll and pitch of the ship, making it impractical to secure boats to it. The boats may, in this situation, be secured in tandem from astern or hoisted aboard for the duration of the blow. In either event, always use fenders and take precautions against lines chafing.

12.9   Handling a Boat under Oars   A boat under oars, if properly handled, possesses much the same maneuverability as a powerboat and, in the case of the whaleboat, considerably more seaworthiness. The following commands apply when handling a boat under oars:

Command	Meaning
Stand by the oars	Lift oars off the thwarts, place blades flat on the forward gunwales, push oars forward until handle is over respective thwart.
Up oars	Lift oars to vertical position. Trim blades fore and aft with handle resting on footings.

Command	Meaning
Shove off the bow	Bowman lets go boat rope or sea painter or hauls in boat painter. Shoves off bow using boat hook.
Let fall	Let oars fall into rowlocks using crook of outboard arm to control the oars. Trim oars horizontally with blades trimmed fore and aft. Bowmen up oars before command of "let fall" or put out oars as soon thereafter as possible.
Give way	Move blades of oars forward and dip about half way into the water and start stroke. At end of stroke, blades are feathered fore and aft and pushed forward and another stroke is made.
Oars	Complete the stroke and level the oars horizontally with the blades trimmed fore and aft.
Back water	Row backwards.
Hold water	Complete the stroke, stop rowing, dip blade about half way into water, and hold water to stop the way on the boat.
Stern all	When rowing in ahead motion, complete the stroke, then commence to back-water, gradually increasing the depth of immersion of the blades.
Way enough	When rowing in ahead motion, complete the stroke, raise oars with crook of elbow to about 30 degrees, swing blades forward, and place oars in the boat.
Toss oars	Complete the stroke, come to "oars," raise the oars smartly to the vertical, rest handles on the footings, and trim blades fore and aft.
In bows	The bowmen complete the stroke, swing their oars forward, and boat the oars, then stand by with boat hooks or to receive the sea painter or boat rope.
Boat the oars	From "oars" or from "toss oars," place the oars in the boat with blades forward.
Out oars	Place oars in rowlocks directly from the boated position or from "stand by oars" position.
Stand by to give way	Term used in racing. The blades are pushed to forward position and slightly dipped ready for an instant start.
Give way port, back-water starboard (or vice versa)	The orders are followed to turn the boat without making way ahead or astern.
Give way port, hold water starboard (or vice versa)	This command will result in turning the boat with slight headway.
Trail oars	At this command, the blades of the oars are brought alongside the boat and left trailing in the water, in single-banked boats fitted with swivel rowlocks.

Large boats propelled by oars, such as the whaleboat, are normally steered by a sweep oar. A sweep oar is somewhat larger than an oar used to propel the boat. The coxswain using this oar can steer the boat with a great deal more maneuverability than the standard tiller, dependent on how much leverage is used or how deep the oar is set.

Boats under oars may also be steered by the use of a tiller (rudder); however, except for use in extremely heavy seas or during long periods of time, the tiller possesses no advantages over the sweep oar nor is it as efficient.

12.10 Handling a Boat under Sail It is beyond the scope of this book to describe the handling of the numerous yachts, pleasure craft, and small commercial vessels which use sail as motive power. Ship's boats are workboats. They are not designed to sail and none carry sails except incidentally. Reasons of stowage forbid the use of false keels and special ballast. Because of this, ship's boats must depend upon their beam for stability and always have a tendency to make leeway unless fitted with a centerboard. An attempt will be made to give an elementary explanation of the principles of handling boats under sail with the hope that it will be sufficient for use in an emergency.

12.11 Terms Used The direction of the wind is that from which it blows. To *windward* is into the wind; to *leeward* is down the wind. A *lee shore* is the shore to leeward. The *weather side* is that side exposed to the wind; the *lee side* is the opposite side. Naturally a boat heels away from the wind, so that the lee side is *down* and the weather side *up*. When the rudder is amidships the tiller or helm* is also. The coxswain may put his tiller up to windward and have *weather helm*, or if he puts it down he has *lee helm*. When a boat turns her head into the wind, as if she were going to tack, she is said to *luff*. The opposite of this is *wearing away*.

When sailing with the wind on one side, a puff of wind may strike the sail, causing the boat to heel and possibly capsize. To prevent this, the coxswain may luff by putting his helm down until she turns into the wind; the sails then cease to *draw*, and the boat comes back to an upright position.

It may be necessary in a heavy squall to let the sheets go; therefore, in a small boat *never belay the sheets*. A sheet is a line that controls the foot of a sail. (Fig. 12.9)

When a sheet is hauled in and the boom or foot of the sail is nearly fore and aft, the sheets are said to be *hauled aft*. In *setting the jib aback* or *backing the foresail*, the weather sheets are *flattened aft*. This may be required to give more turning effect in tacking and is also done in

---

* While the terms "helm" and "tiller" have been officially banned in connection with modern ships, they are still applicable to sailboats and will be used here in accordance with original practice.

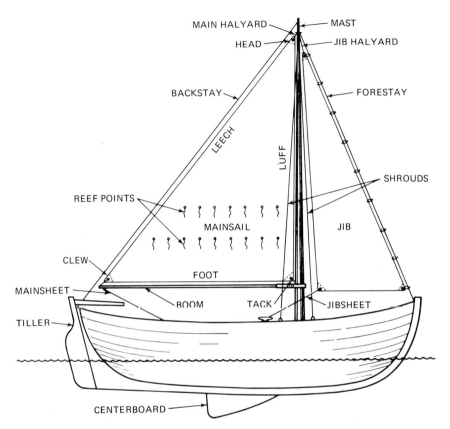

MAIN HALYARD
MAST
HEAD
JIB HALYARD
BACKSTAY
FORESTAY
LEECH
LUFF
SHROUDS
REEF POINTS
MAINSAIL
JIB
CLEW
FOOT
MAINSHEET
BOOM
TACK
JIBSHEET
TILLER
CENTERBOARD

Fig. 12.9 Typical Merchant Marine lifeboat with sail rigged.

heaving to. To bring the sails more nearly parallel to the centerline of the boat they are *trimmed in;* the opposite is *easing off* or *starting the sheets.*

A boat cannot sail directly into the *eye of the wind,* but depending on the boat and rig, sails at an angle of from four to six points from it. She must thus make a zigzag course upwind on *tacks.* This process is called *beating to windward.* She is said to be sailing *close-hauled* or *on the wind* on each of these tacks.

A sailboat is said to be on the *starboard tack* when the wind is coming over the starboard side, and the *port tack* when the wind is coming over the port side. When a boat is not sailing as close to the wind as possible with advantage, she is said to be *sailing free.* When the true wind is within two points on either quarter, she is said to be *running* before the wind. If, when sailing free, the wind is still forward of the beam, she is said to be on a *close reach;* if the wind is from abaft the beam, she is said to be on a *broad reach*. The *apparent wind* is the wind striking the sails which is generated by a combination of the boat's speed through the water and the *true wind*. In obeying the Rules of the Road the prevailing or true wind fixes the respective **obligations of sailing vessels. (Fig. 12.10)**

Tacking is bringing the boat on the opposite tack, head through the wind. *Wearing* consists in turning the boat from one tack to the other tack, stern through the wind. During this procedure, as the wind

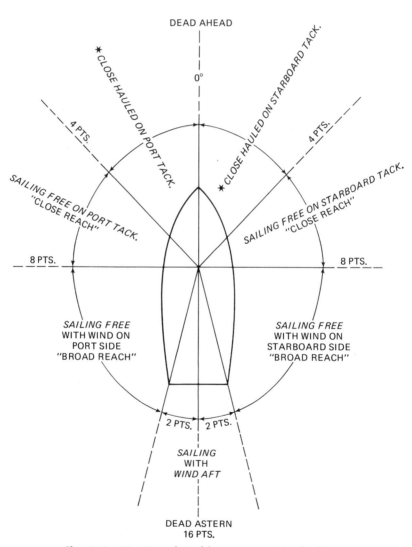

Fig. 12.10 Direction of wind for various points of sailing.

comes aft and the sails are trimmed flat, the boom is carefully and intentionally allowed to swing to the opposite side. The boom is then said to have been *"jibed"* over. Should the boat be sailing free and alter her course so as to bring the wind on the opposite side, carrying the stern through the wind, she has been "jibed," such as "jibing around a buoy."

Trim   To do her best under sail, a boat must be trimmed in accordance with her build and rig. To effect this condition, the trim of the boat and sails must be altered, as necessary, to meet the varying conditions of sailing.

In sailing on the wind, a properly designed and trimmed boat should carry a slight weather helm; that is, she should have a slight tendency to come into the wind. If too much weight is carried forward, the boat trims by the head, the stern rises, offering less lateral resistance aft to the water. The bow being deeper offers greater lateral resistance to the water, and in addition has the increased pressure of the bow wave on the bow. These forces form a couple tending to cause the boat to luff, which, to counteract, necessitates an excessive weather helm. Too much weight aft causes a corresponding tendency to fall off.

If the sails are too flat forward, lee helm is necessary to counteract the tendency to fall off; if too flat aft, weather helm is necessary.

In addition, as the boat heels, the forward component of the force of the wind on the sail acting on the center of effort is displaced to leeward of the keel line, which produces a leverage which tends to make the boat luff. This tendency is especially noticeable in a tall sloop rig, which endeavors to *"work out from under"* when struck by a sudden gust as she is making headway close-hauled.

When running before the wind, weights should be carried aft to decrease yawing, but this may decrease the speed if overdone.

After the boat has been under way for some time, the sail or halyards may stretch, or in wet weather, may shrink. This calls for appropriate setting up or slacking off on the halyards to correct the set of the sail.

12.12   Close-hauled—on the Wind   On the wind, a boat should carry a little weather helm. The sails should be kept well full, sheets not too flat, but everything drawing and the boat alive. It is a common mistake to get the sheets so flat that the boat, while pointing high, actually makes a course to leeward of that which she would make if kept away a little with sheets eased accordingly; and it is of course clear that, if kept away, her speed will be greater than when jammed up into the wind in the hope of stealing a fraction of a point.

A boat of good draft with a deep keel and centerboard, and yachts designed for racing, with fin-keels 10 feet below their normal water line, will lie amazingly close to the wind with little leeway. Ship's boats, however, are not constructed on yachting lines and cannot be held up in the same way. The shape of the sail when close-hauled is very important; the leech should be almost flat, and some boats, to accomplish this, have battens which fit in pockets in the leech of the sail. A little curve or belly should be allowed in the luff. The cut of the sails, the way they are laced to the yards and booms, and the tautness of the halyards all affect the shape of the sails when drawing.

The sails being properly set, the luff of the sails is kept just short of trembling, with weather helm enough to let the helmsman "feel" that she wants to come into the wind. As the wind will vary more or less (in apparent, if not real, direction), it is necessary to be watchful and bring her up or keep her away from time to time in order that she may always be at her best. The sails should be kept fuller in rough than smooth water, as it is more important that the boat be kept *going* so as to be always under command of the rudder. If a heavy breaking sea is seen bearing down upon her, she should be luffed to meet it and kept away again as soon as it has passed. If she loses way she becomes helpless at once. It is dangerous to be caught by a heavy sea on the beam; and, if the course to be made in rough water would bring the boat into the trough, it is the best plan to run off for a time with the sea on the quarter, then bring her up with it on the bow, and so make good the course desired without actually steering it at any time.

For a moderate squall, the boat should be luffed sufficiently to shake the sails without spilling them, thus keeping enough headway to retain control. If the wind becomes stronger, she must be luffed more decidedly and the sheets eased off. The sheets may, of course, be let go, and in an emergency this must be done at once, in addition to putting down the helm. For this reason it is a universal rule in boat sailing that the sheets should never be belayed or left untended in any weather.

12.13 Sailing Free   A boat sails her fastest on this point of sailing. The tendency to luff is strong, especially if the wind is fresh and the boat or sails are improperly trimmed. In a squall the situation is quite different from that in sailing close-hauled. Here the wind cannot be spilled by a touch of the tiller and the only prudent thing to do is to slack the sheets while luffing. In this procedure care must be taken not to jam the helm down hard for it causes the boat to heel dangerously to leeward, and as it turns into the wind the lee quarter and rail may go under, the end of the boom trip in the water, and the boat capsize.

The same thing may happen in jibing if the boat is allowed to fill away too quickly on the new tack. The force of the wind would be much reduced by running off, but the trouble with this is that, if it comes too strong, there is no recourse but to lower the sail, and the chances are that it will bind against the shrouds and refuse to come down. Moreover, there is always danger that the wind will shift in the squall, and the mainsail may jibe with dangerous force.

The gaff-headed rig has the advantage over the tall triangular rig on this point of sailing, but the gaff-headed mainsail must be tended more carefully, as the efficient angle to the apparent wind exists within narrower limits than that of the jib-headed rig. In general, in sailing free the gaff-headed rig must be trimmed closer than a jib-headed rig in order to maintain its most efficient angle. This requires close watching of the apparent wind at all times. Underwater resistance may be somewhat reduced by partially raising the centerboard, if the boat be so equipped.

The tall jib-headed rig gains power as the wind hauls forward and the low gaff-headed rig gains power as the wind draws aft.

12.14 Running before the Wind In a fresh breeze, this is the most dangerous point of sailing, because of the chance of an unintentional jibe. The danger increases if the boat yaws. From this follows the rule to keep the weight fairly well aft, though never at the extreme after end when running before the wind. Very careful steering is required; and, if the sea is heavy, the boom may jibe in spite of all the care that can be taken unless lashed to the lee rail or shroud by a "lazy guy."

Squalls are not as dangerous before the wind as when close-hauled or reaching, unless they are accompanied by a shift of wind. To reduce sail quickly in a gaff-headed boat, to meet this emergency, the peak of the mainsail may be dropped.

In running before the wind, the foresail is sometimes set on the side opposite the mainsail, a temporary boom being rigged by using a boat hook or an oar. A boat sailing in this way is sailing "wing and wing."

If the sea is rough, it is well to avoid running with the wind dead aft. To make a course directly to leeward, the wind may be brought first on one quarter and then on the other, the mainsail being clewed up or the peak dropped each time the course is changed, if the breeze is strong enough to make jibing dangerous.

A serious danger in running before a heavy sea is that of "broaching to." The boat will yaw considerably, the rudder will often be out of water, and the sails will be becalmed in the trough of the sea. The situation here is much like that of a boat running in a surf; and, as in that case, the yawing will be reduced by keeping the weights aft and by steering with an oar. The jib should always be set with the sheet flat aft. It helps to meet and pay her off if she flies to, against the helm. A drag towed over the stern is also helpful.

Another danger in running is that the boom may dip as she rolls and thus capsize the boat.

12.15 Tacking   In tacking, the same principles apply to a boat as to a ship. An after sail tends to bring her head into the wind and a head-sail to keep her off; but all sails, so long as they draw, give her head-way and so add to the steering power of the rudder.

It is clear that a short full boat will turn to windward better than a long narrow one and will require a much shorter distance for coming around. Thus a short boat is preferable to a long one for working up a narrow channel.

When about to tack, the coxswain should let her fall off a little to fill the sails and gain good headway, and he should watch for smooth water and avoid luffing into a breaking wave. The rudder should not be suddenly put hard over, but should be put over enough to have a good effect at first and then more and more as the boat swings; by the time the boat is swinging rapidly the rudder should be over about 30 or 35 degrees and held there.

Under ideal conditions, a boat, close-hauled but with good way on, shoots into the wind as the tiller is eased down, making a good reach to windward and filling away on the new tack, without a moment losing headway. The main boom is hauled amidships in a two-masted boat and nearly amidships in a single-masted boat, and as the jib and the foresail lift, their sheets are let go. The boat comes head to wind and as she pays off on the new tack the sheets are hauled aft and she is steadied on her course. Under less favorable conditions, such as a heavy head sea or a very light breeze, tacking is not so simple.

If the boat gets in "irons," the jib sheet must be held out on the old lee bow to pay her head around. Care must be taken not to make a "back sail" of the mainsail. If she gathers sternway, the rudder is shifted, and if necessary, an oar is gotten out to help her around. The statement is sometimes made that it is lubberly to use an oar in a boat under sail. The lubberly part is the getting into a position where an oar is needed.

Carrying the weights forward is favorable for tacking, but when a boat has sternway she may be helped around by putting a few of the crew on the (new) lee quarter, where, by increasing the immersion of the full lines of the counter, they may add to the resistance and cause the bow to fall off.

Attention may again be called to the fact that in squally weather a boat is in a dangerous position whenever she is without headway, because she can be neither luffed nor kept away in the event of being struck by a heavy gust. If, through ignorance or carelessness, the sheets are belayed at such a time, the danger is greatly increased.

12.16 Wearing In beating to windward, boats ordinarily go about by tacking, because in tacking they turn into the wind and gain ground to windward. In wearing around they turn away from the wind, losing more or less distance to leeward according to circumstances; still it is often possible to wear in winds so strong or water so rough that tacking ship's boats is impossible. It is often necessary to resort to wearing when maneuvering in close quarters, such as clearing a dock or avoiding a collision.

In wearing, the helm is put up and the mainsheet eased off in order to help in bearing away and to get the maximum effect of the mainsail in increasing headway. When the wind comes nearly aft the sheets are rounded in smartly in such a manner that both the sail and the stern pass through the wind at the same time. As the sails jibe over, the sheets are eased off slowly and gradually. Care should be taken at this point, especially with a sloop rig, that the boat not be allowed to come up on the new tack too quickly, as this may bring about a dangerous heel to leeward.

The details of the maneuver may vary considerably, according to the conditions of wind and sea and peculiarities of the boat as to rig and trim. In boats of more than one mast, it is best to sail dead before the wind, trim in the sails, jibe them, and ease them out on the new tack in the order of jib, foresail, and mainsail.

In a fresh breeze, as jibing is dangerous, the mainsail should be doused, brailed up or the peak dropped before the wind comes aft, and set again in time to bring her to the wind on the new tack.

12.17 Remarks on Jibing A sail is "jibed" when it is allowed to swing from one side to the other, the wind being aft or nearly so, and the sail full first on one side and then on the other. This may be done intentionally, as in wearing or in simply changing course, or it may come unexpectedly from a shift of wind or from the yawing of the boat. As it necessarily involves a violent swing of the sail, it puts a heavy strain upon the spars and rigging; it endangers everyone in its path and causes the boat to lurch more or less steeply to leeward. At this point the boat shows a strong tendency to luff on the new tack, and if not met with the rudder the boat may be knocked down and capsized.

It is important in jibing that the sails be trimmed flat before the stern of the boat is brought into the wind, and after the boom has jibed over, the sheets should be started slowly and gradually. The trimming of the sheets should be so timed with the swinging boat that the helmsman does not have to check his swing and wait for the sails to be trimmed in, nor should the boat be allowed to run with the sheets flat aft. In either case the boat loses speed, and loss of speed is loss of control.

12.18 Reefing When an open boat begins to ship spray and water over the lee rail, it is time to reef. A boat that is decked over may run with her lee rail awash; but when an open boat heels her gunwale close to the surface of the water, it must be remembered that a fresher puff may bear the gunwale lower without warning, and that the moment it dips, the boat will almost certainly fill and capsize.

The details of reefing will depend upon the rig, but a few general **rules may be laid down. The crew should be stationed before begin**ning, and should all be required to remain seated. The boat is then luffed, but not to the point where steerageway and control are lost. One hand lowers the halyards of each sail as much as necessary, another hauls down on the luff and shifts the tack. The sheet is hauled in a little to let the men get hold of and gather the foot. The clew earing, followed by the points, are then passed, and the halyards manned. The sail is then hoisted and the sheets trimmed as the boat fills away on her course.

If the boat has more than one sail, it is a good plan to reef them one at a time.

Handling Boats in a Surf

The proper handling of boats in a surf is an art in itself, calling for special judgment and skill that can be acquired only by practical experience. Some groups of seamen, such as fishermen along the New Jersey coast and the U.S. Coast Guard, have every opportunity to acquire this skill through experience and, in addition, are equipped with boats specially designed for the purpose. They are thus often able to take boats successfully through a surf so dangerous that it would be disastrous for the ordinary boat handler.

Amphibious operations require landings to be made regularly on beaches where more or less surf may be expected, and landing craft are designed especially for this work. In addition, their crews must be specifically trained for this type of work.

Due to the hazards of the sea any seaman is likely to find it necessary to take almost any kind of ship's boat or raft ashore through a surf. He may have a green or exhausted crew whose lives as well as his own depend on his performance; therefore it behooves each of us to learn all he can of the subject both by study and by actual experience whenever opportunity offers.

A surf never looks as dangerous from seaward as it is, especially from a small boat. When there is any possibility of a surf, a beach should be approached with caution, and care should be taken to remain well outside the breakers until ready to make the attempt at running the surf. If there is any possibility of help from the shore, it should be awaited before running a heavy surf. If no help is available and it is necessary to run the surf unaided, two principles should be kept in mind. First, the boat *must* be kept end on to the surf to avoid broaching and capsizing. Second, the boat must be able to meet and resist the breakers to keep them from driving her toward the beach out of control or, in extreme cases, driving her under or throwing her end over end.

Methods of running the surf vary with the height of surf, type of beach, set of current, weather, type and trim of boat, gear available, and experience and condition of crew. The means and methods to be used must be decided after a consideration of these factors which by their nature preclude the statement of other than general principles. Although there are various methods for handling boats in a surf and accomplishing a landing successfully, only the one considered safest and simplest is discussed here.

12.19 Landing through a Surf   The most important consideration for the inexperienced coxswain is the necessity for remaining outside the breakers for a long enough time to study the surf carefully. Care must be exercised to ensure that the boat is kept far enough outside the outermost line of breakers to avoid being caught unexpectedly by a sea. When this is done, one will find that the large seas come in a more or less regular sequence, usually three or four in a series. Then follows a period of smaller seas during which there is a period of build-up. It is during this time that the entrance into the line of breakers must be made.

Having determined the period of the seas and decided on the run in, wait until the last sea of the large series breaks just inshore of the boat and then turn so as to present the bow seaward and back in. As each succeeding wave overtakes the boat, it may be necessary to pull ahead to meet it. With this method the oarsmen are normally faced so that the coxswain may best use them to control the speed and direction of the boat. Too much emphasis cannot be placed on the full utilization of the oars in steering the boat. It is possible for the boat to be kept headed directly into the seas by having first one side and then the other give way as may become necessary. As each sea passes, "stern all" and gain more distance toward the beach. With each overtaking sea the boat will be carried shoreward a considerable distance, even though the oarsmen are pulling against it. If even the smaller seas are of dangerous size, it will be necessary to impart a great deal of way to the boat in order to give it sufficient inertia to overcome the power of the sea and avoid broaching.

Broaching is most apt to occur when the seaward end of the boat is lifted by an onrushing wave, depressing the shoreward end in the relatively calm, motionless water which is immediately in front of the wave. We have, under these circumstances, one end of the boat deeper than the other and embedded in stationary water while the other end has a tremendous force acting on it. It is apparent that this force applied to one side or the other of the seaward end of the boat will create a powerful turning moment, one arm of which is equal to about the length of the boat. Thus, it is obvious that a great amount of power is necessary to overcome the forces which tend to cause broaching.

Considering the weight of the boat constant, since buoyancy is also a paramount feature, this power can be met only by rowing strongly against each oncoming wave. Weights should be located in the bow (seaward end) of the boat, but not in the extreme end. Oarsmen should use a short, fast, powerful stroke so that they may back-water as each sea passes with as little delay as possible.

It should now appear that the seaward end of the boat is the most important and the one on which adverse forces are apt to be most dangerous. Hence, it follows that, if there were some means of holding the bow steady while the overtaking seas pass, the problem would be less difficult. In practice there are two very handy devices for accomplishing this. These are the *drogue* and the *surf-line*.

A drogue is a conical-shaped bag about 2 feet wide across the mouth and 4½ feet long. It is towed mouth foremost by a 2½-inch line which is secured to the mouth by means of a bridle. A small line known as the tripping line is made fast to the apex, or pointed end. When towed mouth foremost, the drogue fills with water and offers considerable resistance; when towed by means of the tripping line, the resistance becomes negligible and the drogue passes through the water easily.

When a drogue is used in a boat landing through a surf, it must be carefully tended by men in the bow so that there is always a strain on the towing line when a sea overtakes the boat. When the sea passes it is desirable to "stern all," and the tripping line is hauled taut so that the drogue passes easily through the water. The coxswain and men tending the drogue must be alert to slack the tripping line well in advance of the arrival of the next wave in order to allow it to fill with water and exert the greatest resistance to keep the bow pointed sea-ward. A drogue is especially recommended when there is any current setting parallel to the beach.

A surf-line consists of a 2½- or 3-inch line made fast to an anchor just beyond the outermost line of breakers. This line should be about 150 fathoms long. The line which is coiled in the boat free for running is payed out by men in the bow so that there is always a strain on it when the boat is overtaken by a sea; as the sea passes, the line is again payed out.

A surf-line exerts a more positive force on the bow of a boat land-ing through a surf, but it is not recommended when there is any appreciable current setting parallel to the beach. The reason for this is, of course, that the farther the boat progresses (i.e., the longer the scope), the more it will be carried down by the current. Hence, there will actually come a time when the boat will be carried broadside to the waves or nearly so and be in grave danger of capsizing. Another disadvantage of the surf-line is that it actually stops the progress of the boat toward the beach each time the men in the bow hold it to permit a sea to pass under the boat.

12.20 Landing Craft (LCVP) The most interesting and important phase of LCVP operation is the run to the beach. In the surf, the coxswain and crew are really put to the test. There are a number of factors to be kept in mind when the student coxswain goes into the surf for the first time. These will be discussed roughly in the order in which they occur during a landing operation.

The coxswain should make certain that each crew member is in his place as he makes ready for the run. It is necessary that all men wear life jackets when the LCVP or LCM is launched. There may be no time to slip them on in an emergency. Even a champion swimmer can drown quickly if he happens to be knocked out for a moment in an accident, as when a boat turns over.

As the beach is approached, the rolling ground swell which begins to rise several hundred yards out from the shore determines the size of the surf. Once inside the breaker line, course should not be changed. Therefore, the boat should be lined up with the spot on the beach where it is to be landed. This should be done before the boat enters the surf.

The LCVP, handled by an expert, can cope with a 12-foot surf, but a 6- to 8-foot surf is high enough to cause plenty of trouble, especially for the beginner. Regulate the speed of the boat so that it rides in to the beach *just behind the crest of a comber.* If the boat is right on the crest it will be set down *hard* on the sand when the wave crashes and ebbs.

The boat should be kept *at right angles to the surf.* The LCVP is likely to broach if this rule is not observed. Usually the surf goes in parallel to the beach and if you hit the sand head-on the boat will ground safely.

The exact spot at which the coxswain aims his boat should be chosen with care. The LCVP was designed primarily to run aground on a sand beach. Any large stones or outcropping of rocks that might damage hull or ramp should be spotted in advance. Both coxswain and forward lookout will need to keep a sharp eye open for underwater obstacles.

If the boat should run aground on a sandbar some distance from the beach, the engine should be run slowly in forward speed until the hull is floated partly free by the next breaker. When the boat has this flotation, the engine speed should be increased. If the boat is not freed, the engine speed should be cut and an attempt made when the next incoming wave lifts the boat.

It is unwise to assume that the water is shallow all the way to shore if the boat grounds some yards out. Unless word is received from the beach party, the unloading of troops should not be attempted. The water may be 10 feet deep a few yards inshore from a sandbar that has stalled the boat.

After clearing all bars, the LCVP should be run on the beach at a good speed to ensure a good hold on the sand. When properly beached, the boat is at right angles to the surf and its keel is grounded along its entire length. In this position the boat is not likely to broach while loading or discharging cargo.

The engine should be kept turning over at about 1200 rpm to hold the boat well up on the beach. Avoid letting the screw face wildly. Idle down when water recedes and the screw loses its bite between breakers.

Should the engine fail or some mishap occur when the boat is within the surf-line but not aground, the first thing to do is drop a stern anchor. This helps to hold the stern at right angles to the breakers if the line is payed out carefully. *Do not snub* the line, but let the boat surge toward the beach with each comber. Only when the boat touches the beach is the anchor line snubbed to prevent broaching. The flow of the tide is something to take into consideration if the boat will be beached for any length of time.

Fig. 12.11 Beaching an LCVP.

Several precautions may be taken to keep from broaching. *First,* be sure that the breaking seas are kept dead astern. Otherwise the stern will fall off to port or starboard as the water dashes against it. *Second,* drive well up on the beach so that the entire length of the keel is aground. *Third,* speed up the engine in forward gear as incoming waves float the boat. *Fourth,* see that the antibroaching lines are **thrown to the beach party at once. Figure 12.11 (A, B, C) shows how** these lines are used to prevent broaching.

No hard and fast rule can be laid down for the use of the anti-broaching lines. The coxswain must think and act intelligently to allow for wind, different types of beaches, and other factors influencing broaching. Usually, however, it is wise to line up the bow with some object on the beach. Then it is immediately apparent if the bow or stern is moving. If this happens, the rudder should be put *in the direction in which the stern is swinging.* Then the engine should be speeded to drive higher on the beach to bring the stern around. Sometimes, if the surf is not high, it is possible to free the broached boat by engine power alone.

When retracting from the beach the coxswain tackles the most difficult part of the landing operation. It is during retraction that the beginner at boat handling is likely to broach or damage the rudder, screw, or skeg.

The coxswain will be most successful in getting away from the shore and safely beyond the breaker line if he observes the following:

1. The rudder should be set amidships before attempting to retract. In the LCVP this may be done by running the engine about half speed ahead. The discharge current or wash from the screw will force the rudder into an amidships position.
2. The bow should be lined up with an object on the beach. If this is done it will be easier to note any swing of the boat soon enough to correct the movement and hold her straight.
3. The engine should be shifted into reverse and a wave to float the hull should be awaited. When flotation is achieved the engine should be accelerated. Nearly always the boat will move backward a short distance.
4. When the wave recedes the engine should be prevented from racing needlessly as the screw loses its bite in the water; this will prevent the rudder and skeg from digging into the sand upon which they rest.
5. If the bow begins to swing, the steering wheel should be turned *in the direction of the swing.* This should bring the bow back. The wheel should then be turned back before this return swing

is completed or the bow will move too far and require more maneuvering.

6. Once the LCVP is floating free and has passed any outer sand-bars, it should be backed at right angles to the surf until outside of the breaker line.

7. Once through the breakers, and when the boat is on the crest of a wave, the rudder should be put over hard, and the engine shifted into forward and accelerated. This will cause the boat to pivot quickly and take the next sea on the bow.

12.21 Beaching and Retracting with the LCM   Most of the general rules laid down for running in to the beach in the LCVP are observed when piloting the larger tank lighter. The boat is kept at right angles to the surf and is driven ashore just behind the crest of a wave. It should be grounded well up on the beach along the entire length of the keel and the engines kept running with enough speed to hold the boat firmly beached while loading or unloading.

Once the coxswain is familiar with his boat, the tank lighter is easier to retract than the smaller, single-screw LCVP. This is due to the fact that the twin-screw design gives better control over the bow's tendency to fall off to port or starboard when backing through the surf. in retracting, the LCM's rudders are put amidships, both engines are reversed, and she is backed off slowly.

If the bow falls off to starboard there is no need to spin the wheel. The coxswain simply speeds up the port engine in reverse until the swing is corrected. Ease off on the throttles, however, as soon as the bow begins to come back to starboard. Otherwise it might continue its swing and fall off to port.

Like the LCVP, the tank lighter can broach in a few seconds. Because of her greater size, the LCM is apt to be more difficult to salvage. The same precautions to be followed with the LCVP help to keep the LCM at right angles to the surf.

12.22 The Motor Lifeboat   Prudent seamanship requires that a boat always be kept ready for immediate use as a lifeboat. Aboard all men-of-war and many passenger liners a boat of the motor whaleboat type is used as the ready lifeboat.

Men-of-war, if so equipped, have two of their boats rigged as ready lifeboats, one on either side to expedite lowering. Smaller men-of-war and most auxiliaries have only one boat rigged as a lifeboat. Passenger liners like large men-of-war have two small boats rigged, normally situated on either side forward of the boat deck. The sea painter is

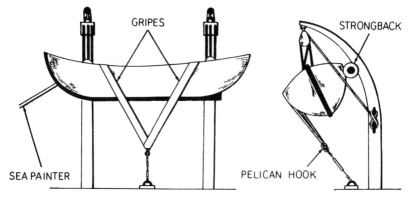

Fig. 12.12 Ready lifeboat.

kept rigged, and it becomes only a matter of releasing the gripes before the boat can be lowered. Most Navy lifeboats are rigged for
lowering by radial davits as shown in Fig. 12.12 whereas most merchant ships use gravity davits. It must be pointed out that boats of the
Merchant Marine are in themselves lifeboats and, as such, are rigged
for immediate use. Thus, with but few exceptions all boats aboard
merchant ships may be used as ready lifeboats with no special preparations.

Since the gravity davit does not require that the boat be swung out
to facilitate speed in launching, only the use of the radial davit will
be discussed in any detail. As a general rule the davits are swung outboard and the boat is griped against a spar spanned between the davit
arms called a *strongback* or *pudding spar.* The boat is griped up
against two puddings (fenders) built up around the spar. The V-shaped
gripes (made of line or wire covered with canvas to prevent chafing)
have their upper ends shackled to eyes in the strongback or pudding
spar or to each davit head. The lower end of the V is attached to the
deck, which is joined by means of a turnbuckle equipped with a
pelican hook. The turnbuckle is used to take up any slack and keep
the boat snug against the puddings. The pelican hook is used for
quick release.

In order that the weight of the boat does not rest upon the falls,
wire pendants called preventers are run from the davit heads to the
hoisting eyes of the boat. These pendants are also equipped with
pelican hooks to facilitate quick release. Aboard auxiliaries and merchant ships, the lifeboat generally rests upon chocks directly beneath
the davit. To secure this boat for sea in its chocks, clamps equipped
with a turnbuckle are used. The lower end is secured to the deck and
the clamp is fitted over the gunwale. Several quick turns of the turn-

buckle are all that is required to release the clamp and have the boat ready for instantaneous lowering.

Helicopter Operations

12.23 The Helicopter at Sea The helicopter is of marked significance to mariners, performing a variety of useful or vital services in its capacity of a physical link between ships and between ship and shore. Some of the many tasks regularly performed offshore by helicopters are:

At-sea pickup and transport of emergency medical cases.
Search and rescue.
Transport of supplies and personnel.
Icefield reconnaissance.
Planeguard duty for navy aircraft carriers.
Anti-submarine search and attack.
Coast and Geodetic Survey support.
Minefield reconnaissance and minesweeping.

A responsible mariner will inform himself of helicopter capabilities, limitations, and requirements, for he can expect to work closely with this unique tool at some stage, perhaps on short notice.

Life or health is frequently at stake in helicopter operations. Those awaiting help may be jeopardized by the failure, delay, or inefficiency of a helicopter mission. Participants or bystanders may be endangered by an accident, not necessarily a crash, during operations with a helicopter. Consequently, knowledge of and adherence to prescribed operating and safety procedures, and the development of informed judgment are required of those working with or near helicopters.

12.24 Helicopter Types In general configuration, the two most common types are the following.

Single rotor—having two or more large horizontal rotor blades rotating about a single vertical axis near the helicopter center of gravity. There is also a small vertical sidefacing rotor at the tail used to counteract the torque effects of the large rotor and to provide control about the yaw axis.

Tandem rotor—having two sets of horizontal blades. One set of blades (one rotor) is placed near each end of the fuselage. These rotors rotate in opposite directions, thus no vertical anti-torque propeller is required.

Helicopters may be either single-engine or multi-engine. The transition from reciprocating engines to gas turbine engines in recent years

Fig. 12.13 An HH 3F twin-turbine helicopter gives crewmen a lift with the heavy aids to navigation daymark they are assembling for an offshore site. The Coast Guard's new fleet of HH 3Fs are equipped for supporting world-wide navigational aids, border patrol, law enforcement, and oceanographic and geodetic research. Their primary work of search and rescue is facilitated by the unique airborne navigational computers they carry. *(Official U.S. Coast Guard photograph.)*

Fig. 12.14 The HH 52A, known also as the S 62, has a maximum speed of 100 miles an hour, a cruising speed of 98 miles an hour, and a loading capacity of more than 3000 pounds. A versatile aircraft, the HH 52A can operate from water, land, ice, snow, swamp, mud, or practically any other surface. *(Official U.S. Coast Guard photograph.)*

has markedly improved helicopter performance. (See Figs. 12.13 and 12.14).

12.25 Helicopter Characteristics Helicopters perform many demanding tasks under difficult conditions. However, they are as vulnerable to misuse as any complex machine. Respect for their characteristic limitations is as important as proper use of their capabilities.

Lift for flight is achieved by the speed of rotation of the rotor, rather than the forward speed of the vehicle as in the conventional airplane. Consequently hovering, sidewards, and backwards flight are possible, within definite limits.

Helicopters are characterized by relatively slow airspeed. While top speeds well in excess of 150 knots can be reached by modern helicopters, many older models cruise at speeds of 65 to 85 knots. The most frequent and critical helicopter operations take place at very slow speeds and low altitudes. These include takeoff and landing, hovering, and flight operations around a ship.

In case of failure of an engine in flight, a twin-engine helicopter may be able to use the remaining good engine to continue flight or to make a powered landing. A single-engine helicopter must land in the event of engine failure. However, under most flight conditions the helicopter can be brought to a controlled landing, by the process of "autorotation." This is a maneuver in which the helicopter's forward motion, descent, and proper pilot action cause the rotors to continue to turn, and so produce enough lift for "gliding" flight.

Modern helicopters of moderate to large size, particularly those operated by the U.S. Coast Guard and the U.S. Navy, are equipped for instrument flight, and can operate over water in weather of moderate severity. Older helicopters and the smaller models of current helicopters have very limited ability to operate at night over the water or under conditions of low visibility. Unless equipped with the proper **instruments and radios for instrument flying, the best helicopter pilot is running a great risk when he undertakes helicopter flight without a visible horizon.**

The useful operating range of a specific helicopter is primarily influenced by the wind velocity and the rate of fuel consumption, which depends upon the engine power setting used. Range and endurance vary with specific helicopter models and the conditions under which the helicopter is operated. Sustained high-speed flight or sustained hovering markedly reduce flight endurance because of high power settings. A typical endurance figure for normal flight conditions, however, would be about two to three hours, with another hour available in some cases by the use of auxiliary fuel tanks. Hovering, slow flight, and lateral flight are valuable helicopter characteristics. Sideward and backward flight are limited to a few knots airspeed, except that the tandem rotor helicopter can accomplish sideward flight of up to about 30 knots. A helicopter normally must hover facing into the wind since, with the wind abeam or wind aft, slow ground speed or hovering is possible only in very light wind conditions.

In the hovering condition, the action of the rotors pushes air downwards to the surface. The air then flows outward and circulates back into the rotors from the top. This downwash has considerable velocity and its effects should be anticipated by those working with helicopters. For personnel working near or under a hovering helicopter on a deck, the wearing of helmet and goggles is advisable. Debris and loose articles of clothing are hazards in the vicinity of a hovering helicopter. Objects may be blown overboard or low-density objects, such as hats, can be captured by the recirculating air pattern and pulled into the helicopter blades, causing damage. When hovering over the water, downwash blows spray at high velocity, which can reduce the efficiency of personnel in a boat under or near the helicopter. A further potential hazard exists with regard to turbine-powered helicopters, where the ingestion of foreign objects into the engine's air intake is almost certain to result in engine failure. Shipboard personnel must be aware of this hazard and make every effort to reduce the foreign object damage (FOD) potential.

Many modern helicopters are amphibious, capable of landing in the water in light to moderate sea states. If some lift is being provided by the rotors, considerable waterborne stability is provided. Conversely, with no rotor lift waterborne stability is reduced. In this conditions, if the helicopter rolls or pitches very much the tips of the rotor blades may touch the water.

For operations where landing is not possible or desirable, the helicopter will normally use a powered hoist, carrying 50 to 100 feet of strong, flexible steel cable. A hook at the free end of the cable permits the attachment of devices such as a net, basket, Stokes litter, light cargo in a bag, or a harness or sling for lifting a man into the helicopter. Some helicopters are rigged with external cargo hooks underneath, at the center of gravity, for the attachment of heavy cargo in cargo nets or on pallets in slings.

A common device for hoisting able personnel to and from the helicopter is a sling which attaches to the hoist cable hook. This is a loop of webbing, sometimes padded into a horsecollar shape. The bight of the loop should always be placed at the back of the man to be hoisted, with the ends passing under each arm up to the hook. A common and dangerous mistake occurs in placing the bight in front, over the chest.

12.26 Wind Wind velocity and turbulence are major factors in helicopter operations and must be taken into account at all times by the pilot and by shipboard personnel working with a helicopter. The presence or absence of relative wind can determine or limit the helicopter's ability to take off or hover safely with a heavy load. This is particularly true in hot, humid weather which reduces helicopter performance.

A helicopter can fly in forward flight with somewhat more load than it can safely support in hovering flight, because of increased lift provided by the relative wind created by the helicopter's forward motion. In a practical sense, this means that under some conditions a helicopter is able to maintain station over the deck of a ship only if the ship maneuvers to provide the necessary relative wind velocity. With insufficient wind velocity, the helicopter may not be able to hover, or may operate with inadequate margin of safety to properly cope with turbulence or an emergency.

The relative wind with respect to the ship should, if possible, satisfy several conditions. Preferably it should provide a clear, overwater, upwind approach for the helicopter to the position at which the ship-helicopter operation, such as hoisting a man, will take place. To minimize turbulence, the wind should reach the helicopter after having passed around as little superstructure as possible. The wind direction should permit the helicopter to face into the wind, or nearly so, while maintaining its hover over the ship. This helicopter heading should permit a clear view of the ship by the pilot and the hoist operator, both of whom are normally stationed on the helicopter's right-hand side, so that they can have adequate visual reference for accurate positioning over the deck. If a clear deck or level space exists aft for helicopter operation, it can be seen that these conditions are well satisfied by the ship taking an upwind course and speed which establishes the relative wind about 10 to 30 degrees on the port bow, with relative velocity of over 10 knots. The helicopter pilot and the hoist operator then have the ship in full view during approach and hover. If the helicopter must operate at a point other than the after end of of the ship, a relative wind close to broad on the ship's beam is generally preferable, to permit a clear approach. In the case of a ship dead in the water less flexibility exists and the pilot must determine whether safe operations are possible.

When the helicopter is traveling point to point, wind direction affects performance and navigation. A helicopter cruising at 60 knots airspeed on a course directly into a 30-knot wind can achieve, at most, one half its no-wind range, and has a ground speed of only 30 knots. Any crosswind component reduces range, even for a round-trip flight, because of the necessity to crab into the wind to maintain the desired track. Wind effects on helicopter ground speed must be kept in mind by controlling personnel of a ship from which a helicopter operates.

12.27   Emergency or Occasional Operations with Helicopter   The ship which does not regularly operate with a helicopter should nevertheless anticipate the possibility and be prepared. The most probable occurrence will be the necessity to transfer an individual between the ship and an airborne helicopter by helicopter hoist. If a U.S. Coast Guard helicopter is involved, the ship can expect to be contacted on radio (HF, VHF, or UHF), and briefed by the pilot as to his intentions and requirements for ship actions. Such a brief set of instructions obviously is no substitute for previous indoctrination of ships' personnel. If the helicopter is unable to establish radio contact, the degree of urgency and pilot's discretion will determine whether or not a message drop, large writing on a blackboard, or other communication will permit enough information exchange for the personnel transfer or other mission to be safely accomplished. Fuel limitations may preclude time-consuming attempts to communicate at length by other than radio, or to engage in prolonged hovering over the ship. Consequently, ship action which immediately demonstrates familiarity with helicopter operations by steering a good course and by manning the appropriate deck area with properly equipped personnel saves valuable time and may make the difference between mission success and failure.

12.28   Sustained Operations with Helicopter   A ship which is to operate a helicopter from its deck should prepare, with the help of the helicopter pilot, a "Helicopter Operations Bill" which details stations and defines duties and responsibilities for various operations; including launch, land, refuel, and emergencies such as deck crash, fire, and man overboard. Explicit safety precautions should be part of the bill or issued as a separate directive for wider promulgation.

12.29   Safety Precautions   Implicit in the foregoing description of helicopter characteristics and limitations have been the basic precautions to be observed in operating with helicopters. Listed below are some specific procedures and precautions.

  A. *Preparations for receiving helicopters for hovering transfer:*
    1. A red flag prominently displayed at the landing or hovering area indicates that the ship is not ready to receive the helicopter, and an approach should not be commenced until a green flag is displayed. A green flag indicates that the ship **is ready to receive the helicopter. (Fig. 12.15.)**

2. Provide a clear deck, free of loose gear and free of any projection on which a hook, basket, litter, or line may foul.
3. Remove or rig out of the way: stays, booms, whip antennae, loose halyards, and other obstructions which may endanger **the helicopter in the hover position.**
4. Clear from the vicinity all exposed idle personnel. High-velocity blade fragments, in case of accident, can endanger bystanders.
5. Have a lifeboat manned and, if possible, rigged out.
6. Have medical, fire, and rescue parties stationed.
7. If able personnel are to be transferred, have them in life jackets and briefed in procedure.
8. Have the helicopter hoist detail properly trained, clothed, and equipped. A pair of bolt cuttters should be readily available for emergency use. An electrician's grounding tool should be available to ground the cable from the helicopter.

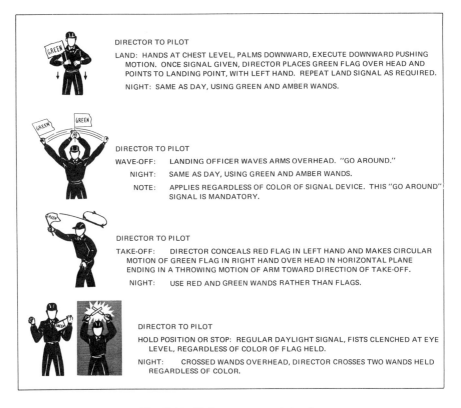

Fig. 12.15 Helicopter control signals.

Large amounts of static electricity build up in the helicopter due to blade rotation and a man can get a bad jolt from **touching the cable, basket or litter.**

9. If a stretcher (Stokes litter) patient is to be transferred, have a light free-running tending line attached to one end of the litter. This is hand-tended under very light tension to orient the litter. DO NOT SECURE LINE TO SHIP. Attach a hoisting bridle to the litter with the short lines at the head, so that the head will ride high.

10. Under penalty of causing the helicopter to crash, NEVER attach the helicopter hoist cable (or any line from heli-copter) to the ship, or allow it to become fouled. Should this inadvertently occur, notify the pilot and cut the cable *imme-diately* with bolt cutters or heavy cable cutters. The cable is tough stainless and will not yield to a light tool. The only exception to immediate cable cutting is the case where there is no doubt that the pilot knows the situation and is able to hover low to keep slack in the cable until it is freed.

11. Do not attempt to hook on to the hoisting hook until slack exists in the hoist cable sufficient to accommodate unex-pected relative motion between helicopter and the deck which can be caused by a pitching deck or by helicopter motion in turbulent air.

12. The helicopter should spend as little time over the deck as possible. When not actually performing hoist maneuvers, the pilot should normally move abeam to windward so as to avoid hitting the ship in case of loss of power.

13. Personnel who operate under the helicopter should be trained or briefed for maximum efficiency so as to minimize hover time and time spent under the helicopter.

14. Personnel should be aware of the static electricity hazard associated with the helicopter hoisting operations. Deck per-sonnel should either allow the hook or hoist to touch the deck first, or ground it by using a "deadman's stick."

B. *Launch, land, and on-deck operations:*
A ship operating a helicopter regularly will have detailed instruc-tions available from the helicopter detachments. Some basic precautions are:

1. Caution in moving helicopters aboard ship, or in moving ob-jects near the helicopter, is necessary to avoid damage. The helicopter is very vulnerable to collision and to thrown or falling objects (such as tools, or a baseball).

2. Due to possible existence of turbulent winds over the deck, and deck motion, the helicopter should always be checked and securely tied down on the deck, and if possible spotted facing into the wind.

3. Helicopters should not be fueled with their engine running except in emergency.

4. Personnel should not be allowed to walk under rotors during rotor engagement or shutdown due to blade flapping at low rpm.

5. Personnel should never approach a helicopter on deck while the rotors are turning unless the plane director on deck and the pilot are aware of their presence and permission is granted to approach.

6. Only qualified personnel should be allowed around helicopters, particularly when operating.

7. Fire extinguishers should be manned when starting engines and during all refueling operations.

8. **Launch and recovery cannot be attempted safely while the ship is in a turn.**

9. The pilot is responsible for ensuring that *all* tiedowns are off before lifting the helicopter off. Failure to do so results in an almost certain crash.

C. *Joint rescue operations:*

When a helicopter and surface vessel (ship or boat) jointly engage in a rescue attempt of personnel in the water, maximum coordination is essential. Otherwise mutual interference can result to the detriment of those awaiting rescue, and with hazard to both the helicopter and surface vessel. In no event should competition be permitted to develop. The first to arrive at the exact site of rescue should normally be in charge of the operation. The superior speed and rescue capability of a trained helicopter team should be recognized in most instances. The helicopter and surface vessel may be able to perform rescues simultaneously, or the helicopter's superior search capability utilized. Alternatively, one or the other might better stand by, ready to render assistance, but remaining clear so as to provide ample maneuvering room to the other. When standing clear, the surface vessel should be aware of the helicopter requirement, normally, to make an upwind approach to a point of rescue and should avoid blocking the approach and takeoff path.

Ice Seamanship

With the increasing activity in both the Arctic and Antarctic, an understanding of ice seamanship in its broad sense is becoming more important. The heightened activity includes the finding of oil, gas, and minerals in the Arctic in commercial quantities, the advent of tourism in the Antarctic, and the support of polar science and research plus Naval training in strategic ice-pack areas.

13.1 General In sea-ice areas today a vessel either operates singly or is aided by icebreaker escort. Generally, an unreinforced ship should never attempt to negotiate more than three-tenths of ice concentration by itself, and this estimation depends upon how the ice is disposed. In other words, if it is necessary to break through ice other than the smallest sizes or brash ice, icebreaker assistance is usually required. A vessel with an ice classification, with the increased power and built-in protection from ice damage, has far greater capability in the ice than this. The trend now is to employ only ice-classified vessels and to request icebreaker escort for only the most difficult ice passages, that is, about six-tenths concentration and above. The characteristics of the ice—its hardness, temperature, thickness, amount of snow cover, and salt content—and how it is disposed should be taken into account.

13.2   Polar Ice   Two kinds of ice confront the mariner in the polar regions: (1) icebergs of land origin, and (2) field ice of sea origin (Fig. 13.1.)

Icebergs, composed of frozen moisture from the atmosphere, are of huge bulk and deep draft, the latter being from four to eight times its height, depending upon its shape and density. In clear weather, the outlines of an iceberg can be readily detected by eye. In any kind of visibility, the ship's radar is capable of picking up icebergs, but if many icebergs are in the vicinity during poor visibility, care should be taken to plot continually the position of each in relation to that of the ship or a dangerously close iceberg may be overlooked.

Icebergs should never be approached close aboard by any vessel except, at times, by an icebreaker. During the years before the advent

Fig. 13.1   U.S. Navy icebreaker GLACIER clearing ice from McMurdo Sound channel which leads to main U.S. logistic station in the Antarctic. (*Official U.S. Navy photograph.*)

of radar, many ships were sunk by striking icebergs at high speed during reduced visibility. As a result of the sinking of the *Titanic* by an iceberg in the western North Atlantic in 1912, the International Ice Patrol, financed by maritime interests of many nations and operated by the U.S. Coast Guard, was organized. The positions and tracks of icebergs that present dangers to shipping in the Atlantic are continuously plotted by ships and planes of the Coast Guard. Ships are alerted through broadcasts and notices published by the U.S. Navy.

Icebergs may be avoided by vessels, but field ice, which is composed of frozen seawater, must be crossed or negotiated. This is accomplished most efficiently by traversing the weakest sections of ice or choosing those courses that will take the ship through the areas of highest water-to-ice ratio. As field ice is so important to polar operations, an understanding of its development, distribution, physical characteristics, movements, deterioration, and mechanics is necessary.

Sea ice is never a solid, homogenous mass, except in sheltered sounds and embayments. Rather, it is constantly being broken into floes as variations in temperature, wind, and current create cracks and channels. These same forces propel the sections or pieces of ice apart and together in an accordion-like manner that alternately increases and decreases pressure in the pack.

The term "icebreaking" is actually a misleading term of how a passage is opened through sea ice; the mechanics of the process are better described as "ice displacement." Ice forward of the icebreaker is shoved aside to accommodate the underwater portion of the vessel. Where the ice coverage is too solid to permit lateral displacement, it is necessary to shove the ice over and under adjacent layers.

Only those pieces of ice too large to be readily shoved aside are broken. Breakage is accomplished either by the shock of impact or by cleaving action, in which the bow rises up and cuts through because of weight and the leverage applied at the bow section by the buoyancy of the depressed stern. The broken pieces must still be forced into nearby ice-free areas or the icebreaker will be impeded in its progress. Occasionally, ice is forced under the hull to be caught in the propeller stream and driven astern. Under such circumstances, a piece of ice may become entangled with a propeller, sometimes resulting in a broken blade or shaft. The friction of the ice against the under part of the vessel may also bring the icebreaker to a halt.

The cushioning effect of snow can prevent the upraised bow from returning to the water or ice-free area beneath the icebreaker hull. As a counter-measure, liquid ballast (usually sea water) can be transferred laterally between heeling tanks to impart a rolling motion to the ice-breaker, breaking the snow's sticky grip. Sometimes, however, even this method, combined with the sudden application of full-astern power, is of little use. In such cases, depending upon the situation, explosives or just waiting until a shift in tide or wind direction may be the only course of action remaining.

13.3 Icebreaker Techniques   An icebreaker, with the aid of its heli-copters searching ahead, attempts to locate the easiest paths through the jigsaw-puzzle pattern of ice floes. Ease of transit, however, is not the only criterion. Compromises must be made in order that the courses taken never stray further than 45° from a direct one to the destination, unless, of course, such a course is only of very short duration.

With its barrel-like hull and no keels to impinge against ice, an ice-breaker rolls hideously in rough seas. Before the advent of anti-roll devices, everyone boasted of a record roll at one time in the 60°-range. But in the ice, where the vertical movement of the seas is dampened, an icebreaker ride is an entirely different affair. While in light to moderate ice, there is an almost imperceptible rising and lowering of the bow as the vessel rides up to break the larger floes. The ride and motion are pleasant.

If charging and backing tactics must be employed due to heavy ice conditions or pressure, the effect is like riding a freight train over a broken track. When in solid, homogeneous ice, where these tactics are employed, the bridge controllers are advanced to full ahead (with all diesel-generators on the line). The engines respond with a roar, the ship charges ahead, and momentum builds up. Bow metal grinds against hard ice, and the ship slows. The bow rises sharply as the icebreaker comes to a complete stop after an advance of about one length. The propellers are then reversed and the ship backs off for another charge. It is a slow operation that, although necessary, is hard on machinery.

13.4 Basic Channel-Cutting Methods   To cut a channel through an area of fast-ice (homogeneous or solid) in a sound or embayment, either of two basic methods may be used, but first a plan should be evolved that will take into account the general effect of wind, tide, and access into a desired location. For an excellent example where the yearly cutting of a channel through fast-ice is always necessary by icebreakers, let us take the situation at McMurdo Sound in the Antarctic. There, two or three icebreakers are employed to carve a channel in December that will accommodate thin-skinned supply ships scheduled to come later. The 25- to 40-mile-long channel is cut in the shape of a huge V with the open end to the north at the entrance and its center axis aligned as much as possible in the direction of the prevailing southerly winds with due regard given to the Coriolis effect. This will facilitate the escape of the broken ice, or brash. In spite of these precautions, clogging of the channel by ice rubble sometimes reaches serious proportions. The ice-breakers themselves may have difficulty negotiating the ice-conglomerate that accumulates when northerly winds blow or when there are extended periods of calm. At such times, the situation can be improved only by the slow process of attrition wherein the icebreakers work up and down the channel, breaking large ice chunks into smaller ones and stirring up the ice debris with screw currents to promote melting.

If only one icebreaker is available to carve the channel—perhaps because its partner is occupied in reworking ice that is clogging the channel—it should alternately charge the ice at a 30° to 40° to port of the axis and then to starboard, employing a third blow straight ahead along the axis.

The other basic method requires two icebreakers. They make two straightforward, parallel cuts, about three ship-widths apart. The intervening ice breaks up under this attack, yielding a channel of greater width than does the herringbone pattern method. It also has the advantage of being about three times as fast as the single-ship approach.

13.5 Preparation for a Polar Cruise   *Preparing the Crew*   Initiate a polar training program for the crew, including damage control procedures, the effects of low temperatures upon materials, the classification of sea ice, ice terminology, survival instructions and precautions, and ice and sea life reporting. Employ such references as reports of previous expeditions and operations, ice atlases, and sailing directions of the areas where the ship will be operating. Polar shiphandling and operation manuals, books, and films together with instructions for the operation of shipboard equipment in cold weather and ice observing and reporting techniques are other valuable aids for the program.

Navigational Aids   The navigator should obtain up-to-date charts of the areas to be navigated, including the latest information on pertinent topographic features, points of land, prominent peaks, islands, and other configurations of harbors or operational areas. He should realize that celestial navigation during the summer months depends solely upon altitude sights of the sun, and that piloting is performed mainly by use of radar and the gyro compass in lieu of lighthouses and other customary navigational aids.

Ice atlases portray average ice conditions for each month of the year and are valuable, not for depicting conditions during a certain year, but for showing the trend of ice growth and deterioration throughout the year. From studying them, one will see that the maxi-

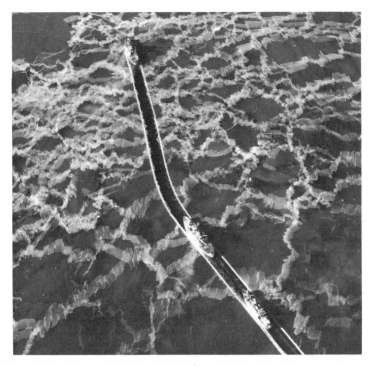

Fig. 13.2 *U.S.S. Edisto, U.S.S. North Wind,* and *R.R.S. John Biscoe* transit pack off Palmer Gerlasche Strait. *(Official U.S. Navy photograph.)*

mum growth in distribution or area covered is attained during March and September for the Arctic and Antarctic respectively, and that the sea-ice areas have reached the greatest shrinkage in September and March for the Arctic and Antarctic respectively. This is because the cumulative effect of the sun or lack of sun has reached its maximum at these times. Usually polar operations are conducted early in the summer season before much disintegration has occurred. The only advantage of early operations is that if a vessel experiences trouble, one has the assurance that conditions will inevitably become better. The disadvantage, however, is that a vessel may be damaged needlessly by heavy ice.

Sailing Directions, which can be obtained from the U.S. Defense Mapping Agency Hydrographic Center at Suitland, Maryland, give general information on ice conditions together with useful advice on piloting, currents, meteorology, flora and fauna, and natives (if any). Sailing Directions also give an account of ship exploration within an area of region. The principal help provided by Sailing Directions lies in the description and photographs of navigational landmarks and warning of navigational hazards of an area. The Antarctic Sailing Directions of the U.S. Hydrographic Center are unusually descriptive in information on whaling, sealing, and exploration, and even provide the ingredients for an acceptable trail ration. The Sailing Directions of other countries, particularly Canada for the Arctic, and Argentina, Chile, and Great Britain for the Antarctic provide additional information of value. Some of the charts produced by these countries, too, may be of a more convenient scale for navigating.

Before reaching sea-ice areas, one should be thoroughly knowledgeable about ice reporting and forecasting. In this regard, "Ice" Messages, Ice Forecasts, facsimile presentations, and information which has been compiled previously on operations in the same area can be most helpful.

Current and future ice conditions are developed for the Arctic by Canada and the United States and to some extent for the Antarctic by the latter country. In the past, ships operating in these regions together with need-to-know operational bases are informed of these data by on-the-spot "Ice" Messages, daily 48-hour operational forecasts, twice-weekly 5-day forecasts, twice-monthly 30-day forecasts, and one long-range forecast for the entire season. Ice charts sent by facsimile broadcast provide a visual portrayal of ice conditions. The use of satellite photos of the ice areas also has proved of value in recent years, indicating where general areas of sea ice and open water exist.

Preparing the Vessel While the ship is in drydock examine all underwater openings to ensure that they are unobstructed and that the individual valves work efficiently. As ringbolts, scupper guards, and other hull projections may be damaged by sea ice, remove these if possible.

Provide timbers, joists, lumber, and iron cut to various shapes and sizes, an assortment of nuts and bolts, packing and washer material, oakum, quick-drying cement and other patch material for repairing holes and fractures to the shell plating. For a steel vessel the most useful equipment is a portable welding outfit. Further needs are diving equipment, ice anchors and explosives.

To combat cold, snow, topside ice, and sea ice, provide special stores consisting of cold-weather clothing and footwear, ice axes, explosives, detonators, fuses, anti-freeze liquid, hardwood mallets, heavy hammers, snow shovels, extra storage batteries, and sufficient storage battery acid for cold-weather operations (125 percent normal allowance). If the ship's mission is to operate in the Antarctic, carry the following mooring equipment aboard: 8-foot long wooden planks or sections of telephone poles ("deadmen"), 6-foot long manila or steel wire straps for use with the deadmen, hardwood toggles or fids for use as mooring triggers, shovels and ice chisels for digging holes in the bay ice, and a number of spars or telephone poles to serve as fenders when mooring against an ice edge. Never store supplies, equipment, or cargo against the sides of the vessel in a hold so as to deny access in the event of damaged plating.

Ship's gear and equipment should be examined and placed in top operating condition for the difficult voyage ahead, the gyro compass, fathometer(s), and radar(s) being of utmost importance in this regard. The magnetic compass should be compensated.

To determine whether the vessel meets ice strengthening and power requirements, reference should be made to the ice classification rules provided by an appropriate classification society as described in the following section.

13.6   Ice Classification of Vessels   With the exception of naval vessels or vessels operated by military or quasi-military agencies, ships are classified with regard to their ice-navigating capabilities by the various classification societies. Thus, the classification society known as Lloyds' Register of Shipping (British) assigns the classification mark 100A1 with the addition of 1, 2, or 3 to differentiate between the various graduations of ship operating ability and safety in ocean-ice areas. Likewise, the classification society known as Det Norske Veritas (Norwegian) assigns the classification mark 1A1 with the addition of "Is A," "Is B," or "Is C." Other classification societies assign similar classification marks and additions although the American Bureau of Shipping, due to the fact that all major ports in the United States are warm-water ports, assigns the classification mark A1(E) and grants a certificate showing that the ship has "ice strengthening" in obedience of certain prescribed construction rules.

In general, ice classification regulations apply to ship construction, strength, and engine power as follows:

Shell plating: Shell plating at icebelt to be thicker than standard plating by various percentages over 100 percent.

Frame spacing, stringers, and strength members: Intermediate frame spacing to be accomplished in specific areas of a ship; stringers and strength members to be fitted in specific areas of a ship.

Propeller, shafts, etc.: Propellers to be of cast steel or other material of equal strength. Diameters and thicknesses of propeller and shafts to be increased over standard by various percentages over 100 percent.

Rudder head, pintles, etc.: Diameters and cross sections to be increased by various percentages over 100 percent of standard.

Engine horsepower: Horsepower to be above standard by various ratios.

Side and bottom valves: Side and bottom valves to be fitted with steam connections to keep from freezing and to remove ice if choked.

Shape of bow and stern: Suitable for navigation in ice in accordance with classification assignment.

13.7   Topside Icing   On the voyage into high latitudes the first indication that there is a difference from operations in more temperate climates may be the freezing of spray on the topside of the vessel. Such a phenomenon occurs when the wind is strong enough to blow spray from wave crests and from the water stirred up by the passage of the ship. It may also occur during fog (including "frost smoke") in freezing temperatures. This kind of icing, sometimes known as "glaze ice," has high density and great powers of adhesion.

Ice tends to form high up on the ship, on masts and rigging, resulting in loss of freeboard and stability. Therefore a vessel with increased freeboard and metacentric height together with minimum topside area in the form of masts, rigging, and superstructure offers the great-

Fig. 13.3   Two U.S. Coast Guard Icebreakers using railroad-track method for cutting ice channel into McMurdo Sound, Antarctica. (*Official U.S. Navy Photograph.*)

est margin of safety in this regard. When a large area of ice builds up, particularly around and ahead of the foremast, it may act as a sail and hamper the ship's maneuverability.

Typical conditions for the formation of glaze ice are temperatures of 20 to 25 degrees F with a Force 6 and above wind, and sea temperatures of 30 to 34 degrees F. If air temperatures fall below 0 degrees F (−17.7 degrees C) the ice cannot adhere because it will strike the ship in the form of small, dry crystals.

There are a number of ways to reduce the effects of this kind of icing. One is by reducing the high topside area upon which the ice will adhere. Thus a tripod mast may substitute for a normal mast and rigging, and light alloys or fiber glass may replace normal construction materials. Another aid is the elimination of as much rigging as possible. Wire ropes may replace rails, and all movable rigging such as derricks or cranes should be lowered to their extreme extent. Electric coils may be installed in important apparatus.

When serious icing conditions prevail, a course downwind should be taken if possible so as to reduce substantially the amount of spray being driven over the ship.

Many ice-removal methods may be employed when glaze ice has accumulated on the ship. The most common method is by manual means, by using mallets, chippers, clubs, scrapers, shovels, and stiff brooms. Care should be observed not to damage underlying metal surface. Other methods, though less effective, are: hot-air heaters, rock salt (corrosive to metal surfaces), and ice-phobic coatings or anti-icers.

13.8 Operations and Navigation in Sea-Ice Areas Before entering the ice, the ship should be trimmed down by the stern in order to prevent low-riding ice from striking propeller(s). When the approach is made to an ice boundary for the first time, care should be taken to enter the perimeter in the lee as much as possible, particularly if there are growler-size chunks or pieces of heavy ice bobbing up and down from waves or a stiff wind. Usually by skirting around long ice tongues or choosing entry at a point which derives protection from ice to windward, entry may be made safely. A thorough preliminary reconnaissance through observations from the crow's nest and use of the radar will be an aid in this respect. Remember that the effect of wind and swell decreases in proportion to the distance from the the ice edge. Retracting the pitometer sword prior to ice entry is recommended.

After ice entry is made, the conning officer will be required to make innumerable decisions about speed and course. If the situation requires it, the best way for him to view the ice conditions ahead is to position himself as high in the ship as possible. He will see that the channels between individual ice floes never follow a straight line and that some end up in cul de sacs. Choosing the correct channel and maintaining a course that will keep the vessel as clear of ice contact or breaking through the least ice possible is a job that will keep him occupied constantly. Although many course changes will be necessary, he must remember not to allow the vessel to stray too far from the desired base course or he may find the vessel actually doubling back on its track. A good rule to follow is never to permit the course to vary more than 45 degrees from the base course.

In order to get the "feel" of the ship when navigating in ice, proceed at a very slow speed at first, then work up to a greater speed when the reaction of the ship in ice becomes better known. Choose weak sections in the ice and approach at a slow speed. When contact is made, increase power. If it is necessary to strike an ice floe, never hit it a glancing blow as this will swing the bow in the direction of least resistance and tend to swing the vulnerable propeller(s) toward the floe. If heavy ice halts the ship, the rudder should be kept amidships and the propeller(s) turning over "ahead." This evolution should clear the ice astern so that the ship will be able to back down for another attempt at going ahead.

Never enter dense field-ice areas with a single ship without icebreaker assistance if it can be avoided. Plane and helicopter reconnaissance is a great help in selecting navigable areas before they are actually reached by a vessel. "Water sky" is another aid that has been employed frequently in both the Arctic and Antarctic. This is the dark appearance on the underside of a cloud layer due to the reflection of a surface of open water surrounded or bounded by ice. When the underside of a cloud layer produces a yellowish-white glare, the phenomenon is known as "ice blink." Thus the selection of a base course towards "water sky" rather than "ice blink" ensures that the ship will approach open water or light ice concentrations.

If the ship becomes involved in heavy ice and cannot move in any direction, one or more of the following procedures may be employed for getting free:

1. Go full speed astern, then full speed ahead. By putting the rudder first to one side and then to the other, it may be possible to get the stern to move slightly to one side so that the bow will shift a little. If this occurs, going astern should release the vessel from the grip of the ice.
2. Sally the ship by having the crew run first to one side then to

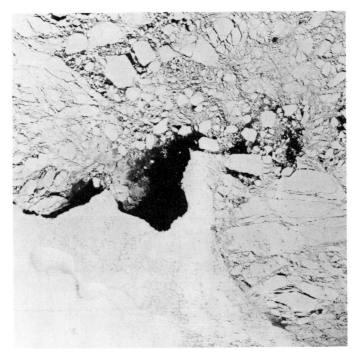

Fig. 13.4 Satellite photograph of ice conditions aid ship penetration of ice surrounding Antarctic continent. (*Official U.S. Navy photograph.*)

the other on signal. However, this will be ineffective for a large ship. Shifting heavy weights and ballast are other alternatives and swinging out boats on booms helps in heeling the ship.

3. If the foregoing methods fail, bury a large spar or deadman in the ice on the quarter or astern, then winch the ship sternwards by purchases with the engines put on full astern.

4. Employ explosives as a last resort, planting charges at strategic points of ice pressure just off the bows. "Shaped charges" are useful for creating holes through the ice to enable the explosive charge to be placed beneath the ice surface. Close down radio transmissions to avoid prematurely setting off explosions. Have the crew seek cover during the blast and have engines on full ahead.

Because of the numerous course and speed changes during ice operations, accurate dead reckoning is almost impossible. Automatic dead-reckoning devices cannot be employed due to the impracticability of introducing an accurate speed component (ice damages the propeller of a "speed log"); therefore reliance must be placed on either a "Dutchman's log" or use of the radar. In the first method the speed is estimated by noting the time taken for the ship's stern to come abreast of a chip of wood thrown overboard from the ship's bow. Then with the formula $S = D/100T$, the ship's speed S in knots may be estimated, using D as the length of the ship in feet, and T as the noted time in minutes for the observations. However, the ship's radar will be far more accurate in estimating speed.

Because of the constant daylight, celestial positioning during the summer months when ice operations become practicable is entirely dependent upon altitude sights of the sun, the position being obtained by crossing sun lines, taken at intervals at least two hours apart. However, each set of observations should consist of at least three or more integrated sextant observations so that a mean may be determined.

The magnetic compass, due to the low horizontal component of the earth's magnetism—being zero magnitude at the magnetic poles—has little value for navigation in the polar regions although it is surely better than nothing if the gyro compass fails. Although the gyro compass loses its directive force at the geographic poles and is subject to errors, it is still invaluable for bearing reference and the ship's course. It should be checked against sun azimuths several times daily and corrected in accordance with latitude versus speed tables or diagrams.

13.9 Escort by Icebreakers   Escort by icebreaker(s) is necessary for cargo or similar ships, especially those ships not having an ice classification, when traversing field-ice areas greater than three- or four-tenths ice concentration. The resulting formation may consist of a single icebreaker–escort and one ship, an icebreaker and several ships, or two or more icebreakers and several ships.

Icebreakers perform escort duties in either one of two ways: (1) aiding vessels over only very difficult stretches of ice, as in the St. Lawrence approaches during the height of winter, or as in the Soviets' North Sea Route during summer; or (2) remaining with vessels during the major portion of the polar voyage as is necessary in the high latitudes of the Arctic Polar Basin and the Antarctic seas.

The objective of the ice convoy is to get the vessels which make up its composition through a stretch of ice in the fastest time, yet in a safe manner. Basic considerations in the success of any ice convoy are, first, the prevailing ice conditions, and second, the type and number of vessels to be conducted by the icebreakers. This means that an ice convoy should be formed basically of ships which because of their dimensions, construction, and engineering allow them to operate safely with the ice convoy in prevailing ice conditions.

As the leading vessel in an ice convoy and the others dispersed behind it in column, the icebreaker must set the course and speed of the convoy. It must select those courses which will get the convoy through the weakest sections of ice in the general direction of the convoy's destination. This it can accomplish through helicopter help or by conning from its crow's nest or high con. Compromises must usually be made in turning to new courses, making them gradual enough and straight enough so the following ships will have little difficulty in conforming. The character and pattern of ice floes and the fact that the icebreaker, due to its relatively short length, tends to follow the path of least resistance, make the channel behind the icebreaker a meandering one that is often difficult for long ships to follow. Another difficulty is that the ice-free path cleared by the wide beam of the icebreaker, while at first adequate, tends to close rather quickly, making it necessary for the following ships to keep closed-up.

Before icebreaker-escort operations commence, the captain of the icebreaker should be cognizant of the following characteristics of each vessel to be escorted: length, turning radius, tonnage as loaded, draft, horsepower, steam or diesel, direct or electric drive, turbine or engine, number of propeller shafts, special ice-strengthened features included in the ice classification of a vessel, maneuverability aids such as a variable pitch propeller(s) and bow thruster, and ice experience of captain or master. Such data will determine the vessel's position in a multiple-ship ice convoy and be of help to the icebreaker captain in knowing how a vessel will respond to various ice situations.

A vessel must be subject to the orders given by the captain of the icebreaker, obeying them promptly without question. It must maintain its position in a formation to the best of the conning officer's ability, and he must not allow the vessel to venture into the ice on its own accord. Vessels are to be guided by voice and whistle signals if so prescribed, repeating them to acknowledge that they are understood and will be executed. Convenient whistle signals are: 1 short blast—Stop; 1 long blast—Come Ahead; several short blasts—Back. Vessels should be ready in all respects for towing and should have repair facilities for possible ice damage. They should promptly notify the icebreaker captain of ship damage, engine casualties, besetment, or difficulty in maintaining proper station in the ice convoy.

Once the ice convoy is under way, the following thumb rules are helpful:

1. In making course adjustments to remain in proper station, be careful not to swing the amidships section or the stern of the ship against heavy ice. These are the vulnerable portions of the ship.

Fig. 13.5 USS EDISTO transits ice pack off Antarctic peninsula near Gerlasche Strait. (*Official U.S. Navy photograph.*)

2. Employ aids for maintaining station in the formation. A stadimeter, radar, or a range finder will help the ship handler in this respect.
3. When a formation turn is made, start the ship swinging so that the vessel's bow will turn just inside the kick of the ship ahead, ensuring that the ship will remain in the cleared channel at the completion of the turn. (All course changes should be as gradual and minimal as possible.)

In the event a vessel is brought to a stop because of ice, and attempts to extricate itself prove fruitless, the only recourse is to await help from an icebreaker. In most cases the icebreaker will halt all other ships in the convoy with the advice that they keep headed on course (with no way) if possible. After an initial survey of the situation, the captain of the aiding icebreaker will either back down to break the ice just ahead of a vessel if it is stopped by a concentration of ice just ahead of the bow, or clear the ice from the lee side of the vessel if it is more seriously blocked from maintaining progress. In any case, just before the icebreaker begins to move the critical piece of ice that blocks progress, the engines of the beset vessel should be put on ahead full in order to take advantage of release from pressure when it comes.

The following precautions should be observed by the icebreaker breaking out a beset ship:

1. When employing the backing-down method to free a ship's bow from ice, the icebreaker must be careful not to allow her powerful screw currents to turn the bow of the other ship away from the desired course, and to observe caution not to place its own propellers and rudder against heavy ice.
2. In clearing ice from the lee side of a beset ship, the icebreaker should be aware of the danger presented by the bow of the other ship blowing against the icebreaker's side. Also, the icebreaker must avoid pushing heavy ice chunks against the thinner hull of the ship it is aiding.

When towing a vessel of an ice convoy, the techniques are much the same as in conventional towing arrangements except that the towed ship must be towed either in the icebreaker's stern notch or at a short scope (50 to 100 feet) of the towing hawser. This is necessary so that ice closing behind the icebreaker's stern does not hinder the progress of the tow.

The notch method is recommended only for light-tonnage vessels in which the bow is relatively low. Larger ships with higher bows impose too much of an impediment on the stern when turning and the bows will not remain in the notch satisfactorily. In the notch method the bow of the tow is brought into the notch by the towing engine and snugly secured against chafind gear. To help prevent the tow's bow from jumping or swinging out of the notch, two preventer lines should be taken from the tow's bow, from either side, and then crossed at the notch and secured to bitts on either quarter of the icebreaker.

The short-scope method, which has been found to be the most satisfactory in the majority of cases, permits towing at a distance of 50 to 100 feet behind the icebreaker's stern, but with the added danger of the tow overriding the icebreaker if the latter suddenly strikes heavy ice or incurs an engine casualty. The powerful propeller wash from the icebreaker will tend to prevent damage by swinging the tow's bow to one side or other and also by slowing the momentum of the tow. In some cases it may be necessary for the tow to back down full and to swing clear of the icebreaker's stern promptly, so ready communications or whistle signals should be set up beforehand.

13.10   Anchoring and Mooring   The only difference in anchoring and mooring in ice-cluttered waters as compared to that in ice-free waters is the degree of readiness required to weigh anchor on short notice. When operating in areas off the ice shelves of the Antarctic, which include about 75 percent of the periphery of that continent, the extreme depths will preclude the possibility of anchoring. Low sections of the ice shelf or stretches of fast or bay ice, which is smooth, thick, and exists in one unbroken strip, fortunately provide convenient piers against which to moor.

Because many of the embayments and harbors in the polar regions have never been charted, the selection of an anchoring site depends upon the results of preliminary soundings conducted by boats sent ahead of the ship on the way in to an anchorage. A further precaution in entering such an anchorage would be letting the anchor out to about 10 fathoms and holding it there while the ship cruises slowly ahead.

For mooring a ship to an ice edge, the employment of ice anchors is not advised during the summer months. Their bearing surface is small and usually not sufficient to hold in soft summer ice. Experience has shown that deadmen, when employed as in Fig. 13.6, provide greater holding power and make weighing easier and quicker with the toggle release. When laying out the deadmen, it is very important for the trench for each deadman to be slotted at an angle so that the pull on a mooring line will tend to bury the deadman ever deeper in the ice. Once the deadmen have been positioned in their trenches, cover each with snow and small pieces of ice, and if freezing air temperatures prevail, pour fresh water over the ice conglomerate so that it will quickly freeze.

When the ship is satisfactorily moored against a straight, crack-free ice edge, all overboard discharges from the ship should be either blanked off or diverted to spread down the ship's sides by the use of canvas or wooden overlays otherwise the erosive effects of the streams of water on ice alongside in the vicinity of a hatch may render a site unsafe for unloading or loading.

The best way of ensuring that the ice remains safe during unloading operations is to post an ice patrol with responsibilities for continuous examination of access roads and ice in unloading zones. Members of this patrol should have full authority for keeping areas as clean and free of trash, oil, and foreign mater as possible. This prevents the increased melting effect of the sun on dark material. Metallic objects will often melt their way so deeply into the ice that they cannot be recovered.

Large amounts of cargo should never be allowed to accumulate in

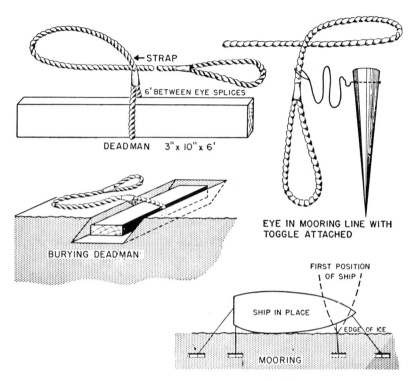

STRAP

6' BETWEEN EYE SPLICES

DEADMAN   3" x 10" x 6'

BURYING DEADMAN

EYE IN MOORING LINE WITH
TOGGLE ATTACHED

FIRST POSITION
OF SHIP

SHIP IN PLACE

EDGE OF ICE

MOORING

Fig. 13.6 Mooring to ice shelf.

one location on the ice because of the possibility of sudden ice break-up.

Roads, particularly when air temperatures are above freezing, become dark and rutted deeply from embedded foreign matter and continued use. For this reason, frequent changing of routes or access roads over an ice surface may be necessary.

The ice patrol should not only maintain a log or journal, noting every development and detail relating to the strength and safety of the ice in the proximity of a ship, but should also be fully cognizant of "ice mechanics" regarding cracks and anomalies of the ice.

13.11 Boat Operations   The following rules should be observed when operating boats with internal combustion engines in the polar regions:

1. The first boat ashore should carry survival gear for all personnel to be landed.
2. Check fuel, lubricating oil, and boat equipment each time before leaving the ship. Fill fuel tanks full to prevent condensation and freezing.

3. When operating in sea ice, station a bow lookout who can warn of nearby ice.
4. Use caution when approaching ice. Proceed at slow speed, avoiding as much as possible any contact with ice. If contact is unavoidable, push against the ice at a slow speed so that the piece of ice will be swung to one side.
5. Warm up engines very slowly. Keep engine heaters in place when the boat is not in use. Maintain circulation water to a minimum, just enough to prevent overheating of engines. When a boat is hoisted out of the water, drain the engine block. If an engine has a closed circuit cooling system, ensure that the cooling liquid does not freeze by adding anti-freeze liquid if necessary.
6. After a landing is made, never shut down the engines. Coxswains should never leave their tillers unattended. When there is drifting ice about, the boat should always be ready to move quickly.
7. When a boat goes into the water ensure that the drain plugs are in place. When a boat is hoisted out of the water, likewise make sure that the drain plugs are out of the drain holes. The drain plugs may be frozen in place unless these chores are performed each time.

Reference is suggested to Captain E. A. MacDonald's (USN, Ret.) *Polar Operations,* published by the United States Naval Institute, Annapolis, Maryland.

PART

III

Oceanography and the Weather

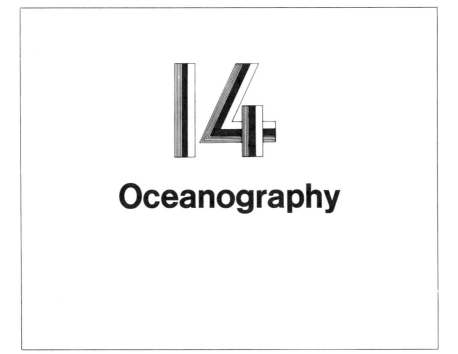

Oceanography

The seaman encounters and must deal with more facets of nature than do people in any other occupation. To be an efficient, safe sailor he must understand the fundamental processes of the oceans. This means involvement in many scientific disciplines.

At the surface of the oceans, where his operations are affected by winds, sea state, heat exchange, currents, and weather, he joins with the meteorologist. The shape of the ocean floor, the beaches, the harbors, and the types of anchoring ground involve geology. Chemistry and physics enter when he deals with the nature and behavior of seawater and pollution of the sea. Navigation is based on astronomy. Mathematics is involved in nearly every theoretical aspect and practical application of oceanography.

The mariner needs to know oceanography if he is to use the ocean environment to his own best advantage. The ability to locate currents, predict storms, avoid fog, or prevent marine life from eroding the underwater portions of the hull makes the mariner's life at sea safer and more comfortable as well as enabling him to perform such basic tasks as transporting passengers, hauling cargo, launching aircraft, hunting submarines, catching fish, or just sailing for enjoyment more effectively.

Safety at sea is always the first consideration of mariners, but the number of ships lost or damaged at sea is often forgotten. Insurance records show that well over 200,000 ships have sunk or run aground in the past 100 years; approximately 2000 ships of all types are lost or damaged each year. A better knowledge of oceanography might have done much to reduce losses due to storms, ice, inadequate charts, and oceanic phenomena affecting safe navigation of ships.

The magnitude of our shipping effort, with a U.S. merchant fleet of approximately 1300 ships of over 1000 tons, points up the importance of oceanography. The industry provides employment for over 200,000 people and contributes $5 billion annually to the U.S. economy.

Size, Shape, and Composition of the Oceans

14.1 Bottom Topography and Size   The three oceans—Atlantic, Pacific, and Indian—cover 70.8 percent of the earth's surface to an average depth of two miles. In scale, the depth would be but a coat of varnish on a 24-inch diameter globe of the world, but from man's viewpoint, the oceans are tremendous. Satellite photographs of the earth emphasize the relative smallness of land masses in relation to the much larger oceans.

The world's oceans are contained by land in a common pattern. Starting at the shore line (see Fig. 14.1), the bottom slopes very gently over the continental shelf out to the shelf break. The average width of the continental shelf is 42 miles, but it varies from less than a mile off

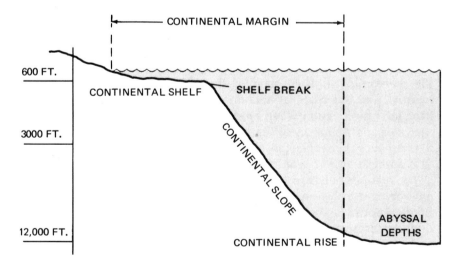

Fig. 14.1 Ocean margin topography.

the California coast to 800 miles off northern Siberia. The shelf break depth varies from 165 to 1500 feet, with an average depth of about 430 feet, although the depths most commonly used for defining the outer edge of the continental shelf is 100 fathoms or 200 meters because these contour lines are shown on most marine charts and these depths are normally very close to the shelf break area. (Legal definition of the maximum shelf depth and of the boundaries of the deep ocean floor is being studied and debated at length in the United Nations General Assembly; valuable rights to bottom exploration and exploitation are at stake.)

At the edge of the shelf break, the bottom drops steeply along the continental slope until it reaches the abyssal plain, the bottom of the ocean basin.

Submarine canyons are a permanent feature on the shelf and slope. Many equal the Grand Canyon in size. Some canyons are associated with rivers, like the Congo Canyon; some are seaward from bays, like the huge Monterey Canyon; some canyons have no apparent continental topographic connection.

The central floors of the ocean basins range from 11,000 to 18,000 feet in depth. In some places the floors are remarkably flat; elsewhere, except for the ridges, the deep-sea floor consists mainly of low hills a few hundred feet high. The ocean basins are divided by broad, rounded mountain ranges, 600 to 1200 miles wide and over 6000 miles long. The Mid-Atlantic Ridge winds down the center of the Atlantic from Iceland to the Southern Ocean. It bends eastward south of the Cape of Good Hope and extends into the center of the Indian Ocean. In the Pacific, a similar ridge extends nearly from Antarctica to lower California.

In the Pacific Ocean, deep trenches occur on the seaward sides of the island chains and along the base of the continental slopes. These trenches are often thousands of miles long and only 12 to 20 miles wide. They are the deepest parts of the oceans; the Marianas Trench is the deepest at 36,204 feet. Fourteen Pacific Ocean trenches are deeper than 21,000 feet. The Atlantic Ocean has only two; the Indian Ocean, one.

The deep-sea floor is pimpled with isolated volcanoes and volcanic ridges. Some of these rise above the sea surface as volcanic islands; others are covered with a thick pile of limestone, consisting of skeletons of reef corals and other marine animals and plants. These are the coral atolls of the Pacific and Indian oceans. Volcanoes that do not break the sea surface are called seamounts. Most have conical or irregular shapes but many, called guyots, have broad, flat tops— almost surely planed off by waves sometime in the past hundred mil-

Fig. 14.2 Atlantic Ocean floor. (*Courtesy* National Geographic *Magazine. Copyright 1968 National Geographic Society.*)

lion years either when the water level was lower or before the seamounts sank—we do not know which.

Figure 14.2 illustrates the irregularity of the earth's surface under the ocean waters.

14.2 Exploring and Working at the Ocean Bottoms   Knowledge of the shape and composition of the ocean bottoms is important to both the scientist and the mariner. The scientist deduces when and how the oceans were formed, their chemical composition, and gravity and magnetic variations. The mariner and commercial organizations use the information for navigation, type of holding ground available for anchoring, laying and operating cable, oil exploration, operation of sonar equipment, and many other purposes.

Mapping the ocean bottoms has evolved from the old lead sounding technique to use of modern echo sounders. The sounders measure the depth of the water by determining the time taken for sound waves to travel from the ship to the bottom and return. Precision Depth Recorders plot the bottom profile. Echo sounders also give good indications of the type of bottom and character of the layers underneath. For example, the recorded profile will indicate whether the bottom is mud, sand, or rock, and it can penetrate short distances into the bottom to portray the thickness of the various sediment or rock layers.

The nature of the ocean bottom is determined mainly by taking cores, or by collecting grab and dredge samples. The first reliable deep-ocean cores were taken by the Challenger Expedition in the early 1870s. These penetrated only two feet, but provided 85,000 years of geological history. It was 1945 before cores over 100 feet were obtained. In 1961, a Project *Mohole* test drill went to 1030 feet (10 million year sediments). In 1970, the drilling ship *Glomar Challenger* drilled to a record 3321 feet. This was done in water 20,146 feet deep; the drill string was 20,752 feet long.

Although coring and collecting grab and dredge samples will continue to be a most important means of geological exploration in the deep ocean basins, future exploration of the shallower ocean regions may be made by men working directly near the bottom in deep submergence vehicles (DSV) (Fig. 14.3).

These are several vehicles routinely used by industry and the Navy to do work down to a few thousand feet; the work involves such projects as underwater construction, cable inspection, and bottom searches. In deeper water, there are DSVs of the *Alvin, Trieste,* and *Aluminaut* classes. *Alvin* located the lost nuclear weapon off Palomares, Spain in 2500 feet of water. *Trieste II* worked at 8500 feet in the *Thresher* search, and at over 10,000 feet in the *Scorpion* search. *Trieste I* was used to explore the Challenger Deep at 36,000 feet. In vehicles such as these, and the more sophisticated models of the future, scientists will be able to hover over, observe, and retrieve specimens with a selectivity never anticipated a few years ago.

Water and Its Role in Shaping the Environment

Water is an amazing chemical compound, with more unique properties than any other substance. Our lives depend upon water—our bodies are 80 percent and our blood 92 percent water. But the dependency goes beyond the mere need to drink water; the unique qualities of water influence the environment and thus our way of life

Fig. 14.3   Deep submergence vehicles *Autec* and *Turtle*.

in many ways. Here we shall discuss those unique characteristics which are important in oceanography and to the environment.

Water has more capacity to absorb heat than any solid or liquid except ammonia. Great amounts of heat are stored in seawater without large changes in temperature over a short time. Thus, the climates of land areas close to large bodies of water will not change rapidly as is the case in areas farther inland. Ocean currents transfer great amounts of heat around the world, influencing climates of land masses adjacent to the currents' paths. An example of how this works might be to compare the severe climate of central Asia with that of the British Isles. The latter is mild because of the prevailing westerly winds from and over the North Atlantic Ocean.

Water has the highest latent heat of vaporization of any substance; it takes over five times the amount of heat to change a volume of water from liquid to vapor than is required to raise the same amount of water from solid to liquid. This is an extremely significant factor in the world heat budget because it allows the transfer in the atmosphere of enormous quantities of heat over the earth's surface. Each gram of water that evaporates acquires 540 calories of heat. This latent or "stored" heat is released to the surrounding air when the water vapor condenses and falls as rain. To maintain the heat balance in earth and atmosphere, 30 to 40 inches of water must evaporate and precipitate per year over the world. This computation agrees well with world rainfall estimates.

Water's latent heat of fusion is the highest of all liquids except ammonia. This is the heat required to change a substance from the solid to the liquid state. Eighty calories must be removed from a gram of water of 0 degrees C to change it to ice, which is almost as much heat as is needed to raise the same gram of water from the freezing to the boiling point. Water's high heat of fusion has the effect of a thermostat at the freezing point, since so much heat must be released to freeze a given mass of water without changing its temperature.

Another unique property of water arising from its peculiar molecular structure is its density change with temperature change. Fresh water gradually increases in density with decrease in temperature until, at 4 degrees C, maximum density is reached. With further cooling the process is reversed and density starts to decrease. At 0 degrees C the decrease is most pronounced, and the ice that forms will suddenly increase its volume by 10 percent over the volume of the original water. This quality of not having its most dense structure as a solid occurs in only a few elements in nature. The fact that ice floats is important in protecting biological life in rivers, lakes, and oceans from severe cold.

Water in Motion

There are clear distinctions between sea, swell, and breakers, although all are manifestations of energy moving through water with an undulatory motion.

Waves are generated in four basic ways in the open sea: by changes in atmospheric pressure; by wind acting on the water's surface; by seismic disturbances, such as earthquakes; and by tidal attractions of the sun and moon.

14.3 Wind Waves   An idealized wind wave can be represented by a sine curve, as shown in Fig. 14.4. Wavelength is the distance between two successive wave crests; height is the vertical distance from trough to crest; period is the time in seconds required for two suc-

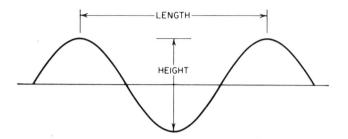

Fig. 14.4 Elements of waves.

cessive wave crests to pass a point. Speed of the wave in knots is given by the formula:

$$\text{Velocity (knots)} = \frac{L \text{ (feet)}}{T \text{ (seconds)}} \times 0.6$$

where L wavelength and T = period.

The idealized wave described above probably never occurs in nature. Waves in generating area are most confused. They seem to appear and disappear at random, and there is no obvious pattern to the sea surface. The sea and its randomness can be described mathematically by the sum of an infinite number of infinitesimal sine waves, each with a different period, length, and direction. It is from this mathematical description that forecasting methods have been developed.

The confused, random picture might be expected, since the waves are generated by winds which are far from constant in speed or direction, and the waves in the immediate generation area are further confused by swell coming from one or more other generation areas.

It should be kept in mind that waves in the open sea are not masses of moving water. The wave shape moves, while the individual water particles describe circular motions but remain essentially in place with little forward movement.

Wave heights are determined by the winds, whose energy as applied to wave production is determined by three parameters: wind speed, wind duration, and fetch. Fetch is the distance over the open sea that the wind blows without a significant change in direction.

For each wind speed there is a maximum amount of energy that can be transferred to the sea surface. Energy application beyond this maximum results in breaking waves and energy dissipation to heat. When energy input equals energy dissipation, the waves stop growing and the sea is at its fully developed state. To reach this stage, minimum values of both fetch and duration are required. Table 14.1 gives

**Table 14.1 Minimum Fetch and Duration Required for a Fully Developed
Sea with Various Wind Speeds, and Wave Characteristics
of the Fully Developed Seas**

| Wind Speed (knots) | Wave Heights | | | Period Length | | Min. Fetch (miles) | Min. Duration (hours) |
| | Avg. | Highest | | Avg. (sec) | Avg. (ft) | | |
		1/3	1/10				
10	1.1	1.8	2.3	2.7	27	10	2.4
20	4.6	7.3	9.3	5.4	111	75	10
30	10.3	16.4	20.8	8.0	250	280	23
40	18.2	29.1	37.0	10.7	444	710	42
50	28.4	45.5	57.8	13.4	700	1420	69

typical values for the requirements, and shows characteristics of a
fully arisen sea. Note the tremendous increase in both fetch and duration required to get a fully developed sea as the wind speed is increased. Because of size and shape, normal weather systems will only
rarely support development of fully developed seas for wind speeds
over 40 knots. The Antarctic is the only region in the world where high
wind speeds can operate with unlimited fetch. The severe and frequent storms in the Roaring Forties take advantage of this; the infamous heavy seas of Cape Horn are one result.

One interesting and dangerous phenomenon among the wave
families is the occasional appearance of a giant, which may be nearly
twice the height of the significant wave heights (the average of the
highest 1/3 of the waves) for that particular sea state. A sea of 30-foot
waves might spawn a rogue wave of nearly 60 feet, sometimes with a
nearly vertical face. There have been hundreds of recorded cases of
sudden, unexpected steep, giant waves which capsized or pitchpoled
yachts, washed men and cargo overboard, and damaged ships.

The highest wave ever reliably reported was 112 feet, measured
from the U.S.S. *Ramapo* in the Pacific Ocean.

14.4 Swell When waves have left the generation area, and either
other waves no longer interfere with them or the wind stops blowing,
they move off in a regular undulating motion and smooth out so they
begin to look like our idealized wave. Now they are called swell (or
swell waves). Swell moves from the generating area at a constant
speed and with gradually diminishing height. If not interfered with by
land, swell can travel thousands of miles. Surfers at a Southern California beach may be riding waves that were generated by storms
southeast of New Zealand.

14.5 Breakers—Surf When waves reach an area where depth of bottom is half the wavelength, the waves begin to "feel bottom" and a transformation takes place. Wave speed decreases, so that the crests move closer together. Energy of the crests is inversely proportional to wave speed, so wave height increases, which increases wave steepness. When steepness approaches 1/7 (height to wavelength), the waves become unstable and break.

In practice, breaker height is rarely more than twice the height of the waves approaching from deep water, but a long-period swell and the right beach gradient can produce tremendous breakers of four to five times the height of the originating swell. The famous surfing beaches in Hawaii provide regular samples of this relationship. Obstacles such as sharp cliffs and precipitous islands accentuate the severity of the surf, which may reach heights of 100 feet in such situations.

14.6 Seismic Sea Waves The seismic-generated sea wave is called a tsunami (often mistakenly called a tidal wave). This wave generates from a submarine earthquake or volcanic eruption and moves out from the generation area at speeds up to 500 miles per hour. Because of their long wavelengths of the order of 100 miles and their small heights, usually 1 to 2 feet, tsunamis are rarely observed at sea. But, in some cases, tsunamis increase markedly in size in coastal areas, causing great damage and loss of life. These cases are attributed to some resonant conditions for particular frequencies in the tsunami. In one Hawaiian case, waves crested at 55 feet.

In V-shaped bays, the problem is worse. A famous Japanese tsunami had a height of 10 feet at the mouth of a bay and over 70 feet at the head of the same bay. An earlier tsunami reached 93 feet, with 6 to 8 waves at intervals between 7 and 34 minutes.

Tsunamis have traveled enormous distances; one that started in Chile was recorded in Japan, more than 10,000 miles away.

14.7 Tides and Tidal Currents Tides and tidal currents are caused by variation in gravitational attractive forces of the sun and moon on the earth and its water skin. The moon's effect is much greater than the sun's because, although much smaller, it is much closer to the earth.

Here is how Newton's equilibrium tide theory, simplified, explains the action of the gravitational forces.

The ocean area facing the moon receives more gravitational pull (GP) than does the earth, while the water on the opposite side of the earth receives the least. Thus, water is pulled away from the earth on the moon side; the earth is pulled toward the moon, but less than the water on the moon's side; the earth is pulled away from the water opposite to the moon. We end up with two water bulges on opposite sides of the earth, or a high tide on both sides of the earth. (Fig. 14.5.) The sun's gravitational force acts in the same way as the moon's.

If earth, sun, and moon are all in a straight line, we would expect and get maximum tidal ranges; these are called spring tides. When sun and moon are at right angles, not working together, the smaller-than-average neap tides result. Spring and neap tides occur every 14 days, which is one-half the period of revolution of the moon about the earth.

Tide forecasting is not as simple as it might seem. The factors of earth's rotation about its axis, earth's revolution about the sun, the moon's revolution about the earth, and the tilt of the earth in relation to sun and moon are readily calculated. But the problem becomes most complicated by factors such as varying water depth, varying ocean basin size and shape, and unique coastal configuration.

Tidal currents, the horizontal motion involved with tides, are significant and must be accounted for in navigation in confined areas. Currents of 10 knots occur in Seymour Narrow, Alaska; 4 knots occur in the Golden Gate entrance to San Francisco Bay.

Tidal range varies from less than an inch to a mean spring range of 44.6 feet in the Bay of Fundy in Canada. The Severn River in England has a 43-foot spring range. Topography accounts for the wide variation.

14.8 Currents   Ocean currents form a system of great rivers within the world's oceans. Currents are found at all depths and moving in all directions, but a general worldwide pattern prevails.

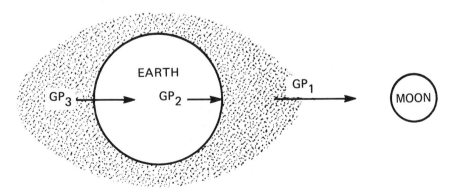

Fig. 14.5 Double bulge produced by the moon.

The primary current-generating forces are wind and density differences in water, the effects of which are modified by water depth, underwater topography, basin shape, land masses, and deflection from the earth's rotation. The current pattern is really two basic systems superimposed.

One system starts with the uneven latitudinal heating of the earth. Equatorial waters acquire more heat from the sun than do waters at higher latitudes. These warmer waters become less dense and spread out over the surface toward the poles. Thus, a giant convection cell is set up, where water sinking at the poles flows toward the equator, rises in equatorial regions, and then flows poleward again after heating.

The surface winds now enter the picture. They have more effect on the surface flow than the uneven heating effect.

The pattern of mean surface winds in the Northern Hemisphere is northeast (NE Trades) from 0 to 30 degrees north, southwest from 30 to 60 degrees north and northeast again from 60 degrees north to the pole. The Southern Hemisphere presents a mirror image of this system.

These winds, in the climatic average, break into cellular patterns. At high latitudes, there are low-pressure centers, such as the Icelandic and Aleutian Lows; there are high-pressure centers above the subtropics of all oceans, such as the Azores High. The surface ocean currents follow the pattern of cellular flow quite well. In the ocean basin of the Northern Hemisphere, there is a large clockwise circulation centered in the subtropics, and a counterclockwise circulation in the subpolar zone. In lower latitudes, a cold current flows equatorward in the eastern part of the ocean, while a warm current moves poleward along its western edge. In higher latitudes, the warm current, after crossing the ocean to the east, flows poleward along the eastern side of the basin; cold water is carried to lower latitudes in the west. Figure 14.6 shows average surface currents of the world's oceans. Figure 16.11, section 16.7, shows mean winds. The close similarity in flow pattern is readily apparent.

The magnitude of some of the current systems might be considered. The Gulf Stream, probably the most famous of all currents, moves with speeds of from half a knot to over three knots. It transports water at the rate of 30 billion gallons per second, which is more than 65 times the amount of water moved by all the rivers of the world combined.

14.9 Current Measurements   The easiest and most obvious way of measuring a surface current is to put a floating object in water and

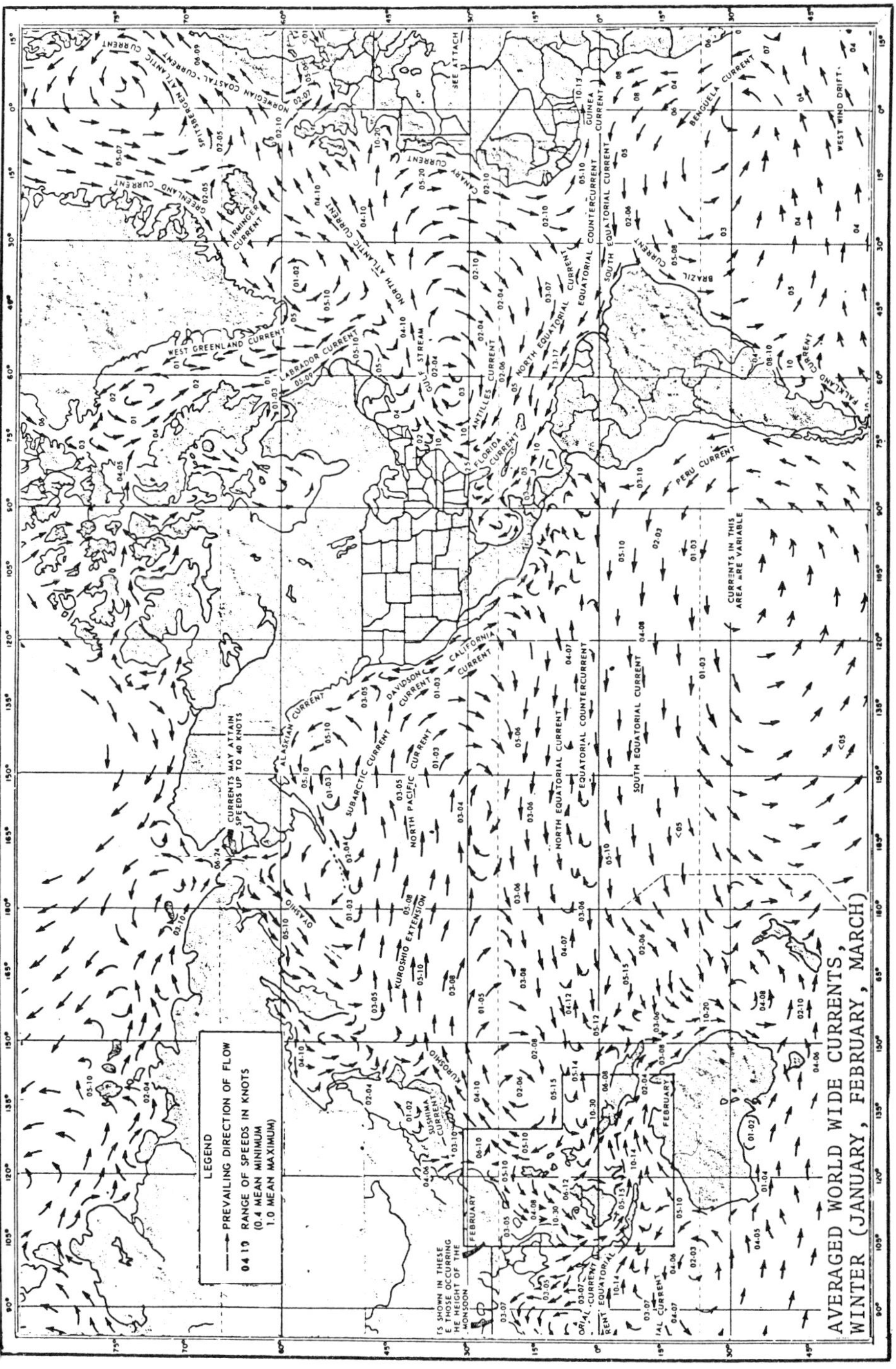

Fig. 14.6 World currents.

observe how far and how fast it drifts. The romantic "message in a bottle" is an example. This method can be refined by putting a radio transmitter or radar reflector on the floating object. A still more sophisticated variation is to put two large electrodes in the surface water to measure the electric potential developed by the moving conductor (sea water) within the earth's magnetic field.

Various current meters have been used to measure currents. The newer devices utilize the speed of sound in two directions to determine currents; sound speed is measured in one direction and compared with sound speed in the opposite direction. The difference between the two is the speed of water movement.

Currents at mid-level between the surface and bottom can be measured by devices like the Swallow float. This device, which floats at a particular density level, is preset and tracked with acoustic gear. The Swallow float was used in the discovery of the Cromwell countercurrent in the equatorial Pacific; this undercurrent flows east to west almost at the equator.

Temperature Structure of the Oceans

A knowledge of the temperature structure of the oceans is important in the fishing industry, in antisubmarine warfare, and particularly in weather forecasting and climatology.

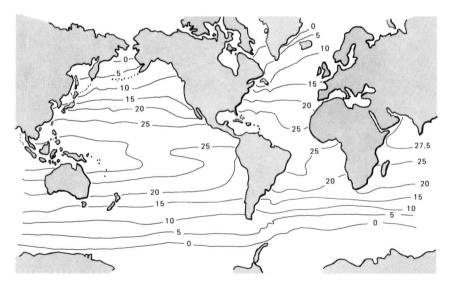

Fig. 14.7 Average yearly ocean surface temperature (degrees C).

14.10   Surface Temperatures   The global sea suface temperature pattern, on an average yearly basis, is shown in Fig. 14.7. From this, we see the effect of the greater heat input in equatorial regions; the sea surface temperature gradually decreases toward the poles. The process that keeps temperatures from being equal at equal latitudes throughout the world is transfer of heat by currents. Figure 14.7 shows deviations from the ideal pattern. One is the kinking of isotherms along oceanic edges. The western North Atlantic shows warmer waters farther north than would be expected. This contrasts with the eastern North Pacific, where the isotherms show colder water farther south than might be expected. These displacements are caused by permanent ocean currents.

A second deviation is the packing of the isotherms at higher latitudes, so the rate of change in surface temperatures increases with latitude toward the poles.

14.11   Temperature Variation with Depth   The oceans are three-layered in their vertical temperature structure. In the surface region, there is a layer of relatively warm water called the mixed layer. Below this is the main thermocline, where the temperature decreases rapidly with depth. In the bottom layer, the deep layer, there are constant and cold temperatures. In higher latitudes, the deep layer extends all the way to the surface. Figure 14.8 shows typical winter temperature variations with depth at three latitudes.

At high and low latitudes there is no marked seasonal water temperature change. In mid-latitudes, in spring, there is a gradual warming of the surface layer, and a seasonal thermocline develops. The

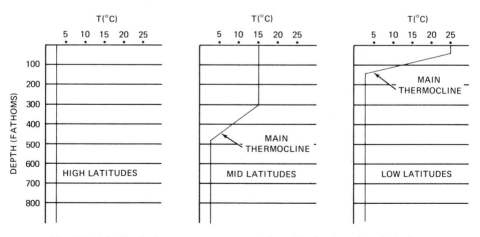

Fig. 14.8   Idealized winter temperature variation with depth at three latitudes.

warming takes place in the upper few hundred feet, and results in a seasonal thermocline becoming superimposed on the main thermocline. The seasonal thermocline reaches its maximum depth in fall.

Superimposed on the seasonal variation is a daily variation in temperature, called the diurnal thermocline. These, typically, may be as much as 1 to 2 degrees in magnitude and 20 to 30 feet in depth.

14.12   Measuring Temperature in the Oceans   Surface water temperature is measured by taking readings of a thermometer which is exposed to the water as it enters the ship's cooling water intake. These measurements are often not too accurate because of poor location of the thermometer and because of the gross scale (2 to 5 degree graduations) of the thermometers used. A more accurate method is to haul a bucket of water aboard and measure the water's temperature with a simple thermometer. Sea surface temperature measurements by satellite, using infrared sensors, are coming into general use; they will be of particular value in those ocean areas of few or no ship reports.

Most measurements of temperature below the surface are made with the bathythermograph (BT). The conventional BT consists of a temperature-sensitive sensor which causes a stylus to move as the temperature changes and a pressure-sensitive sensor which causes a carriage to move at right angles to that caused by the temperature variation. As the device is lowered into the water, pressure and temperature variations cause motion of the carriage and stylus, resulting in a plot of temperature versus depth. The BT may be used to depths of 900 feet. The ship must slow down to 10 knots for optimum results.

The conventional BT is gradually being replaced by a much more accurate expendable XBT. This device is dropped over the side, and it telemeters the temperature information along a very thin wire to a recorder on the ship. The sink rate of the unit is known, so instrument depth may be determined as a function of time. At the end of the drop, the wire breaks and the XBT sinks to the bottom. XBTs which measure down to 2500 feet are now available, and 5000-foot instruments are under development.

For deeper and more accurate temperature determinations, primarily for scientific use, other instruments are used. The Nansen bottle is the basic device. It is, very simply, a piece of pipe with a valve at each end, with two reversing thermometers attached. The Nansen bottles are fastened at spaced intervals to a wire cable and lowered into the water by means of a special oceanographic winch capable of paying out or hauling in 36,000 feet of wire cable.

When the entire cast has been lowered into the water, a messenger (small brass weight) is attached to the cable and released. When it hits the first bottle it trips a latch, which causes the Nansen bottle to flop down into the reversed position, thereby releasing the bottle's messenger. This new messenger travels down the wire to release the latch on the second bottle. The process continues until all bottles have been reversed.

When the bottle is reversed, both valves close, trapping a water sample. At the same time, the column of mercury in the reversing thermometers separates at a restricted region, thus preventing any subsequent change in temperature reading. One of the thermometers is protected against pressure; the other is not. The unprotected one will have a higher reading than the other, and the difference in readings is related to the depth. Thus, the water temperature at the sample depth is obtained, as is the depth at which the sample was taken.

In addition to reversing thermometers, another temperature-measuring instrument has come into use in recent years. This is the thermistor chain, a long cable containing a great number of temperature-sensitive devices called thermistors. The chain is towed behind a ship, and readings at 100 to 200 different depths are relayed to the ship.

Practical Results from Oceanography

The application of oceanographic knowledge produces many practical results that affect the entire American economy. Here, we shall discuss some of those advances useful to a mariner.

14.13 Improved Charts   Our maps of the ocean floor are about equal in accuracy and degree of detail to the maps of the land surface of the earth published 200 years ago, but improvements have been marked in the last 20 years. Before 1935, charts gave spot depths which were obtained by hand lead. With the advent of the continuous recording echo sounder, complete profiles of the bottom could be made. Echo sounders can be put on anything from small power boats to aircraft carriers, so it is routine for the more popular harbors to be well sounded.

There have been increased requirements in navigation charts, primarily by submarines. Before 1940, detailed depth knowledge to 50 feet was sufficient. During World War II, detailed knowledge to 500 feet became necessary. Now, with modern deep-diving submarines capable of traveling submerged at speeds over 25 knots, it is necessary to show every possible mountain peak or other danger to submerged navigation. This means that the entire ocean area must be accurately charted.

14.14 Ice Predictions   Construction of the Distant Early Warning Net (DEW Line) in the late 1940s involved ice operations for many ships. Ice damage exceeded $1 million a year during the early operations. At that time, the U.S. Naval Oceanographic Office started a prediction program based on aerial observations and environmental factors such as currents, winds, and rates of ice formation. The program was taken over by the Naval Weather Service when it became operational, and highly accurate forecasts of ice conditions are now available. The predictions enable planners to say when ships should leave U.S. harbors in order to be able to conduct ice-free operations, and how long the ships can stay in the Arctic or Antarctic without fear of being iced in. On voyages into areas where ice packs may be driven toward shore by strong winds, forecasters advise on timing and evasion— when to proceed, when and where to seek shelter.

Commercial interest in ice forecasting has mounted tremendously with the oil discovery on the North Slope of Arctic Alaska. Operations there must be supplied, and products must be moved to either U.S. coast. The icebreaker/tanker *S.S. Manhattan* made the pioneering voyage in an effort to see if oil could be moved through the North-west Passage to the lucrative East Coast ports. All activities connected with the North Slope oil operations made evident the need for accurate ice forecasting.

14.15 Weather Predictions   The oceans furnish almost 100 percent of the precipitation that falls on land in the form of rain, hail, or snow. They play a major role in keeping the temperature of our planet within the narrow limits necessary for human existence.

A description of oceanic conditions is a vital ingredient in weather forecasting models. Ocean temperature structure, composition and movement of ocean currents, and heat exchange between the ocean and the atmosphere are all taken into account in preparing forecasts. Forecast accuracy on a global scale has improved a great deal with the use of oceanic parameters on a synoptic basis.

Further refinement of the heat exchange computations will be necessary to develop medium and long-range forecasting capability. Every type of ocean operation, surface and subsurface, will benefit immensely when good, extended forecasts are available.

The reports on weather and sea state made regularly by ships at sea form the foundation of existing forecasting methods. These reports will be just as important to the more sophisticated, long-range, future methods.

14.16 Optimum Track Ship Routing   Optimum Track Ship Routing (OTSR) is a system that clearly illustrates effective combination of the disciplines of meteorology and oceanography to produce a proven, useful operational forecasting product. Scientific OTSR was developed to the operational stage by the U.S. Naval Oceanographic Office. It was turned over to the Naval Weather Service for fleet use in 1958. There are several commercial organizations which provide OTSR service for the merchant fleet.

The goal of OTSR is to recommend routes which will result in least steaming time en route consistent with the most favorable weather available, and will avoid areas of possible storm damage. All oceans are covered by the service.

Action starts with a request from the ship, naming ports, operating speed, dates, and other pertinent information. The voyage must exceed 1500 miles to make routing worthwhile, hence it is usually transoceanic.

The weathermen who do the routing know the ship characteristics as related to various types of seas, so a destroyer and a large tanker traveling at the same time to the same port might get different routing instructions. The ship router bases his work on three types of charts: detailed weather and oceanographic analyses for the day of departure; prognostic sea state charts out to three days; and prognostic charts showing locations of storm centers and storm tracks from three days out to the port of destination. From these, he issues a recommended route to the ship.

Once a day, the ship sends back a situation report, including position, state of the sea, and weather, and perhaps comments on that day's routing results. The ship router updates his weather and sea state charts each day and modifies the ship's track as necessary. The routers look for such things as moderate, following swell (worth up to a knot in speed made good); avoidance of sea conditions of danger; and least time en route.

It is difficult to make a precise evaluation of the program, but one survey by MSC showed an annual saving of about $1 million. Three-fourths of this was attributed to shorter sailing times; the remainder to maintenance and damage avoided. Other evaluations show an average reduction of voyage time of 10 percent. The U.S. Merchant fleet makes over 7000 voyages a year in which OTSR would be applicable.

14.17 Search and Rescue   There are many times when search and rescue procedures must be used at sea. Search involves finding drifting life rafts or lifeboats, small boats dead in the water, and sometimes people adrift in life jackets.

Forecasting techniques have been developed which can give fairly accurate positioning of the object of the search. The forecast ingredients are: average sea current, local wind current, shape and size of the lost object, and local winds to develop leeway data.

Forecasts are made of the search target position for specified time intervals following time zero. The error probability for each starting search position is given, which helps in the decision as to the type of search pattern to be used.

14.18 Improved Fish Catch The fishing industry is important to the U.S. economy; about $2 billion worth of sea produce a year is harvested. It is of even greater importance to foreign countries whose people consume almost three times as much fish per capita as does the United States.

The Bureau of Commercial Fisheries (BCF) has had and now has an aggressive research program on how marine life is affected by the oceanic environment. Much is known now about how fish react to varying temperatures, how food supplies for fish are generated by ocean currents, and how spawn are affected by temperature and currents. To put this knowledge to use in directing fishing fleets to the best fishing areas, or in forecasting good and bad fishing years, detailed knowledge of the ocean temperature structure and current must be available. Forecasts of changes are required, so fishermen can be told when and where to move.

Variation in temperature structure affects sound propagation in the oceans, just as it affects fish behavior, so it was only natural that BCF and the Navy submarine hunters would join together on the problem. Ideas and information are exchanged. Operationally, the results have been very successful. A few examples should be examined.

Fish are very temperature-sensitive. The optimum temperature for albacore fishing is between 17 and 19 degrees C. During normal years, the bulk of the albacore catch is taken from the fishing area off Southern California. In 1967, sea surface temperatures were anomalously warm off California and Oregon. As a result, the albacore fishing area shifted farther north, and the bulk of that year's catch was taken well off Oregon (Fig. 14.9). Had the fishing not been directed into this area, the year would have been disastrous for the West Coast tuna fleet.

Figure 14.10 illustrates another effect of temperature variations on fishing.

14.19 Wave Forecasts Sea and swell analyses and forecasts are a fundamental requirement for a wide range of civil and military applications. Wave information is used in all marine operations, in strategic

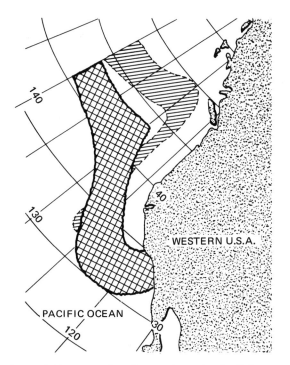

Fig. 14.9 Optimum fishing areas for albacore (cross-hatched) for an average August.

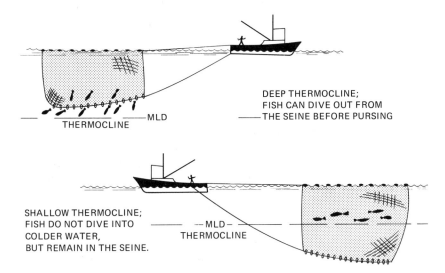

Fig. 14.10 Schematic example of the effect of different mixed layer depth on purse seining for pelagic fish.

and tactical planning, design of ships and other platforms both surface and subsurface, shore line structure, shore line control, and coastal safety. As exploration and exploitation activities in the oceans increase, wave information will be of increased importance.

There are several forecasting methods in common use today. They give essentially the same results if the same surface wind forecast is used. The forecast method is based upon a knowledge of how wind and water react to each other, how energy from the wind is transferred to water, how energy in the waves is dissipated and at what rate. Knowing these things (there are still some only partially solved problems in these areas), the forecaster starts his work with a surface wind forecast. From the wind charts, he outlines fetch areas over which the winds blow at approximately constant speed. He knows the length of time the wind has blown over the area, and his forecast tells him how much longer it can be expected to blow. Using the numbers from fetch length, wind duration, and wind speed, the forecaster enters nomograms with these as arguments, and reads off the expected wave heights and wave periods. Swell forecasts are made, using wave heights and periods as basic input.

14.20   Antisubmarine Warfare (ASW) Environmental Prediction   An ocean search for an enemy submarine is a problem similar to searching for a person in a completely darkened room, with the hunted person being able to move at will—as quietly as possible, of course! The enemy submarine beneath the surface can be seen from the air only to depths to 300 feet; light has only shallow penetration below the ocean surface. There is no scent. Noise can be minimized by moving slowly. Modern submarines are agile. If the hunter comes close, dodging maneuvers are effective. If the hunter is closing in, the prey can run at high speed—out the door of the darkened room and (maybe) off to safety.

The purpose of the ASW environmental prediction system is to provide fleet commanders and ASW units with forecasts of oceanographic conditions for use in finding enemy submarines, for routing convoys through areas where their detection by enemy submarines will be least likely, and for making weapons settings. These forecasts can be used for submarines as well.

Figure 14.11 shows the complexity of the antisubmarine warfare environment with which ASW forecasters must deal. The sketch portrays the major oceanographic problems in the detection, identification, localization, and destruction of submarines. Starting from left to right, the first column shows a typical bathythermograph trace of temperature versus depth. The temperature is constant down to a

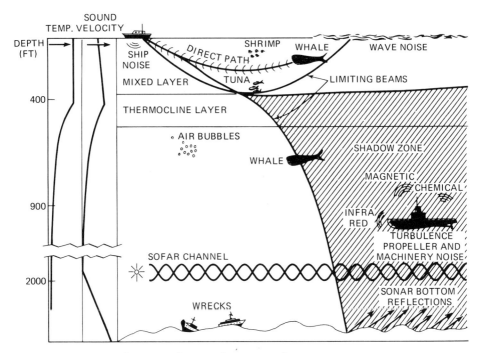

Fig. 14.11   The antisubmarine warfare environment.

maximum of 400 feet. This zone is the mixed layer. The temperature then normally decreases sharply until it reaches the nearly constant temperature of deep water (about 35 degrees F). This region is the main thermocline.

The second column shows a plot of sound velocity versus depth. Sound velocity increases in the mixed layer because of the increased pressure, but as temperature decreases in the thermocline so does sound velocity. At about 2000 feet in depth the pressure effect exceeds the temperature effect and the sound velocity begins to increase again. The point of minimum sound velocity is the axis of another sound layer called the SOFAR (Sound Fixing and Ranging) Channel. Sound is very effectively trapped in this channel, and small explosions have been heard for distances up to 12,000 miles.

In Figure 14.11 the sketch to the right shows various noise sources in the oceans: own ship's noise, marine life, machinery noise from the submarine, and surface wave noise. Whales or large fish can give a sonar return simulating a submarine. In the thermocline, sound beams are for the most part bent upward, giving a large area below which the submarine can hide.

Direct-path sonar beams can pick up submarines in the mixed layer, but these beams are channeled within this duct or else bent down toward the bottom, leaving a shadow zone where energy does not penetrate. Longer ranges into the shadow zone can be obtained through bottom reflection of the sound (called bottom bounce), but use of this technique requires detailed knowledge of the bottom including slope, bottom composition, and nature of the sedimentation layers under the ocean bottom.

The submarine puts energy into the water in the form of machinery and propeller noise but also gives off chemical, infrared, magnetic, and other detectable signals which resemble those of bottom wrecks, large fish or whales, air bubbles, and distant surface ships. The problem of separating the submarine's signal from the confusion of the background noise is formidable. When we consider that the submarine can change depth at will and can evade at speeds in excess of most surface ships, the problem of locating a high-speed evading target in three dimensions is most difficult.

Sonar equipments, the "ears" in the search for submarines, show wide variance in the distance at which they can pick up targets that are putting out the same signal strength. Environmental effects account for the wide variation; these effects are what must be forecast.

The Fleet operators do not want to make computations based on unending volumes of sea surface temperatures, temperature profiles, and layer depth predictions. They want answers to the question, "At what range will *my* sonar system acquire a target in my immediate area *today?*" So, the Naval Weather Service has devised a system for providing forecast detection ranges for each of the several sonar systems now in use. The approach is to combine a full array of oceanographic analysis fields into composite propagation loss profiles for a series of point locations which are representative of predetermined acoustical regimes. Each regime is an area reasonably homogeneous as to water mass, bathymetry, and bottom bounce acoustical loss. Both power-limited and ray path-limited ranges are predicted; the selection depends upon the spatial relationship of the transducer and target, whether they are in the same layer, lie across a layer boundary, or are both in a duct. Range variability which might be expected with each regime is also calculated. The system is adaptable to both active and passive detection systems.

The acoustic ranges are presented in two parts. Acoustic Sensor Range Prediction (ASRAP) is for the support of fixed-wing aircraft, the P3/S3 squadrons. Ship Helicopter Acoustic Range Prediction System (SHARPS) is for the support of other Fleet users.

14.21 Harbor Flushing and Oil Spills   Harbor pollution is a problem of great and growing concern. Pollution may be caused by such things as industrial wastes, sewage, oil spills, and pesticides. Detailed flushing studies have been made of all major harbors in order to minimize harmful effects and to institute pollution control measures.

Anyone who has lived on a boat tied up at a marina knows that when the tide goes out it takes all of the garbage with it. Unfortunately, 12 hours later when the tide comes in so does most of the garbage that was removed on the last tide. The same effect will be had with nuclear or any other form of harbor pollution. The first tide will take out most of the pollution, but each succeeding tide will bring in a little and take out a little. Some areas of a harbor may be completely free of pollution after the first tide. Other areas, because of currents or other conditions, may retain serious levels of contamination for days or even weeks.

Flushing studies involve extensive investigations of all oceanographic conditions of a harbor: tidal information, currents, changes in bottom depth, nature of the bottom, location of eddies and backwaters, and similar data. From these studies tables can be prepared to show how long it would take a harbor to become completely free of pollution.

Methods have been developed which forecast with precision the movement of harbor or offshore oil spills. These forecasts identify the area of maximum threat from the oil spill, thus permitting containment action to be taken most effectively.

Oceanic Phenomena

There is a wealth of information contained in the oceans, much of which is of practical importance to mankind. Some practical applications have been described above. But in addition to their utilitarian aspects, the oceans provide a vast source of intellectual knowledge useful to other sciences. For example, the coming and going of the Ice Ages can be traced by analyzing marine fossils.

We know with a fair amount of certainty that the average ocean temperature was about 85 degrees F some 200,000 years ago but that 25,000 years later it had dropped to 70 degrees F. This temperature drop was due to the Ice Age, but the method of tracing the extent of the glaciers by determining the temperature of the oceans thousands of years ago is a triumph of the scientific technique.

In 1947 Professor Harold Urey discovered that the ratio of oxygen-18 to oxygen-16 in shells and skeletons of marine animals can be correlated with the temperature in which the shells were formed. A difference of one hundredth of one percent (.01%) in the ratio of oxygen-18 to oxygen-16 in the carborates of the shells corresponds with a temperature difference of 1 degree F. By measuring the ratio difference in different layers of bottom cores, oceanographers can trace fluctuations in the ocean's temperatures back thousands of years. This use of radioisotope techniques also enables oceanographers to tell that a fossil mollusk from a core was born millions of years ago in the spring when the water temperature was 72 degrees F, that it lived for about five years, and that it died in late summer.

14.22 Deep Scattering Layer   The deep scattering layer (DSL) was discovered by the U.S. Navy during World War II in connection with acoustical research. False-bottom recordings from echo sounders appeared regularly; these recordings were shown to be closely correlated with the vertical movements of "layers" or concentration of tiny marine organisms such as plankton. The layer rises at night and sinks by day, which suggests that members of the plankton family are light-sensitive, and live in layered colonies at depths related to light intensity. The biological composition of the layers, to this day, has not been fully identified.

The most plausible suggestion is that the DSL consists of a whole society of marine animals, that their vertical movements are triggered by changes in light intensity, and that the predator-prey relationships prevail. Large fish eat small ones; small fish eat still smaller fish; the process continues until we reach the very small plankton. This aggregation appears as a "layer" on the echogram. The DSL is of interest both to the marine biologist and to sonar operators.

14.23 Internal Waves and Dead Water   Whenever two layers of different density meet at an interface, there is a possibility that waves will be created between the two layers. The most striking case of wave action occurs at the interface between the atmosphere and ocean where the density difference between air and water is a maximum.

The oceans, however, consist of other layers of different density. Whenever there are changes in temperature or salinity there are interfaces along which wave action can and frequently does occur. Within the ocean medium itself these waves are called internal waves. Their effect was known for hundreds of years during sailing ship days as dead water. However, it was not until this century that the laws governing dead water were understood.

If the keel of a ship happens to be at the depth coinciding with the interface of two density layers, the ship's motion may set up internal waves. When this occurs so much energy from the ship's forward motion is used to generate the waves that nothing is left for forward motion of the ship. The result is that the ship is stopped dead in the water despite full sails and winds of 5 to 10 knots.

This was a not infrequent occurrence during sailing ship times and at least once affected the course of history. In the battle of Actium, Marc Anthony's fleet was stopped by internal waves, which contributed greatly to his defeat. Octavius won the battle and went on to become the Emperor Augustus, the first of the Roman Emperors.

The internal waves can easily be observed by taking temperature versus depth readings as frequently as possible at any stationary point (see Fig. 14.12). A plot of the temperature readings versus depth will show that any one value (say 50 degrees F) will vary in depth with each reading. The amplitude of the depth changes in a temperature reading is the amplitude of the wave. The time interval between readings when a temperature value occurs at the same depth is the period of the wave.

The phenomenon of internal waves has an application for a slow-moving submarine making an attack at periscope depth. Should an internal wave be generated, the submarine could be stopped by it in the dead water, or could broach and expose the conning tower. Either event could be disastrous.

A submarine can trim its buoyancy so that it can "rest" on a density layer, move slowly, and remain undetected by surface craft. But internal waves along the density interface could cause trouble. A submarine crossing from dense to less dense water would suddenly become heavy and would start to sink—requiring the prompt pumping of ballast overboard. There are some who think that several submarine losses have been caused by situations like this.

14.24 Upwelling and El Niño   When prevailing winds blow along a shore, there is a mass transport of water in upper layers to the right

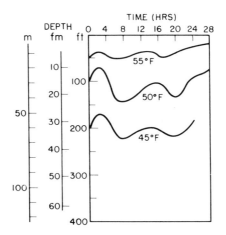

Fig. 14.12 Internal waves from a plot of isothermal variation.

of the wind direction in the Northern Hemisphere. As the water is moved offshore in the surface layer, pressure forces water in the subsurface layers to rise. The process is called upwelling.

Upwelling is important because it provides a constant circulation whereby nitrogenous decay products from dead marine life are brought from the bottom to the surface. This fertilizes the ocean area involved, providing nourishment for marine life over wide ocean areas.

One of the most important areas for upwelling is along the west coast of South America between the shore line and the northward-flowing Humboldt Current. The upwelling brings up phosphates and other minerals from lower depths which in turn nourish plankton and fish life of all sorts. Birds come from long distances to feed on the fish, and the islands where the birds nest are filled with bird droppings (guano). A third of a million tons of guano are sold yearly as high-grade fertilizer. In the same area fishermen catch upwards of 100,000 tons of anchovies as well as substantial catches of larger species feeding on the anchovies. But every so often conditions change and the Humboldt Current meanders from its normal course.

When it does this, upwelling stops and a warmer current moves in from the north. The result is catastrophic. The fish population moves out to sea with the current, leaving the birds without a source of food. Up to 25 million birds may die in the famine, with the hydrogen sulfide from their decaying bodies so thick that ships' hulls are turned black. This particular phenomenon is called the Callao Painter, but the overall phenomenon causing the upwelling to stop is called El Niño, and it is one of the most destructive oceanographic conditions in existence.

14.25 The Red Tide The same atmospheric conditions which affect the prevailing winds causing the Humboldt Current to wander further out to sea are also responsible for another destructive occurrence known as the Red Tide. When upwelling stops, cool waters are no longer brought to the surface. The surface layers become heated, which brings about a bloom of tiny red-colored plankton. The plankton become so thick that the water actually takes on a reddish hue—hence the name Red Tide.

The result of the Red Tide is that millions of fish are suffocated by the tiny organisms clogging their gills. Their dead bodies are thrown up along miles of beaches with a stench that carries for miles. Although not as economically destructive as El Niño, the Red Tide does cause severe hardships along the coasts where it occurs. Only a few years ago it occurred off the coast of Florida with the unhappy result that hundreds of resort towns were forced to close down until the tide had passed and its debris was cleared away.

14.26 The Black Sea   There is one last phenomenon to discuss and that is the hydrogen sulfide content of the Black Sea between Russia and Turkey. The Black Sea is a very large salt water lake whose only opening is through the Straits of the Dardanelles.

The sill between the Black Sea and the Aegean is very shallow and narrow, so there is a minimum exchange of water between the two seas. This lack of exchange has a very harmful effect: It prevents any reasonable amount of upwelling, so as marine life on the surface dies it sinks to the bottom where it remains to decay.

Over a period of hundreds of years the decayed matter gave off hydrogen sulfide gas and used-up oxygen which completely destroyed all bottom life. The hydrogen sulfide layer begins at a few hundred feet in depth and continues to the bottom. In this region there is no life in the Black Sea.

From a naval point of view the Black Sea poses a very interesting problem. When mixed in water, the hydrogen sulfide gas has a corrosive effect on metals as can be seen from the Callao Painter effect during El Niño, mentioned above. A submarine operating for extended periods in the hydrogen sulfide zone would run the serious risk of ruined hull fittings with an attendant risk to the ship and its crew.

Environmental Pollution[1]

The oceans, containing a volume of water amounting to 318 million cubic miles, were thought at one time to be an inexhaustible dumping ground. Recent experience has indicated otherwise. Extreme caution is now exercised before permitting the offshore dumping of dredge spoil, of garbage, of radioactive wastes. In fact, the offshore dumping of anything that can impair the environment is viewed as a problem.

Terrestrial pollution is closely related to oceanic pollution. Water moves to streams either overland or through the ground to be discharged eventually to the ocean. In its seaward path water can leach stockpiled wastes, or it can be a vehicle for any waste discharged into a stream.

Environmental pollution does not stop with the contamination of water. The solid waste problem, the pollution of air, and the effect of noise all affect the environment. This realization has resulted in legislation requiring a study of the impact on the environment prior to approval of activities that may eventually result in pollution.

Pollution is population dependent. A density of one person per square mile permits an approach to waste disposal that must be denied to a

[1]John F. Hoffman, Ph.D., P.E., Professor, Dept. of Environmental Sciences, U.S. Naval Academy.

population density of a thousand persons per square mile. Pollution problems in undeveloped countries are different than those in developed countries. Underdeveloped countries have sanitation problems and crop problems. Developed countries have these, plus problems arising from affluence. The wealth of a country can be seen in its Gross National Product (GNP). The Gross National Product for any one year is the sum of goods and services produced and sold in that year. Pollution arises from both the manufacture of products and their transportation in the air, on the land and on the ocean.

In the forty two years following 1930 the GNP of the United States has increased more than twelve-fold while the population has less than doubled. From 1960 to 1972 the GNP increased one hundred percent while the population increased less than 15 percent. It does not stretch the imagination to conceive of the variety and amounts of wastes generated by the industries that support the rate of change of production. Much of the pollution from these wastes ends up in the ocean.

15.1 The Hydrologic Cycle   Important to the various aspects of water pollution is the hydrologic cycle. The hydrologic cycle, an unending chain of events, is depicted in Fig. 15-1.

Precipitation, which includes rain, snow, hail, etc. falls on the land. Part runs off overland to streams, part seeps into the ground to become ground water, and part is evaporated. Stream flow terminates in the ocean.

Evaporation is a continuous process. Plants and trees use water stored in the soil to distribute soluble nutrients throughout the plant structure.

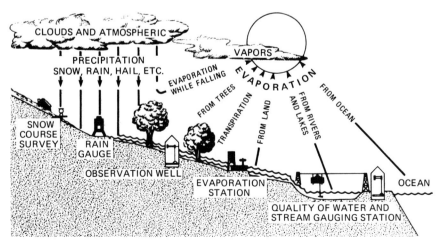

Fig. 15.1 The hydrologic cycle.

This water then evaporates from the leaves in a process called transpiration. Water also evaporates from the soil surface, the surfaces of plants that intercept precipitation and from water bodies such as rivers and lakes.

Stream flow, one of the most important factors influencing oceanic pollution, has two components. One is the baseflow, which represents seepage from ground water storage and accounts for stream flow during periods when there is no precipitation. The other is overland runoff which occurs during times of precipitation and of snow melt. A knowledge of stream flow is of such extreme importance in water supply and waste disposal that the U.S. Geological Survey, Department of Interior, maintains a nationwide network of stations to measure stream flow continuously. The equipment at one of these stations is shown in Fig. 15-2. As the result of the efforts of the U.S. Geological Survey, data concerning the volume of water discharged annually into the oceans that bound the United States is being amassed, as well as data concerning the annual amounts of chemical salts and of suspended silt, clay, etc. that are being similarly discharged.

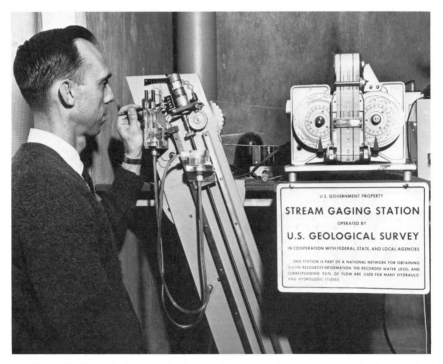

Fig. 15.2 U.S. Geological Survey Equipment for automatically measuring the flow in the Potomac River at the Little Falls pumping station. (*Photograph courtesy U.S. Geological Survey.*)

Stream flow is usually below average during the summer months due to the effects of evaporation. As a result, the concentration of any pollutant discharged to a stream at a constant rate of flow throughout the year, such as sewage, would be increased during periods of low flow. Where serious stream pollution can occur as the result of low seasonal stream flow storage reservoirs are built for the purposes of increasing the flow during these times.

15.2   Ecology   One of the primary concerns in the pollution picture is the impact that pollution has on the ecology of both the water and terrestrial environments. Ecology is basically the study of the structure and function of nature. It is involved with the basic elements together with the inorganic and organic compounds within the environment; the plants utilizing nutrients, water, carbon dioxide and solar energy to synthesize plant material; the animals that subsist on the plants and, in many cases, on other animals; and the bacteria and fungi that decompose wastes and convert them back to the basic elements and inorganic and organic compounds.

Pollution can disturb this balance. Shown in Table 15-I are the important factors necessary for the successful continuance of this balance together with the disrupting effects of pollution.

Important to both the fresh water and sea water environment is the food web. Shown in Fig. 15-3 is a diagram indicating the interdependency of the various marine organisms necessary to produce a herring. Bacteria are consumed by tiny protozoa, which in turn are

Table 15-1   The Relationship of Pollution to Important Factors in the Water Environment

Factor	Function	Disrupting Agent
Light	food web mobility	silt-dredging, land erosion colored chemicals humic acids
Temperature	reproduction food web metabolism	industrial and power plant discharges, sudden changes in air temperature, overland runoff
Dissolved oxygen	metabolism	biodegradation of organic material
Plankton	food web oxygen production	oil, chemicals, organic wastes, water temperature, self-annihilation

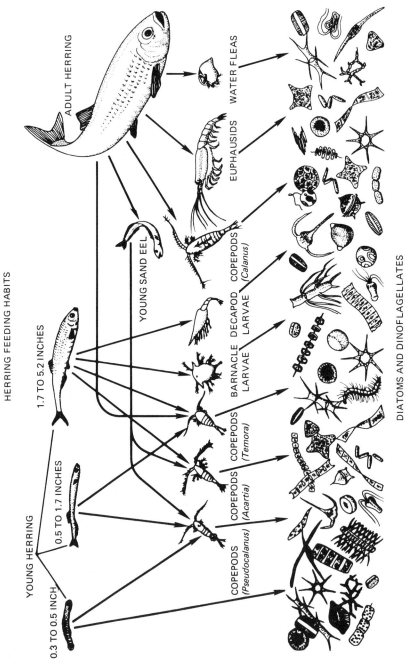

Fig. 15.3 The food web. (From *The Life of the Ocean*, pp. 54–55, McGraw-Hill Book Co.)

consumed by various other organisms including larger protozoa. Protozoa are consumed by fish fry. Fish fry are consumed by larger fish and other creatures and so on. Pollution in an environment may be passed through the food web. For example, if DDT enters the water environment through contaminated mosquitoes which are consumed by fish fry, the ultimate effect would be to contaminate the organs of fish-eating birds and affect their reproduction.

Vital to the water environment is dissolved oxygen. Some organisms, such as carp, can survive in water containing relatively little dissolved oxygen; others, like trout, require more. In the natural course of events aquatic animals survive and propagate in a compatible environment. Pollution can change this. Aquatic organisms that are mobile can move out of the polluted environment. Those that cannot, such as oysters and clams may succumb to the pollution.

A measure of the degree of pollution in an environment is the biochemical oxygen demand (BOD). This is quantified by a standard laboratory test in which the dissolved oxygen contents of two water samples are measured five days apart. The difference between the two oxygen contents is the oxygen consumed by the decomposing organisms present.

Alteration of certain chemical compounds has the same effect. The difference in dissolved oxygen contents in this latter case, however, is termed chemical oxygen demand (COD). The addition of certain classes of pollutants to water bodies pose special problems. Accordingly, oil pollution, heavy metal pollution, thermal pollution and radiological pollution are discussed in slightly greater detail below.

15.3   Oil Pollution   Oil pollution in the ocean arises from a number of sources. Among these are the discharge of bilge water at sea, accidental spills at sea, leaks from industrial plants and the willful discharge of spent oil to streams and rivers.

Oil spills in fresh water bodies and in the oceans have a number of effects. Oil coats the gills of fish and inhibits the interchange of oxygen with the blood; oil coats small organisms and essentially eliminates them from the food web; oil settles to the bottom blanketing fish eggs and bottom dwelling organisms; decomposition of oil by bacteria depletes the supply of dissolved oxygen; oil impairs the solution of oxygen from the atmosphere; oil flavors fish to render it unplatable; oil washed onshore is unsightly and destructive and birds that have feathers coated with spilled oil cannot fly.

Tests by the American Petroleum Institute indicate that as little as 200 gallons per square mile produces a film on the water surface 12 millionths of an inch thick which is characterized by bright bands of color.

Owing to the problems created, it is desirable to remove oil as rapidly as possible after the spill is discerned. Various methods of coping with oil spills exist. Sludge formers, such as clay, cause the oil to sink. However, this approach transfers the problem from the water surface to the bottom of the ocean. Emulsifiers break up the oil mass into fine droplets and enables dispersal. The increased surface area enables more rapid decomposition by bacteria.

In polar regions decomposition in the water environment takes place at a very slow rate. Other means are necessary to cope with spills. One of these is to burn the oil floating on the surface. Straw or tiny glass beads spread on the oil surface act as wicks to facilitate combustion. This, however, transfers the problem to one of air pollution.

When the sea is sufficiently calm, "skimmers" and mechanical corrals can be used. These are particularly useful in harbors. Booms floating on the surface, towed by boats, localize the spill and permit pumping the oil to storage. Shown in Fig. 15-4 is a mechanical boom. A recently developed method that appears to hold promise is an endless-belt squeegee. A plastic foam belt absorbs the oil as it passes through the oil spill. The oil-ladened belt is then put through a wringer and the oil squeezed out.

Fig. 15.4 A lightweight aluminum boom for containing oil spills. (Photograph by Reynolds Metal Company.)

15.4   Heavy Metal Pollution   Heavy metal pollution generally occurs from the discharge of industrial wastes into rivers or into the ocean, although the leaching of ore bodies is also a source. The heavy metal contaminants usually consist of one or more of the following: copper, zinc, lead, chromium, cadmium, mercury, iron, arsenic, and manganese. The tolerance of aquatic organisms for these pollutants in their dissolved state is relatively low compared to the tolerance of the human body to compounds such as sugar and table salt.

Frequently, these metals occur as insoluble sediments as in the case of Chesapeake Bay and the Rhine River. Unless some action takes place to cause these sediments to be dissolved, no harmful results take place because of their presence. On the other hand, heavy metals in solution may be discharged directly from industrial plants and are much more poisonous to the water environment.

15.5   Thermal Pollution   The demand for electric energy in the United States roughly doubles every ten years. In 1970, 1524 billion kilowatt hours of electric energy were utilized; by 1990 it is estimated that 5852 kilowatt hours of electricity will be required to fulfill the needs of the nation.

Electric power is produced by steam driven turbines turning electric generators. The steam is produced from water using the heat released by nuclear reactions or by the combustion of gas, oil, or coal. The former fuel source gives rise to the term nuclear power plant. The latter fuel source gives rise to the term fossil fuel plant.

In the case of both nuclear power plants and fossil fuel power plants large amounts of condenser cooling water are required. However, part of the heat from fossil fuel plants is discharged to the atmosphere through smoke stacks, whereas many nuclear power plants use water exclusively for condenser cooling.

Electric power plants are relatively inefficient and it is not unusual to have two watts of heat discharged to a river, estuary, or the ocean for every one watt of electricity generated. The large volume of water necessary for cooling requires that plants be located adjacent to these water bodies.

Two effects are produced by the use of water for condenser cooling. One effect is the cooking of the tiny animals involved in the food web in the proximity of the hot metal walls of the cooling system. The second effect is to change the temperature of the water body to which the cooling water is discharged. The federal government permits only a rise of five degrees Farenheit above the natural water temperature. However, even this temperature increase may magnify the predominance of certain bacteria and parasites which are kept in check at lower temperatures. Thermal barriers may be created because of temperature differences. The temperature of the body of a fish is only about one degree above the water in which he swims. Sudden penetration into markedly different temperature zones produces a shock. Another effect arises from the fact that the concentration of oxygen dissolved in water is reduced at higher temperatures. If pollution in the water from other sources produces a large biochemical oxygen demand a critical condition may be imposed. Additionally, higher than natural water temperatures may alter the life and breeding habits of certain aquatic animals such as the Chesapeake Bay oyster.

There are some measures to cope with the thermal discharges from industrial plants. Perhaps the most recent is the location of power plants off shore in the ocean surrounded entirely by water. Plans are underway to accomplish this off the coast of New Jersey within the next few years. Another method of discharging the heat is by the use of spray ponds, lagoons and canals; the purpose of these is to increase the water area exposed to the atmosphere. Cooling towers are also a useful means of heat exchange by exposing spent cooling water flowing through piping to an updraft of cooling air. Unfortunately, as can be seen in Fig. 15-5, these structures are huge and may be up to 500 feet high and 500 feet in diameter. In some cases, cooling towers have reportedly created local fogs.

At the present time research is being undertaken to utilize waste heat for oyster and flounder cultivation and for desalination of salt water. The major problem involved is making the processes economically feasible.

15.6 Radiological Pollution   Radiological pollution of the water environment arises from the presence of radioactive salts in water. These salts cause changes within animal tissue and results in the damage or the destruction of the cells.

Natural background radiation results from cosmic rays as well as from radioactive compounds in the soil. They have little effect on the human body. Artificial sources of radioactivity include luminous dials and medical and dental x-rays. Excessive exposure of the human body to x-rays may be harmful.

One important characteristic of some unicelled aquatic plants, some fish, and some insects is the ability to concentrate certain elements within their body. One commonly encountered example is the seaweed kelp from which we obtain iodine by leaching the ash after roasting. If these are radioactive salts, a problem can result. For example, oysters and clams obtain their food by straining out tiny floating plants from water that is being passed through their bodies. If these plants contain con-

Fig. 15.5 Cooling tower of Trojan Nuclear Power Plant on the Columbia River near Prescott, Washington. (EPA—Documerica, Gene Daniels. Courtesy U.S. Environmental Protection Agency.)

centrated radioactive salts, the oysters or clams will become radioactive themselves.

A case in point is the plutonium production plant at Hanford, Washington. More than 60 radioactive salts have been determined as entering the Columbia River from this plant. The major radioactive salts entering the ocean environment via the Columbia River are radioactive chromium salts and radioactive zinc salts. Levels of radioactive zinc greater than those in the environment have been detected in some sea animals off the coast of Oregon at depths of over 9,000 feet.

There are three methods of disposal of radioactive materials. Soluble salts can be diluted and dispersed to the environment. Liquids can be concentrated by evaporation and stored in containers such as buried glass-lined steel tanks. At one time it had been the plan to sink these containers in the deeper parts of the ocean. At present, however, this has been abandoned. The third method is to store short-lived materials temporarily awaiting their decay and then discharge the material to the environment.

15.7 Pesticides   The increasing population in the world has necessitated an increase in food production. Pesticides have done much towards helping to increase farm and ranch yield by the prevention of plant and animal diseases and the control of crop predators.

The term pesticide includes insecticides, herbicides, fungicides, fumigants, and rodenticides. Of the five the most commonly encountered pesticides are insecticides. The most publicized insecticide is DDT, one of a group of insecticides called chlorinated hydrocarbons. Persistence in the environment is one of the major differences between chlorinated hydrocarbons and other insecticides; they do not readily decompose.

Known effects of DDT and the related compounds DDD and DDE are the thinning of bird eggshells to the point that the bird population is diminished. Also noted is the interference with the production of tiny single-celled plants which help to maintain the oxygen concentration in the ocean as well as play a part in the food web.

15.8 Offshore Dumping   The ocean forms a very convenient dumping place. Waste towed sufficiently far offshore from the point of origin and dumped, will not be returned by currents, and will sink out of sight; no odors, no noise. Industrial wastes, municipal sewage and sludge both treated and untreated, coal wastes, fly ash, munitions, etc., disposed of in this fashion have had a telling effect on the oceanic environment.

The effects, although local in impact, have been noted world wide. Total depletion of dissolved oxygen due to decomposition results in the predominance of certain types of bacteria. This type of bacteria obtains its oxygen from oxygen-bearing chemical salts. One product formed is hydrogen sulfide which has the odor of "rotten eggs," and produces an environment in which neither plants nor aquatic animals can survive. Another product formed is methane which when exposed to sunlight is altered to carbon monoxide.

Dumped wastes, in some cases, are so poisonous that even bacteria cannot survive and the bottom of the ocean becomes stagnant with no decomposition taking place at all.

Dumping can destroy commercial fishing operations. For example, china clay waste dumped off the coast of Cornwall, England, in areas of commercial lobster fishing, destroyed this fishery. Blanketing the submerged growths of seaweed eliminated the food supply of the lobsters.

Deep draft ships necessitate deeper shipping channels in the vicinity of ports. Disposal of the dredge spoil arising from deepening these channels is a problem. The spoil may contain oily wastes, heavy metals, pesticides and organic materials.

One way of coping with the spoil in the nearshore area is to build and fill a diked disposal area. Valuable real estate is created while solving the problem. One such diked disposal area is Craney Island, located in the proximity of the harbor of Norfolk, Virginia. A considerable saving is effected by the disposal of dredge spoil locally compared with the previous disposal of spoil 20 miles offshore.

15.9 Solid Waste Disposal   Control of the trash explosion in the United States is expensive and difficult. Four pounds of solid waste is generated each day by every person in the United States. The total daily amount for the nation is 400,000 tons.

Solid waste consists of plastics, metals, cardboard and paper and organic materials. It is not without a redeeming trait, however, for the value of garbage is around $13.50 per ton based on recoverable waste.

In our modern society there are three acceptable ways of handling the solid waste problem. These are: sanitary landfill, incineration and pyrolosis. The latter method seems to hold a lot of promise. Experiments are also being conducted which involve the bailing of solid wastes and dumping them in the ocean.

Sanitary landfill is an engineered operation. Sites are located in areas remote to the city served. Refuse from collection trucks is dumped into a wide, deep, sloping trench excavated by bulldozers. Earth is placed over each layer of garbage and compacted in a continuous operation. By the close of each day all the garbage dumped has been covered with a layer of soil.

Incineration involves the burning of waste materials in a combustion chamber. Metals are usually recovered and sold. Uncontrolled burning results in a smoky emission. However, oxygen injected into the process enables complete combustion and helps to reduce smoke. Water flowing through piping embedded in the combustion chamber wall is converted to steam in some processes. The sale of this steam helps to defray the cost of incinerator operation.

Pyrolosis involves the heating of waste in the absence of air to temperatures ranging from 900°F. to 2000°F., breaking down organic materials in a smokeless process. Recoverables in the overall process are oil, ferrous metals, tin and aluminum. Steam produced in the process is sold. Pre-processing the waste also yields shredded paper for use as fuel.

The area occupied by these plants is small and they can be centrally and conveniently located within a city contrasted with the remote location of sanitary landfills. Small units are adaptable for shipboard use.

15.10   Air Pollution   As the affluence of America increased, so has the growth of industry and the number of automobiles. These increases were accompanied by increases in the discharge of a variety of harmful gaseous pollutants. The most widespread of the harmful gaseous emissions are hydrogen sulfide, sulfur dioxide, sulfur trioxide, carbon monoxide, nitrogen oxides and hydrocarbons. These gases are essentially colorless. However, fine particles of soot, minerals, and various metallic dusts add the undesirable characteristics of color, irritation and clogging to the emissions. Low level winds distribute emissions in coastal areas to the ocean near shore. High level winds distribute them world wide to remote parts of the oceans.

Secondary products result from the interaction of some of the various gases. Exposure of certain emissions to sunlight gives rise to photochemical smog. Some secondary chemical products formed are ozone, formaldehyde and sulfuric acid.

Sources of air pollution are transportation (planes, automobiles, trucks, ships, and trains); fuel combustion in stationary sources (power plants, heating plants, steam plants, etc.); industrial processes and solid waste disposal (incinerators, garbage dumps, leaf burning). A variety of other sources exist but are relatively insignificant. Power plants and motor vehicles together in 1970, accounted for more than fifty percent of the total emissions of carbon monoxide, hydrocarbons, nitrogen oxides and sulfur oxides. Automobiles discharge their exhaust at ground level; power plants discharge stack emissions high in the air.

Effects associated with air pollution are: reduced visibility, structural metal corrosion, fabric disintegration, crop damage, asthma, emphysema, and lung cancer.

The seriousness of air pollution from the human body aspect can be realized by considering the case of London where, in the period December 5–9, 1952, 4,000 deaths occurred in excess of the number to be expected. In Donora, Pennsylvania, October 27–31, 1948, twenty deaths and 5900 illnesses occurred in an industrial town of 14,000. A number of other similar cases are on record.

Air pollution is best controlled at the source. Pollution control devices on automobiles for carbon monoxide, nitrogen oxides and hydrocarbons are required by the Clean Air Act of 1970. Electric precipitators in smoke stacks and fabric filters remove particulates from both industrial processes and power plants. Scrubbers, which are water sprays, dissolve gases as the polluted air flows through the spray and help control sulfur dioxide.

New concepts appearing on the horizon may enable the utilization of the vast quantities of high sulfur oil and coal that exist in the world. While processes exist that can reduce the percent of sulfur in the fossil fuels, the approach is still in an advanced developmental stage. Fuel switching may be another answer, at least for the near future. In this approach a pollution sensing network is established in a region together with a network of meteorological instruments. When the predicted weather conditions indicate that emissions will be rapidly dissipated the fuel used in a power plant or an industrial process is switched from a low sulfur fuel to a high sulfur fuel. Subsequent adverse weather predictions result in a switch back to a low sulfur fuel.

15.11 Noise Pollution   In recent years a gradual awareness has arisen that sound can be a pollutant that effects adversely our sensibility as well as pleasing it. Sound is a series of pressure waves in air that is funneled by the outer ear to the ear drum causing it to vibrate. A small coupling of bones called the hammer, anvil, and stirrup attached to the inside of the ear drum transmits the vibrations through the nerve system to the brain.

The measure of sound level is based on the decibel. The decibel is a relationship between the pressure of a given sound on the ear drum and the pressure at which sounds first become detectable by the ear. A wide difference in pressures can be tolerated by the human ear. In fact, the maximum pressure that the ear can temporarily withstand before malfunctioning is more than 500 million times the threshold pressure at which the detection of sound first takes place. The sound level, measured by the decibel scale varies from 0 decibels at the threshold of hearing to 180 decibels at the maximum pressure. The threshold of pain is about 120 decibels.

Shown in Table 15-2 are the sound levels produced by various activities. Noise effects man's behavior and can result in a loss in work

Table 15-2   Sound Pressure Levels for Sounds of Various Origins.

Decibels	Origin of Sound
0	Sound becomes audible
60	Conversational speech
75	Automobiles
90	Heavy trucks
110	Automatic punch press
120	Pneumatic chipper—threshold of pain

capacity, a disruption of rest and sleep, annoyance, and a general mental stress. Some studies suggest that the blood pressure and the heart action may be also directly or indirectly effected.

15.12 Legal Controls   During the early 1960's it became very evident that existing federal and state laws concerning pollution were not complete enough nor stringent enough to cope with the growing pollution problems. Accordingly, the federal government took the lead and The Congress passed the National Environmental Policy Act of 1969 setting the stage for evaluating the pollution problem. On December 2, 1970 the Environmental Protection Agency (EPA) was established.

As early as 1963 The Congress passed the first of the Clean Air Acts which authorized financial assistance to the state and local governments for the initiation and improvement of control programs. Amendments passed in 1965 gave the federal program authority to curb motor vehicle emissions and, in 1967, required, among other things, the governors of individual states to establish air quality standards. In 1970 the final grouping of Clean Air Act Amendments were signed into law after almost a decade of evaluation.

A series of water laws enabled the beginning of the long trip back. In 1956 the Federal Water Pollution Control Act was passed providing for federal and state cooperation in river basin planning, and in establishing federal grants for the construction of waste treatment facilities. Water quality standards were to be established for all interstate and coastal waters by January 1, 1972 as the result of the Water Quality Act of 1965. And finally, the monumental task of restoring America's waters was initiated by virtue of the Water Quality Improvement Act of 1970.

Noise pollution is the most recent enemy being attacked. The Noise Pollution and Abatement Act of 1970 directed that substantial research be undertaken to study a wide range of problems concerning the harmful effects of noise. In 1971, the EPA set up its own Office of Noise Abatement and Control for these purposes. The Noise Control Act of 1972 enables the establishment of federal noise emission standards for products that are to be distributed in interstate commerce.

The above-mentioned laws form merely the framework for actions that will correct the pollution problem. A number of other recent laws supplement this framework to make it a workable approach. Enthusiasm for repairing and maintaining the environment is high, but it should be remembered that the price of obtaining this goal is also high. This cost must eventually be borne by the taxpayer.

15.13 Ocean Pollution   Up to now the major emphasis of this chapter has concerned the impact of terrestrially generated pollution on the oceans. Another source exists, however, and that is pollution that arises from activities that take place upon the ocean itself.

In regard to pollution the ocean may be viewed as being divided into two zones, the nearshore province and the deep ocean province. The nearshore province extends from the shore to a point where the depth is about 100 fathoms, the hundred fathom line. Included in this province are harbors, estuaries, and bays. The deep ocean is the rest of the ocean area.

The width of the nearshore province varies, but averages about 10 miles. There is considerable variation however, and much greater and much narrower distances are in evidence. The nearshore province is small, about 10 percent of the total ocean area, but it is the region where most of the wealth of the sea is extracted: oil, sulfur, seafood, metals, etc.

Economic development of this region results in a simultaneous increase in pollution. Its proximity to the shore ranks it as the first area to be impacted as terrestrial pollution is delivered to the ocean through rivers. Furthermore, it is the scene of coastal shipping and ships, both large and small, contribute to the problem. This shipping problem carries over as a major problem to the deep ocean as well.

Smoky stack emissions from the incomplete combustion of fuel, solid wastes from the packaging of goods consumed enroute, galley wastes resulting from food preparation, oily waters contained in bilges, oil spills during fuel transfers, human wastes, and the flaking of anti-fouling paint pollute the oceanic environment.

Where dilution can take place easily and completely, aided by the mixing action of wind and currents, the impact is lessened. Incomplete dilutions increase the impact locally. For those waste products not broken down by the environment, the only function of the ocean is that of a storehouse of large but definitely limited capacity. Shown in Fig. 15.6 is a photograph of a folded newspaper resting on the bottom of the western part of the Atlantic Ocean at a depth of more than 15,000 feet. Thor Heyerdahl in the report of his epic-making voyage in the "Ra" across the Atlantic Ocean from northern Africa indicated long stretches of sea covered with oil refuse, plastics and other nondecomposable material. What does not decompose or otherwise decay in the ocean must accumulate.

Pollution by ships, unless controlled, can be expected to intensify with time. Increases in shipping tonnage results in an increase in the number of sea passages. Imports to and exports from the United States have risen from 160 million tons in 1950 to 540 million tons in 1970, slightly less than quadrupling in twenty years. Added to this, in 1970, is 240 million tons of coastwise shipping. Worldwide, in 1970, international shipping accounted for the transportation of 2865 million tons of goods.

Fig. 15.6 Folded newspaper resting on bottom of the ocean.

The concentration of shipping and the maintenance dredging of ship channels intensifies the pollution of estuaries and harbors. Oil spills that occur during the offloading of tankers are said to comprise the largest single source of harbor oil pollution.

Pollution is created by the large number of small pleasure craft. Heads (toilets) are discharged into estuaries and embayments. In many cases, complete and rapid dilution of the waste cannot take place due to wind and tidal action. Disease-producing bacterial and viruses dwelling in the human intestines may occur at these times in unsafe concentrations. Shellfish and persons engaged in water sports exposed to these viruses and bacteria may become infected.

Much research is going into the problem of the control of oceanic pollution. Part of the solution is to control pollution on the land before it can reach the ocean through rivers. Part of it is to control pollution discharged from ships. The U.S. Navy is pursuing an intensive investigation of waste incineration, oil separation from bilge water, and the at-sea-containment of waste to be discharged to inport disposal systems as means of coping with the problem.

The following list of Do's and Don'ts concerning oceanic pollution has been recommended by the U.S. Naval Ship Systems Command:

Industrial and Chemical Wastes

DO: Store hazardous waste materials (mercury, solvents, etc.) in suitable containers for ultimate shore disposal.

DON'T: Discharge these materials overboard or into ship drains.

Solid Wastes

DO: Use incinerators for combustible trash.

DO: Make sure trash discharged overboard will sink.

DON'T: Discharge any solid trash overboard within 50 miles of land.

Oil and Oily Wastes

DO: Observe all regulations concerning handling of fuel oils and prevention of fuel oil discharges.

DO: Report all accidental oil discharges.

DO: Inspect oil storage tanks weekly for signs of leakage.

DO: Inspect oil lines, transfer equipment and any other oil-related gear for leaks periodically.

DON'T: Allow oil to accumulate in bilges or boilers.

DON'T: Fill fuel oil tanks above the 95% full level.

DON'T: Discharge oily wastes overboard or into ship bilges.

The Atmosphere
and Its Circulation

16.1 Introduction   Man lives at the bottom of an ocean of air, the atmosphere, whose state changes by the day, the hour, even the minute. The state of the atmosphere at a given time and location is what man calls weather. Climate is what he calls a description of weather conditions for an area over a period of years. Meteorology is the science which deals with the nature of the atmosphere, its changes, and reasons for the changes.

During the present century, meteorology has developed along sound scientific and mathematical lines so that today much is known not only about local conditions as they exist in many parts of the world but about the causes of weather as well. Experience has always been and still is necessary in forecasting weather, but modern developments have done much to put the subject more nearly on a sound scientific basis.

The weather section of this volume is directed to those who, although not undertaking to be their own forecasters, should be able to understand the advice of the professional in order to make full use of existing weather facilities, to interpret conditions in the absence of information, to develop the ability to supplement official broadcasts with personal observations, and to make intelligent decisions on the basis of existing information. This section, therefore, will present some of the fundamental modern concepts of the physical processes which cause weather, along with descriptive weather information, which will afford a basis upon which to build further knowledge through observation and reference to literature on the subject.

The *United States Coast Pilots* and the *Sailing Directions* published by the National Ocean Survey and Navy Department, respectively, contain much descriptive material of the weather and climate to be found along our coasts and in many parts of the world. Such subject matter should be read by those operating in the areas concerned. Also the monthly *Pilot Charts* published by the Hydrographic Center of the Navy Department contain a mass of useful information concerning prevailing winds, fog, ocean currents, and average weather conditions. On the backs of many of these charts are special articles on such topics as hurricanes, waterspouts, fog at sea, icebergs, and other phenomena.

The *U.S. Navy Marine Climatic Atlas of the World* is a series of studies which presents meteorological and oceanographic information for the surface and upper-air over the ocean areas of the world. Users will find this series of publications most helpful in weather studies of and operations over the ocean areas.

16.2 The Atmosphere   The atmosphere, the mixture of gases which surrounds and is bound to the earth by gravitational attraction, extends to an indefinite height. It is still dense enough at 600 miles above the earth to yield auroral effects; the extreme upper limit would be 18,600 miles, where a gas molecule would no longer be held in orbit by the earth's gravitational attraction.

The atmosphere is divided by its vertical temperature structure into layers, forming a series of concentric shells, as shown in Fig. 16.1. From the standpoint of meteorology, the two significant layers are the troposphere, where the temperature averages 1 degree F lower with each 300 feet of added height; and the stratosphere, so called because it tends to remain layered, or stratified, without rapid upward or downward mixing. The troposphere and stratosphere are separated by the tropopause, the level at which temperature stops decreasing with height. The tropopause is higher over the equator than at the poles, higher in summer than in winter, and higher over stormy areas than over regions of settled weather.

Other features of the troposphere are:

1. It has both horizontal and vertical air circulation.
2. It is the region to which are confined such phenomena as storms,

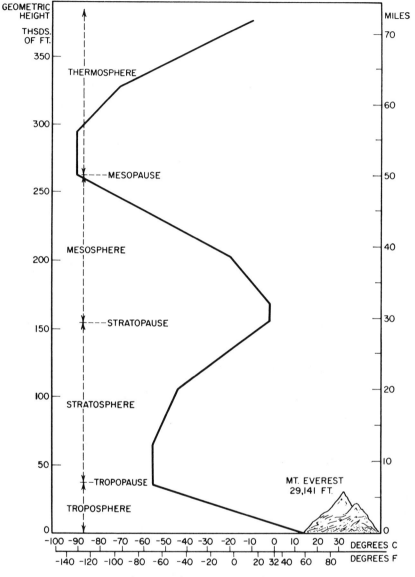

Fig. 16.1   The upper atmosphere.

precipitation, changing weather conditions, and nearly all clouds.
3. About three-fourths of the mass of the atmosphere is contained in the troposphere.
4. Its average upper limit is about 7 miles above the earth's surface, but it varies from about 10 miles at the equator to about 5 miles at the poles.

5. It contains water vapor in varying amounts from less than 1 percent up to 5 percent by volume.
6. It is compressed and therefore quite dense as compared with the stratosphere. In the lower levels of the troposphere atmospheric pressure is approximately 1 inch of mercury less at each 1000-foot interval above the earth's surface.
7. Flying conditions may be poor. Icing, rough air, poor visibility, cloud ceilings, and thunderstorms are common in the troposphere.

Essential characteristics of the stratosphere are:

1. A nearly constant temperature exists for a considerable distance upward from the base of the stratosphere, after which the temperature increases with height.
2. Vertical air motion occurs only in shallow waves, although strong winds exist.
3. Very little water vapor is found in the stratosphere; clouds are virtually nonexistent.
4. Favorable flying conditions prevail.

16.3 Composition of Air   Figure 16.2 shows the approximate percentages by volume of the principal constituents of the air. Throughout the troposphere, air is composed of a mixture, not a chemical compound, of about 77 percent nitrogen, 21 percent oxygen, 1 per-

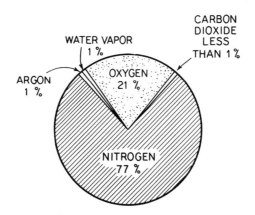

Fig. 16.2 Air—a mixture of gases. Nitrogen predominates; each has a function, but water vapor is the most important in weather and climate phenomena. The percentages by volume are indicated, but the percentage of water vapor may vary from less than 1 percent to about 5 percent.

cent water vapor, 1 percent argon, and less than 1 percent carbon dioxide. There are traces of a number of other gases, dust, smoke, and salt particles, which are important in weather processes. Each atmospheric constituent except argon is important: oxygen to animal life and combustion, nitrogen as a dilutant for oxygen, carbon dioxide to plants, and water vapor in the formation of various weather phenomena.

It is now believed that the gaseous constituents of the stratosphere and their percentages are the same as in the troposphere, with the exceptions of water vapor and ozone. Water vapor is virtually nonexistent in the stratosphere. Ozone (triatomic oxygen) is concentrated in very small but still significant amounts in the layer 12 to 20 miles above the ground. Because of its radiation absorption capacity, it is important to the radiation balance of the upper atmosphere, and protects living things on the earth from excessive ultraviolet radiation from the sun. It does, however, present serious problems for high-flying aircraft because of danger from ozone poisoning and decay of such materials as rubber.

Air even at high levels and far inland contains large numbers of salt particles which have been carried away from the sea by the winds. These, together with other so-called hygroscopic particles, such as soot and smoke, provide important nuclei necessary for the formation of raindrops. Such particles also affect the visibility and are a factor in sky coloring.

The amount of water vapor air can hold varies with the temperature; water vapor usually composes only about 1 percent of the air, but it may be present in an amount ranging anywhere from near nothing to 4 or 5 percent by volume. When air temperature increases 20 degrees F, the capacity of the air for water vapor approximately doubles; therefore, air at 80 degrees F can hold 16 times as much as air at 0 degrees F.

Air is considered saturated when it contains the maximum possible amount of vapor at the existing temperature. The term is rather misleading, as saturated air, even at warm temperatures, never consists of more than a small percentage of water vapor by volume. Relative humidity is the ratio of the amount of water vapor actually measured to that which the air could hold at saturation at existing temperature. When relative humidity reaches 100 percent, the air has attained its dewpoint temperature. This is the lowest temperature to which air can be cooled, at constant pressure, before condensation begins.

16.4 Heating and Cooling of the Atmosphere   Heat is transferred in three ways: by *radiation,* by *conduction,* and by *convection.* The sun sends forth a constant flow of energy which reaches the outer limits of our atmosphere in the form of short-wave radiation. From 35 to 40 percent of this incoming radiation is reflected back to space, while the remainder, except for a small part absorbed in the atmosphere, is absorbed by and heats land and water at the earth's surface. Some of this earth-trapped energy is reradiated as long-wave radiation. Part of it heats the atmosphere; the remainder returns to space. Water vapor and carbon dioxide, the principal heat-absorbing constituents of the atmosphere, absorb the outgoing long-wave radiation more readily than the incoming short-wave, causing the atmosphere to act as a heat trap like the glass of a greenhouse.

The loss of energy from the earth's surface and atmosphere must balance incoming solar radiation, or we would be faced with the chilling prospect of trying to survive on an earth which would get colder or, worse, an earth turned incandescent, since the temperature would rise on an average of around 3 degrees F per day if all the solar radiation were trapped and none reflected.

Radiation is not the only means by which the atmosphere is heated. Air in immediate contact with warmer water or land surfaces is heated by means of conduction. Conduction alone is effective in heating only that portion of the atmosphere which is adjacent to the earth. Convection can carry heated portions of surface air to upper levels of the troposphere. When a mass of air at the earth's surface becomes heated by conduction, it expands and becomes lighter per unit volume. It is then underrun by surrounding colder, heavier air and is pushed upward. It rises and its heat, acquired at the earth's surface, is carried to higher levels. The colder air from above, which replaces it at the surface, is heated in turn and eventually rises to upper levels. Examples of convection, conduction, and radiation are shown in Fig. 16.3.

16.5 Atmospheric Pressure   Air is light, but the total weight of the atmosphere is enormous. If the weight of all the air were replaced by the same weight of ordinary water, the globe would be covered with a layer 34 feet deep.

At sea level, the average pressure exerted by the atmosphere amounts to 14.7 pounds per square inch, or a column of air one inch in cross section extending from sea level to the upper limit of the atmosphere weighs 14.7 pounds. Pressure decreases with height in the atmosphere; at 18,000 feet it is only about half the sea level pressure, one quarter at 36,000 feet.

The atmospheric pressure due to oxygen decreases proportionately with height, so that man has normal respiration only to about 13,000 feet. At 30,000 feet, he will become unconscious in little more than

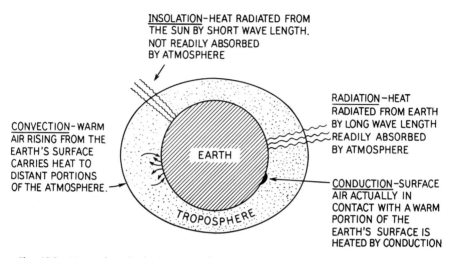

Fig. 16.3 Means by which the atmosphere may receive heat: radiation, conduction, and convection.

a minute. Near 52,000 feet and higher, man, in a manner of speaking, drowns in his own water vapor, because at this height and at normal body temperature the lungs become filled with carbon dioxide and water vapor; there is not enough pressure for any oxygen to enter the lungs. Above 63,000 feet, the pressure is so low that body liquids begin to boil at ordinary blood temperature.

In meteorology, atmospheric pressure is usually expressed in terms

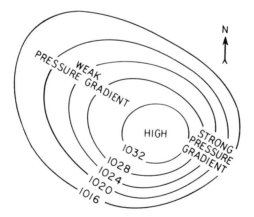

Fig. 16.4 An area of high pressure centered at "high." In the southeast quadrant of this "high," the isobars are close together, and the pressure gradient is known as strong; at the center and to the northwest, the gradient is weak.

of the length in inches of a mercury column or in millibar units. These units will be considered later in connection with barometers. Fourteen and seven-tenths pounds per square inch is equivalent to 29.92 inches of mercury or to 1013.25 millibars.

Atmospheric pressure at any location constantly changes, and it varies from place to place. These variations in pressure values are due to changes in temperature. When air is warmed, it expands, becomes less dense, and the atmospheric pressure is reduced. Conversely, when air becomes cold, it contracts and becomes heavier. Areas covered by cold masses of air will record higher atmospheric pressure readings.

Lines drawn on a map through points on the earth having the same atmospheric pressure are known as isobars. These lines of equal pressure show the distribution of the pressure force. Horizontal pressure gradient refers to the decrease of pressure per unit distance in a horizontal direction perpendicular to the direction of the isobars. In Fig. 16.4 the isobars are seen to be spaced closer together in the southeast portion of the high pressure area than in the northwest section. When isobars are close together, the situation is known as a steep or strong pressure gradient.

16.6 Wind Speed and Direction—Causes   Speed of the wind is determined primarily by the pressure gradient. Strong gradients cause strong winds; the horizontal pressure gradient force is inversely proportional to the isobar spacing.

For any given pressure gradient the wind blows stronger over water areas than over land because of reduced friction. Hills, trees, buildings, and similar objects retard the speed of the wind more than do water surfaces. The earth's frictional effect can be detected as high as 3000 feet with strong winds and exceptionally rough terrain, but ordinarily the effect does not exist at heights over 1500 feet above land and water surfaces.

Wind direction depends chiefly upon the direction of the pressure gradient and the rotation of the earth. Let us first consider the effect of the pressure gradient. Figures 16.5(a) and (b) show the tendency of air to flow from a high pressure area to a section where the pressure is lower. This flow of air we know as wind, and it tends to blow parallel to the pressure gradient, i.e., at right angles to the isobars. However, due to the rotation of the earth, the wind is deflected to the right in the northern Hemisphere and to the left in the Southern Hemisphere.

Wind deflection caused by the earth's rotation is known as the *Coriolis effect*. Figure 16.6(a) shows a disk rotating to the left counterclockwise. Let us assume that air starts to move in a straight line from

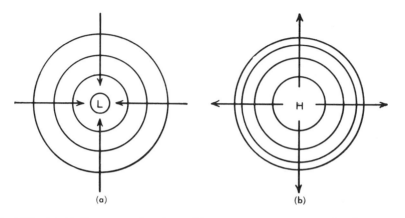

Fig. 16.5 (a) Air flows toward regions of low pressure. Were it not for the apparent deflective force due to the earth's rotation, air would tend to flow directly toward points where pressures are the lowest. (b) Air flows away from regions of high pressure. Wind direction would be parallel to the gradient as shown, were it not for the earth's rotation.

A toward points B and C, with B located just off the edge of the disk, C located at the edge of the disk. Assume, also, that point C on the disk rotates 30 degrees to the left during the time that it takes the air to move from A to B. Figure 16.6(b) shows the curved path which the air would take over the rotating disk to reach B. To see this clearly, cut a disk of paper and fasten it with a thumbtack at the center to a board.

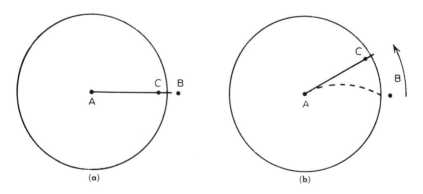

Fig. 16.6 Coriolis force demonstrated. (a) Air starts to move from point A, located on a disk which is rotating counterclockwise, toward point B, which is located just off the disk. As the air leaves point A it is also headed toward point C on the edge of the disk. (b) The disk rotates through an angle of 30 degrees as the air moves across the disk from A to B. The air, because it is headed toward B, does not reach point C. Though the air moves directly from A to B its path appears as a curved line to an observer on the disk.

Make an X on the board just off the disk. Place a pencil point at the center of the disk and draw a line slowly toward X, at the same time rotating the disk slowly in a counterclockwise direction. The pencil line will curve as in (b).

The plane of the horizon of an observer located any place in the Northern Hemisphere rotates toward the left with reference to a point in space. Therefore the plane of the horizon may be likened to the plane in (b), and air in motion in any direction on the earth north of the equator is deflected to the right. In the Southern Hemisphere wind from any direction is deflected toward the left. This is because the observer's horizon in the Southern Hemisphere rotates in a clockwise manner, or toward the right.

The Coriolis force is perpendicular to and directly proportional to the pressure gradient. It is strongest in polar regions but is zero at the equator. At intermediate latitudes it varies as the sine of the latitude.

A third effect of importance in determining wind speed and direction is friction. Friction retards air movement; the degree depends upon the nature of the surface over which the air is moving. It is least over water and greatest over mountainous terrain (Fig. 16.7).

Friction causes surface winds to flow across the isobars toward low pressure instead of parallel, as they would do when pressure gradient and Coriolis forces are in balance. Figure 16.8 shows the effect of friction. It acts in a direction opposite to the actual wind and slows it down. The Coriolis force is proportional to wind speed so, with friction entering the picture, it is not able to balance the pressure gradient force. Instead, the pressure gradient force is balanced by the force resulting from the combined friction and Coriolis forces, and the actual wind blows across the isobars toward lower pressure. Since friction decreases with height, we would expect (and find) that the winds gradually turn with height until, above the friction layer, they blow along the isobars. Speed increases gradually as friction decreases.

16.7 General Winds of the Earth   Uneven heating of the earth's surface causes differences in atmospheric pressure which, in turn, cause winds. Equatorial regions of the earth receive considerably more heat than do the polar areas. Figure 16.9 illustrates the effect of direct and oblique rays. This excess of heat at the equator is the basis of a definite world wind pattern. On a nonrotating globe of homogeneous surface the system would be simple. The atmosphere, having been warmed and expanded over the hot equatorial belt, would flow poleward at the higher levels of the troposphere. This would tend to increase polar surface atmospheric pressures. Air then would tend to

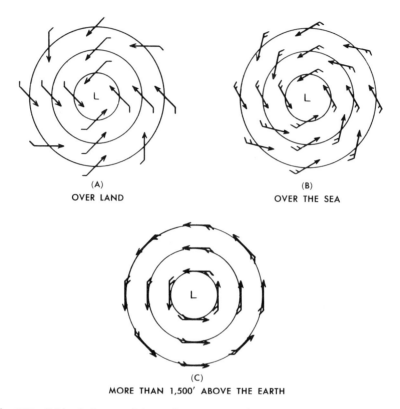

(A)
OVER LAND

(B)
OVER THE SEA

(C)
MORE THAN 1,500' ABOVE THE EARTH

Fig. 16.7 With similar conditions of pressure gradient, wind velocities are greater over the sea than over land; at elevations above 1500 feet wind velocities are greater than at the surface. It is also apparent from the figures that the wind blows parallel to the isobars at elevations above 1500 feet; it makes an angle of 10 to 20 degrees over the sea; over the land the wind makes an angle with the isobars which averages about 30 degrees.

flow away from the poles and along the earth's surface to the equatorial girdle of lower pressure. This simple circulation is shown in Fig. 16.10. Such a circulation is impossible because of the influence of the earth's rotation. The world wind system is further complicated by the contrasting temperatures of continents and oceans and by many other local causes which will be considered in order. Refer now to Fig. 16.11.

16.8 The Doldrums The girdle of low atmospheric pressure in the region of the equator where the trade winds from the Northern and Southern Hemispheres converge, is known as the doldrums or Meteorological Equator. This zone shifts slightly north and south with the

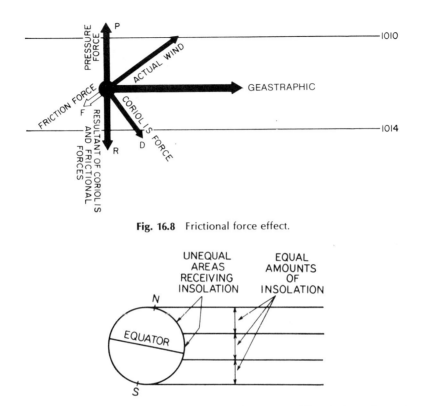

Fig. 16.8 Frictional force effect.

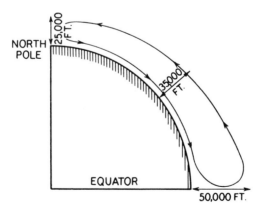

Fig. 16.9 The sun's rays reach the earth's surface more obliquely in polar regions than in the tropics. This causes unequal heating of the earth's surface. It will be noted that equal amounts of insolation affect unequal areas of the earth's surface.

Fig. 16.10 Theoretical pattern of wind circulation due to the unequal heating of the earth's surface. Actually this scheme is considerably modified because of the rotation of the earth, the influence of oceans, continents, and other factors. (*After Rossby.*)

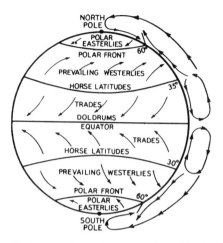

Fig. 16.11   General pattern of world winds.

seasons, and its mean position is somewhat north of the equator. It is characterized by light and variable surface winds and frequent calm conditions. Warm temperatures and associated rising air currents are quite general. Cloud types are the bulging, piled-up cumulus, and cumulonimbus (thunderhead). The air is sultry, and showers and thunderstorms are frequent. The sky is often overcast. Average annual rainfall is heavier than that of any other latitudinal belt.

16.9   Subtropical High-Pressure Belt or Horse Latitudes   In considering the world wind system, conditions which exist in the Northern Hemisphere will be described first, then differences found in the Southern Hemisphere.

Air rising over the doldrums flows poleward in the high levels of the troposphere, but it does not blow directly north. The Coriolis effect causes it to be deflected to the right, and it becomes a southwest wind. In fact, at about latitude north 35 degrees it is supposed that the deflecting effect of the earth's rotation causes the wind at high levels to blow approximately from west to east, although the wind circulation at high levels is not nearly as well understood as conditions at the earth's surface. This deflection of the wind to the right causes the air to tend to pile up at about 35 degrees north latitude. The result is a ring of high pressure which extends around the earth at that latitude. The cooling of the air as it flows northward at high levels and its consequent shrinking and sinking contribute to the high-pressure belt. This region is characterized by descending air currents and cloudless skies. At the earth's surface the winds are light and variable. The weather is generally fine; air humidity is comparatively low. This is in marked contrast to weather in the doldrums. It was from the persistent fine weather that the horse latitudes were so named, because horses had to be thrown overboard from sailing ships when lack of rain, combined with slow sailing in the light winds, caused water supplies to run low.

16.10 The Trade Winds   With surface pressure conditions high at the horse latitudes and low in the doldrums we would expect to find wind blowing from the high- to the low-pressure region. This is precisely what happens. The trade winds blow from the horse latitudes to the doldrums and are the most persistent in direction and force of any wind belt in the world. Captains of early sailing vessels, particularly Christopher Columbus, learned to take advantage of the trade winds on their voyages to the New World. Were it not for the rotation of the earth, the trade winds would blow directly from north to south. The deflective effect, however, turns them to the right so that they become the northeast trade winds.

16.11 The Prevailing Westerlies   Surface air also flows northward from the high-pressure region of the horse latitudes. The Coriolis effect deflects it to the right so that it becomes a southwesterly wind. The prevailing southwesterlies of the temperate zone, or middle latitudes, are not nearly so consistent as the trades of lower latitudes. This is because the region of the prevailing westerlies includes the paths of many storms throughout the year; these storms are associated with winds from all points of the compass. Only occasionally are the trades interrupted by storms, the hurricanes which occur only during a portion of the year.

16.12 The Polar Cap of High-Pressure, and Prevailing Northeasterlies
Wind at the higher levels of the atmosphere flows poleward where it descends and tends to build up a region of high pressure at the earth's surface. Winds at surface levels therefore tend to blow southward but are deflected toward the right by the Coriolis effect and become the prevailing northeasterlies of the polar regions.

16.13 The Southern Hemisphere   The Coriolis effect in the Southern Hemisphere causes deflection of moving air to the left instead of to the right as in the Northern Hemisphere. Hence, trades south of the equator blow from the southeast rather than from the northeast; prevailing westerlies are from the northwest rather than southwest. Southern polar region winds blow from the southeast instead of from the northeast. The Southern Hemisphere is predominantly a water surface, and without the complicating effects caused by large land masses, the prevailing winds are not only much more constant in direction but they have higher average speeds than the Northern Hemisphere. The area of prevailing westerlies of the Southern Hemisphere is known as the *Roaring Forties* because of the comparatively high speeds in the general area between latitudes 40 and 50 degrees south.

16.14   The Jet Stream   The jet stream was discovered toward the end of World War II, when American bombers flying to Japan encountered headwinds which often caused them almost to stand still with relation to the ground. Studies since then, along with reports from high-level flights, have established the fact that the winds in the upper troposphere of each hemisphere are normally concentrated into relatively narrow bands of strong winds called jet streams. There are centered just below the tropopause (30,000 to 60,000 feet) in mid-latitudes, but both latitudinal position and height vary considerably. The jet streams resemble rapidly flowing, meandering rivers, flowing between banks of relatively stagnant air. The average wind direction in jets is from west to east, but an individual jet will usually show north-to-south wave patterns, often of large amplitude. Wind speeds of up to 300 knots have been measured in jet streams, but the speed is more often in the 100 to 150 knot range. These jet streams play an important role in the development and movement of surface storms, and they are associated with clear air turbulence.

16.15   Heating and Cooling of Land and Water   The general pattern of global wind circulation at the earth's surface is considerably modified by the uneven heating of the continents and oceans. During the daytime, land areas are usually much warmer than they are at night. This is because the heat which is absorbed during the day penetrates only a short distance and is readily reradiated to open space. The balance between incoming and outgoing heat occurs at about two hours past noon. After that time land areas lose heat by radiation faster than they receive heat from the sun. Likewise there is a considerable annual variation in land temperatures; they are much colder during winter than in summer.

The effect of the sun's heat upon ocean surfaces is much different from that on land because of the heating qualities of water. Water is a good absorber because the heat can be mixed mechanically through a thicker layer than land, which must rely upon slower molecular processes. Water is a good heat conductor, so it is effective in moderating the atmosphere. Water has a heat capacity two or three times that of land, so it can absorb great amounts of heat without heating to the high daytime ground temperatures of a desert and, conversely, it can give up comparable amounts without getting cold. Water evaporates continuously from the oceans, a heat loss which keeps oceans from getting too warm in summer.

16.16 Permanent and Semipermanent High and Low Centers   In winter the continental land masses of North America, Asia, and Europe are much colder than the waters of the north Atlantic and Pacific oceans (Fig. 16.12; see also Fig. 16.13). The result of this is the building up of high-pressure areas over the continents and low-pressure centers over the adjacent oceans. The *low* which lies between Canada and the Scandinavian peninsula is known as the *Icelandic low*. The counterpart low area in the Pacific is known as the *Aleutian low*. These low areas are associated with much cloudiness, rain, drizzle, sleet, snow, fogginess, and strong winds. The stormy weather of these regions is not unlike stormy weather of any other section, but it is more widespread, persistent, and intense.

It must be borne in mind that the Aleutian and Icelandic lows do not represent a continuation of one and the same low-pressure area. Rather, they are regions where low-pressure systems form or arrive from other places to remain for a time. Later the lows may move on or die out and are replaced by other lows. The Aleutian and Icelandic centers shift to various positions and are at times replaced by high-pressure areas.

Semipermanent high-pressure areas in the Northern Hemisphere are located in the Atlantic near the Azores and in the Pacific off the coast of California. A lesser center is found in the vicinity of Bermuda. In the Southern Hemisphere semipermanent high centers are located in the Pacific west of Chile, the Atlantic west of Africa, and the Indian Ocean. These high centers represent intensifications of the ring of high pressure which lies between the trades and the prevailing westerlies in both the Northern and Southern Hemispheres.

The semipermanent lows and highs affect the general scheme of global wind circulation and have a decided effect on the weather in many parts of the world. They also have a direct relation to the direction and velocity of the currents of the oceans. Having considered the general pattern of world wind circulation, pressure, and heat distribution, we shall now look at the seasonal winds.

16.17 The Monsoon Winds   Monsoon winds develop in response to the annual variation in temperature between continents and oceans. These differences in temperature and therefore in pressure cause semi-

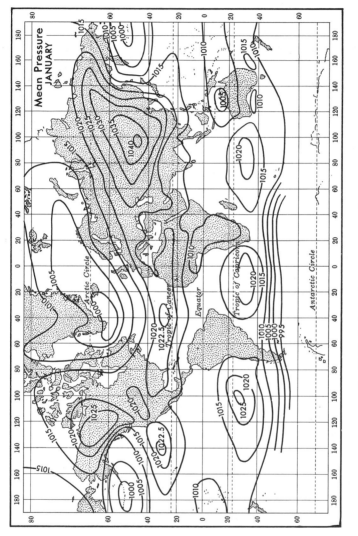

Fig. 16.12 Isobars of mean pressure for January.

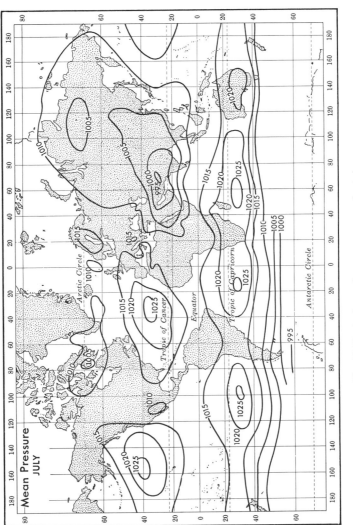

Fig. 16.13   Isobars of mean pressure for July.

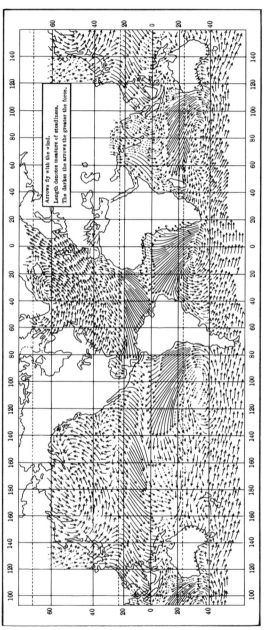

Fig. 16.14 Ocean winds, January and February.

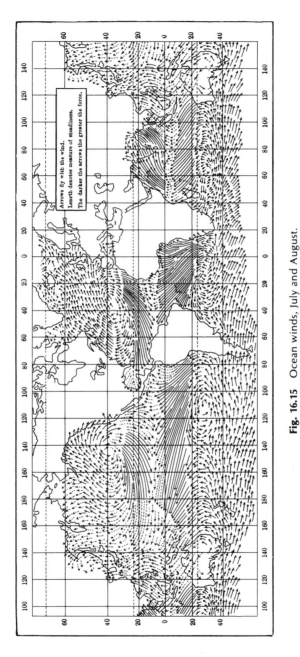

Fig. 16.15 Ocean winds, July and August.

annual reversals in the wind direction in the areas affected. The results are quite marked in the Indian Ocean, China Sea, and south and southeastern Asia (Fig. 16.14 and 16.15). During the winter season air flows outward from the interior of the continent of Asia toward the regions of lower pressure which prevail over the warm waters of the Indian Ocean and Australia. In India and southeastern Asia the winds then prevail from the northeast and are dry because of their origin and their descent on the southern slopes of the east-west Himalaya range; it is the season of fine weather in that part of the world and extends from October to April. After the winds cross the equator, they are deflected toward the left and become northwest winds.

During the warmer portion of the year conditions are reversed. The southeast trades south of the equator cross to the Northern Hemisphere and are then deflected toward the northeast, becoming the winds of the southwest monsoon of south and southeast Asia. It is then that the wind flows from the relatively high-pressure area of Australia and the Indian Ocean to the area of low pressure which prevails over the continent of Asia. As the moist ocean winds reverse themselves and move inland over India and adjacent sections, they bring heavy squalls, rains, and occasional cyclones (like Atlantic hurricanes). The summer monsoon usually occurs from May to September. During this season there is considerable local variation in winds and rain, but, in general, it is the rainy season for that part of the world. In areas where the winds are deflected for considerable distances upward by the Himalayas, very heavy rainfall is reported. Cherrapunji, India, has an average annual rainfall of 35½ feet, and most of it comes during the summer monsoon.

Many other parts of the world have similar seasonal reversals in wind direction which are often associated with dry and rainy seasons. A mild monsoon wind reversal is noted in the states bordering the Gulf of Mexico, and there are monsoon-type winds in Australia, Central and South Africa, and South America.

16.18   Land and Sea Breezes   In the tropics and particularly during the warmer seasons of higher latitudes, the land during the day is commonly warmer than adjacent water. This applies not only to coastal sections but to inland lakes as well. Air overlying the land is heated, it expands, and is pushed upward by cooler air which flows onshore from the surface of adjacent water. Such sea breezes may penetrate inland for distances of 25 miles or more, although they extend only a few hundred feet above the ground. On inland lakes the effect usually prevails for distances of only a few miles. Over land surfaces at night, loss of heat by radiation causes land surfaces to become cooler than water surfaces, and a reversal of the wind direction takes place. The contrast between land and water temperatures at night is not as great as during the day; therefore the nighttime land breeze is usually not as strong as the sea breezes of daytime.

16.19 Mountain and Valley Breezes   During the daytime convectional currents tend to rise over mountains because of heating of mountainsides and summits. A general flow of air takes place up the valleys. At night radiation brings about chilling of the mountain slopes with the resultant chilling of the adjacent air. The cool, dense air then drains down the valleys. Winds of quite high velocity are sometimes noted, particularly in narrow canyons.

16.20 Gravity or Drainage Winds   During the cold season, strong high-pressure areas of dense, cold air build up over plateaus and inland areas sheltered by mountains. Usually, the air will seep down the slopes and come to the coast as a gentle or moderate breeze. But an approaching low-pressure center may cause the cold air to be accelerated through the mountain gaps and valleys to arrive at the coast with strong, gusty winds. The effect is most pronounced when the cold air must pass through a narrow valley, or through an opening where several valleys converge. The *Santa Ana,* of Southern California, is the most common example of destructive gravity winds in the United States. The most widely known wind of this type is the *bora,* a cold, north-northeasterly wind which blows over the northern shores of the Adriatic. Winds over 80 mph, with gusts to 135, have been recorded in *boras.* Other well-known gravity winds are the *mistral* of southern France, *Northers* in the Gulf of Mexico, *Tehuantepecers* and *Papagayoes* on the west coast of Mexico and Central America.

Clouds, Thunderstorms, Stability, and Fog

17.1 Introduction A knowledge of the various kinds of clouds, how they form, and what they mean is an indispensable tool to those at sea or in the air, or to anyone who must deal with the weather and its changing conditions. Because clouds offer visual evidence of conditions which exist in the atmosphere and of changes which are taking place, they also afford an indication of coming weather conditions, particularly if they are observed at intervals to note changes in structure or type which may be taking place.

Aviators soon learn to know the clouds which are associated with rough air and smooth air and the kinds which cause their planes to be coated with ice.

Clouds, as seen from the earth's surface, are divided into three groups according to structure and height. *Cirrus* clouds, of the high family, are feathery and silk-like; *stratus* are the layer clouds which form a more or less uniform flat mass over most or all of the sky; *cumulus* are the heap-shaped, lumpy masses. In height above ground, *cirrus* clouds occur only in the upper troposphere; *stratus* are only at low levels, while certain stratiform clouds are present only in the middle troposphere. *Cumulus* clouds may extend from near the ground to the *cirrus* level.

The principal types of clouds are grouped by height as follows: *Cirrus, cirrostratus, cirrocumulus*—20,000 to 40,000 feet; *altostratus, altocumulus*—8000 to 20,000 feet; *stratus, stratocumulus, nimbostratus*—below 8000 feet. Except for the low-cloud genera, the others tend to be higher in the tropics than at higher latitudes.

Cloud forms are divided into ten genera. In addition, there are many subtypes and combinations, but these need not be discussed here. The International Cloud Atlas, published by the World Meteorological Organization, contains detailed descriptions and excellent photographs of all cloud forms.

Figure 17.1 describes nine of the cloud genera. *Nimbostratus* is not included because it is too difficult to photograph. It is a low, amorphous, and rainy layer of a dark gray color usually nearly uniform; it is feebly illuminated, seemingly from inside. When it gives precipitation, it is in the form of continuous rain or snow. But precipitation alone is not sufficient to distinguish the cloud which should be called *nimbostratus* even when no rain or snow falls from it. There is often precipitation which does not reach the ground; in this case the base of the cloud is usually diffuse and looks wet on account of the general trailing precipitation, and it is not possible to determine the limit of its lower surface.

17.2 What Do Clouds Mean?   Cloud types, by themselves, are significant only if consideration is given to the method and timing of their development, to the structural changes that are taking place, and particularly to the sequence in which they occur.

Cirrus clouds may be the first sign of an approaching storm, but to have detection significance, they must increase in number and be succeeded by cirrostratus clouds. Cirrostratus, if a storm is approaching, must thicken and be succeeded by altostratus. Altostratus clouds are succeeded by nimbostratus and the precipitation which started with the altostratus continues—often with fog present. Stormy conditions are present with both altostratus and nimbostratus. The end of these conditions is signaled by breaks in the low clouds and patches of blue sky to the west. Storms in mid-latitudes generally move from west to east, so their approach is indicated by clouds from the west, their retreat by clearing conditions in the west.

Cumulus clouds mark the tops of rising air currents, caused by horizontal temperature differences at the earth's surface. Air may also be started upward when deflected by a hill or mountain or by encounter

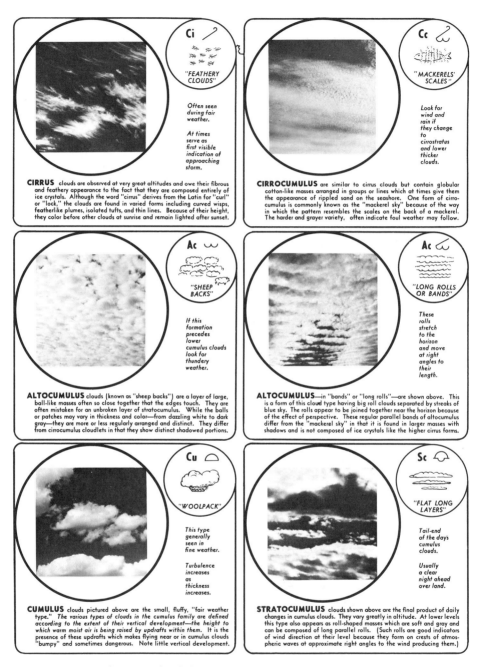

Ci

"FEATHERY CLOUDS"

Often seen during fair weather.

At times serve as first visible indication of approaching storm.

CIRRUS clouds are observed at very great altitudes and owe their fibrous and feathery appearance to the fact that they are composed entirely of ice crystals. Although the word "cirrus" derives from the Latin for "curl" or "lock," the clouds are found in varied forms including curved wisps, featherlike plumes, isolated tufts, and thin lines. Because of their height, they color before other clouds at sunrise and remain lighted after sunset.

Cc

"MACKERELS' SCALES"

Look for wind and rain if they change to cirrostratus and lower thicker clouds.

CIRROCUMULUS are similar to cirrus clouds but contain globular cotton-like masses arranged in groups or lines which at times give them the appearance of rippled sand on the seashore. One form of cirrocumulus is commonly known as the "mackerel sky" because of the way in which the pattern resembles the scales on the back of a mackerel. The harder and grayer variety, often indicate foul weather may follow.

Ac

"SHEEP BACKS"

If this formation precedes lower cumulus clouds look for thundery weather.

ALTOCUMULUS clouds (known as "sheep backs") are a layer of large, ball-like masses often so close together that the edges touch. They are often mistaken for an unbroken layer of stratocumulus. While the balls or patches may vary in thickness and color—from dazzling white to dark gray—they are more or less regularly arranged and distinct. They differ from cirrocumulus cloudlets in that they show distinct shadowed portions.

Ac

"LONG ROLLS OR BANDS"

These rolls stretch to the horizon and move at right angles to their length.

ALTOCUMULUS—in "bands" or "long rolls"—are shown above. This is a form of this cloud type having big roll clouds separated by streaks of blue sky. The rolls appear to be joined together near the horizon because of the effect of perspective. These regular parallel bands of altocumulus differ from the "mackerel sky" in that it is found in larger masses with shadows and is not composed of ice crystals like the higher cirrus forms.

Cu

"WOOLPACK"

This type generally seen in fine weather.

Turbulence increases as thickness increases.

CUMULUS clouds pictured above are the small, fluffy, "fair weather type." The various types of clouds in the cumulus family are defined according to the extent of their vertical development—the height to which warm moist air is being raised by updrafts within them. It is the presence of these updrafts which makes flying near or in cumulus clouds "bumpy" and sometimes dangerous. Note little vertical development.

Sc

"FLAT LONG LAYERS"

Tail-end of the day's cumulus clouds.

Usually a clear night ahead over land.

STRATOCUMULUS clouds shown above are the final product of daily changes in cumulus clouds. They vary greatly in altitude. At lower levels this type also appears as roll-shaped masses which are soft and gray and can be composed of long parallel rolls. (Such rolls are good indicators of wind direction at their level because they form on crests of atmospheric waves at approximate right angles to the wind producing them.)

Fig. 17.1   Cloud chart. (*Courtesy of* All Hands *Magazine.*)

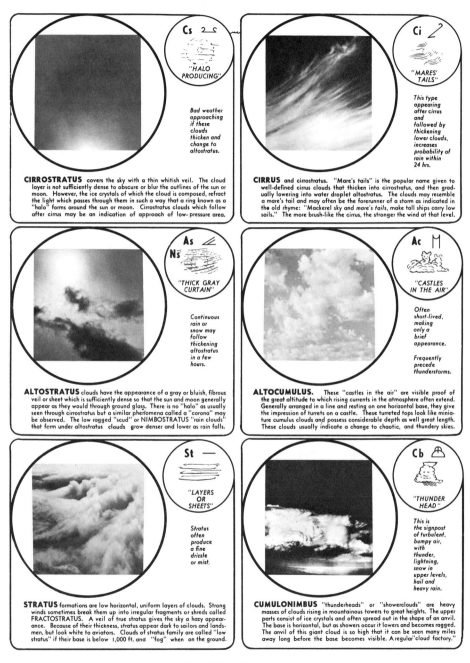

Cs

"HALO PRODUCING"

Bad weather approaching if these clouds thicken and change to altostratus.

CIRROSTRATUS covers the sky with a thin whitish veil. The cloud layer is not sufficiently dense to obscure or blur the outlines of the sun or moon. However, the ice crystals of which the cloud is composed, refract the light which passes through them in such a way that a ring known as a "halo" forms around the sun or moon. Cirrostratus clouds which follow after cirrus may be an indication of approach of low-pressure area.

Ci

"MARES' TAILS"

This type appearing after cirrus and followed by thickening lower clouds, increases probability of rain within 24 hrs.

CIRRUS and cirrostratus. "Mare's tails" is the popular name given to well-defined cirrus clouds that thicken into cirrostratus, and then gradually lowering into water droplet altostratus. The clouds may resemble a mare's tail and may often be the forerunner of a storm as indicated in the old rhyme: "Mackerel sky and *mare's tails*, make tall ships carry low sails." The more brush-like the cirrus, the stronger the wind at that level.

As
Ns

"THICK GRAY CURTAIN"

Continuous rain or snow may follow thickening altostratus in a few hours.

ALTOSTRATUS clouds have the appearance of a gray or bluish, fibrous veil or sheet which is sufficiently dense so that the sun and moon generally appear as they would through ground glass. There is no "halo" as usually seen through cirrostratus but a similar phenomena called a "corona" may be observed. The low ragged "scud" or NIMBOSTRATUS "rain clouds" that form under altostratus clouds grow denser and lower as rain falls.

Ac

"CASTLES IN THE AIR"

Often short-lived, making only a brief appearance.

Frequently precede thunderstorms.

ALTOCUMULUS. These "castles in the air" are visible proof of the great altitude to which rising currents in the atmosphere often extend. Generally arranged in a line and resting on one horizontal base, they give the impression of turrets on a castle. These turreted tops look like miniature cumulus clouds and possess considerable depth as well great length. These clouds usually indicate a change to chaotic, and thundery skies.

St

"LAYERS OR SHEETS"

Stratus often produce a fine drizzle or mist.

STRATUS formations are low horizontal, uniform layers of clouds. Strong winds sometimes break them up into irregular fragments or shreds called FRACTOSTRATUS. A veil of true stratus gives the sky a hazy appearance. Because of their thickness, stratus appear dark to sailors and landsmen, but look white to aviators. Clouds of stratus family are called "low stratus" if their base is below 1,000 ft. and "fog" when on the ground.

Cb

"THUNDER HEAD"

This is the signpost of turbulent, bumpy air, with thunder, lightning, snow in upper levels, hail and heavy rain.

CUMULONIMBUS "thunderheads" or "showerclouds" are heavy masses of clouds rising in mountainous towers to great heights. The upper parts consist of ice crystals and often spread out in the shape of an anvil. The base is horizontal, but as showers occur it lowers and becomes ragged. The anvil of this giant cloud is so high that it can be seen many miles away long before the base becomes visible. A regular "cloud factory."

Fig. 17.1 (*Continued*)

with a colder and denser air mass. Whether or not an air current continues to ascend depends upon its temperature as compared with the temperature of the surrounding air.

If cumulus clouds form early on a summer morning, it means that the air is quite moist and convection has begun. This means that the clouds are likely to become more numerous by afternoon, build up to high levels, and by the middle of the afternoon thunderstorms are likely. If cumulus clouds do not appear until late in the morning, it means that the air has little water vapor. The afternoon would have comparatively few clouds; the bases of these would be high, but their tops would not reach to the great heights of cumulonimbus clouds.

In the late afternoon if the air is stable, the afternoon cumulus clouds will gradually disappear, and by evening the sky will be clear. If the air, however, is unstable, the clouds will continue to build up to great heights even during the evening, and thunderstorms are likely then even at night.

An examination of the weather and operational significance of the ten principal cloud types will now be made.

Cirrus clouds arranged in filaments or strands, scattered and not increasing (mares' tails), have no meaning as related to weather, except to signify that any bad weather is far distant. Cirrus in thick patches, often anvil-shaped, mean that showery weather is near. These clouds are associated with and formed from the tops of thunderstorms. Cirrus clouds shaped like hooks or commas signal the approach of a warm front, almost certainly if followed by cirrostratus clouds. Also, they indicate the presence and location of jet streams. None of the cirrus types have significance for flight operation except for what use may be made of the jet stream identification.

Cirrostratus clouds, when in a continuous sheet and increasing, signify the approach of a warm or occluded front with attendant rain, snow, and stormy conditions. If the clouds are not continuous and increasing, it signifies that a storm is passing to the south of the observer and no bad weather will occur. Other than reduced visibility within the clouds, cirrostratus have no flight significance.

Cirrocumulus clouds are rare, and are of mixed significance. In some areas they foretell good weather; in others, bad. Good weather areas are England, New England, and along the west coast of the United States. Bad weather areas are southern Europe, particularly Italy. These clouds have no significance in the tropics. They have no flight operational significance except that they are somewhat more turbulent than cirrus and cirrostratus.

Altostratus clouds are the most reliable weather indicator among the cloud family, and the greatest help to the single-station forecaster.

They nearly always indicate frontal overrunning, and impending rain or snow of the steady all-day type, if the overcast cloud layer progresses continually over a station and thickens. Another important aid given by altostratus clouds is the detection of new storm development, particularly at sea where reports are few. Altostratus clouds will often signal formation of a low long before it is apparent from the surface-level isobars or wind. Flight conditions in altostratus are usually not prohibitive. Turbulence is generally light, and icing is serious only if prolonged flight through the cloud is required. What is important to pilots and surface observers is the indication of approaching rain and the warm front, with associated low ceilings, poor visibility, and possibly heavy icing in lower clouds.

Altocumulus clouds, in general, are indicative of instability at high levels, but are significant only when followed by thicker, high-cloud forms or cumuliform lower clouds. When arranged in parallel bands, these clouds are found in advance of warm fronts, on the forward and lateral edges of altostratus sheets, and near the axis of the jet stream. North of this banded type, altostratus and precipitation may be expected, and if the altostratus is moving southward, precipitation may be expected at the given station. When altocumulus occurs in the form of turrets rising from a common flat base, it is frequently the forerunner of instability in a deep layer, with heavy showers and thunderstorms. For flight operations, altocumulus clouds are characterized by only mild turbulence, and only light to moderate icing. When associated with thunderstorms, of course, flight hazards increase markedly.

Stratocumulus clouds which form from degenerating cumulus clouds are usually followed by clearing at night and fair weather. The roll stratocumulus, with its washboard-looking undersurface, is characteristic of the cold seasons over both land and water, where the air is cooled from below and mixed by winds of 15 knots or more. This cloud yields no more than light precipitation of the drizzle type— possibly fine snow. Stratocumulus will persist for long periods under proper air-to-land or air-to-sea temperature relations. Stratocumulus rarely presents serious flight hazards. It is thin, so a flight path can be chosen above or below the cloud layer. It does cause icing, which must be taken into account during takeoffs and landings, or when operational situations require prolonged flight in the cloud layer. Also, visibility may be seriously reduced in the stratocumulus drizzle or snow.

Stratus clouds have little weather significance. They indicate an inversion at low levels, a few hundred feet above the surface. Other than light drizzle, no stratus precipitation can be anticipated except that from higher clouds when the stratus forms ahead of a warm front. In this case, the rain supersaturates the cold air, stratus, then fog, will form. On continental west coasts, such as California, the absence of stratus in summer is more significant than when it is present. It implies offshore flow and higher maximum temperatures—80s and 90s instead of the usual 60s to 70s. Stratus clouds are a serious hazard to flight because of the low ceilings, but represent no hazard to surface operations.

Nimbostratus clouds are of little help as a forecasting device, since the bad weather is already at hand when these dark clouds with their heavy rain or snow are overhead. It can be assumed, once nimbostratus has formed, that existing wind and weather conditions will persist for several hours. For flight operations, nimbostratus offer hazard because of occasional heavy turbulence, low ceilings, and heavy icing. The stormy conditions which accompany nimbostratus clouds make surface operations difficult.

Cumulus clouds, when detached and with little vertical development, are called "fair weather cumulus" and have practically no effect upon flight operations. When cumulus clouds swell and have considerable vertical development, with dome-shaped protuberances forming a cauliflower-like pattern at the top of the cloud, there are deep layers of instability. Shower and thunderstorm development is likely, but this can only be forecast with assurance through knowledge of the height of the freezing level and high-level inversions. This type of cumulus cloud is very turbulent, and above the freezing level, can cause the heaviest aircraft icing. However, since cumulus clouds usually cover only about 25 percent of the sky, they can easily be circumnavigated. They affect surface operations only by the gusty winds which occur in the showers.

Cumulonimbus clouds, which may extend from near the surface to as high as 65,000 feet, represent the greatest layer thickness of instability to be found in the atmosphere. The immediate implication of a cumulonimbus which has developed to the thunderstorm stage is heavy rain, lightning, gusty winds, and possibly hail. It is the most dangerous cloud for flight operations because turbulence may cause loss of control or structural damage. Tornadoes are associated with thunderstorms and derive their energy from them.

17.3 How Clouds Form   Clouds result chiefly from ascending air currents. When air rises, it encounters regions of lower pressure, and expands. If not saturated with water vapor, expanding air cools at the rate of 5.5 degrees F for each 1000 feet of rise above the earth. If a current of air rises sufficiently high, its temperature will eventually decrease to a value at which the air will be saturated with water vapor. Any further temperature decrease will cause some of the water vapor to be condensed into cloud particles.

17.4   Adiabatic and Saturation Adiabatic Rates   The cooling rate of 5.5 degrees F per 1000 feet for rising and expanding unsaturated air is known as the adiabatic, or dry, rate of cooling. An adiabatic cooling process is one in which no heat is added or taken away from the mass of air by exchange with the environment; the air cools only because of expansion.

Descending air is compressed and warmed at the dry adiabatic rate of 5.5 degrees F per 1000 feet. Warming of the air keeps the relative humidity below 100 percent, so the dry adiabatic rate will always apply to descending air.

If rising air cools to the dew point and condensation starts, a cloud will appear. This signals a release of the heat of condensation, which is about 600 calories per gram of water vapor condensed. If the parcel continues to rise, the cooling rate will now be about 2.7 degrees F for every 1000 feet of ascent. The 5.5 degree F cooling rate for un-saturated air is balanced against the 2.8 degree F heating rate from heat of condensation. The 2.7 degree F cooling rate is known as the wet adiabatic, or saturation adiabatic.

Foehn, or Chinook Winds   These winds illustrate the effects of the adiabatic heating and cooling of air. A foehn is a warm, dry wind which blows down the side of a mountain range. When atmospheric pressure conditions are higher on one side of a range than on the other side, air is caused to flow upward, over, and down the range toward the area of lower pressure on the leeward side. An example of these conditions is found in the Rockies when pressure is high over the north Pacific and low in the northern plains states. Fairly warm, moist air then flows inshore and ascends to higher ground. If at first the air is not saturated, it cools at the dry adiabatic rate of 5.5 degrees F for each 1000 feet rise in elevation. Once it becomes saturated, clouds form and the cooling rate decreases to about one-half the dry adiabatic rate. Under these conditions rain or snow is very likely. Once the air reaches the region overlying the backbone of the Rocky Mountain range, it begins its descent at the dry adiabatic rate to the sections of eastern Montana and Wyoming, where it is known as a chinook wind and is much warmer and drier at any elevation than at a corresponding elevation on the western slope. This is, of course, due to the net cooling rate on the windward slope being less than the heating rate on the lee slope. The chinook wind is so pronounced at times that it has rapidly and completely melted and evaporated heavy

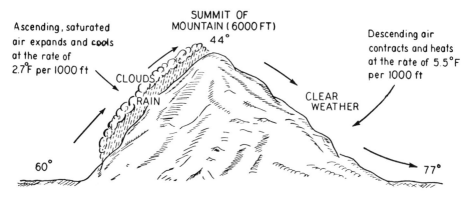

Fig. 17.2 The formation of a chinook wind. Saturated air at a temperature of 60 degrees F ascends a mountain range. Clouds and rain occur on the windward slopes. Upon reaching the summit the temperature of the air has decreased to 44 degrees F. Descent on the leeward slopes results in the warming of the air so that its temperature is increased to 77 degrees F, 17 degrees F higher than at the corresponding level before ascent.

blankets of snow east of the Rockies. Figure 17.2 illustrates the formation of a chinook wind.

In Europe this type of wind is known as a *foehn*. It is common on the north slope of the Alps. Warm, moist winds from the Mediterranean are forced to ascend the southern slopes of the Alps when pressure is low over central Europe. As the wind descends to lower ground north of the Alps, it becomes the warm, dry *foehn*.

The discussion of the chinook wind illustrated one type of cloud formation, by orographic ascent. Three further examples of cloud formation are as follows:

1. Convection   Consider the case of cumulus clouds which form over an island during the daytime. The land areas become warmer than the surrounding water surfaces. The warm land heats the overlying air and causes it to expand and become less dense. It is then pushed upward by cooler, denser air which flows inshore from the colder sea surfaces. If the rising air current continues to ascend, it will eventually cool to the dew point or temperature where its water vapor causes saturation of the air. The relative humidity then is 100 percent, and any further rising and cooling of the air results in the condensation of some of the water vapor into visible cloud particles. Cumulus clouds have flat bases. This is apparent if they are viewed from an airplane or in a diagonal direction from the earth. The flat base marks the elevation at which the rising air current cooled to the dew point. Typical cumulus clouds have rounded, domelike, clear-cut tops. Their tops (Fig. 17.3) mark the height of the ascending air currents which caused the clouds. At elevations below the cumulus cloud base the air was cooling at the dry adiabatic rate. Throughout the cloud

Fig. 17.3 Cumulus (Cu). (*Official U.S. Navy photograph.*)

mass the rising air column cools at the wet, or saturation adiabatic, rate. Cumulus clouds, once formed, may be carried horizontally for considerable distances by the winds, but without the support of rising currents they eventually tend to return to the invisible vapor form from which they had their genesis.

2. *Overrunning Air Currents*   Now consider what happens when a current of cool air from the east converges with a current of warm air moving from the south. As you look at Fig. 17.4, note that you are facing west with north to the right and south to the left. The current of cool air is moving away from you as indicated by the circle with a

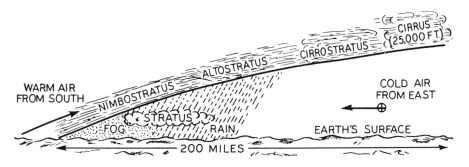

Fig. 17.4 A vertical cross-section through the air looking west. The cirrus clouds shown may be 25,000 feet above the earth's surface, and 200 miles north of the place where the warm current began its ascent over the cooler wedge of air.

cross representing the tail of an arrow moving with the wind. The southern current is warmer and therefore lighter than the easterly current. When these currents meet, they do not tend to mix. The warmer current is deflected upward by the heavier, denser air as indicated in the figure. The figure actually shows what is known as a **warm front. Fronts, together with air masses, are discussed in Chapter 19.**

Many types of clouds are formed when an air current overruns another, rises, expands, and cools adiabatically. Four types—cirrus, cirrostratus, altostratus, and nimbostratus—are shown in Fig. 17.4.

3. Turbulence Figure 17.5 shows how clouds may be formed because of turbulence. Wind blowing over the earth's surface, particularly over rough terrain, causes upward and downward currents up to 1500 to 2000 feet above the surface and sometimes higher. Obviously if the air contains much water vapor, adiabatic cooling of the rising air currents may result in the air temperature reaching its dew point and the formation of clouds. The cloud types are either stratus or stratocumulus and are usually not rain-producing. The tops of these clouds ordinarily do not extend to elevations more than about 4000 feet above the ground. Turbulence due to surface friction does not often exist above this level. If the air is unstable, the tops may extend to any height.

Wind speed often determines whether clouds or fog will form. As we shall see later, gentle or light winds often produce fog when flowing over

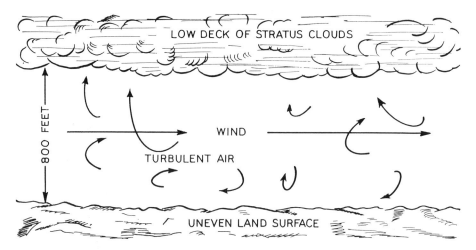

Fig. 17.5 Stratus. These clouds may form when fresh to strong winds of high humidity blow over rough terrain. Friction with the ground surfaces causes upward air currents which expand, cool, and produce stratus or stratocumulus clouds.

cold surfaces. If the wind velocity is moderate to strong, friction of air and ground so stirs up the air that clouds are more likely to form than fog.

17.5 Stability, Instability, and Conditional Instability: Inversions

Why are cumulus cloud tops low and rather flat on some days, whereas at other times the tops grow to great heights, sometimes building up to the great cumulonimbus cloud masses? The stability condition of the air is the answer to these questions, and the processes involved are as follows:

If a volume of air rises for any reason, as, for instance, in one of the ways described in the formation of clouds, it can do one of three things after the initial force which started it upward is removed. It may remain at the height to which it was forced; it may sink back to a lower level; or it may continue its journey upward. What it does de-

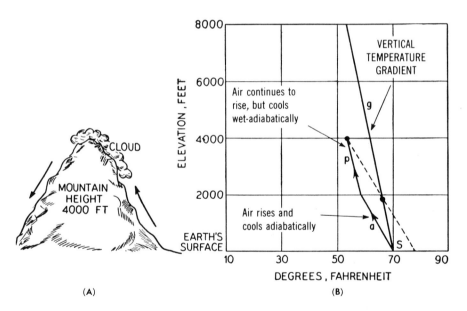

Fig. 17.6 Stable. (A) shows a current of air rising over a mountain. It expands and cools at the adiabatic rate (5.5 degrees F/1000 feet) until it reaches an elevation of 2000 feet where the air becomes saturated. Rising from 2000 to 4000 feet it cools at the wet adiabatic rate (about 2.7 degrees F/1000 feet). Now refer to graph (B). Let us assume that line g represents the existing vertical temperature gradient. Line a shows the rate of decrease in the temperature of the rising air current as it cools at the adiabatic rate. Line p shows the rate of decrease of the temperature of the rising air current as it cools at the wet adiabatic rate. Looking back at (A) it will be noted that the mountain forces the air current only to a height of about 4000 feet. Referring again to (B) it will be noted that at all heights the temperature of the rising column is less than its environment, and therefore stable. Hence upon reaching the leeward side of the mountain the air current will tend to descend.

pends on the stability of the air. If the air is in a condition of neutral stability, the particle remains at the elevation to which it was pushed; if the air is stable, it will tend to drop back; but if the air is unstable, it will continue its journey upward.

It will be recalled from Chapter 16 that the temperature of the atmosphere on the average is 1 degree F colder at each 300 feet of elevation above the earth. This is only an average condition and is known as the lapse rate, or vertical temperature gradient. The existing lapse rate at any place and time may be either greater or less than 1 degree F per 300 feet. Sometimes the temperature is warmer at increased elevations; such a condition is known as an *inversion.*

Conditional instability is the term applied to air that is stable when cooling takes place at the adiabatic rate, but unstable when it occurs

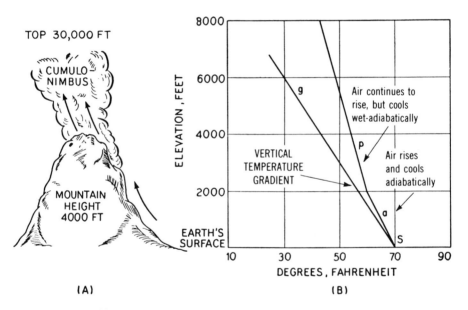

(A)   (B)

Fig. 17.7 Unstable. Again, (A) shows a current of air ascending a mountain slope. Expansion and cooling occur at the adiabatic rate up to 2000 feet where the dewpoint is reached and a cloud base forms. Above 2000 feet cooling takes place at the wet adiabatic rate. Referring to (B) we note that the existing vertical temperature gradient is represented by line g. This temperature gradient is steeper than the one shown in Fig. 17.6. Lines a and p show the rate of temperature decrease while the air column is cooling at the adiabatic and wet adiabatic rate, respectively. It will be noted that at any height the temperature of the rising air column (shown by line a-p) is greater than the air through which it is rising (shown by line g). Therefore, once the air begins to ascend the mountain slope it will tend to continue upward as long as it continues to be warmer than its environment.

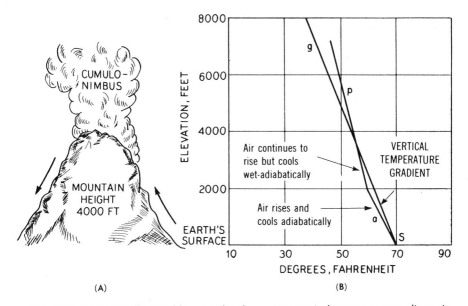

(A)   (B)

Fig. 17.8 Conditionally unstable. Note that the existing vertical temperature gradient g is steeper than in 17.6, but not so steep as in 17.7. Air having this type of temperature gradient is stable for air columns rising and cooling at the wet adiabatic rate. In this particular case as air ascends the mountain slope at 2000 feet it has expanded and cooled to the dewpoint where a cloud base forms.Between 2000 and 4000 feet the rising air column expands and cools at the wet adiabatic rate. If the air column rises to just above 4000 feet, it will be warmer than its environment and will continue upward. Had the air column contained less moisture it would have continued to a higher elevation than 2000 feet at the adiabatic rate, and cumulonimbus might not have formed.

at the saturated adiabatic. Conditional instability is quite common and is the basis of much of our cloudiness and precipitation.

Figures 17.6, 17.7, and 17.8 graphically illustrate stable, unstable, and conditionally unstable conditions; flat cumulus and cumulonimbus clouds are shown on the appropriate diagrams. In Fig. 17.6 it will be noted that the cloud top does not extend to a great height because the air column which forms the cloud does not tend to continue upward beyond the level to which it is forced by the mountain. In Fig. 17.8 the cloud top reaches high because its air column continues to rise after being forced to 4000 feet by the mountain. In Fig. 17.7 any slight upward motion of the air at S will result in a rising air column; the column will continue to rise as long as it is warmer than its environment.

Figures 17.9(A) and (B) show low and high temperature inversions, respectively. Inversions at the earth's surface as in Fig. 17.9(A), de-

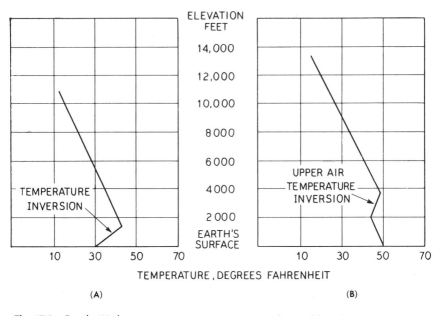

Fig. 17.9 Graph (A) shows a temperature inversion at the earth's surface. Surface inversions are characterized by stability and poor visibility; common at night, they are often associated with ground fog. Graph (B) shows an upper air inversion, the base of which is known as a "lid." It is difficult for air from below to penetrate the base of a lid; any smoke, fog, dust or haze present tends to spread out at the base of an upper air inversion.

velop at night over land surfaces because of radiation of heat from the earth when skies are clear and winds are light. Ground fog is often the result. Inversions at levels above the earth's surface act as lids above which air rising from below finds it difficult to penetrate. This condition causes a spreading out at the base of the upper air inversion of smoke and other restrictions to visibility.

Inversions near the earth's surface are important not only because of their relation to fog but also to air pollution, a problem which increases linearly with increasing population density. In areas like coastal Southern California, for example, there are persistent inversions which trap man-made pollutants. The topography, which allows for no low-level escape to the east, aggravates the problem. Health and economy are adversely affected. Occasionally, lethal smogs have developed when a strong inversion and light winds have persisted for several days. Notable examples occurred in Donora, Pennsylvania, in 1948, and in London in 1952. In these cases, a dense fog combined with smoke and other pollutants and became concentrated to the toxic level.

17.6   The Thunderstorm   Thunderstorms are spectacular, violent local storms produced by cumulonimbus cloud and are characterized by squalls, gustiness, turbulence, heavy showers, thunder and lightning, and often hail, which can be as large as four inches in diameter. The strong and gusty surface winds are of serious concern to surface craft and to aircraft on the ground; the strong vertical currents in and below the cumulonimbus cloud offer danger in flight. Up and down drafts may be so strong as to put dangerous strains and stresses on a plane's structure, or cause loss of control in large aircraft. Visibility is invariably poor in a thunderstorm, ceilings are low, and landings difficult to make. Airplanes may also be seriously damaged by hail; lightning may affect radio antennae, Pitot tubes, and other protruding equipment; icing of the plane's surfaces and fuel system is likely.

Thunderstorms form in a number of ways, but all require warm, **unstable air of high moisture content, and some type of lifting or trigger** action. The air parcel must be lifted to a point where it is warmer than the surrounding air, after which it will continue to rise freely until, at some point aloft, the air parcel has cooled to the temperature of the surrounding air. Lifting may occur in several ways, as by heating, mountains, or fronts.

17.7   Life Cycle of the Thunderstorm   The life cycle of the thunderstorm is short, often lasting only from one to two hours, and consists of three stages. In the *cumulus* stage, the cloud is warmer than the outside air, so the cloud air is accelerated upward. There are only updrafts within the cloud at this stage. These updrafts increase with elevation, and the cloud builds rapidly to heights well above the freezing level. During this process, cloud droplets, raindrops, and snowflakes accumulate rapidly in the cloud. When the heavier elements of this accumulation can no longer be supported by the updrafts, water begins to fall through the cloud. Frictional drag exerted by the water turns the updraft into a downdraft, and heavy rainfall reaches the ground. This is the beginning of the mature stage of the thunderstorm.

In the mature stage, there are updrafts and downdrafts side by side within the cloud. The falling rain and snow, coming from the colder air aloft, cools the downdraft, which spreads out horizontally over the ground as a cool pool of air. Sharp, strong gusts are characteristic of the arrival of the downdraft at the ground; gusts of over 80 knots have been recorded. During the mature stage, the downdrafts gain over the updrafts and the storm reaches the dissipating stage. During this stage, the cloud exhausts its water supply, the rain intensity decreases, and finally the cloud dissolves into irregular lumps or scud at low levels and dense patches and streaks of cirrus at high levels.

The above description applies to a single thundercloud. Generally, there are several of these cells in a cluster, with each cell from 1 to 6 miles in diameter. The stage of development of these cells will vary from young to old. There is a strong tendency for new cells to form on the forward side of the downdraft of an old cell, so the life span of a cluster will be much longer than the life of an individual thunderstorm.

17.8 Thunderstorm Patterns Thunderstorms occur in more or less distinct patterns, which can be grouped into the air mass and frontal varieties.

Air mass thunderstorms form within a uniform mass of air which has the necessary warm, humid, and unstable air required for storm development. They occur over land or water almost anywhere in the world, although rarely at high latitudes. Their formation is caused by heating of the air at the surface, so over land they occur most frequently in the afternoon hours, usually on hot, sultry days when winds are light. Strong winds prevent thunderstorm formation by breaking up the vertical currents. Over the oceans, thunderstorms are more frequent at night, because the sea surface temperatures remain almost as warm at night as during the day.

However, temperatures at the upper levels over the ocean drop a considerable amount throughout the night because of radiation. This results in the same type of temperature contrast between the warm surface air and the cooler upper air as is found over the land during summer afternoons. Many persons who have gone to sea may recall clear days and evenings which have been followed by showers before daybreak. While thunderstorms are most common during the warmer seasons over land, they occur at sea with greater frequency during colder months.

Another way in which air mass thunderstorms form is known as *orographic*. Thunderstorms occur quite commonly on the windward slopes of mountains. The upward deflection of the air by the mountains furnishes the trigger action which may result in thunderstorm activity. Even in relatively flat country, such as the middle western states, thunderstorm activity may break out when air ascends only a few hundred feet in the vicinity of low rolling hills.

Frontal thunderstorms occur along warm and cold fronts and prefrontal squall lines. They occur at any time of day or night. Both warm and cold front thunderstorms result when moist, warm, unstable air is forced to rise over the cold wedges of air lying beneath the frontal surfaces. Line squall thunderstorms form anywhere from 50 to 300 miles ahead of cold fronts under special atmospheric conditions. These thunderstorms are similar to those in a cold front, although tending to be a little more intense and menacing in appearance. Tornadic activity sometimes occurs along with line squalls. Frontal thunderstorms usually form in a line along the leading edge of the front.

17.9 Forecasting and Tracking Thunderstorms   Thunderstorms are forecast by use of data from upper air soundings; the essential problem is that of determining the stability of the air mass (Figs. 17.6, 17.7, and 17.8), and whether or not there will be enough heating or lifting to release the instability. Forecasting thunderstorms is beyond the scope of the layman, although he can often anticipate air mass thunderstorms with accuracy by observing the degree and time of development of cumulus clouds in his vicinity (Section 17.2).

Once formed, thunderstorms are tracked by reports from the network of weather stations, and particularly by radar stations.

17.10 Tornadoes   Although the tornado is the least extensive of all storm types, it is the most violent and sharply defined. Tornadoes occur in other parts of the world but are most common in the United States, particularly in the plains and southern areas. "Tornado Alley," from Oklahoma north-northeast to Iowa, has more tornadoes than any other area in the world. Tornadoes average only a few hundred yards in diameter and move at 25 to 40 knots along paths which range from a few hundred feet to 300 miles in length and average 25 miles. In the Northern Hemisphere the wind of the tornado almost always whirls counterclockwise, and speeds approach 400 miles per hour. The tornado may be recognized by its funnel-shaped cloud which builds downward from a cumulonimbus cloud. A mammatus sky—one with many dark bags hanging down from cloud base—often gives warning of impending tornado formation; it is also known as a tornado sky.

The tornado funnel may or may not reach ground but does little damage unless it does so. The pressure within a tornado is very low, and a building literally explodes when struck, because the normal pressure within a building pushes the walls and ceiling outward toward the region of the tornado's low pressure. A 20 by 40 foot house, for example, would have a 68-ton outward force exerted on the roof during an overhead passage of an average-sized tornado. The violent winds then complete the structure's destruction and scatter parts in every direction. The cloud mass is one of condensed vapor, though it also contains much dust and debris picked up along its journey.

17.11 Waterspouts Tornadoes over water are called waterspouts. They are not as violent as tornadoes, but have capsized boats and damaged property when they moved over land. The waterspout is composed of water droplets formed by condensation, not of sea water drawn up by the funnel, although some sea spray is carried aloft as is shown by unusually salty rainwater following passage of a waterspout. The extremely low pressure at the center of a waterspout is shown by the creation of a mound of water perhaps two feet high at the center.

17.12 Fog Fog is a cloud with its base at or very near the ground. Although the substance of fog is the same as that of a cloud, the processes of cloud and fog formation are different. Clouds form chiefly because air rises, expands, and cools. Fog results from the cooling of air which remains at or near the earth's surface. This lowering of air temperature may occur in a number of ways, as described under the following fog types:

Advection Fog These fogs form when warm air sufficiently high in water vapor content flows over cooler land or water surfaces. The cool surface chills the overrunning air, and water vapor of the air tends to condense on particles of dust, smoke, or salt even before the relative humidity reaches 100 percent. The fog may be light, moderate, or dense, depending upon the amount of vapor that condenses. Dense fog is likely if the relative humidity value approaches 100 percent.

Tropical air moving northward in winter will encounter ground that is near freezing, often snow covered. If wind speeds are 15 knots or more, the cooled air is mixed through a layer some 1000 feet thick. An inversion forms at the top of the mixed layer, and a stratus deck forms first near the top. As the tropical air continues northward, the mixed layer becomes saturated at lower and lower levels until the stratus layer finally reaches the surface. The fog layer is very thick and persists day and night in contrast to radiation fog.

Summer advection fog is rare over land in summer, but at sea it is very common when warm, moist air is advected over cold currents in high latitudes. Favored regions for fog formation, summer or winter, are those where cold and warm ocean currents are adjacent to one another.

Radiation or Ground Fog This fog type is a nighttime, over-land phenomenon. At night there is only outgoing radiation at the earth's surface, so the topsoil temperature gradually decreases, as does the temperature of the air in contact with it. Cooling raises the relative humidity of the air, until at some point during the night, the relative humidity becomes high enough for condensation to occur and a mist forms at the ground. This deepens and thickens into a fog. Light winds, clear skies, moist air, and long nights are the requirements for formation of radiation fog. It is a shallow fog through which the sky is usually plainly visible, but it makes aircraft landings and takeoffs difficult; it obscures landmarks to some extent, thus complicating navigation. Sometimes it forms soon after sunset; at other times it may require a sustained drop in temperature throughout the night before forming.

Radiation fog usually burns off within an hour or so after sunrise. If mixed with smoke, which is particularly common in winter, it forms a greasy "smog" (smoke and fog) which may not be dissipated until later in the morning.

Steam Fog or Arctic Sea Smoke   Steam fog occurs when very cold air passes over much warmer water. The difference in vapor pressure causes rapid evaporation from the water surface into the air, soon filling the air with fog. Steam fog is usually very shallow, and looks like tufts of whirling smoke coming out of the water. If there happens to be an inversion not too far above the water surface, the air between the surface and the inversion will fill with steam and become a dense fog. Steam fog is most common with arctic regions, but also occurs frequently over inland bodies of water, lakes and rivers, when cold fall and winter air moves southward.

Frontal Fogs   Fog sometimes forms ahead of warm fronts and behind cold fronts when the rain falls from the warm air above the frontal surfaces into the colder air beneath. Evaporation from the warm raindrops causes the dewpoint temperature of the cold air to rise until condensation on existing nuclei takes place. If the winds are strong, or the cold air unstable, stratus or stratocumulus clouds will form instead of fog.

Inversion Fog.   This type of fog is typical of the subtropical west coasts, California, for instance. Upwelling of cold water is common along west coasts, and the air over this cold water acquires low temperatures and high relative humidity. Above the cool, moist layer lies a temperature inversion which keeps the moist air from rising. Fog forms, as in the advection process, and is very frequent offshore. At night, as the land cools, the fog works inland.

Ice Fog   Ice fogs occur at temperatures of −30 degrees C or colder, and are found most frequently in inhabited areas. Aircraft running up their engines in temperatures −40 degrees C or lower will quickly cause an airport to be covered with ice fog. Even reindeer, after some exercise, find themselves surrounded with ice fog caused by evaporation of body liquids which condense and freeze in the bitterly cold air.

17.13 Fog at Sea   Fog is rare at the equator and in the trade-wind belt except along the coasts of California, Chile, and northwest and southwest Africa. On the other hand, it is a common phenomenon of middle and high latitudes, particularly in spring and early summer. The Newfoundland Banks is a region where the Gulf Stream and the Labrador current meet. When warm air from the Gulf Stream overruns the cold water of the Labrador current, dense fog banks result. Likewise, in the northwestern Pacific, fog is common off the coast of Asia where warm air of the Japanese current overruns the cold Kamchatka current. During spring and summer, warm, moist air currents which flow from land to sea produce fog over coastal water areas. A shift in wind direction tends to drift the fog back over adjacent land areas. During fall and early winter, air blowing from sea to land tends to produce fog over coastal sections. Such fog may drift to sea with a reversal of the wind direction.

In the north Pacific Ocean and Bering Sea wide areas of dense fog are common, and at times the fog may extend to elevations of 4000 feet or more. It is caused by air moving northward from high-pressure areas which are centered in the Pacific Ocean at about latitude 35 to 40 degrees north. The air reaches its saturation temperature in passing over the colder waters to the north. Chilling of the air also increases its density so that there is no tendency of the air to rise and clear. Fog may persist in the Aleutian area when winds are quite strong. When fog-laden wind flows around and over land obstructions, clear spots may be found to leeward; the sun is not effective in burning off this type of fog. During fall and spring months, fog is at a minimum in the Aleutians; in winter, arctic sea smoke is common, and it may at times build up to elevations of several thousand feet above the surface.

17.14 Weather Modification   Of mankind's many dreams for improving his lot upon earth, few have been as widespread and persistent as that of controlling weather. It was not until World War II that it was demonstrated in the laboratory that clouds could be modified and some precipitation produced by scientific means. Since then, greatly increased research activity in the field of weather modification has demonstrated that we still do not have enough knowledge of fundamental atmospheric processes and cloud physics to know how to bring about successful weather modification. The potential benefits to mankind are great; of primary interest are the ability to increase precipitation, to dissipate low stratus and fog, and to modify severe weather, particularly thunderstorms and tropical cyclones.

We must learn how to reap the benefits of weather modification while, at the same time, avoiding activity which might affect the climatic controls of heat-moisture balances, and general atmospheric and oceanic circulations. Action founded on lack of understanding, which might affect climates, has too many potential hazards—such as flooding of heavily populated coastal plains, turning fertile areas into deserts, and destruction of insect and animal life.

The foundation of weather modification experiments to date involves attempts to alter the life cycle of a cloud or a cloud system by seeding with such substances as water, dry ice, silver iodine, carbon black, and other chemicals. The object is (1) to cause the small cloud droplets to coalesce and reach a size large enough to fall to earth or (2) to seed that part of the cloud composed of supercooled water droplets (droplets still in liquid form but in equilibrium at temperatures below freezing). The seeding agent provides nuclei upon which the supercooled droplets collect and are transformed to ice particles. These ice particles, because of vapor pressure differences between ice and water droplets, collect neighboring water droplets and grow to a size large enough to fall toward or to the ground.

While progress in weather modification has not been rapid, these statements can be made with accuracy:

1. Under specialized conditions, and to a limited degree, rainfall can be increased from individual cumulus clouds.
2. Clouds can be modified by artificial means, either increased in size or dissipated. Areas of supercooled clouds 30 by 70 miles in size have been dissipated.
3. Evaporation processes can be altered over water surfaces, and there is evidence that this might be possible over land covered with vegetation.
4. There is evidence that modification of the electrical charge in the lower atmosphere may affect precipitation from cumulus clouds.
5. We can see and measure the serious results of altering the atmosphere by man-made air pollution.

Various interesting weather modification studies are in progress.

Project STORMFURY, a DOD–NOAA effort to modify hurricanes by seeding, may have succeeded in reducing wind speeds at seeding altitudes in one 1969 hurricane by about 33 percent. Other studies include triggering release of energy in the high atmosphere by suitable catalysts applied on atomic oxygen and free radicals, and determining the effect of atomic testing upon atmospheric processes. Within the next decade, it seems almost certain that man will have a considerable degree of success in his efforts at small scale weather modification.

Weather Elements, Instruments, and Reports

18.1 Introduction In order to determine and describe the conditions of the atmosphere or weather at a given time and place, various weather elements must be observed and measured. The reports of the observations are quickly made available for the use of seamen, airmen, forecasters, and others concerned. The values of some elements are estimated or determined visually; others are measured with the aid of instruments, some of which are carried aloft thousands of feet by balloons in order to determine pressure, temperature, moisture, and wind conditions in the vertical.

18.2 Clouds Cloud observations include notations as to the types which are present, proportion of the sky that they cover, and height of bases. Twenty-seven variations of the ten basic cloud genera can be recorded. For example, cumulus clouds may be of the relatively flat-topped type of fair, settled weather; or their tops may extend to a considerable height, thereby indicating unstable atmospheric conditions with the possibility of storminess. When cloud types and their variations are observed and reported adequately, many useful inferences may be drawn concerning present weather conditions and imminent changes. This is particularly true at sea, where weather reports are scarce.

18.3 Visibility   By visibility is meant the greatest horizontal distance in a given direction at which it is just possible to see and identify with the unaided eye (a) by day, a prominent dark object at the horizon and (b) at night, a known light source. Each weather station maintains a "visibility weather chart" which shows distance and direction of various permanent landmarks or other reference points used in determining visibility. In open seas the determination of visibility is much more difficult; the usual point of reference being the horizon.

There is a definite relationship between general weather conditions and the visibility. When the air is warmer than the underlying surface, it tends to be stable, and poor surface visibility due to fog, haze, smoke, drizzle, or dust may prevail. Poor visibility is often associated with clouds of the stratus type. If the surface is warmer than the overlying air, horizontal visibility at the surface tends to be good. This is because particles that restrict visibility are carried upward by the surface air, which expands and rises when heated by the warm surface. Any clouds present would be the cumulus type. Fog and falling snow are two of the most serious restrictions to visibility, because visibility can deteriorate so rapidly with the occurrence of either. Fog may be anticipated when the temperature and dewpoint values are approaching each other. This is especially true when the air has considerable foreign matter present, such as dust, smoke, and haze. Visibility is of prime importance in navigation at sea and to landing aircraft.

18.4 State of the Weather   A weather report always includes a reference to the state of the weather. This, in general, refers to the existence, imminence, or absence of precipitation, but obstructions to vision are also included in this part of the code. It is possible to record and report 100 different states of the weather, ranging from cloudless skies to heavy thunderstorms with hail. Other conditions which can be reported with existing weather codes include low fog, haze, distant lightning, smoke, and various degrees of fog, rain, snow, showers, drizzle, squalls, etc. Definitions of some of the more frequently reported state-of-weather elements follow.

Dust   This consists of minute earth particles which are picked up and carried along by the wind. Distant objects have a more or less grayish or tan appearance, depending on the amount of dust present.

Although there is always some dust in the air, appreciable amounts are usually of local origin. Blowing dust is reported when sheets or clouds of it are carried along in a strong wind.

Haze   Haze is composed of very finely divided particles of matter from land areas or of salt particles from the sea. They are much smaller than dust particles. Haze gives distant objects a pale blue or sometimes yellow appearance. At a distance the details of objects disappear, and the objects stand out in silhouette fashion.

Smoke   Particles resulting from combustion are known as smoke. Except for its odor it might be confused with fog, dust, or haze, especially in light amounts. It is common in the vicinity of cities, especially to leeward of industrial areas. It gives a reddish tinge to the sun's disk at sunrise and sunset.

Hydrometeors are defined as water in solid or liquid form falling through the air. The following types are noteworthy in meteorology:

Drizzle   Drizzle is composed of minute liquid droplets so numerous they seem to fill the air. This form of precipitation originates in stratus clouds or fog. Drizzle particles seem to float in the air and appear to follow even slight motion of the air. Drizzle is characteristically associated with poor visibility. When the droplets instantly freeze to objects which they strike, they are known as freezing drizzle.

Rain   Rain is drops of water larger than drizzle falling from clouds. The drops are usually sparser than those of drizzle. When they freeze to objects, the condition is known as freezing rain.

Sleet   In the United States sleet is defined as frozen raindrops. In England and in the International Weather Code, as well as in popular press vernacular, a mixture of rain and snow is known as sleet.

Hail   Hail is almost exclusively a phenomenon of violent or prolonged thunderstorms. Hail consists of ice balls or stones with diameters ranging from $\frac{1}{5}$ inch to 4 inches or more, which fall either detached or fused in irregular lumps. They may be transparent or composed of alternate clear and opaque, snowlike layers.

Snow   This form of precipitation from clouds consists of white or translucent ice crystals mainly in branched hexagonal shapes often mixed with simple ice crystals.

Showers   This form of precipitation is associated with cumuliform clouds and is characterized by beginning and ending suddenly. Showers, usually of short duration, often occur in a series with periods of fair conditions between individual shower periods. Unstable atmospheric conditions are indicated by showers, and the form of precipitation may be either snow or rain. Snow showers are sometimes known as *snow flurries*.

18.5 Atmospheric, or Barometric, Pressure The value of the atmospheric pressure is one of the most important elements in reporting and forecasting the weather. It is particularly significant when considered in connection with the direction and speed of the wind and cloud types and sequences. Average pressure values reveal much regarding the prevailing or climatic characteristics of a region. Pressure variations are not for the most part perceptible to human senses. Pressure is the one element that cannot be estimated; its value must be determined instrumentally. Pressure-measuring instruments in common use are the mercurial barometer, the aneroid barometer, and the barograph.

The *mercurial barometer* has been the world-wide standard at land stations, but most ships and stations now use the *aneroid* type. Mercurial barometers are direct-reading, but corrections are applied for temperature, gravity, and elevation above sea level; also, each instrument has an individual correction which must always be applied. The mercurial barometer is essentially a glass tube with one end closed. It is filled with mercury and inverted so that the open end projects into a well or cistern. The top of the mercury in the tube will then lower until the column just balances a column of the atmosphere of the same cross section as that of the mercury. The height of the mercury column as measured from the top of the liquid in the cistern is an expression of the atmospheric pressure. When the atmospheric pressure increases, the mercury rises; a decrease in atmospheric pressure causes the column to decrease in height. In nautical terminology, the mercurial barometer was commonly called "the glass," a contraction of "weather glass." High pressure was known as a "high glass," low as a "low glass." A high glass was associated in general with fair weather conditions, whereas a low glass often meant cloudiness, rain, increased windiness, and stormy conditions in general.

The scale on European mercurial barometers is usually in terms of

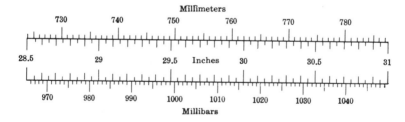

Fig. 18.1 The relationship between the millimeter, inch, and millibar scales. European barometers are commonly fitted with millimeter scales, while instruments in the United States and England are read in inches. The millibar unit is used on weather maps.

millimeters; in the United States, inches are used. Readings may be made to thousandths of an inch by means of a vernier scale. The value in inches is converted to units of millibars. This unit has been adopted in scientific meteorological work because it represents a force, whereas mercury in inches is a unit of length. Isobars on weather maps are drawn in terms of millibars rather than inches. A millibar is equivalent to 1000 dynes per square centimeter; 1000 millibars are equivalent to 29.53 inches of mercury. The standard pressure of 29.92 inches equals 1013.25 millibars (see Fig. 18.1).

The aneroid barometer (Fig. 18.2) is a small, convenient instrument operating on a principle different from that of the mercurial type. It

Fig. 18.2   Aneroid barometer. (*Courtesy of Taylor Instrument Companies.*)

consists essentially of a corrugated metallic chamber or cell exhausted of air. The cell is prevented from collapsing by means of a strong steel spring. One side of the cell is arranged so that it responds to variations in atmospheric pressure by expanding and contracting. This motion is magnified by a system of levers and chains and transmitted to a hand on the dial of the instrument. Temperature differences are compensated for by means of a bimetallic link of brass and steel. It is necessary occasionally to test and compare aneroid barometers with standard mercurial instruments.

Barographs (Fig. 18.3) are instruments which afford a continuous record of atmospheric pressure and consist of two units. First, the motion of a series of small aneroid cells is magnified and transmitted to a pen by means of a system of levers and chains. Second, a card mounted on a drum is rotated slowly on a vertical axis by means of a clock mechanism. The pen traces a continuous record of the barometric pressure on the card. The barograph is a most useful instrument because it not only shows the present reading but, even more important, whether or not pressure values are rising or falling and the rate of changes. One of the most significant elements of a weather report is the *pressure tendency* during the three-hour period prior to the report. The tendency includes both the character of pressure change, i.e., whether the pressure is rising or falling, etc., and the net amount in tenths of millibars of such change. The barograph trace

Fig. 18.3 Microbarograph. (*Courtesy of Friez Instrument Div., Bendix Aviation Corp.*)

shows the pressure tendency at a glance. The barograph, like all aneroid barometers, must be compared frequently with standard mercurial instruments. The card on the drum may record the pressure for four or seven days, depending on the type of barograph in use. Figure 18.4 shows a typical barograph trace. It will be noted that pressure values are indicated along the vertical scale, whereas time units are marked off on the horizontal scale. The time lines are curved because the pen that records pressure value is pivoted at the aneroid unit.

18.6 Temperature   Air temperature is measured by thermometers or other devices, graduated in degrees Fahrenheit (freezing 32 degrees, boiling 212 degrees) or, by many nations, in degrees Centigrade, or Celsius (freezing 0 degree, boiling 100 degrees). To be representative, air temperatures near the surface must be measured under conditions where there are no influences on the thermometer except the free air. Hence, thermometers at land stations are exposed in white shelters which have insulated roofs and louvered sides and are raised five to six feet off the ground. At sea, temperature measurement in a shelter is not satisfactory because at any one location in the ship, conditions are not always the same. For example, at one time heat may issue up from below decks to affect the thermometer; at other times the prevailing wind may carry the heat in the other direction. There is also the problem of temperature differences on leeward and weather sides. Temperature and humidity measurements are made aboard ship with the sling psychrometer (Section 18.7) or the portable aspiration thermometer. The latter consists of a tubular shield, artificially ventilated by means of a mechanically driven fan attached to the top of the instrument. The *aspiration* thermometer may be taken to any part of the ship for readings, and it is not affected by the direct rays of the sun.

The *thermograph* is an instrument which affords a continuous record of the air temperature. A commonly used thermograph is one which uses a bimetallic strip as the reactor. Two thin, curved sheets of metal of widely different thermal expansion are welded together. When the temperature changes, the two metals expand unequally, and the curvature of the strip changes. This change is transferred through levers to a pen which moves up and down on a card which is wrapped around a drum. The drum is driven slowly around a vertical axis by a clock mechanism. The values shown by such an instrument are subject to error, but if the thermograph is compared frequently with a good mercurial thermometer, the errors may be determined and corrected.

A *maximum* thermometer shows the highest temperature which

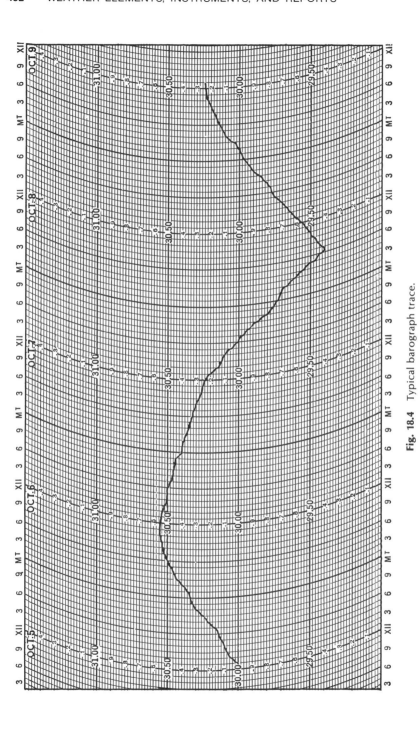

Fig. 18.4   Typical barograph trace.

occurred since the instrument was last read and set. It is similar to an ordinary thermometer except that the bore has a constriction in it just above the bulb, like the clinical or fever thermometers used by doctors. When the mercury in the bulb warms and expands, mercury will flow past the constriction and rise in the bore, but mercury will not flow back into the bulb when the temperature decreases. To force the mercury back into the bulb it is necessary to whirl or shake the thermometer.

A *minimum* thermometer shows the lowest temperature which occurred since it was last read and set. This is an alcohol thermometer with a small glass index which looks like a two-headed pin in the alcohol column. The top of the alcohol, the meniscus, holds the pin at the top by surface tension. As the alcohol retreats with lower temperature, the index is dragged down. Then, as the temperature rises, the liquid leaves the index, which remains with its outer end still showing the lowest temperature reached.

18.7   Dewpoint and Relative Humidity   The water vapor content of the air may be obtained by means of *psychrometer* readings. The psychrometer consists of two thermometers, one of which is called the *dry-bulb,* the other, the *wet-bulb.* There is no difference in the two thermometers, but the bulb of one is fitted with a piece of cloth. This instrument may be carried to any part of the ship to obtain suitable exposure. When a reading is desired, the cloth on the wet-bulb thermometer is moistened. The psychrometer is then whirled. If the air is saturated with water vapor, as during a dense fog, there will be no evaporation from the wet-bulb, and the two thermometers will read the same. When the air is not saturated, evaporation will take place from the wet-bulb. The evaporation is associated with cooling, and the reading of the wet-bulb will be lower than the reading of the dry-bulb thermometer. For any given air temperature, the greater the difference in the dry- and wet-bulb readings, the lower will be the dewpoint and relative humidity. In order to get the dewpoint and relative humidity values it is necessary to look up their values in tables of dewpoint and humidity. The dry-bulb temperature and the difference between the dry- and wet-bulb readings are the two arguments which are used in entering the tables. The aspiration psychrometer, described in Section 18.6, is gradually replacing the sling psychrometer, described above, for humidity measurements.

A continuous record of relative humidity is made by means of a *hygrograph.* The recording pen is actuated by a unit of human hairs which expand and contract with changing humidity conditions. Values are recorded by the pen on a card which is mounted on a revolving drum driven by a clock mechanism. The idea of using human hair as a humidity indicator is not new. An old American Indian saying was, "When the locks of the Navajoes turn damp in the scalp house, surely it will rain," which fits in with the increased humidity usually found as a low pressure center approaches.

18.8   Wind Direction   The wind direction is the direction *from* which the wind blows. For example, a wind blowing from the northwest toward the southeast is known as a northwest wind. The direction may be estimated or it may be determined by means of a wind vane. *Wind vanes* point toward the direction from which the wind is blowing. Vanes may be wired to an indicator in the weather office or some other location so that the wind direction may be known at a glance. In most weather offices, a permanent record is made of the readings.

In order to estimate the wind direction by the appearance of the sea, the crests of the small ripples are considered to be perpendicular to the wind direction. In strong winds the foam streaks show the wind direction reliably. At night and during heavy rains when the ripples cannot be seen, it may be necessary to note the apparent direction of the wind. This is the direction from which the wind seems to blow; it is the resultant of the true wind and the ship's movement. Wind vanes on board ship also register the apparent wind. To determine the true wind direction and velocity from the values of the apparent wind direction and force and the true course and speed of the vessel, one of several methods may be used—the plotting or maneuvering board, the true wind computer, tables, or direct-reading instruments.

18.9   Wind Speed   Wind speed may be estimated or it may be measured by means of an *anemometer*. It is expressed in knots, miles per hour, meters per second, or in Beaufort force numbers. The Beaufort scale of wind force, shown in Table 18.1, is useful in estimating wind forces. Experienced seamen become expert at estimating wind speed and direction by observing waves, funnel smoke, flags, and even sounds. This is fortunate, since 90 percent of the wind information from ocean areas comes from merchant ships with no wind observation equipment.

18.10   Upper Air Winds   Some shore and ship meteorological stations are equipped to determine the direction and force of the wind at various heights above the earth's surface. This information is important to airmen for navigation and fuel consumption planning. Forecasters are also interested in upper air wind data because it indicates sources of air masses and other processes that determine cloudiness, precipitation, and other weather conditions.

Pilot balloon (PIBAL) observations are used to get upper air wind data. Small rubber ballons are inflated with hydrogen or helium so that they have a definite rate of ascension. After a balloon is released, it is watched through the telescope of a theodolite, an instrument that resembles a surveyor's transit. By means of scales on the theodolite, the azimuth and the vertical angle of the balloon are determined at one-minute intervals. The balloon has an assumed rate of ascension based on atmospheric density and vertical wind velocity, so its height is known within reasonable accuracy at all times. Therefore by means of trigonometry, the height, together with the azimuth and vertical angle reading, is used to compute the wind speed and direction through each successive layer.

For example, let us suppose that a 30-inch balloon is inflated so that it has an ascension rate of 600 feet per minute. If the balloon goes straight up after release, it is obvious that calm conditions prevail at the elevations corresponding to that portion of the balloon's journey. If after 2 minutes the balloon is located south of the 600-foot observation we know that a north wind is blowing between 600 and 1200 feet.

A pilot balloon observation terminates once the balloon gets out of sight because of clouds or distance. During World War II, when wind information at high levels and above cloud layers became of critical importance, balloons were equipped with radar targets (reflectors), and tracking was done by radar. This method of obtaining accurate upper air winds has been generally replaced by tracking the signal from a radiosonde transmitter with radio direction-finding equipment. **Wind measurements obtained by these two methods are called RAWINS. Aboard ship the radar reflector method is most frequently used. Ship's course and speed must be considered.**

18.11   Ceiling   The ceiling is the vertical distance between the earth's surface and the lowest layer of obscuring phenomena, such as clouds, that covers more than one half of the sky. The ceiling value is important in aviation. Ceiling values may be estimated or they may be measured. Previous ceiling values, weather trends, and conditions reported from surrounding areas, must be considered in estimating ceilings. Aircraft reports are an important source of ceiling information; these are obtained in "let downs" or in level flight at the base of cloud decks.

Table 18.1 Beaufort Scale of Wind Force

Beaufort No.	Knots (mph)	Description	Effect at Sea	Effect Ashore
0	Less than 1	Calm	Sea like a mirror.	Smoke rises vertically.
1	1–3 (1–3)	Light air	Ripples with the appearance of a scale are formed but without foam crests.	Does not move wind vanes, but wind direction shown by smoke drift.
2	4–6 (4–7)	Light breeze	Small wavelets, still short but more pronounced; crests have a glassy appearance and do not break.	Wind felt on face; leaves rustle; ordinary vane moved by wind.
3	7–10 (8–12)	Gentle breeze	Large wavelets. Crests begin to break. Foam of glassy appearance. Perhaps scattered white horses.	Leaves and small twigs in constant motion; wind extends light flag.
4	11–16 (13–18)	Moderate breeze	Small waves, becoming longer; fairly frequent white horses.	Raises dust and loose paper; small branches are moved.
5	17–21 (18–24)	Fresh breeze	Moderate waves, taking a more pronounced long form; many white horses are formed. (Chance of some spray.)	Small trees in leaf begin to sway; crested wavelets form on inland waters.
6	22–27 (25–31)	Strong breeze	Large waves begin to form; the white foam crests are more extensive everywhere. (Probably some spray.)	Large branches in motion; whistling heard in telegraph wires; umbrellas used with difficulty.
7	28–33 (32–38)	Moderate gale (high wind)	Sea heaps up and white foam from breaking waves begins to be blown in streaks along the direction of the wind. Spindrift begins.	Whole trees in motion; inconvenience felt in walking against wind.
8	34–40 (39–46)	Fresh gale	Moderately high waves of greater length; edges of crests break into spindrift. The foam is blown in well-marked streaks along the direction of the wind.	Breaks twigs off trees; generally impedes progress.
9	41–47 (47–54)	Strong gale	High waves. Dense streaks of foam along the direction of the wind. Sea begins to roll. Spray may affect visibility.	Slight structural damage occurs (chimney pots and slate removed).
10	48–55 (55–63)	Storm	Very high waves with long overhanging crests. The resulting foam in great patches is blown in dense white streaks along the direction of the wind. On the whole the surface of the sea takes a white appearance. The rolling of the sea becomes heavy and shocklike. Visibility is affected.	Seldom experienced inland; trees uprooted; considerable structural damage occurs.
11	56–63 (64–73)	Violent storm	Exceptionally high waves. (Small and medium-sized ships might for a long time be lost to view behind the waves.) The sea is completely covered with long white patches of foam lying along the direction of the wind. Everywhere the edges of the wave crests are blown into froth. Visibility affected.	Very rarely experienced; accompanied by widespread damage.
12	Above 63 (73)	Hurricane	The air is filled with foam and spray. Sea completely white with driving spray; visibility very seriously affected.	

Many shore stations are equipped with ceilometers, which are instruments used to determine ceiling conditions both at night and during daylight hours (see Fig. 18.5). The height of the cloud base is determined by trigonometry from the known baseline and the projector beam angle.

18.12 Ocean Surface Temperature Observations from ships at sea include the temperature of the water at the surface. This is obtained by a thermometer reading at the condenser intake or by measuring

Table 18.1 Beaufort Scale of Wind Force *(Cont.)*

Wind and Sea Scale for Fully Arisen Sea[a]

Wind Speed (knots)	Wave Height—Feet Average	Significant Average 1/3 Highest	Average 1/10 Highest	Average Period	Average Wave Length	Minimum Fetch (nautical miles)	Minimum Duration (hours)	Average Wave Height[b] (maximum)
0	0	0	0	—	—	—	—	—
2	0.05	0.08	0.10	0.5	10 in.	5	18 min	
5	0.18	0.29	0.37	1.4	6.7 ft	8	39 min	
8.5	0.6	1.0	1.2	2.4	20	9.8	1.7 hrs	2(3)
10	0.88	1.4	1.8	2.9	27	10	2.4	
13.5	1.8	2.9	3.7	3.9	52	24	4.8	3½(5)
16	2.9	4.6	5.8	4.6	71	40	6.6	
18	3.8	6.1	7.8	5.1	90	55	8.3	
19	4.3	6.9	8.7	5.4	99	65	9.2	6(8½)
20	5.0	8.0	10	5.7	111	75	10	
22	6.4	10	13	6.3	134	100	12	
24.5	8.2	13	17	7.0	164	140	15	9½(13)
26	9.6	15	20	7.4	188	180	17	
28	11	18	23	7.9	212	230	20	
30.5	14	23	29	8.7	258	290	24	13½(19)
32	16	26	33	9.1	285	340	27	
34	19	30	38	9.7	322	420	30	
37	23	37	46.7	10.5	376	530	37	18(25)
40	28	45	58	11.4	444	710	42	
42	31	50	64	12.0	492	830	47	
44	36	58	73	12.5	534	960	52	23(32)
46	40	64	81	13.1	590	1110	57	
48	44	71	90	13.8	650	1250	63	
50	49	78	99	14.3	700	1420	69	
51.5	52	83	106	14.7	736	1560	73	29(41)
54	59	95	121	15.4	810	1800	81	
56	64	103	130	16.3	910	2100	88	
59.5	73	116	148	17.0	985	2500	101	37(52)
>64	>80	>128	>164	18	~	~	~	45(−)

[a] To attain a fully arisen sea for a certain wind speed, the wind must blow at that speed over a minimum distance (fetch) for a minimum time (duration). When winds are 50 knots or more, the required fetch and duration for a fully arisen sea rarely occur. The wave heights shown in the last column, "Average Wave Height" represent what will be found on the average at given wind speeds.
Wave heights refer only to wind waves, and swells from distant or old storms are nearly always superimposed on the wind-wave pattern.
Practical Methods of Observing and Forecasting Ocean Waves, Pierson, Neuman, James, H.O. Pub. 603, 1955.
[b] H.O. 118A.

the temperature of the water brought on deck in a bucket. Sea surface temperatures are also provided by infrared sensors on satellites. Water temperature is important in the forecasting of fog, clouds, mixed layer depth, and other phenomena.

18.13 Marine Automatic Weather Stations   To fill the gaps in key ocean areas, seagoing automatic weather stations are being developed. The U.S. Navy pioneered one version called NOMAD (Figure 18.6) which was tested in the Alaskan Gulf, Gulf of Mexico and off the Virginia Capes.

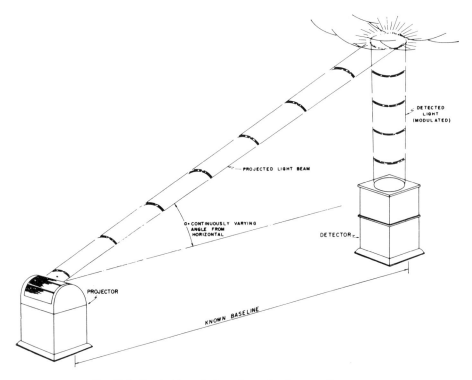

Fig. 18.5 Typical installation of rotating beam ceilometer.

The Gulf of Mexico test included successful use of a nuclear device to provide power for radio transmissions and instrument operation.

These automatic stations relay weather observations every six hours, and every hour if the winds are over 21 knots. Winds, temperature, and pressure are now included in the reports, with humidity to be added later.

Later model buoys will provide oceanographic as well as meteorological information, water temperatures from 24 selected levels between the water surface and a depth of 1000 feet. Also, an inertial device is being developed to provide information on wave and swell height.

The National Oceanic and Atmospheric Administration (NOAA) has charge of the national buoy program, and is actively engaged in research and development in cooperation with other maritime nations and the World Meteorological Organization.

18.14 Temperature, Humidity, and Pressure at High Levels The *radiosonde* is an instrument which is used to obtain the pressure, temperature, and humidity at various levels above the earth's surface.

Fig. 18.6   Naval oceanographic meteorological automatic device (NOMAD)

Only a limited number of land stations and ships are equipped to make this type of weather observation known as a RAOB. The instrument consists of a container with elements for determining the pressure, temperature, and humidity of the upper air and with a battery-operated radio transmitter by means of which the measurements are transmitted to a receiver located at the meteorological station. The instrument is carried aloft by a free balloon to heights consistently near 100,000 feet and many times between 100,000 and 150,000 feet. When the balloon bursts, the radiosonde descends by means of a parachute.

Information obtained by means of RAOBs is made use of immediately in the preparation of weather maps and charts.

Weather reconnaissance flights often use a *dropsonde* to obtain upper air data. This instrument is similar to the radiosonde and is parachuted to the earth from the aircraft. The aircraft orbits within signal reading distance of the dropsonde and collects the data transmitted in a manner similar to that of the radiosonde receiver.

18.15   Rocketsondes   As the space age emerges, the requirements for high-level atmospheric information increase rapidly. Environmental factors are of importance in the design, launching, and reentry of missiles and space systems. For design of missiles and space systems, information is needed as to the mean conditions of density, temperature, and wind in the 100,000 to 350,000 foot layer. (Radiosondes and Rawins give the information from surface to 100,000 feet.) Research for systems of the future require that the level be raised to 600,000 feet.

Meteorological and geophysical satellites provide atmospheric information in the horizontal at flight level. Rockets provide density, wind, and temperature information in the vertical—reliably to 200,000 feet, less reliably above this. Temperature and density to 100,000 feet are obtained from bead thermistors. Between 100,000 and 200,000 feet two methods are employed. In one, a sphere of known displacement is inflated at about 250,000 feet. It reaches terminal velocity after falling to 200,000 feet, and is tracked by precision radar to collapse-point near 100,000 feet. Density is calculated from the rate of descent, temperature from the density, and winds are read directly. Another method uses a parachute, ejected at high levels and carrying bead thermistors. Here, the temperature is a direct input, density is computed from temperature and, again, winds are determined directly from the radar track.

Above 200,000 feet, the measurement problem increases in difficulty. Methods under development include (1) measurements by a ram air gauge; (2) release of small grenades at 2-mile intervals, which make it possible to determine time of travel and direction of sound waves; and (3) falling spheres (as already described).

18.16 Weather Satellites   The newest means of obtaining information about the state of the atmosphere is from weather satellites, which operate in two ways. Some circle the earth at altitudes over 400 miles and transmit pictures of the earth and its cloud cover along a path 750 to 1000 miles wide. Others are placed in an earth-synchronous orbit at about 22,000 miles high over the equator; they are stationary with respect to a chosen longitude, and provide pictures of almost half of the earth. Figure 18.7 illustrates how the cloud patterns of whole storms can now be seen. In addition to daylight pictures, weather satellites are equipped with infrared radiometers which, by sensing the differences in heat radiation from the earth and the clouds, make it possible to determine cloud patterns at night.

Research on how to obtain maximum use of satellite data is progressing well. Previously, the meteorologist's methods were based upon looking upward at cloud systems from scattered observation points; now, he must learn to use continuous data with a view from the top.

Fig. 18.7 The earth as seen by the applications technology satellite from an altitude of 22,240 statute miles. *(Courtesy of NASA.)*

Already, operational use can be made of the pictures which show configuration and location of extratropical and tropical cyclones, presence or absence of clouds, and location of jet streams. Vertical temperature structure of the atmosphere and sea surface temperatures are other operationally useful satellite products. Hurricanes and typhoons have been discovered and tracked by satellites in a few cases. The particular value of satellites in tropical areas is the discovery of hurricanes and typhoons in the incipient stage. Reconnaissance aircraft can then be sent to the suspicious areas to make a thorough investigation. Research is now under way, the results of which may make it possible to use satellite observations to determine with accuracy the intensity of storms, cloud thickness, state of the sea, and surface winds, and to be able to monitor movement and changing configuration of ice packs. A further use of weather satellites will be as collectors and transmitters of data from outlying manned or automatic weather stations, weather and oceanographic buoys, and instrumented balloons floating freely at known atmospheric levels.

18.17   Transmission of Weather Observations   By international agreement, the ships of all maritime nations use the same code for the transmission of weather reports by radio. A coded ship weather message consists of a series of seven, or more five-digit numbers, the number of groups depending upon whether an abbreviated, or a full message is sent. Coded reports from ships differ slightly from land station messages because ships must report their position by latitude and longitude. Ship reports usually consist of the first seven groups of a full weather message. This is known as an abbreviated message, and the symbols of these groups are as follows:

99	$L_aL_aL_a$	$Q_cL_oL_oL_oL_o$	$YYGGi_w$	Nddff	VVwwW	PPPTT	$N_hC_Lh C_MC_H$
99	384	31587	28183	61820	94100	11558	44620

The top line shows the symbols that stand for the data which is to be coded and transmitted by radio. The second line is the coded message ready to be transmitted as six numbers of five digits each. The meaning of the symbols and the digits shown in the sample report above is as follows:

99	Indicator for recognition of a ship weather report
$L_aL_aL_a$	The latitude of the ship when the observation was made; 384 is the code for 38.4 degrees
Q_c	Quarter of the globe to which ship's latitude and longitude refer: 7 = N and W; 1 = N and E; 5 = S and W; 3 = S and E
$L_oL_oL_oL_o$	The longitude; 1587 is the code for 158.7 degrees
YY	The day of the month based on GMT; 28 is code for 28th day of the month
GG	The Greenwich Mean time at which the observation was taken, to the nearest hour on the 24 hour scale; 18 is the code for 1800 GMT
i_w	Wind units and method of determination indicator; 3 is code for wind speed estimated in knots
N	Total amount of cloud; 6 means that six-eighths of the sky is covered by clouds.
dd	The true direction, in tens of degrees, from which the wind is blowing; 18 means that the wind is blowing from 180 degrees.
ff	The wind speed in knots; the number 20 in the code stands for the wind speed in knots.
VV	The visibility or horizontal distance at which objects can be seen in daylight or at which lights can be seen at night; 94 stands for ½ nautical mile (1000 meters).
ww	The present weather at the time of observation; the figure 10 stands for light fog, visibility 1000 meters (1100 yards) or more.
W	Past weather; the digit 0 means that the weather within the six-hour period immediately preceding the observation was clear, or only a few clouds were present.
PPP	The barometric pressure, in millibars and tenths (initial 9 or 10 omitted). The values refer to sea level and include all corrections for index errors, temperature and gravity; 115 stands for 1011.5 millibars.

TT	The air temperature, in whole degrees Centigrade (Celsius).
N_h	Fraction of celestial dome covered by low clouds. If there are no low clouds, report that fraction covered by middle clouds.
C_L	Clouds of types stratocumulus, stratus, cumulus, and cumulonimbus; 4 refers to stratocumulus formed by the spreading out of cumulus; cumulus also often present.
h	The height of base of low cloud above the sea (or ground); 6 means 3500 to 5000 feet.
C_M	Clouds of types altocumulus, altostratus, and nimbostratus; 2 stands for thick altostratus or nimbostratus.
C_H	Clouds of types cirrus, cirrostratus, and cirrocumulus; 0 means that there are no high clouds present.

18.18   The Use of Weather Reports

Ship and land stations, regardless of location, observe and record weather conditions simultaneously every six hours, starting at midnight Greenwich time. The reports are transmitted by landline or radio to collection and control centers, and there further relayed so as to reach all users in the shortest possible time. These reports are used for the preparation of weather charts, from which forecasts are made. The forecasts are transmitted on assigned frequencies and at specified times to any party that can receive the broadcast. In addition to forecasts, a general description of the weather map is also broadcast, along with selected surface reports from which a ship may prepare its own weather map if it so desires. Advancements in radio facsimile have made it possible to broadcast facsimiles of the current weather maps in picture form. Many merchant ships and a great number of military ships are equipped to copy this form of transmission.

Complete weather broadcast schedules for various parts of the world are contained in the following publications: Worldwide Marine Weather Broadcasts, issued jointly by NOAA and the Navy; Marine Weather Services Charts, published by NOAA; and Information for Shipping, Publication No. 9. TP 4 (Volume D) published by the World Meteorological Organization.

18.19   Plotting Reports on the Weather Map

Persons who regularly receive and decode reports soon learn to do so with very little reference to code tables. An element—for example, wind force—always occupies the same position in the same code group. If a weather element is missing for any reason, the observer who makes up the report

NOTE: For a more complete description of marine weather codes and observational practices consult the NOAA Publication: Weather Service Observing Handbook No. 1: Marine Surface Observations.

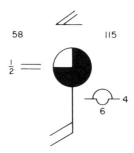

Fig. 18.8 Abbreviated weather message as it would be entered on a weather map.

at the point of origin always fills in the space which the element would ordinarily occupy in the message with the solidus (1).

Figure 18.8 shows the station model used for plotting on a weather map the data of the ship's report appearing on page 584. First, the position of the ship is located on the chart, and a small circle is drawn there. The various weather elements of the report are then arranged at definite positions with reference to the circle. By using the same position for the same element each time there is then no question as to what element a figure represents. The circle is usually filled in first to represent the amount of the sky that is covered by clouds. Next, the arrow shaft is drawn to represent the wind direction. The shaft is always extended toward the direction from which the wind blows. The wind force is represented by feathers or barbs at the end of the shaft. One half of a barb stands for 5 knots, and one long barb stands for 10 knots. In Fig. 18-8 the wind force is 20 knots. Once the arrow shaft is drawn, the other elements may be recorded. If the arrow were to be drawn in last, it might extend through some of the other data with the danger of obliterating part of them.

Symbols are used to depict the wind direction and force, cloud forms, the present and past state of the weather, and the amount of clouds covering the sky. Coded figures represent the amount of sky covered by low clouds. The elements represented directly by figures are the temperature, visibility and the pressure (tens and units of millibars).

18.20 Criteria for Wind Warnings *Wind Warning Terminology in Common Usage by NOAA and the U.S. Navy* Warnings of winds associated with closed cyclonic circulations of tropical origin are expressed in the following terms:

Types of Warning	*Corresponding Wind Speed*
Tropical depression	Winds up to 33 knots
Tropical storm	Winds between 34 and 63 knots
Hurricane/typhoon	Winds of 64 knots or greater

Warnings of winds associated with weather systems located in latitudes outside tropical regions, or by systems of tropical origin other than closed cyclonic circulations, will be expressed in the following terms:

Types of Warning and Advisory	Corresponding Wind Speed
Small craft advisory	Winds up to 33 knots (use in coastal and inland waters only)
Gale warning	Winds between 34 and 47 knots
Storm warning	Winds of 48 knots or greater

Wind Warning Terminology Used by NOAA for Coastal Warning Displays   Warnings of winds for coastal display purposes are issued by NOAA in accordance with the following criteria:

Types of Warning	Corresponding Wind Speed
Small craft warning	Winds up to 33 knots
Gale warning	Winds between 34 and 47 knots
Storm warning	Winds between 48 and 63 knots
Hurricane warning	Winds of 64 knots or greater

Weather of the
Middle Latitudes

19.1 Introduction The middle latitudes of the Northern Hemisphere, lying between tropical and polar regions, have a temperate climate that is favorable to man.

There are more people in the mid-latitudes, and there is more "weather." Weather patterns in the tropics and in polar regions tend to occur in more or less dependable patterns, which is not the case in the middle latitudes.

In the region of the middle latitudes masses of air moving northward from the tropics and southward from polar regions tend to converge and create various types of weather fronts. The reaction of these air masses with each other and with the land and water surfaces of the earth causes the constant weather changes which characterize the middle latitudes of both hemispheres. Widespread areas of low and high pressure drift eastward in the prevailing westerlies of these latitudes, alternately bringing changes in weather conditions.

This chapter deals with the air masses, fronts, and high- and low-pressure systems of the middle latitudes. The preparation and use of weather maps are described, and general principles for forecasting weather from surface weather maps and from local indications are given. In addition to the surface weather maps, professional meteorologists construct and use many other maps, charts, and graphs which show pressure, humidity, temperature, and wind conditions in the upper portions of the atmosphere. These data are used in forecasting and in aircraft operation. The recent development of new instruments and techniques for gathering and interpreting atmospheric conditions at various elevations above the earth's surface has enabled the meteorologist to gain a better understanding of present weather conditions and to forecast changes more effectively than would be possible with only the use of the surface weather map.

19.2 The Meaning and Classification of Air Masses   An air mass is a large body of air whose physical properties, particularly temperature and moisture distribution, are nearly homogeneous in the horizontal. One of the most important elements of forecasting is recognizing the various air masses in the weather picture, determining their characteristics, and predicting their behavior.

When a large body of air remains for some time over a locality, it acquires the characteristics of that region. For example, air that stands for several days or weeks over northern Canada during the winter becomes cold. It will have low moisture content, both because of its coldness and because of the absence of water at the earth's surface from which vapor could be received. It would be described as a cold, dry mass of polar continental air, and the region where it acquired those characteristics is known as the source region (Fig. 19.1). On the other hand, a body of air which stagnates over the Gulf of Mexico for some time acquires the warmth of those waters, and it will acquire a large content of water vapor because of the ready evaporation induced by the large capacity of warm air for vapor. Such a body of air would be known as a warm, moist mass of tropical air. In this case the source region, the Gulf of Mexico, is tropical maritime.

Air masses are classified according to their sources, which may be arctic, polar, tropical, or monsoon. They are further classified as to their moisture content. Masses whose source regions are over the ocean are known as maritime air masses and are moist or high in water vapor content. Those originating over land areas are known as continental masses and are relatively dry or low in water vapor content. A further classification depends on whether an air mass, once it starts to move about, is warmer or colder than the surface over which it is moving. For example, a mass which moves northward over the Gulf states from the Gulf of Mexico would be classed as a warm mass in winter because land surfaces of those states in winter are colder than the waters of the Gulf. However, in summer

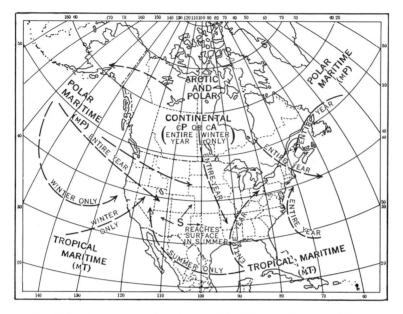

Fig. 19.1   Air mass types that visit the United States. *(Courtesy of CAB.)*

the mass would be classed as cold because then the land surfaces are warmer than the water surfaces.

19.3   Weather in Warm and Cold Air Masses   Warm and cold air masses may occur in either summer or winter months. Weather associated with these air masses is a function of the temperature differential between the air mass and the underlying surface. A cold air mass will absorb heat and moisture from below, the lapse rate will steepen, and heat and moisture will be conducted to higher levels. The typical weather associated with a cold air mass is good visibility, turbulent and gusty winds, cumuliform clouds, showers, and, in severe cases, thunderstorms. Conversely, a warm air mass will surrender heat to the surface, and the coldest air is found in the layers near the ground or water. This stable stratification means that there is no tendency for the air to rise and mix, and the associated weather consists of layer-type clouds, fog, drizzle, poor visibilities, and steady or calm winds.

19.4   Oceans, Ocean Currents, and Weather   The oceans and their currents have a very strong stabilizing influence on temperatures over most of the world. The oceans can stabilize temperatures because of water's great specific heat capacity.

The moderating influences of the oceans are carried around the world by air masses and ocean currents. Figure 19.2 shows the general pattern of ocean currents throughout the world. Comparison with Figures 19.14 and 19.15 shows that the direction of flow of ocean currents tends to coincide with the prevailing winds of the world.

Ocean currents distribute huge quantities of warm and cold water over thousands of miles. The warm currents prevent the great north-south temperature contrasts we would have otherwise. In the North Atlantic, the Gulf Stream is a predominant feature. Its cold counterpart is the Labrador Current, which starts in the Arctic Ocean, and passes south and southeastward past the Grand Banks, thence to the mid-Atlantic states of the United States. In the North Pacific, the current system is quite similar. The Japan Current brings warm water toward the Gulf of Alaska, and there is a cool current along the east coast of Asia. In the Southern Hemisphere, the cold polar current is mainly from east to west, although there are numerous branches along the west coasts of South Africa and South America. The general effect in the Northern Hemisphere is to have cold east coasts, warm west coasts north of 40 degrees N, warm east coasts, cool west coasts south of this latitude.

The Gulf Stream illustrates how ocean currents affect weather and climate. It flows through the Straits of Florida, where it unites with the Antilles Current. The combined current flows northward at three to four knots along the Atlantic coast, then up to Nova Scotia and Newfoundland. The Gulf Stream air masses usually do not penetrate the East Coast because of the prevailing westerly winds, but the warm waters of the Gulf Stream serve as an active breeding ground for many of the severe storms which cause heavy rains, snows, and strong winds over the Seaboard states. Also, the Gulf Stream serves as a path for many hurricanes.

At the Grand Banks of Newfoundland, where the Gulf Stream meets the cold Labrador Current, the world-famous fogs occur. Soon after this, the Gulf Stream current divides into several branches. One flows toward the west coast of Greenland, where it greatly modifies the climate of the southwest coast—so much so that Eric the Red led his fellow Norsemen there to settle. Another branch flows toward Iceland, where it mellows the climate somewhat before losing itself in the Norwegian Sea. The main branch of the Gulf Stream passes straight eastward, dividing again soon. The southern branch turns southeastward, skirting the coasts of southwest Europe and Africa as a cold current before returning to the tropics to start the long journey over again. The northern division of the current, hurried along by the strong winds of the Icelandic Low, washes the shores of west and

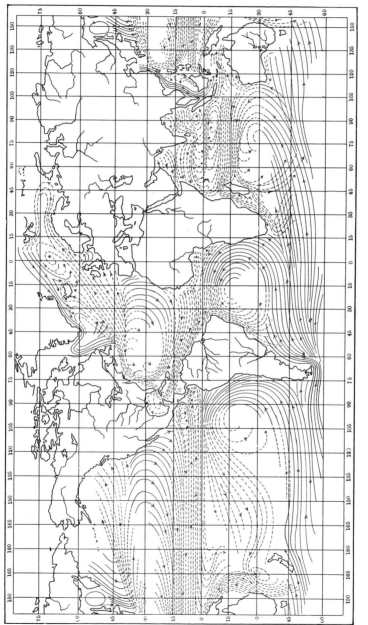

Fig. 19.2 Ocean currents—cold, solid lines; warm, dotted lines (Courtesy of NOAA.)

northwest Europe with the warmest waters to be found anywhere at latitudes this high. The current goes into the North Sea and along the west coast of Norway, contributing a strong mellowing influence on Norway's climate, and throwing off eddies of warm water into the Norwegian Sea to influence the weather there. The current then goes past North Cape as far as Murmansk, so famous in World War II as an ice-free port. One branch of the current keeps the west coast of Spitzbergen ice-free in summer, a coast only 800 miles from the North Pole. Even after the current sinks below the fresher waters of the Arctic Sea, it still provides enough heat through the ice to make the area much warmer than comparable Antarctic latitudes.

19.5 Fronts   Adjacent air masses with different qualities of temperature and humidity do not tend to mix readily. The cold masses are heavy and the warm masses light, so the warmer of two converging currents tends to overrun the colder. The polar front is the surface between the converging southwesterly winds of middle latitudes and the prevailing northeasterlies of polar regions. The latter form a wedge over which the winds from the south ascend. A frontal surface, then, is the boundary between two masses of air of dissimilar properties. A surface front is the area where this boundary intersects the ground. In general, there are four kinds of fronts: cold, warm, occluded, and stationary. All types are watched closely on weather maps because it is along them that the poorest weather conditions occur, and frequent and rapid changes from one type of weather to another take place in their vicinity.

19.6 Warm Fronts   Figure 19.3 shows a west-east, vertical cross section through the atmosphere. To the right is a mass of cool air which

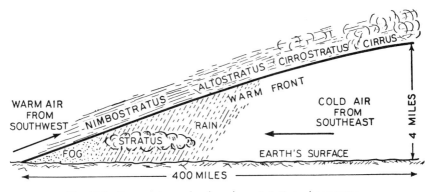

Fig. 19.3 Temperature, cloud, and precipitation phenomena.

is flowing from the southeast; on the left is a warm air mass flowing from the southwest. As the currents are converging, the warm stream is forced to ascend the cool barrier. It is assumed that the system as a whole is drifting from west to east, as is customary for atmospheric disturbances in the temperate zone of middle latitudes. It is further assumed that the warm current has a reasonably high relative humidity. The slope of the wedge is exaggerated in the figure in order to show clearly the processes involved. Actually the ratio of slopes of warm fronts averages about 1 mile in the vertical to 100 miles horizontally, but will sometimes be as high as 1 to 300 miles. As the warm air stream rises over the wedge of cold air, it expands and cools adiabatically, which results in the formation of the various cloud types shown.

The figure shows a situation which is quite typical of warm fronts that occur in the United States and other portions of the middle latitudes. Warm front areas often cover hundreds of square miles—in fact, whole states or groups of states. Cloud ceilings are low because of the presence of nimbostratus clouds over wide areas, and visibilities may be poor due to the presence of rain or drizzle and fog. Where temperatures in the cloud and rain areas are near freezing, icing on aircraft is prevalent.

Warm front flying is generally smooth, except when unstable warm air is involved. In this case, thunderstorms and other turbulent clouds will form in the warm air above the frontal surface. In fact, any cloud type may appear along a warm front under various conditions. During late fall and early spring, frozen rain (sleet) may form in the rain curtain under the front when raindrops falling from above are frozen in the cold air of the wedge.

19.7 Cold Fronts   A west-east, vertical cross section through the atmosphere showing a typical cold front of the middle latitudes appears in Fig. 19.4. At the left in the figure is shown a wedge of cold air advancing from the northwest. It is underrunning and forcing upward a stream of warm, moist air that flows from the southwest. The system is drifting toward the east. As in the illustration of the warm front, the wedge is exaggerated so that the principles involved will stand out clearly. Cold fronts are usually steeper than warm fronts, with slopes ranging from 1/50 to 1/150. Even when the slopes are similar to those of warm fronts, the leading edge of the cold front is much steeper because of the effect of surface friction on the advancing cold air.

As in the case of the warm front, weather is poor along the cold front, but it is a different type of weather, because the greater steep-

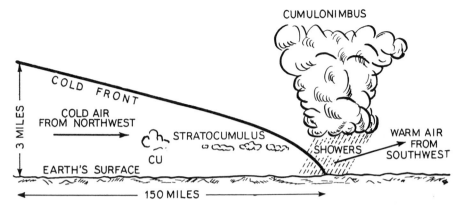

Fig. 19.4 Cold front wind, temperature, cloud, and precipitation phenomena.

ness and speed of the cold front makes it act more violently in forcing the warm air upward, with resulting formation of clouds and precipitation. Warm air is nosed upward by the leading edge of the cold wedge, and cumulus rather than stratus clouds form. The cloud tops commonly reach quite high and often develop into cumulonimbus. Precipitation types are rain showers and often heavy hail or snow flurries. Cold front cloud and precipitation areas are narrow horizontally as compared with those of the warm front. The air is usually rough up to an elevation of 6000 feet, and it may be turbulent to heights of 20,000 feet or more when thunderstorms are present, which is quite common. At levels where the temperature is at or below freezing, aircraft icing will be encountered, and visibilities and ceilings are unfavorable for contact flight in the cloud and precipitation region.

In the cold air immediately behind the front, stratocumulus or cumulus clouds often prevail over mountainous or moist areas. They form as the cold air moves rapidly over ground previously heated by the presence of the warm air ahead of the front.

Before considering occluded fronts let us examine an extratropical cyclone and note the relationships which exist betweeen various kinds of air masses and fronts which may be found in an extratropical cyclone, or low.

19.8 Extratropical Cyclones   Figure 19.5 shows the air masses, fronts, clouds, precipitation, and winds which are a part of an extratropical cyclone, also known as a depression, low-pressure area, or simply as a low. The figure represents an idealized model as visualized by the Norwegian meteorologist J. Bjerknes, and it shows the low in one particular stage of its development. The center sketch shows a

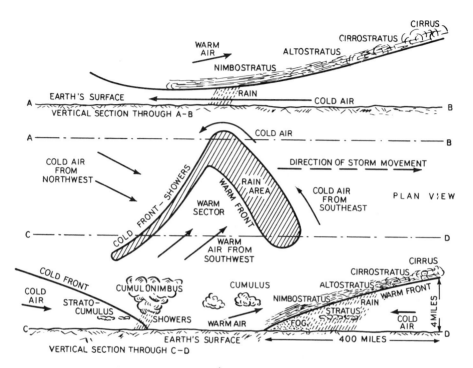

Fig. 19.5 A plan view and two vertical sections of an extratropical cyclone. Hatched portions in the plan view show where rain is occurring. *(After Bjerknes.)*

plan view. At the top of the figure appears a vertical section of the low taken through the line A–B; the bottom diagram is a vertical section taken through the line C–D. Looking back at the plan view we note the warm front where warm air from the so-called warm sector is converging and ascending with cold air to the right. A cold front exists where cold air at the left is under-running air in the warm sector. A broken arrow pointing to the right at the middle of the figure indicates that the entire formation, that is the low, is moving toward the right, or east. The shaded portion shows where rain is occurring. Cloud types are not shown in the plan view.

The vertical section through C–D, which is shown on the lower portion of the figure, helps to explain what is happening in the upper air. It will be noted that cumulonimbus clouds are shown at the cold front; altocumulus clouds also are often present there. In the cross section through A–B the warm air does not touch the earth's surface but is riding up over the cold air which is sweeping around toward the west. If we look back at the middle and lower views, the broad area of rain at the warm front and the narrow band of rain along the cold front are evident.

19.9   Formation and Occlusion of Extratropical Cyclones   The life history of a depression is shown in Fig. 19.6. A stationary front such as the polar front is shown in (a) with cold air flowing toward the west while warm air flows toward the east. In (b) the front has ceased

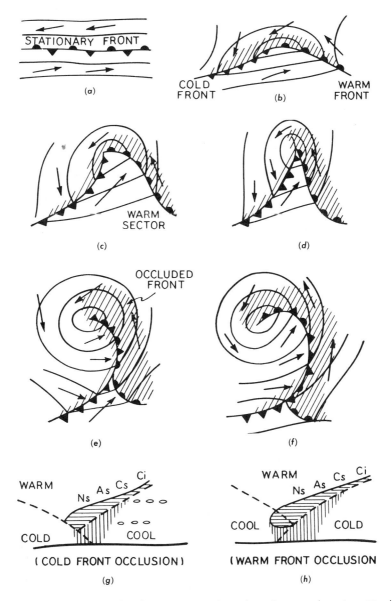

Fig. 19.6 Development of a depression. Horizontal section, or plan view. Hatched areas are precipitation areas.

to be straight, possibly because pressure is being exerted at the left side of the figure by a mass of cold air to the north. A definite cold and warm frontal system has developed, and the arrows show that the wind has commenced to blow in a counterclockwise direction around a center of lower pressure. The hatched areas indicate that cloudiness and precipitation have begun. This development is known as a wave that has formed along the stationary front, and the wave will move from left to right along the front in much the same manner as an ocean wave. The cyclone has reached a normal stage of development in (c). The cold front advances faster than the warm front, and in (d) has overtaken the warm front in the vicinity of the center of the depression; the dying-out or occlusion of the cyclone has begun. The process from this stage onward resembles, in fluid motion, the breaking of an ocean wave. Further occlusion has taken place in (e) and (f); under these conditions cloudiness and precipitation continue but in diminishing amounts. Occlusion, if it continues, results in the obliteration or filling up of the depression.

Two distinct types of occluded fronts are shown in (g) and (h). When the cold front caught up with the warm front, the air in (g) to the left was colder than that at the right, and therefore it underran the latter as shown. The warm sector has been squeezed above the ground level. Precipitation continues at and behind the surface front, and it is chiefly that of the showery type such as is found along cold fronts. In (h), which shows the warm-front type of occlusion, the air to the left is not as cold as that at the right. The cool air, therefore, is shown to be rising over the cold air, and precipitation continues at and ahead of the surface front; it is the steady rain or drizzle typical of warm fronts.

19.10   Extratropical Cyclone Weather   Assume that the low shown in Fig. 19.7 is moving east-northeast at 600 miles per day, and that the center passes north of the ship at point A. The first indication of the approaching storm is a falling barometer, which will continue to fall, and more rapidly, until the warm front passes. Along with the pressure fall, cirrus clouds usually appear, and these thicken in a few hours to cirrostratus. If the overruning air is unstable or turbulent, cirrocumulus will occur along with the cirrostratus, forming the "mackerel sky" so often mentioned in sailing-ship lore. Winds are southerly and increasing. The waves start to build up, along with the wind, and are superimposed on a southwesterly swell moving out from the area of the storm center.

When the warm front is about 300 miles away, altostratus clouds are predominant; sometimes they are mixed with altocumulus. Precip-

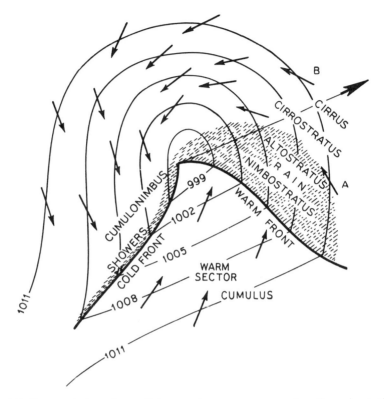

Fig. 19.7 Extratropical cyclone. Rain or showers are occurring throughout the shaded area.

itation, rain or snow, can start at any time when the warm front is 200 to 300 miles distant. Winds and waves continue to increase, with the winds backing more and more into the southeast. After the precipitation starts, the rain or snow becomes heavier, the clouds thicker and lower (becoming nimbostratus, and sometimes stratocumulus). Often, there is low stratus or fog when falling rain saturates the cold air underneath the front, and there may be cumulonimbus clouds above the front. Winds and waves continue to build, winds up to 45 knots in a strong storm, and waves 25 to 35 feet with an occasional high one up to 50 feet.

As the warm front passes, the winds shift from southeast to southwest; the temperature rises rapidly; cloudiness decreases or vanishes altogether; precipitation stops; the barometer steadies and remains so through the warm sector. Winds will usually be lighter and seas lower.

As the cold front approaches, the southerly wind flow increases and

Fig. 19.8 Cold front cloud. *(Official U.S. Navy photograph.)*

high cumuliform clouds will darken the horizon to the west and northwest (Fig. 19.8). When the front arrives, there are heavy showers, often thunderstorms, strong gusty winds, and confused seas. The wind shifts sharply from south or southwest to a direction between west and north; the barometer rises rapidly; the temperature drops sharply. Usually, there is rapid clearing behind the cold front. Waves will now come from the northwest and increase rapidly—sometimes up to 35 feet in six hours. The seas will then subside gradually, although it will sometimes be two days before they drop below 10 feet.

Suppose now that the low center passes south of a ship located at point B. Figure 19.7 shows that point B will not encounter the warm and cold fronts, so the weather sequence will be quite different from that at point A. The first indications of the approach of the low are cirrus clouds, a shift in wind direction to the east, and a downward trend of the barometer. As the low moves closer, cirrostratus clouds replace the cirrus, the wind continues from the east, and the barometer contines downward. Presently altrostratus clouds replace cirrostratus clouds, and steady, light rain begins; the wind continues from the east; the barometer falls further. As the low progresses east-northeastward, the wind shifts to northeast and then to north, with nimbostratus clouds replacing the altostratus. Eventually the wind shifts to northwest; the barometer begins to rise; the sky gradually clears; the precipitation ceases. The low has passed to the eastward, and fine, clear weather prevails.

The description above is of an idealized low. Actually, lows vary as much as people do. Some are of large diameter, well over 1000 miles; some are small, 400 to 500 miles. Some have heavy precipitation; other have little. Cloud forms may not follow the conventional pattern. However, wind, temperature, and pressure nearly always follow a predictable pattern, particularly at sea.

19.11 Distribution and Movement of Lows   Extratropical cyclones (lows) form along fronts, and hence occur with greatest frequency in the higher mid-latitudes where the cold and warm air masses meet along the Polar and Arctic fronts. In the Northern Hemisphere, there is a maximum frequency of lows at 50 degrees N in winter, 60 degrees N in summer. In the Pacific, there is a broad band of frequent cyclone activity from southeast Asia to the Gulf of Alaska. In the cold season, these storms become very intense, and usually move northeastward to accumulate in the Gulf of Alaska. Some storms which form on the mid-Pacific polar front take a more southerly track and reach the coast as far south as Southern California.

On the Atlantic side, the most favored region for low development is the Virginia Coast and general area east of the southern Appalachians. These, often called Hatteras storms, are frequently very intense. They move northeasterly along the Gulf Stream and eventually stagnate near Iceland, or in the waters between Greenland and Labrador.

Figure 20.1a shows preferred tracks of mid-latitude lows.

The rate of movement in summer is about 500 miles per day; in winter it is somewhat faster, probably averaging 700 miles in 24 hours, but there are many variations. At times an extratropical cyclone may slow down and remain stationary over an area, while at other times a section of the country may be subjected to a series of lows which move along quickly one after the other. They are more stormy and sharply defined in winter than in summer.

19.12 Anticyclones   Anticyclones (Fig. 19.9) are areas of high pressure; their name is derived from the fact that the wind within them blows clockwise and outward, opposite to that of cyclones.

The subtropical anticyclones, centered around the world at 30 degrees latitude, are very persistent at all times of the year. They move little or not at all. The migratory anticyclones, or highs, alternate with

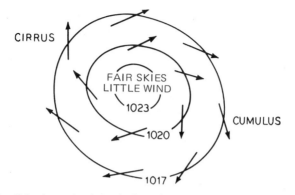

Fig. 19.9 An anticyclone, high, and associated weather elements.

lows in a regular parade across the oceans and across the United States. In North America, the likely regions for initial development of highs are Alaska and western Canada to the east of the Rocky Mountains. These highs move southeastward toward the Atlantic Coast, lose their identity as they reach the warm Atlantic waters and become absorbed in the subtropical anticyclone.

Cool or cold and fair weather is typical of migrating highs.

Their rate of movement and size are fairly comparable to those of lows. Many highs which invade the United States may be thought of as atmospheric mountains of cold, dense air which have broken away from their northern source regions to drift southward in order to lessen the pressure which builds up in polar areas.

19.13 Preparation of Surface Weather Maps Surface weather maps are prepared four or more times daily at forecasting centers. The technical methods involved are beyond the scope of this book, but enough has been presented to this point to enable the reader to understand and use an already prepared surface chart. These charts are available in daily newspapers, and at sea they are available over several types of broadcasts. Some ships even plot their own weather charts.

The surface weather map does not show conditions that exist in the upper air, such as the direction and velocity of the wind at various heights, cloud levels, turbulence, regions where airplane icing may occur, air stability, temperature and humidity values, and other phenomena important to the forecaster and airplane pilot. Therefore, in addition to the surface map, auxiliary maps and diagrams are prepared. The most useful of these are the constant pressure charts, which depict conditions at several selected upper levels along a constant pressure surface. For example, the 500-millibar charts show wind, temperature, and humidity conditions along this pressure surface, which varies between about 16,500 feet and 19,500 feet. The constant pressure charts are used in forecasting to determine movement of weather systems, wind flow at high levels, jet stream location and intensity, and the development and intensity of pressure systems.

Electronic computers are replacing man on most hand plotting and analysis jobs. In the past decade, there has been rapid advance in the numerical forecasting field, and numerical upper air charts are now of a quality which can be equaled on a routine basis only by a few top analysts.

19.14 Preparation of a Forecast   Once all the weather charts are analyzed, the forecaster has several things to consider before he makes up a forecast. These include:

1. Displacement of fronts and pressure systems.
2. Deepening and filling of pressure systems.
3. Development of new pressure systems and their influence on the existing pattern.
4. Properties of existing air masses, and the changes which might occur with displacement.
5. Local influences, such as mountains, bodies of water, and industrial activity.

Formulas have been developed by meteorologists to solve the problems outlined above. Some of these are derived from theoretical studies which attempt to describe the state of the atmosphere in mathematical terms.

Empirical rules are derived from local observations. Climatological rules must be invoked, and finally the forecaster injects an experience factor.

19.15 Use of Weather Maps and Forecasting at Sea   The seaman can do much to help himself by using weather information, even if it is only what he can see or measure from his own bridge. Before radio came into use, the master of a ship had to rely on what conclusions he could draw from the appearance of the sky, movement of upper clouds, backing and veering of the wind, pressure changes, changes in the state of the sea, and changing visibility. Many seamen became, and are, relatively expert at forecasting weather changes relying simply upon their own observations; naturally, without knowing the state of the upstream weather, there are bound to be some disappointing results (they occur even when forecasters do know the upstream weather). Lacking other information, a seaman can improve upon his local knowledge by asking another ship or two in the general area to send position, present weather, barometric reading, and wind direction and force. With this, he can make a two- or three-point sketch, which will give him a rough estimate of the pressure pattern, intensity of the pressure systems in his area, and possibly, location of fronts.

Normally, ships can copy broadcasts which give them other ships' weather reports, weather maps in coded form, as well as forecasts of weather conditions for the area of concern. Some ships are equipped with radio facsimile equipment, and can copy a great variety of weather and oceanographic charts.

If a ship has forecasts available, it usually need not make its own, since the weather offices ashore have many more reports with which to work, and professional meteorologists to do the forecasting. However, there are many situations where a ship will be in an area which is not adequately covered, and it will be to the ship's advantage to use its own observation, a weather map and to apply forecasting rules. Some of the more reliable rules for use at sea are listed below:

1. Rule of persistence. This involves extrapolating into the future the same rates of movement and changes in intensity of pressure systems which have occurred in the past. The rule is quite reliable for up to six hours, with a gradual loss of reliability thereafter.

2. Troughs of low pressure tend to move with an eastwardly component to the position of the preceding ridge of high pressure, but the speed of movement is quite variable.

3. Lows with a warm sector tend to move in a direction parallel to the warm sector isobars and with a speed of about 80 percent of the warm sector winds.

4. When a low has a large "open" warm sector, deepening may be expected.

5. Rate of deepening will usually increase with the narrowing of the warm sector (**cold front approaching the warm front**) and decrease when the occlusion process is going on.

6. When a low has nearly occluded, it moves less rapidly, and with very large occluded lows, the movement is very slow and irregular.

7. Small lows caught in the circulation of a large system tend to follow the main system.

8. A large low with no fronts will tend to move in the direction of the strongest winds in the circulation.

9. Frontal depressions tend to occur in families, each low following approximately the path of its predecessor but displaced somewhat towards a lower latitude.
10. Lows tend to move around large, warm highs in the direction of the air flow around their boundaries.
11. Occluded cyclones tend to weaken slowly or fill, particularly over a relatively cool surface.
12. Ridges of high pressure between lows tend to move in the same direction and the same speed as the lows themselves.
13. Speed of fronts is determined largely by the wind component perpendicular to the front.
14. A front parallel to the isobars moves slowly or is stationary.
15. Frontal precipitation increases in intensity as the wind shift across the front becomes sharper.
16. Weather activity of cold fronts in subtropical latitudes is more active than in warm fronts. This condition is reversed in polar latitudes.

After the above rules have been applied, and the shipboard forecaster has developed an idea as to what the future weather map will look like, he is ready to make a forecast.

From his knowledge of the weather, gained by study and experience, the mariner uses his prognostic map and his own weather observations to determine future weather conditions. If there is a low approaching, the forecaster determines where the center will pass in relation to his own position and applies typical low-pressure center weather conditions as appropriate. Approaching cold and warm fronts are treated similarly. If the forecaster has temperature readings of air and water for the area, he can estimate the probability of fog occurrence. From the isobaric pattern, he can calculate wind speed and direction. These will provide the necessary information to make a forecast of sea state.

The Tropical Cyclone

20.1 Introduction Tropical cyclones are atmospheric systems, of tropical origin, in which the barometric pressure steadily decreases from the periphery to a minimum at the center, and where the winds spiral inward from all sides (counterclockwise in the Northern Hemisphere). When winds of the cyclonic circulation reach a strength of 64 knots or more near the center, the cyclone will, depending upon its location, be called a hurricane (Atlantic, Gulf of Mexico, Eastern Pacific), a typhoon (Western North Pacific), a baguio (Philippines), willy-willy (Western Australia), or simply a cyclone (Indian Ocean). Tropical storms are the same atmospheric phenomenon, but of lesser intensity—34 to 64 knots.

Mature tropical cyclones are extraordinarily violent. They usually do not involve as large an area as many temperate zone storms, nor do they have the sharply-concentrated, irresistible force of tornadoes. But, they are the most dangerous and destructive of all storms. From hurricanes alone, in an active season, damage may approach two billion dollars, and hundreds, often thousands, of lives and homes are destroyed. Some coastal cities have been destroyed, never to be rebuilt.

Ships at sea must make every effort to avoid tropical cyclones of hurricane or typhoon intensity.

Even a well-found ship in some cases may be in danger of foundering. Masts and superstructures are vulnerable because of the extreme violence of wind and sea. Personnel may be lost overboard or injured by objects adrift. Lifeboats, airplanes, and other exposed objects are most certain to be carried away by the wind and sea. The prudent seaman will find it well worth while to study the nature of the tropical cyclone and to avoid it if possible. Many ships at sea have never encountered a tropical cyclone; if ordinary precautions are used, most ships should never have to pass through a violent one.

20.2 Areas Affected   Regions in which tropical cyclones form and move are shown in Fig. 20.1A and 20.1B. Tracks are shown in the Pacific and Indian oceans both north and south of the equator and in the north Atlantic Ocean. It will be noted that in the Atlantic Ocean south of the equator the tropical cyclone is entirely absent. These storms are unknown in the Arctic and Antaractic oceans.

Generally, tropical cyclones form over the ocean in latitudes between 5° and 20° north and 5° and 20° south. Once formed they may travel distances of hundreds or even thousands of miles before losing their force and finally dissipating; they are the most persistent of all storms, sometimes living three to four weeks. Many tropical cyclones move near to or cross over continental coastal areas, but South America, Europe, and Africa are free from such visitations. In North America the east and west coasts of Mexico and the Central American countries and the states of the Gulf and Atlantic coasts may be affected. China, Japan, India, and the northwestern and northeastern portions of Australia are other regions subject to the tropical cyclone.

Tropical cyclones of the eastern North Pacific may be encountered from May through December off the western coasts of Mexico and Central America. Hurricanes of this region are as violent but usually not so large as those of the North Atlantic.

In the western North Pacific the tropical cyclone may occur during any month of the year, though the months of greatest frequency for this storm in that region are July, August, September, and October. There are over twice as many tropical cyclones per year in the Western Pacific as in the Atlantic, and more or these become giant storms.

20.3 Frequency of Tropical Cyclones   Tropical storms and hurricanes occur with greatest frequency during August, September, and October in the Atlantic. Figure 20.2 shows monthly frequency of an 83-year sample, excluding 2 tropical storms and 1 hurricane in February and

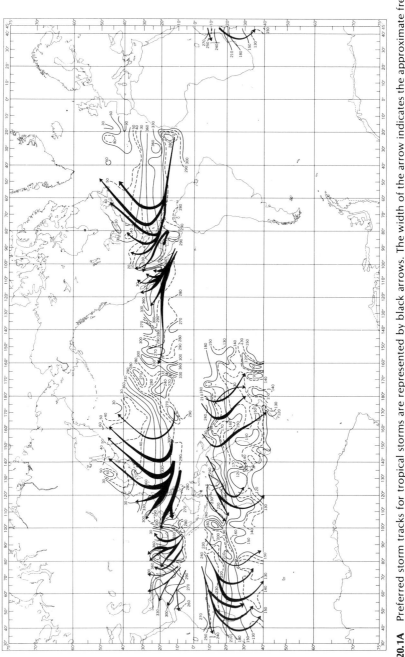

Fig. 20.1A Preferred storm tracks for tropical storms are represented by black arrows. The width of the arrow indicates the approximate frequency of storms; the wider the arrow the higher the frequency. Isolines on the base map show the resultant direction toward which storms moved (Isogons). Data for the entire year have been summarized for this figure. (*Mariners' Worldwide Climactic Guide to Tropical Storms at Sea,* U.S. Navy.)

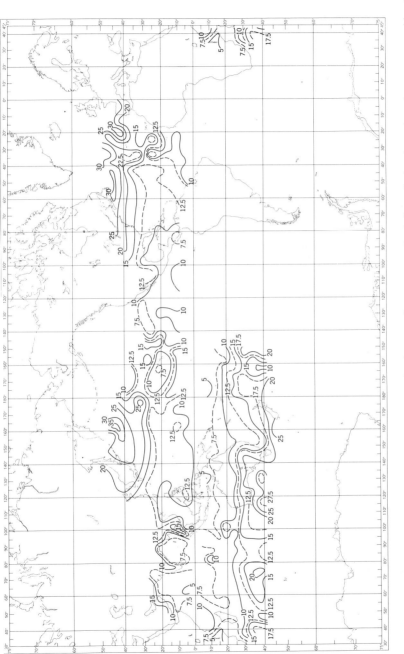

Fig. 20.1B Average speed of storm movements (in knots). In this figure scalar mean speeds of all tropical cyclones have been computed for the entire year. (*Mariners' Worldwide Climactic Guide to Tropical Storms at Sea*, U.S. Navy.)

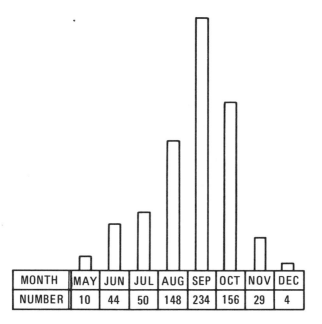

MONTH	MAY	JUN	JUL	AUG	SEP	OCT	NOV	DEC
NUMBER	10	44	50	148	234	156	29	4

Fig. 20.2 The total number of tropical storms and hurricanes, in the North Atlantic is shown by months for the period 1886–1969.

March. Figure 20.3 shows the annual frequency of the same sample; the number per year is quite erratic, ranging from 1 to 21. This figure also shows that there was a maximum, on the average, in the early part of the period, then another starting in the early 1930s. The latter increased frequency has tended to maintain itself ever since, and there are more hurricanes. The average number of hurricanes during the 83-year period is 4, but it is 5 for the past 30 years, and 6 for the past 10 years. This increased number of tropical storms and hurricanes is associated with a gradual warming of the atmosphere and sea during the period. Figures 20.4A and 20.4B trace paths of hurricanes through two preferred "windows" centered at 15°N–71°W and 28°N–86°W.

Tropical cyclones of the Bay of Bengal and the Arabian Sea are more likely to be encountered during May and October than in other months, whereas the season for tropical cyclones of the South Pacific and South Indian Ocean extends from September to May, with the months of January, February, and March having the greatest frequencies.

20.4 Formation of the Tropical Cyclone   It is fortunate that typhoons, hurricanes, and other tropical cyclones are comparatively few in number as compared with their nontropical cousins. With the

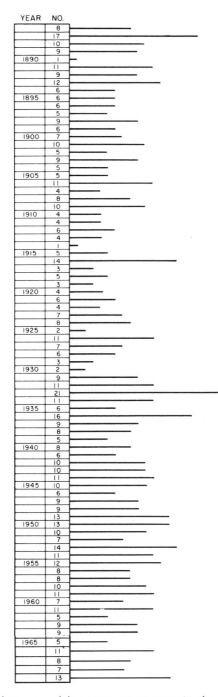

Fig. 20.3 Tropical storm and hurricane occurrences in the North Atlantic for the period 1886–1969.

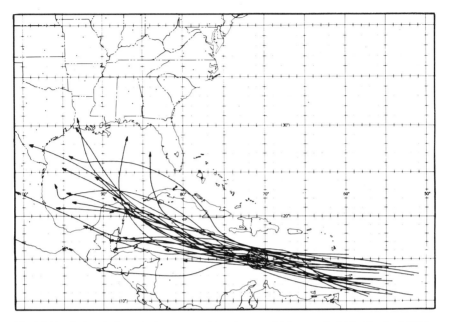

Fig. 20.4A Paths of all tropical storms and hurricanes which passed within 75 mi. of 15°N., 71°W., July 16 through Sept. 20, 1886–1970. (From Hope and Neumann.)

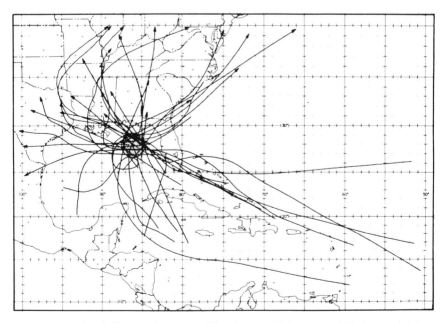

Fig. 20.4B Paths of all tropical storms and hurricanes which passed within 75 mi. of: 28°N., 86°W., July 16 through Sept. 20, 1886–1970. (From Hope and Neumann.)

latter, there are often as many on the weather map in one day as there are hurricanes in a season or two.

Meteorologists have not been able to unravel the mysteries of tropical cyclone formation, although the tropical cyclone is the nearest thing to a simple heat engine to be found among atmospheric disturbances. Day after day, in tropical regions, conditions look just right for cyclones to form from existing disturbances in the trade wind belt —temperatures of air and water warm enough, plenty of moisture, winds of the right speed. Yet, only once in ten times are tropical cyclones born from these fertile-looking patterns, and when they do form the manner varies from storm to storm.

The mean latitude of storm formation moves poleward in the first half of the season and then retreats equatorward. Early- and late-season cyclones form mostly in the belt from 5 to 15 degrees in the Northern Hemisphere, at the height of the season between 10 and 25 degrees. In the Atlantic, there is some cyclogenesis between 25 and 30 degrees N, with a northern limit of 35 degrees N. The great majority of tropical cyclones undergo their principal development in the northeast trade wind current, and not in the doldrums or equatorial trough, as had been thought for so many years.

In addition to the north-south shift of tropical cyclone formation, there is an east-west pattern, particularly so in the Atlantic. Here, a majority of early season (May and June) storms originate in the Gulf of Mexico and western Caribbean. In July and August, the areas of most frequent origin shift eastward, and by September they are located over the large area from the Bahamas southeastward to the Lesser Antilles, and thence eastward to south of the Cape Verde Islands, near the coast of Africa. After mid-September, the principal areas of origin shift back to the western Caribbean and Gulf of Mexico.

20.5 Tropical Cyclone Movement   Tropical cyclones are notorious for their erratic movement. There is a general similarity of movement in the early stages of storm development along the ESE-WNW axis, and all cyclones have a tendency to move eventually toward higher latitudes. But, there is no longitudinal regularity in any turn to the north, and in all track samples there are benders, loopers, double loopers, and wobblers. Also, tropical cyclones have sudden accelerations (as much as 1500 percent in 24 hours), and sudden decelerations; sometimes storms stop suddenly and hold position within a 50-mile circle for as much as three days.

The mean speed of tropical cyclone movement south of 30 degrees N varies, by areas, between 12 to 16 knots. Occasionally, when the subtropical highs are exceptionally strong, hurricanes and typhoons will move toward the west at 20 to 25 knots south of 30 degrees N.

North of 30 degrees N, speed of storm movement is much less predictable. The speed range is from 0 to 60 knots, and acceleration can be pronounced. Disastrous and unexpected results have occurred when hurricanes that were loafing along off the Virginia Capes have suddenly spurted and roared up the coast, sometimes at speeds as high as 70 knots.

Hurricanes and typhoons favor movement over the warmest waters. The Gulf Stream is a good example.

20.6 General Nature The average mature tropical cyclone has an area of hurricane-force winds (64 knots or 75 mph) of a little over 100 miles in diameter, and gale-force (34 to 64 knots) winds over an area 400 miles in diameter. In large hurricanes, these areas may be over 200 miles for hurricane-force winds and 600 miles for gale-force. In a few huge Pacific typhoons, the area of hurricane-force winds has exceeded 300 miles, with gale-force winds covering an area over 1500 miles in diameter. The correlation between maximum winds at the center and the diameter of strong wind area is poor; a gale-force wind 600 miles from the hurricane center does not necessarily mean that winds near the center will be of remarkably high speed. Small storms may be the strongest. For instance, the infamous Florida Keys hurricane in 1935, the most intense on record, had a path of destruction only 40 miles wide.

The strongest winds of hurricanes and typhoons have probably never been measured, because wind measuring devices are not designed to stand much more than 125 knots, after which they stop functioning or are blown away. Reconnaissance planes have often reported winds in the 130 to 150 knot (150 to 175 mph) range; actual measurements at land stations have been made as high as 150 knots; and in the Florida Keys hurricane mentioned above, engineers estimated that the winds must have been in the 170 to 215 (200 to 250 mph) range to account for the damage done.

An estimate of the maximum surface wind in a cyclone is obtained by the empirical formula

$$V_{max} = K\sqrt{1010 - P_c}$$

where:

V_{max} = maximum sustained surface wind speed in knots
K = constant, given variously by several authors as 14, 15, or 16
P_c = central (minimum) pressure of the cyclone in millibars

A feature of the wind which helps to account for much of the damage is its gustiness. Momentary gusts exceed the steady winds by 30 to 50 percent, so a wind of 100 knots may have momentary gusts to 150 knots.

Winds in a tropical cyclone do not blow in circles centered around the eye; instead, they angle in anywhere from 20 to 30 degrees all the way from the outer limits of the storm circulation up to the wall of the eye. The angle grows less and less as the eye is approached and the winds blow stronger. At the wall of the eye, the winds do blow in a circle. The 20 to 30 degree inflow accounts for the fact that birds, butterflies, and helpless ships may drift into the eye of a tropical cyclone.

It is typical for the strongest winds to occur to the right of the direction of motion, looking downstream. On the right side the forward motion of the storm is added to the observed wind velocity and on the left it is subtracted.

The steepest pressure gradients in the world, barring tornadoes, occur in tropical cyclones in lower latitudes. One ship in the Caribbean experienced a pressure fall of 1.34 inches (40.50 millibars) in 20 minutes. In the 1935 Florida Keys hurricane, one estimate gave a pressure gradient of 1 inch in 6 miles. The lowest sea-level barometric pressure readings for the whole world have been recorded in hurricanes and typhoons. The lowest reading at sea was 26.18 inches (886.56 millibars); the land record is 26.35 inches.

The eye of the tropical cyclone is unique among atmospheric phenomena. At the edge of the eye, the winds are at their strongest. Then, within a distance of as little as a few hundred feet, it is possible to have the winds fall off from 100 knots to 10. In the eye, the dense, dark clouds are gone, although there are usually some low clouds present. The average diameter of the wind eye is about 14 miles, but it can be as small as 4 miles and as large as 100.

The strong winds of tropical cyclones generate some of the highest of ocean waves. In an average hurricane, waves of 35 to 40 feet are common; in giant storms, they build to 45 to 50 feet, and there have been reports of waves 60 to 90 feet in height. The highest waves are found on the right side of the storm along the direction of movement because the stronger winds are found here and they have a longer time in which to push upon the water, since waves and storm are moving in the same direction.

Waves move more slowly than the winds which create them, but still move much faster than the tropical cyclone itself. As the waves move out of the storm area, at perhaps 45 to 50 knots, they become swells and continue on ahead of the storm for hundreds or even thousands of miles. A characteristic of hurricane or typhoon swells is their long period of 2 to 4 per minute, as contrasted with the normal 10 to 15 per minute.

Rainfall is heavy in tropical cyclones. Over water, it has been calculated that there should be a fall of about 11 inches at any one location during the passage of a hurricane. Over land, because of the added lifting effect, tremendous amounts of rainfall are recorded, like the 49.13 inches in 24 hours at Paishih, Taiwan, or the 96.5 inches in 4 days in Jamaica.

Tropical cyclones live longer than any other storms. Their average life is 9 days, but many have lived 3 to 4 weeks, and the record-breaker logged 5 weeks during a grand tour from Africa to the Bahamas to Cape Hatteras to the Azores.

20.7   Hurricane Advisories and Storm Signals   During the hurricane season, the U.S. Navy, NOAA, and U.S Air Force work together to provide the coastal areas of the United States and shipping interests with timely storm warnings. NOAA is responsible for warning civil interests and merchant shipping, the Navy is concerned with its coastal activities and ships at sea, and the Air Force has the responsibility of Air Force and Army installations in the critical area.

The Department of Defense is assigned reconnaissance responsibility and is frequently called upon to investigate areas of possible hurricane formation. Once a tropical storm is located, the hurricane hunter planes give it almost a 24-hour-per-day examination, sifting out all the facts on surface and upper winds, state of the sea, pressure, the eye, and storm location. Without this reconnaissance information, the forecast centers would not be able to forecast any better than they did thirty years ago. Small storms would be missed for days or forever; intensities would be misjudged; movement forecasts would be very inaccurate. Hurricane recon is a difficult, dangerous job, but one that has saved many lives and prevented much damage.

A similar arrangement is in effect in the Pacific, except that typhoon warnings are issued for all civil and military interests from the Joint Typhoon Warning Center (Navy and Air Force), located in the Navy's Fleet Weather Central, Guam.

Weather satellites play an increasingly important role in the discovery of incipient tropical cyclones, and in tracking them in their later and more destructive stages. Satellite information is still not detailed enough to replace that obtained by aircraft, but the future holds great promise of satellites doing the whole job of detection and tracking.

In addition to hurricane and storm communiqués by radio, a system of flags and lights (Fig. 20.5) is displayed at many coastal points along the United States seacoasts when winds dangerous to navigation are

SMALL CRAFT, GALE, WHOLE GALE AND HURRICANE WARNINGS

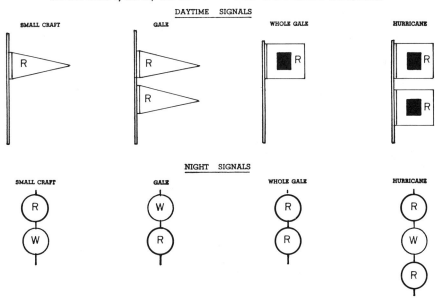

Fig. 20.5 Storm and hurricane wind displays.

forecast for any coastal section. Explanations of the various warnings follow:

Small Craft Warning   One red pennant displayed by day and a red light over a white light at night indicate that winds up to 38 miles an hour (33 knots) and/or sea conditions dangerous to small craft are forecast for the area.

Gale Warning   Two red pennants displayed by day and a white light above a red light at night indicate that winds ranging from 39 to 54 miles an hour (34 to 48 knots) are forecast for the area.

Whole Gale Warning   A single square red flag with a black center displayed during daytime and two red lights at night indicate that winds ranging from 55 to 73 miles an hour (48 to 63 knots) are forecast for the area.

Hurricane Warning   Two square red flags with black centers displayed by day and a white light between two red lights at night indicate that winds 74 miles an hour (64 knots) and above are forecast for the area.

20.8 Locating a Tropical Cyclone by Local Signs   *First Indications*
The long-period, heavy swell of the hurricane arrives well before its

clouds. The first clouds directly connected with the hurricane circulation are cumulonimbus (thunderstorm). There are active bands of these along a line several hundred miles ahead of the storm; the distance varies with the size of the storm. Following these, and the day before the storm arrives, the tropical pattern is out of phase. The thunderstorms of the day before are missing. The usual cumulus clouds are suppressed. There are bright skies and above-normal temperatures. Then, the barometer starts to drop, and the wind may come from an unusual direction. In the trades a north wind is a most unusual direction and generally a danger sign.

Convincing Signs A drop in barometric pressure of 3.4 millibars (0.10 inches) or more within a 24-hour period, particularly if it occurs over a period of 3 to 6 hours, is significant in relation to the approach of a tropical cyclone. It should be kept in mind in this connection that in the tropics there is a very regular, twice-daily rise and fall in barometric pressure over a range of 2 millibars (0.06 inch).

It is significant when there is an increase in wind speed of 25 percent or more in a limited area in the normal trade wind flow, especially if the wind flow changes cyclonically, say from easterly to a more northerly direction. Also, any wind south through west to north is a danger signal.

The significant cloud pattern starts with cirrus. These seem to converge in the direction from which the storm is approaching, a characteristic most noticeable at sunrise and sunset. The cirrus clouds are followed by cirrostratus, the producer of solar and lunar halos, and of brilliant ruby and crimson skies at sunrise and sunset. Next come the altostratus, often mixed with altocumulus. The steady rain accompanying the altostratus is another indication, as the rain in the tropics is usually the showery type. As the center gets closer, the clouds change at lower levels to cumulus congestus; the barometer falls more rapidly; the wind increases; the seas grow mountainous; finally, an ominous black wall of clouds approaches, called the "bar" of the storm.

20.9 Ships in a Hurricane The following rules apply in handling ships at sea (see Chapter 9):

1. Determine the bearing, distance and track of the cyclone from the official warnings, or from your own calculations if there are no warnings. From this information, you can plan how best to avoid the dangerous semicircle on the right side of the cyclone, looking downstream in the direction of movement. Relationship to shoal water must be considered in the planning.

2. If near a cyclone and you have no warnings, determine its bearing by (a) the direction from which the swells are arriving and (b) by adding 115 degrees to the direction from which your observed true wind is blowing.
3. If the wind gradually hauls to the right (clockwise) the ship is in the dangerous semicircle. If it hauls to the left, you are in the safe or navigable semicircle. See Fig. 20.6.
4. If the wind remains steady in direction, increases in speed, and the barometer continues to fall, you are directly in the path of the storm.
5. Use your radar if available. A continuous knowledge of the center position is helpful in maneuvering.
6. Do not try to outrun or cross the "T" of a mature tropical cyclone; it usually means trouble. The main difficulty arises from the front-running swells, which build rapidly in size with the approach of the center. These can cut down ship speed by several knots, while the storm keeps roaring along, or speeds up.
7. If Sea Surface Temperature charts are available, avoid the areas of warmest waters. When tropical cyclones are moving slowly, at 10 knots or less, they tend to use such warm areas as a path.
8. If the ship is actually caught in a cyclone circulation, even the fringes, these steps should be taken:

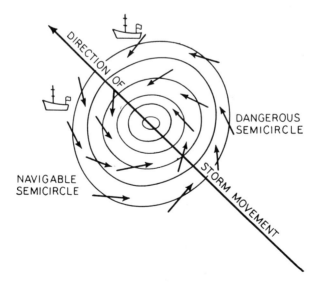

Fig. 20.6 A ship hove-to in the dangerous semicircle will note the wind to shift to the right (clockwise); the wind will shift to the left (counterclockwise) if the ship is in the navigable semicircle.

a. If you are dead ahead of the center, bring the wind on the starboard quarter (160 degrees relative) and make best speed on this course. This will take the ship away from the center most quickly and into the safe semicircle. When well within this semicircle, bring the wind 130° relative and continue best speed.
b. If the ship is in the safe or navigable semicircle, bring the wind on the starboard quarter (130 degrees relative) and make the best speed.
c. If in the dangerous semicircle, bring the wind on the starboard bow (45 degrees relative) and make as much headway as possible.

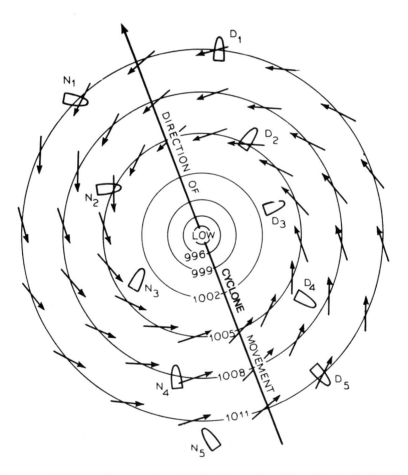

Fig. 20.7 This figure illustrates the rules for lying to by sailing ships in the Northern Hemisphere. Note that the wind draws aft in the cases of both vessels N and D.

d. If behind the cycone center steer best riding course which maintains an opening with the center, remembering the tendency of the cyclone to eventually curve northward and eastward.

20.10 Sailing Ships (Northern Hemisphere)   (See Fig. 20.7) While making a preliminary study of the storm, sailing ships should be hove to on the starboard tack. If the wind shifts to the right, the ship is in the dangerous semicircle but on the proper tack. Then it may attempt to work away from the track of the storm center, close-hauled on the starboard tack. If it is necessary to heave to, do so on the same tack.

If the wind hauls to the left while hove to on the starboard tack, the ship is in the navigable semicircle and heading away from the track of the storm center. In this case the wind should be brought on the starboard quarter and then run as long as possible. If it is necessary to heave to, do so on the port tack; try to make as little headway as possible.

If the wind direction remains the same while hove to on the starboard tack and the barometer falls steadily, it is likely that the ship is ahead and in the path of the hurricane. This is true if we assume that the storm is circular in shape rather than elliptical. The ship should run with the wind on the starboard quarter and hold the compass course thus noted until the barometer begins to rise.

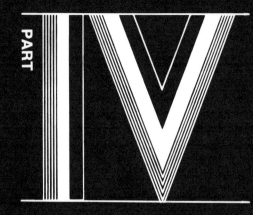

Rules
of the Road

Introduction to the
Rules of the Road

21.1 History The need for uniform Rules of the Road arose when steam vessels with higher speeds than sailing vessels appeared on the trade routes of the world. The modern Rules date from 1863 in which year Great Britain and France adopted uniform regulations for the prevention of collisions at sea.

The Congress of the United States approved a law on April 29, 1864, containing Rules similar to those already adopted by Great Britain and France. About 1885, Belgium, Denmark, Germany, Japan, and Norway accepted the same Rules as Great Britain, France, and the United States.

The President of the United States called in 1889 a conference of all maritime nations to draw up rules and regulations for the safety of lives and property at sea. The conference approved the International Rules of the Road, 1889, which were accepted and used by all maritime nations until a 1948 revision was adopted and put into effect in 1954.

An international conference was held in the spring of 1960. As an outgrowth of this conference, the 1948 Rules were changed in many ways. The most significant revision concerned conduct in restricted visibility. A new rule was adopted to provide for safe navigation by a vessel which detects another vessel outside of visual or audible range. Though not mentioning radar specifically, this rule—when considered together with the annex entitled "Recommendations on the Use of Radar Information as an Aid to Avoiding Collisions at Sea"—resolved several important questions which existed concerning a vessel navigating with the aid of radar.

The effective date of the 1960 International Rules was September 1, 1965. They were enacted by the United States as Public Law 131, 88th Congress, on September 24, 1963, and declared effective on the date indicated by Presidential proclamation. Other countries by similar process made the rules effective on the same date.

The most recent revision of the International Rules is an outgrowth of an international conference held in London in 1972 under the auspices of the Intergovernment Maritime Consultative Organization (IMCO). The International Regulations for Preventing Collisions at Sea, 1972, will become effective sometime after January 1, 1976; one year after a sufficient number of nations have approved the revision.

The rules have been reorganized in the 1972 revision and a number of editorial improvements are evident. The rules provide: (a) better guidance in determining safe speed, and risk of collision (b) recognition of vessels constrained by draft and air-cushion vessels (c) regulations concerning operation in or near traffic separation schemes adopted by IMCO (d) technical details for lights, shapes and sound signalling devices in separate annexes (e) new sound signals for the overtaking situation in narrow channels (f) a number of changes concerning lights, shapes, and fog signals.

The International Rules have made provision for any local rules that nations may wish to exercise in waters under their jurisdiction that are not part of the High Seas. In U.S. Waters such a code has been established known as the *Inland Rules of the Road.*

The Inland Rules of the Road were approved by Congress on June 7, 1897, and made effective October 7, 1897. There have been some later additions and amendments. However, they are in need of further revision and should be made more uniform with the International Rules.

The line of demarkation between the waters under the International and the Inland Rules was originally set forth by the Secretary of the Treasury under the Act of February 19, 1895. Some changes and additions have been made since that time. The Commandant of the U.S. Coast Guard is now charged with the determination of this boundary line, which is shown on all charts.

The boundary line for seaplanes on the water is not the same as that for vessels. Public Law 131 states that the International Rules of the Road "shall not apply . . . with respect to aircraft in any territorial waters of the United States." Civil Air Regulations in 14 CFR Parts 3 and 60 apply to seaplanes on the water in United States territorial waters. These regulations conform to the Inland Rules for vessels.

The Statutory Rules for the Great Lakes and Western Rivers were enacted by Congress on February 8, 1895, and May 21, 1948, respectively.

The Pilot Rules (3) for Inland Waters, for the Great Lakes, and for the Western Rivers were originally issued by the Board of Supervising Inspectors for Steam Vessels, Department of Commerce, under the Acts of June 7, 1897, February 8, 1895, and R.S. 4412, respectively. The authority to issue Pilot Rules has now been transferred to the Commandant of the Coast Guard by Executive Order 9083 of February 28, 1942, effective March 1, 1942, and reaffirmed by subsequent Reorganization Plans. The three Pilot Rules supplement the Inland, Great Lakes and Western Rivers Rules, but they do not supersede those statutory Rules. The Pilot Rules have the force of statute, but they are not "judicially noticed." They must be proved in court. Courts can and have ruled certain Pilot Rules void because they conflicted with the statutory Rules.

21.2 Various Rules of the Road

1. International Rules of the Road, agreed to internationally and enacted by Congress. These rules are applicable on the High Seas and on all water joining the High Seas, unless covered by local rules.
2. In the United States local rules are:

   a. The Pilot Rules for Inland Waters prescribed by the Commandant of the U.S. Coast Guard for the above Inland Waters.
   b. The Great Lakes Rules enacted by Congress for use on the Great Lakes and connecting and tributary waters as far east as Montreal.
   c. The Pilot Rules for the Great Lakes issued by the Commandant of the Coast Guard.
   d. The Western Rivers Rules, enacted by Congress and effective on the Red River of the North, Missisippi River, and waters tributary to the latter.
   e. The Pilot Rules for Western Rivers, by the Commandant of the Coast Guard.
   f. General Regulations of the Corps of Engineers, Department of the Army, applicable to the Great Lakes.
   g. The Motor Boat Act of 1940, applicable to every vessel propelled in whole or in part by machinery and not more than 65 feet in length, except tugboats and towboats propelled by steam. It is effective in all U.S. waters.
   h. Miscellaneous U.S. Statutes, i.e., Stand-by Act; Wreck Act; Death on High Seas Act; Naval Lights Act; Anchorage Act of March 3, 1899; Bridge-to-Bridge Radiotelephone Act (1973).

    i.   Panama Canal Rules.
    j.   Hawser Rules for tows in Inland Waters, prescribed by Commandant of the Coast Guard.
    k.   Anchorage Regulations issued by the Corps of Engineers, Department of the Army.
    l.   Statutes of the several states of the United States.
    m. Decisions of the U.S. courts.
    n.   Customs accepted by the courts.

3. In foreign countries local rules are not as extensive as are U.S. Inland Rules and, generally speaking, International Rules are in force. Some local rules are made, usually in addition to the International rules, and details may be found in Sailing Directions. However, extensive local rules do exist in, for example, the Suez Canal and Kiel Canal.

21.3 Risk of Collision   The International Rules and the Inland Rules prescribe certain "Steering and Sailing Rules" which must be followed when two vessels are approaching each other ". . . so as to involve risk of collision. . ." Justice Longyear, in the MILWAUKEE, said, "Risk of collision begins the very moment when the two vessels have approached so near each other and upon such courses that by a departure from the rules of navigation . . . , a collision might be brought about."

    The Inland Rules state: "Risk of collision can, when circumstances permit, be ascertained by carefully watching the compass bearing of an approaching vessel. If the bearing does not appreciably change, such risk should be deemed to exist." This caution might be extended to the distance where the two approaching vessels are so far apart that either one or both could change course or speed without affecting the other vessel. It is reasonable to state that risk of collision is involved when "the bearing does not appreciably change" and when the approaching vessels are so close that the movements of one does affect the other and when "by a departure from the rules of navigation . . . a collision might be brought about."

21.4 Ability to Maneuver   Both Rules are based, *in part*, on the premise that certain vessels are unable to maneuver as quickly and as easily as other types of vessels. The more maneuverable is required, therefore, to keep clear of the less maneuverable. An example is the rule which requires power-driven vessels to keep out of the way of sailing vessels except when the sailing vessel overtakes the power-driven vessel. There is a Rule for each case.

21.5 Burdened and Privileged Vessels   The terms *burdened* and *privileged* vessels are often used to indicate the vessel which must give way and the vessel which must hold its course and speed when there is risk of collision. The terms are expressive but misleading because each vessel is required by the Rules to act in a certain manner. For example: "When two power-driven vessels are crossing so as to involve risk of collision, the vessel which has the other on her own starboard side shall keep out of the way" (Int. Rule 15). "Whereby any of these Rules, one of the two vessels is to keep out of the way, the other shall keep her course and speed. . . ." (Inland Article 21.)

21.6 Obedience in Time.   It is important that the Rules be obeyed in time to avoid the immediate risk of collision, to give the other vessel an opportunity to understand the situation, and take proper action. "The Rules must be obeyed when the vessels are far enough apart to adopt these manuevers deliberately and safely."

21.7 Shifting Responsibility   The courts have ruled, in many cases, that, when two vessels are approaching each other so as to involve risk of collision, the original responsibilities under the law cannot be changed by the subsequent movements of either vessel until the collision is so imminent that both must take appropriate action under Article 27 or Rule 20 or until the risk of collision exists no longer. In other words, no subsequent change in bearing or distance, after risk of collision is involved, will alter the fact that one of the vessels must keep clear and the other hold her course and speed. Of course, the time may come when there is no right of way and, therefore, each vessel must take measures to avoid the collision which is imminent. When the risk of collision exists no longer, the Rules apply no longer and a different situation may then arise.

21.8 Assumptions   In order that a collision may be avoided after risk of collision exists, it is necessary that the movements of one vessel—the privileged one—must be known so that the other vessel—the burdened one—may change her course and speed, if necessary, to keep clear. A vessel has the right to assume that the other vessel will obey the Rules of the Road, will be navigated with care and attention, will keep to its own side of a channel, etc. However, the assumption does not hold when it is evident that the other vessel is not being navigated with care and attention. For example, a privileged vessel in a crossing situation should not hold its course and speed until collision results. Justice Longyear, in the MILWAUKEE, said, "It is true, that, prima facie, each has the right to assume that the other will obey the law. But this does not justify either in shutting his eyes to what the other may actually do, or in omitting to do what he can to avoid an accident, made imminent by the acts of the other."

21.9 Rule 2, Art. 27—General Prudential Rule This rule does not apply in every case where it suits the convenience of the vessel to use it. On the contrary, the other Steering and Sailing Rules should be strictly adhered to, in most cases. But the object of the Rules is to prevent and not cause collisions. There have been and will be many different situations. In order to cover *all* situations, Rule 2 and Article 27 were added. They should be obeyed where collision is imminent and where both vessels must take further action to avoid collision. Until this point is reached, the other Steering and Sailing Rules should be applied.

2.10 Customs in U.S. Waters Customs must be proved in each case; they must not conflict with the statutes and regulations; and they must be reasonable in view of a particular, permanent, local condition. Some customs have been accepted by the courts, whereas some have not. "Moreover, each vessel has the right to assume that the other will conform to the requirements of an established usage, and must govern her own conduct accordingly"—Justice Wallace in the ALASKA.

21.11 Jurisdiction When collision between vessels occurs in navigable waters used in interstate commerce, the case can be heard in the federal courts sitting as courts in admiralty. The district courts are the trial courts, the circuit courts hear appeals, and the Supreme Court may hear the final appeal. If the collision occurs on waters wholly within a state, the state courts have sole jurisdiction. If the collision occurs on waters in or between two states which empty into the sea, there is concurrent jurisdiction. Either the federal or state court may hear the case.

When a vessel runs into a pier or bridge through negligence or bad seamanship, the admiralty courts have no jurisdiction. On the other hand, if a bridge or draw damages a vessel due to improper construction or operation, the case can be heard by an admiralty court.

21.12 Legal Personality A merchant ship is liable *in rem* (against a thing) for the faults of her master, officers, or men (perhaps a lookout) operating the ship. She can be sued in an admiralty court, attached, and sold to satisfy a judgment. The owners are not otherwise liable in such suits unless they have contributed to the fault by neglect, privity, or knowledge.

The Sovereign cannot be sued because one of her vessels, i.e., a naval vessel, has collided with a merchant vessel unless she has granted such privilege. Congress has approved such proceedings, but a naval vessel cannot be seized and thus placed out of commision or sold to satisfy a judgment.

21.13 Court Decisions in U.S. Waters   Article 29 of the Inland Rules requires precautions to be taken *in addition* to the observance of the other rules—these additional precautions may be expected because (1) they are the ordinary practice of a good seaman (2) they are required by the special circumstances of the case. Because the Inland Rules have not been significantly revised for years, and many of the rules have been construed together with Article 29, a familiarity with court interpretations is necessary in order to properly conduct a vessel in U.S. inland waters.

21.14 Unequal Fault, Equal Responsibility   U.S. courts have held that where both vessels are in fault in a collision the liability of each vessel is one-half of the total loss. However, if the fault of one is great and that of the other is minor, nonstatutory, and noncontributory, the courts may not inquire fully into the minor fault or they may disregard it and order the full costs to be paid by the vessel with the major fault.

21.15 Pertinent Statutes   *Anchorage Act*   A vessel has a right to anchor. The only question is, where can she anchor legally? Certain water areas are designated by the Secretary of the Army as anchorages. It is improper, although not unlawful, to anchor outside of these areas in restricted waters, save in an emergency. A vessel has a right to anchor in large, navigable water areas such as Chesapeake Bay or on soundings off the Coast. The Anchorage Act of March 3, 1899, states: "It shall not be lawful to tie up or anchor vessels or other craft in navigable channels in such a manner as to prevent or obstruct the passage of other vessels or craft. . . ." The trend of judicial opinion has been to permit anchorage in a channel, "but to forbid them [vessels] from doing so in such a manner as to obstruct said channels or render their navigation difficult or dangerous." Channels are primarily for traffic and not for anchorage. It is sometimes necessary to anchor in a narrow channel—in a thick fog— but the anchorage should be shifted to an authorized anchorage ground as soon as possible. While the vessel remains in the narrow channel, every precaution to prevent collision should be taken such as: (a) use a short scope of chain, (b) keep power on the anchor engine (c) station a watch in the engine room and keep steam up to the throttle, (d) station a watch on the bridge, (e) post extra lookouts.

Of course, if the channel is well lighted, marked, and wide and there is plenty of room for other vessels to pass, a vessel may remain at anchor there without violation of the statute. An example is the Hudson River off 96th Street, New York. Even so, she should anchor to one side of the channel, and be particularly careful that: (a) her anchor lights are showing, (b) a trained lookout is posted, (c) proper signals are sounded in a fog, and (d) the anchor ball is hoisted by day.

Attention is called to Article 11 of the Inland Rules which permits the Secretary of the Army to designate "special anchorage areas" where vessels not more than 65 feet in length may anchor and "not be required to carry or exhibit an anchor light." Such areas are usually near yacht clubs or marinas and are intended primarily for pleasure craft, secured for the night. However, the Inland Rules permit nondescript craft, such as barges, canal boats, or scows to anchor in these anchorages with but one anchor light irrespective of the length of the vessel or, if in a group, the length of the group.

After the vessel has anchored in accordance with her legal rights, she must exhibit the proper lights at night, sound correct fog signals when necessary, and post a watch on deck. Sufficient trained lookouts must be stationed to inform the officer in charge of the ship of the approach of other vessels or objects which might require action.

An anchored vessel is presumed to be without fault if a moving vessel collides with her unless the moving vessel can prove that the collision "was the result of inevitable accident" or that the anchored vessel was in fault. The moving vessel must proceed lawfully in moving through an anchorage ground. Tides and current do not excuse her.

The anchored vessel may be found in fault if she has failed to anchor in a legal position, show the proper lights, or sound the proper fog signals. She may also be found in fault if she: (a) anchors without necessity in a narrow channel; (b) swings to the tide and obstructs the channel substantially; (c) anchors on a frequented compass course when a safer anchorage is available; (d) fails to move from a channel when possible; (e) fails to move when warned that her position is dangerous; (f) anchors where approaching vessels rounding a point sight her suddenly and belatedly; (g) fails to veer chain or use her helm when such action might prevent a collision, the moving vessel having done all in her power to avoid a collision; (h) anchors so close to another anchored vessel as to foul her when swinging; (i) fails to shift anchorage when dragging dangerously close to another anchored vessel. The vessel which anchored first should warn the one who anchored last that the berth chosen will foul the former's berth.

Vessels which drag should take every measure possible to stop dragging, such as dropping a second anchor. Anchored vessels are not required to keep steam up unless weather, ice, or good seamanship demands it. An anchored vessel is not required to take unusual precautions to avoid collisions with moving vessels.

A moored vessel alongside a wharf may be found in fault if she projects into the channel and thereby obstructs it and contributes to a collision. A slight projection may not cause her to be found at fault if passing vessels can pass her safely using reasonable care. If the moored vessel unnecessarily obstructs the slip in which she is secured so that other vessels using the slip cannot evade collision by exercising reasonable care, she may be found at fault. A moored vessel alongside a wharf or slip is not required to show anchor lights, to sound fog signals, or to post a lookout. She must, however, house her anchors in the usual, secure manner so that passing vessels will not be damaged by them. In some areas she may be required by custom or local regulation to show a white light at each projection or extremity, and normally should of her own accord in congested waters.

Finally, anchorage may be regulated by state or local authorities, provided such ordinances or laws do not conflict with federal statutes and maritime law as interpreted by U.S. courts.

Stand-by Act   Congress passed the "Stand-by Act" on September 4, 1890. This statute states, in part: "That in every case of collision between two vessels it shall be the duty of the master or person in charge of each vessel, if and so far as he can do so without serious danger to his own vessel, crew and passengers, to stay by the other vessel until he has ascertained that she has no need of further assistance, and to render to the other vessel, her master, crew and passengers such assistance as may be practicable and as may be necessary in order to save them from any danger caused by the collision, and also to give to the master or person in charge of the other vessel the name of his own vessel and her port of registry, or the port or place to which she belongs and also the name of the ports and places from which and to which she is bound. . . ."

Reports of Collisions   With few exceptions, U.S. vessels which have sustained or caused any accident involving loss of life, material loss of property, or any serious injury to any person, or have received any material damage affecting their seaworthiness or efficiency, are required to report the accident within five days or as soon thereafter as possible to the commander of the Coast Guard District where the vessel belongs or where the accident took place. (Act June 20, 1874, as amended by Reorganization Plan 3.) This is usually done by means of a written report to the nearest officer-in-charge, Marine Inspection.

Exceptions to the foregoing are primarily public vessels, such as Navy and Coast Guard ships, and small vessels numbered by the individual states under the Coast Guard supervised Federal Boating Act of 1958. If numbered by a state, and power-driven, a vessel usually reports directly to the state by which it is numbered (i.e., registered).

Motor Boat Act of 1940   The Act of April 25, 1940 applies to every vessel in U.S. waters propelled in whole or in part by machinery and not more than 65 feet in length, except tugboats and towboats propelled by steam. In its amended form the act prescribes lights and sound devices and other safety equipment for such vessels and provides penalties for reckless or negligent operation of any vessel subject to U.S. laws.

Prior provisions for numbering (i.e., registering) motorboats were superseded by the Federal Boating Act in 1958.

Log Books The Act of February 27, 1877, as revised, requires that: "Every vessel making voyages from a port in the United States to any foreign port, or, being of the burden of seventy-five tons or upward, from a port on the Atlantic to a port on the Pacific or vice versa, shall have an official log book; and every master of such vessel shall make or cause to be made therein, entries of the following matters, that is to say: "First. . . .

"Twelfth. In every case of collision in which it is practicable to do so, the master shall, immediately after the occurrence, cause a statement thereof, and of the circumstances under which the same occurred to be entered in the official log book."

Wreck Act, March 3, 1899 The act empowers the Secretary of the Army to remove any sunken boat, water craft, raft, or other similar obstruction, which has existed for a period longer than thirty days, from any river, lake, harbor, sound, bay, canal, or other navigable waters of the United States.

Death on the High Seas Act, March 30, 1920 The act permits the personal representative of a decedent to maintain a suit for damages in the district courts of the United States, in Admiralty, for the exclusive benefit of the decedent's wife, husband, parent, child, or dependent relative against the vessel, person, or corporation which is liable for the wrongful act, neglect, or default resulting in the death of the decedent.

Naval Vessels Lights Act The Act of September 24, 1963, prescribing the International Rules of the Road, 1960, and the Acts of March 5, 1948, and December 3, 1945, provide that the several Rules of the Road for International and Inland waters, the Great Lakes, and the Western Rivers shall not apply to any vessel of the Navy or of the Coast Guard, insofar as they pertain to lights, where the Secretary of the Navy, Secretary of the Treasury, or such official or officials as either may designate, shall find or certify that, by reason of special construction, it is not possible with respect to such vessels or class of vessels to comply with the statutory provisions as to the number, position, range of visibility, or arc of visibility of lights. The lights of any such exempt vessel or class of vessel shall, however, comply as closely to the requirements of the statutes as feasible. A notice of such finding or modification and of the character and position of the lights displayed must be published in the Federal Register and in the Notice to Mariners."

Sea Manners   The expression is understood by seamen to mean a consideration for the other vessel and the exercise of common sense under certain conditions when vessels meet. A tug with a tow is difficult to maneuver. A large ship is more difficult to maneuver than a smaller one. A convoy or a formation of naval vessels is more difficult to maneuver than a single ship. All of these vessels are required to obey the Rules of the Road. No vessel is exempt. If a vessel disobeys the Rules, she is liable. Accordingly, seamen are not advised to disobey the Rules of the Road to show sea manners, but to obey them. The Rules of the Road apply when there is a risk of collision. Before that moment, there is enough time and plenty of opportunity for a single vessel to avoid a tug with tow, a convoy, or a formation of naval ships. Small vessels can keep clear of large ones.

The rules caution sailing vessels against hampering large power-driven vessels in narrow channels, and prohibit power boats under 65 feet from hindering large vessels navigating a narrow channel. These are but two common cases calling for sea manners. Sea manners should be applied where conditions indicate, and in all waters.

LIGHTS AND SHAPES

22.1 Introduction The basic purpose of lights is to warn vessels of the presence or approach of other vessels, and to aid in determining the course and target angle (the relative bearing of your own vessel from the target) of vessels underway. White lights are visible at a greater range than colored lights, and many vessels carry two white lights on the fore and aft centerline, the masthead and after range lights. These lights serve not only to aid in the determination of course and target angle, but immediately give an indication of any *change* in course.

By observing the lights or shapes displayed by an approaching vessel, the mariner can determine which vessel has the responsibility to keep out of the way of the other. As will be discussed in later chapters, this responsibility will be determined by the different right of way categories, or the approach situation between vessels in the same category.

The application of the International lights and shapes rules is stated in Rule 20:

INTERNATIONAL RULE 20—APPLICATION (OF PART C)

(a) Rules in this part shall be complied with in all weathers.
(b) The rules concerning lights shall be complied with from sunset to sun-

514

rise, and during such times no other lights shall be exhibited, except such lights as cannot be mistaken for the lights specified in these rules or do not impair their visibility or distinctive character, or interfere with the keeping of a proper look-out.

(c) The lights prescribed by these rules shall, if carried, also be exhibited from sunrise to sunset in restricted visibility and may be exhibited in all other circumstances when it is deemed necessary.

(d) The rules concerning shapes shall be complied with by day.

(e) The lights and shapes specified in these rules shall comly with the provisions of Annex I to these regulations.

When subject to the International Rules lights are *required* to be shown in restricted visibility as well as at night. Lights may also be shown any other time when deemed necessary.

ARTICLE 1 OF THE INLAND RULES STATES:

Art. 1. *The rules concerning lights shall be complied with in all weathers from sunset to sunrise, and during such time no other lights which may be mistaken for the prescribed lights shall be exhibited.*

While the Inland Rules do not mention the use of lights during the day, common sense and good seamanship would dictate that lights be displayed any time a vessel is being navigated in conditions of restricted visibility.

In the International Rules certain lights are required only when a vessel is underway and "making way through the water." Making way refers to motion that is a result of a vessel's propelling machinery (or sails), including the motion after the engines are stopped—up to the time when a vessel is actually dead in the water. The Inland Rules make no such distinction, and vessels must display the same lights at all times when underway, even if dead in the water.

22.2 Lights and Shapes—International Rules

22.2.1 Definitions—International Rules:

INTERNATIONAL RULE 21—DEFINITIONS

(a) "Masthead light" means a white light placed over the fore and aft centerline of the vessel showing an unbroken light over an arc of the horizon of 225 degrees and so fixed as to show the light from right ahead to 22.5 degrees abaft the beam on either side of the vessel.

(b) "Sidelights" means a green light on the starboard side and a red light on the port side each showing an unbroken light over an arc of the horizon of 112.5 degrees and so fixed as to show the light from right ahead to 22.5 degrees abaft the beam on its respective side. In a vessel of less than 20 metres in length the sidelights may be combined in one lantern carried on the fore and aft centerline of the vessel.

(c) "Sternlight" means a white light placed as nearly as practicable at the stern showing an unbroken light over an arc of the horizon of 135 degrees and so fixed as to show the light 67.5 degrees from right aft on each side of the vessel.

(d) "Towing light" means a yellow light having the same characteristics as the "sternlight" defined in paragraph (c) of this rule.

(e) "All round light" means a light showing an unbroken light over an arc of the horizon of 360 degrees.

(f) "Flashing light" means a light flashing at regular intervals at a frequency of 120 flashes or more per minute.

The terms "range light" or "after range light" will be used in this text rather than the terminology used in the International Rules; "a second masthead light abaft of and higher than the forward one." Where a towing vessel is required to show two or three masthead lights in a vertical line they will be termed "towing masthead lights" in this text.

22.2.2 Power-Driven Vessel Underway—International Rules:

All power-driven vessels are required to show a masthead light, sidelights (10 point) and a sternlight (12 point). A 20 point range light is required for vessels 50 meters and upward in length, and optional for vessels less than 50 meters in length. In addition to the aforementioned lights, an air-cushion vessel operating in the non-displacement mode is required to show a flashing yellow light (32 point). The flashing light must flash at regular intervals at a frequency of 120 flashes or more per minute, a frequency significantly higher than that of lighted aids to navigation.

A power-driven vessel of less than 7 meters in length and whose maximum speed does not exceed 7 knots may show one 32 point white light in lieu of the lights prescribed above for a larger power-driven vessel. Such a vessel shall, if practicable, also exhibit sidelights.

22.2.3 Power-Driven Vessel Engaged in Towing—International Rules
All power-driven vessels engaged in towing must show sidelights (10 point) and a sternlight (12 point). A 20 point range light is optional for vessels less than 50 meters in length, and required for vessels 50 meters and upward in length. Vessels towing astern must display a yellow towing light (12 point) in a vertical line above the sternlight.

A vessel towing astern, when the length of the tow (measured from the stern of the towing vessel to the after end of the tow) exceeds 200 meters, is required to show three masthead towing lights (20 point). Vessels towing astern with the length of the tow 200 meters or under, vessels towing alongside and vessels pushing ahead show two masthead towing lights. A diamond dayshape is required only when the length of the tow exceeds 200 meters.

"A vessel engaged in a towing operation such as renders her unable to deviate from her course" shall show the lights required for a vessel towing astern and in addition shall show three 32 point lights in a vertical line where best seen, red—white—red. In the daytime a ball—diamond—ball is required in a vertical line where best seen (shown in addition to the diamond when length of tow exceeds 200 meters). The red—white—red lights are not required for vessels less than 7 meters in length.

When a pushing vessel and a vessel being pushed ahead are rigidly connected in a composite unit they shall show the lights prescribed for a power-driven vessel.

22.2.4 Vessels Being Towed—International Rules
A vessel or object being towed astern is required to show sidelights and a sternlight, and when the length of tow exceeds 200 meters, a diamond shape where it can best be seen. Where from any sufficient cause it is impracticable for a vessel or object being towed to show sidelights and a sternlight, "all possible measures shall be taken to light the vessel or object towed or at least indicate the presence of the unlighted vessel or object."

A vessel being pushed ahead, not being part of a composite unit, is required to show sidelights at the forward end. A vessel being towed

INTERNATIONAL
Towing (length of tow exceeding 200 meters)

INTERNATIONAL
Towing (length of tow not exceeding 200 meters)

alongside is required to show a sternlight and sidelights at the forward end.

22.2.5 Sailing Vessel Underway—International Rules:

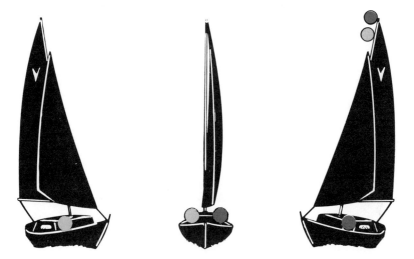

A sailing vessel is required to show sidelights and a sternlight, and may in addition show red over green (32 point) lights at or near the top of the mast.

A sailing vessel less than 12 meters in length may combine the sidelights and sternlight in one lantern carried at or near the top of the mast where it can best be seen. The red over green lights may not be shown with such a combined lantern.

A sailing vessel less than 7 meters in length shall, if practicable, show sidelights and a sternlight or the combined lantern, "but if she does not, she shall have ready at hand an electric torch or lighted lantern showing a white light in sufficient time to prevent collison."

Vessel Under Oars

25 (d) (ii) A vessel under oars may exhibit the lights prescribed in this rule for sailing vessels, but if she does not, she shall have ready at hand an electric torch or lighted lantern showing a white light which shall be exhibited in sufficient time to prevent collision.

Vessel Under Sail and Power

25 (e) A vessel proceeding under sail when also being propelled by machinery shall exhibit forward where it can best be seen a conical shape, apex downwards.

22.2.6 Vessel Engaged in Fishing—International Rules:

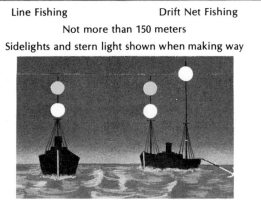

Line Fishing   Drift Net Fishing
Not more than 150 meters
Sidelights and stern light shown when making way

Trawler
Sidelights and stern light shown when making way

A vessel engaged in fishing or trawling, whether underway or at anchor, shall exhibit only the lights and shapes described below.

A vessel when engaged in trawling, by which is meant the dragging through the water of a dredge net or other apparatus used as a fishing appliance, is required to show green over white 32 point lights. A vessel 50 meters and upward in length is required to show an after range light which is *higher* than the green light; the range light is optional for a vessel less than 50 meters in length. A vessel engaged in trawling is required to show sidelights and a sternlight only when making way through the water.

A vessel engaged in fishing, other than trawling, is required to show red over white 32 point lights. When there is outlying gear extending more than 150 meters horizontally from the vessel, a 32 point white light must be displayed in the direction of the gear. A vessel engaged in fishing is required to show sidelights and a sternlight only when making way through the water.

A vessel engaged in fishing or trawling is required to show two cones, point to point; a vessel less than 20 meters in length may substitute a basket. A vessel engaged in fishing, other than trawling, with outlying gear extending more than 150 meters horizontally from the vessel must also show a cone point up, in the direction of the gear.

A vessel engaged in fishing in close proximity to other vessels may exhibit the additional signals described in Annex II to the International Rules.

A vessel when not engaged in fishing shall not exhibit the lights and shapes described above, but only those prescribed for a vessel of her length.

22.2.7   Vessel Not Under Command—International Rules:

Carries side and stern lights,
if making way through water.
Vessel not under command

A vessel not under command is required to show red over red (32 point) lights in a vertical line where best seen. In addition, sidelights and a sternlight are required only if making way through the water. By day two balls must be shown in a vertical line where best seen.

The lights prescribed for a vessel not under command are not required for vessels less than 7 meters in length.

22.2.8   Vessel Restricted in Her Ability to Maneuver—International Rules:

INTERNATIONAL
SHIP ENGAGED IN
SPECIAL OPERATIONS,
SUCH AS CABLE-LAYING
BUT NOT FOR SHIP
NOT-UNDER-COMMAND

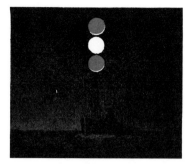

A vessel restricted in her ability to maneuver (special operations), except a vessel engaged in minesweeping, is required to show three 32 point lights in a vertical line where best seen, red—white—red. A vessel making way through the water must also show a masthead light, range light, sidelights and a sternlight (the range light is optional for a vessel less than 50 meters in length). During the day three shapes must be displayed in a vertical line where best seen, ball—diamond—ball.

When at anchor, the red—white—red lights or ball—diamond—ball shapes are shown in addition to the light(s) or shape for a vessel at anchor.

The lights prescribed for a vessel restricted in her ability to maneuver are not required for vessels less than 7 meters in length.

22.2.9 Vessel Engaged in Dredging or Underwater Operations—International Rules:

A vessel engaged in dredging or underwater operations, when restricted in her ability to maneuver, is required to show three 32 point lights in a vertical line where best seen, red—white—red. When an obstruction exists, she must also show red over red 32 point lights on the obstructed side and green over green lights on the clear side (all displayed below the red—white—red lights). Such a vessel, when making way through the water, must also show a masthead light, range light, sidelights and a sternlight (the range light is optional for a vessel less than 50 meters in length).

During the day the ball—diamond—ball shapes must be displayed in addition to two balls in place of the red lights on the obstructed side and two diamonds in place of the green lights on the clear side. These are also the only day shapes shown when at anchor.

Such a vessel, when at anchor, shows only the red—white—red lights, and if an obstruction exists, the two red and two green lights.

Whenever the size of a vessel engaged in diving operations makes it impracticable to exhibit the shapes described above, a rigid replica of the International Code flag "alpha" not less than one meter in height shall be exhibited. Measures shall be taken to ensure all-round visibility.

A vessel less than 7 meters in length is not required to show the above described lights.

22.2.10   Vessel Engaged in Minesweeping—International Rules:

A vessel engaged in minesweeping is required to show three 32 point green lights, one at the foremast head and one at each end of the fore yard. She is also required to show all the other lights prescribed for a power-driven vessel of her length. During the day three balls are shown in the same position as the three green lights. The lights and shapes indicate that it is dangerous to approach closer than 1000 meters astern or 500 meters on either side.

A vessel less than 7 meters in length is not required to show the above described lights.

22.2.11   Pilot Vessel—International Rules:

All vessels engaged in pilotage duty and underway are required to show white over red (32 point) lights in a vertical line at or near the masthead, sidelights and a sternlight.

A pilot vessel at anchor is required to show the white over red lights in addition to the anchor light(s) or a ball during the day. A pilot vessel when not engaged on pilotage duty shall exhibit the lights or shapes prescribed for a similar vessel of her length.

22.2.12 Vessel at Anchor or Aground—International Rules:

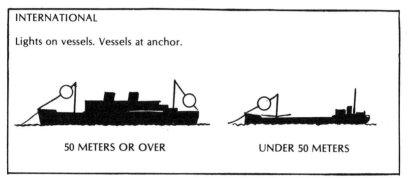

INTERNATIONAL

Lights on vessels. Vessels at anchor.

50 METERS OR OVER   UNDER 50 METERS

A vessel at anchor is required to show two white lights (32 point), one in the fore part of the vessel and the other near the stern and lower than the forward light. A vessel less than 50 meters in length may substitute one white light (32 point) where best seen. Vessels of 100 meters and upward in length are required to illuminate their decks with working lights or equivalent (optional for smaller vessels).

A vessel aground is required to show the anchor lights for a vessel of her length and two red lights (32 point) in a vertical line where best seen.

A vessel less than 7 meters in length, when at anchor or aground, not in or near a narrow channel, fairway or anchorage, or where other vessels normally navigate, shall not be required to exhibit the lights or shapes described above.

22.2.13 Vessel Constrained by Her Draft—International Rules:

A vessel constrained by her draft is required to show all the lights for a power-driven vessel of her length, and *may* in addition show three red lights (32 point) in a vertical line, or a cylinder, where best seen.

22.2.14 Seaplanes:

Where it is impracticable for a seaplane to exhibit lights and shapes of the characteristics or in the positions prescribed in the rules of this part she shall exhibit lights and shapes as closely similar in characteristics and position as is possible.

22.3 Lights and Shapes—Inland Waters
22.3.1 Definitions—Inland Waters:

MASTHEAD LIGHT

Art. 2. *A seam vessel when underway shall carry—*
(a) On or in the front of the foremast, or if a vessel without a foremast then in the fore part of the vessel, a bright white light so constructed as to show an unbroken light over an arc of the horizon of twenty points of the compass, so faced as to throw the light ten points on each side of the vessel, namely, from right ahead to two points abaft the beam on either side, and of such character as to be visible at a distance of at least five miles.

Range Light A white light abaft of and higher than the masthead light. It is in line with (forms a range) if the vessel is seen from dead ahead. It is a 32 point light, except for seagong steam vessels which may show a 20 point light.

Sternlight A 12 point white light showing 6 points from right aft on each side. In inland waters, it is required only when there is no other light visible from aft.

Sidelights A red light on the port side, and a green light on the starboard side. Both are 10 point lights showing from dead ahead to two points abaft the beam on their respective sides.

Towing Masthead and Towing Range Lights Two or more lights of the same character as the 20 point masthead light or the 32 point range light.

Amber Pushing Lights Two amber lights displayed in a vertical line at the stern showing over the same arc as would a 12 point sternlight.

Double Frustum of a Cone A shape formed by placing two frustums base to base.

22.3.2   Steam Vessel Underway—Inland Waters:

A seagoing steam vessel is required to show a masthead light (20 point), sidelights (10 point) and a sternlight (12 point). The after range light is a 20 point light, and is optional regardless of the length of the vessel. This reference to a "seagoing" steam vessel permits vessels in this category to show the same lights in inland waters which they would show when subject to the International Rules. The Motorboat Act of 1940, which changes the lighting requirements for certain steam vessels not more than 65 feet in length, contains similar provisions.

Steam vessels, except seagoing vessels and ferryboats, are required to show a masthead light (20 point), sidelights (10 point) and a 32 point after range light.

Double-end ferryboats show sidelights and two 32 point range lights at the same height. Another light may be shown above the range lights for the purpose of distinguishing different ferryboat lines from each other.

22.3.3   Steam Vessel Towing or Pushing—Inland Waters

A steam towing vessel may display her towing lights either forward or aft. If displayed forward, they will all be of the same character as the 20 point masthead light—"towing masthead lights." If displayed aft, they will all be of the same character as the 32 point range light—"towing range lights." A sternlight is required if no other light is visible from aft.

Towing astern—towing range lights

A steam vessel towing astern and displaying towing range lights is required to show 3 towing range lights and sidelights.

Towing astern—towing masthead lights

A steam vessel towing astern and displaying towing masthead lights is required to show 3 towing masthead lights and sidelights. She may show a 32 point after range light, but if she does not, she must show a sternlight. In lieu of the sternlight a small white light may be used for the tow to steer by, but it shall not be visible forward of the beam.

Towing alongside or pushing
ahead—towing range lights

A steam vessel displaying towing range lights when towing alongside or pushing ahead is required to show 2 towing range lights (32 point) and sidelights.

Towing alongside or pushing ahead—towing masthead lights

A steam vessel displaying towing masthead lights when towing alongside or pushing ahead is required to show 2 towing masthead lights (20 point) and sidelights. When towing alongside a 32 point after range light may be shown, but if the range light is not shown, a sternlight is required. When pushing ahead, two amber lights must be displayed in a vertical line at the stern; a 32 point after range light may be shown in a vertical line above the amber lights.

22.3.4 Vessels Being Towed—Inland Waters:

Art. 5 *A sailing vessel underway and any vessel being towed, except barges, canal boats, scows, and other vessels of nondescript type, when in tow of steam vessels, shall carry the same lights as are prescribed by article 2 for a steam vessel underway, with the exception of the white lights mentioned therein, which they shall never carry.*

22.3.5 Sailing Vessel Underway—Inland Waters:

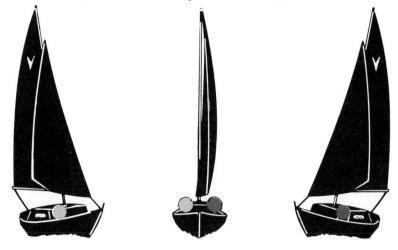

Art. 5. *"A sailing vessel underway and any vessel being towed, except barges, canal boats, scows, and other vessels of nondescript type when in tow of steam vessels, shall carry"* sidelights and a sternlight.

22.3.6 Fishing Vessels—Inland Waters:

INLAND TRAWLING, DREDGING, FISHING WITH DRAG NETS OR LINES

Art. 9. (a) *Fishing vessels of less than ten gross tons, when underway and* <u>*when not having their nets, trawls, dredges, or lines in the water,*</u> *shall not be obliged to carry the colored side lights; but every such vessel shall, in lieu thereof, have ready at hand a lantern with a green glass on one side and a red glass on the other side, and on approaching to or being approached by another vessel such lantern shall be exhibited in sufficient time to prevent collision, so that the green light shall not be seen on the port side nor the red light on the starboard side.*

(b) All fishing vessels and fishing boats of ten gross tons or upward, when under way and <u>*when not having their nets, trawls, dredges, or lines in the water,*</u> *shall carry and show the same lights as other vessels under way.*

(c) All vessels, when trawling, dredging, or fishing with any kind of drag nets or lines, shall exhibit, from some part of the vessel where they can be best seen, two lights. One of these lights shall be red and the other shall be white. The red light shall be above the white light, and shall be at a vertical distance from it of not less than six feet and not more than twelve feet; and the horizontal distance between them, if any, shall not be more than ten feet. These two lights shall be of such a character and contained in lanterns of such construction as to be visible all around the horizon, the white light a distance of not less than three miles and the red light of not less than two miles.

§80.32a Daymarks for Fishing Vessels with Gear Out   All vessels or boats fishing with nets or lines or trawls, when underway, shall in daytime indicate their occupation to an approaching vessel by displaying a basket where it can best be seen. If the vessels or boats at anchor have their gear out, they shall, on the approach of other vessels, show the same signal in the direction from the anchor back towards the nets or gear.

22.3.7 Dredge—Inland Waters   A stationary dredge is required to

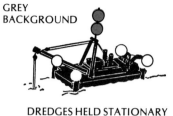

GREY
BACKGROUND

DREDGES HELD STATIONARY
(LIGHTS)

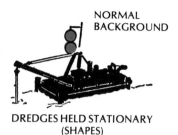

NORMAL
BACKGROUND

DREDGES HELD STATIONARY
(SHAPES)

show two red 32 point lights in a vertical line where best seen, and a white light at each corner. Scows alongside must have a white light on each outboard corner. A dredge working in a channel must have its anchors marked by buoys. At night the location of the buoys must be shown either by red lights on the buoys or by throwing light on them from the dredge when other vessels are passing. Pipelines attached to dredges must be lighted by a single row of amber lights, and the discharge end, or both sides of an opening in a channel, by two red lights in a vertical line. The dayshape for a stationary dredge is two red balls in a vertical line where best seen.

A self-propelled dredge underway and engaged in dredging operations shall display three 20 point masthead lights, white—red—red, sidelights, an after range light (32 point), and two red lights in a vertical line at the stern (12 point). By day she shall show two black balls in a vertical line where best seen.

GREY
BACKGROUND

SELF PROPELLED SUCTION DREDGES
(LIGHTS)   UNDERWAY—DREDGING

SELF PROPELLED SUCTION DREDGES
(SHAPES)   UNDERWAY—DREDGING

A self-propelled dredge underway and engaged in dredging operations shall display three 20 point masthead lights, white—red—red, sidelights, an after range light (32 point), and two red lights in a vertical line at the stern (12 point). By day she shall show two black balls in a vertical line where best seen.

A non-self-propelled dredge which is underway and engaged in dredging operations while being pushed ahead shall display the sidelights normally required for a barge towed by being pushed ahead. In addition the dredge and towboat, lighted as a single vessel, must show all the lights described in the preceding paragraph for a self-propelled dredge. The dredge and towboat are treated as a single vessel for the purpose of dayshapes and must carry two black balls in a vertical line where best seen.

22.3.8 Vessel Alongside or Moored Over a Wreck—Inland Waters

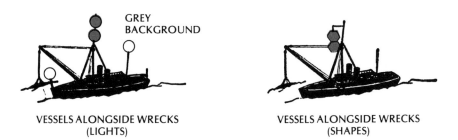

VESSELS ALONGSIDE WRECKS
(LIGHTS)

VESSELS ALONGSIDE WRECKS
(SHAPES)

Steam vessels, derrick boats, lighters, or other types of vessels made fast alongside a wreck, or moored over a wreck which is on the bottom or partly submerged, or which may be drifting ... are required to display a dayshape of two double frustums of cones, both red, in a vertical line where best seen. By night this situation shall be indicated by two red lights (32 point) displayed in a vertical line where best seen, in addition to a white light at the bow and stern of each outside vessel or lighter.

22.3.9 Submarine Construction, Etc.—Inland Waters Vessels

VESSELS MOORED OVER SUBMARINE CONSTRUCTION
(LIGHTS)

VESSELS MOORED OVER SUBMARINE CONSTRUCTION
(SHAPES)

moored or anchored and engaged in laying cables or pipe, submarine construction, excavation, mat sinking, bank grading, revetment or other bank protection operations... are required to display three red lights (32 point) in a vertical line where best seen. Anchors must be marked by buoys if working in a channel. At night the location of the buoys must be shown either by red lights on the buoys or by throwing light on them from the plant when other vessels are passing. Where a stringout of moored vessels or barges engaged in the operations crosses a channel, the stringout shall be marked by a horizontal row of amber lights, and each side of the opening with three red lights.

22.3.10   Vessel Towing a Submerged or Partly Submerged Object— Inland Waters   A vessel towing a submerged or partly submerged object, such tha. no signals can be displayed on the object being towed, shall display four towing lights in lieu of the regular towing lights. A vessel so engaged and displaying towing range lights is required to show four 32 point towing range lights in a vertical line, white—red— red—white, and sidelights.

A vessel displaying 20 point towing masthead lights is required to show four such lights in a vertical line, white—red—red—white, and

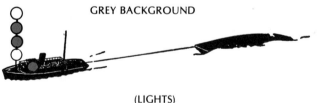

GREY BACKGROUND

(LIGHTS)
VESSELS TOWING SUBMERGED OBJECTS

(SHAPES)
VESSELS TOWING SUBMERGED OBJECTS

sidelights. She may in addition show a 32 point after range light, but if she does not, she must display a 12 point sternlight.

When engaged in towing a submerged object during the day, two double frustums of cones, black and white horizontally striped over red, must be displayed where best seen.

22.3.11 Pilot Vessel On Station—Inland Waters A steam pilot

| Steam Pilot Vessel | | Sailing Pilot Vessel |
| At Anchor | Under Way | At Anchor on Duty |

(Shows Flare-up at Intervals)

vessel on station and not at anchor is required to show white over red (32 point) lights at the masthead, and sidelights. She shall also show a flare-up light or flare-up lights at short intervals, which shall never exceed 15 minutes. When on station and at anchor she shows the white over red lights and a flare-up light or flare-up lights, but not the sidelights. When not engaged on her station on pilotage duty, she shall carry the same lights as other steam vessels.

A sailing pilot vessel (which is rare) does not show the red light at the masthead, and is required to show sidelights only when approaching other vessels. A pilot vessel of such a class as to be obliged to go alongside of a vessel to put a pilot on board, may show the white light instead of carrying it at the masthead, and may combine the sidelights in a single lantern.

22.3.12 Vessel at Anchor or Aground—Inland Waters A vessel

less than 150 feet in length at anchor or aground is required to carry one 32 point white light forward. A vessel 150 feet or upward in length is required to carry two 32 point white lights, with the forward light at least 15 feet higher than the light at or near the stern.

II (c) The Secretary of the Army may, after investigation, by rule, regulation, or order, designate such areas as he may deem proper as 'special anchorage areas'; such special anchorage areas may from time to time be changed, or abolished, if after investigation the Secretary of the Army shall deem such change or abolition in the interest of navigation. When anchored within such an area—

(1) a vessel of not more than sixty-five feet in length shall not be required to carry or exhibit the white light required by this article;

(2) a barge, canal boat, scow, or other nondescript craft of one hundred and fifty feet or upward in length may carry and exhibit the single white light prescribed by paragraph (a) of this article in lieu of the two white lights prescribed by paragraph (b) of this article; and

(3) where two or more barges, canal boats, scows, or other nondescript craft are tied together and anchored as a unit, the anchor light prescribed by this article need be displayed only on the vessel having its anchor down.

§ **80.25   Vessels Moored or at Anchor**   Vessels of more than 65 feet in length when moored or anchored in a fairway or channel shall display between sunrise and sunset on the forward part of the vessel where it can best be seen from other vessels one black ball not less than two feet in diameter.

22.3.13   Vessel Employed in Hydrographic Surveying—Inland Waters

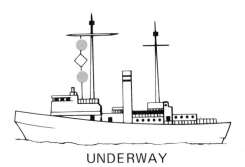

UNDERWAY

AT ANCHOR

Vessels of the National Ocean Survey, while actually engaged in hydrographic surveying and underway, shall display three dayshapes in a vertical line where best seen, green ball—white diamond—green ball. No special lights are shown when underway at night. These special signals do not give the surveying vessel the right of way over other vessels.

When engaged in surveying operations and at anchor in a fairway, such vessels shall display from the mast two black balls in a vertical line by day, and two red lights in a vertical line by night. A flare-up light must also be available to attract attention when necessary.

22.3.14   Coast Guard Vessel Handling or Servicing Aids to Navigation:

§ 80.33a   Warning signals for Coast Guard vessels while handling or servicing aids to navigation.

(a) Coast Guard vessels while engaged in handling or servicing an aid to navigation during the daytime may display from the yard two orange and white vertically striped balls in a vertical line not less than three feet or more than six feet apart, and during the nighttime may display, in a position where they may best be seen, two red lights in a vertical line not less than three feet nor more than six feet apart.

(b) Vessels, with or without tows, passing Coast Guard vessels displaying this signal, shall reduce their speed sufficiently to insure the safety of both vessels, and when passing within 200 feet of the Coast Guard vessel displaying this signal, their speed shall not exceed 5 miles per hour.

22.4   Miscellaneous Provisions—International and Inland:
22.4.1   Distress Signals:

INTERNATIONAL RULE 37—DISTRESS SIGNALS

When a vessel is in distress and requires assistance she shall use or exhibit the signals prescribed in Annex IV to these regulations.

ANNEX IV TO THE INTERNATIONAL RULES DISTRESS SIGNALS

1. The following signals, used or exhibited either together or separately, indicate distress and need of assistance:
(a) a gun or other explosive signal fired at intervals of about a minute;
(b) a continuous sounding with any fog-signalling apparatus;
(c) rockets or shells, throwing red stars fired one at a time at short intervals;
(d) a signal made by radiotelegraphy or by any other signaling method consisting of the group ... — — — ... (SOS) in the Morse Code;
(e) a signal sent by radiotelephony consisting of the spoken word "Mayday";
(f) the International Code Signal of distress indicated by N.C.;
(g) a signal consisting of a square flag having above or below it a ball or anything resembling a ball;
(h) flames on the vessel (as from a burning tar barrel, oil barrel, etc.)
(i) a rocket parachute flare or a hand flare showing a red light;
(j) a smoke signal giving off orange-colored smoke;

(k) slowly and repeatedly raising and lowering arms outstretched to each side;

(l) the radiotelegraph alarm signal;

(m) the radiotelephone alarm signal;

(n) signals transmitted by emergency position-indicating radio beacons.

2. The use or exhibition of any of the foregoing signals except for the purpose of indicating distress and need of assistance and the use of other signals which may be confused with any of the above signals is prohibited.

3. Attention is drawn to the relevant sections of the International Code of Signals, the Merchant Ship Search and Rescue Manual and the following signals:

(a) a piece of orange-coloured canvas with either a black square and circle or other appropriate symbol (for identification from the air);

(b) a dye marker.

INLAND ARTICLE 31—DISTRESS SIGNALS

Art. 31. When a vessel is in distress and requires assistance from other vessels or from the shore the following shall be the signal to be used or displayed by her, either together or separately, namely:

In the daytime—

A continuous sounding with any fog-signal apparatus, or firing a gun.

At night—

First. Flames on the vessel as from a burning tar barrel, oil barrel, and so forth.

Second. A continuous sounding with any fog-signal apparatus, or firing a gun.

22.4.2 Signals to Attract Attention:

INTERNATIONAL RULE 36—SIGNALS TO ATTRACT ATTENTION

If necessary to attract the attention of another vessel, any vessel may make light or sound signals that cannot be mistaken for any signal authorized elsewhere in these rules, or may direct the beam of her searchlight in the direction of the danger, in such a way as not to embarrass any vessel.

INLAND ARTICLE 12—SIGNALS TO ATTRACT ATTENTION

Art. 12. Every vessel may, if necessary, in order to attract attention, in addition, to the lights which she is by these rules required to carry, show a flare-up light or use any detonating signal that cannot be mistaken for a distress signal.

22.4.3   Additional Station or Signal Lights:

INTERNATIONAL RULE 1(c)

(c) Nothing in these rules shall interfere with the operation of any special rules made by the Government of any State with respect to additional station or signal lights or whistle signals for ships of war and vessels proceeding under convoy, or with respect to additional station or signal lights for fishing vessels engaged in fishing as a fleet. These additional station or signal lights or whistle signals shall, so far as possible, be such that they cannot be mistaken for any light or signal authorized elsewhere under these rules.

INLAND ARTICLE 13—NAVAL LIGHTS AND RECOGNITION SIGNALS

Art. 13. *Nothing in these rules shall interfere with the operation of any special rules made by the Government of any nation with respect to additional station and signal lights for two or more ships of war or for vessels sailing under convoy, or with the exhibition of recognition signals adopted by shipowners, which have been authorized by their respective Governments, and duly registered and published.*

TITLE 32, CODE OF FEDERAL REGULATIONS

PART 707—DISTINCTIVE LIGHTS AUTHORIZED FOR SUBMARINES

§ 707.1   Display of distinctive lights by submarines.

(a) In accordance with Rule 13(a), International Rules and Article 13, Inland Rules, the Secretary of the Navy has authorized the display of a distinctive light by U.S. Naval submarines in international water and in the inland waters of the United States. The light will be exhibited in addition to the presently prescribed navigational lights for submarines.

(b) The normal navigational lights of submarines have been found to be easily mistaken for those of small vessels when in fact submarines are large deep draft vessels with limited maneuvering characteristics while they are on the surface. The newly authorized light is expected to promote safety at sea by assisting in the identification of submarines.

(c) U.S. submarines may therefore display an amber rotating light producing 90 flashes per minute visible all around the horizon at a distance of at least 3 miles, the light to be located not less than 2 feet, and not more than 6 feet, above the masthead light.

(Sec. 1 (art. 13), 30 Stat. 99, sec. 4 (rule 13(a)), 77 Stat. 203; 33 U.S.C. 182, 1073(a)) [30 F.R. 11173, Aug. 31, 1965, as amended at 32 F.R. 8589, June 15, 1967]

22.4.4   Vessels of Special Construction or Purpose:

INTERNATIONAL RULE 1(e)

(e) Whenever the Government concerned shall have determined that a vessel of special construction or purpose cannot comply fully with the provisions of any of these rules with respect to the number, position, range or arc of visibility of lights or shapes, as well as to the disposition and characteristics of sound-signalling appliances, without interfering with the special function of the vessel, such vessel shall comply with such other provisions in regard to the number, position, range or arc of visibilty of lights or shapes, as well as to the disposition and characteristics of sound-signalling appliances, as her Government shall have determined to be the closest possible compliance with these rules in respect to that vessel.

INLAND ARTICLE 30—LIGHTS ON UNITED STATES NAVAL VESSELS AND COAST GUARD CUTTERS

Art. 30. *The exhibition of any light on board of a vessel of war of the United States or a Coast Guard cutter may be suspended whenever, in the opinion of the Secretary of the Navy, the commander in chief of a squadron, or the commander of a vessel acting singly, the special character of the service may require it.*

"Lights for Coast Guard Vessels of Special Construction" are listed in Part 135 of Title 33, Code of Federal Regulations. Navigational light waivers for the Department of the Navy are listed in Part 706 of Title 32, Code of Federal Regulations. Both can be found in CG-169.

22.4.5   Lights for Small Vessel in Bad Weather—Inland Waters:

Art. 6. *Whenever, as in the case of vessels of less than ten gross tons, underway during bad weather, the green and red side lights cannot be fixed, these lights shall be kept at hand, lighted and ready for use; and shall, on the approach of or to other vessels, be exhibited on their respective sides in sufficient time to prevent collision, in such manner as to make them most visible, and so that the green light shall not be seen on the port side, nor, if practicable, more than two points abaft the beam on their respective sides. To make the use of these portable lights more certain and easy the lanterns containing them shall each be painted outside with the color of the light they respectively contain, and shall be provided with proper screens.*

22.4.6   Lights for Small Rowing Boats, Rafts, and Other Craft Not Provided For—Inland Waters:

Art. 7. Rowing boats, whether under oars or sail, shall have ready at hand a lantern showing a white light which shall be temporarily exhibited in sufficient time to prevent collision.

Art. 9. (d) Rafts, or other water craft not herein provided for, navigating by hand power, horse power, or by the current of the river, shall carry one or more good white lights, which shall be placed in such manner as shall be prescribed by the Commandant of the Coast Guard.

Responsibilities
Between Vessels—
Right of Way

23.1 Right of Way Between Different Categories of Vessels   This
section will consider the right of way between different categories of
vessels underway, namely:

Category	International Rules Special Light Array	Inland Waters Special Light Array
not under command	red over red	—
restricted in ability to maneuver (includes minesweeper)	red—white—red (3 green lights)	various
constrained by draft	red—red—red	—
engaged in fishing includes trawling	red over white green over white	red over white red over white
sailing vessel	red over green (optional)	NONE
power-driven/steam vessel includes: pilot vessel towing vessel	NONE white over red towing masthead lights	NONE white over red towing masthead OR towing range lights

The only categories mentioned by the *Inland Rules* for the purpose of determining right of way are steam vessel, sailing vessel and vessel engaged in fishing:

—STEAM VESSEL must keep out of the way of a SAILING VESSEL
—SAILING VESSEL must keep out of the way of a VESSEL ENGAGED IN FISHING

The above provisions also hold true in the *International Rules*, but they are only a subset of a comprehensive hierarchy for "responsibilities between vessels." Note that the *Inland Rules* do not give a vessel engaged in fishing the right of way over a steam vessel, however, a 1974 court decision gives the right of way to fishing vessels.

The *Pilot Rules for Inland Waters* contains regulations governing vessels which pass a floating plant working in a navigable channel. The term "floating plant" includes dredges, derrick boats, snag boats, drill boats, pile drivers, maneuver boats, hydraulic graders, survey boats, working barges, and mat sinking plant. The *Pilot Rules* also prescribe lights and shapes for various types of floating plants. There is no special array common to all types, however, most floating plants display two or three red lights in a vertical line (see Chapter 22). The regulations for passing a floating plant will be covered in a later section.

Rule 18 of the *International Rules* provides the following hierarchy of "responsibilities between vessels." Except where Rule 9 (Narrow Channels), Rule 10 (Traffic Separation Schemes), or Rule 13 (Overtaking Situation) otherwise require, all vessels shall keep out of the way of vessels in all categories which are listed above the category pertaining to their own vessel:

(1) Vessel not under command, vessel restricted in her ability to maneuver (including a vessel engaged in minesweeping operations)
(2) Vessel constrained by her draft
(3) Vessel engaged in fishing
(4) Sailing vessel
(5) Power-driven vessel

23.2   Exceptions to Right of Way Provisions Between Categories   The *Inland Rules* make the following exceptions to the right of way provisions discussed in the previous section:

—"In narrow channels a steam vessel of less than sixty-five feet in length shall not hamper the safe passage of a vessel which can navigate only inside that channel." (Art. 25)
—"This rule shall not give to a sailing vessel the right to hamper, in a narrow

channel, the safe passage of a steam vessel which can navigate only inside that channel." (Art. 20)

—"This rule shall not give to any vessel or boat engaged in fishing the right of obstructing a fairway used by vessels other than fishing vessels or boats." (Art. 26)

—"Notwithstanding anything contained in these rules every vessel, overtaking any other, shall keep out of the way of the overtaken vessel." (Art. 24)

The exceptions above also hold true in the *International Rules,* but the International Rules contain additional provisions which are no included in the Inland Rules.

RULE 9—NARROW CHANNELS

(b) A vessel of less than 20 metres in length or a sailing vessel shall not impede the passage of a vessel which can safely navigate only within a narrow channel or fairway.

(c) A vessel engaged in fishing shall not impede the passage of any other vessel navigating within a narrow channel or fairway.

(d) A vessel shall not cross a narrow channel or fairway if such crossing impedes the passage of a vessel which can safely navigate only within such channel or fairway. The latter vessel may use the sound signal prescribed in Rule 34(d) if in doubt as to the intention of the crossing vessel.

(g) Any vessel shall, if the circumstances of the case admit, avoid anchoring in a narrow channel.

RULE 10—TRAFFIC SEPARATION SCHEMES

(a) This rule applies to traffic separation schemes adopted by the organization.

(h) A vessel not using a traffic separation scheme shall avoid it by as wide a margin as is practicable.

(i) A vessel engaged in fishing shall not impede the passage of any vessel following a traffic lane.

(j) A vessel of less than 20 metres in length or a sailing vessel shall not impede the safe passage of a power-driven vessel following a traffic lane.

23.3 Sailing Vessel Approaching Sailing Vessel—International Rules:

RULE 12—SAILING VESSELS

(a) When two sailing vessels are approaching one another, so as to involve risk of collision, one of them shall keep out of the way of the other as follows:

(i) when each has the wind on a different side, the vessel which has the wind on the port side shall keep out of the way of the other;

(ii) when both have the wind on the same side, the vessel which is to windward shall keep out of the way of the vessel which is to leeward;

(iii) if a vessel with the wind on the port side sees a vessel to windward and cannot determine with certainty whether the other vessel has the wind on the port or on the starboard side, she shall keep out of the way of the other.

(b) For the purposes of this rule the windward side shall be deemed to be the side opposite to that on which the mainsail is carried or, in the case of a square-rigged vessel, the side opposite to that on which the largest fore-and-aft sail is carried.

23.4   Sailing Vessel Approaching Sailing Vessel—Inland Waters

SAILING VESSELS

Art. 17. When two sailing vessels are approaching one another, so as to involve risk of collision, one of them shall keep out of the way of the other as follows, namely:

(a) A vessel which is running free shall keep out of the way of a vessel which is closehauled.

(b) A vessel which is closehauled on the port tack shall keep out of the way of a vessel which is closehauled on the starboard tack.

(c) When both are running free, with the wind on different sides, the vessel which has the wind on the port side shall keep out of the way of the other.

(d) When both are running free, with the wind on the same side, the vessel which is to the windward shall keep out of the way of the vessel which is to the leeward.

(e) A vessel which has the wind aft shall keep out of the way of the other vessel.

When the average boat sails with the wind broad on her bow, she is beating (close-hauled). Most vessels will be close-hauled when the wind is from a direction within five points of dead ahead. A vessel has the wind aft when she is running before the wind, with the wind from a direction within two points of dead astern. "Running free" in the Inland Rules (in contrast to its popular usage in sailing today) includes close reach, beam reach and broad reach.

Approach Situations Between Power-Driven/ Steam Vessels In Sight

24.1 General Provisions—International and Inland

24.1.1 Risk of Collision The privileged or burdened status of two power-driven/steam vessels approaching each other is determined by the approach situation—meeting, crossing or overtaking. For any of the three approach situations to exist, two vessels must be approaching so as to involve risk of collision and they must be in visual contact, which does not include tracking by radar. The situations apply in fog and other conditions of restricted visibility, *but only after the vessels have sighted each other.*

INTERNATIONAL RULE 7—RISK OF COLLISION

(a) Every vessel shall use all available means appropriate to the prevailing circumstances and conditions to determine if risk of collision exists. If there is any doubt such risk shall be deemed to exist.

(b) Proper use shall be made of radar equipment if fitted and operational, including long-range scanning to obtain early warning of risk of collision and radar plotting or equivalent systematic observation of detected objects.

(c) Assumptions shall not be made on the basis of scanty information, especially scanty radar information.

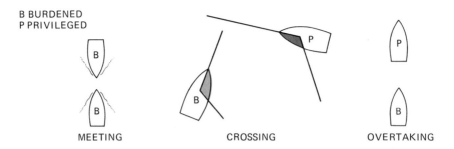

B BURDENED
P PRIVILEGED

MEETING   CROSSING   OVERTAKING

(d) In determining if risk of collision exists the following considerations shall be among those taken into account:

(i) such risk shall be deemed to exist if the compass bearing of an approaching vessel does not appreciably change;

(ii) such risk may sometimes exist even when an appreciable bearing change is evident, particularly when approaching a very large vessel or a tow or when approaching a vessel at close range.

INLAND STEERING AND SAILING RULES—PRELIMINARY

Risk of collison can, when circumstances permit, be ascertained by carefully watching the compass bearing of an approaching vessel. If the bearing does not appreciably change, such risk should be deemed to exist.

Rule 7 contains items of good seamanship which should be followed in inland waters as well. Bearings of approaching vessels must be compass bearings (true or magnetic), not relative bearings.

24.1.2 Whistle Signals:

INLAND ARTICLE 18, RULE IX

Rule IX. *The whistle signals provided in the rules under this article, for steam vessels meeting, passing, or overtaking, are never to be used except when steamers are in sight of each other, and the course and position of each can be determined in the day time by a sight of the vessel itself, or by night by seeing its signal lights. In fog, mist, falling snow or heavy rain storms, when vessels can not see each other, fog signals only must be given.*

INLAND ARTICLE 28—BACKING SIGNAL

Art. 28. *When vessels are in sight of one another a steam vessel underway whose engines are going at full speed astern shall indicate that fact by three short blasts on the whistle.*

INTERNATIONAL RULE 34—MANOEUVRING AND WARNING SIGNALS

(a) When vessels are in sight of one another, a power-driven vessel underway, when manoeuvring as authorized or required by these rules, shall indicate that manoeuvre by the following signals on her whistle:

—one short blast to mean "I am altering my course to starboard";

—two short blasts to mean "I am altering my course to port";

—three short blasts to mean "I am operating astern propulsion."

(b) Any vessel may supplement the whistle signal prescribed in paragraph (a) of this rule by light signals, repeated as appropriate, whilst the manoeuvre is being carried out:

(i) these light signals shall have the following significance:

—one flash to mean "I am altering my course to starboard";

—two flashes to mean "I am altering my course to port";

—three flashes to mean "I am operating astern propulsion";

(ii) the duration of each flash shall be about one second, the interval between flashes shall be about one second, and the interval between successive signals shall be not less than ten seconds;

(iii) the light used for this signal shall, if fitted, be an all-round white light, visible at a minimum range of 5 miles, and shall comply with the provisions of Annex I.

The International Rules require a power-driven vessel to give the one and two short blast signals when a vessel of any type or category is in sight. They are rudder-action signals, intended to inform other vessels that a change of course is being executed.

The one and two short blast signals in inland waters are signals of proposal-agreement in the meeting and overtaking situations. They do not signal a change in course or intention to change course, but they enable vessels to agree on which side they will pass. Section 80.03 of the Pilot Rules contains the following statements: "one short blast of the whistle signifies intention to direct course to own starboard"; "two short blasts of the whistle signify intention to direct course to own port." The two statements are in conflict with the Inland Rules which govern the meeting and overtaking situations, and are therefore invalid. The Inland Rules prescribe no signals for the crossing situation; the proper use of signals is derived partially from the Pilot Rules and partially by the rulings of U.S. courts. This will be discussed in greater detail in section 24.4.

The three short blast backing signal in both the International and Inland Rules is given by a power-driven/steam vessel when a vessel of any type or category is in sight. In the International Rules it is required when the engines are going astern at any speed. The courts have ruled that vessels in inland waters should sound three short blasts when backing at less than full speed or when making sternway.

24.1.3 Danger/Doubt Signal:

INLAND ARTICLE 18, RULE III

Rule III. *If, when steam vessels are approaching each other, either vessel fails to understand the course or intention of the other, from any cause, the vessel so in doubt shall immediately signify the same by giving several short and rapid blasts, not less than four, of the steam whistle.*

INTERNATIONAL RULE 34(d)

34(d) When vessels in sight of one another are approaching each other and from any cause either vessel fails to understand the intentions or actions of the other, or is in doubt whether sufficient action is being taken by the other to avoid collision, the vessel in doubt shall immediately indicate such doubt by giving at least five short and rapid blasts on the whistle. Such signal may be supplemented by a light signal of at least five short and rapid flashes.

The Inland danger signal is prescribed only for steam vessels. The International signal of doubt is not restricted to power-driven vessels, but the vessels must be in sight of each other. The courts have ruled that the Inland danger signal may be used in restricted visibility when vessels are not in sight of each other. In both waters, the signal is required by the vessel in doubt, which may be *either* a burdened or privileged vessel.

24.1.4 Burdened Vessel Duties

INTERNATIONAL RULE 16—ACTION BY GIVE-WAY VESSEL

Every vessel which is directed by these rules to keep out of the way of another vessel shall, as far as possible, take early and substantial action to keep well clear.

INTERNATIONAL RULE 8—ACTION TO AVOID COLLISION

(a) Any action taken to avoid collision shall, if the circumstances of the case admit, be positive, made in ample time and with due regard to the observance of good seamanship.

(b) Any alteration of course and/or speed to avoid collision shall, if the circumstances of the case admit, be large enough to be readily apparent to another vessel observing visually or by radar; a succession of small alterations of course and/or speed should be avoided.

(c) If there is sufficient sea room, alteration of course alone may be the most effective action to avoid a close-quarters situation provided that it is made in good time, is substantial and does not result in another close-quarters situation.

(d) Action taken to avoid collision with another vessel shall be such as to result in passing at a safe distance. The effectiveness of the action shall be carefully checked until the other vessel is finally past and clear.

(e) If necessary to avoid collision or allow more time to assess the situation, a vessel shall slacken her speed or take all way off by stopping or reversing her means of propulsion.

INLAND ARTICLES 22 AND 23—BURDENED VESSEL DUTY

Art. 22. Every vessel which is directed by these rules to keep out of the way of another vessel shall, if the circumstances of the case admit, avoid crossing ahead of the other.

Art. 23. Every steam vessel which is directed by these rules to keep out of the way of another vessel shall, or approaching her, if necessary, slacken her speed or stop or reverse.

The International Rules contain items of good seamanship which should also be observed in inland waters.

24.1.5 Privileged Vessel Duties:

INTERNATIONAL RULE 17—ACTION BY STAND-ON VESSEL

(a) (i) Whereby any of these rules one of two vessels is to keep out of the way, the other shall keep her course and speed.

(ii) The latter vessel may, however, take action to avoid collision by her manoeuvre alone, as soon as it becomes apparent to her that the vessel required to keep out of the way is not taking appropriate action in compliance with these rules.

(b) When, from any cause, the vessel required to keep her course and speed finds herself so close that collision cannot be avoided by the action of the give-way vessel alone, she shall take such action as will best aid to avoid collision.

(c) A power-driven steam vessel which takes action in a crossing situation in accordance with sub-paragraph (a) (ii) of this rule to avoid collision with another power-driven vessel shall, if the circumstances of the case admit, not alter course to port for a vessel on her own port side.

(d) This rule does not relieve the give-way vessel of her obligation to keep out of the way.

INLAND ARTICLE 21—PRIVILEGED VESSEL DUTY

Art. 21. Where, by any of these rules, one of the two vessels is to keep out of the way, the other shall keep her course and speed.

The provision in Rule 17(b) above applies in inland waters by court interpretation of Article 27, the "General Prudential Rule."

24.1.6 Approaches in a Narrow Channel:

INTERNATIONAL RULE 9—NARROW CHANNELS

(a) A vessel proceeding along the course of a narrow channel or fairway shall keep as near to the outer limit of the channel or fairway which lies on her starboard side as is safe and practicable.

(d) A vessel shall not cross a narrow channel or fairway if such crossing impedes the passage of a vessel which can safely navigate only within such channel or fairway. The latter vessel may use the sound signal prescribed in Rule 34(d) if in doubt as to the intention of the crossing vessel.

(g) Any vessel shall, if the circumstances of the case admit, avoid anchoring in a narrow channel.

INLAND ARTICLE 25—NARROW CHANNELS

Art. 25. *In narrow channels every steam vessel shall, when it is safe and practicable, keep to that side of the fairway or midchannel which lies on the starboard side of such vessel.*

24.2 Overtaking Situation

24.2.1 Overtaking Situation Defined Rule 13 of the International Rules Clearly defines the overtaking situation:

INTERNATIONAL RULE 13—OVERTAKING

(a) Notwithstanding anything contained in the rules of this Section any vessel overtaking any other shall keep out of the way of the vessel being overtaken.

(b) A vessel shall be deemed to be overtaking when coming up with another vessel from a direction more than 22.5 degrees abaft her beam, that is, in such a position with reference to the vessel she is overtaking, that at night she would be able to see only the sternlight of that vessel but neither of her sidelights.

(c) When a vessel is in any doubt as to whether she is overtaking another, she shall assume that this is the case and act accordingly.

(d) Any subsequent alteration of the bearing between the two vessels shall not make the overtaking vessel a crossing vessel within the meaning of these rules or relieve her of the duty of keeping clear of the overtaken vessel until she is finally past and clear.

Article 24 of the Inland Rules contains the same provisions as Rule 13, although it assumes that the doubtful situations addressed by Rule 13(c) occur only by day. The differences arise in the conduct and signals required of vessels during the passing.

The rules do not prescribe the side on which the overtaking vessel should pass. In confined waters, good seamanship suggests that the passing shall be to port if safe and practicable, since the vessel ahead is required to keep to the starboard side of a fairway or channel. The overtaken vessel may be forced to move to starboard if she meets another vessel end on. Such a move to starboard might be awkward, if not dangerous, to the overtaking vessel trying to pass to starboard.

In situations where the overtaken vessel gives a whistle signal of agreement to the other vessel's proposal, such agreement should not be given when it is dangerous to pass. The overtaken vessel similarly should not agree to an overtaking proposal if she herself is planning a maneuver, such as a turn to make a berth or pick up a pilot.

An overtaking vessel must anticipate changes of course by the overtaken vessel for the purpose of following the channel or avoiding rocks, shoals or other vessels. Sailing vessels, in particular, must be given a wide berth in order that they may make the necessary tacks to follow a channel.

24.2.2 Overtaking Situation in the International Rules   The overtaking situation in *open waters* under the International Rules is very simple. The overtaking (burdened) vessel sounds one or two short blasts if she turns right or left to avoid the overtaken (privileged) vessel. The privileged vessel maintains course and speed.

The overtaking situation in restricted waters is modified by the Narrow Channel Rule:

INTERNATIONAL RULE 9(e)

(i) In a narrow channel or fairway when overtaking can take place only if the vessel to be overtaken has to take action to permit safe passing, the vessel intending to overtake shall indicate her intention by sounding the appropriate signal prescribed in Rule 34(c)(i) [two prolonged blasts followed by one short blast to mean "I intend to overtake you on your starboard side" OR two prolonged blasts followed by two short blasts to mean "I intend to overtake you on your port side."] The overtaken vessel shall, if in agreement, sound the appropriate signal prescribed in Rule 34(c)(ii) [one prolonged, one short, one prolonged and one short blast, in that order] and take steps to permit safe passing. If in doubt she may sound the signals prescribed in Rule 34(d) [signal of doubt, five or more short blasts].

(ii) This Rule does not relieve the overtaking vessel of her obligaton under Rule 13.

The overtaking vessel should not attempt passing until an agreement is reached, nor does agreement relieve her of her obligation to keep out of the way until well past and clear. Note that the signals are *not* limited to power-driven vessels.

24.2.3 Overtaking Situation In Inland Waters   Article 18, Rule VIII, applies only to a steam vessel overtaking another steam vessel:

> Rules VIII. *When steam vessels are running in the same direction, and the vessel which is astern shall desire to pass on the right or starboard hand of the vessel ahead, she shall give one short blast of the steam whistle, as a signal of such desire, and if the vessel ahead answers with one blast, she shall direct her course to starboard; or if she shall desire to pass on the left or port side of the vessel ahead, she shall give two short blasts of the steam whistle as a signal of such desire, and if the vessel ahead answers with two blasts, shall direct her course to port; or if the vessel ahead does not think it safe for the vessel astern to attempt to pass at that point, she shall immediately signify the same by giving several short and rapid blasts of the steam whistle, not less than four, and under no circumstances shall the vessel astern, attempt to pass the vessel ahead until such time as they have reached a point where it can be safely done, when said vessel ahead shall signify her willingness by blowing the proper signals. The vessel ahead shall in no case attempt to cross the bow or crowd upon the course of the passing vessel.*

The overtaking vessel is not permitted to pass the vessel ahead until the overtaken vessel answers with the same signal. "The signal of an overtaking vessel must be repeated if not responded to, and the possibility of collision avoided, if necessary, by slackening speed or changing course." The privileged vessel is not obligated to maintain course and speed until she agrees to the proposal of the overtaking vessel.

24.3 Meeting Situation

24.3.1 Head-On Situation Defined   The head-on situation is defined by Rule 14 of the International Rules:

INTERNATIONAL RULE 14—HEAD-ON SITUATION

(a) When two power-driven vessels are meeting on reciprocal or nearly reciprocal courses so as to involve risk of collision each shall alter her course to starboard so that each shall pass on the port side of the other.

(b) Such a situation shall be deemed to exist when a vessel sees the other ahead or nearly ahead and by night she could see the masthead lights of the other in a line or nearly in a line and/or both sidelights and by day she observes the corresponding aspect of the other vessel.

(c) When a vessel is in any doubt as to whether such a situation exists she shall assume that it does exist and act accordingly.

The "head and head" situation is defined very similarly in Article 18 and Section 80.4 of the Pilot Rules:

Art. 18. Rule I. *When steam vessels are approaching each other head and head, that is, end on, or nearly so, it shall be the duty of each to pass on the port side of the other; and either vessel shall give, as a signal of her intention, one short and distinct blast of her whistle, which the other vessel shall answer promptly by a similar blast of her whistle, and thereupon such vessels shall pass on the port side of each other.*

The foregoing only applies to cases where vessels are meeting end on, or nearly end on, in such a manner as to involve risk of collision; in other words, to cases in which, by day, each vessel sees the masts of the other in a line, or nearly in a line, with her own, and by night to cases in which each vessel is in such a position as to see both the sidelights of the other.

It does not apply by day to cases in which a vessel sees another ahead crossing her own course, or by night to cases where the red light of one vessel is opposed to the red light of the other, or where the green light of one vessel is opposed to the green light of the other, or where a red light without a green light or a green light without a red light, is seen ahead, or where both green and red lights are seen anywhere but ahead.

The International Rules have improved upon the definition of the head-on situation by including the sighting of the masthead and range light in a line or nearly in a line—with or without the sidelights. Since the white lights are often in view for some time before the sidelights are visible, it is prudent to maneuver before the colored lights are within range.

A meeting situation is generally considered to exist if the appropriate aspect of the other vessel is sighted within one point of the bow. The provision in Rule 14 to treat borderline cases as meeting situations is also good seamanship in inland waters.

The definition of a meeting situation is more strictly applied in open waters than in restricted waters. Two vessels which are travelling in opposite directions in a narrow, crooked channel will eventually pass in a meeting situation even though they initially sight each other on crossing courses.

24.3.2 Head-on Situation in the International Rules   In a head-on situation both vessels are burdened and required to alter course to starboard in order to pass port to port. No mention is made of a starboard to starboard pasage, which implies that such a passage is only proper when there is no risk of collision.

Changes of course must be accompanied by the appropriate one and two short blast signals while the vessels are in sight of each other.

24.3.3 Head-on Situation in Inland Waters   In a head and head situation both vessels are burdened and required to alter course to starboard in order to pass port to port. The whistle signals are signals of proposal and agreement. One vessel sounds one shot blast to propose a port to port passage; the other vessel agrees to such a passage with the same signal. This exchange of signals is required by the Pilot Rules whenever the CPA (closest Point of Approach) is within one-half mile, including situations where the vessels pass safely with no course change required by either. In this latter case, the vessels may not actually be within the definition of head and head if only the red light is visible.

Unless it is necessary to avoid immediate danger, a vessel should not alter course until her whistle of proposal has been answered. If the other vessel crosses your signal, or makes a proposal with which you do not agree, the courts require that you sound the danger signal and stop your engines, and reverse if the proximity of the vessels require it. A vessel which answers two short blasts with the danger signal, and then sounds one short blast without stopping or reversing, is guilty of cross signals—even if the original proposal was an improper one. After stopping, signals must be exchanged before the vessels pass each other. The same procedure is recommended when the other vessel does not answer your proposal, rather than repeating the signal.

24.3.4 Starboard-to-Starboard Meeting in Inland Waters (not within the definition of head and head)   When vessels are meeting within the definition of "head and head," a port to port passage is required. The Inland Rules prescribe signals for a starboard to starboard passing, and the Pilot Rules require that the signals be exchanged whenever the CPA is within one-half mile. In this situation each vessel will have only the green sidelight of the other in sight.

Inland Rules: *But if the courses of such vessels are so far on the starboard of each other as not to be considered as meeting head and head, either vessel shall immediately give two short and distinct blasts of her whistle, which the other vessel shall answer promptly by two similar blasts of her whistle, and they shall pass on the starboard side of each other.*

24.4 Crossing Situation

24.4.1 Crossing Situation Defined   The crossing situation is defined by Rule 14 of the International Rules:

INTERNATIONAL RULE 15—CROSSING SITUATION

When two power-driven vessels are crossing so as to involve risk of collision, the vessel which has the other on her own starboard side shall keep out of the way and shall, if the circumstances of the case admit, avoid crossing ahead of the other vessel.

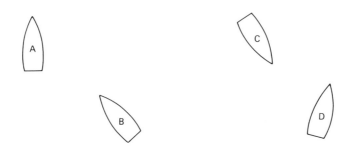

The *Inland Rules* contain the same provisions in Articles 19 and 22. The crossing situation is any approach situation which is neither a meeting nor an overtaking situation. In the diagram above, if vessel B is in any doubt as to whether she is overtaking or crossing vessel A, she is required by the rules to assume that she is overtaking and keep out of the way. If vessel D is in any doubt as to whether she is meeting or crossing vessel C, she should assume that it is a meeting situation and alter course to starboard for a port to port passing (this is a requirement in the International Rules which is not mentioned in the Inland Rules).

24.4.2 Crossing Situation in the International Rules   In a crossing situation, the vessel which has the other on her own starboard hand is burdened and required to sound the appropriate one, two or three short blasts as she maneuvers to keep out of the way.

The privileged vessel is required to maintain course and speed. Rule 17 gives the circumstance under which a privileged vessel is *required* to depart from the requirement to maintain course and speed (paragraph (b)), and the circumstance under which she *may* depart from that requirement (subparagraph (a)(ii)).

RULE 17—ACTION BY STAND-ON VESSEL

(a)(i) Where by any of these rules one of two vessels is to keep out of the way, the other shall keep her course and speed.

(ii) The latter vessel may, however, take action to avoid collision by her manoeuvre alone, as soon as it becomes apparent to her that the vessel required to keep out of the way is not taking appropriate action in compliance with these rules.

(b) When, from any cause, the vessel required to keep her course and speed finds herself so close that collision cannot be avoided by the action of the give-way vessel alone, she shall take such action as will best aid to avoid collision.

(c) A power-driven vessel which takes action in a crossing situation in accordance with sub-paragraph (a)(ii) of this rule to avoid collision with another power-driven vessel shall, if the circumstances of the case admit, not alter course to port for a vessel on her own port side.

(d) This rule does not relieve the give-way vessel of her obligation to keep out of the way.

If the privileged vessel departs from the requirement to maintain course and speed, she must accompany all maneuvers, including a maneuver in extremis, with the appropriate one, two or three short blasts.

24.4.3 Crossing Situation in Inland Waters   The use of whistle signals in the crossing situation is unlike that in the overtaking and meeting situations, where the signals were a proposal by one vessel, and an agreement by the other, on which side they would pass. The Inland Rules do not prescribe signals for the crossing situation, but certain provisions of the Pilot Rules combined with court rulings forms a rather complex set of directives.

A very important point to remember is that the failure of one vessel to sound a one short blast signal does not, by itself, excuse the other from her obligation under the Inland Rules—the burdened vessel is still required to keep out of the way and avoid crossing ahead, and the privileged vessel is required to maintain course and speed.

Paragraph 80.03(a) of the Pilot Rules says that "when two steam vessels are approaching each other at right angles or obliquely . . . one short blast of the whistle signifies intention . . . of steam vessel which is to starboard of the other to hold course and speed." The courts have held that this signal is not required but permissive. Although use of the one-blast signal by the privileged vessel is permissive—if the signal is given at all, it must be given in a timely manner:

If signals are to be of any value, they must be given with an allowance of a sufficient time to exchange signals and agree on a passing, taking into consideration the speed, power and apparent agility of the vessels.

The privileged vessel is required to depart from the requirement to maintain course and speed when "in extremis."

A steamer, when the privileged vessel, in crossing is not required to change course or reverse to avoid collision until it becomes evident that the other vessel will not or cannot keep out of the way.

24.4.4 Pilot Rules Modify Rules of Crossing:

§ 80.7 Vessels approaching each other at right angles or obliquely.

(a) When two steam vessels are approaching each other at right angles or obliquely so as to involve risk of collision, other than when one steam vessel is overtaking another, the steam vessel which has the other on her own port side shall hold her course and speed: and the steam vessel which has the other on her own starboard side shall keep out of the way of the other by directing her course to starboard so as to cross the stern of the other steam vessel, or, if necessary to do so, slacken her speed or stop or reverse.

(b) If from any causes the conditions covered by this situation are such as to prevent immediate compliance with each other's signals, the misunderstanding or objection shall be at once made apparent by blowing the danger signal, and both steam vessels shall be stopped and backed if necessary, until signals for passing with safety are made and understood.

Paragraph (a) above eliminates the possibility of the burdened vessel avoiding the other by turning left without crossing ahead of the privileged vessel.

Paragraph (b) contains the more significant modification of the rules of crossing. This modification was validated by a Supreme Court decision in 1940:

We think that Inspectors' Rule II [Pilot Rules, Section 80.2] should be read in connection with their Rule VII [paragraph 80.7(b)] and that both should be construed in the light of the statutory provision in Article 27 . . . We hold these rules are not essentially inconsistent with the statute and are valid.

The only point which requires clarification is what constitutes a "misunderstanding or objection." A "misunderstanding" occurs when cross signals are sounded—"answering one whistle with two, and answering two whistles with one." An "objection occurs if one vessel makes a proposal which is unacceptable to the other, as when a burdened vessel sounds an illegal two-blast signal, which is a proposal to cross ahead of the privileged vessel. A circuit court of appeals, commenting on the 1940 Supreme Court decision mentioned earlier, makes it clear that the privileged vessel cannot cross a two-blast signal nor maintain speed in such circumstances:

There can be no doubt that the Supreme Court meant to hold that in a crossing case, when the holding-on vessel gets two blasts from the giving-way vessel, which are unacceptable to her, she must neither cross the signal, nor keep her speed, but must at least stop her engines, and if necessary back, "until signals for passing with safety are made and understood" . . .

Rule VII [Section 80.7(b)] is explicit; it forbids any agreement other than an assent to the proposal, until after the vessels have at least stopped their engines. They may not undertake to agree while they remain underway.

24.5   Whistle Signals For Narrow Channels
24.5.1   Bend Signal

INLAND ARTICLE 18, RULE V

Rule V. *Whenever a steam vessel is nearing a short bend or curve in the channel, where, from the height of the banks or other cause, a steam vessel approaching from the opposite direction can not be seen for a distance of half a mile, such steam vessel, when she shall have arrived within half a mile of such curve or bend, shall give a signal by one long blast of the steam whistle, which signal shall be answered by a similar blast given by an approaching steam vessel that may be within hearing. Should such signal be so answered by a steam vessel upon the farther side of such bend, then the usual signals for meeting and passing shall immediately be given and answered; but, if the first alarm signal of such vessel be not answered, she is to consider the channel clear and govern herself accordingly.*

INTERPRETATIVE RULINGS—INLAND RULES

SUBPART 86.10—STEERING AND SAILING

§ 86.10-1   Bend signal and subsequent meeting situation.

Article 18, Rule V, and Article 18, Rule IX, of section 1, of the Act of June 7, 1897, as amended (33 U.S.C. 203), must be read together and followed after a bend signal is answered and the word "immediately" as used in Rule V shall be construed to require the exchange of sound signals for passing immediately upon sighting the other vessel.

INTERNATIONAL RULE 9(f)

(f) A vessel nearing a bend or an area of a narrow channel or fairway where other vessels may be obscured by an intervening obstruction shall navigate with particular alertness and caution and shall sound the appropriate signal prescribed in Rule 34(e).

INTERNATIONAL RULE 34(e)

34(e) A vessel nearing a bend or an area of a channel or fairway where other vessels may be obscured by an intervening obstruction shall sound one prolonged blast. Such signal shall be answered with a prolonged blast by any approaching vessel that may be within hearing around the bend or behind the intervening obstruction.

The bend signal is prescribed only for steam vessels in the Inland Rules. The International bend signal is not limited to power-driven vessels.

24.5.2   Inland "Slip Whistle":

INLAND ARTICLE 18, RULE V

When steam vessels are moved from their docks or berths, and other boats are liable to pass from any direction toward them, they shall give the same signal as in the case of vessels meeting at a bend, but immediately after clearing the berths so as to be fully in sight they shall be governed by the steering and sailing rules.

The courts have required that the long blast signal be given by a vessel leaving her dock or berth even when such a vessel is in sight of other vessels. When a vessel is not fully in sight, the slip whistle must be sounded repeatedly as long as the vessel is hidden from view. Note that this signal is not prescribed for use by an anchored vessel which is getting underway.

The courts have ruled that a vessel moving from her dock or berth is in "special circumstances" until settled on her course.

24.5.3   Passing Floating Plant in Navigable Channels—Inland Waters:

NOTE: The term "floating plant" as used in Sections 80.26 to 80.31a, includes dredges, derrick boats, snag boats, drill boats, pile drivers, maneuver boats, hydraulic graders, survey boats, working barges, and mat sinking plant.

§ 80.26   Passing signals.

(a) Vessels intending to pass dredges or other types of floating plant working in navigable channels, when within a reasonable distance therefrom and not in any case over a mile, shall indicate such intention by one long blast of the whistle, and shall be directed to the proper side for passage by the sounding, by the dredge or other floating plant, of the signal prescribed in the local pilot rules for vessels underway and approaching each other from opposite directions, which shall be answered in the usual manner by the approaching vessel. If the channel is not clear, the floating plant shall sound the alarm or danger signal and the approaching vessel shall slow down or stop and await further signal from the plant.

(b) When the pipeline from a dredge crosses the channel in such a way that an approaching vessel cannot pass safely around the pipeline or dredge, there shall be sounded immediately from the dredge the alarm or danger signal and the approaching vessel shall slow down or stop and await further signal from the dredge. The pipeline shall then be opened and the channel cleared as soon as practicable: when the channel is clear for passage the dredge shall so indicate by sounding the usual passing signal as prescribed in paragraph (a) of this section. The approaching vessel shall answer with a corresponding signal and pass promptly.

(c) When any pipeline or swinging dredge shall have given an approaching vessel or tow the signal that the channel is clear, the dredge shall straighten out within the cut for the passage of the vessel or tow.

§ 80.27   Speed of vessels passing floating plant working in channels.

Vessels, with or without tows, passing floating plant working in channels, shall reduce their speed sufficiently to insure the safety of both the plant and themselves, and when passing within 200 feet of the plant their speed shall not exceed five miles per hour. While passing over lines of the plant, propelling machinery shall be stopped.

§ 80.28   Light-draft vessels passing floating plant.

Vessels whose draft permits shall keep outside of the buoys marking the end of mooring line of floating plant working in channels.

24.6   Traffic Separation Schemes—International Rules

INTERNATIONAL RULE 10—TRAFFIC SEPARATION SCHEMES

(a) This rule applies to traffic separation schemes adopted by the organization.

(b) A vessel using a traffic separation scheme shall:

(i) proceed in the appropriate traffic lane in the general direction of traffic flow for that lane;

(ii) so far as practicable keep clear of a traffic separation line or separation zone;

(iii) normally join or leave a traffic lane at the termination of the lane, but when joining or leaving from the side shall do so at as small an angle to the general direction of traffic flow as practicable.

(c) A vessel shall so far as practicable avoid crossing traffic lanes, but if obliged to do so shall cross as nearly as practicable at right angles to the general direction of traffic flow.

(d) Inshore traffic zones shall not normally be used by through traffic which can safely use the appropriate traffic lane within the adjacent traffic separation scheme.

(e) A vessel, other than a crossing vessel, shall not normally enter a separation zone or cross a separation line except:

(i) in cases of emergency to avoid immediate danger;

(ii) to engage in fishing within a separation zone.

(f) A vessel navigating in areas near the terminations of traffic separation schemes shall do so with particular caution.

(g) A vessel shall so far as practicable avoid anchoring in a traffic separation scheme or in areas near its terminations.

(h) A vessel not using a traffic separation scheme shall avoid it by as wide a margin as is practicable.

(i) A vessel engaged in fishing shall not impede the passage of any vessel following a traffic lane.

(j) A vessel of less than 20 metres in length or a sailing vessel shall not impede the safe passage of a power-driven vessel following a traffic lane.

24.7   Bridge-To-Bridge Radiotelephone—U.S. Waters

PART 26—VESSEL BRIDGE-TO-BRIDGE RADIOTELEPHONE REGULATIONS

Sec.
26.01   Purpose.
26.02   Definitions.
26.03   Radiotelephone required.
26.04   Use of the designated frequency.
26.05   Use of radiotelephone.
26.06   Maintenance of radiotelephone; failure radiotelephone.
26.07   English language.
26.08   Exemption procedures.
26.09   List of exemptions. [Reserved]
26.10   Penalties.

AUTHORITY: The provisions of this Part 26 issued under 85 Stat. 146; 33 U.S.C.A. secs. 1201–1208; 49 CFR 1.46(o) (2).

§ 26.01 Purpose.—(a) The purpose of this part is to implement the provisions of the Vessel Bridge-to-Bridge Radiotelephone Act. This part—

(1) Requires the use of the vessel bridge-to-bridge radiotelephone;

(2) Provides the Coast Guard's interpretation of the meaning of important terms in the Act;

(3) Prescribes the procedures for applying for an exemption from the Act and the regulations issued under the Act and a listing of exemptions.

(b) Nothing in this part relieves any person from the obligation of complying with the rules of the road and the applicable pilot rules.

§ 26.02 Definitions.—For the purpose of this part and interpreting the Act—

"Secretary" means the Secretary of the Department in which the Coast Guard is operating;

"Act" means the "Vessel Bridge-to-Bridge Radiotelephone Act," 33 U.S.C.A. sections 1201–1208;

"Length" is measured from end to end over the deck excluding sheer;

"Navigable waters of the United States inside the lines established pursuant to section 2 of the Act of February 19, 1895 (28 Stat. 672), as amended," means those waters governed by the Navigation Rules for Harbors, Rivers, and Inland waters (33 U.S.C. sec. 151 et seq.), the Navigation Rules for Great Lakes and their Connecting and Tributary Waters (33 U.S.C. sec. 241 et seq.), and the Navigation Rules for Red River of the North and Rivers emptying into Gulf of Mexico and Tributaries (33 U.S.C. sec. 301 et seq.);

"Power-driven vessel" means any vessel propelled by machinery; and

"Towing vessel" means any commercial vessel engaged in towing another vessel astern, alongside, or by pushing ahead.

§ 26.03 Radiotelephone required.—(a) Unless an exemption is granted under § 26.09 and except as provided in subparagraph (4) of this paragraph, section 4 of the Act provides that—

(1) Every power-driven vessel of 300 gross tons and upward while navigating;

(2) Every vessel of 100 gross tons and upward carrying one or more passengers for hire while navigating;

(3) Every towing vessel of 26 feet or over in length while navigating; and

(4) Every dredge and floating plant engaged in or near a channel or fairway in operations likely to restrict or affect navigation of other vessels: *Provided,* That an unmanned or intermittently manned floating plant under the control of a dredge need not be required to have separate radiotelephone capability;

Shall have a radiotelephone capable of operation from its navigational bridge, or in the case of a dredge, from its main control station, and capable of transmitting and receiving on the frequency or frequencies within the 156–162 Mega-Hertz band using the classes of emissions designated by the Federal Communications Commission, after consultation with other cognizant agencies, for the exchange of navigational information.

(b) The radiotelephone required by paragraph (a) of this section shall be carried on board the described vessels, dredges, and floating plants upon the navigable waters of the United States inside the lines established pursuant to section 2 of the Act of February 19, 1895 (28 Stat. 672), as amended.

§ 26.04 Use of the designated frequency.—(a) No person may use the frequency designated by the Federal Communications Commission under section 8 of the Act, 33 U.S.C.A. section 1207(a), to transmit any information other than information necessary for the safe navigation of vessels or necessary tests.

(b) Each person who is required to maintain a listening watch under section 5 of the Act shall, when necessary, transmit and confirm, on the designated frequency, the intentions of his vessel and any other information necessary for the safe navigation of vessels.

(c) Nothing in these regulations may be construed as prohibiting the use of the designated frequency to communicate with shore stations to obtain or furnish information necessary for the safe navigation of vessels.

NOTE: The Federal Communications Commission has designated the frequency 156.65 MHz for the use of bridge-to-bridge radiotelephone stations.

§ 26.05 Use of radiotelephone.—Section 5 of the Act states—

(a) The radiotelephone required by this Act is for the exclusive use of the master or person in charge of the vessel, or the person designated by the master or person in charge of the vessel, or the person designated by the master or person in charge to pilot or direct movement of the vessel, who shall maintain a listening watch on the designated frequency. Nothing contained herein shall be interpreted as precluding the use of portable radiotelephone equipment to satisfy the requirements of this Act.

§ 26.06 Maintenance of radiotelephone; failure of radiotelephone.—Section 6 of the Act states—

(a) Whenever radiotelephone capability is required by this Act, a vessel's radiotelephone equipment shall be maintained in effective operating condition. If the radiotelephone equipment carried aboard a vessel ceases to operate, the master shall exercise due diligence to restore it or cause it to be restored to effective operating condition at the earliest practicable time. The failure of a vessel's radiotelephone equipment shall not, in itself, constitute a violation of this Act, nor shall it obligate the master of any vessel to moor or anchor his vessel; however, the loss of radiotelephone capability shall be given consideration in the navigation of the vessel.

§ 26.07 English language.—No person may use the services of, and no person may serve as a person required to maintain a listening watch under section 5 of the Act, 33 U.S.C.A. section 1204 unless he can speak the English language.

§ 26.08 Exemption procedures.—(a) Any person may petition for an exemption from any provision of the Act or this part;

(b) Each petition must be submitted in writing to U.S. Coast Guard (M), 400 Seventh Street SW., Washington, DC 20590, and must state—

(1) The provisions of the Act or this part from which an exemption is requested; and

(2) The reasons why marine navigation will not be adversely affected if the exemption is granted and if the exemption relates to a local communication system how that system would fully comply with the intent of the concept of the Act but would not conform in detail if the exemption is granted.

§ 26.09 List of exemptions. [Reserved]

§ 26.10 Penalties.—Section 9 of the Act states—

(a) Whoever, being the master or person in charge of a vessel subject to the Act, fails to enforce or comply with the Act or the regulations hereunder: or whoever, being designated by the master or person in charge of a vessel subject to the Act to pilot or direct the movement of a vessel fails to enforce or comply with the Act or the regulations hereunder—is liable to a civil penalty of not more than $500 to be assessed by the Secretary.

(b) Every vessel navigated in violation of the Act or the regulations hereunder is liable to a civil penalty of not more than $500 to be assessed by the Secretary, for which the vessel may be proceeded against in any District Court of the United States having jurisdiction.

(c) Any penalty assessed under this section may be remitted or mitigated by the Secretary, upon such terms as he may deem proper.

This amendment shall become effective January 1, 1973.

Law in Fog
and Restricted
Visibility

The conduct of a vessel in fog must be determined by adherence to requirements in the following general areas:

(1) Navigation lights
(2) Speed
(3) Obtaining early warning of risk of collison

(4) Action to avoid an approaching vessel which has been detected only on radar
(5) Action to avoid an approaching vessel whose fog signal has been heard, but the vessel has not been visually sighted
(6) Fog signals

The area of navigation lights was the subject of Chapter 22.

The International Rules state that Rule 19, Conduct of Vessels in Restricted Visibility, "applies to vessels not in sight of one another when navigating in or near an area of restricted visibility." United States courts have also required vessels to comply with the rules of fog when near a fog bank, even though the vessel has not herself entered it.

Restricted visibility has been carefully defined in the International Rules to include "any condition in which visibility is restricted by fog, mist, falling snow, heavy rainstorms, sandstorms or any other similar causes." The omission of the phrases "or any other similar causes" from the Inland Rules is not significant, as the courts will apply the rules to such conditions not specifically mentioned in Article 15, as has already happened in a case where visibility was restricted by smoke.

25.1 Speed in Fog

INTERNATIONAL RULE 6—SAFE SPEED

Every vessel shall at all times proceed at a safe speed so that she can take proper and effective action to avoid collision and be stopped within a distance appropriate to the prevailing circumstances and conditions.

In determining a safe speed the following factors shall be among those taken into account:

(a) By all vessels:

(i) the state of visibility;

(ii) the traffic density including concentrations of fishing vessels or any other vessels;

(iii) the maneuverability of the vessel with special reference to stopping distance and turning ability in the prevailing conditions;

(iv) at night the presence of background light such as from shore lights or from back scatter of her own lights;

(v) the state of wind, sea and current, and the proximity of navigational hazards;

(vi) the draught in relation to the available depth of water.

(b) Additionally, by vessels with operational radar:

(i) the characteristics, efficiency and limitations of the radar equipment;

(ii) any constraints imposed by the radar range scale in use;

(iii) the effect on radar detection of the sea state, weather and other sources of interference;

(iv) the possibility that small vessels, ice and other floating objects may not be detected by radar at an adequate range;

(v) the number, location and movement of vessels detected by radar;

(vi) the more exact assessment of the visibilty that may be possible when radar is used to determine the range of vessels or other objects in the vicinity.

Article 16 of the Inland Rules requires that all vessels (including sailing vessels) "go at a moderate speed, having careful regard to the existing circumstances and conditions." The term moderate speed has not been popular nor particularly useful to the mariner, and has been subject to a great deal of interpretation in U.S. courts. The main result of this interpretation is what is known as the "half-distance rule"—*a vessel should proceed at a speed which enables her to stop in half the distance of the visibility before her.* Additionally, if the current and visibility are such that a vessel must go at a speed faster than that required by the half-distance rule in order to maintain bare steerageway, she shall anchor (or not get underway in the first place). The courts in the United States have also made it clear that radar is not an excuse for exceeding moderate speed. U.S. courts have also ruled that a fog bank must be searched with radar, and a vessel shall reduce speed or stop if necessary until it has been done. The greater the speed at which a vessel is travelling, the greater should be the range setting of her radar.

25.2   Obtaining Early Warning of Risk of Collision

INTERNATIONAL RULE 5—LOOKOUT

Every vessel shall at all times maintain a proper lookout by sight and hearing as well as by all available means appropriate in the prevailing circumstances and conditions so as to make a full appraisal of the situation and of the risk of collision.

INTERNATIONAL RULE 7—RISK OF COLLISION

(a) Every vessel shall use all available means appropriate to the prevailing circumstances and conditions to determine if risk of collision exists. If there is any doubt such risk shall be deemed to exist.

(b) Proper use shall be made of radar equipment if fitted and operational, including long-range scanning to obtain early warning of risk of collision and radar plotting or equivalent systematic observation of detected objects.

(c) Assumptions shall not be made on the basis of scanty information, especially scanty radar information.

(d) In determining if risk of collision exists the following considerations shall be among those taken into account:

(i) such risk shall be deemed to exist if the compass bearing of an approaching vessel does not appreciably change;

(ii) such risk may sometimes exist even when an appreciable bearing change is evident, particularly when approaching a very large vessel or a tow or when approaching a vessel at close range.

Rules 5 and 7 make it very obvious that radar is not a substitute for a "proper lookout by sight and hearing." The Inland Rules do not mention radar at all, but the U.S. courts have ruled that radar is not an excuse for non-compliance with the Inland Rules (lookouts are required). The courts have also ruled that dependable radar equipment must be turned on and intelligent and reasonable use made of it. A vessel rigging her booms in such a way as to greatly impair use of her radar was found guilty of gross negligence.

The radar plot required by the International Rules includes a radar deflection plotter fitted over the scope, as well as plotting directly on the scope. "Systematic observation" includes the plotting teams used on most naval vessels as well as computerized collision avoidance systems which process radar bearing and range data and display information on a cathode ray tube.

25.3   Avoiding Radar Contacts

INTERNATIONAL RULE 19(d)

(d) A vessel which detects by radar alone the presence of another vessel shall determine if a close-quarters situation is developing and/or risk of collision exists. If so, she shall take avoiding action in ample time, provided that when such action consists of an alteration of course, so far as possible the following shall be avoided:

(i) an alteration of course to port for a vessel forward of the beam, other than for a vessel being overtaken.

(ii) an alteration of course towards a vessel abeam or abaft the beam.

INTERNATIONAL RULE 8—ACTION TO AVOID COLLISION

(a) Any action taken to avoid collision shall, if the circumstances of the case admit, be positive, made in ample time and with due regard to the observance of good seamanship.

(b) Any alteration of course and/or speed to avoid collision shall, if the circumstances of the case admit, be large enough to be readily apparent to another vessel observing visually or by radar; a succession of small alterations of course and/or speed should be avoided.

(c) If there is sufficient sea room, alteration of course alone may be the most effective action to avoid a close-quarters situation provided that it is made in good time, is substantial and does not result in another close-quarters situation.

(d) Action taken to avoid collision with another vessel shall be such as to result in passing at a safe distance. The effectiveness of the action shall be carefully checked until the other vessel is finally past and clear.

(e) If necessary to avoid collision or allow more time to assess the situation, a vessel shall slacken her speed or take all way off by stopping or reversing her means of propulsion.

The U.S. courts have made similar requirements in ruling that the radar bearing of an approaching vessel which remains fairly constant is indicative of a collision course and requires immediate and radical avoidance action by the observing vessel.

25.4   Actions When a Fog Signal is Heard

INTERNATIONAL RULE 19(e)

(e) Except where it has been determined that a risk of collision does not exist, every vessel which hears apparently forward of her beam the fog signal of another vessel, or which cannot avoid a close-quarters situation with another vessel forward of her beam, shall reduce her speed to the minimum at which she can be kept on her course. She shall if necessary take all her way off and in any event navigate with extreme caution until danger of collision is over.

The requirements of the Inland Rules (Article 16) are slightly different:

A steam vessel hearing, apparently forward of her beam, the fog signal of a vessel the position of which has not been ascertained shall, so far as the circumstances of the case admit, stop her engines, and then navigate with caution until danger of collision is over.

U.S. courts have maintained a very strict interpretation of Article 16—the engine must be *stopped* when a fog signal is heard apparently forward of the beam—regardless of the apparent distance of the signal.

In the International Rules, a vessel must slow to *bare steerageway*, except where it has been determined (by radar) that a risk of collision does not exist. The use of radar does not excuse a vessel in inland waters from the requirement to stop her engines when a fog signal is heard.

Care must be taken in determining "that a risk of collision does not exist." Such a determination can only be made with certainty with a radar which is properly tuned and not degraded by sea return or thunderstorms.

25.5   Fog Signals   Neither the rules nor the courts have attempted to give a distance which defines restricted visibility for the purpose of sounding fog signals. Textbook writers have long recommended the required visibility of sidelights as a guideline, which is presently two

miles in inland waters and three miles for vessels of 50 meters and upward in length in the International Rules.

The Inland Rules prescribe three types of devices for sounding signals in restricted visibility: whistle (or siren), fog horn and bell.

Art. 15. *All signals prescribed by this article for vessels underway shall be given:*
1. By "steam vessels" on the whistle or siren.
2. By "sailing vessels" and "vessels towed" on the fog horn.
The words "prolonged blast" used in this article shall mean a blast of from four to six seconds' duration.
A steam vessel shall be provided with an efficient whistle or siren, sounded by steam or by some substitute for steam, so placed that the sound may not be intercepted by any obstruction, and with an efficient fog horn; also with an efficient bell. A sailing vessel of twenty tons gross tonnage or upward shall be provided with a similar fog horn and bell.

Note that sailing vessels and vessels towed are to sound signals on a fog horn, and that sailing vessels are not required to have a whistle.

The International Rules also prescribe three types of devices for sound signals: whistle, bell and gong (use of the fog horn was dropped from the latest revision). The equipment now required is determined entirely by the *length* of a vessel, not by sailing/power-driven vessel status. The size of the vessel will be indicated by the frequency and audibility of the whistle signal, with the signals sounded by larger vessels being generally of lower frequency and greater audibility than those of smaller vessels.

INTERNATIONAL RULE 33—EQUIPMENT FOR SOUND SIGNALS

(a) A vessel of 12 metres or more in length shall be provided with a whistle and a vessel of 100 metres or more in length shall, in addition, be provided with a gong, the tone and sound of which cannot be confused with that of the bell. The whistle, bell and gong shall comply with the specifications in Annex III to these regulations. The bell or gong or both may be replaced by other equipment having the same respective sound characteristics, provided that manual sounding of the required signals shall always be possible.

(b) A vessel of less than 12 metres in length shall not be obliged to carry the sound signalling appliances prescribed in paragraph (a) of this rule but if she does not, she shall be provided with some other means of making an efficient sound signal.

The following table summarizes the fog signals prescribed in both sets of rules.

Key: — prolonged blast 4–6 seconds	Bell	5 second rapid ringing
short blast	Gong	5 second rapid sounding
"blast" on foghorn, unspecified duration	S	distinct stroke on bell

	International[1] Signal/Interval	Inland Signal/Interval
Power-driven/steam vessel making way through the water	— 2 minutes	— 1 minute
Power-driven/steam vessel underway but stopped	— — 2 minutes	no special signal—same as steam vessel underway making way
Vessel not under command	—.. 2 minutes	no such category in inland waters, sound signal for class of vessel
Vessel restricted in her ability to maneuver	—.. 2 minutes	no such category in inland waters, sound signal for class of vessel
Vessel constrained by her draft	—.. 2 minutes	no such category in inland waters, sound signal for class of vessel
Vessel engaged in fishing	—.. 2 minutes	no special signal, sound signal for class of vessel
Vessel engaged in towing or pushing	—.. 2 minutes	—.. 1 minute
Vessel towed (or the last vessel in a tow, if manned)	—... 2 minutes	—.. 1 minute (optional) on fog horn
Sailing vessel	—.. 2 minutes	on fog horn, 1 minute: 1 blast starboard tack 2 blasts port tack 3 blasts wind abaft beam

Vessel at anchor < 100 m.	Bell	1 minute	Bell[4] 1 minute
≥ 100 m.	Bell Gong	1 minute	Bell[4] 1 minute
may in addition sound	. —.	as required[2]	
Vessel aground < 100 m.	SSS Bell SSS	1 minute	danger or distress signal
≥ 100 m.	SSS Bell SSS Gong	1 minute	danger or distress signal
may in addition sound	"appropriate whistle signal"[3]	as required	

[1](a) Pilot vessel may in addition sound 4 short blasts as an identity signal (sound as required).

(b) A vessel of less than 12 m. in length shall not be obliged to give the above-mentioned signals but, if she does not, shall make some other signal at intervals of not more than two minutes.

[2]Used by a vessel at anchor to give warning of her position and of the possibility of a collision to an approaching vessel.

[3]See Appendix A.

[4]Not required in a "special anchorage area" by a vessel of not more than 65 feet in length, or a barge, canal boat, scow or other nondescript craft.

The Inland Rules lack a signal to be given by a vessel aground, and the courts have held that the at-anchor signal is *not* a proper signal for a vessel aground. It is proper for a vessel aground to sound a distress signal, but only if actually requiring assistance. The danger signal may be used to warn other vessels.

Under the Inland Rules the danger signal may be sounded when in doubt as to the course or intention of the other vessel, even though she is not in sight in the fog. The International signal of doubt is permitted only when vessels are in sight of one another.

The Inland Rules allow but do not require a vessel towed to sound the same signal as the towing steam vessel. A tow in inland waters need not sound a fog signal at all times in a fog, but it should do so when the circumstances make it desirable to indicate its location. The tow should sound it when it is in crowded waters or when the tow is long. When a tow is anchored, proper signals must be given by each vessel (at least by each vessel on the outside of a tier). The tug, if present, is responsible. If the tug is not present, the tow is responsible.

Vessels moored at the end of a pier have been required by U.S. courts to "make some noise with a horn, a bell, a gong, or the like." All vessels in a nest are required to give signals within the statutory interval.

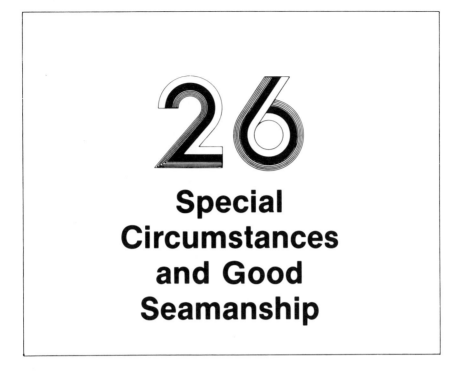

Special Circumstances and Good Seamanship

26.1 Special Circumstances Requiring a Departure from the Other Rules Article 27 of Inland Rules, the "General Prudential Rule," and Rule 2(b) of the International Rules provide for cases where special circumstances may require a departure from the other rules in order to avoid "immediate danger." It is not implied that the other rules do not apply to close-quarters situations. The meaning is that in some situations, in the face of *immediate danger*, obedience to a rule may *cause* a collision.

General Prudential Rule

Art. 27. *In obeying and construing these rules due regard shall be had to all dangers of navigation and collision, and to any special circumstances which may render a departure from the above rules necessary in order to avoid immediate danger.*

Rule 2—Responsibility

(b) In construing and complying with these rules due regard shall be had to all dangers of navigation and collision and to any special circumstances, including the limitations of the vessels involved, which may make a departure from these rules necessary to avoid immediate danger.

26.1.1 In Extremis   Vessels are "in extremis" whenever the vessels are in such close proximity, regardless of the cause, that adherence to a rule is certain to cause a collision. The rules do not tell a vessel in extremis to turn left or right, or to back down; the vessels must "take such action as will best aid to avoid collision."

The International Rules provide for a maneuver by the privileged vessel in extremis—U.S. courts have construed Article 27 in the same manner.

RULE 17—ACTION BY STAND-ON VESSEL

(b) When, from any cause, the vessel required to keep her course and speed finds herself so close that collision cannot be avoided by the action of the give-way vessel alone, she shall take such action as will best aid to avoid collision.

26.1.2 Vessel Unable to Comply With the Rules—Inland Waters
In inland waters there are no special lights or shapes for a vessel not under command or restricted in her ability to maneuver to advertise her plight. In such situations, a vessel should sound the danger signal to warn the other vessel of her inability to abide by the rules. A privileged vessel is required to stop upon hearing the danger signal.

A vessel in special circumstances will often sound two short blasts signalling her desire to cross ahead of a privileged vessel in a crossing courses situation. Although the two-blast signal is not legal in a crossing situation, the crossing rules do not apply in special circumstances. The privileged vessel, recognizing the special circumstances, would be justified in answering the two-blast signal with the same signal and maneuvering to keep out of the way.

26.1.3 Approach of a Third Vessel   A vessel may approach two (or more) other vessels in such a way that she is privileged with respect with one, and burdened with respect to the other. If she cannot abide by the steering and sailing rules by handling the approaches one at a time, special circumstances should be deemed to exist.

26.1.4 Situations Not Covered by the Rules   There are some situations for which the rules provide no specific guidance as to how to maneuver with respect to the other vessel. Examples include "approach situations" where one or both vessels are entering a slip, maneuvering around piers, or backing. In each case there is a vessel which is not on a steady course. Even though both sets of rules provide a signal for a vessel backing, and the Inland Rules provide a signal for a vessel leaving her slip, there are no directions on how to maneuver if an approaching vessel cannot be avoided without one of them taking action. Such situations are "special circumstances," and the rules for meeting, crossing or overtaking do not apply.

Article 27 has also modified the requirement for the privileged vessel. U.S. courts have ruled that the privileged vessel is legally maintaining course and speed when maneuvering for the following reasons:

(1) "stopping her engines and checking her speed preparatory to landing"

(2) "following a channel course that of necessity curves around bends"

(3) stopping to pick up a pilot

(4) making "such necessary variations in her course as will enable her to avoid immediate danger arising from natural obstructions to navigation."

26.1.5 Departure from the Rules by Agreement   There are two situations in inland waters where departure by (whistle-signal) agreement can occur. The first is a meeting situation which is meeting "head and head." Vessels who agree to pass starboard to starboard in a head and head situation, by the exchange of two-blast signals, place themselves in special circumstances. Vessels similarly place themselves in special circumstances in a crossing situation when the vessels agree, by the exchange of two-blast signals, to the crossing of the privileged vessel's bow. If a collision results, the vessel proposing the departure is certain to be found at fault, unless departure was necessitated by immediate danger. The proposal is not binding on the other vessel, and she may be found at fault for the agreement.

26.2 Good Seamanship   Special circumstances may also require precautions *in addition to* those specified in the rules. The mariner is also required to take precautions dictated by the ordinary practice of seamen. Article 29 of the Inland Rules, the "Rule of Good Seamanship," is similar in wording to Rule 2(a):

Rule of Good Seamanship

Art. 29. *Nothing in these rules shall exonerate any vessel, or the owner or master or crew thereof, from the consequences of any neglect to carry lights or signals, or of any neglect to keep a proper lookout, or of the neglect of any precaution which may be required by the ordinary practice of seamen, or by the special circumstances of the case.*

RULE 2—RESPONSIBILITY

(a) Nothing in these rules shall exonerate any vessel, or the owner, master or crew thereof, from the consequences of any neglect to comply with these rules or of the neglect of any precaution which may be required by the ordinary practice of seamen, or by the special circumstances of the case.

Any condition which causes a deviation from the norm may require additional precautions. The following factors may necessitate additional precautions:

(1) adverse weather conditions
(2) unusual conditions of loading or trim
(3) failure or degradation of any equipment important to safe navigation
(4) traffic density
(5) proximity of navigational hazards
(6) availability of external aids to navigation
(7) transport of dangerous cargo or cargo which poses a threat to the environment

The following list contains specific actions which may be required by good seamanship. Refer also to the discussion of the Anchorage Act in Chapter One. (All quotations are from U.S. court rulings on the Inland Rules.)

(1) Speed in good visibility
    (a) must comply with local regulations
    (b) must not create swell or suction which would cause damage to other vessels
    (c) must be such that our vessel is completely under control
(2) Vessels must not pass unnecessarily close to pier ends
(3) Vessels must be properly manned and steered
(4) Vessels must not navigate with defective equipment
(5) Vessels have the "responsibility to utilize available weather reports so that it can operate in manner consistent with foreseeable risk."
(6) Vessels moored must have sufficient mooring lines.
(7) "A navigator is chargeable with knowledge of the maneuvering capacity of his vessel. He is bound to know the character of his vessel and how she would turn in ordinary conditions."
(8) "When a vessel is known to be about to enter or leave a dock, other vessels should keep well clear and avoid embarrassing her maneuvers."
(9) "In waters well frequented by small tows...the law requires that a ship should have a competent person standing by in the forecastle ready at a moments notice to let go the anchors."

(10) Where two steamers about to meet are running one with and the other against the tide, if it be necessary that one or the other should stop in order to avoid a collision, the one proceeding against the tide should stop.

26.2.1   Proper Lookout—Inland Waters   The courts have given legal meaning to the term "proper lookout." Again we quote:

(1) "Lookout is person who is specially charged with duty of observing lights, sounds, echoes, or any obstruction to navigation."

(2) "Lookouts, who must be kept on all vessels, must be persons of suitable experience, properly stationed on vessel, and actually and vigilantly employed in the performance of that duty."

(3) "Lookout should be placed as low and as far forward as possible." This is a requirement in clear weather as well as in fog if failure to comply can result in any one of the following:
  (a) the lookout does not have a clear, unobstructed view
  (b) the lookout's ability to hear signals is impaired
  (c) the lookout will sight a danger earlier if placed forward (as when leaving a blind slip)

(4) "Lookout . . . should have no other duties."

(5) The circumstances will dictate the number of lookouts required. The number must be sufficient to detect any reasonably foreseen danger from any direction.

(6) A lookout astern is required when backing.

(7) Lookouts must have a direct and positive means of communicating what they observe to the conning officer. A lookout cannot wear headphones, as his ability to hear signals would be impaired.

26.2.2   Proper Lookout—International Rules

RULE 5

LOOKOUT

Every vessel shall at all times maintain a proper lookout by sight and hearing as well as by all available means appropriate in the prevailing circumstances and conditions so as to make a full appraisal of the situation and of the risk of collision.

RULE 7

RISK OF COLLISION

(a) Every vessel shall use all available means appropriate to the prevailing circumstances and conditions to determine if risk of collision exists. If there is any doubt such risk shall be deemed to exist.

(b) Proper use shall be made of radar equipment if fitted and operational, including long-range scanning to obtain early warning of risk of collision and radar plotting or equivalent systematic observation of detected objects.

(c) Assumptions shall not be made on the basis of scanty information, especially scanty radar information.

(d) In determining if risk of collision exists the following considerations shall be among those taken into account:

(i) such risk shall be deemed to exist if the compass bearing of an approaching vessel does not appreciably change;

(ii) such risk may sometimes exist even when an appreciable bearing change is evident, particularly when approaching a very large vessel or a tow or when approaching a vessel at close range.

Radar for Collision
Avoidance

The International Rules make it clear that a quick look at the radar is not enough:

INTERNATIONAL RULE 7(c)
Assumptions shall not be made on the basis of scanty information, especially scanty radar information.

The reason is that observation of only the direction of relative motion (DMR) can be misleading. Consider the following two examples where the positions of a radar contact have been marked with a grease pencil at six minute intervals. Our own vessel is heading north at 20 knots. Radar presentation is stabilized, north-up. In Example One, if the range rings were at two mile intervals, the speed of relative motion (SRM) would be 40 knots, and the contact would be on a course nearly reciprocal to our own at a speed of approximately 20 knots. If the range rings were at one mile intervals, the SRM would be 20 knots, and the contact would be dead in the water. With the range rings at 1000 yard intervals,

577

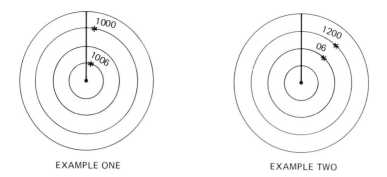

EXAMPLE ONE   EXAMPLE TWO

the SRM would be 10 knots, and we would be overtaking a vessel proceeding at approximately 10 knots.

The vector diagrams below illustrate two possibilities for Example
Two.

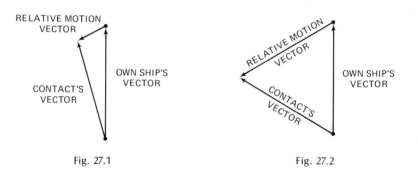

Fig. 27.1   Fig. 27.2

Figure 27.1 illustrates a case with a low SRM (represented by the length
of the relative motion vector). The situation is one where our own
vessel is gradually overtaking another. Figure 27.2 illustrates a case
with a high SRM, where the contact's course is nearly at a right angle
to our own.

In the two examples given, knowledge of the speed of relative
motion was required to differentiate between the possibilities represented by the direction between the two radar positions marked
on the scope. Rough estimates may be made by comparing our own
speed with the SRM. The International Rules require "systematic observation of detected objects—the positions must be related to time
in order to determine the speed of relative motion.

A radar contact's course, speed, CPA range and CPA bearing can
be obtained by transferring data to a maneuvering board or radar

plotting sheet. With some sacrifice in accuracy, the same information can be obtained by methods used directly on the radar scope or reflection plotter. In many circumstances, the loss of accuracy is insignificant when the result is more timely action. In addition, less attention is directed away from the scope where new contacts or changes of course by contacts might be observed. By simply extending the direction of relative motion past the center of the scope, the range and bearing of the closest point of approach (CPA) may be obtained.

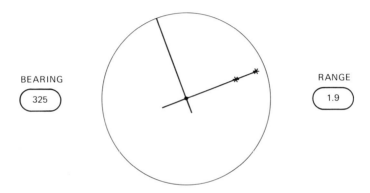

BEARING

325

RANGE

1.9

The course and speed of a contact may be estimated by constructing a small triangle, using the relative plot as one side. In Fig. 27.3 below, the contact's position has been marked at six minute intervals.

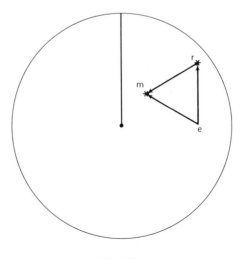

Fig. 27.3

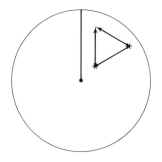

Fig. 27.4

The length of the *er* side of the triangle, the vector for own ship's course and speed, is 1/10 of our speed in knots (for a triangle with each side representing miles traveled in 6 minutes). The length of the vector must be measured using the range scale in use on the radar scope. The direction *e-r* is parallel to the heading marker. The *em* side of the triangle represents the contact's course and speed. The contact's speed is obtained by measuring the length of the *em* vector and multiplying by 10. An alternate method of constructing the same triangle is shown in Fig. 27.4.

A similar method is called the "ladder method." It allows the observer to make an approximate solution quickly and then refine the solution after more observations. The "ladder" represents the distance own ship travels from the time of the first observation used. The contact's course is obtained in the same manner as in the pre-

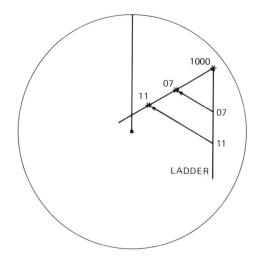

Fig. 27.5

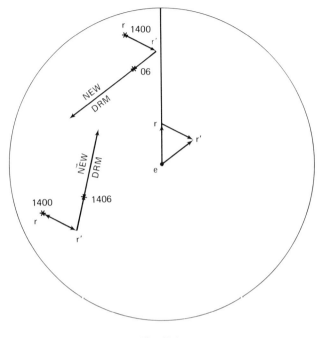

Fig. 27.6

vious method described. Note that in Fig. 27.5, each solution for the contact's speed involves taking the distance traveled over different time intervals (7 and 11 minutes in the example).

The effect of a planned course change can be calculated by another method used directly on the scope or reflection plotter. In Fig. 27.6, the relative plot with 6 minute intervals is employed. The length of *er* and *er'* represent distance traveled in six minutes. The vector *rr'* represents the planned course change by own ship. By the construction shown, the new direction of relative motion (DRM) after the course change may be obtained. Note that this method does not require previous solutions of contacts' courses and speeds.

Appendices

Appendix 1

Rope and Cordage

Rope is a term which includes both fiber and wire rope. Seamen, however, ordinarily refer to fiber rope as line and wire rope as rope or wire. More exactly, a line is a piece of rope, fiber or wire, which is in use or has been cut for a specific purpose, for example, lifeline, heaving line, lead line. There are, nevertheless, a few lines with the word *rope* in their titles—wheel rope, foot rope, bell rope.

A1.1 Fiber Rope Fiber rope is made from natural fibers (manila, hemp, sisal, cotton) and synthetic or man-made fibers (nylon, polyester, polypropylene).

1. Manila Manila made from the fibers of the Abaca plant is the strongest and the most expensive of the natural fibers. The strength of fiber ropes depends in part on the lengths of the individual fibers; Manila has the longest natural fibers, some being over three feet in length. It has long been the standard of strength for fiber rope, and line made of other natural fibers is rated in percentages of the strength of manila.

Manila is the most common natural fiber line used aboard ship. For uses such as towlines, mooring lines, and boatfalls where great strength is required manila has largely been replaced by synthetic fiber lines.

2. Sisal Sisal, made from the agave plant is a common natural fiber line used on shipboard. Of the natural fibers it is next in strength to manila, being rated at 80% of manila's strength. Sisal is commonly mixed with manila and the rope obtained is called composite line. Composite line is rated at 90% of manila of the same size. Sisal is less expensive than manila but it is brittle and fibers break readily when worked around an edge. It is also very stiff and difficult to work with, especially when wet.

3. Hemp Hemp rope made from the fiber of the stalk of the hemp plant, is now used only for "small stuff." Usually it is tarred. Aboard ship the most commonly used hempen cordages are marline and ratline. Marline, two-stranded, left-lay, and tarred, is used for seizing, worming, and serving ropes. Untarred marline is used for sennit, braided cord, and fabric made of flat, plaited yarns. When greater bulk and strength are required, houseline and roundline (3-strand, right-lay, tarred), are employed. Seizing stuff (3-strand, right-lay, tarred), furnished in four sizes ranging from ½ to 1 inch in circumference, is used in place of tarred marline when better weather resistance and greater strength are required.

Ratline (3-strand, right-lay, tarred) in sizes ranging from ¾ to 1½ inches in circumference is used for lashings, servings, and the snaking on small ships such as destroyers. Snaking is the netting between the gunwales and one of the lifelines, intended to keep objects from washing overboard.

4. Cotton   Cotton line, made from the fibers of the cotton plant, may be of 3-strand, right-lay or of braided construction. A hollow braided (without core) line, called *signal halyard,* was formerly used to fly signal flags. In the Navy, nylon now serves that purpose, because it resists weather and stack gases much better. Other braided cotton lines with cores are used for heaving lines, lead lines, and so on. Various sizes of 3-strand, right-lay cotton

Fig. A1.1   Eight-inch nylon hawser faked down. *(Official U.S. Coast Guard photograph.)*

lines are used for fancy work and lashings. The best known of these is "white line."

5. *Nylon* Nylon (Fig. A1.1) is a synthetic fiber of great strength, elasticity, and resistance to weather. It comes in twisted, braided, and plaited construction, and it can be used for almost any purpose except for lashings, highlines, and other purposes where its slippery surface is detrimental.

Nylon is expensive, costing almost three times as much as manila of the same size. It has several advantages over manila, however. It is almost three times as strong and lasts five times as long. Then too, its greater strength permits using a line about two-thirds as large. For these reasons, nylon is more economical. In the Navy, the use of nylon is authorized for towlines, mooring lines, boat falls, and signal halyards.

One feature of Nylon which is a disadvantage in some applications is its elasticity. Under load it will stretch up to forty percent of its original length. This stretch is only evidenced in the standard three stranded nylon line and not in the double braided or plaited lines. A degree of elasticity of this amount is not desirable in a line to be used as a boat fall or for a boom guy purchase.

Nylon rope of twisted construction is available in sizes up to 12 inches in circumference and as double-braided nylon lines (Fig. A1.2) up to 6½ inches in circumference. Double-braided line consists of an outer portion, or cover, of tightly braided fibers and a closely braided core. Approximately 50 percent of the strength is in the core. Size-for-size, double-braided line is about 1.2 times as strong as twisted nylon.

Nylon line in 8 stranded plaited construction is available in sizes up to 12 inches circumference. It is only slightly less strong than the double braided line and stands up to hard usage and abrasion better. Eight stranded synthetic lines are becoming increasingly popular with merchant marine users.

6. *Other Synthetics* Dacron has about 80% of the strength of nylon but will only stretch a bout ten per cent of its original length. Polyethelene and polypropylene are only half as strong as nylon size for size but they float in water, a feature that makes them desirable for use in the towing industry. Also size for size they are twenty five percent lighter than nylon making them very easy to handle.

A1.2 Construction of Fiber Rope The steps in constructing twisted or plain laid fiber rope are about the same, regardless of the type of fiber used. The fibers are combed smooth; an emulsion of oils is added to soften, lubricate, and preserve them; and then the fibers are spun into yarns or threads (Fig. A1.2). Threads are twisted into strands, and the strands are twisted into rope. Ropes are twisted together to form cables. Threads are twisted to the right, and successive twists are taken in opposite directions. Although most rope used aboard ship is 3-strand, right-lay, some 4-strand and some left-lay ropes are manufactured. In a right-lay rope, the twist of the strands is to the right.

Large line is measured by circumference, but small stuff (i.e., line 1½ inches in circumference and smaller) is identified by the number of threads. The largest small stuff is 24-thread. Large line (starting with 1¾ inches) is manufactured in ¼-inch graduations.

(A) Double-braided
Nylon Rope.

(B) Rope in Coil.

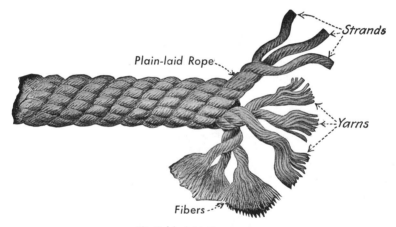

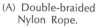

Plain-laid Rope

Strands

Yarns

Fibers

(C) Cable-laid Rope.

(D) Cross Section, Three-strand Rope.

Fig. A1.2 Fiber rope.

Braided ropes may be hollow-braid, stuffer-braid, solid-braid or double-braid. As stated before, hollow-braid rope has no core; it is, essentially, a hollow tube. Stuffer-braid rope has a yarn core, with the cover braided about it. Solid-braid ropes are usually manufactured of large yarns tightly braided around each other, forming a hard, relatively stiff rope that will not kink, snag, or swell in water. The double-braid rope is described in the subsection on nylon rope.

Plaited rope is made of eight strands (four right-twist and four left-twist). The strands are paired and plaited as in a 4-strand sennit.

A1.3 Care of Natural-Fiber Rope   Unlike metal, fiber has not a permanent elastic limit within which it can be worked indefinitely. Therefore, no attempt should be made to put a maximum strain on a rope that has seen continuous service under a moderate strain or on one that has once been close to the breaking point. The safety of a rope decreases comparatively rapidly with use, dependent to some extent upon the amount of strain. This is due to the fact that the fibers slip a small amount under each strain in spite of the twisting.

Rope tends to contract when wet, and unless allowed to do so freely, may be injuriously strained. It is for this reason that running gear is slacked in damp weather. On the other hand, advantage may be taken of this tendency for tautening lashings by wetting the rope.

Never:
1. Stow wet or damp line in an unventilated compartment or cover it so that it cannot dry. Mildew will form and weaken the fibers.
2. Subject line to intense heat or unnecessarily allow it to lie in the hot sun. The lubricant will dry out, thus shortening the useful life of the line.
3. Subject a line to loads exceeding its safe working load. To do so may not break the line, but individual fibers will break, reducing the strength.
4. Allow line to bear on sharp edges or run over rough surfaces. The line will be cut or worn, reducing the strength and useful life.
5. Scrub line. The lubricant will be washed away, and caustics in strong soap may harm the fibers.
6. Put a strain on a line with a kink in it.
7. Try to lubricate line. The lubricant you add may do more harm than good.
8. Let wear become localized in one spot.
9. Unbalance line by continued use on winch in same direction.

Always:
1. Dry line before stowing it.
2. Protect line from weather when possible.
3. Use chafing gear (canvas, short lengths of old fire hose, etc.) where line (or wire) runs over sharp edges or rough surfaces.

4. Slack off taut lines when it rains. Wet lines shrink, and if the line is taut, the resulting strain may be enough to break some of the fibers.
5. Coil right-laid rope to the right (clockwise).
6. Inspect a line before using it. Overworked or overstrained line will have a bristly surface. Mildew can be seen, and it has a peculiar, unpleasant odor. Untwist the line so that the inner parts of the strands can be seen. If they have a dull grayish look, the line is unsafe.
7. Give line the care it deserves—someday your safety may depend on it.
8. Use chafing gear or occasionally "freshen the nip" to prevent or reduce localized wear.
9. Reverse turns on winches periodically to keep out the kinks.
10. Lay right-laid lines clockwise on reels or capstans and left-laid lines counterclockwise until they are broken in.
11. When opening a new coil of line, place the coil so that the end is at the bottom. Cut the stoppers and pull the end up through the tunnel. The line should uncoil counterclockwise.

A1.4   Care of Nylon Rope   Most of the tips for the care of natural-fiber rope should be observed with nylon line. However, nylon is not subject to mildew, and it may and should be scrubbed if it becomes slippery because of oil or grease.

A coil of nylon rope, unlike other fiber rope, is not opened by pulling the end up through the eye of the coil. It should be unreeled in the same manner as wire rope.

Normally, plain-laid nylon rope is right-handed and should be coiled on capstans and reels in a clockwise direction. Cable-laid nylon rope is left-laid and should be coiled on capstans or reels in a counterclockwise direction.

Constantly coiling twisted nylon rope in the same direction tends to tighten the twist or unbalance the lay. To alleviate this condition, such rope should occasionally be coiled down against the lay. Braided nylon, having no lay, can be coiled down or coiled on a gypsy head in either direction without becoming unbalanced. One manufacturer recommends stowing braided line in a figure eight, but points out that this is not a rigid requirement.

Nylon differs from other fiber ropes in that it stretches under load, yet recovers to its normal size when tension is removed. With rope and cable-laid nylon, a stretch of one-third its length is normal under safe working loads. A stretch of 40 percent of its length is the critical point, and it parts at 50 percent stretch. With double-braided nylon, the critical point is reached when the line is stretched 27 percent. It parts when the stretch is 30 percent. This elongation may at times be a disadvantage, but it can be halved by doubling the lines. Nylon rope can stand repeated stretching with no serious effect.

Sharp, cracking noises, caused by readjustment of the strands, are heard when applying a load to new cable-laid hawsers. Wet hawsers under strain emit steamlike vapor. Nylon rope that has been under heavy strain may develop glazed areas where it has worked against bitt and chock surfaces.

This condition may be caused by paint or the fusing of the fibers. In either case, the effect on the rope's strength is negligible.

Plain-laid nylon has a tendency to elongate around bitts when loaded. To minimize this extension, take a round turn around the part of the bitts nearest the chock before making figure eights.

New cable-laid nylon hawsers tend to be stiff and difficult to handle. To alleviate this condition, put the cables under tension for 20 minutes at 30 percent extension; for example, 100 feet when under tension would measure 130 feet.

Nylon rope can hold a load even though a considerable amount of the yarns has been abraded. Where such a condition is excessive but localized, the chafed section may be cut away and the ends spliced together.

When nylon lines become iced-over in use, they should be thawed carefully at moderate temperatures and drained before stowing.

If a nylon line becomes slippery because of oil or grease, it should be scrubbed down. Spots may be removed by cleaning with light oils such as kerosene or diesel oil.

Because nylon rope, on parting, is stretched 50 percent of its length, it parts with a decided snapback. Keep your men and yourself out of the direct line of pull when heavy strains are applied.

Do not use a single part of plain-laid rope for hauling or hoisting any load which is free to rotate. Where one part of rope is essential, use cable-laid hawsers.

Do not stow nylon rope in strong sunlight. Cover it with paulins. In stowage, keep it away from heat and strong chemicals.

Employ only nylon rope stoppers for holding nylon hawsers under load.

Do not use wire or spring-lay rope in conjunction with nylon rope in the same chock or on bitts or bollards.

Extreme care should be exercised when easing out nylon line around bitts and cleats under heavy load. Nylon's coefficient of friction is lower than that of manila, and it may slip on easing out, so keep an extra turn on the bitt or cleat.

When rigging nylon or other rope for heavy strains, do not attach fairlead blocks or other equipment to padeyes or other fittings that have not been tested for the load. Untested padeyes have pulled away under heavy strain and injured and killed men in the vicinity.

Persons used to the audible protests of natural fiber lines under heavy loads must be particularly careful to train themselves to notice and rely on nylon's visible signs of warning—elongating and decreasing in diameter.

When nylon hawsers are employed on capstans for heavy towing or impact loading, take six turns on the capstan and two turns over-laying the last four turns. This method reduces the hazard of sudden surges.

The previous remarks concerning unreeling, storage, and cleaning of nylon rope apply to other synthetic fiber, ropes as well. Other synthetics do not have nylon's coefficient of elasticity however, and with them stretch should not exceed manufacturer's recommended limits. Like double braided line the eight stranded plaited lines may be coiled down either to the left or right as desired.

A1.5   Wire Rope   In order to understand this discussion on wire rope, the reader must first know the terms used.

Nominal breaking strength—The nominal breaking strength is the value on which designs should be based.

Acceptance breaking strength—The acceptance breaking strength is the minimum value on which compliance with the specification is determined.

Bright wires—Bright wires are wires in ropes or strands that are uncoated.

Core—The core is the foundation member (a twisted fibrous material, a wire strand, or an independent wire rope) or a wire rope around which the strands are laid.

Filler wires—Filler wires are small-diameter auxiliary wires for supporting and positioning main wires. Filler wires are sometimes included in the actual wire count and identification of the rope construction.

Galvanized (or coated) wire ropes and strands—Galvanized wire ropes and strands are wire ropes or strands made of zinc-coated (galvanized) wires.

Galvanized (zinc-coated) wires—In the manufacture of "galvanized" rope wire, the wire is zinc-coated at finished size.

Lang lay—In a lang lay wire rope the direction of lay of the wires in the strand and of the strand in the rope is the same. As a result the rope has an appearance that the wires are diagonal to the axis of the rope. The wires and the strands may run to the right—"right lang lay" (commonly called lang lay); or to the left—"left lang lay" (on specific orders only).

Lay—The word "lay" is used by the wire rope industry in two different ways

  a. The lay is the manner in which the wires in a strand or the strands in a wire rope lay (twisted).
  b. The lay is the distance parallel to the longitudinal axis in which a wire makes a complete turn (spiral or helix) about the axis of the strand or a strand about the axis of the rope. It is also called the lay length or the pitch.

A1.6   Construction of Wire Rope   Wire rope is composed of three parts—wires, strands, and core. The basic unit is the wire. A predetermined number of wires of proper size are fabricated in a uniform geometric arrangement of definite pitch or lay to form a strand of required diameter. The required number of strands are then laid together symmetrically around a core to form the rope.

Cores are of three general types: fiber, wire strand, and independent wire rope. The core affords support to the strands wound about it. Fiber cores are adequate for most types of service, because they not only provide the necessary foundation, but also add to the flexibility and elasticity of the rope. For service where high operating pressures are encountered or in cases where resistance to heat, additional strength, or minimum stretch is a prerequisite, either a strand core or an independent wire rope core is recommended.

Most wire rope is made of steel, but some is made of phosphor-bronze. Much of the steel rope is galvanized. Other variations in construction are in the numbers of wires in the strands and the strands in the rope. Some of the more common types of ropes and their uses follow. (See also Fig. A1.3.)

Galvanized-Wire Rope Galvanized-wire rope should be used if the rope is likely to corrode because of the presence of moisture, as for the standing rigging of a ship. Because the zinc coating is rapidly removed by wear, it should not, in general, be used for hoisting.

Uncoated-Wire Rope Uncoated-wire rope should be used where it is protected from moisture, as in a building, and for more or less continuous

6 Strands of 12 wires (6 × 12)

6 Strands of 24 wires (6 × 24)

6 Strands of 19 wires (6 × 19)

6 Strands of 37 wires (6 × 37)

Wire Rope Unlaid, Showing Hemp Core

Fig. A1.3 Types of wire rope.

hoisting. It may be used instead of galvanized-wire rope, where it is exposed to moisture, as for derrick guys, if a protective coating is applied to the rope at regular intervals.

Phosphor-Bronze Wire Rope Phosphor-bronze wire rope has lower strength than steel-wire rope; therefore the working loads should be lower. The sheaves should also be larger than those for steel rope. It is nonmagnetic and is used on small vessels.

(The numbers of wires and strands in a rope are indicated by a designation such as 6 × 19, that is, six strands of nineteen wires each.)

Six by Seven Only the galvanized type is specified. This construction is the stiffest of all the varieties. It is not suitable for general hoisting, but is applicable mainly for permanent standing guys.

Six by Nineteen When made of ungalvanized steel wire, this rope is principally used for heavy hoisting, and is of great strength, particularly useful on derricks and dredges. It is the stiffest and strongest construction of the types listed which are suitable for general hoisting purposes.

Six by Twenty-four This construction has almost the same flexibility as the 6 × 12 construction, but is stronger. It is used primarily in the larger sizes, where the strength of a 6 × 12 rope of the same size will not be satisfactory, and where extreme flexibility is the major consideration.

Six by Thirty-seven When made of ungalvanized steel wire, this construction is very flexible, making it suitable for cranes and similar machinery where sheaves are of necessity smaller than desirable. It may be used for heavy hoisting especially when conditions are unusually severe.

Six by twelve This construction of the fiber core of each strand as well as the fiber core of the rope itself is more flexible than 6 × 37 or 6 × 19 but not nearly as strong.

Spring-lay A special type of wire rope is spring-lay, a combination of wire and fiber. It is designated as 6 × 3 × 19, because it is composed of six main strands laid around a fiber core. Each main strand consists of three preformed wire strands and three fiber strands laid alternately around a fiber center. The function of the fiber parts is to provide a cushion for the wire strands, resulting in a rope having great flexibility and elasticity.

Spring-lay is normally used for mooring lines and, on tugboats, for alongside towing and berthing vessels.

Because it is a combination of wire and fiber, rules for the care of both wire and fiber rope apply when dealing with spring-lay. Uncoil it in the same manner as wire rope.

Spring-lay is spliced the same as wire rope.

A1.7 Care of Wire Rope Wire rope needs better care than hemp or manila and far better care than it generally receives on shipboard. It should be kept on a reel when not in use. A single kink in the finest wire rope practically ruins it at once. In receiving a line and transferring it from one reel to another, care should be taken to unreel it, instead of slipping off the successive bights over the end of the reel. Fig. A1.4 illustrates the right way and the wrong way of dealing with wire rope under various conditions.

A wire hawser should be gone over thoroughly every month or two with a standard lubricant preservative. It is important that the lubricant, whatever its composition, be thin enough to penetrate into interstices of the rope and yet have consistency enough to adhere to the wire for a reasonable length of time, after which it should be renewed. Care must be taken to ensure covering the rope all around. A hawser used for towing should be relubricated after use while being reeled up.

Wherever wire rope is to be worked over a sheave, the diameter of the sheave and the speed of running become very important factors. The larger the sheave and the lower the speed, the better. All manufacturers of wire rope prescribe a minimum diameter for sheaves, and their guaranteed breaking strains and estimated safe-working loads are for these minimum diameters and for moderate speed. High speed increases the wear upon the rope, not only by the friction on the sheaves but still more by the friction of the wires upon each other.

The diameter of the sheave over which the rope is worked should never be less than 20 times that of the rope itself; and the less flexible the rope, the larger should be the sheave.

It is important that the score of the sheave be of such size as to carry the rope without excessive play and, above all, without friction against the sides of the score. Metal sheaves are not required to be lined with wood or leather.

TO TAKE ROPE FROM COIL

Right Way   Wrong Way

TO MEASURE DIAMETER

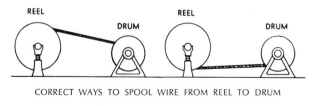

CORRECT WAYS TO SPOOL WIRE FROM REEL TO DRUM

Fig. A1.4 Handling wire rope.

Fig. A1.4a   Incorrect way to remove wire rope from a reel. (*Photograph courtesy of Bethlehem Steel Corporation.*)

Fig. A1.4b   Correct way to uncoil wire rope. (*Photograph courtesy of Bethlehem Steel Corporation.*)

Fig. A1.4c   Correct way to remove wire rope from a reel. (*Photograph courtesy of Bethlehem Steel Corporation.*)

Fig. A1.4d   A second correct way to remove wire rope from a reel. (*Photograph courtesy of Bethlehem Steel Corporation.*)

Fig. A1.4e The incorrect way to uncoil wire rope. (*Photograph courtesy of Bethlehem Steel Corporation.*)

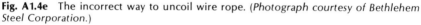

The turns of the rope should never be allowed to overlap on the drum of the winch.

As the wear of the rope over a sheave increases more rapidly with the speed than with the load, it is better, when an increased output is demanded, to increase the load rather than the speed.

By far the most unfavorable conditions to which wire rope can be subjected are those when it runs over sheaves that give it a reverse bend like the letter S. It passes over one sheave with a bend to the right and immediately swings around another with a bend to the left.

Wire rope should be condemned when the outside wires are worn down to one half their original diameter, or when it is apparent from broken wires or other abnormal indications that it has been subjected to excessive strain, or to a sharp bend resulting in a pronounced kink. Wire rope should be replaced whenever the total number of fishhooks (broken wires) in one lay exceeds four percent of the total number of wires in the rope. For example a 6 × 19 wire rope contains 114 individual wires; if 5 broken wires are encountered in one lay of the rope, replace it. (One lay is the length of rope needed for one strand to complete one spiral around the rope.) Figure A1.5 shows the results of improper care.

Table A1.1   Ropes of Twisted Construction

Size Circumference (inches)	Minimum Breaking Strength (pounds)—Fiber Type				
	Natural		Synthetic		
	Sisal	Manila	Poly-propylene	Polyester	Nylon
¾	480	600	1,100	1,500	1,500
1	800	1,000	1,700	2,500	2,500
1⅛	1,080	1,350	2,150	—	3,000
1¼	1,400	1,750	2,500	—	4,500
1½	2,120	2,650	3,700	5,000	5,500
1¾	2,760	3,450	4,800	—	7,000
2	3,520	4,400	6,000	8,000	8,400
2¼	4,320	5,400	7,000	—	11,500
2½	5,200	6,500	9,000	13,000	14,000
2¾	6,160	7,700	11,000	—	16,000
3	7,200	9,000	13,000	18,500	22,000
3½	9,600	12,000	16,500	25,000	28,500
3¾	10,800	13,500	19,500	—	33,000
4	12,000	15,000	21,500	31,000	37,500
4½	14,800	18,500	26,000	—	46,000
5	18,000	22,500	32,000	48,000	57,000
5½	21,200	26,500	38,000	—	68,000
6	24,800	31,000	44,000	68,000	81,000
6½	—	—	50,000	—	90,000
7	32,800	41,000	60,000	88,000	110,000
8	41,600	52,000	75,000	110,000	137,000
9	51,200	64,000	94,000	140,000	170,000
10	61,600	77,000	115,000	165,000	200,000
11	72,800	91,000	—	—	240,000
12	84,000	105,000	—	—	280,000

Table A1.2 Ropes of Braided Construction

Size Circumference (inches)	Minimum Breaking Strength (pounds)			
	Double-Braid Nylon	Poly-propylene	Plaited Polyester	Nylon
¾	1,650	—	—	—
1	2,750	—	—	—
1⅛	3,300	—	—	—
1¼	5,000	—	—	—
1½	6,650	—	—	—
1¾	8,300	—	—	—
2	11,000	—	—	—
2¼	15,000	—	—	—
2½	17,500	—	—	—
2¾	20,800	—	—	—
3	25,000	14,000	22,300	27,000
3½	35,000	16,800	27,800	33,500
3¾	40,000	—	—	—
4	45,000	23,000	37,000	46,500
4½	60,000	28,500	47,200	56,500
5	70,000	34,000	55,000	70,000
5½	90,000	40,000	63,000	82,800
6	100,000	48,000	80,500	98,000
6½	120,000	—	—	—
7	—	61,000	100,000	131,000
8	—	81,500	133,000	170,000
9	—	105,000	168,000	212,000
10	—	118,000	195,000	245,000

Table A1.3 Comparison of Breaking Strengths for Various General Purpose Wire Ropes (Uncoated)[a]

Rope Type	Rope Size (inches) Breaking Strength (pounds)							
	1/4	3/8	1/2	5/8	3/4	1	1 1/4	1 1/2
6 × 7, IPS/FC	5290	11,720	20,600	31,800	45,400	79,400	122,000	172,000
6 × 19, IPS/FC	5480	12,200	21,400	33,400	47,600	83,600	129,200	184,000
6 × 19, IPS/WSC or IWRC	—	13,120	23,000	35,800	51,200	89,800	138,800	197,800
6 × 19, CRS/IWRC or IWRC	—	15,100	26,000	41,200	58,800	103,400	159,800	228,000
6 × 19, CRS/IWRC	—	—	22,800	35,000	49,600	85,400	129,400	180,500
6 × 37, IPS/FC	5180	11,540	20,400	31,600	45,200	79,600	123,000	175,800
6 × 37 and 6 × 61 IPS/WSC[b] or IWRC[b]	5560	12,400	22,000	34,000	48,600	85,600	132,200	189,000
6 × 37, CRS/IWRC	—	—	20,400	31,300	44,400	77,300	118,300	166,000
8 × 19, IPS/FC	4700	10,480	18,460	28,600	41,000	72,000	111,400	158,800
6 × 37 and 6 × 61, EIPS/WSC or IWRC	6400	14,280	25,200	39,200	55,800	98,200	152,200	216,000
6 × 91, EIPS/IWRC	—	—	—	—	—	—	—	—

See page 638 for footnote.

Table A1.3   Comparison of Breaking Strengths for Various General Purpose Wire Ropes (Uncoated)[a] (Cont.)

Rope Type	Rope Size (inches) Breaking Strength (pounds)						
	1¾	2	2¼	2½	2¾	3	3½
6 × 7, IPS/FC	—	—	—	—	—	—	—
6 ×19, IPS/FC	248,000	320,000	400,000	488,000	584,000	—	—
6 × 19, IPS/WSC or IWRC	266,000	344,000	430,000	524,000	628,000	—	—
6 × 19, EIPS/WSC or IWRC	306,000	396,000	494,000	604,000	722,000	—	—
6 × 19, CRS/IWRC	—	—	—	—	—	—	—
6 × 37, IPS/FC	238,000	308,000	386,000	472,000	568,000	670,000	898,000
6 × 37 and 6 × 61, IPS/WSC or IWRC[b]	256,000	330,000	414,000	508,000	610,000	720,000	966,000
6 × 37, CRS/IWRC	—	—	—	—	—	—	—
8 × 19, IPS/FC	—	—	—	—	—	—	—
6 × 37 and 6 × 61, EIPS/WSC or IWRC	292,000	380,000	478,000	584,000	700,000	828,000	1,110,000
6 × 91, EIPS/IWRC	—	—	—	554,000	666,000	786,000	1,054,000

[a] Subtract 10 percent for zinc-coated (galvanized) wire rope.
[b] 6 × 61 rope available only in sizes 2 inches and above and only in regular lay.

LEGEND: IPS—Improved Plow Steel.   FC—Fiber Core.
          E—Extra, as EIPS.   WSC—Wire Strand Core.
          CRS—Corrosion-resistant Steel.   IWRC—Independent Wire Rope Core.

Table A1.4 Breaking Strengths of Various Marine Wire Ropes

Rope Type	Rope Size (inches) Breaking Strength (pounds)										
	1/4	3/8	1/2	5/8	3/4	1	1 1/4	1 1/2	1 3/4	2	2 1/4
Marine											
6×6, IPS/FC[a]	—	9,960	17,520	27,000	38,600	67,600	—	—	—	—	—
6×12, GIPS/FC	3,020	6,720	11,820	18,320	26,200	46,000	71,200	101,400	136,600	176,400	—
6×12, PhB/FC	1,470	3,220	5,640	8,740	12,240	—	—	—	—	—	—
6×24, GIPS/FC	—	9,540	16,800	26,000	37,200	65,600	101,400	144,600	195,000	252,000	—
Spring Lay											
6×3×7, G	—	—	8,940	13,900	19,920	—	—	—	—	—	—
6×3×19, G	—	—	—	—	—	35,000	54,400	77,800	105,400	137,000	212,000

[a] Subtract 10 percent for zinc-coated (galvanized) wire rope.

LEGEND: IPS—Improved Plow Steel.   PhB—Phosphor Bronze.
G—Galvanized.   FC—Fiber Core.

WALL ROPE WORKS
NEW BEDFORD CORDAGE CO.
BEVERLY, NEW JERSEY 08010

	NATURAL FIBERS				NYLON FILAMENT TYPE		POLYESTER FILAMENT TYPE			
	MANILA		SISAL				DACRON		ESTERLON	
DESCRIPTION	3' to 6' long leaf fibers from the Abaca plant, a close relative of the Banana, spun into yarns and twisted into rope.		2' to 4' long leaf fibers from the Agave Sisalana plant which resembles the century plant, spun into yarn and twisted into rope.		Made from Hexamethalene diamine and adipic acid, which are made from coke, air and water, from petroleum products and or from Furfural, an agricultural by-product. This compound is extruded through fine orifices to form fine filaments (6 denier) twisted into rope. Figures below apply to Nylon 6 6 Nylon 6 (Golden Nyline) behaves very similarly, but is more sensitive to heat and exhibits more elongation.		Polyester fiber is made from Ethylene Glycol, used in large quantities as an anti-freeze, and terephthalic acid, a chemical made from petroleum. Dacron is the trade name for duPont's polyester fibers. This is extruded to 5.8 denier filaments, twisted into yarn, plied and twisted into rope.		Esterlon is our trade name for ropes made from polyester fiber other than duPont's. This is extruded to 6.8 denier filaments, twisted into yarn, plied and twisted into rope.	
ROPE DIAMETER	1"	2"	1"	2"	1"	2"	1"	2"	1"	2"

STRENGTH CHARACTERISTICS										
Tensile Strength Dry (For comparisons of other sizes, see tensile strength tables for each type of rope)	9,000 lbs.	31,000 lbs.	7,200 lbs.	24,800 lbs.	25,000 lbs.	92,000 lbs.	22,000 lbs.	80,000 lbs.	20,000 lbs.	65,000 lbs.
Recommended Factor of Safety	5	5	5	5	9	9	9	9	9	9
Working Strength	1,800 lbs.	6,200 lbs.	1,440 lbs.	5,000 lbs.	2,890 lbs.	10,000 lbs.	2,450 lbs.	8,900 lbs.	2,220 lbs.	7,200 lbs.
Wet Strength Compared to Dry Strength	Up to 120%	Up to 120%	Up to 120%	Up to 120%	90 – 95%	90 – 95%	100%	100%	100%	100%
Strength per unit of Weight, or "Breaking Length" (Tensile strength lbs. per ft.)	33,000	29,000	26,700	23,000	96,000	97,000	72,000	64,000	65,000	55,000
Ability to absorb shock loads, expressed as foot-pounds of energy absorbed per pound of rope. DRY / WET	1,800 / 1,120	1,800 / 1,120	1,400 / 950	1,400 / 950	15,660 / 15,000	15,660 / 15,000	7,300 / 7,300	7,300 / 7,300	6,800 / 6,800	6,800 / 6,800
Repeat Loading Characteristics	POOR	POOR	POOR	POOR	GOOD	GOOD	EXCELLENT	EXCELLENT	GOOD	GOOD
Individual Filament or Fiber Strength (Grams per Denier)	5.0 – 7.0	5.0 – 7.0	4.0 – 5.0	4.0 – 5.0	8.0 – 9.0	8.0 – 9.0	7.5 – 9.0	7.5 – 9.0	6.5 – 8.5	6.5 – 8.5

WEIGHT & DENSITY CHARACTERISTICS										
Pounds per 100 Ft.	27.0	108.0	27.0	108.0	26.0	95.0	30.5	118.0	30.8	118
Specific Gravity of Fiber	1.5 – 1.6	1.5 – 1.6	1.25	1.25	1.14	1.14	1.38	1.38	1.38	1.38
Ability to Float	No	No	No	No	No	No	No	No	No	No

ELASTICITY – STRETCH										
Permanent Elongation at Working Loads (20% of Breaking Strength)	4.8%	4.8%	4.9%	4.9%	8.0%	8.0%	6.2%	6.2%	6.0%	6.0%
Working Elasticity (Temporary stretch under load) at Working Loads (20% of Breaking Strength)	5.0%	5.0%	5.0%	5.0%	16.0%	16.0%	5.9%	5.9%	6.5%	6.5%
Elongation at 100% Load (at break) for broken-in ropes	13%	13%	13%	13%	35%	35%	20%	20%	22%	22%
Individual Filament or Fiber Elongation	2 – 3%	2 – 3%	2 – 3%	2 – 3%	16 – 18%	16 – 18%	10 – 12%	- - -	12 – 14%	12 – 14%

SURFACE CHARACTERISTICS										
Coefficient of friction, new ropes on steel. Rendering qualities – Ability to ease out smoothly under load over bitts	Excellent		Excellent		Poor		Good.		Good.	
Hand (Feeling of rope to the touch)	Some harshness due to hairs. After use considerable harshness due to broken fiber ends.		Fairly harsh due to nature of fiber and hairs. After use quite harsh due to broken fiber ends.		Smooth. After use becomes fuzzy with a softer feel.		Smooth & Hard. Not slippery. After use becomes fuzzy with a softer feel.		Smooth & Hard. Not slippery. After use becomes fuzzy with a softer feel.	

WATER ABSORBED INTO FIBER										
(Some water will be held between fibers of all ropes)	Up to 100% of weight of rope		Up to 100% of weight of rope		Up to 9%		Less than 1%		Less than 1%	

RESISTANCE TO ROT, MILDEW & ATTACK BY MARINE ORGANISMS										
(Some marine organisms will attach themselves to any submerged object, including synthetic ropes)	Poor		Very Poor		100% Resistant		100% Resistant		100% Resistant	

DETERIORATION										
Due to aging (stored ropes, ideal conditions)	About 1% per year		About 1% per year		Zero		Zero		Zero	
Due to exposure to sunlight	Some slight		Some slight		Some slight		Almost none		Almost None	

RESISTANCE TO CHEMICALS										
To Acids	Very poor		Very poor		Fair—except to concentrated sulphuric & hydrochloric acids.		Very good to excellent		Very good to excellent	
To Alkalis	Very poor		Very poor		Excellent		Very good—except to concentrated Sodium Hydroxide at high temperatures		Very good – except to concentrated Sodium Hydroxide at high temperatures	
To Solvents	Good		Good		Good		Very good to excellent		Very good to excellent	

WEAR										
Resistance to surface abrasion	Good		Fair		Very Good		Excellent		Excellent	
Resistance to internal wear from flexing	Good		Very Good		Excellent		Very good to excellent		Very Good to excellent	
Resistance to cutting (toughness)	Good		Poor		Excellent		Very good to excellent		Very Good to excellent	

HIGH & LOW TEMPERATURE PROPERTIES										
Melting Point	Loses strength rapidly over 180° F.		Loses strength rapidly over 180° F.		482° F. Progressive strength loss above 300° F.		500° F. Progressive strength loss above 300° F.		500° F. Progressive strength loss above 300° F.	
Low temperature properties	No change		No change		No change		No change		No change	
Flammability	Burns like wood		Burns like wood		Burns with difficulty		Burns with difficulty		Burns with difficulty	

ECONOMICS										
Average comparative service life calling Manila 1.	1	1	0.8	0.8	2 – 5	2 – 5	3 – 6	3 – 6	3 – 5	3 – 5
Comparative cost per pound based on list prices Calling Manila 100	100	100	72	72	226	243	316	337	259	279
Comparative cost per foot based on list prices Calling Manila 100	100	100	72	72	217	214	356	369	294	306
Comparative cost per foot as above allowing for service life factor	100	100	96	96	76	72	93	94	86	87
Comparative cost per 100 lbs. of working strength as above based on Rope Diameter first cost basis (cost per ft/wkg. str.)	100	100	96	96	167	157	304	294	312	375
Comparative cost per 100 lbs. of working strength as above, allowing for service life factor.	100	100	120	120	48	45	68	65	78	93

WDS – 113 Revised – Jan. 73

Specifications Chart

	POLYETHYLENE		POLYPROPYLENE — MONOFILAMENT & PLURAL FILAMENT		POLYPROPYLENE — MULTIFILAMENT		BLENDS — POLY-PLUS		BLENDS — POLYCRON		LST	LST-WB
Description	Made from polymers and copolymers of ethylene, a natural gas or petroleum derivative. This is extruded to 600 denier (12 mil) filaments, twisted into yarn, plied and twisted into rope.		Made from a derivative of propane, a product of natural gas or petroleum. Monofilament is extruded to filaments of 500 denier (12 mil). Plural filament is extruded to filaments of 280 denier (6 mil). These are twisted into yarn, plied and twisted into rope.		Multifilament is extruded to filaments of 6 denier, twisted into yarn, plied and twisted into rope.		100% Polypropylene core with single cover of blended polyester (52%) and polyethylene (48%) both by weight, plied and twisted into rope.		100% Polyethylene core with double cover of Polyethylene yarns veneered with Dacron, plied and twisted into rope. 1.5–16" dia. and larger are identified by a black Polyethylene core.		LST is our trade name for ropes having a cover of polyester and a core of blown Monofilament Polypropylene encased within a sleeve wrap. (Available in 1¼" dia. and larger).	Contains a double cover of Polyethylene Yarns veneered with polyester and a core of blown monofilament Polypropylene yarns enclosed within a sleeve wrap. (Available in 1¾" dia. and larger).
Diameter	1"	2"	1"	2"	1"	2"	1"	2"	1"	2"	2"	2"
	12,600 lbs.	47,700 lbs.	14,000 lbs.	52,000 lbs.	12,600 lbs	47,700 lbs.	15,000 lbs.	56,500 lbs.	14,000 lbs.	60,000 lbs.	73,000 lbs.	65,000 lbs.
	6	6	6	6	6	6	6	6	6	6	8	8
	2,100 lbs.	7,900 lbs.	2,330 lbs.	8,700 lbs.	2,100 lbs.	7,900 lbs.	2,200 lbs.	8,400 lbs.	2,070 lbs.	8,900 lbs.	9,100 lbs.	8,100 lbs.
	100%	100%	102–105%	102–105%	102–105%	102–105%	100%	100%	100%	100%	100%	100%
	66,000	75,500	77,800	75,500	65,600	64,500	69,800	68,000	53,000	63,000	91,000	74,000
	4,600	4,600	9,300	9,300	9,200	9,200	8,600	8,600	8,300	8,300	9,000	8,000
	4,600	4,600	9,300	9,300	9,200	9,200	8,600	8,600	8,300	8,300	9,000	8,000
	FAIR	FAIR	EXCELLENT	EXCELLENT	EXCELLENT	EXCELLENT	VERY GOOD	VERY GOOD	GOOD	GOOD	GOOD	GOOD
	5.5–7.0	5.5–7.0	6.0–7.5	6.0–7.5	5.0–6.5	5.0–6.5	---	---	---	---	5.0–9.0	5.0–9.0
	18.5	72.5	18.0	69.0	19.2	74.0	21.5 (Varies with Rope Size)	83.0 (Varies with Rope Size)	26.5 (Varies with Rope Size)	95.0 (Varies with Rope Size)	80.0 (Varies with Rope Size)	83.6 (Varies with Rope Size)
	.95	.95	.91	.91	.91	.91	Varies with Rope Size	Varies with Rope Size	No	No		
	Yes	Yes	Yes	Yes	Yes	Yes					Yes	Yes
	5.8%	5.8%	3.8%	3.8%	7.5%	7.5%	5.9%	5.9%	4.7%	4.7%	7.0%	6.5%
	5.9%	5.9%	8.9%	8.9%	10.5%	10.5%	7.1%	7.1%	5.1%	5.1%	3–4%	4.5%
	22%	22%	24% (MULTI)	24% (MONO)	36%	36%	27%	27%	21%	21%	20%	20%
	11–14%	11–14%	16–20%	14–18%	22–28%	22–28%	---	---	---	---	---	---
Handling	Good but requires extra wraps.		Poor		Fair		Good		Good		Good.	Good.
	Smooth and very slippery. After use becomes slightly harsh due to broken fiber ends.		Smooth but not slippery. After use becomes harsh due to broken fiber ends.		Smooth & Soft with some natural fuzziness. Remains same after use.		Smooth & Hard. After use bristles and fuzz appear but little harshness.		Smooth & Hard. Not slippery. After use becomes fuzzy but not harsh.		Smooth & Hard. Not slippery. After use becomes fuzzy with a softer feel.	Smooth & Hard. Not slippery. After use becomes fuzzy but not harsh.
	Zero		Zero		Zero		Almost Zero		Almost Zero		Less than 1%	Less than 1%
	100% Resistant		100% Resistant		100% Resistant		100% Resistant		100% Resistant		100% Resistant	100% Resistant
	Zero		Zero		Zero		Zero		Zero		Zero	Zero
	Some black resists best		Some black resists best				Very slight		Almost none		Almost none	Almost none
Chemical resistance	Excellent except to conc. sulphuric		Excellent		Excellent		Good to excellent		Excellent except to conc. nitric		Good	Very good to excellent
	Good		Good		Good		Excellent		Excellent		Very good to excellent	Very good – except to concentrated Sodium Hydroxide at high temperatures
	Good		Good		Good		Good to excellent		Good to excellent		Very good to excellent	Very good to excellent
	Good		Good		Good		Very Good		Very Good		Very Good	Very Good
	Very Good		Very Good		Very Good		Very Good		Very Good		Very Good	Very Good
	Good		Good		Very Good		Very Good		Very Good		Very Good	Very Good
Temperature	280° F. Softens above 250° F. Becomes brittle below –150°F. Burns with difficulty		330° F. Softens above 300° F. No change. Burns with difficulty		330° F. Softens above 300° F. No change. Burns with difficulty		Progressive strength loss above 250° F. Some brittleness below –150°F. Burns with difficulty		Progressive strength loss above 250° F. Some brittleness below –150° F. Burns with difficulty.		Progressive strength loss above 250° F. No change. Burns with difficulty	Progressive strength loss above 250° F. Some brittleness below –150° F. Burns with difficulty.
	2	2	2–3	2–3	2–3	2–3	2½	2½	2–4	2–4	3–5	3–5
	174	171	167	164	237	256	217	216	259	244	239	239
	113	115	111	105	158	164	172	166	253	215	177	186
	78	79	60	60	79	79	77	73	95	80	48	70
	135	124	117	107	135	131	157	133	248	168	131	·143
	68	62	43	43	54	52	63	53	83	56	33	36

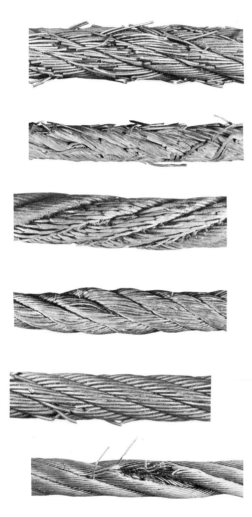

(A) Sheaves too small. This rope was forced to travel continuously over sheaves whose diameters were too small. This caused severe bending fatigue. Result—broken wires, ruined rope.

(B) Drum abrasion and abuse caused this. The rope was scuffed over and over against previous wraps on a flat-faced drum. Its life ended long before it should have.

(C) Kinking caused this. This dog-leg, or kink, was finally straightened out of this rope—but notice the uneven wear at the point where the kink had been. Beware of dog-legs! They're expensive.

(D) Uneven drum winding is a frequent rope-wrecker. This rope was wound unevenly time after time onto a drum. Result—it is crushed and flattened. The service cost of this rope was unnecessarily high. WATCH how the rope winds!

(E) Acids did this. This rope was attacked by high sulfur content in the water and crude oil through which the rope operated. A heavily internally lubricated rope will resist the action for a time.

(F) Foul play "killed" this rope. While in operation, this rope met with an accident that mashed and cut many of its wires. Result— a ruined rope, and many a rope dollar wasted that could have been saved.

Fig. A1.5 Results of improper care. *(Courtesy of Le Tourneau-Westinghouse Co-Operator.)*

Appendix 2

Knotting and Splicing

A2.1 Knots, Bends, and Hitches Except among seamen, the term *knot* is ordinarily used as an all-inclusive term covering the more specific use of knots plus bends and hitches. To be more specific, knots are used to form eyes or to secure a line around a cord or object. Bends are used to secure lines together. Hitches secure lines to, or bend a line around, objects such as a ring, spar, or stanchion. In many cases, however, the functions of knots, bends, and hitches overlap; for example, the versatile bowline can be used for all three purposes.

A2.2 Knots Figure A2.1 shows the more common and useful knots.

Overhand Knot The overhand knot (A) is formed by passing the end of the line over the standing part and through the eye. This knot is seldom used alone, but is the first move in tying a few other knots such as the square knot.

Square Knot The square or reef knot (B) has a multitude of uses, chiefly in lashing situations where the line is passed around an object, heaved taut, and secured.

Bowline The bowline (C) also is a knot with many uses. It is employed whenever a loop is needed, such as in making a temporary eye in a mooring line.

Running Bowline The running bowline (D) can be used when a running eye is needed. It is made by tying a bowline around the standing part.

Bowline on a Bight The bowline on a bight (E) is used when greater strength than that given by a single bowline is necessary or when the end of the line is unavailable. This knot is tied with the line doubled. Form an eye as when making the single bowline, then pass the bight through the eye and around the two loops thus formed.

(A)
OVERHAND KNOT

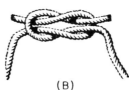

(B)
SQUARE OR REEF KNOT

(C)
BOWLINE

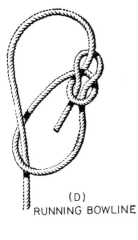

(D)
RUNNING BOWLINE

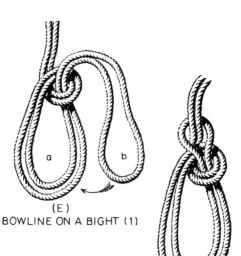

(E)
BOWLINE ON A BIGHT (1)

(E)
BOWLINE ON A BIGHT (2)

(F)
FIGURE −OF−EIGHT
KNOT

(G)
SHEEPSHANK

Fig. A2.1 A few of the more common knots.

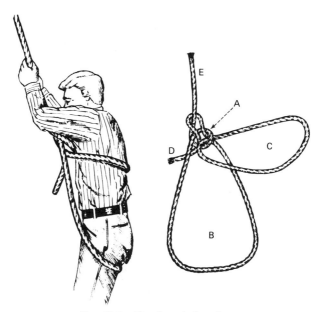

Fig. A2.2 The French bowline.

Figure-of-Eight Knot The figure-of-eight knot (F) is used to prevent a line rove through a block from unreeving. It can also be used temporarily to keep an unwhipped line from unlaying.

Sheepshank The sheepshank (G) is used to shorten a rope or to compensate for a weak spot in a line. The weakened spot should be in the center of the three parallel parts.

French Bowline The French bowline (Fig. A2.2) may be employed to send a man over the side to work when he may have to use both hands, or it can be employed to hoist an unconscious man. The man sits in one eye, and the other goes around his body. The weight of his body in the one eye pulls the other eye taut and keeps the man from slipping out of the knot. The French bowline is tied in the same way as the ordinary bowline except that the end is run through the eye the second time before passing it around the standing part and back through the eye.

A2.3 Bends Bends are used to join two lines together.

Becket or Sheet Bend The becket or sheet bend (Fig. A2.3) is made by passing the end of one line through the eye or bight of the other, around the eye, and under itself. The single becket bend (A) is used with lines of the same, or nearly same, size; the double becket bend (B) is used with lines of different sizes.

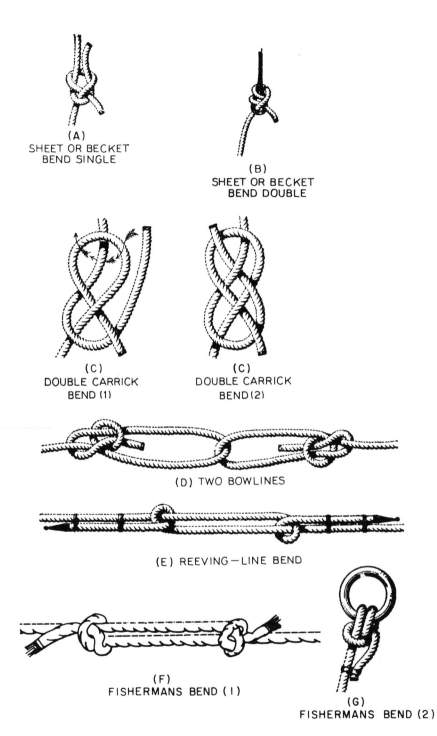

(A)
SHEET OR BECKET
BEND SINGLE

(B)
SHEET OR BECKET
BEND DOUBLE

(C)
DOUBLE CARRICK
BEND (1)

(C)
DOUBLE CARRICK
BEND (2)

(D) TWO BOWLINES

(E) REEVING—LINE BEND

(F)
FISHERMANS BEND (1)

(G)
FISHERMANS BEND (2)

Fig. A2.3 Some useful bends.

Double Carrick Bend   The double carrick bend (C) may be used to join two lines, if the ends are seized to the standing parts after tying the knot. This knot has more applications in fancy work, however. Note that the ends should come out at opposite corners of the knot.

Two Bowlines   Using two bowlines (D) is a convenient way of bending two hawsers together, but they are somewhat bulky. Then too, under great strain, they tend to part where the lines join.

Reeving-Line Bend   The reeving-line bend (E) connects two hawsers in such a way that they will reeve through an opening, offering as little obstruction as possible. It is made by taking a half hitch with each end around the other hawser and seizing the ends to the standing parts.

Fisherman's Bend   There are two different knots called fisherman's bend. One (F) is a variation of the reeving-line bend, but it should not be used on mooring hawsers. It may jam in a chock. It is used on fishlines and other lines that must pass through relatively small openings. The ends need not be whipped to the standing parts. The second fisherman's bend (G) is used for securing a line to a buoy or a hawser to the ring or jew's harp of an anchor. The end should be seized to the standing part.

A2.4   Hitches   Hitches (Fig. A2.4) are used to bend a line to a ring or to or around a spar or stanchion.

Timber Hitch   The timber hitch (A) may be used to haul an object such as a spar that has a fairly rough surface. It cannot be used on metal pipes and rods. To tie, the end is passed around the object, around the standing part, and then several times around itself.

Timber and Half Hitch   Adding a half hitch to the timber hitch (B) gives better control, and the combination is less likely to slip than the timber hitch alone. Unless you can slip the half hitch over the end of the object, tie it before making the timber hitch.

Rolling Hitch   The rolling hitch (C), sometimes called the taut-line hitch, is used when the line is to be bent to a round object or to another, taut, line. It is the basic hitch in one method of passing a stopper (Fig. A2.6). To tie, take a turn around the taut line and pull tight. Take a second turn; this turn must cross the first (Fig. A2.6(B)). Pull taut and add a half hitch.

Two Half Hitches   Two half hitches (D) can be used to bend a line to a ring, spar, or stanchion. When tying, pass the end around the standing part twice—both times in the same direction.

Round Turn and Two Half Hitches   To ensure that the line will not slip along a spar or stanchion when the angle of pull is acute, take a round turn before tying the two half hitches (E).

Clove Hitch   The clove hitch (F) is one of the most useful hitches, and is probably used more often than any other knot to secure the end of a line. It will hold as long as there is a strain on the line, but once the strain is

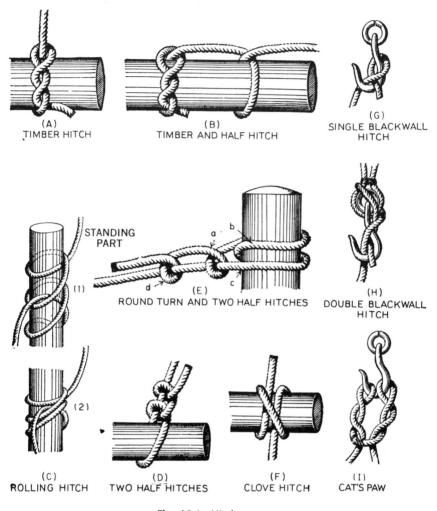

Fig. A2.4 Hitches.

removed, the hitch should be checked and tightened to prevent the end from pulling out when the strain is reapplied. To make the hitch more secure, after tying it, add a half hitch around the standing part.

Blackwall Hitch   The blackwall hitch (G) is used to bend a strap to a hook. To tie, make a loop with the end under the standing part. Slip the loop up over the hook and pull it tight around the back of the hook. The double blackwall hitch (H) is made in the same manner; just lay up a second loop before slipping the line up over the hook. Tighten the double blackwall hitch as shown in the illustration.

Cat's Paw The cat's paw (I) is used to shorten a line. Take two bights, twist them in opposite directions as many times as necessary, and slip them over the hook.

A2.5 Securing the End of a Rope Figure A2.5 shows several knots worked in the end of a rope by unlaying the rope and using the strands. Knots of this kind may be used to keep a rope from unlaying or for ornamental purposes. Before unlaying, place a temporary whipping below the point of the knot.

Wall Knot Form a bight with the first strand (A) and pass the second strand around it. Pass the third strand around the end of the second and through the bight of the first. Pull taut.

Wall and Crown After tying the wall knot, top off with a crown. Lay strand 1 across the wall knot (B) and strand 2 across 1. Number 3 goes over number 2 and under number 1.

Double Wall and Single Crown Tie a single wall and crown, leaving some slack in it. Pass each strand through the wall knot again, following the part nearest (C).

Double Wall and Double Crown Also double the parts of the knot forming the crown (D). This knot also is called the man-rope knot.

Double Matthew Walker Pass strand "a" around the standing part and through itself, thus forming a knot. Pass strand "b" around the standing part and through itself and the knot in strand "a." Strand "c" goes around the standing part and through itself and the knots in strands "a" and "c."

Single Matthew Walker The single Matthew Walker (G and H) is a cross between the wall knot and double Matthew Walker. Each strand goes through itself and one eye formed by another strand.

Laniard Knot The laniard knot (I) is a single Matthew Walker tied in a 4-strand line.

Whipping A whipping prevents a rope from unlaying. To make a temporary whipping, lay a length of stout cord along the line and take several turns around it and the line (J). Lay the other end of the cord along the line (K) and wrap the cord around it and the line. Pull taut (L). The whipping should be about as long as the diameter of the rope.

Sailmaker's Whipping The sailmaker's whipping is made with a sail needle and a length of twine. Push the needle through the line where the inboard end of the whipping will be. Pull all but a short length of the twine through the line. Wrap the twine around its end and the line, as for the temporary whipping. Then pass the needle through a strand close to the end of the turns. Haul taut. Run the needle through the next strand—but at the other end of the whipping. Haul taut. Run the needle through the last strand, again

(A)

WALL KNOT

(B)

WALL AND CROWN

(C)

**DOUBLE WALL AND
SINGLE CROWN**

(D)

**DOUBLE WALL
AND DOUBLE CROWN
OR "MAN ROPE KNOT"**

(E)

**DOUBLE MATTHEW
WALKER (1)**

(F)

**DOUBLE MATTHEW
WALKER (2)**

(G)

**SINGLE MATTHEW
WALKER (1)**

(H)

**SINGLE MATTHEW
WALKER (2)**

(I)

LANIARD KNOT (1)

(J)

(K)

(L)

WHIPPING THE END OF A ROPE

Fig. A2.5 Securing the end of a rope.

at the opposite end of the whipping. Haul taut, and secure the whipping by passing the needle through the rope a couple of times.

A2.6 Passing a Stopper   A stopper is used to hold a line under tension while the hauling part is being transferred from the gypsy head or capstan to the bitts or cleat where the line is to be belayed. There are several ways of passing a stopper. Two methods for stopping fiber line and two methods for stopping wires are illustrated.

The first method (Fig. A2.6(A)) employs the first two turns of a rolling hitch PASSED AGAINST THE LAY OF THE ROPE backed up by a half hitch passed some distance away from the above two turns, as illustrated, to prevent the stopper jamming. Several additional turns are then made around the taut line against the lay to complete the stopper. The second method (B) is used on smaller lines such as boatfalls. Smaller lines tend to take a kink and bind the first hitch of a stopper, making it almost impossible to remove the stopper. For this reason, a half hitch backed up by several turns with the lay is used.

For stopping wire rope a chain stopper should be used. There are two methods by which this can be done as well. The first method (Fig. A2.7(A)) uses a chain stopper with a short length of small stuff bent on the end link. The stopper consists of six or more half hitches made with the chain along the wire. The small stuff on the end is intended to keep the chain stopper taut until the strain is picked up.

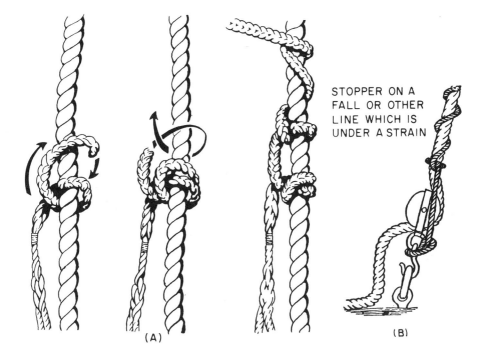

STOPPER ON A
FALL OR OTHER
LINE WHICH IS
UNDER A STRAIN

(A)

(B)

Fig. A2.6   Passing a stopper.

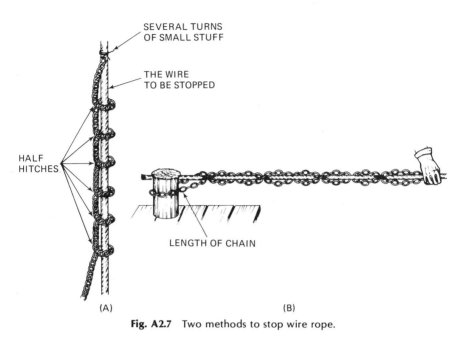

SEVERAL TURNS
OF SMALL STUFF

THE WIRE
TO BE STOPPED

HALF
HITCHES

LENGTH OF CHAIN

(A)   (B)

Fig. A2.7 Two methods to stop wire rope.

The second method (B) is used primarily to stopper wire rope and springlay mooring lines. To apply the stopper a bight of a length of chain is dropped over the bitt or fitting on which the wire is to be belayed. The two ends are then criss-crossed over and under the wire, as shown, at least six times. The ends are held taut by hand or secured by several turns of small stuff until the wire is belayed.

With all the stopper hitches it must be remembered that the strain must be put on the stopper SLOWLY. Throwing the turns off the gypsy so that the stopper abruptly takes the strain might result in a parted stopper at worst or at best a jammed stopper hitch. The command "Back easy" is used to direct that the turns on the gypsy be eased out until the stopper has the strain. When it is ascertained that the stopper has the strain the command "Up behind" is given, directing the turns to be thrown off the gypsy and belayed as quickly as possible.

A2.7 Passing a Strap At times it is necessary to clap a tackle on a rope or the hauling part of another tackle to increase the pull. For this purpose an endless strap or selvage is used in one of the following ways:

First Method In the first method (view (A), **Fig. A2.8**) wrap the strap tightly around the rope. Pass the end toward the direction of pull through the other end, and slip it over the hook.

Second Method In the second method (B), hold the center of the strap against the hawser and wrap both ends around it. The ends cross each other. Slip the hook through both ends.

(A)   (B)   (C)

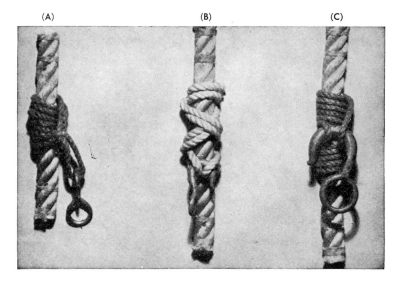

Fig. A2.8 Passing a strap.

Third Method In the third method (C), spread the loop of one end of the strap; wrap the other end around the hawser inside the loop. Slip the hook through both ends.

A2.8 Splicing Twisted Fiber Rope Splices are used to make permanent eyes and permanent repairs in ropes. There are three general types: eye, short, and long. Several variations of the three exist for splicing wire rope.

When splicing fiber rope, the usual practice is to take three or four tucks with each strand. Better-looking but less secure is the taper splice, wherein one tuck is taken with each full strand; half of each strand is cut away and the second tuck taken, and half of the remaining part of each strand is cut away and the third tuck taken.

When splicing large lines, it is a good idea to whip the strands and whip the line at the point to which the strands will be unlaid.

Eye Splice To make an eye splice, unlay the line 6 or more inches, depending on the size of the line. Tuck the center strand under any strand of the rope (Fig. A2.9(A)). Next, tuck the strand to the left of the center strand under the next strand up the line from the strand the center one is under (B). Turn the line over and tuck the last strand under the remaining strand (C). The remaining tucks are made by passing the working strands over one of the standing strands and under the next.

If the line is large it may be necessary to use a fid, a round, pointed tool for opening the strands of fiber rope. Figure A2.10 shows a fid and tools for splicing wire rope.

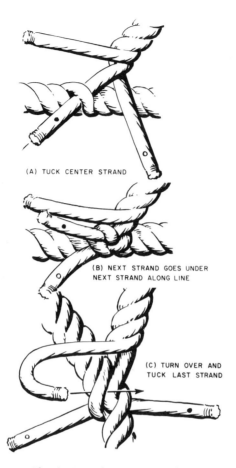

(A) TUCK CENTER STRAND

(B) NEXT STRAND GOES UNDER
NEXT STRAND ALONG LINE

(C) TURN OVER AND
TUCK LAST STRAND

Fig. A2.9   Making an eye splice.

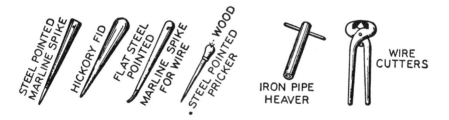

STEEL POINTED
MARLINE SPIKE

HICKORY FID

FLAT STEEL
POINTED
MARLINE SPIKE
FOR WIRE

STEEL POINTED
WOOD
PRICKER

IRON PIPE
HEAVER

WIRE
CUTTERS

TOOLS FOR SPLICING
BOTH FIBER AND WIRE ROPE

Fig. A2.10   Tools for splicing both fiber and wire rope.

SHORT SPLICE (1)   SHORT SPLICE (2)   SHORT SPLICE (3)

Fig. A2.11 Making a short splice

Short Splice   The short splice almost doubles the size of the line at the point of the splice; therefore, it can be used only in line that does not have to pass through a block or other small opening. To make, unlay both ends 6 or more inches. Marry the two ends, with the strands from each end alternating (**Fig. A2.11**). Until one attains some skill in splicing, it is a good practice to seize the strands at the marriage.

Take any strand of either rope and pass it over one strand and under the next. Do the same with the remaining strands of that rope. Take two or more tucks with each strand. Turn the line and take one or two tucks with each strand of the other rope.

Be sure to pull the strands up taut, and do not let the twist out of the strands.

Long Splice   The long splice is used in running rigging, because it does not appreciably enlarge the line and it will pass through blocks and other small openings.

The long splice is begun just like the short splice, except that each end is unlaid for 15 turns, and if the strands are seized together, one strand must be left out (strand 1, line 1). This strand is unlaid and the corresponding strand of the second line (strand 1, line 2) is laid in its place. Twist the strand while laying it in, in order to retain the set of the line. When all but about 6 inches of strand 1, line 2 is laid in, tie an overhand knot with the two number 1 strands (view (A), **Fig. A2.12**). If tied properly, this overhand knot will lie snugly in the groove; otherwise, it will bunch up. Tie the knot as shown in view (A).

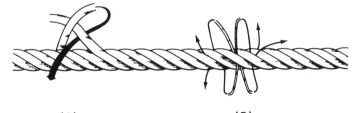

(A)   (B)

TIE AN OVERHAND KNOT   SPLIT STRANDS AND TUCK

Fig. A2.12 Long splice.

After knotting the first pair of strands, cut the seizing and start unlaying a strand of line 2 (strand 2, line 1). Lay in all but about 6 inches of strand 2, line 1 and knot the two number 2 strands.

One of the number 3 strands is then unlaid from 6 to 12 inches from the marriage point, the other number 3 strand laid in, and the two knotted. Then each strand is split. Half is passed over one strand and under the next in one direction (B). The other half of that strand goes over and under in the opposite direction. Thus, four tucks are taken at each knot.

A2.9 Splicing Braided Line The method of splicing a braided line depends upon its construction; indeed, braided line with a solid core cannot be spliced.

Halyard Splice The halyard splice is used on braided line with a hollow core. It is most commonly seen on signal halyards and flags, where it is used to attach snaps and rings. To make the splice (**Fig. A2.13**), unlay about 2 inches of the end and taper it. In a piece of wire several inches long, make an eye in one large enough to take the tapered end of the halyard. Thread the end into this eye. Insert a marline spike, pricker, or other tapered instrument in the side of the halyard, about 1½ inches up from the start of the taper. Work the spike up the center of the halyard about 2 inches and back out the side again. Pull the spike out, but hold the halyard so that you can thread your wire and the end of the halyard through the holes made by the spike. Slip the halyard snap or ring over the end, and thread the wire through the bottom hole and out the top hole. Pull the end through. Discard the wire and pull on the eye and standing part, working the bitter end back inside the halyard. With sail twine and needle, put a whipping around the splice, starting where the end enters the standing part.

Samson Eye Splice Splicing double-braided nylon line is somewhat like splicing signal halyard, because the end must be worked into the center. Because of the braided core, however, procedure differs, and special tools are needed. For line 1½ inches in circumference and below, a fid and a pusher are used (**Fig. A2.14**). For line larger than 1½ inches, pusher and fid are combined in the fid shown in view 1. Stamped on each fid is a number indicating the size of line for which the fid was made. Fids also serve as rules to measure with while splicing, as will be explained. Friction or maskng tape and a soft lead pencil, crayon, or—preferably—a wax marking pencil are needed. Sharp-pointed shears also are handy.

Both of the splices described here, and the line that they are used on, were developed by the Samson Cordage Works of Boston, Massachusetts.

Measure one fid length from the end of the line and mark point T. From T form a bight the size of the eye desired. Mark this as point X (view 2 of **Fig. A2.14**). If the eye is to include a thimble, form the bight around the thimble.

Approximately five fid lengths up the line from X tie a slip knot; pull it tight. This knot is very important, because it prevents slack in the cover

STEP 1:
UNLAY THE STRANDS
ABOUT 4 INCHES. DI-
VIDE THE STRANDS AND
TAPER THE END BY
CUTTING OFF EACH
PART ABOUT 1 INCH
SHORTER THAN THE
OTHER. EITHER SERVE
THE LOOSE STRANDS
OR TAKE SEVERAL
HALF HITCHES.

STEP 2:
INSERT MARLIN SPIKE
AS ILLUSTRATED, TO
MAKE A SMALL HOLE
IN THE HALYARD.

STEP 3:
INSERT WIRE EYE THROUGH
THE HOLE IN THE HALYARD.
PLACE TAPERED END OF
HALYARD INTO THE EYE OF
THE WIRE. PULL THE WIRE
HOOK BACK THROUGH THE
HALYARD, DRAWING THE TA-
PERED END OF THE HAL-
YARD THROUGH THE HOLE.

STEP 4:
THE SPLICE IS NOW MADE.
TO MAKE CERTAIN THAT
THE SPLICE WILL NOT PULL
OUT, YOU CAN, WITH NEE-
DLE AND SAIL TWINE, TAKE
A COUPLE OF TUCKS THROUGH
THE SPLICE.

Fig. A2.13   Halyard splice.

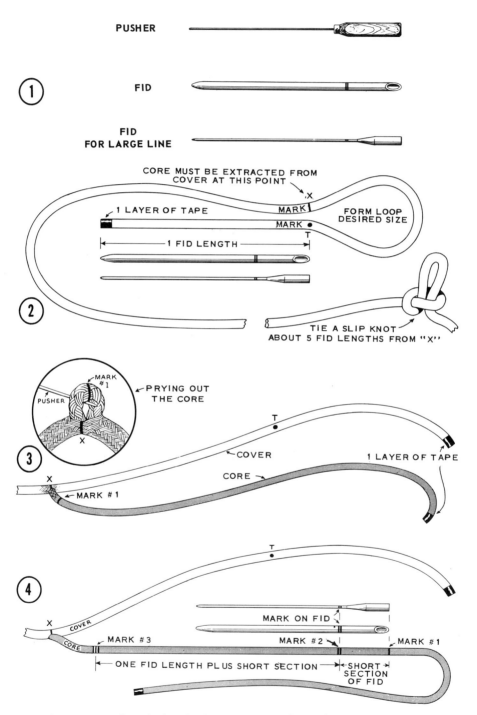

Fig. A2.14 Marking the line for the Samson eye splice in double-braided line.

braid from working too far up the standing part of the line, thus making it impossible to work the slack back down when needed. You must remember that disturbing the relationship between the length of the core and the length of the cover seriously affects the strength of the line. For this reason, the proper relationship must be restored after completing the splice, and this cannot be done if the slack works too far up the standing part.

Bend the line sharply at X, and with the pusher separate the cover strands, exposing the core. Work the pusher into the core and pry out a bight. Put one heavy mark on the core. (See insert, view 3.) This is mark number 1. Pull the core out of the cover, from X to the end of the line. Tape the end.

Grasp the line at X and pull out more of the core. From mark number 1, measure along the standing part a length equal to the short section of the fid. Make two heavy marks. This is mark number 2 (view 4). (Old-style fids are not marked off. Therefore, if you have one of these, use the distance from the end of the word "braid" to the hollowed-out end of the fid.)

From mark number 2, measure in the same direction one fid length plus a short section of the fid, and mark this point with three heavy lines. This is mark number 3.

Run the fid through the core from number 2 to number 3 (view 1, Fig. A2.15). Pinch the taped end of the COVER into the hollow end of the fid. Jam the pusher into the cover where it is tucked into the fid, and holding the core lightly at 3, push the fid and cover through the core. (The hollow end of the fid used with line over 1½ inches in circumference is threaded. Screw the fid onto the cover, and then run the fid and cover through the core.)

Hold the core lightly and pull on the cover until point T emerges at number 3 (view 2).

You now must taper the bitter end of the cover. Beginning at T, count off seven pairs of strands that revolve clockwise. Mark the pair and call this point R. Run the mark completely around the cover, but leave the pair of marked strands distinguishable as shown in the insert of view 3 of Fig. A2.15. Continue marking every seventh pair of clockwise strands until you reach the end of the cover. Now go back to R and count off and mark the fourth pair of strands that run counterclockwise. Then, count off and mark every seventh counterclockwise pair.

Starting at the end of the line, cut and remove every pair of marked strands up to and including those at R (view 4). Sharp-pointed scissors are better than a knife for cutting nylon strands.

The foregoing method of tapering is recommended by the manufacturer, but you may find the following simpler and faster.

Establish point R, then, using an estimated distance equal to about half the circumference of the line, measure off and mark the clockwise strands to be cut. Next, count off four pairs of counterclockwise strands from R and from that point measure off and mark the counterclockwise strands to be cut.

After cutting and removing the strands, grasp the core at 2 and carefully pull on the cover until R emerges at 2.

You now are ready to run the core back into the cover, going from R to X.

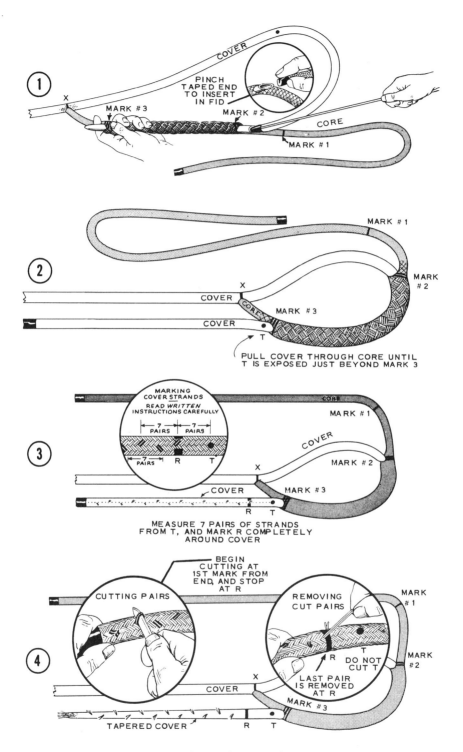

Fig. A2.15 Tucking and tapering the cover.

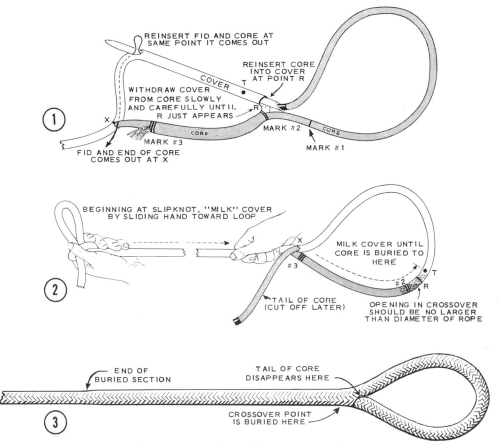

Fig. A2.16   Completing the Samson eye splice.

Depending on the size of the eye, the fid may not be long enough to reach X in a single pass; therefore insert the fid into the cover at R and work it only as far as is convenient and bring it out at any place (view 1, Fig. **A2.16**). Jam the end of the core into the hollow end of the fid and push fid and core through the cover. Repeat this step as many times as is necessary, always reinserting the fid into the place from which it came.

Draw the core through the cover until the parts of the line are two-blocked at the crossover. Then, holding the line tightly at the crossover and working both ways from the crossover, smooth out the braid. The bitter end of the cover will disappear into the core, but there will be a length of the core protruding at X (view 2).

Grasp the line at the slip knot with one hand and with the other milk the cover down over the section of core in the eye. Work gently at first, then more firmly. Continue this until the exposed core and the crossover are entirely buried in the cover. The cover may bunch at the crossover. If it does, tug on the tail of the core until the bunching is eliminated. If you are using a thimble, place it in the eye just before pulling the crossover into the cover. After all the slack has been worked down, points T and X should coincide.

Smooth out the cover around the eye. If the eye is the correct size, cut off the tail of the core and untie the slipknot. If the eye is not the right size, you will have to remake the splice because there is no way to adjust its size. View 3 shows how a completed splice should appear.

Although the core is cut at the fork of the eye, leaving only the cover bridging that point, the strength of the splice is not affected as long as nothing binds the eye on that side while a strain is being applied. With the legs of the eye sharing the load equally, the splice is 100 percent strong.

Samson end for end splice   The same tools and materials required for the Samson eye splice are used for this splice.

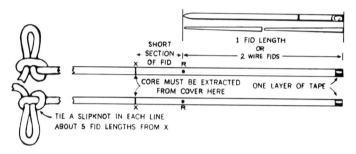

Fig. A2.17   Samson end for end splice—making the measurements.

Tape the end of each rope with one thin layer of tape. Lay two ropes to be spliced side by side and measure one tubular fid length (2 wire fid lengths because wire fid is ½ size) from end of each rope and make a mark. This is point R (Reference.)

From R measure one short fid section length as scribed on the fid; then, mark again. This is Point X where you should extract core from inside cover. Be sure both ropes are identically marked. (Fig. A2.17).

Tie a tight slipknot approximately 5 fid lengths from X.

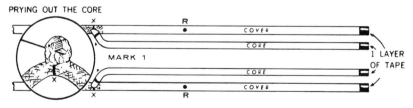

Fig. A2.18   End for end splice—Extracting the cores.

Bend rope sharply at X. With the pusher or any sharp tool such as an ice pick, awl, or marlin spike, spread cover strands to expose core. First pry; then, pull core completely out of cover from X to the end of rope. Put one layer only of tape on end of core. (fig. A2.18).

To assure correct positioning of Mark #1 do the following.

Holding the exposed core, slide cover as far back towards the tightly tied slip knot as you can. Then, firmly smooth cover back from the slip knot towards taped end. Smooth again until all cover slack is removed. Then, mark core where it comes out of cover. This is Mark #1. Do this to both ropes. (Fig. A2.18).

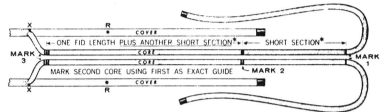

with wire fid double measurements.

Fig. A2.19   Samson end for end splice—marking the cores

Hold one core at Mark #1 and slide cover back to expose more core.

From Mark #1, measure along core towards X a distance equal to the short section of fid* and make two heavy marks. This is Mark #2.

From Mark #2 measure in the same direction *one fid length plus another short section** and make three heavy marks. This is Mark #3. (Fig. A2.19).

Mark second core by laying it alongside the first and using it as an exact guide.

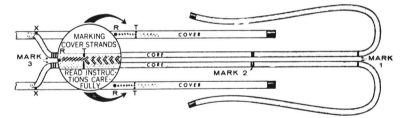

Fig. A2.20   Samson end for end splice—marking the covers for tapering.

Note nature of the cover braid. It is made up of strand pairs. By inspection you can see that half the pairs revolve to the right around the rope and half revolve to the left.

Beginning at R and working toward the taped end of cover, count 7 consecutive pairs of cover strands which revolve to the right (or left). Mark the 7th pair. This is Point T (Fig. A2.20). Make Mark T go completely around cover.

Starting at T and working toward taped cover end *count* and *mark every second right pair* of strands for a total of 6. Again, starting at T, count and mark every second left pair of strands for a total of 6. (Fig. A2.20).

Make both ropes identical.

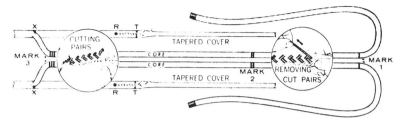

Fig. A2.21   End for end splice performing the Taper

First remove tape from cover end. Starting with last marked pair of cover strands toward the end, cut and pull them completely out (Fig. A2.21). Cut and remove next marked strands and continue with each right and left marked strands until you reach Point T. *Do not cut beyond this point.* (Fig. A2.21).

Retape tapered end.

Cut and remove marked strands on the other marked cover, again stopping at T. Retape tapered end.

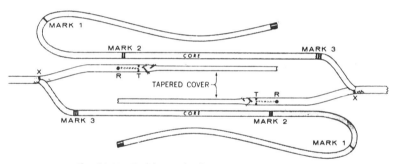

Fig. A2.22   End for end splice-repositioning the ropes.

Reposition ropes for splicing according to diagram. Note how cover of one rope has been paired off with core of the opposite line. *Avoid twisting.* (Fig. A2.22).

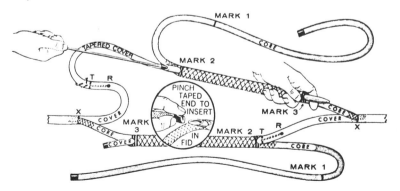

Fig. A2.23   End for end splice—Putting the cover inside the core.

Insert fid into one core at Mark #2 and bring it out at Mark #3. Add extra tape to tapered cover end then jam it tightly into hollow end of fid (Fig. A2.23). Hold core lightly at Mark #3, place pusher point into taped end pushing fid with cover in it from Mark #2 out at Mark #3. When using wire fid, attach fid to cover. Then pull fid through from Mark #2 to Mark #3. Pull cover tail through core until Mark T on cover meets Mark #2 on core. Insert other cover into core in same manner.

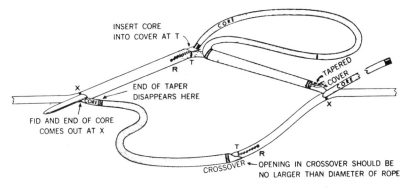

Fig. A2.24   End for end splice—Reinserting the core into the cover.

Now put core back into cover from T to X. Insert fid at T, jam taped core tightly into end of fid. With pusher, push fid and core through cover bringing out at Point X. When using wire fid attach fid to taped core. Then pull fid and braid through from T to X. (Fig. A2.24). Do this to both cores. Remove tape from end of cover. Bring crossover up tight by pulling on core tail and on tapered covered tail. Hold crossover tightly smoothing out all excess braid away from crossover in each direction. Tapered cover tail will disappear at Mark #3. Cut core tail off close to Point X.

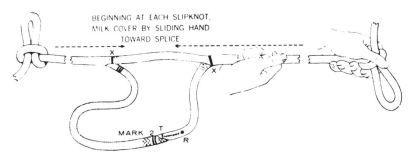

Fig. A2.25   End for end splice—burying the exposed core.

Hold rope at slipknot and with other hand milk cover toward the splice, gently at first, and then more firmly. The cover will slide over Mark #3, Mark #2 the crossover and R. Repeat with the other side of the splice. (Fig. A2.25).

Continue burying until *all cover slack between the knot and the splice* has been removed.

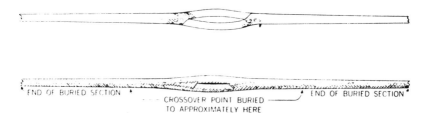

END OF BURIED SECTION

CROSSOVER POINT BURIED
TO APPROXIMATELY HERE

END OF BURIED SECTION

Fig. A2.26   End for end splice—Finishing the splice.

The splice is done when *all* cover slack has been removed and there is an opening in the splice approximately equal in length to the diameter of rope. (Fig. A2.26). If at the opening one side of the splice is noticeably longer than the other side, something is wrong. Check Steps 1-9 and remake if necessary.

Now untie the slip knots.

A2.10   Splicing eight stranded plaited ropes   Eight strand rope is no more difficult to splice than three or four strand, and easier than braided ropes. Anyone who has already mastered other splices should have no difficulty splicing eight strand rope. By splicing in pairs of strands the problem of splicing is immediately reduced by half. An amateurish or even sloppy splice will still give almost maximum efficiency with eight strand ropes. These splicing instructions have been prepared by the Columbian Rope Company for splicing their eight strand "Pli Moor." Included in this section are instructions for an eye, short, and long splice in eight strand plaited line as well as instructions for making a temporary eye splice. The following tools and materials will be needed for these splices: A splicing fid; a roll of plastic or masking tape; a sharp knife; about 8 to 10 inches of twine; and a marking pen or colored chalk.

Eight strand plaited rope is made up of four pairs of strands; two of these pairs turn to the right and the other two pairs turn to the left. In the following figures the two pairs turning to the right have been shaded for simplification. The other two pairs have been left white. From here on they will be referred to as the white and the dark pairs.

If the rope you wish to splice is white it will simplify matters if you use the marker or chalk and color the pairs which turn to the right so that they will conform to the shaded pairs in the illustrations. Count back a distance of about 10 pics (see insert Fig. A2.27) from the end and tie string securely around the rope so it passes directly over the center of both pairs of dark strands. Place the knot of the string so that it is directly on top of one of these pairs. It is important that this knot be tied securely to prevent slipping. Unlay the pairs of strands back to the string making sure not to mix or twist them. Tape the ends of the pairs together as seen in Fig. A2.27.

A. Hold or lay the rope so that the pairs of white strands are on top and bottom with the knot to the right as you look towards the end.

B. Bend the rope over to the desired eye in such a way as to keep the knot inside the loop as shown in Fig. A2.27.

C. Using the fid to make clearance and starting with the darkened pairs, tuck

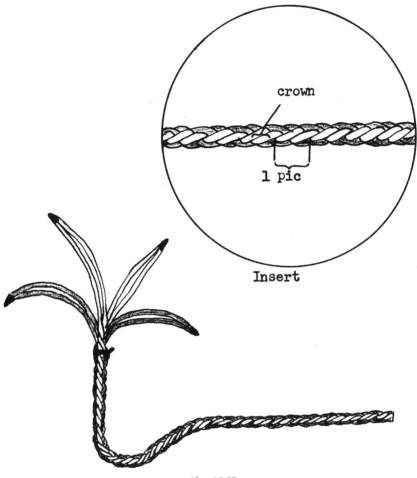

crown

1 pic

Insert

Fig. A2.27

them under the diametrically opposite white pairs as shown in Fig. A2.28. MAKE SURE THAT THE LAY OF THE PAIRS IS NOT DISTURBED. Do not twist them so that the individual strands cross over one another within the pair.

D. Turn the eye over, tuck the white pairs under the diametrically opposite dark pairs as shown in Fig. A2.29 (Note that in Fig. A2.29 the splice is turned over from Fig. A2.28) The white pairs to be tucked should follow the white pairs of the standing part and the black to be tucked should follow the black pairs of the standing part. The ends in the figures have been numbered to help follow their progress.

E. With the first full tuck complete, pull all 4 ends down firmly. Starting with the dark pairs, take another full tuck (a full tuck means inserting all four pairs. By starting with dark pairs you avoid having to go under two pairs at once). The

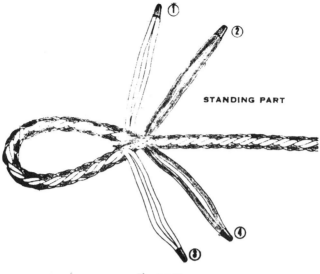

Fig. A2.28

splice should appear as shown in Fig. A2.30. From here on little difficulty should be experienced in completing the splice.

F. Starting with the dark pairs, take at least one more full tuck. With a very soft rope, it may be necessary to take a forth or fifth full tuck.

Fig. A2.29

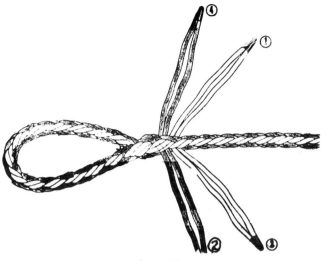

Fig. A2.30

G. Having completed the final tuck select the strand closest to the eye in each pair. Tape this strand close to where it emerges from the tuck and then cut it off as shown in Fig. A2.31.

H. Splice the remaining single strands just as before for another full tuck. The splice should appear as shown in Fig. A2.32.

I. Tape and cut off the remaining four single strands as shown in Fig. A2.33. The eight ends may be heated and fused so that they will not fray; however, caution

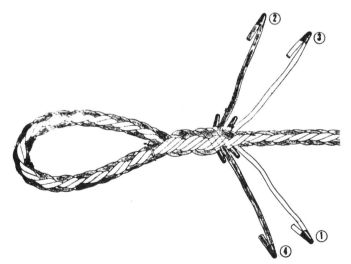

Fig. A2.31

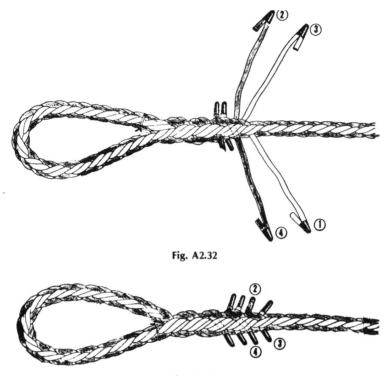

Fig. A2.32

Fig. A2.33

should be used to insure that only the ends are fused and the strands are not damaged.

Short Splice For Eight Stranded Plaited Rope To make a short splice to join the ends of two lengths of eight strand line the same tools and materials are used as in the eye splice discussed previously.

A. Lay the two rope ends that are to be spliced, side by side on a flat surface. Tape the ends as shown in Fig. A2.34.

B. Determine which pairs of strands go to the right and which go to the left. If the rope which is to be spliced is all one color, mark all the pairs which are going to the right with the marker, from the ends back along the rope for a distance of 11 to 12 pics (Fig. A2.26). From here on we will refer to these pairs as dark (going to right) and light (going to left).

Fig A2.34

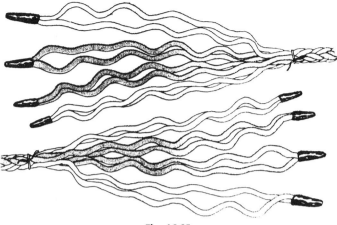

Fig. A2.35

C. Count back from the ends of the rope 10 crowns (see insert Fig. A2.26). At this point mark around the entire rope and tie a string securely around the ropes so that it passes directly over the pairs of dark strands on one rope and over the light strands of the second (Fig. A2.34).

D. Unlay the four pairs of strands of both ropes back to the strings and tape the ends, in pairs, as shown in Fig. A2.35. The undisturbed portion of the ropes above the strings should be laying with the dark strands on top. Throughout the splice these pairs should run parallel and not be allowed to twist over one another.

E. Start to marry the two ropes at the strings in the following manner. (Fig. A2.36).

    1. Bend the two top (dark) pairs back along the rope.

    2. Spread the white strands back at 45 degree angles to the axis of the rope.

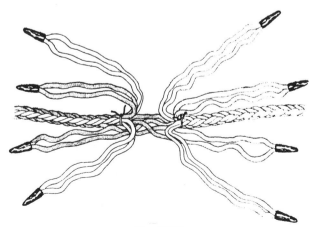

Fig. A2.36

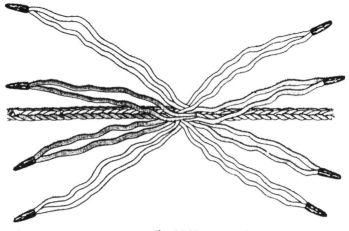

Fig. A2.37

3. Marry the bottom (dark) pairs by inserting the pair from the right between the pair from the left, at the strings.

4. Marry the white pairs. The right pair between the two strands from the left on one side and the left hand pair between the strands from the right on the other side (Refer to Fig. A2.37).

5. Marry the top dark strands. The pair from the left between the pair from the right. The splice should appear as shown in Fig. A2.37.

F. Cut off both strings. Using both hands first grasp the four pairs on the right hand and then the four pairs on the left hand. Pull the marriage up snug and tie a string securely around the entire marriage point as illustrated in Fig. A2.38.

G. Using the fid to make space, start splicing by inserting the white pairs from the left under the dark pairs from the right. Next the white pairs from the right are inserted under the dark pairs from the left. Complete this first tuck by following the same sequence, as above, with the four pairs of dark strands going under the white strands on the opposite side of the marriage. The splice should appear as shown in Fig. A2.39.

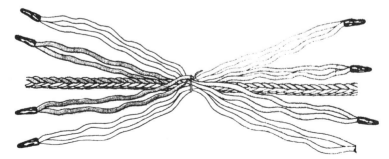

Fig. A2.38

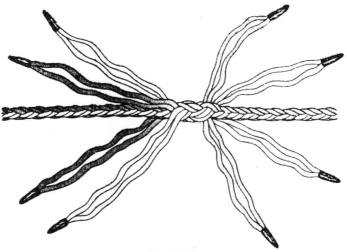

Fig. A2.39

H. Continue splicing pairs as in step (G) for two additional complete tucks. The splice should now resemble Fig. A2.40.

I. Now split the pairs and using only one strand of each pair, make two additional tucks, as illustrated in Fig. A2.41.

J. Tape and cut the ends off about two pics long. Now complete the taping as shown in Fig. A2.42.

This is the finished splice. It should never be used when the spliced work must pass around clear or over a sheave. No matter how poor the first attempt at the

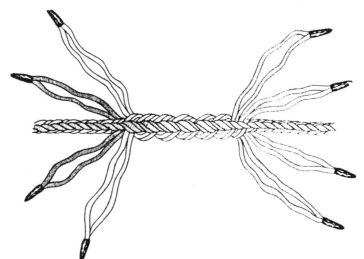

Fig. A2.40

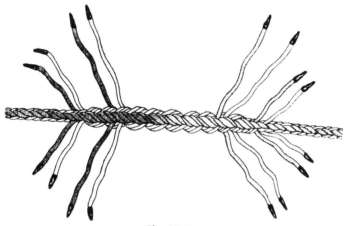

Fig. A2.41

short splice may be, you will find that this splice has a high degree of efficiency. (It is 90-95% as strong as the rope itself.)

Long Splice for Eight Stranded Plaited Rope Whenever it is necessary to splice the ends of two lines together so that the resulting splice can freely pass around cleats and over sheaves a long splice must be used. The following section describes how to make a long splice in eight stranded plaited rope. The tools and materials necessary to accomplish this task are the same as those listed for the eye splice.

A. As shown in Fig. A2.43 lay the two rope ends to be spliced side by side on a flat surface. Taking one rope at a time mark the two pairs of strands going to the right, if necessary, as described in the previous sections. Continue the marking back from the ends of the rope for a distance of 30 Pics. (see insert Fig. A2.26).

B. With the dark strands running along the top of each rope, starting from the ends, count back to the ninth crown (or nine full pics). Mark this point clearly all around the rope. Repeat this for three counts of six pics each and also clearly mark as above. These will be the 3/4, 1/2, 1/4, and center marks as shown in Fig. A2.43.

C. At the center mark of end "A" (Fig. A2.43) SECURELY tie the string around the rope over the crown of the dark strands. With end "B," tie the string between the center mark strands and the next pair so that the string passes over the crown of the white strands as shown in Fig. A2.43.

D. Taking one end at a time unlay the rope back a short distance. Taking each pair of strands, one at a time tape them together at the end. Work the tape so

Fig. A2.42

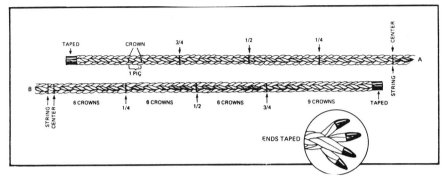

Fig. A2.43

that the end is pointed or conical, (See insert Fig. A2.43), as this will help when the splice begins. Carefully unlay the ropes back to the strings and position the strands as shown in Fig. A2.44.

E. Marry the bottom dark pairs, by inserting the pair from the right between the two strands of the pair from the left at the center mark; DO NOT PULL TIGHT.

F. Marry the white strands, on the side away from you, in exactly the same manner. The two white pairs on the side towards you should be reversed in that the pair from the left should be inserted between the two strands of the pair from the right at the center mark.

G. To complete this initial step marry the top pair of dark strands by inserting the pair from the left through the pair from the right at the center mark.

H. Carefully check your work against Fig. A2.45. If it does not conform, recheck the last three steps. Cut and remove both strings. Taking four pairs of

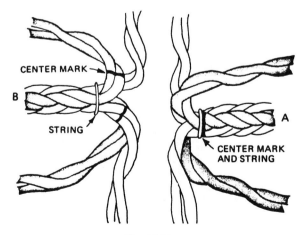

Fig. A2.44

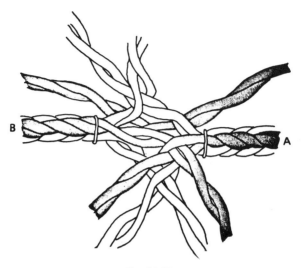

Fig. A2.45

strands in each hand pull all the marriages up tight so that all of the center marks are together.

I. Tie off each of the four marriages individually as pictured in Fig. A2.46. This will take some care to keep them from loosening. The center marks must stay together for a successful splice.

J. Start splicing with the two top (dark) pairs of strands. First cut off the outside pair at the marriage (Fig. A2.47). This should be the pair coming from the right. Now cut the string. Pull the cut ends back from under the white pair. Insert the uncut dark strands (coming from the left) in their place. INSURE THE INSERTED STRANDS ARE LAID IN PARALLEL AND NOT TWISTED ON ONE ANOTHER. (See Fig. A2.48). Continue removing the cut dark strands one pic at a time and inserting the dark pair from the left to the ¾ mark on the strands being inserted.

K. Having reached the ¾ mark, cut the tape holding the two srands from the left. Split the pair into two separate strands. Choose one and its exact counter-

Fig. A2.46

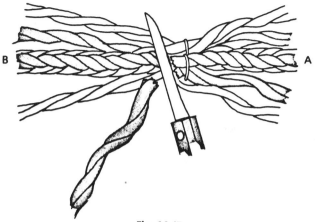

Fig. A2.47

part from the right. Remove the single strand from the right from under the white strands in the same manner as you previously did with the pair. Insert the single strand from the left in its place. Continue removing and inserting for a distance of six more pics. (Fig. A2.49).

L. Return to the center marriage point. Choose the white strand marriage on the side away from you. This time cut off the two strands coming from the left. Cut the string. Then moving in the opposite direction duplicate your actions in step (J) to the ¾ mark and step (K) for six more pics.

M. From this point on the splice is relatively simple. Return to the center marriage and repeat the above procedure with the remaining pairs of white strands working back in the original direction as in step (J). This time go only to the ¼ mark with two strands and to the ½ mark with the single strand.

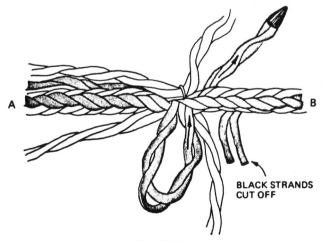

BLACK STRANDS
CUT OFF

Fig. A2.48

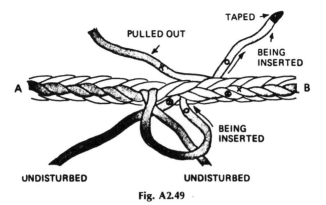

Fig. A2.49

N. With the remaining pair of dark strands work to the left to the ¼ mark with two strands and to the ½ mark with a single strand. The splice should now appear as shown in Fig. A2.50.

O. The ends remaining should be cut off about four pics long. Then tape the ends in a conical manner as shown in Fig. A2.43. Working in the direction that each has been spliced to this point, tuck each end, in turn, up the center axis of the rope for a distance of about three pics. (See Fig. A2.51). Whatever short ends remain should be cut flush.

Temporary Eye Splice for Eight Stranded Plaited Rope The last splice that will be discussed in this section is a temporary splice that can be put in eight strand plaited line quickly and is almost as efficient as the regular eye splice.

To construct this quick eye splice perform the following steps:

A. Determine the size of the eye desired and form a loop as shown in Fig. A2.52(A). Be sure to allow ten to twelve inches of excess to be spliced.

B. Using a fid or other pointed tool, separate the strands so that there is an opening formed by one pair of right turning strands and one pair of left turning strands on either side of the opening. Tuck the excess rope to the point where you have formed the size of the eye desired.

C. Counting down three pics for the top pair of strands, repeat the process in the opposite direction from step (B).

D. Repeat this two more times as shown in Fig. A2.52(A).

E. Pull these loops down until your splice appears as Fig. A2.52(B).

F. Cut off the excess to distance no closer than three inches from the final tuck.

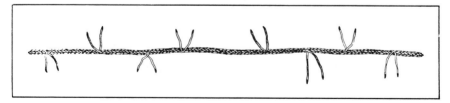

Fig. A2.50

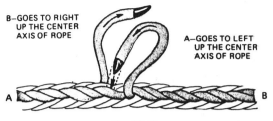

B–GOES TO RIGHT
UP THE CENTER
AXIS OF ROPE

A–GOES TO LEFT
UP THE CENTER
AXIS OF ROPE

Fig. A2.51

While this type of splice is considered to be temporary in nature, it will afford you a good splice.

A2.11 Seizings   At times eyes must be made in the bight of lines where they cannot be spliced. In such circumstances, seizings are used. There are

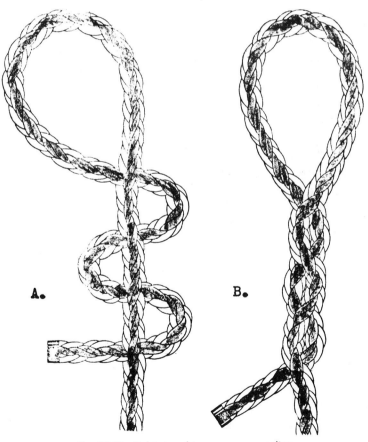

Fig. A2.52 Eight strand temporary eye splice.

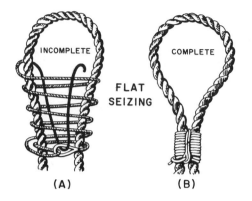

FLAT
SEIZING

INCOMPLETE

COMPLETE

(A)

(B)

(C)
ROUND SEIZING

(D)
ROUND SEIZING

(E)
ROUND SEIZING CROSSED
CLOVE HITCH FINISH

(F)
RACKING SEIZING

(G)
RACKING SEIZING

(H)
THROAT SEIZING

Fig. A2.53 Seizings.

many types of seizings, but the most common are the flat, round, racking, and throat.

Flat Seizing The flat seizing (Fig. 2.53(A)) is light and is used where the strain is not too great. In the flat seizing, a single layer of turns is taken around the two parts of the line. The seizing is secured with a clove hitch over the turns and between the two parts of the line.

Round Seizing   The round seizing (C,D,E) consists of two layers of turns. It is secured in the same way as the flat seizing.

Racking Seizing   The racking seizing is used when the strain on each of the two parts of the line is different. It consists of figure-eight turns around the two parts (F,G) that are secured with a clove hitch in the usual manner.

Throat Seizing   The throat seizing is used where a permanent eye is needed in the bight of a line. It consists of a round seizing applied as shown in view (H). It also is secured with a clove hitch, but the clove hitch goes around both parts of the line instead of between them.

A2.12   Worming, Parceling, and Serving   Worming, parceling, and serving is a method of preserving both wire and fiber rope, although it is more commonly done to wire. Worming (Fig. A2.54) is marline or ratline (depending on the size of the rope) wound along in the grooves of the rope. Parceling is narrow strips of light canvas or cotton cloth spiral-wrapped along the rope. Serving is marline tightly wound on the rope by means of a serving mallet or board. "Worm and parcel with the lay, turn and serve the other way."

A2.13   Seizing Wire Rope   Great care is exercised in the manufacture of wire rope to lay each wire in the strand and each strand in the rope under uniform tension. It the ends of the rope are not secured properly, the original balance of tension will be disturbed and maximum service will not be obtained, because some strands will carry a greater portion of the load than others. Before cutting steel wire rope, it is necessary to place at least three sets of seizings on each side of the intended cut. Each seizing should consist of eight turns of annealed iron seizing wire. The distance between seizing should equal the rope's diameter.

To make a temporary wire rope seizing, wind on the seizing wire uniformly, using strong tension on the wire. After taking the required number of turns as in step 1 in Fig. A2.55, twist the ends of the wires counterclockwise as in step 2. Grasp the ends with end-cutting nippers and twist up the

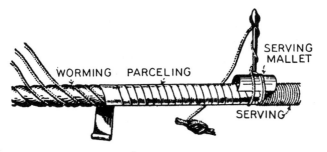

Fig. A2.54   Worming, parceling, and serving.

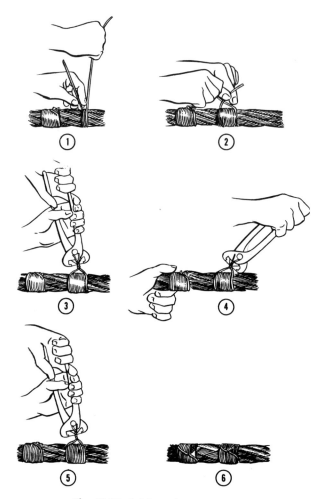

Fig. A2.55 Seizing wire rope.

slack as in step 3. Do not try to tighten the seizing by twisting. Draw up on the seizing as in step 4. Twist up the slack. Repeat steps 4 and 5 if necessary. Cut the ends and pound them down on the rope as in step 6. If the seizing is to be permanent, or the rope is 1⅝ inches or more in diameter, use a serving bar or iron to increase tension on the seizing wire when putting on the turns.

A2.14 Splicing Wire Rope Wire rope usually is six-stranded with a hemp core. Normally, one works the strands separately, but in some splices, pairs may be worked. The work calls for special appliances and for a degree of skill such as can be acquired only by long practice under expert instruction.

Something may be learned from careful description and much more from an occasional visit to a rigging loft; but the facilities which are available on shipboard do not permit doing such work as is possible with a rigger's bench, a turning-in machine, etc. Where a heavy rope is to be bent around a thimble or the parts otherwise brought together for splicing or seizing, a rigger's screw is needed. In the absence of this, a vise may be used, but less conveniently.

In tucking the strands of a splice, the lay of the rope is opened out and the spike left in, holding the strands apart until the tuck has been made. With large wire, it is necessary to haul the strands through with a jigger. After a tuck is taken, the rope is hammered down with a wooden mallet. After the splice is completed, the strands are cut off with a pair of wire cutters.

Liverpool Eye Splice   The Liverpool splice is one of the most common and the easiest of the eye splices to put in. *Never use it, however, in a wire which, when loaded, is free to spin, because it is likely to pull out.*

To find the distance the strands should be unlaid for an eye splice, multiply the diameter of the wire by 36 inches. Find and measure off that distance and put a seizing at that point. Another seizing should be put on just below the point where the first tuck is to be made. Next, cut the end seizings and carefully unlay the strand, whip the ends of each strand tightly with several turns of sail twine or friction tape. Cut out the core, form the eye, and put it in the rigger's screw or a vise, with the unlaid strands on your left. Stretch out the standing part of the wire, lash it, and you are ready to go to work.

When splicing wire, always insert the marlinspike against the lay, but make sure that you do not shove it through the core.

The first strand of the Liverpool goes under three strands, the second under two, and the third under one. They all enter at the same point, but come out at different places as shown in Fig. A2.56.

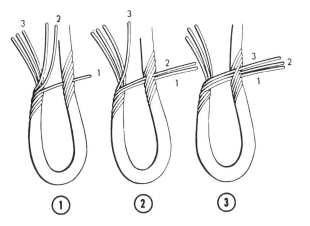

Fig. A2.56   Tucking the first three strands in a Liverpool.

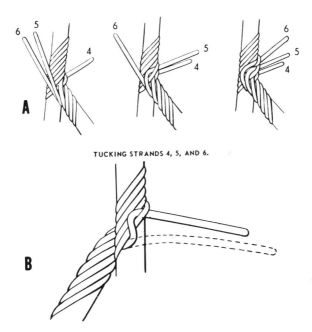

TUCKING STRANDS 4, 5, AND 6.

Fig. A2.57   Start of second round of tucks in the Liverpool splice.

Strands 4, 5, 6 are tucked as shown in part A of Fig. A2.57. The succeeding tucks are made by wrapping each strand back around and under the strand it already is under, as in part B of Fig. A2.57. To avoid kinking the strands on the last tucks, insert the spike and run it up the wire, as in steps 1 and 2 of Fig. A2.58. Follow the spike up with the strand, shove it under the spike, and pull taut. Keeping a strain on the strand, work the spike and strand back around and down together. (See steps 3 and 4, Fig. A2.58.) Hold the strand there and work the spike back up the wire. Follow up with the strand and take the last tuck. Work that strand back down and hold it there. Before pulling out the spike, run it back up until the strands of the standing wire bind the working strand in place. Make the second and third tucks with the remaining strands in the same way.

A locking tuck may be taken after completing the third round of tucks. This decreases the possibility of the splice working out. For this tuck, take every other strand (2, 4, and 6, for example) and pass each of these with the lay over two strands and tuck under the next strand. Each of these strands, therefore, goes over the adjacent working strand (as well as the two strands of the standing part) and locks in in place.

Short Splice   To make a short splice, you need to unlay 2 or 3 feet of each rope, depending on the size of the rope. To find the distance, use the same formula as for the eye splice. Prepare each rope, seizing before unlaying, and whipping each strand. Interlace the strands as is done with fiber

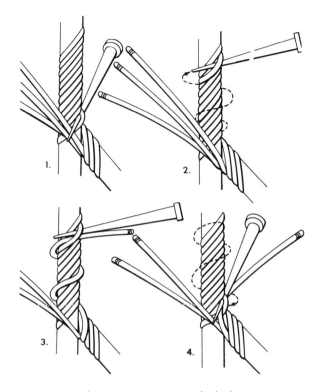

Fig. A2.58 How to avoid a kink.

rope and then seize them. Remove one of the temporary seizings and commence tucking. Tucks go against the lay, over one and under two. Take four
rounds of tucks and then split each strand and bend half of it back out of
the way. The halves bent back are dropped at this point. Take two more
tucks with the other halves. Next, turn your wire and repeat the foregoing
steps in the opposite direction. Beat out the splice with a wooden mallet,
working from the center to the ends and turning the splice as you beat. To
complete the work, cut off the strands and beat down the ends.

Long Splice   The recommended number of feet to make a long splice in
wire is 40 times the diameter of the wire. In other words, a long splice in
¾-inch wire would cover a distance of 30 feet, ½-inch wire would be 20
feet, etc. For purposes of the following description, ¾-inch wire, or a splice
of 30 feet, is used.

Step 1: (See Fig. A2.59.) Measure 15 feet from the ends of each wire and
put on temporary seizings.

Step 2: Cut the end seizings, unlay, and whip the strands. Cut out the
core, interlace the strands, and butt the ends of the rope together solidly and
seize in place.

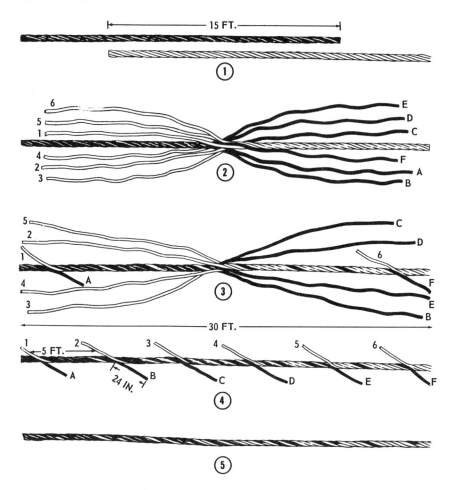

Fig. A2.59 Making a long splice.

Step 3: Cut off the temporary seizing on one rope and start unlaying any one of the strands, laying the opposite strand from the other rope in the groove as you go. Lay in all but 2 feet of this strand and cut off all but 2 feet of the unlaid strand.

Step 4: Repeat step 3, unlaying the strand next to the strand laid in step 3. That gives you a strand laid in each direction as in the figure.

Step 5: Repeat step 3 with the next strand of the first rope, stopping 5 feet short of the meeting point of the first pair. Continue unlaying and laying in successive strands, working first one way and then the other, leaving 5-foot intervals between the meeting points. When all strands are laid in, your splice should look like that in step 5 of the figure.

One method of securing the ends of a long splice is the same as for fiber rope. Tie an overhand knot and pull it taut. Then divide the ends in three parts and tuck them separately as shown in Fig. A2.60.

Fig. A2.60   One method of securing ends of a long splice.

The preferred method of securing the ends is illustrated in Fig. A2.61. Tuck the ends of the strands into the rope, replacing the core. Seize the strands at their meeting point and cut off the end whippings. Untwist the strands so that the "form" or "set" is taken out. Next, build up the strands to the same size as the core. This may be done with successive seizings of seizing wire if it replaces a wire core. If the rope has a hemp core, serve the strands with marline or wrap them with friction tape.

Secure a Spanish windlass on each side of the meeting point as in step 1 in Fig. A2.61. Twist in opposite directions, opening the lay of the rope. Cut

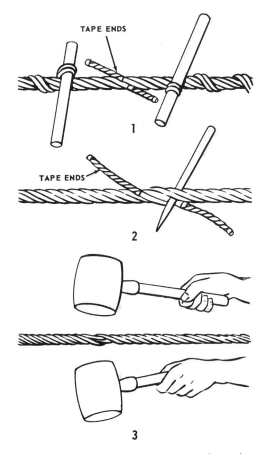

Fig. A2.61.   Preferred method of securing ends in a long splice.

the core and pull out the ends a few inches Shove a marlinespike under two adjacent strands as in step 2. You now can take off the Spanish windlasses. Work the spike along the rope, pulling out the core and laying in the strand until all the strand is in. Then cut off the core at that point and shove the end back in place and pull out the spike. Repeat the process on all the other strand ends. Notice that the strands do not cross before tucking. After securing the ends, beat out the splice as in step 3. A long splice with the ends secured in the manner described does not alter the size of the rope, and will almost defy detection after the rope is in use a short time.

A2.15   Wire Rope Clips   A temporary eye splice may be put in wire by using wire rope clips. The correct and incorrect ways of using these clips are shown in Fig. A2.62. The U-bolt always goes over the bitter end and the roddle on the standing part. Space the clips a distance apart equal to six times the diameter of the wire. After a rope is under strain, tighten the clips again. On operating ropes, tighten the clips every few hours and inspect the rope carefully at points where there are clips. Pay particular attention to the wire at the clip farthest from the eye, because vibration and whipping are dampened here and fatigue breaks are likely to occur.

To obtain maximum strength in the temporary eye splice, use the correct size and number of wire clips. Size is stamped on the roddle between the two holes. The correct number of clips to use for various sizes of wire ropes is shown in the accompanying table.

Size of Rope (inches)	Number of Clips
½	2
⅝	3
¾	3
⅞	4
1	4
1⅛	5
1¼	5
1½	6

INCORRECT

INCORRECT

CORRECT

Fig. A2.62   The correct and incorrect use of wire rope clips.

A2.16   Wire Rope Clamped Splices   In recent years a method of fabricating wire rope eye splices using steel clamps applied under great pressure has been developed. The resulting splices are 100% efficient and have the full strength of the rope itself. They are made at a much lower cost in man hours and much less wire is used because no excess wire for tucking is needed. Splices of this type are widely used for cargo slings and other applications in the marine industry. Many naval amphibious and replenishment ships have the equipment on board to produce these splices. Clamps are available at present to splice wire ropes up to

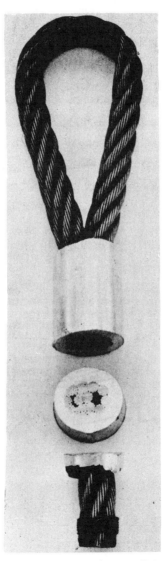

Fig. A2.63   Example of clamped 100% efficient eye splice.

one and one half inches in diameter. In this clamping process the metal clamp is squeezed into the wires and the wires are forced together.

A2.17 End Connectors Various end connectors are used with wire rope to attach ropes to each other, to the ship, and to different assemblies. In the Navy, poured wire rope sockets are required for boat lifting slings, running rigging, and the like where the connection must equal 100 percent of the rope's breaking strength. Fiege connectors can usually be substituted in other uses.

Sockets Sockets are classed as open or closed, depending on whether they are the jaw and pin or loop types. The rope end should be whipped (seized) near the end. Put on an additional seizing at a distance from the end of the rope equal to the length of the basket of the socket (Fig. A2.64). It is very important that the seizings be secure to prevent untwisting of the wires and strands and a resultant unequal tension between the several wires after the socket is attached. Place the rope end upright in a vise. Remove the seizing at the bitter end. Cut out the hemp heart down to remaining

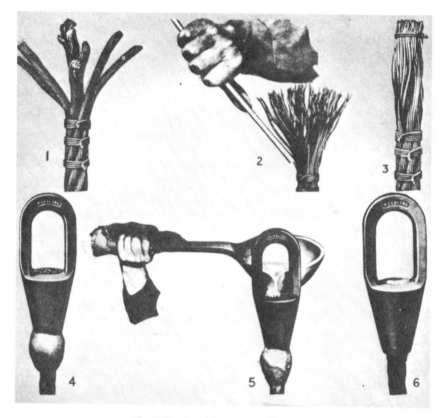

Fig. 2.64 Attaching a poured socket.

seizing. If the heart is wire, allow it to remain. Untwist the strands and broom out the wire. The wires should be separated from each other but should not be straightened. Clean the wires carefully with methyl chloroform from the ends to as near the first seizing as possible; wipe dry. Dip wires into muriatic acid diluted with an equal amount of water. (Carefully pour acid into water; DO NOT POUR WATER INTO ACID.) Use no stronger solution, and take extra care that acid does not touch any other part of the rope. To remove the acid, dip the wires into boiling water containing a small amount of soda. Heat the socket to about 300 degrees. Draw the wires together again with a piece of seizing wire, and force the socket down over them until it reaches the seizing. Free the wires within the socket basket and allow them to spread evenly and naturally. The ends of the wires should be level with the large end of the socket basket. Care should be taken to see that the centerline of the basket is lined up exactly with that of the rope, i.e., that the socket is in a true straight line with the rope, so that when under load each element will sustain its due share. Seal the small end of the socket around the rope with putty, fire clay, or a similar substance. Fill the socket basket with molten zinc. The zinc must not be too hot, particularly

Socket applied showing twisted wires and completed assembly

SLEEVE

Strand passed through sleeve

PLUG

SLEEVE

Wires fanned out for insertion of hollow plug

SLEEVE   PLUG   SOCKET

Plug driven in and wires closed to apply socket

INSPECTION HOLE

CUTAWAY ASSEMBLY

Fig. A2.65 An example of a fiege connector.

on small ropes. From 800 to 850 degrees is the correct temperature. Allow to cool in air or plunge the connector into cool, fresh water. Remove all seizing except the one nearest the socket.

Fiege Connector   Figure **A2.65** shows one type of fiege connector used with ropes with fiber cores and the steps in attaching it. Two seizings are applied at the point where the end of the sleeve will be, the sleeve is pushed down over the wire, the end seizing is cut, and the strands (or wires, depending on the type of plug) are fanned out. Then the core is cut out down to the taper of the sleeve, and the plug is inserted and driven to a solid seat. Finally, the wires are gathered together so that the socket can slide down over them, and the socket is screwed down tight.

Appendix 3

Mechanical Weight-Lifting Appliances

The advent of nuclear power afloat has not relieved seamen of the necessity of having the same fundamental knowledge of ropes, tackles, and weight-handling that was required of their predecessors. True, the weights are heavier, are moved greater distances, and wire rope is used now, but the same principles of mechanical advantage and friction still apply.

Tasks requiring the use of booms, tackles, topping lifts, and other mechanical appliances are the daily lot of seamen. Merchant vessels and Naval cargo ships require the rigging of many different purchases for positioning and steadying the cargo booms and for handling the weights after the booms have been rigged.

Anyone who is concerned with rigging or operating cargo booms should be thoroughly familiar with the forces set up during the operation. To this end, he should consult the manufacturer's tables to determine the strength of the wire or rope used in the standing and running rigging, and he should never exceed these loads. He should inspect all the rigging periodically, replacing worn parts and performing such preventive maintenance as may be specified by the manufacturer. Finally, he should be familiar with the fundamentals of applied mechanics and the effects of acceleration and deceleration on the rigging.

The weight lifting appliances discussed in this appendix include blocks, tackle, shackles, swivels and hooks. Line and wire characteristics are discussed in Appendix 1.

A3.1 Shackles Shackles are used to connect objects together. They may be used to connect one wire eye to another, or a sling to a load, or a hook to a block or a hook to a wire rope eye. The uses of shackles in weight handling and other shipboard applications are too numerous to mention.

The most common shackle in use is the anchor screw pin type. Other types of shackles used on shipboard include round pin and safety type shackles. (Fig. A3.1)

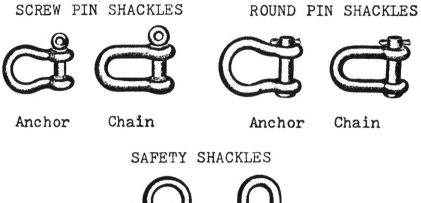

SCREW PIN SHACKLES   ROUND PIN SHACKLES

Anchor   Chain   Anchor   Chain

SAFETY SHACKLES

Anchor   Chain

Fig. A3.1 Types of shackles.

The following formula may be used to estimate the safe working load of a shackle.

Safe working load = 3 D² (expressed in tons)

Where D is the wire diameter of the shackle at the sides. Thus for a one inch shackle the safe working load is $(1)^2 \times 3$ or 3 tons.

Given below is a table listing the test loads at which shackles of various sizes failed:

Test of Shackles

Diameter of metal	Broke at	Remarks
¾ inch	20,700 lbs.	Eye of shackle parted.
⅞ inch	38,100 lbs.	Eye of shackle parted.
1 inch	51,900 lbs.	Eye of shackle parted.
1¼ inches	75,200 lbs.	Eye of shackle parted.
1½ inches	119,980 lbs.	Eye of shackle parted.
1¾ inches	146,400 lbs.	Sheared shackle-pin.
2 inches	196,600 lbs.	Eye of shackle parted.
2½ inches	210,400 lbs.	Eye of shackle parted.

It should be pointed out that for many heavy lifts the substitution of shackles for hooks is desirable since a shackle is about five times stronger than a hook of the same wire diameter.

A3.2 Hooks   The hook is customarily the point in the weight handling appliance where the load is attached. The hook because of its open construction

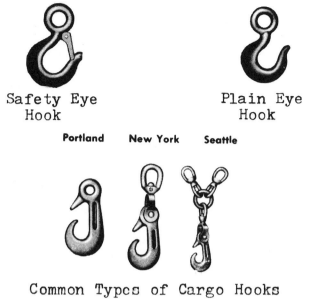

Safety Eye
Hook

Plain Eye
Hook

Portland   **New York**   **Seattle**

Common Types of Cargo Hooks

Fig. A3.2   Various types of hooks.

is usually the weakest part of the appliance or cargo rig. Illustrated in Fig. A3.2 are various types of hooks. The latch across the opening of the safety hook is installed to prevent the load or sling ring from coming out of the hook if the strain is abruptly eased. Mousing a hook with marline or other small stuff accomplishes the same thing. It should be pointed out that mousing of the hook with line will do nothing to prevent the hook from opening out under excessive strain. A formula for estimating the safe working load of a hook is given as:

$$\text{Safe working load} = 2/3\ D^2 \text{ (expressed in tons)}$$

where D is the wire diameter of the hook at the back of the hook below the eye.

The table below illustrates the loads under which hooks of various sizes actually failed.

Test of Hooks

Diameter of metal	Broke at	Remarks
½ inch	2,385 lbs.	
¾ inch	4,130 lbs.	
1 inch	10,315 lbs.	
1¼ inches	14,510 lbs.	Hook partly straightened,
1½ inches	20,940 lbs.	then fractured across
1¾ inches	27,420 lbs.	the back.
2 inches	38,100 lbs.	
2½ inches	55,380 lbs.	

Fig. A3.3 Types of Swivels

A3.3 Swivels   Swivels are used together with shackles, blocks and hooks in weight-lifting appliances. A swivel should be inserted in the makeup of a rig whenever a twist is possible in the rig or load. Two types of swivels are illustrated above. These are the most common types in shipboard use. Swivels are somewhat stronger than shackles of the same size.

A3.4 Blocks   A "block," in the nautical sense, consists of a frame of wood or steel, within which is fitted one or more sheaves (pulleys).

Blocks take their names from the purpose for which they are used, the places they occupy, or from some peculiarity in their shape or construction. They are designated further as single, double, or triple blocks, according to the number of sheaves they have.

The size of the block is determined by the circumference of the rope to be used with it. For rope, the size of the block in inches is three times the circumference of the rope; the diameter of the sheave is twice the circumference of the rope. Thus a block for use with a 3-inch rope would be (3 times 3) a 9-inch block, measured as the length of the cheek, and its sheave would be (2 times 3) 6 inches in diameter.

Because of their greater strength, artificial fiber ropes require blocks of greater strength; therefore, ropes of artificial fiber must not be substituted

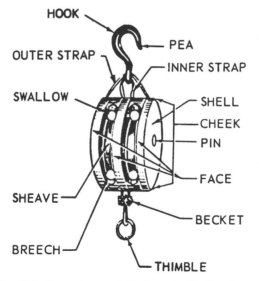

Fig. A3.4 Parts of a wood block used with fiber lines.

for manila or other natural fiber ropes until it has been determined that the blocks are strong enough.

Blocks for use with wire rope are not so well standardized. Wire rope can be made to conform to widely varying specifications. When specifications for blocks are drawn, the advice of the manufacturer should be followed as to diameter of sheave or drum over which the wire is to be rove and the speed of operation (linear speed of the wire). If such advice is not followed, the life of the rope will be materially shortened due to alternate bending and straightening as the wire passes over the sheave (drum).

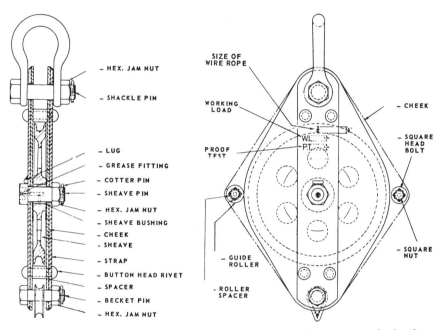

Fig. A3.5   Parts of a diamond type block commonly used with wire rope with a low line speed.

A good rule of thumb to follow in regard to the size of a wire rope block to use is to use a block with a sheave diameter equal to twenty times the diameter of the rope. The diamond type wire rope block and the roller bearing wire rope blocks are illustrated in Fig. A3.5 and A3.6 respectively. In cargo handling rigs the diamond block is customarily used in the makeup of topping lifts and the roller bearing or "speed" block is used as the head and heel block of the boom through which the cargo whip is reeved.

A3.5 Moving Weights Most heavy weight-handling on cargo vessels is done by means of one or more cargo booms. With the use of one boom the weight is lifted from its initial position, the boom is swung until the weight is over its intended position, and the weight is lowered. This method

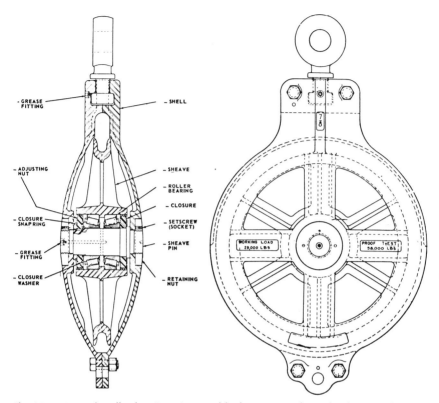

Fig. A3.6   Parts of a roller-bearing wire rope block as commonly used with cargo whips and other applications with high line speed.

is satisfactory only when light loads are being moved because the boom guys must be readjusted as the boom swings.

A more common method is the yard-and-stay rig in which two booms are used. One boom, called the hatch boom, is rigged to plumb (over) the cargo hatch being worked, while the other, or outboard boom is rigged over the side to plumb a lighter or the dock. Two winches and two cargo runners or whips are used, one on each boom. Each runner is attached to a common hook which engages the load. For loading, the winch of the outboard boom hoists the load, or draft, high enough to clear the ship's side or other obstruction. The draft is then "racked" inboard with the hatch boom winch heaving in and the other winch slacking off slowly until the load is entirely supported by the hatch boom. Finally, the hatch boom winch lowers the draft into the hold, with the outboard cargo runner being kept slack. For unloading, the cycle is reversed. See Fig. A3.7.

In any weight-handling operation, speed should be subordinated to safety and smoothness of operation. Jerky movements caused by too-rapid accelera-tion and deceleration put enormous strains on the standing and running

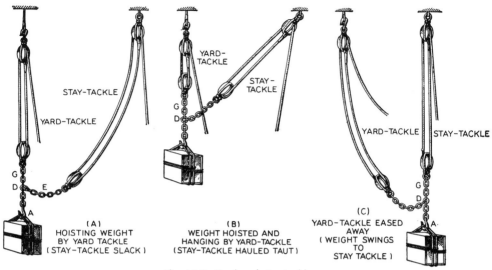

STAY-TACKLE

YARD-TACKLE

G
D E

A

(A)
HOISTING WEIGHT
BY YARD TACKLE
(STAY-TACKLE SLACK)

YARD-
TACKLE

STAY-
TACKLE

G
D

(B)
WEIGHT HOISTED AND
HANGING BY YARD-TACKLE
(STAY-TACKLE HAULED TAUT)

YARD-TACKLE | STAY-TACKLE

G
D

A

(C)
YARD-TACKLE EASED
AWAY
(WEIGHT SWINGS
TO
STAY TACKLE)

Fig. A3.7   Yard-and-stay tackles.

rigging. This could result in the parting of one or more lines and the collapse of the entire rig with resulting damage to the load, the ship, and the operating personnel.

The greatest force must be applied in starting a load, because it is necessary to overcome inertia. Therefore, the force must be applied gradually, lest the strain exceed the safe working load. Speed may be increased once the load is moving.

A3.6   Tackles   An assemblage of ropes (falls) and blocks for the purpose of multiplying force is a tackle. (See Fig. A3.8)

The seaman speaks of "reeving" when he passes ropes around the sheaves of the blocks. These ropes are called "falls." The "standing part" is that part of the fall made fast to one of the blocks. The hauling part is the end of the falls to which force is applied to handle the weight. To "overhaul" the falls is to separate the blocks. To "round in" is to bring the blocks together. The blocks are said to be "chock-a-block" or "two-blocked" when they are tight together.

Tackles are designated either according to the number of sheaves in the blocks that are used to make the tackle, e.g., single, two-fold, three-fold purchase; or according to the purpose for which the tackle is used, e.g., yard tackles, stay tackles, fore-and-aft tackles. Other designations handed down from the past still persist, as luff tackles, gun tackles, Spanish burtons.

A single whip ((A), Fig. A3.9). A single block fixed.

A runner (B). A single block movable.

A whip and runner. A whip hooking to the hauling part of a runner.

Ratio of Weight W to force F Necessary to Raise Weight

	Disregarding Friction	Allowing for Friction
Fig. 1	$F = W$	$\dfrac{F}{W} = \dfrac{11}{10}$
Fig. 2	$\dfrac{F}{W} = \dfrac{10}{20}$	$\dfrac{F}{W} = \dfrac{12}{20}$
Fig. 3	$\dfrac{F}{W} = \dfrac{10}{30}$	$\dfrac{F}{W} = \dfrac{13}{30}$
Fig. 4	$\dfrac{F}{W} = \dfrac{10}{40}$	$\dfrac{F}{W} = \dfrac{14}{40}$
Fig. 5	$\dfrac{F}{W} = \dfrac{10}{50}$	$\dfrac{F}{W} = \dfrac{15}{50}$
In a three-fold pur-chase	$\dfrac{P}{W} = \dfrac{10}{60}$	$\dfrac{F}{W} = \dfrac{16}{60}$
Luff on luff	$\dfrac{P}{W} = \dfrac{10}{120}$	$\dfrac{F}{W} = \dfrac{16}{120}$

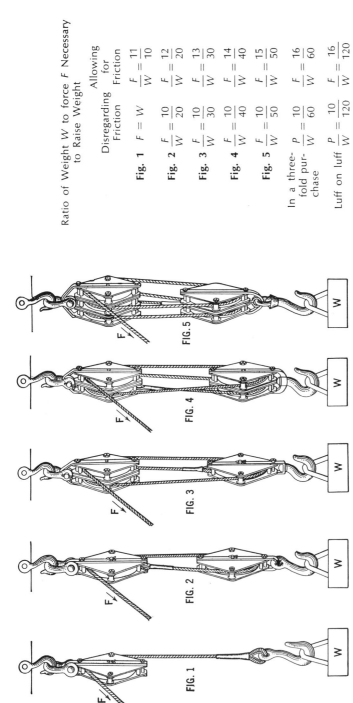

FIG. 1   FIG. 2   FIG. 3   FIG. 4   FIG. 5

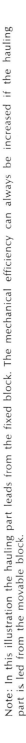

Fig. A3.8 Types of tackles.

Note: In this illustration the hauling part leads from the fixed block. The mechanical efficiency can always be increased if the hauling part is led from the movable block.

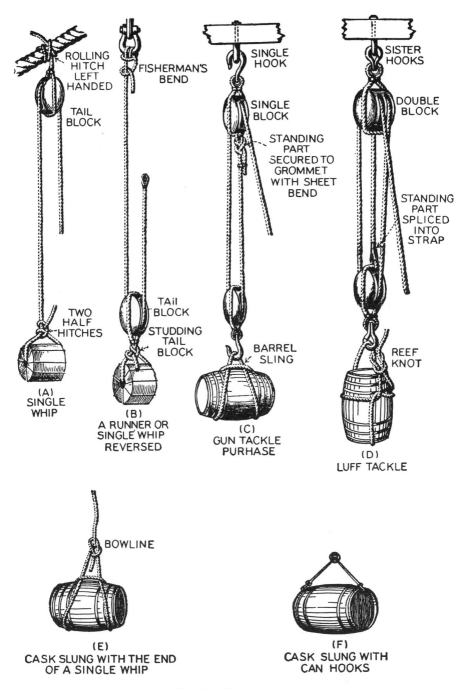

Fig. A3.9 Tackles in use.

A gun tackle purchase (C).

A luff tackle (D). A single and double block; also called a jigger in the Navy.

A luff upon luff. The double block of one luff tackle hooked to the hauling part of another, thus multiplying the power.

A two-fold purchase (Fig. A3.8). Two double blocks.

A double luff. A double and treble block (Fig. A3.8).

A three-fold purchase. Two treble blocks. This is the heaviest purchase commonly used (Fig. A3.10).

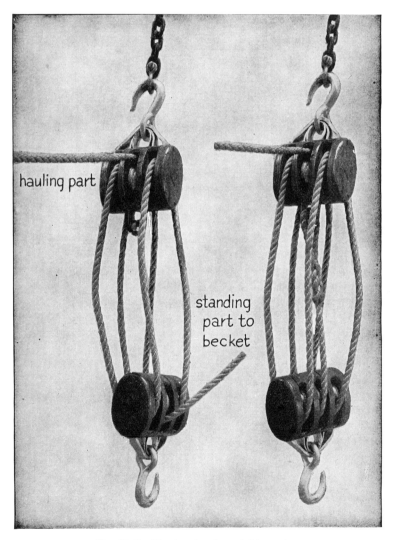

Fig. A3.10 Rigging the three-fold purchase.

Thwartship tackles are used on the heads of boat davits for rigging in. In a more general sense the term is applied to any tackle leading across the deck. Similarly, a tackle for hauling out the backbone of an awning or for any other purpose where it has a fore-and-aft lead is a *fore-and-aft tackle*.

Hatch tackles are used at hatches for hoisting, lowering stores, etc.

Jiggers are small light tackles used for miscellaneous work about the ship. In the Navy this term is usually reserved for the luff tackle.

A *deck tackle* is a heavy purchase, usually two-fold, used in handling ground tackle, mooring ship, and generally for heavy work of any kind about the deck.

Yard-and-stay tackles take their names from their application on ships with masts and yards, where they were used together for transferring stores from a boat alongside to the deck or hatch of the ship. The general principle involved in the "yard-and-stay" is of wide application on merchant ships where a weight is to be lifted from a dock and lowered through a hatch on a vessel.

When working with tackles, it is sometimes necessary to know the mechanical advantage (MA); that is, the "multiplying force of the tackle." The basic formula for work applies here:

$$fD = Wd$$

This formula may be expressed as force times the distance through which it moves equals weight times the distance through which it moves. In any tackle with a movable block, the force is multiplied, and the hauling part moves a greater distance than the weight. In our formula, *d* represents the smaller distance.

In a two-fold purchase, for example, if *f* acting through 4 feet (*D*) moves the weight (*W*) 1 foot (*d*), we can write the fundamental equation:

$$f \times D = W \times d$$
$$f \times 4 = W \times 1, \text{or}$$
$$f = \frac{W}{4}$$

The force has been multiplied four times. If the weight were, say, 100 pounds, the force required to lift it would be:

$$\frac{W}{4} \text{ or } \frac{100 \text{ pounds}}{4} = 25 \text{ pounds}$$

Thus, to find the mechanical advantage of a tackle one could experiment, making the necessary measurements and calculations. A simpler method is to count the parts of the fall at the movable block.

Both of the foregoing methods of finding MA ignore friction in the tackle. Ordinarily, seamen can do the same, but if the power-to-weight ratio is so critical that friction must be considered, add 10 percent of the load for every sheave in the tackle (including fairlead blocks). For example, in a rig with a two-fold purchase and one fairlead block, add 50 percent to the load. Thus, with a 100-pound weight, total load would be 150 pounds. The force needed to lift this load would be:

$$\frac{150}{4} = 37.5 \text{ pounds}$$

A3.7   Chain Hoists   Chain hoists, or chain falls as they are often called, provide a convenient and efficient method for hoisting loads by hand. Chief advantages of chain hoists are that one man can raise a load of several tons, and the load can remain stationary without being secured. The slow lifting travel of a chain hoist permits small movements, accurate adjustments of height, and gentle handling of loads. For these reasons they are particularly

Fig. 3.11   Chain hoists. Left, differential chain hoist; right, spur gear.

useful in machinery spaces, but many times they come in handy on deck, too. There are four general types of chain hoists: differential, spur gear, worm gear, and lever (ratchet). The differential and spur types (Fig. A3.11) are the most common.

The mechanical advantages of chain hoists vary from 5 to 250, depending on their rated capacities, which range from ½ ton to 40 tons. Although the most expensive, the spur gear is the most efficient chain hoist—losing only some 15 percent of the power through friction and other factors. The lever type is suitable only for light tasks.

Ordinarily, chain hoists are constructed with their lower hook as the weakest part of the assembly. This is a precaution, so that the lower hook will start to spread open before the chain hoist itself is overloaded. Under ordinary circumstances, the pull exerted on a chain hoist by one or two men will not overload the hoist.

Chain hoists should be inspected at frequent intervals. Any evidence of spreading or excessive wear on the hook is sufficient cause to require its replacement. If the links of the chain are distorted, this is an indication that the chain hoist has been heavily overloaded and is probably unsafe for further use. Under such circumstances, the chain hoist should be surveyed (discarded).

A3.8 General precautions   In preparing for any lift with weight handling appliances, in addition to insuring that all components are of adequate size to accomplish the desired task, each part should be inspected to determine its condition. Fiber lines should be inspected for signs of excessive wear: fraying, rot, and dryness. The line should be twisted open to expose the interior of the strands. If the interior is grey, dried out and powdery the line is unsafe for use. Wire ropes should be examined for fish hooks, badly worn areas, and kinks. A badly worn wire rope should not be used. (Refer to wire rope wear criteria in Appendix 1.) Wooden blocks should be examined to insure there are no cracked or rotted cheeks, worn pins, or cracked or badly worn metal parts. All metal fittings such as shackles, metal blocks, swivels, and hooks should be carefully examined for any signs of cracks, distortion, excessive wear, and metal fatigue. REMEMBER specifications for gear are given for new components; the actual safe working load of the equipment you plan to use may be far less than this if it is worn or old.

Some excellent general precautions in the usage of weight handling gear are given in the following section.

GENERAL PRECAUTIONS

1. Remember that the giving way of one part breaks and destroys other parts, frequently to an extent not readily repaired, and, furthermore, endangers the men.

2. Heavy weights must never be allowed to drop, even for the shortest distances, but must be lowered to rest with a gentle motion, and at the same time chocked to prevent rolling or sliding.

3. In raising or lowering heavy weights always, whenever possible, closely follow up with blocks or chocks to guard against any possible giving way of jacks or tackle.

4. All motions with heavy weights must be slow, so as not to generate momentum.

5. Supports must have a firm base and cribbing, a level foundation, and be built up vertically.

6. All fittings or appliances used for securing lines must be strong and secure beyond any possibility of carrying away.

7. Be careful at all times to avoid any sudden shocks or strains.

8. Every operation should be done with spirit but without bustle or confusion.

9. Vigilance on the part of the person in charge should be unceasing to see all gear is rigged, handled, and operated correctly.

10. Do not permit men to step on a taut fall, or to get in positions of danger, such as under weights, in the bight of a running rope, or at the end of a taut rope or cable which might give way.

11. Special precautions must be taken in wet weather when the material is slippery.

12. Overhaul tackle as frequently as necessary, keep free from rust, corrosion and dirt and keep well oiled and operating freely.

13. Always insure that decks are adequately shored to withstand the additional stresses of handling heavy weights.

14. Overloading decreases the strength of rope materially. Rope should never be loaded beyond one-third of its breaking load.

15. Keep wire rope well coated with a preservative lubricant. Keep wire free of kinks or sharp bends.

Index